The Stranger from Paradise

The Stranger from Paradise

A Biography of William Blake

G.E. Bentley, Jr

*"I have very little of Mr. Blake's company;
he is always in Paradise"*

Published for the Paul Mellon Centre
for Studies in British Art by

Yale University Press
New Haven and London

Copyright © 2001 by G.E. Bentley, Jr
First published in paperback in 2003

Set in Ehrhard 6 by Fakenham Photosetting, Norfolk
Printed in China through Worldprint

For information about this and other Yale University Press publications, please contact:
U.S. Office: sales.press@yale.edu   www.yale.edu/yup
Europe Office: sales@yaleup.co.uk   www.yale.co.uk

ISBN 0–300–08939–2 (hbk)
ISBN 0–300–10030–2 (pbk)
Library of Congress Card Number 00–111810

A catalogue record for this book is available from the British Library.

10 9 8 7 6 5 4 3 2

Endpapers: details from Blake, "Chaucer's Canterbury Pilgrims" (1810). See Pl. 108.
Fitzwilliam Museum, Cambridge.

For B.B.B.

INVICTA

Contents

Illustrations

The originals are on paper unless otherwise specified.

Plates between pages 292 and 293

Figures

Items from the collection of G.E. Bentley, Jr have been photographed by Adrian Oosterman Oostudio Photography

Abbreviations

BB	G.E. Bentley, Jr, *Blake Books* (Oxford: Clarendon Press, 1977)
BBS	G.E. Bentley, Jr, *Blake Books Supplement* (Oxford: Clarendon Press, 1995)
Blake	*Blake: An Illustrated Quarterly*
BR	G.E. Bentley, Jr, *Blake Records* (Oxford: Clarendon Press, 1969), the source of all dated biographical references to Blake unless otherwise identified
BR (2)	*Blake Records*, second edition (New Haven and London: Yale University Press 2003) which incorporates *Blake Records* (1969), *Blake Records Supplement* (1988) and extensive contemporary references to Blake discovered after 1987. *BR*(2) is cited here only for references which do not appear in *BR* or *BRS*.
BRS	G.E. Bentley, Jr, *Blake Records Supplement* (Oxford: Clarendon Press, 1988)
Butlin	Martin Butlin, *The Paintings and Drawings of William Blake* (New Haven & London: Yale University Press, 1981)
Cunningham	Allan Cunningham, "William Blake", *The Lives of the Most Eminent British Painters, Sculptors, and Architects*, Second Edition (London: John Murray, 1830) (*BR* 476–507)
Gilchrist	Alexander Gilchrist, *Life of William Blake, "Pictor Ignotus"* (London: Macmillan, 1863), Vol. I
Malkin	B.H. Malkin, *A Father's Memoirs of His Child* (London: Longman, Hurst, Rees, & Orme, 1806), xvii–xli (*BR* 421–31)
Robinson	[Henry Crabb Robinson], "William Blake, Künstler, Dichter, und Religiöser Schwärmer", *Vaterländisches Museum*, I (January 1811) (*BR* 432–55, in German and English)
Smith	John Thomas Smith, "Blake", *Nollekens and His Times* (London: Henry Colburn, 1828), II (*BR* 455–76)
Tatham	Frederick Tatham, MS "Life of Blake" (*c.* 1832) (*BR* 507–35)
Visions (C)	*Visions of the Daughters of Albion* Copy C; the copy identifications derive from *BB*.
WBW	*William Blake's Writings*, ed. G.E. Bentley, Jr (Oxford: Clarendon Press, 1978), the source of all references to Blake's writings unless otherwise identified

A superscript number identifies an endnote (giving the source of information) to be found at the end of the book. A superscript symbol identifies a note at the foot of the page giving supplementary information. Essays whose author is not identified are by G.E. Bentley, Jr. For descriptions of the biographies here, see Appendix 1: Principal Biographies of Blake.

Acknowledgements

For half a century I have been wrestling with the spirit of William Blake, with the protean shapes of Blake's myth and the factual Laocoon of his life. And I have enjoyed it all. If I could believe that this biography is worthy of him, I would feel that I had won his blessing.

Research for *The Stranger from Paradise* has been carried out particularly in Toronto and Ottawa; in Mears, New York, and San Marino; in Oxford, London, Chichester, Durham, Edinburgh, York, Felpham, and Middleton-in-Teesdale; in Beijing; in Auckland; and in Canberra. It has been supported by fellowships from the Social Sciences and Humanities Research Council of Canada (1995–98) and Hatfield College, Durham (1996). If this book is worthy, its worth is significantly due to such institutional generosity.

The fraternity of Blake scholarship has been wonderfully generous to me. For unflagging council and friendship, I am grateful particularly to Professor Robert N. Essick and Professor Joseph Viscomi.

For very particular favours, I thank Sarah Bentley, Mr Martin Butlin, Mr Keri Davies, Mr Kimball Higgs, Mrs Heather Howell, Mr Jeffrey Barklay Mertz, Professor Terry L. Meyers, Mr Paul Miner, Professor Dennis Read, Professor Roussel Sargent, Margaret Sharmon, and Dr Gerald Vaughan.

And above all, I owe more than thanks to Dr E.B. Bentley, who believes in this book and its author beyond reason and who has assisted me in every library and study in which the work has been done. With the verdant world of ideas and facts I feel at home and at ease. With the sterile brutes of electronic technology, however, I am a stranger and astray. For the patience to cope with computer failure in a Michigan cottage and in a Beijing apartment, with printer recalcitrance in an Oxfordshire village and an Italian palace, with the wrong-size paper in Durham and Canberra, I am entirely dependent upon Dr E.B. Bentley. She accomplishes through patience, persistence, and love what is impossible to those, like myself, who will not read the directions or ask idiot questions. For the coaxing of these electronic brutes, like some slow beast slouching towards Bethlehem to be born, I owe everything to Beth. Also my love.

Dutch Boys Landing
Mears, Michigan
23 August 1999

Genealogies

The genealogies of the families of the poet (Blake family) the poet's wife (Boucher–Butcher) and the first husband of his mother (Armitage family) derive from *Blake Records*, second edition (?2002).

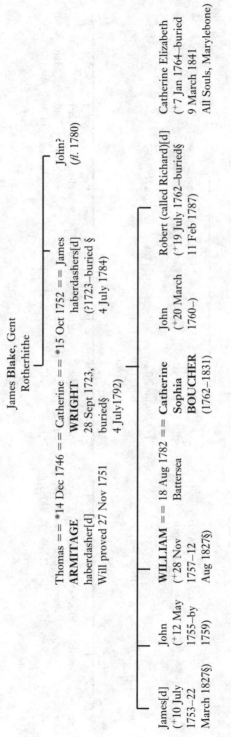

BLAKE

James **Blake**, Gent
Rotherhithe

Thomas == == *14 Dec 1746 == Catherine == == *15 Oct 1752 == James   John?
ARMITAGE   **WRIGHT**   haberdashers[d]   (*fl.* 1780)
haberdasher[d]   28 Sept 1723,   (?1723–buried §
Will proved 27 Nov 1751   buried§   4 July 1784)
                                4 July1792)

James[d]   John   **WILLIAM** == 18 Aug 1782 == **Catherine**   John   Robert (called Richard)[d]   Catherine Elizabeth
(+10 July   (+12 May   (+28 Nov   Battersea   **Sophia**   (+20 March   (+19 July 1762–buried§   (+7 Jan 1764–buried
1753–22   1755–by   1757–12   **BOUCHER**   1760–)   11 Feb 1787)   9 March 1841
March 1827§)   1759)   Aug 1827§)   (1762–1831)   All Souls, Marylebone)

Sources

[d] 28 Broad Street, Golden Square

* St George's Chapel, Mayfair; much of this information derives from Keri Davies, "William Blake's Mother: A New Identification", *Blake*, XXXIII
   (1999), 28, 39, 41.

+ St James, Westminster

§ Bunhill Fields

BOUCHER–BUTCHER

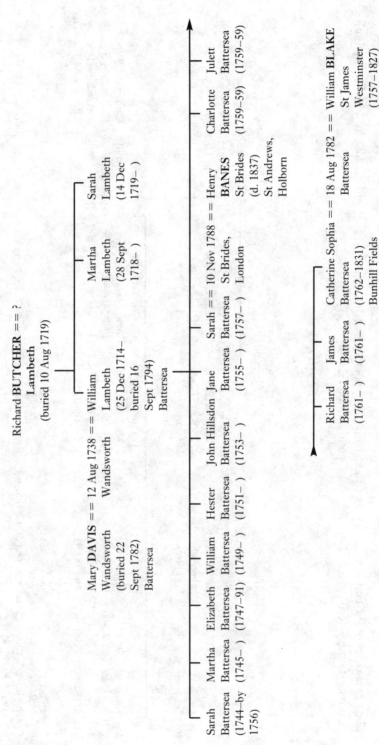

Richard **BUTCHER** == ?.
Lambeth
(buried 10 Aug 1719)

Mary **DAVIS** == 12 Aug 1738 == William Lambeth
Wandsworth Wandsworth (25 Dec 1714–
(buried 22 buried 16
Sept 1782) Sept 1794)
Battersea Battersea

Martha Sarah
Lambeth Lambeth
(28 Sept (14 Dec
1718–) 1719–)

Sarah Martha Elizabeth William Hester John Hillsdon Jane Sarah ==
Battersea Battersea Battersea Battersea Battersea Battersea Battersea Battersea
(1744–by (1745–) (1747–91) (1749–) (1751–) (1753–) (1755–) (1757–)
1756)

Sarah == 10 Nov 1788 == Henry **BANES**
Battersea St Brides, St Brides
(1757–) London (d. 1837)
St Andrews,
Holborn

Charlotte Julett
Battersea Battersea
(1759–59) (1759–59)

Richard James Catherine Sophia == 18 Aug 1782 == William **BLAKE**
Battersea Battersea Battersea St James
(1761–) (1761–) (1762–1831) Westminster
Bunhill Fields (1757–1827)
Bunhill Fields

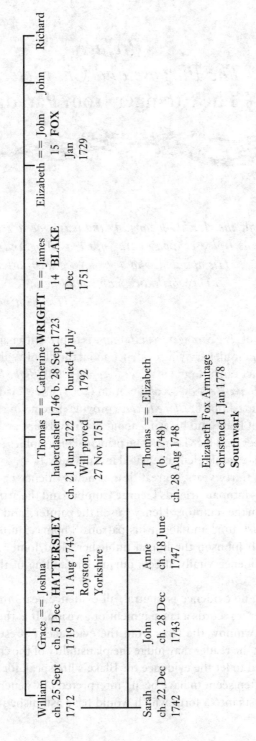

ARMITAGE

Richard Armitage
farmer of Cudworth, Yorkshire

Thomas == Catherine **WRIGHT** == James **BLAKE**
haberdasher 1746 b. 28 Sept 1723   14 Dec 1751
ch. 21 June 1722   buried 4 July 1792
Will proved
27 Nov 1751

Elizabeth == John **FOX**   John   Richard
15 Jan 1729

William   Grace == Joshua **HATTERSLEY**
ch. 25 Sept   ch. 5 Dec   11 Aug 1743
1712   1719   Royston,
Yorkshire

Sarah   John   Anne
ch. 22 Dec   ch. 28 Dec   ch. 18 June
1742   1743   1747

Thomas == Elizabeth
(b. 1748)
ch. 28 Aug 1748

Elizabeth Fox Armitage
christened 1 Jan 1778
Southwark

b. = born in London
ch. = christened in Royston, Yorkshire

Preface
The Purpose and Character of
The Stranger from Paradise

*Tell me the Acts, O historian, and leave me to reason upon
them as I please; away with your reasoning and your rub-
bish. . . . His opinion, who does not see spiritual agency, is
not worth any man's reading . . . .*

[*Descriptive Catalogue ¶77*]

The purpose of *The Stranger from Paradise* is to present a narrative incorporat-
ing all the significant surviving evidence about the life of William Blake. Almost
all this evidence can be found in *Blake Records* (1969), *Blake Records Supplement*
(1988), and *Blake Records*, second edition (2003). New evidence in the forth-
coming second edition of *Blake Records* provides fascinating information about
the families of Blake and his wife, about his friendships and patrons, his professional career, and his visions. The principal biographies of Blake from 1806
to 1998 are listed and briefly evaluated in Appendix 1.

In the last thirty years, a great deal of new evidence has been discovered
about Blake's intimate friends George Cumberland the artist and dilletante,[1]
John Flaxman the sculptor,[2] Henry Fuseli the painter,[3] and Thomas Stothard
the book-illustrator[4] and about his patrons Thomas Butts the government
clerk,[5] Joseph Johnson the liberal publisher,[6] and John Linnell the artist.[7]
This new evidence vitally affects our understanding of the life of William
Blake.

Of course, no evidence is neutral; all evidence bears the bias of the witness, whether it records a tax-payment or a vision. It is the jury of posterity
which must winnow the facts from the evidence. I present extensive evidence so that the reader may judge the plausibility of the conclusions I offer.

I have tried to let the evidence for Blake's life speak for itself. Blake's life
and works often seem to have been "interpreted" by generations of scholars
and enthusiasts into a form which would have astonished the man himself.

Blake has been variously claimed as an Irishman and a Cockney, a Marxist and a mystic, a Mason and a neo-Platonist and a Gnostic—and even as a conventional believer in the Church of England. It is time to let the unmediated evidence for Blake's life speak for itself, purged as far as possible of the myths that have been industriously spun around him since his works and his genius were rediscovered by Alexander Gilchrist and displayed in 1863 in his *Life of William Blake, "Pictor Ignotus"*.*

---

* According to *BB* 25,

> Its effect was thunderous. Never has an important literary reputation been posthumously established so instantaneously and effectively. ... Gilchrist's title. *"Pictor Ignotus"*, had not been mere showmanship. Blake *had* been unknown, and Gilchrist's *Life* made him sensationally well known. From 1863 on Blake at last took his place in literary and artistic history as one of the great figures of the Romantic Movement.

For previous biographies of Blake, see Appendix 1.

Introduction
Paradise and the Beast

The Stranger from Paradise is epitomized by the quotation on the title page: "I have very little of Mr. Blake's company; he is always in Paradise."*

This is the language of radical religious Dissent, of what pious prelates deplored as Enthusiasm. The Beast and the Whore derive from Revelation. She is the woman whom John saw sitting "upon a scarlet-colored beast", "And upon her forehead was ... written Mystery, Babylon the Great, the Mother of Harlots, and the Abomination of the Earth" (Revelation xvii, 3, 5) (see "The Great Red Dragon and the Beast from the Sea" and "The Whore of Babylon" Pls 5, 75).

Blake writes of "Religion hid in War, a Dragon red & hidden Harlot"[1] and of "Babylon ... Calld natural religion",[2] "Babylon, the rational morality".[3] The Whore and her Beast represent the state church and temporal power which are among us everywhere. "I behold Babylon in the opening streets of London".[4] All laws and codes "given under pretence of divine command" represent "The Abomination that maketh desolate, i.e State Religion".[5]

Blake probably learned such language at the knees of his Dissenting parents.

Such radical Dissenters were not rare in Blake's time, and of course they survive and diversify into the twenty-first century. Their language is read-

---

* Catherine Blake's comment (*c.* 1810) to Seymour Kirkup (*BR* 221). Blake wrote of himself: "The artist is an inhabitant of that happy country", i.e., Eden (*Descriptive Catalogue* ¶74).

ily adaptable to political agitation, to the uses of those who wish to change the forms of government rather than to destroy or ignore all forms of government. Had Blake been merely an Enthusiast, turning his back upon "the fiends of commerce"[6] and upon the "Lord Chancellor" who is "The Prince of darkness",[7] or had he been merely a political radical like Tom Paine and Pigsmeat Spence, focusing upon the evils of the world rather than upon the glories of heaven, he would scarcely be remembered today as more than a footnote to history.

But Blake transmuted his native language of religious Enthusiasm into the language of art, and he interfused the revolutionary Christian vision that was his birthright with the English literary vision in which he immersed himself during his adolescence and the neo-classical artistic vision into which he grew in manhood. Together they transformed an arcane religious Enthusiasm into a new gospel of art, a gospel which remains other-worldly and fundamentally spiritual. Christ and the Bible are still the centre of Blake's vision, but they are so transformed that both fellow Enthusiasts and members of the Church of England would scarcely recognize them.

> The Vision of Christ that thou dost See
> Is my Visions greatest Enemy[.]
>
> ("Everlasting Gospel", Notebook p. 33)

In a similar transformation, Blake made an engraving of the Laocoon, and then he added inscriptions. In these inscriptions the Trojan priest and his two sons struggling with an avenging serpent are transmogrified into Jehovah and his two sons Adam and Satan attacked by the serpents of Good and Evil. And round the design he wrote a series of aphorisms demonstrating his mature concept of Christianity:

> Jesus & his Apostles & Disciples were all Artists. . . .
>   A Poet a Painter a Musician an Architect: the Man Or Woman who is not one of these is not a Christian[.]

For Blake, paradise was the human imagination, and he spent most of his time there. He believed in it firmly, and he acted unhesitatingly and consistently on his belief. His greatest achievement in his poetry and his designs is to carry us with him into such an imaginative world.

Blake deserves to be remembered with honour not primarily because of his transmutation of Christianity but because of his transmutation of art. In words and images, in sounds and shapes as diverse as his early *Songs of Innocence* (1789) and his late *Illustrations of The Book of Job* (1826), he shows us how,

To see a World in a Grain of Sand
And a Heaven in a Wild Flower[,]
Hold Infinity in the palm of your hand
And Eternity in an Hour[.]

("Auguries of Innocence" from the Ballads [Pickering] Manuscript)

It is in the glories of sight and sound, in the divine vision preserved in time of trouble, that Blake lives for us most truly.

His life is more than an illumination of his own poetry and designs. It bears the shape of great art itself. From his youthful vaulting ambitions in painting, engraving, poetry, and music, through his mature flirtation with the Goddess Fortune, to his joyful return to the vision and confidence of his youth, Blake's life provides a pattern of noble self-sacrifice and wise self-understanding which inspired admiration and love in his generation and in ours. There are many who love the man not only beyond his powerful designs and exquisite poetry but in spite of them. There is little evidence that his youthful disciples understood or even read his poetry, but they came to the House of the Interpreter as to a shrine; the artist Samuel Palmer used to kiss the bell-pull when he came to Blake's "enchanted rooms".[8]

In part the young men were worshipping the serenity which they found there, for all his life Blake lived in visionary realms of gold. What mattered to Blake was not the "hole" "I live in . . . here" but the "beautiful mansion" which "God has . . . for me elsewhere".[9] Once at an evening party a beautiful, pampered little girl was presented to him, "a poor old man, dressed in such shabby clothes": "*H*e looked at her very kindly for a long while without speaking, and then stroking her head and long ringlets said 'May God make this world to you, my child, as beautiful as it has been to me'."[10]

He devoted his life to "my visionary studies" so that he could "converse with my friends in Eternit*y*, See Visions, Dream Dreams & prophecy & speak Parables".[11] He was overwhelmed by inspiration, and in a letter of 23 October 1804 he wrote: "Dear Sir, excuse my enthusiasm or rather madness, for I am really drunk with intellectual vision whenever I take a pencil or graver into my hand . . .". Twenty-three years later, on 12 April 1827, when he was ill in bed, he wrote to his old friend George Cumberland: "I have been very near the Gates of Death & have returned very weak & an Old Man feeble & tottering, but not in Spirit & Life not in The Real Man The Imagination which Liveth for Ever. In that I am stronger & stronger as this Foolish Body decays." He subjected his foolish body to his will and devoted both to the service of God. He said, "I cannot consider death as any thing but a removing from one room to another",[12] and his own death was in joyful song. As young George Richmond wrote on 15 August 1827: "Just before he died His Countenance became fair—His eyes brighten'd and He burst out in Singing of the things he Saw in Heaven[.] In truth He Died like a Saint . . .".

Blake's life has power to move an unGodly age through its example of the self-devoted, God-intoxicated man who transformed London's "dirty streets Near where the dirty Thames does flow"[13] into the paradise of the imagination. He demonstrates the triumph of the human spirit over the Realm of the Beast.

Blake's life has the power to move us as do his poetry and his art. It is this power which may justify an account of the Stranger from Paradise in the Realm of the Beast.

CHAPTER I

1720–1772: God at the Window

God ... put his head to the window[1]

William Blake's Christian life began in grandeur and glory when he was christened at the noble marble baptismal font in the majestic new parish church of St James's, Westminster.

He was born at 7:45 p.m.[2] on Monday 28 November 1757 in the parish of St James's, one of the most prosperous, fashionable, public-spirited, and democratic parishes in the kingdom. When the area was developed after the Restoration of Charles II in 1660 and the Fire of London in 1667, it was laid out methodically and handsomely, with straight streets and elegant squares such as Berkeley Square and St James's Square and Golden Square, near where the Blakes lived.

Christopher Wren designed the church to dazzle (Pl. 1). Its great vaulted hall and gallery supported by Corinthian columns could accommodate two thousand worshippers, and its massive organ-case and beautiful limewood reredos and wonderful marble baptismal font were all carved by Grinling Gibbons. The pedestal of the font represents the Tree of Life with Eve offering Adam the apple, and the bowl shows the Ark and the Baptism of

Christ (Pl. 2). When the church was completed and consecrated in 1684, in the lifetime of Blake's grandparents, all that taste and money could do sanctioned the services in St James's.

The parish and its church were magnets to aristocrats and artists, to politicians and poets. The Earl of Chesterfield, the letter-writer and patron, was christened there in 1694, as were William Pitt in 1708, later Prime Minister, and the children of James and Catherine Blake.

Christening

When James and Catherine Blake brought William, their third son then two weeks old, to be christened on Sunday 11 December 1757,* they were probably accompanied by their first son James, then a little over four years old, by their second son John, two and a half, by the child's grandfather James Blake from across the river in Rotherhithe, and by his mother's parents Mr and Mrs Wright, as well as by the child's god-parents. And among the ordinary Sunday congregation of clergymen in surplices and wigs, gentlemen wearing lace and swords, ladies with powdered hair, combed children, and babies in white gowns,† there were friends and acquaintances and customers of the Blakes' little haberdashery shop a few minutes walk to the north. The six beadles may have been carrying their handsome new silver-headed staves of office[3] as they led in the vicar and the choir.

The solemn setting and the sonorous service were impressive: "Suffer the little children to come unto me . . . for such is the kingdom of God"[4] (Pl. 3). But perhaps the setting and service did not greatly impress the little Blake family group assembled there. William Blake rarely again participated in such august ceremonies or in such distinguished company. He was familiar with the affairs of the church and the parish,‡ and his father and his brother did extensive business with the St James parish Work House and School of Industry. But there is no evidence of the Blake family at services in St James's, Piccadilly, aside from christenings.

---

* There may be some uncertainty as to whether Catherine Blake was present at the christening. In the Church of England women were expected to be "churched", normally two weeks after child-birth, before they attended public worship again. However, Dissenters like the Blakes often objected to and neglected such survivals of Jewish and Catholic ritual in the services of the Church of England, and some priests refused to perform services for women who had not been churched.

† Seven other babies were christened in St James's that day.

‡ On the death in June 1825 of Gerrard Andrewes, who had for long been the Rector of St James's, Blake expressed his sorrow and his conviction that "Every Death is an improvement of the State of the Departed."

From the Shadows to the Light: Blake's Family

No augury of excellence, no precedent of promise illuminates the obscurity of William Blake's origins. His parents left no footprints in the sands of time except when they stepped into a city guild hall to be apprenticed or into church to be married, when they voted and paid their taxes, christened their children, and died. So inconspicuous are they that we do not even know the dates and places of their birth, the names of their mothers,* or whether they had siblings.

The earliest information about Blake's family is that his grandfather James Blake, a "Gentleman" of Rotherhithe, was sufficiently prosperous in July 1737 to pay the very large sum of £60 to apprentice his son James Blake to Francis Smith as a draper. The boy was probably born about 1723, for the normal age of apprenticeship was fourteen.

When the younger James Blake finished his seven-year apprenticeship in 1744, he moved to a substantial house at 5 Glasshouse Street, near Oxford Street, Westminster (Pl. 7), which he took over from John Blake, perhaps his brother. The house was probably used for both a residence and a hosiery and haberdashery shop shared at first with John Blake (1743) and then with Mr Butcher (1751), perhaps his cousin.

James Blake was a gentle, amiable man of "easy habits & . . . moderate desires, moderate Enjoyments, & . . . by his Sons description, a lenient & affectionate Father, always more ready to encourage than to chide".† He was a "devout man"[5] and a Dissenter, and, like many Dissenters, his political sympathies were liberal. At the 1749 election, "James Blake Glasshouse S.t Hosier" voted for the anti-court candidates Earl Percy and Lord Clinton,‡ as did his fellow-hosier Thomas Hermitage (i.e., Armitage) of 28 Broad Street,[6] who may well have been an acquaintance.

Thomas Armitage had married Catherine Wright on 14 December 1746 at St George's, Hanover Square, a casual wedding-factory much patronized by Dissenters,§ and both bride and groom were probably Dissenters. They moved into 28 Broad Street, Golden Square, in 1748, and when Thomas

---

* Peter Ackroyd, *Blake* (1995), 20 says that Blake's maternal grandfather was "a hosier", but as he identifies Blake's mother as "Catherine Hermitage" rather than Catherine Wright (her maiden name) or Catherine Armitage (her first married name), we may wonder about the accuracy of the unidentified source of his information about her father.

† Tatham (*BR* 508). According to Gilchrist, Blake in later years rarely spoke of his father or mother (*BR* 48).

‡ *BR* 551. In the 1780 and 1784 elections James Blake voted for the Whig James Fox and wasted his second vote. William Blake was a more extreme Dissenter than his father and brother, for they voted while he did not, though he was eligible to do so.

§ See *BR* (2). Some reasons given by Dissenters for avoiding a church wedding, "that priestly usurpation", were expressed by John Linnell to explain his own wedding without benefit of clergy in 1817—see below, p. 366.

made his will on 20 July 1751 he identified himself as a "Haberdasher and Hosier" of St James, Westminster. The Armitages had no children, and when Thomas died a little later in 1751 he left "the rest residue and remainder of my estate", consisting chiefly of his house and business, to "my said Wife Catherine Armitage". The will was proved on 27 November 1751.[7]

The death of Thomas Armitage must have left his young widow in difficulty. Her chief property was the house and hosiery shop, and at best she had taken only a subsidiary role in the business. She could scarcely have known the Company of Drapers and the masculine world of the financial City, and she probably knew little of which merchants supplied reliable goods or how to tell the best prices. As a woman, even as the widow of a draper, it would have been difficult for her to drive bargains and insure the performance of her bargains in the male world of commerce.

The natural place for her to turn for assistance was to friends of her late husband who were in the same line of business. Among these was young James Blake, who had his own hosiery and haberdashery shop in Glasshouse Street, just on the other side of Golden Square. He probably started helping her not long after her husband's death in the latter part of 1751.

Eleven months after she had proved her late husband's will, Catherine Armitage married James Blake on 15 October 1752 at St George's, Hanover Square, in a brisk ceremony—there were fifteen weddings before noon at the church that day. When they were married, Catherine was thirty and James was twenty-nine, early middle age by the standards of the time.

James Blake took over the hosiery and haberdashery shop at 28 Broad Street. There he and Catherine did a "respectable Trade"* selling gloves and stockings; they had at least enough business to appear respectable to the wise guardians of the poor in St James Parish who repeatedly employed James Blake to supply goods for the parish workhouse and school of industry.[8]

The resources of the little shop must have been strained when Catherine Armitage and James Blake were married. Under the terms of her first husband's will, Catherine was required, if she remarried, to pay from her inheritance £20 to her late husband's brother William, £10 each to his brothers Richard and John and his sisters Elizabeth Fox and Grace Hattersley, and £20 to his nephew and namesake Thomas Armitage, the son of his brother William.[9] Catherine and James Blake must have been persons of courage to assume this £80 debt at the beginning of their marriage.

---

* Tatham (*BR* 508); it is unlikely that James Blake was, as Tatham says, "well to do" and "of substantial Worth" except in moral terms. James Blake died before Tatham was born, and Tatham's information about him probably came from William Blake's widow, whose impoverished childhood may have made a modest competence seem like "substantial Worth".

By the time she was forty-two in 1764, Catherine Blake had borne six children. This is a modest-sized family by the standards of the period; what is remarkable about the family is that only one child died in infancy. From the birth of her first child in 1753 to the adolescence of her last about 1790, Catherine Blake's chief occupation and joy must have been the care of her children, comforting their infant sorrows and rejoicing in their infant joys. For twelve years she had babies in long clothes. Even with help from servants and her husband, she must have been house-bound for much of that period.

Catherine was a tender and sympathetic mother,[10] more inclined to overlook faults than to punish them, especially in her charming, wayward son John. However, she was capable of beating her children under severe provocation such as a wilful lie.[11] In particular, her strange son William "was privately encouraged by his mother" to make designs, and in "the solitude of his room" he used to "make drawings, and illustrate these with verses, to be hung up together in his mother's chamber".[12]

Blake's natural playmates in his childhood were his three brothers and his sister. His eldest brother, James, was four years older than William; John was two years younger;* Robert was four years younger; and Catherine Elizabeth, the baby of the family, was six years younger.

Blake's eldest brother James was born on 10 July 1753, just nine months after his parents were married. When he was fifteen, he was apprenticed on 19 October 1765 to Gideon Boutoult of the Needlemakers' Company. Boutoult, the son of a weaver of Southwark, was probably a Huguenot.[13] On the completion of his apprenticeship he became a member of the firm called "Blake & Son, Hosiers & Haberdashers, 28 Broad-str. Carnaby-mar".[14] He grew up to be "an humble matter-of-fact man", "an honest, unpretending shop-keeper in an old-world style, ill calculated for great prosperity, in the hosiery or any other line ... adhering to knee-breeches, worsted stockings, and buckles".[15] He long retained the stigmata of his childhood among Dissenters, and even in middle age he "would at times *talk Swedenborg*, talking of seeing Abraham and Moses".† For many years, he and Blake rubbed along together well enough. In September 1800 James went to tea with Blake at the home of Blake's patron Thomas Butts, and Blake wrote

---

* An earlier "John Blake, son of John [*sic*] & Catherine", was born on 12 May and christened on 1 June 1755 at St James's, Westminster. If, as seems likely, this is the child of James and Catherine Blake, he must have died before the christening of "John Blake Son of James & Catherine" on 31 March 1760. They were probably named after their uncle(?) John Blake who had shared a house with Blake's father at 5 Glasshouse Street in 1743 and apparently moved to Hog Lane in 1778–88 (*BR* 551, 556–7).

† Gilchrist (*BR* 2); he is unlikely to have "talked Swedenborg" much before 1789 when the first New Jerusalem (Swedenborgian) Church was founded.

Gilchrist had apparently talked to "ladies, yet living [*c. 1860*], friends of Blake's, [*who*] remember to have made their little purchases of gloves and haberdashery" "At James Blake's shop" before it closed in 1812 (*BR* 3).

James a long, confiding letter on 30 January 1803 about his troubles with his patron William Hayley at Felpham. In September 1803, when the Blakes moved from Felpham back to London, William and Catherine Sophia Blake stayed for a time with James and Catherine Elizabeth Blake at 28 Broad Street,[16] and James allowed his shop and home to be used to show Blake's private exhibition in 1809-10 and his Canterbury Pilgrims engraving in 1810.[17]

In later years, however, differences grew between Blake, with "his head ... in the clouds amid radiant visions", and James with his head "bent downwards, and studying the pence of this world".[18] James "pestered his brother the Artist with timid sentences of bread & cheese advice",[19] and after James retired on a little annuity in 1812 to Cirencester Place, "they did not even speak".*

Blake's younger brother John, born on 20 March 1760, was apparently a charming and promising boy—at least he charmed his parents, whose "favourite" he was. He was also "dissolute disreputable", and self-pitying. Though William repeatedly "remonstrated" with his parents over their indulgence to John, he "was often told to be quiet, & that he would bye & bye beg his bread at Johns Door".[20] There was plainly rivalry among the Blake children for their parents' favour, and the others resented John's strong pre-eminence in his parent's affections.

Blake's youngest brother and his favourite was Robert, born on 19 June 1762.[†] He was an "amiable & docile" boy[21] "much beloved by all his companions" such as J.T. Smith.[22] William thought of Robert as a fellow spirit and even as a spiritual guide, and years later in his *Milton* he made mirror images of "William" and "Robert" receiving the inspiration of Milton (Pls 4A–B).

Catherine Elizabeth Blake, born on 7 January 1764, the baby of the family and the only girl, was six years younger than Blake and would have been only eight years old when he moved out as an apprentice. She helped her mother in the house, and after the deaths of her parents in 1784 and 1792 she became the housekeeper of her bachelor brother James who "supported

---

* Gilchrist (*BR* 3). James Blake was buried in Bunhill Fields on 2 March 1827, but the poet's letters give no hint that he was mourning a brother then.
† Robert is probably the son of James and Catherine Blake born on 19 June 1762 and christened "Richard" at St James's, Westminster.
  By a remarkable coincidence, a Robert Blake, born on 4 Aug 1767, was admitted to study engraving at the Royal Academy on 2 April 1782, and *BR* (20 and *passim*) tentatively assumed that this was Blake's brother. However, Frederick Tatham says that when Robert was buried on 11 Feb 1787 he was "24 Years of age" (*BR* 510), and this corresponds exactly with the age of the boy christened Richard Blake in June 1762 but not with that of Robert Blake the student-engraver at the Royal Academy born in April 1767. See Aileen Ward, "Who Was Robert Blake?", *Blake*, XXVIII (1995), 84–9.

his only Sister".[23] She helped William when he moved to Felpham in 1800 and visited him there repeatedly. When she was a young woman, Blake's friend Thomas Butts thought her "charming",[24] but with advancing years and persistent spinsterhood she became "somewhat shy and proud; with precise old-maidish ways", "decidedly a *lady* in demeanour".[25]

There were other members of the family as well, who must have come for family festivities and whom the Blakes probably visited in fine weather. Blake's paternal grandparents lived across the Thames in Rotherhithe, near the great docks, and his maternal grandparents named Wright may have lived in the parish of St George's, Hanover Square, where Catherine Wright lived when she married Thomas Armitage in 1746. Catherine Wright may have had siblings and nephews and nieces as well; Blake had a cousin in Hampstead[26] and an aunt who was buried in Bunhill Fields[27] who are probably on his mother's side of the family. He apparently had an uncle named John Blake who lived in Glasshouse Street, Westminster, in 1743 and in Hogg Lane, Soho,* in 1778-88, and a cousin named Stephen Blake, haberdasher, who was at 28 Broad Street in 1783 and 1784. William Blake probably knew the siblings of his mother's first husband: William Armitage and his son Thomas, Richard and John Armitage, and Elizabeth Armitage Fox and Grace Armitage Hattersley.

The Dissenting Tradition and Blake's Family

Both Read the Bible day & night
But thou readst Black where I read white[28]

Blake's parents raised their children in the Dissenting tradition† of private devotion and private Bible reading rather than public catechism and public worship. But we do not know their church or creed. Like most Dissenters, they believed that all truth lies in the Bible and that the proper interpreter of that truth is the individual conscience, not the priest or the church. The term

---

* John Blake of 32 Hogg Lane was a Breaches Maker, according to his Sun Fire Assurance policy No. 477751.

† According to Crabb Robinson in *Vaterländisches Museum* (1811): "Blake nicht zur bischöflichen Kirche, sondern von Geburt zu einer dissentirenden Gemeinde" (Blake belongs not to the established church but by birth to a dissenting sect) (*BR* 440, 452). Blake was buried in the Dissenting Burial Ground at Bunhill Fields (Aug 1827), as were his father James (1784), his brother Robert (1787), his mother Catherine (1792), his brother James (March 1827), his aunt, and his wife Catherine Sophia (1831).

No early biographer identifies the church to which the Blakes belonged. E.P. Thompson, *Witness Against the Beast* (1993) makes an intriguing but tentative and inconclusive case for the Muggletonians.

used in the eighteenth century for extreme Dissent like this was Enthusiasm, and Blake identified himself as an "Enthusiastic hope-fostered visionary".*

Such Enthusiasts believed that Christ came to release man from the Covenant of the Law, from the "Priest & King Who make up a heaven of our misery",[29] so that "henceforth every man may converse with God & be a King & Priest in his own house".† They believed that all institutions, beginning with the Church and the State, were tyrannical attempts to bind to Satan's Kingdom the souls which Christ had come to free, for "Christ hath redeemed us from the curse of the law" (Galatians iii, 13); as Blake wrote, "One Law for the Lion & Ox is Oppression".‡ Christ

> His Seventy Disciples sent
> Against Religion & Government[30]

For the Muggletonians, "the Devil Reason" "always blasphemed and fought against God",[31] and Blake wrote of "The Great Satan or Reason" ("Laocoon"):

> Serpent Reasonings us entice
> Of Good & Evi*l*, Virtue & Vice
>
> (*For the Sexes* pl. 19, ll. 7–8)

Many Enthusiasts may have felt as Inflammable Gas does in *An Island in the Moon*: "Id see the parsons all hangd[;] a parcel of lying—",§ and Blake wrote that "All Penal Laws ... are cruelty & Murder".[32]

Such Enthusiastic beliefs were the essence of William Blake's credo. He did not attend public worship in St James's, Piccadilly, or anywhere else for the last forty years of his life,** from 1787 to 1827: "I have ... sought to

---

* Letter of 26 Nov 1800. In 1806, Malkin referred to Blake's "Enthusiastic and high flown notions on the subject of religion" (*BR* 424), and on 11 Aug 1800 William Hayley wrote: "I cannot write the word Enthusiasm without recollecting that worthy Enthusiast, the ingenious Blake".

† Annotation (1798) to Watson's *Apology for the Bible* (1798) p. 9. In his letter of 12 April 1827, Blake wrote of "The Mind in which every one is King & Priest in his own House".

‡ *Marriage* pl. 24, ¶90 (note that two of the four faces of the Living Creature seen by Ezekiel i, 10, represented a lion and an ox). Blake wrote of "The Abomination that maketh desolat*e*, i.e State Religion, which is the Source of all Cruelty" (annotation to Watson's *Apology for the Bible* p. 25). He refers to the world as "Satan's Kingdom" in his note (1798) on the title page of Bacon's *Essays* (1798).

§ *Island in the Moon* Chapter 4. In his Notebook p. 103 Blake wrote:

> An answer to the parson
> "Why of the sheep do you not learn peace [?]"
> "Because I dont want you to shear my fleece"

** Smith (*BR* 458); Crabb Robinson wrote in 1811: "wir nicht glauben, dass er sich regelmässig zu irgend einer christlichen Kirche halte" ("we do not believe that he goes regularly to any Christian church") (*BR* 440, 452).

worship God truly—in my own house, when I was not seen of men".[33] "His greatest pleasure was derived from the Bible,—a work ever in his hand",* and he "warmly declared that all he knew was in the Bible".[34] "The book of Revelation ... may well be supposed to engross much of Mr. Blake's study",† as with most such Enthusiasts. "The Bible, he said, was the book of liberty."[35] He read the Bible not just for doctrine or Truth; even in old age he was deeply moved by it: "on one occasion, dwelling upon the exquisite beauty of the parable of the Prodigal, he began to repeat a part of it; but at the words, 'When he was yet a great way off, his father saw him,' he could go no further; his voice faltered, and he was in tears."[36]

Of course like all the more extreme Dissenters, such as John Bunyan, Blake did not read the Bible merely in its literal or its orthodox senses. "He understands by the Bible the Spiritual Sense For as to the natural sense that Voltaire was commissioned by God to expose."[37] For Blake, as for Swedenborg, the true Bible, "the Books of the Word", excluded Job, Proverbs, the Song of Solomon, the Apocrypha, the letters of St Paul, and about a quarter of the Protestant canon.[38]

Some of Blake's conclusions from his reading of the Bible would have been regarded as heresy by almost any church.‡ He said that the Atonement "is a horrible doctrine"[39] and that Christ "was wrong in suffering himself to be crucified".[40] He asserted that "he did not believe in the *omnipotence* of God",[41] and he believed that Christ "*is the only God ...* And so am I and so are you".[42]

It was not only in their dependence upon the Bible and their neglect of the Church that such Enthusiasts differed from members of the Church of England and from many other Dissenters. They rejected not only the vanities of the world but all the ways of the world together. For them, as for Blake, the world is ruled by the Beast and the Whore, the age of miracles is still with us, and the Apocalypse is now.

Blake was, he said, "the companion of Angels", and with them as with his dead brother Robert "I converse daily & hourly in the Spirit".§ Miracles were familiar to him, and he wrote: "I live by Miracle".** For Blake, "Satan

---

* Smith (*BR* 467). Hayley said that Blake was "a most fervent admirer of the Bible", and J.T. Smith asserted that "his Bible was every thing with him" (*BR* 106, 458).
† Smith (*BR* 426). Blake made many splendid pictures based on the Book of Revelation, including some sensational ones of The Beast and the Whore (see Pls 1–5).
‡ Crabb Robinson (*BR* 439, 452) says that "Blake's religiöse Meynungen schienen diejenigen eines rechtgläubigen Christen zu seyn" ("Blake's religious opinions appear to be those of an orthodox Christian"). However, he had not then met Blake, his conclusion seems to be based chiefly on *Descriptive Catalogue* (1809), and it is contradicted by other evidence he presents.
§ Letter of 6 May 1800. He wrote on 12 Sept 1800 that "Angels stand round my Spirit in Heaven", and on 7 Oct 1803 he said: "if on Earth neglected I am in heaven a Prince among Princes".
** Letter of 26 Aug 1799. "*If* you do not find that you have both done such miracles & lived by such you do not see as I do.... I can & do work such as both astonish & comfort me & mine" (marginalium to Watson, *Apology* p. 13).

... is father & God of this World[,] The Accuser",[43] and "The Prince of darkness is a Gentleman & not a Man[;] he is a Lord Chancellor" like Francis Bacon,[44] the ruler of the realm where "The Beast & the Whore rule without control". For Blake, the Beast and the Great Red Dragon are heroic, monstrous forms with the horns and crowns of civil and religious power (Pl. 5).

The more extreme Dissenters such as the Muggletonians rejected not only the state and the state church but all churches and all church-ritual. They believed, as Blake did, that "The outward ceremony is Antichrist".[*] The extravagantly naive Little Vagabond in *Songs of Experience* complains that,

the Church is cold,
But the Ale-house is healthy & pleasant & warm . . . .

But if at the Church they would give us some Ale,
And a pleasant fire our souls to regale;
We'd sing and we'd pray all the live-long day,
And never once wish from the Church to stray.

The naive little stray was not extravagant by the standards of Dissenters such as the Muggletonians. Because they might be harassed socially and even legally under the Conventical Act if they gathered in their own churches, they met for worship in a private room in an ale-house. There they sat by the pleasant fire and talked of Godly subjects and sang hymns of their own composition set to popular tunes, so that neighbours would overhear pub-songs, not church-tunes.[†] It is not the church which sanctifies the congregation for such Dissenters but the pious congregation which sanctifies the place—even if the place is an ale-house. Whether or not Blake's family worshipped thus, he had clearly heard of and respected the practice.

Some of the most unusual beliefs among Dissenters were held by the Muggletonians, a dwindling band of determined worshippers clinging to a faith first articulated during Cromwell's time a century before. They believed that Jesus "*is the only God*", as Blake did,[45] and consequently that

---

[*] "Laocoon". In *Jerusalem* pl. 91, ll. 12–14, Los urges men to

overthrow their cup,
Their bread, their altar-table, their increase & their oath:
Their marriage & their baptism; their burial & consecration.

[†] See E.P. Thompson, *Witness Against the Beast* (1993), 58. In the middle of the eighteenth century, the Muggletonians met at The Blue Boar and the Nag's Head in Aldersgate Street, at The Gun in Islington, and in The Hampshire Hog off Goswell Street (Thompson, *Witness*, p. 67), and there were "Muggletonian meetings" in Barnaby Street and Old Street Square (according to Henry Chamberlaine, *A New and Compleat History and Survey of the Cities of London and Westminster* [London: J. Cooke, (1770)], 615). The first session of the general conference of the New Jerusalem Church on 13 April 1789, attended by William and Catherine Blake, was held in a public house.

God ceased to exist between the death of Jesus and His resurrection. They "believe that that outcast [serpent-]angel ... did enter into the womb of Eve", and Blake shows the Serpent-Satan wrapped round Eve as if in copulation in his colour-print of "Satan Exulting over Eve" (1795) (Pl. 6) and his watercolour of "The Temptation and Fall of Eve" for *Paradise Lost* (1808) (Pl. 105). In this coupling, Satan "died and quickened again in the womb of Eve ... [*and*] Eve brought forth her first born the son of the devil", Cain, who was the father of the reasonable line of temporal power, while Adam was the father of Abel and the faithful race of spiritual power.[46] In Blake's *Jerusalem* (pl. 73, ll. 35–40), Rahab and Tirzah ("Thou Mother of my Mortal part") create the line of temporal power, "Satan Cain Tubal Nimrod Pharoh Priam" through the English monarchs, while "Los Creates Adam Noah Abraham Moses Samuel David Ezekiel", the line of spiritual power, and in his "Laocoon" Blake wrote of Jehovah's "two Sons Satan & Adam".

Throughout Blake's writings we hear of "Priests in rustling scales" and their "Lies and Priestcraft".[47] For instance, he described the worldly Bishop Watson as "a State trickster" and "an Inquisitor",[48] and he wrote:

> The King & the Priest must be tied in a tether
> Before two virgins can meet together*

For the cynical Dissenter, the Church of England was a place where

> the gates of this Chapel were shut,
> And "Thou shalt not" writ over the door ...
> And Priest in black gowns were walking their rounds,
> And binding with briars my joys & desires.
>
> ("The Garden of Love" from *Experience* [*Songs* pl. 44])

Almost certainly Blake derived the essence of this credo of Enthusiasm from his family.

For Blake, the world is an alien environment, a realm ruled by the Beast and the Whore. Natural causes and their effects are illusions: "We who dwell on Earth can do nothing of ourselves, every thing is conducted by Spirits" (*Jerusalem* pl. 3). We live "not by Natural but by Spiritual power alone", for "every Natural Effect has a Spiritual Cause" (*Milton* pl. 26, ll. 40, 44). As for the Blakes,

> We eat little, we drink less;
> This Earth breeds not our happiness.[49]

---

* Notebook p. 106. In his annotations (1798) to Bacon's *Essays* (1798) p. 38, he says that "Every Body hates a king".

Blake was continually sustained by "The Bread of sweet Thought & the Wine of Delight",[50] and even in sorrow and want he wrote: I "rejoice in the exceeding joy that is always poured out on my Spirit".[51] Like the Eternals in *Milton*, he was sometimes "Drunk with the Spirit",[52] with "enthusiasm or rather madness, for I am really drunk with intellectual vision".[*]

When he wrote

The Angel that presided oer my birth
Said "Little creature formd of Joy & Mirth
Go live without the help of any Thing on Earth"

(Notebook p. 32)

he did not mean that his parents neglected him or that he found no friend. Rather, he meant that "This World is too poor to produce one Seed",[53] that our only sources of joy and mirth lie within us, in the mind, rather than outside us, on the earth. Blake's parents were loving and giving, but they could not give him the heavenly beauty and spiritual peace which is to be found only within us, in Christ, or, as Blake came to call Him, in the Human Imagination.

The Blake Home in Broad Street

The neighbourhood of Golden Square where Blake grew up was notable for artists and folk of modest fashion. The painter Jean Etienne Liotard lived at the sign of the Two Yellow Lamps in Golden Square (1754); Matthew Bramble in Smollett's *Humphry Clinker* (1760) brought his family to Mrs Norton's lodging in Golden Square; the great anatomist John Hunter resided in Golden Square (1763), as did the fashionable painter Angelica Kauffmann (about 1767), and David Hartley (1797), whose edition of his father's *Observations on Man* (1791) Blake illustrated.

In Broad Street itself, the very successful Italian stipple-engraver Francesco Bartolozzi and his apprentices lived in 1768–74; the Swiss painter Henry Fuseli was at the corner of Broad Street and Poland Street in 1777–81; the engraver Francis Chesham lodged at 37 Broad Street in 1777 and at 33 Broad Street in 1778; the rising young engraver James Heath was at Broad Street, Carnaby Market, in 1780,[†] and R. Playe published caricatures at 37

---

[*]   Letter of 23 Oct 1804. William Carey described him as a "rapt Enthusiast" (*BR* 246), and in his letter of 25 April 1803 Blake wrote: "I see the face of my Heavenly Father[;] he lays his Hand upon my Head & gives a blessing to all my works. . . . Excuse my perhaps too great Enthusiasm."

[†]   Heath's address is given in the subscription list of the *New and Complete Universal History of the Holy Bible*, ed. Edward Kimpton (?1781). Heath's engraving after Francis Wheatley of the Gordon "Riots in Broad Street" (1780) is not set in Broad Street, Golden Square, as Peter Ackroyd believes (*Blake* [1995], 74), but in the Broad Street in the City (see Pl. 8).

Broad Street in 1784. John Varley, the ebullient painter and astrologer, lived in Broad Street about 1805, and his pupil William Mulready lived with him.

Antonio Canaletto, the great Venetian painter, lodged in 1749 with Mr Wiggan, the cabinetmaker in Silver Street, one street south of Broad Street,[54] the painter George Dawe, son of the engraver Philip Dawe, was born in 1781 in Brewer Street nearby; and Isaac Pocock, a student of the sculptor John Flaxman, lodged in Brewer Street.

In such a neighbourhood it was natural that the father of a boy with artistic gifts should think that honour and a respectable living could be gained in the world of art.

As was usual for tradesmen, James Blake and his family lived above the shop. The Blake house at 28 Broad Street (Pl. 7) consisted of four floors and a basement at the corner of Broad and Marshall Streets, and it shared walls with buildings to the North and East. Because it was on the corner, it did not have access to the open area behind the other houses (Pl. 8).

The land had only recently been developed, and James Blake could remember the time when the area was skylark fields. The row of houses on the north side of Broad Street, begun in 1733–34,[55] was built in a modestly ambitious style, with panelled rooms and balustrades and room for servants. The neighbourhood and the style of buildings were solidly bourgeois.

James Blake's shop was entered through an ornamental portico supported by wooden columns like "the gate of a little temple".* In the front, on the Broad Street side, as on the three floors above, there were three large windows,† and along the Marshall Street side there were two windows— until Pitt's window-tax made windows an expensive luxury, and James Blake walled in one window on each of the three upper floors. In the ground-floor windows were displayed the most alluring goods of the little

---

* M. Rouquet, *The Present State of the Arts in England* (London, 1755), 120, describing the ornamentation of London "shops, particularly the mercers" introduced "Within these few years". In 1790 James Blake was given "leave to ... erect Stone Columns in the stead of those [Columns of Wood] now placed before his House" at 28 Broad Street.

† On the lower floors, the Blakes' windows had segmented arches, unlike the windows of their neighbours. In 28 Broad Street, as

> In most houses the ground storey has been altered by the insertion of a shop- or public-house front in the early or mid nineteenth century [Pl. 7] ... The majority [*of the interiors in Broad Street*] have the standard plan of a single front room on each floor with a smaller room and a dog-legged staircase behind it, a closet sometimes projecting beyond the back room.... The rooms on the first three floors ... were originally, lined with simple rebated panelling in two heights finished with a moulded dado-rail and a box-cornice.... The staircases have moulded closed strings fixed into column, newels with big rectangular heads having moulded tops, and the turned balusters supported a moulded handrail.
>
> (*Survey of London Volume XXXI: The Parish of St James Westminster Part Two: North of Piccadilly* [London: The Athlone Press, 1963], 204–5])

hosiery shop and, in 1809, Blake's great engraving of the Canterbury Pilgrims.[56] Inside was a large room about 20′ x 20′, panelled in the early Georgian style.* On the Marshall Street side were two fireplaces on each floor, with a box for holding the coal that was shipped down from Newcastle. The north and east walls of the ground-floor shop were presumably lined with shelves to hold the goods for sale, and along at least one side there would have been a counter, behind which James Blake waited on his customers.

The three upper floors, where the family lived, were of the same floor dimensions as the shop, but they were low-ceilinged and divided into two or three rooms per floor. Probably the kitchen and the parlour were on the floor above the shop and the sleeping quarters on the top two floors, five or six bedrooms. The window through which God put his head in 1760 (see below) was probably one of the children's rooms on the top floor.

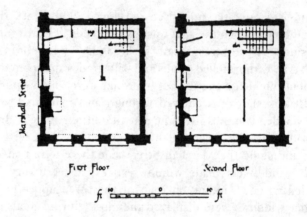

First Floor   Second Floor

When James and Catherine Blake were first married, they must have had space to spare, and their shop-assistants and maidservants could have slept on the top floor and still left room to rent to casual lodgers. As their brood of children grew to five, the space for servants and lodgers and goods for sale must have come under increasing pressure.

From a child's point of view, an enormous advantage of the house-over-the-shop was that both parents were always at home. Food and comfort were no farther away than a cry, and the shop itself must have been a familiar play-place when business was slow. The counter served as a drawing-

---

* At any rate, it was big enough to accommodate Blake's "Ancient Britons", 14′ × 10′, when it was exhibited there in 1809–10.

board, and the great windows provided a moving panorama of the crowded street, sedan-chairs bringing ladies to buy gloves, great rough shire-horses pulling old-fashioned hay-wains and manicured high-stepping ponies for the new-fangled curricles of the gentry, processions of shining charity-school children in their cherished uniforms, and grimy chimney-sweeps in their top hats. And on a summer's day, when the windows were thrown open, there would have been the sounds of iron-shod hooves on the cobblestones, street-vendors crying their wares, church-bells tolling the hours and the services, and mourning doves from Golden Square not far away.

Infancy and Childhood

The infant Blakes were probably laid to sleep in cradles of the kind shown in *Songs of Innocence* (Pl. 9) while their mother sang them traditional nursery rhymes:

> The sow came in with the saddle,
> The little pig rocked the cradle,
> The dish jumped o' top of the table
> To see the brass pot swallow the ladle.
> The old pot behind the door
> Called the kettle a blackamoor.
> "Odd bobbs" said the gridiron, "can't you agree?
> I'm the head constable, bring them to me."[57]

Some of the songs were almost entirely innocent of adult meaning, though none the less entrancing to an infant ear:

> This frog he would a wooing ride
>   Kitty alone Kitty alone
> This frog he would a wooing ride
>   Kitty alone & I
> Sing cock I cary Kitty alone,
>   Kitty Alone Kitty alone
> Cock I cary Kitty alone
>   Kitty alone & I

> (*Island in the Moon* Chapter 9)

When they were old enough to escape long dresses and adult supervision, the children played in the nearby streets and in the "very small, but neat" enclosure "with grass platt, and gravel walks ... surrounded with handsome iron railings"[58] in Golden Square. The smaller children would have played Hoodman Blind[59] and rolled hoops with a stick across the cobblestones and whipped their tops in the dirt and knelt on the ground playing marbles and the older ones would have climbed trees for birds-nests, flown kites, and played cricket in the street.[60] Joe's experience in *An Island in the Moon* (?1784) of bowling his cricket ball "on a turd"[61] has the ring of first-hand experience. And in horse-drawn London, turds would have been everywhere.

As a boy Blake was small and sturdy, remarkable first for his fiery hair and then for his compelling grey eyes.* As a young man, and probably as a boy, he "was short, but well made, & very well proportioned", with "a large head & wide shoulders ... his forehead was very high & prominent over the Frontals. His Eye most unusually large & glassy, with which he appeared to look into some other World." His yellow-brown hair "stood up like a curling flame, and looked at a distance like radiations".†

Such schooling as the young Blakes had was probably at their mother's knee (as we see on the title page of *Innocence*), for most Dissenters distrusted schools outside their sect, and Blake disbelieved in education entirely: "It is the great Sin[.] It is eating of the tree of the knowledge of good & evil."[62] He rejoiced in his escape from such moral taskmasters:

Thank God I never was sent to School
To be Flogd into following the Style of a Fool

(Notebook p. 42)

and he heartily sympathized with "The School Boy" in *Songs of Innocence* who mourned:

to go to school in a summer morn,
O! it drives all joy away:
Under a cruel eye outwor*n*,
The little ones spend the day

As the Blake children grew older, they could wander farther afield and find more adult sights and pleasures. Sheep and cattle were driven through the streets of London to Smithfield Market, and cocks crowed in the met-

---

* The colour of his eyes is given by Samuel Palmer (*BR* 291 n2). T.F. Dibdin wrote that in 1816 "his eyes [*were*] blue, large, and lambent" (*BR* 242). The unsympathetic Southey wrote on 8 May 1830: "his eyes [*had*] an expression such as you would expect to see in one who was possessed".

† Tatham (*BR* 529, 518). For Tatham's imagined version of Blake as a young man, see Geoffrey Keynes, *The Complete Portraiture of William & Catherine Blake* (London: The William Blake Trust, 1977).

ropolitan thoroughfares. Pigeon breeders cherished their broods on rooftops, and excited crowds of boys and men gathered round cock-fights. Grimy coal-men carried on their backs hundred-weight sacks suspended from bands round their foreheads, and costermongers cried their apples and potatoes from barrows on street corners. On the ever-fascinating river there were wherries and fishing-smacks and barges and fishermen on the banks, and at ebb tide there was the excitement of the water racing between the pillars of London Bridge with little boats careening down the crests. There were the raucous fishwives at Billingsgate Market and the hubbub among the vegetable sellers at Covent Garden and the meat stalls at Smithfield. Horses were everywhere, with public liveries and private stables and the great mail coaches rumbling to the country on Tuesdays, Thursdays, and Saturdays. At night the old men of the parish watch patrolled the cobbled streets with their rattles crying "Ten O'Clock and All's Well", and in the grander neighbourhoods link-boys with torches guided late-goers through the darkened streets to give warning of and to footpads. Puppet-players set up their stages from packs on their backs, jugglers tossed flashing knives to gather crowds, and at the great commercial gardens of Vauxhall and Ranelagh there were stunning fireworks. On festivals such as May Day there would be morris dancing behind the hobby-horse and chimney-sweeps parading in costume. On great occasions, such as the opening of Parliament, the King would ride through the streets in his gold and glass carriage surrounded by the silver, shining horse guards.

Probably few Londoners bothered to see their own sights, such as the Tower of London where Colonel Blood almost succeeded in stealing the Crown Jewels in 1671 and Buck House where George II lived and Wren's fine new cathedral at St Paul's, built after the great Fire of London in 1667. But they would all know the square mile of The City once within the Roman walls, the commercial heart of the spreading empire, and the great thoroughfares of the Strand near the Thames and fashionable Oxford Road and Pall Mall, and St Paul's Churchyard, the centre of the publishing world. The empire of law centred on the Inns of Court with their warrens of ancient offices and the gowned and wigged dignitaries who pursued their wordly craft there. Nelson's column and the National Gallery in Trafalgar Square and Regent Street and the British Museum on Bedford Square were all coming imperial triumphs of George III, but the city that made them possible was vibrant and grimy and alive all round the young William Blake.

For public entertainment there were plays at Covent Garden and Drury Lane and Italian operas and ballets, and in the streets and at fairs there were sword-swallowers and wire-dancers and Punch-and-Judy shows. Occasionally a prodigy would appear, a strong man or a fat woman or a boy from the South Pacific or a two-headed calf, and occasionally one might see the ancient spectacle of a Dancing Hare playing on a drum or a Learned Pig who could spell any word given to him and read the mind of any lady in the audience.[63]

There was very little in the way of public sports, but private sports proliferated.

For the wilder spirits there were bare-knuckle boxing matches and bear-baiting and public houses that advertised: "DRUNK FOR A PENNY; DEAD DRUNK AND STRAW TO SLEEP ON TUPPENCE".[64] There were ladies of the night and girls of the embankment and visits to Bedlam to see the poor, mad folk confined in straw and chains. And from time to time, a well-advertised cavalcade would clatter out from the great, gloomy prisons of the King's Bench and Newgate and the Clink across the river in Southwark, carrying condemned and trussed men, women, and boys through the crowded streets to be hanged in public at Tyburn, where Oxford Road meets Hyde Park, near where the Blakes lived. And after the drum-roll and the last drop, hawkers worked their way among the 'prentices and pickpockets and bloodthirsty gentlemen selling the Last Dying Speeches of the grim figures dangling from the gibbets.

Blake's city and his neighbourhood entered into his imagination, and he co-opted Golden Square and its little gated garden* into his city of the New Jerusalem. Once, when he was a child, Blake heard a traveller describing the wonders of a foreign city, and he broke in: "Do you call *that* splendid? . . . I should call a city splendid in which the houses were of gold, the pavement of silver, the gates ornamented with precious stones."† In his earliest poetry he wrote of "golden London, And her silver Thames",[65] and in mature years he said that "Heaven opens . . . on all sides her golden Gates".[66]

> And now the time returns again:
>   Our souls exult & Londons towers
> Recieve the Lamb of God to dwell
>   In Englands green & pleasant bowers.
>
> (Jerusalem pl. 77)

The earliest portals of paradise which Blake saw were probably the gates to the garden of Golden Square.

"This World . . . of Imagination & Vision"[67]

From his earliest childhood Blake saw visions. When he was four years old, God put his head to the window and set the child screaming,[68] and once "his mother beat him for running in & saying that he saw the Prophet Ezekiel under a Tree in the Fields."‡ Later, when he was eight or ten, one day as he was walking on Peckham Rye, near Dulwich Hill in the Surrey countryside not far from his grandfather's residence in Rotherhithe (Pl. 10), he saw "a tree filled with angels, bright angelic wings bespangling every bough like stars". When he told this story at home, it was "only through his mother's intercession . . . [*that he escaped*] a thrashing from his honest father, for

---

* A 1754 plan of Golden Square shows a tree-less and shrub-less octagon with a statue in the middle and a gravel circle around it (*Survey of London Volume XXXI: The Parish of St James Westminster Part Two: North of Piccadilly* [London: The Athlone Press, 1963], 145 and pl. 120b).

† Gilchrist (*BR* 7). Clearly this is a heavenly city. Cf. *Jerusalem* pl. 85, ll. 22–3, in which Jerusalem says: "I see thy Gates of precious stones; thy Walls of gold & silver".

‡ Tatham (*BR* 519); "the Fields" suggests that Blake was far from home when he saw Ezekiel. Blake reports a conversation with Ezekiel in *Marriage* pl. 12: "The Prophets Isaiah and Ezekiel dined with me, and I asked them . . .".

telling a lie". Another time, on a summer morning he saw "the hay-makers at work, and amid them angelic figures walking".*

Clearly both parents were concerned by Blake's stories of seeing visions,[69] though the fault may have lain not in seeing the visions but in speaking of them. Blake spoke familiarly of visions as if they were common-places, as indeed they were to him: "when he said *my visions* it was in the ordinary unemphatic tone in which we speak of trivial matters that every one understands & cares nothing about . . .. Of the faculty of Vision he spoke as One he had had from early infancy—He thinks all men partake of it—but it is lost by not being cultiv^d."[70]

Blake's visions were not cloudy nothings; they were minutely organized, as were the visions of the biblical prophets:

> The Prophets describe what they saw in Vision as real and existing men whom they saw with their imaginative and immortal organs; the Apostles the same; the clearer the organ the more distinct the object. A Spirit and a Vision are not, as the modern philosophy supposes, a cloudy vapour or a nothing: they are organized and minutely articulated beyond all that the mortal and perishing nature can produce. He who does not imagine in stronger and better lineaments, and in stronger and better light than his perishing mortal eye can see does not imagine at all. The painter of this work asserts that all his imaginations appear to him infinitely more perfect and more minutely organized than any thing seen by his mortal eye.
>
> (*Descriptive Catalogue* ¶68)

And in his Vision of the Last Judgment he wrote:

> I assert for My Self that I do not behold the outward Creation & that to me it is hindrance & not Action[;] it is as the dirt upon my feet, No part of Me.
>   "What" it will be Question'd "When the Sun rises, do you not See a round Disk of fire somewhat like a Guinea[?]"
>   O no no I see an Innumerable company of the Heavenly host crying "Holy Holy Holy is the Lord God Almighty"[71]

On 6 May 1800 Blake wrote to console William Hayley on the death of his only son:

---

* Gilchrist (*BR* 7), calling the Peckham Rye angels "his first vision". Gilchrist says his authority is Blake himself ("as he will in after years relate"), but the story probably came through Catherine Blake and Tatham. In any case, the vision of God at the window is earlier. And see Addenda, below.

I know that our deceased friends are more really with us than when they were apparent to our mortal part. Thirteen years ago I lost a brother & with his spirit I converse daily & hourly in the Spirit & See him in my remembrance in the regions of my Imagination. I hear his advice & even now write from his Dictate. . . . even in this world . . . I am the companion of Angels.* May you continue to be so more & more & to be more & more perswade*d*, that every Mortal loss is an Immortal Gain. The Ruins of Time builds Mansions in Eternity.

This is the language of Enthusiasm.

The Boy with the Pencil

From his earliest childhood, Blake showed a passion and a capacity for art. This had been remarked by the time he was three years old[72] and still infantile in elocution and locomotion. His father wanted him to be "educated for his own business" as a hosier, learning sums and accounts and a handsome hand for writing bills and calculations of bolt-length and price-per-yard and profit-margins. However, the boy "neglected the figures of arithmetic", "drew designs on the backs of all the shop bills, and made sketches on the counter".[73]

The child, like the man, was daring and impetuous, not to say head-strong. Everything he did was done with whole-hearted determination, from climbing trees to refusing to go to an ordinary school to persisting with his drawings in shop and field.

By the time he was ten, he was old enough to be of some use in the little hosiery shop, carrying parcels and delivering messages and even lending a hand in showing goods to customers when his father was busy. One chore was probably fetching fish oil from the vestry of St James's Church for the lamp which had to be lit outside the shop on moonless nights.[74]

For Blake there was no allure in the arts of the haberdasher's apprentice, who must learn

to handle a yard with great dexterity, to wind tape neatly upon the ends of my fingers, and to make up parcels with exact frugality of paper and pack thread; . . . the true grace of a counter bow, the careless air with which a small pair of scales is to be held between the fingers, and the vigour and sprightliness with which the box, after the ribband has been cut, is returned to its place.[75]

---

* "I am under the direction of Messengers from Heaven Daily & Nightly" (letter of 10 Jan 1802).

Such simple chores were distasteful to him when all he wanted to do was to draw.

His indulgent father therefore agreed that he was never likely to make a shopman and allowed him to enroll in the Drawing School of Henry Pars[*] near Beaufort Buildings in the Strand a mile or so from Broad Street. For a boy of only ten and a father in only a modest way of business, this was a large indulgence, both foregoing the boy's service and paying his fees.

But there was yet a greater sacrifice to be made. Dissenters like James Blake were eager Bible readers and vigorous disputants. They sang hymns lustily and sometimes wrote them; they reproved the works of the Beast in private and in print; and they kept to themselves and to their trades. They did not buy profane pictures and statues or go to public plays and concerts, and they did not perform in public in painting or on stage for the followers of the Beast and Whore. James Blake's scruples as a Dissenter must have been strained when he indulged his wilful, determined son by allowing him, indeed paying substantial sums to enable him, to become first an art student and then an apprentice engraver.

At Henry Pars's Drawing School, boys were trained to copy prints of famous paintings and casts of classical statues. They began by "copying drawings of Ears, Eyes, mouths, & Noses"[76] and a head and finally a whole human figure—the human figure being the fundamental measure of all art, as the Greeks and neo-classicists taught and as Blake always believed. Such copying was the principal method of teaching, one which Blake clearly performed well. "Copying Correctly . . . is the only School to the Language of Art."[77] He kept all his life a sketchbook he made when he was fourteen, and he probably used it for teaching his brother Robert as he did, many years later, when he was teaching the wife of his patron John Linnell.[†]

The most admired art was that of the Greeks and Romans, and the students at Henry Pars's Drawing School may have had special advantages in learning about and seeing such art. Henry's younger brother William was already making the drawings in Italy and Greece which brought a flood of new information about classical sculpture and architecture to an eager audience throughout Europe, and some of these dis-

[*] Malkin (*BR* 422). "This school was established by Mr. William Shipley, in the year 1755" to train "Youths of genius" in drawing and to introduce them to "masters of the several Arts and Manufactures, in which Elegance of Taste and Correctness of Drawing are required"; the boys have obtained "many of the premiums for Drawings, offered by the Society for the Encouragement of Arts, Manufactures, and Commerce" ([Thomas Mortimer], *The Universal Director*, Part I [1763], 21).

[†] On 20 Oct 1825, Blake brought to Mrs Linnell in Hampstead "a Sketch Book, of Copy from Prints & which he made when about 14^{yrs} old" (*BRS* 113), in 1771. This sketch-book is not known to have survived; probably it disappeared in Tatham's holocaust of Blake's papers.

coveries may have filtered through to the excited little boys in Henry Pars's Drawing School.

Doubtless the boys were also taught some of the principles of perspective and the properties of oil colours and appropriate subjects and techniques of landscape painting, but probably these were of negligible attractiveness to the ten-year-old Blake. They certainly were to the man, who scarcely made a person-free landscape in his life and who came to abominate the use of oil.

Of course Pars's Drawing School could provide only copies in the way of models, and it was very important for the boys to see fine originals as well. At the very best, engravings translate designs in one medium such as oil paintings into a new system of representation, without colours and with solid shadows represented by parallel lines and cross-hatching. Before the founding of the Royal Academy in 1769 and the National Gallery fifty years later, there was very little in the way of publicly accessible art except in the great churches such as Westminster Abbey and St Paul's Cathedral and St James's, Westminster.

But some collectors were generous in allowing their pictures and sculptures to be seen by the public. For most such collections, it was desirable that the public should be well-dressed gentlemen and ladies, and usually the visitors were expected to make an appointment and to present a suitable douceur to the butler who admitted them.*

These conditions were normally impossible for schoolboys, but the Duke of Richmond gave permission for the boys at Pars's School to draw in his Gallery.[78] By such means "Blake, very early in life, had the ordinary opportunities of seeing pictures in the houses of noblemen and gentlemen, and in the king's palaces".[79]

But casts at Pars's Drawing School and paintings in the houses of noblemen were only temporary expedients. What was needed by a serious student like the ten-year-old Blake was constant access to good models. Therefore "His father bought for him [*casts of*] the Gladiator, the Hercules, the Venus of Medicis, and various heads, hands, and feet."[80]

Perhaps the casts of classical sculpture were bought from the cast-maker John Flaxman at the Sign of the Golden Head, New Street, Covent Garden. There William could have met the vendor's precocious son John,† who was

---

* According to Anon., *English Connoisseur* (1766), I, viii: "many of the collections of the great are ever open to the inspection of the curious ... it must be lamented that some are not accessible without difficulty and interest". A newspaper of 1764 said that "The fawning, cringing addresses to those who have it in their power to show them, together with their gaping expectations of what you will give them, is very disagreeable" (W.T. Whitley, *Artists and their Friends in England, 1700–1799* [1928], I, 167).

† Tatham says that Blake and Flaxman "had known each other from boyhood" (*BR* 521), though J.T. Smith says that Blake "became acquainted with Flaxman" "After leaving his instructor" Basire in 1779 (*BR* 456).

 Perhaps plaster-figure makers and modelers of the 1770s hired out statues as B. Papera of 16 Marylebone Street, Golden Square, did thirty years later; in 1804 Sarah Harriet Burney wrote: "By subscribing a shilling a week to Papara, the Plaisterman, I got what busts or whole length figures I pleased" (*The Letters of Sarah Harriet Burney*, ed. Lorna J. Clark [Athens & London: University of Georgia Press, 1997], 56, 58).

two years older than Blake and who was already eagerly preparing to be a sculptor. The deep friendship between the two men when they reached manhood may have begun in these early years of hope and promise for each of them.

The casts probably included not only The Dying Gladiator, the Hercules Farnese, and the Venus de Medici but also the Apollo Belvedere and the Dancing Faun, for, years later, when he was painting his "Ancient Britons", Blake's friends advised him to "take the Apollo for the model of your beautiful Man and the Hercules for your strong Man, and the Dancing Faun for your Ugly Man".[81] And when Blake copied the "Hercules Farnese", the "Venus de Medicis", and the "Apollo Belvedere" in 1815 for Rees's *Cyclopaedia*, he may have been working at home from his own models.*

It was not only casts which the young artist bought.

The same indulgent parent soon supplied him with money to buy prints; when he immediately began his collection, frequenting the shops of the print-dealers, and the sales of the auctioneers. Langford called him his little connoisseur; and often knocked down to him a cheap lot, with friendly precipitation. He [*bought and*] copied Raphael and Michael Angelo, Martin Hemskerck and Albert Durer, Julio Romano, and the rest of the historic class, neglecting to buy any other prints, however celebrated. His choice was for the most part contemned by his youthful companions, who were accustomed to laugh at what they called his mechanical taste.[82]

One can imagine the fiery eagerness with which the fire-haired boy ransacked print shops such as William Wynne Ryland's in the Strand and John Boydell's in Cheapside and haunted auction houses such as Christie's and Langford's. A boy twelve or fourteen years old† among the hardened dealers and elegant connoisseurs must indeed have been a notable phenomenon.

The little house above the shop in Broad Street, with seven or eight small rooms for two adults and five children, cannot have had much space to

---

*   The Apollo Belvedere is apparently the model for David in "David and Saul" (1780–85) (Butlin #118) and for Apollo in "The Overthrow of Apollo" (*c*. 1815) for Milton's "Nativity Ode" (Butlin #542 4), while the Hercules Farnese is the basis for Lot in "Lot and His Daughters" (tempera, 1799–1800) (Butlin #381) and for Giant Despair in "Christian and Hopeful Escape from Doubting Castle" for *Pilgrim's Progress* (1824–27) (Butlin #829 26).

Hogarth's *Analysis of Beauty* (1753) pl. 1 represents a jumble of statues including Hercules Farnese, Venus de Medici, Apollo Belvedere, and Laocoon.

†   Abraham Langford (1711–74) died when Blake was sixteen, so Blake must have made a mark in the print-auction rooms before 1774. Blake kept his prints through all his moves until he sold them in 1821.

spare, and the modest hosiery business is unlikely to have supported much in the way of luxuries beyond food and clothing and furniture. The prints which the young Blake bought, and his statues, must have absorbed a disproportionate amount of family space and of family income.

Blake's predilection for the *Cinquecento* masters was early and emphatic. In his indignant annotations to the conventional Royal Academy lectures of Sir Joshua Reynolds, Blake wrote: "I am happy I cannot say that Rafael Ever was from my Earliest Childhood hidden from Me. I Saw & I Knew immediately the difference between Raphael & Rubens[.]"*

It was only during Blake's lifetime that Michelangelo became the standard of the dedicated and inspired artist of the sublime. For Blake, however, Michelangelo and Raphael were from his boyhood the touchstones of taste. In his *Descriptive Catalogue* (1809) ¶3 he wrote: "The eye that can prefer the Colouring of Titian and Rubens to that of Michael Angelo and Rafael, ought to be modest and doubt its own powers." He admired Michelangelo's self-dedication as much as his genius, and, according to his disciple Samuel Palmer, "He loved to speak of the years spent by Michael Angelo, without earthly reward, and solely for the love of God, in the building of St. Peter's ...."[83] Blake's enthusiasm was so great and so public that in later years he was referred to by at least one of his friends (C.H. Tatham) as "Michael Angelo <u>Blake</u>".[84]

Blake's indulgent father provided him with money for more than prints and casts, for even as a boy Blake had a significant collection of books. Such a breadth of reading so deeply absorbed at such an early age is prodigious. Who encouraged him in proclivities so unusual in a Dissenting family, and where did he get such books? Genius is inherent, but it must be fostered or lost, and books must be bought. And he had no school education, no formal fostering of his knowledge and taste.

Perhaps his mother nurtured her strange son's passion for poetry as she had his delight in drawing. Certainly nothing we know of his pence-counting father suggests a love of literature. The volumes of Chaucer and Shakespeare and Milton over which the boy pored may have come from her family. Her son's knowledge of contemporaries like Burke and Chatterton and Macpherson might have been picked up from current fashions, but the Elizabethan volumes such as Francis Bacon's *Tvvo Bookes* and Ben Jonson's *Masque in Honour of Lord Haddington's Marriage* were far from the fashions

---

* Marginalium to Reynolds, *Works* p. xiv. The unfashionable nature of Blake's allegiance to the masters of the *Cinquecento* is indicated by a story told by John Linnell in his autobiography (p. 26) about "a dealer who was so bitter upon this point that he said to me one day when I had asserted my belief that fine color was to be found in M. Angelo's frescoes—'I'll tell you what' he said. 'I think Michael Angelo was a pinkyfied son of a bitch'[.]"

of the 1770s. Blake's impressive, indeed prodigious self-education may have been protected and encouraged by his mother.

Blake read widely and not merely on the religious subjects one might expect from his Dissenting family. He immersed himself in the Bible of course, and he read the works of his contemporaries Dr Johnson and Thomas Chatterton and Macpherson's Ossian and Thomas Gray. But he also absorbed Chaucer and Spenser and Milton and John Donne and the Metaphysical poets, as his earliest poetry shows. Shakespeare's "Venus and Adonis", his "Tarquin and Lucrece", and his sonnets, which at the time were "little read, were favourite studies of Mr. Blake's early days. So were Jonson's Underwoods and Miscellanies."[85] Probably from a very early date he owned Bysshe's *Art of English Poetry*[86] and Bishop Percy's *Reliques of Ancient English Poetry* (1765). He knew and admired the works of Bishop Berkeley and of Jacob Behmen or Boehme, and he bought books on art such as *A Political History of the Years 1756 and 1757* (?1757) with 75 caricatures (dated by Blake 29 May 1773) and Raphael's *Historia del Testamento Vecchio* (1698) (signed "W Blake 1773").[87]

He was familiar with the foundations of eighteenth-century philosophy, with Bacon's *Tvvo Bookes: Of the Proficience and Aduancement of Learning* (1605) and Locke's *Essay on Human Understanding* and Newton, and Burke's *Philosophical Enquiry into the Origin of our Ideas of the Sublime and Beautiful* (1756).*

He not only read these books, but he annotated them as well, which indicates the indulgence of his family in permitting him to deface such expensive works:

> I read Burkes Treatise when very Young[;] at the same time I read Locke on Human Understanding & Bacons Advance[ment] of Learning[;] on Every one of these Books I wrote my Opinions ... [of] Contempt & Abhorrence. ... They mock Inspiration & Vision[.] Inspiration & Vision was then & now is & I hope will always Remain my Element[,] my Eternal Dwelling Place.
>
> (*Marginalia to Reynolds's Discourses* p. 244)

While yet a boy, he was impressively widely read and even learned.

At the same time that he was studying at Pars's Drawing School and buying prints and casts and books and poring over them, he was writing poetry. His earliest surviving poetry was written when he was eleven,[88] and

---

* In his *Island in the Moon* (Chapters 8–9), Blake quotes Joseph Addison, *Cato* (1713), James Hervey, *Theron and Aspasio* (1755), Henry Wootton, *Reliquae Wottonianae* (1685), and he cites there James Hervey, *Meditations and Contemplations* (1746–47), Homer, Pliny (with a pretend quotation), William Sherlock, *A Practical Discourse upon Death* (1689), Robert South, and Edward Young, *Night Thoughts* (1742–47).

it would be surprising if he had not written earlier poems which were discarded. The earliest verse we can identify is the song beginning "How sweet I roam'd", which "was written before the age of fourteen" and which his friend Benjamin Heath Malkin compared to "The Hue and Cry after Cupid" in Ben Jonson's *Masque in Honour of Lord Haddington's Marriage.*[*] Certainly the Elizabethan echoes are marked:

> How sweet I roam'd from field to field,
>   And tasted all the summer's pride,
> 'Till I the prince of love beheld,
>   Who in the sunny beams did glide!
>
> He shew'd me lilies for my hair,
>   And blushing roses for my brow;
> He led me through his gardens fair,
>   Where all his golden pleasures grow.
>
> With sweet May dews my wings were wet,
>   And Phœbus fir'd my vocal rage;
> He caught me in his silken net,
>   And shut me in his golden cage.
>
> He loves to sit and hear me sing,
>   Then, laughing, sports and plays with me;
> Then stretches out my golden wing,
>   And mocks my loss of liberty.
>
> (*Poetical Sketches*, 10)

Marriage as a cage and love as a tempter and betrayer are sophisticated concepts for a boy of twelve or thirteen.

Blake's four years at Pars's Drawing School, from the age of ten to fourteen, confirmed him in his conviction that his happiness and his genius lay in making beautiful shapes. His masters plainly saw promise of accomplishment in him, and they and the boy persuaded his father to allow him to continue with his art. The greatest question must have been how to reconcile his compulsion to draw pictures with the necessity of earning a living.

---

[*]   Malkin (*BR* 428). "How Sweet" was quoted in print by Malkin and J.T. Smith and in MS by Crabb Robinson and Frederick Tatham (*BR* 428–9, 457, 224n3, and 513).

Rambles in Surrey

From his childhood, Blake was a great rambler, and as soon as he was free of constant parental supervision he probably began to explore for himself, finding first the ramifications of his own neighbourhood, and then those of the nearby squares and markets, and finally reaching into the countryside itself, which was then not very far away, across the silver Thames in Surrey. These rambles may well have included calls upon members of his family, such as his grandparents in Rotherhithe and others in Battersea.*

Blake's pleasantest memories were always with the Surrey side of London. "In his youth he and his Wife would start in the Morning early, & walk out 20 miles & dine at some pretty & sequestered Inn & would return the same day home having travelled 40 miles.... Blake has been known to walk 50 Miles in the day...."[89] He would walk through the countryside south of the city of London (Pl. 10) "to Blackheath, or south-west, over Dulwich and Norwood hills,† through the antique rustic town of Croydon, ... to the fertile verdant meads of Walton-upon-Thames; much of the way by lane and footpath."[90]

In his last years, Blake went often to visit his young friend and patron John Linnell in Hampstead, to the north of London, but the northern suburbs did not agree with him. On 31 January 1826, he wrote: "When I was young Hampstead Highgate Hornsea Muswell Hill & even Islington & all places North of London always laid me up the day after & sometimes two or three days with precisely the same Complaint...." It was in the villages and countryside of Surrey that he felt at home. His later poetry has fond reminiscences to "the Vale of Surrey" and "another pleasant Surrey Bower":[91]

The Surrey hills glow like the clinkers of the furnace

(*Milton* pl. 4, l. 14)

Los & Enitharmon rose over the Hills of Surrey

(*Milton* pl. 44, l. 31)

The little Villages of Middlesex & Surrey hunger & thirst

(*Jerusalem* pl. 30, l. 25)

---

* Gilchrist (*BR* 21) says Blake had relatives in Battersea, Frederick Tatham says that Catherine Boucher in Battersea "lived near his father's house" (*BR* 481), and when Blake was married to her he was recorded as "of the Parish of Battersea" (*BR* 21, 22), indicating that he had been there at least four weeks. For a list of Blakes living then in Battersea (none known to be related to the poet), see *BR* 22 n1.

† See Addenda, below.

Surrey and Sussex are Enitharmons chambe*r*,
Where I will build her a Couch of repose . . . .

(*Jerusalem* pl. 83, ll. 25–6)

But by 1772, when he was fifteen, it was time to make a decision about his future. His rambling childhood days were over.

CHAPTER II

1772–1779: The Visionary Apprentice

Engraving is the profession I was apprenticed to[1]

The Wrong Master

"Father, I do not like the man's face: *it looks as if he will live to be hanged*".[2]

This was a strange conclusion to a business interview. It was even stranger because the boy was only fourteen years old.

James Blake and his son had been talking to Mr Ryland about whether Ryland would take the boy as an apprentice.

William Wynne Ryland, a debonair artist, engraver, and print-seller, had studied in France under François Boucher, and on his return he had established in England the French chalk or stipple manner of engraving. His success was extraordinary, he became Engraver to the King, and his fees were huge—Ryland had charged £100 to take an apprentice just eight years before.[3]

But there was more to it than that. Ryland's print-selling business had gone bankrupt only a few months before, in December 1771, a fact notorious in the print trade. Ryland must have been hard pressed for cash in the spring of 1772.

A decade later, he was so desperately pressed that he turned his professional calligraphic skills to forgery. You may think that engravers to the King are not usually forgers, and sometimes indeed they are not. But the jury was persuaded that Ryland had forged bills on the East India Company for the colossal sum of £7,114, and he was sentenced to death. On 29 August 1783 he was hanged on Tyburn Tree.* The event may have left its mark on Blake in his frequent references to "Tyburns fatal Tree" "on Tyburns brook among the howling Victims".[4]

James Blake must have thought that serving an apprenticeship under such a paragon of fashion and fortune would set up his perplexing young son for life, and he was willing to cope with the expense.† How strange to break off because the boy did not like the man's face (Pl. 11).

Blake's father cannot have known that Mr Ryland would live to be hanged, but he heeded his son's objection to Ryland's ominous face and took the boy elsewhere. It was well that he did so. In later years, William Blake had a deep aversion to fashionable stipple engraving, because, he said, it softened and blurred the sharp, distinct outlines of a design. His prejudice may have begun with his encounter with the fashionably indistinct Mr Ryland.

The choice of a master was far more important than merely finding a good teacher, for the master became a surrogate father. For seven years, seven days a week, the boy lived and worked with his master, ate his master's food, and slept in his master's house, often sharing a bed with the master's son. The domestic character of the master was as important as his professional skill and his ability and inclination to impart it. The boy's adolescence would be tolerable or intolerable depending upon his master and his master's family. Blake's instant and intense antipathy to Ryland was a very important consideration, whatever its basis.

The Right Master

Instead, James Blake took his son to call on James Basire at 31 Great Queen

---

* See Addenda below.

† Tatham (*BR* 510–11), echoed by Cunningham (*BR* 478), says that

> a painter of Eminence was proposed & necessary applications were made, but from the huge premium required, he requested with his characteristic generosity that his Father would not on any account spend so much money on him, as he thought it would be an injustice to his brothers & sisters; he therefore himself proposed Engraving as being less expensive & sufficiently eligible for his future avocations.

It seems likely that Tatham's "painter of Eminence" requiring a "huge premium" and Gilchrist's eminent, grasping stipple-engraver cum artist are the same individual.

Street, near Covent Garden, where they could "easily find the House by the name *Basire* on the door".[5] James Basire, Citizen and Stationer, was a distinguished topographical and antiquarian engraver in mid-career; he had been apprenticed in 1745 and began taking apprentices of his own in 1765. He was the principal engraver to the Society of Antiquaries and the Royal Society, and their voluminous publications provided him with abundant work, sufficient to enable him to take on thirteen apprentices from 1765 to 1799. Shortly before the Blakes called on him, in 1771, his engraving of Benjamin West's "Pylades and Orestes" had made a great stir. He was a gentle, meticulous man, and young Blake must have perceived at once that *he* would not live to be hanged (see Pl. 12).

James Basire and James Blake agreed on the terms of apprenticeship, and this time the boy did not object. Therefore, on Tuesday 4 August 1772, when the Court of Assistants of the Stationers' Company held its monthly meeting, "James Basire of Great Queen Street Lincolns Inn ffields Engraver", "James [Blake] of Broad Street Carnaby Market Hosier", and young William Blake assembled at 9:30 a.m. with other masters, boys, fathers, and guardians before the gowned officers of the Court of the Company in Stationers' Hall near St Paul's Cathedral. There William Blake was formally apprenticed to James Basire as an "Engraver [*for*] seven years [*for a*] Cons[*ideratio*]ⁿ [*of*] £52.10.—paid by his ffather" to Basire plus a Stationers' Hall fee of 9s.6d. and a stamp-duty of £2.12.6.

The indenture stated in carefully legalistic terms that for seven years

the said Apprentice his said Master faithfully shall serve, his Secrets keep, his lawful Commandments every where gladly do.... He shall not waste the Goods of his said Master, nor lend them unlawfully to any. He shall not commit Fornication, nor contract Matrimony within the said Term. He shall not play at Cards, Dice, Tables, or any other unlawful Games, whereby his said Master may have any Loss. With his own Goods or others, during the Said Term, without License of his said Master he shall neither Buy nor Sell. He shall not haunt Taverns, or Play-Houses, nor absent himself from his said Master's Service Day nor Night unlawfully ... And the said Master ... his said Apprentice in the same Art and Mystery which he useth, by the best Means that he can, shall Teach and Instruct, or cause to be Taught and Instructed, finding unto his said Apprentice, Meat, Drink, Apparel, Lodging, and all other Necessaries, according to the Custom of the City of *London*, during the said Term. And to the true performance of all and every the said Covenants and Agreements either of the said Parties binds himself unto the other by these Presents. *In witness* whereof, the Parties above-named to these Indentures interchangeably have put their Hands and Seals the

[*Fourth*] Day of [*August*] in the [*thirteenth*] Year of the Reign of our Sovereign Lord King [*George the Third*] of *Great Britain*, &c. and in the Year of our Lord 17[*72.*]

One copy of the indenture was kept by the master and one by the father or guardian of the boy.

It was probably on the date of the indenture, 4 August 1772, that Blake's mother helped him pack up his clothes and books and prints and statues, and move from 28 Broad Street, Golden Square, into his new home with his new foster-father at 31 Great Queen Street, Covent Garden.

Basire lived in a substantial seventeenth-century building refaced in Georgian times and painted green. Almost across the street was the Free Mason's Tavern. The painters Godfrey Kneller, Thomas Hudson, and Joshua Reynolds (as an apprentice) had lived in the same street, as did the dramatist Richard Brinsley Sheridan, and close by was the staid and august Lincoln's Inn with its wigged and gowned attorneys and Covent Garden with its vegetable markets and theatres.

If Blake was allowed to bring prints and books to his new home, he was given a rare privilege, for apprentice-space was always very limited. A sign that he was given this privilege may be found in his purchase of the Abbé J.J. Winckelmann's *Reflections on the Painting and Sculpture of the Greeks* (1765) which he inscribed with adolescent hubris "William Blake, Lincoln's Inn", as if he were a member of the dignified legal Inns of Court.

Basire and the Antiquarian Society were well suited to one another, for Basire's style was old-fashioned line-engraving, the style of Dürer and Marcantonio, rather than the flashier and more fashionable stipple or mezzotint or (later) lithography. His forte was the accurate representation of old buildings and monuments. When a Roman mosaic floor was uncovered, or a fourteenth-century mural found under the whitewash on a church wall, the eager antiquaries called on Basire to record it. His subjects were from the past and mostly English. Authors who wanted accurate illustrations of *Sepulchral Monuments of Great Britain* or *An Analysis of Ancient Mythology* or *Ancient Monuments in Westminster Abbey* or *The Antiquities of Athens* turned first to James Basire.

And his apprentices of course learned his methods and followed his virtues. All his life, Blake's engraving style was described as old-fashioned, hard and dry, what he called "the Style of Alb Durers Hist[o]ries & the old Engravers".[6] This was the style he had learned as an apprentice, and his greatest triumph in line-engraving, his *Illustrations to the Book of Job* (1826), is manifestly derived from his tutelage by Basire.

The Engraving Studio

Basire's studio seemed a chaos of curious tools and strange smells. There were racks of gravers for engraving and etching-needles for etching and burnishers for smoothing the copper and hammers for correcting mistakes by pounding the back of the copper. Nearby were an oil-stone for sharpening gravers and needles, wax and feathers for smoothing wax, candles for smoking plates, varnish, and a magnifying glass. In a cupboard were the expensive thin sheets of copper and pots of aquafortis, and on a counter was a burner for heating wax and plates and varnish (Pl. 13). Each engraver had a little round sand-bag on which to rest the copperplate, so that he could turn the plate on an angle, and a screen to keep out the glare of direct sunlight reflected from the polished copper.

And then there was all the apparatus for taking proofs and checking on the progress of the engraving. The bulkiest object in the room was the heavy wooden rolling-press with its great arms for pulling the plate beneath the roller and its blankets for making minute adjustments to the pressure. Beneath a shelf holding pots of solid ink was a counter with a marble slab for rolling out the oily black printing-ink. On the slab were dabbers for inking the plates and dirty rags for wiping off excess ink, and in another cupboard was the expensive handmade paper for pulling proofs. And near the ceiling were lines for pinning up the drying prints (Pl. 14).

There seemed to be ink everywhere, on the marble slab and the copper-plates and oily rags and on the apprentices's hands,[*] noses, eyebrows, smocks, and ears, making them look like printer's devils. Everything they touched might turn black until the littlest of the boys was soundly smacked and made to clean his hands with turpentine and heavy soap before going to another job.

And over everything hung the intoxicating smell of aquafortis biting into the copper as it was etched.

In short, it was the orderly chaos of work. Blake lived with this chaos for the rest of his life and turned it into beauty. Later in life, as a practising engraver, "his rooms were clean and orderly; everything was in its place. His delightful working corner had its implements ready—tempting to the hand. The millionaire's upholsterer can furnish no enrichments like those of Blake's enchanted rooms."[7]

One of the earliest lessons the dreamy, impulsive apprentice had to learn was the necessity of patience and perseverance. As he wrote later, "Engraving is Eternal work".[8]

---

[*]   Tatham speaks of books he acquired from Blake which were "dirtied by his graving hands" (*BR* 41 n4), though the surviving copies do not exhibit these printers' stigmata.

The Engraver's Craft

For almost a year, Blake was Basire's only apprentice. He learned to grind gravers and planish plates and pulverize ink and dampen the paper for pulling proofs. These were the most rudimentary skills of his trade, but, far from bridling at such fundamental drudgery, Blake learned under the kindly tutelage of Basire to take pride in all the facets of his craft. He later wrote with the scorn of a trained professional that the very successful engraver William Woollett "I know did not know how to Grind his Graver ... he has often proved his Ignorance before me at Basires by laughing at Basires Knife tools &c ridiculing the Forms of Basires other Gravers till Basire was quite dashd & out of Conceit with what he himself knew ..." (Public Address, Notebook pp. 46–7). The images of the smithy in Blake's poetry, such as "The Tyger", may be connected with beating copper at an engraver's studio.

When the young apprentice was allowed to take up a graver, with the knob in the heel of his hand and his forefinger along the top of the blade, he was taught to push the tool away from him in straight lines, adjusting the copper on the sand-bag to alter the direction of the cut. By changing the angle of the blade, he could make the incision broad or narrow. He learned to represent shading by hatching and cross-hatching the plate, or by the newer method of dot-and-lozenge, which gave an appearance less regular and mechanical than cross-hatching, and most intricate of all were twisting worm-lines, a specialty of Basire's studio.

Blake was justifiably proud of the craft he learned in Basire's shop, and he wrote once: "I defy any Man to Cut Cleaner Strokes than I do or rougher where I please."[9]

Blake also learned to etch a copperplate with acid. The first step was to cover a copperplate evenly with wax so that the etching needle could draw through it, thus exposing the metal surface which was to be bitten with acid. Years later, when he was working with the amateur engraver George Cumberland, Blake explained to him what would have been known to any apprentice:

As to laying on the Wax it is as follows
   Take a cake of Virgins Wax ... & stroke it regularly over the surface of a warm Plate (the Plate must be warm enough to melt the Wax as it passes over)[,] then immediately draw a feather over it & you will get an even surface which when cold will recieve any impression minutely[.]
Note[:] The danger is in not covering the Plate <u>All over</u>[.] ...
   The pressure necessary to roll off the lines is the same as when you print, or not quite so great.

(Letter of 6 Dec 1795)

By 4 August 1772, when Blake joined the household in Great Queen Street, Basire had already taken two apprentices. The first of them, Thomas Ryder, was within a fortnight of completing his term, and the second, John Ward, apprenticed just two years before, had been "turned over by Consent of proper parties [*on 7 April 1772*] to Samuel Sonsby of White Cross Street Citizen and Joiner for the Remainder of his Term".[10]

One of Blake's early exercises was to copy a drawing by Salviati of the Centurion in Michelangelo's fresco of "The Crucifixion of St Peter", a burly, bearded, melancholic figure with crossed arms and downcast brows. Almost as soon as the young Blake had been shown the uses of Basire's tools, when he was fifteen, he engraved the design, later inscribing it "Engraved when I was a beginner at Basires".

The work is a prodigious accomplishment for a beginner. The highlights of the wave-crests, the variety of textures on rocks and sky and clothing, the modelling on the arms and legs demonstrate a flexibility of technique and a confidence of stroke far beyond what one might expect from a beginner with a graver. It is a work of extraordinary promise.

But characteristically Blake transmuted the significance of the subject. He adapted the design of the Roman Centurion to suit Joseph of Arimathea, the disciple of Jesus who buried Him in the cave-tomb, and he incorporated the legend used in Malory's *Morte D'Arthur* (1485) and Spenser's *Faerie Queene* (1596) that Joseph had come to England bearing a cruet of Christ's blood (the Holy Grail) which he buried in the wattle church he founded at Glastonbury. Still later Blake identified Joseph as an archetype of the Christian artist and the suffering prophets who "wandered about in sheepskins and goatskins ... (Of whom the world was not worthy)" (Hebrews xi, 37–8). And about 1810 he inscribed the final state of the print (Pl. 15):

> JOSEPH of Arimathea among The Rocks of Albion
> Engraved by W. Blake 1773 from an old Italian Drawing
> This is One of the Gothic Artists who Built the Cathedrals in what we call the Dark Ages Wandering about in sheep skins & goat skins of whom the World was not worthy[;] such were the Christians in all Ages
> Michael Angelo Pinxit

Thus in his adaptation (*c.* 1810) of his earliest surviving engraving (*c.* 1773), Blake demonstrated the idiosyncratic Dissenting Christianity, the fascination with syncretic mythology, the focus upon England or Albion as the centre of psychic energy, and the extraordinary originality which were to mark all his greatest works in poetry and design for the rest of his life. The print is also an indication of his life-long habit of preserving and expanding his ideas over many years, reading ever deeper significance into them. As he wrote in his Notebook:

Reengraved Time after Time[,]
Ever in their Youthful prime
My Designs unchangd remain

(p. 87)

Since the image on a copperplate appears backwards when printed, all the images on the copper had to be reversed if they were to come right on paper. One of the most difficult skills to be learned by the apprentice engraver was reversed or mirror writing for titles and signatures. There were, of course, specialist Writing-Engravers who created calligraphic title pages and who perfected the crude letters scratched on the copper by the design-engraver, but all engravers had to have the rudiments of the skill. Blake worked hard at learning mirror-writing, practising on blank pages of his *Island in the Moon* and elsewhere. His own works in Illuminated Printing are, of course, all written in mirror-writing on the copper, with occasional tiny mistakes at first.* In time he became a master at the art, as may be seen in his inscriptions to his *Illustrations of the Book of Job* (1826) (Pl. 20). He challenged his reader by leaving some marginal verses in *Jerusalem* in mirror-writing (see Fig. on p. xvii), and his letters sometimes blossom into foliage or tiny figures as on the title page of *Songs of Innocence* (1789) (see Fig. on p. 17 [right]). According to John Linnell, "The most extraordinary facility seems to have been attained by Blake in writing backwards",[11] and Blake's friend George Cumberland praised "the talents of a <u>Blake</u>, who alone excels in that art".†

At Basire's, the boy met the artists and engravers and authors who were creating the great age of English book illustration. One day within a year or so of Blake's moving into Great Queen Street, Oliver Goldsmith, poet, novelist, literary man-of-all-work, and Professor of Ancient History at the newly founded Royal Academy, "walked into Basire's.... The boy—as afterwards the artist was fond of telling—mightily admired the great author's finely marked head as he gazed up at it, and thought to himself how much *he* should like to have such a head when he grew to be a man."[12]

One can easily enough understand the boy's enthusiasm for the great

---

* In *There is No Natural Religion*, for instance, the imprint on the frontispiece is backwards, and later Blake changed his mind as to which side of the letter "g" should have the serif at the top.
† George Cumberland, "Hints on various Modes of Printing from Autographs", *Journal of Natural Philosophy, Chemistry, and the Arts*, XXVIII (Jan 1811) (*BRS* 65). Blake had helped Cumberland with the inscriptions to the plates in Cumberland's *Thoughts on Outline* (1796).

author's literary character, but his admiration for Goldsmith's physiognomy is more idiosyncratic. Goldsmith's face (Pl. 16), marked by small-
pox, with a heavy brow over anxious eyes, a protuberant upper lip and
receding jaw, struck most contemporaries as being "course and vulgar", as
Boswell said,[13] like that of a low mechanic such as a journeyman tailor,
rather than "finely marked". Blake's judgments of physiognomy, like many
of his other judgments, were often perplexing to his contemporaries.

The boy is likely to have seen a good many of the authors for the Society
of Antiquaries such as the distinguished architectural antiquary Richard
Gough and the enterprising linguistic antiquary Jacob Bryant and the energetic radical antiquary Thomas Hollis for whose works Basire signed many
engravings, some of them drawn or engraved by his apprentice William
Blake. And young Blake certainly met the great engravers of the time, for
Basire was on friendly terms with many of them. Through Basire, Blake
learned their capacities and their secrets, and his conclusions did not always
match those of his master.

> I knew the Men [William Woollett & Robert Strange] intimately from
> their Intimacy with Basire my Master* & knew them both to be heavy
> lumps of Cunning & Ignorance as their works Shew .... Wool[/]etts best
> works were Etchd by [*his apprentice*] Jack Brown[*e.*] Wool[/]ett Etchd
> very bad himself. Stranges Prints were when I knew him all done by
> Aliamet & his french journeyman .... I also knew something of Tom
> Cooke who engraved after Hogarth ....
>
> (Public Address, Notebook pp. 55, 57, 60)

And he rejoiced when he found that some of Basire's professional friends
agreed with Basire and his apprentice that the basis of both engraving and
all linear art is drawing: "Gravelot once Said to My Master Basire 'de
English may be very clever in deir own opinions but dey do not draw de
draw' ".[14] As Blake said, "Engraving is drawing on Copper & Nothing
Else".[15]

Drawing in Westminster Abbey

Unlike many engravers' apprentices beginning their term, Blake was
already a trained and moderately accomplished draughtsman when he
began at Basire's, and he could be trusted to make accurate copies. Very

---

* Woollett was presumably the godfather of Richard Woollett Basire who was christened while Blake
  was an apprentice to Basire.

early in his apprenticeship, he may have been set to copying prints or objects in the exact size needed for the commissioned engraving.

Blake worked happily as Basire's only apprentice for almost a year. Then, on 3 August 1773, Basire took on James Parker, the son of Paul Parker of St Mary le Strand, corn chandler. Parker was not a boy as Basire's other apprentices were, for he was already a young man—he was about twenty-two when he came to live with Basire. He must have been eager to become an engraver, but he is unlikely to have been as docile as those who began at the age of fourteen or fifteen, and he must have found it hard to be junior in skill and seniority to a boy only two-thirds his age. He was a careful, methodical man (Pl. 17), and in later years he and Blake became both friends and partners in a print-shop.

But at first there was friction between the apprentices which destroyed the harmony in the engraving-studio:

Blake, not chusing to take part with his master against his fellow apprentices, was sent out to make drawings.* This circumstance he always mentions with gratitude to Basire, who said that he was too simple and they too cunning.

He was employed in making drawings from old buildings and monuments, and occasionally, especially in winter, in engraving from those drawings. This occupation led him to an acquaintance with ... Gothic monuments.... He saw the simple and plain road to the style of art at which he aimed, unentangled in the intricate windings of modern practice. The monuments of Kings and Queens in Westminster Abbey, which surround the chapel of Edward the Confessor, particularly that of King Henry the Third, the beautiful monument and figure of Queen Elinor, Queen Philippa, King Edward the Third, King Richard the Second and his Queen,† were among his first studies. All these he drew in every point he could catch, frequently standing on the monument, and viewing the figures from the top. The heads he considered as portraits; and all the ornaments appeared as miracles of art, to his Gothicised imagination. He then drew Aymer de Valence's monument, with his fine figure on the top

---

* Malkin's account (echoed by all Blake's biographers) begins: "Two years passed over smoothly enough [*1772–74*], till two other apprentices were added to the establishment, who completely destroyed its harmony."

 However, the only other apprentice during Blake's term (Aug 1772–Aug 1779), except for the first and last fortnights, was James Parker, and he joined exactly one year after Blake did. Malkin's information seems to come from Blake himself, and it is rash to ignore or correct him, but his account of the strife caused by the "two other apprentices added to the establishment" of Basire's shop "Two years" after Blake's apprenticeship does not correspond with other verifiable facts.

† These heads are enumerated in the order they appear in Gough's *Sepulchral Monuments*, Vol. I, Part I (1786).

[Pl. 18]. Those exquisite figures which surround it, though dreadfully mutilated, are still models for the study of drapery ... to enumerate all his drawings ... would lead me over all the old monuments in Westminster Abbey, as well as over other churches in and about London.[16]

The Society of Antiquaries gave Basire commissions to make engravings for Richard Gough's *Sepulchral Monuments of Great Britain*, and Basire sent his apprentice to make sketches in Westminster Abbey and elsewhere, a very heavy responsibility for a sixteen-year-old boy. As a representative of such august authority, Blake was given permission to draw from scaffolding in the Abbey, and between services he was largely left alone in the cool vaulted solitude: "one day ... he saw ... The aisles and galleries ... suddenly filled with a great procession of monks and priests, choristers and censer-bearers, and his entranced ear heard the chant of plain-song and chorale, while the vaulted roof trembled to the sound of organ music."* The procession of choristers, with the plain-song echoing and diminishing as they move towards the altar, seems magical in such a setting whether it is vision or reality.

But if his spirit was exalted by such scenes, it was sorely tried by the cold, by the ruinous state of some of the monuments, and by the extreme difficulty of seeing the high tomb-covers from a vantage point. As he struggled to do justice to these marvels of art, his concentration was distracted by boys from Westminster School who used the Abbey as their chapel and who had a freedom there forbidden to others. Naturally they were intrigued by the studious young artist perched high above the monument, and then perplexed, and then tempted, until

one of them ... having already tormented him ... got upon some pinnacle on a level with his Scaffold in order better to annoy him. In the Impetuosity of his anger, worn out with Interruption, he [*Blake*] knocked him off & precipitated him to the ground, upon which he fell with terrific Violence. The young draughtsman made a complaint to the Dean, who kindly ordered that the Door should be closed upon them & they have never since been allowed to extend their tether to the Interior of the Abbey.†

---

* Paraphrase by Oswald Crawfurd, "William Blake: Artist, Poet and Mystic", *New Quarterly Magazine*, II (1874) (*BR* 13). The introductory passage says that the vision is one which "he afterwards records", but Blake is not known to have recorded this story. However, Gilchrist (*BR* 13) tells a somewhat similar tale, which may have been the basis for Crawfurd's: "Shut up alone with these solemn memorials of far off centuries—for, during service and in the intervals of visits from strangers, the vergers turned the key on him,—the Spirit of the past became his familiar companion. Sometimes his dreaming eye saw more palpable shapes from the past: once a vision of 'Christ and the Apostles,' as he used to tell ...".

† Tatham (*BR* 513); the Westminster boys were not permitted in the Abbey except for services, but schoolboys often do what is not permitted. The School has no record or tradition of such an incident.

When Sir Joseph Ayloffe was permitted to open the fourteenth-century tomb of Edward I in Westminster Abbey for an hour on 2 May 1774, he suggested that Basire should record the scene, and Basire entrusted his sixteen-year-old apprentice William Blake to make drawings of what was discovered. This was a serious responsibility and a wonderful opportunity, and Blake's was the only hand which recorded "The Body of Edward y.ᵉ 1.ˢᵗ as it appeared on first opening the Coffin" and "The body as it appeared when some of the vestments were remov'd."[17] Such an opportunity could never recur, for the body crumbled to dust upon being unwrapped.*

Blake's experiences with the monuments in the Abbey and in Gothic churches round London profoundly impressed the earnest apprentice, and their echoes stayed with him throughout his life, determining his style and his subjects and his sympathies. Many years later his young disciple Samuel Palmer wrote: "In Westminster Abbey were his earliest and most sacred recollections. I asked him how he would like to paint on glass, for the great west window, his 'Sons of God shouting for Joy,' from his designs in the *Job* [Pl. 19]. He said, after a pause, 'I could do it!' kindling at the thought."[†]

Blake's drawings from the monuments in Westminster Abbey are marvels of accuracy and beauty and were praised by contemporaries such as Thomas Stothard.[‡] And the engravings from the drawings may also have been made by Blake, though of course Basire signed them to authenticate them as from the studio of a master.

Blake's solitary hours among the Gothic monuments in Westminster Abbey confirmed his conviction that "Gothic is Living Form ... Eternal Existence", while "Grecian is Mathematic Form ... in the Reasoning Memory".[18] The flaming pinnacles and soaring arches of Gothic art haunted his designs from "The Meeting of a Family in Heaven" (1805) for Blair's *Grave* (1808) to the *Illustrations of The Book of Job* (1826) (Pl. 19). Figures outstretched on a tomb recur frequently in his designs, from the title page of *Songs of Experience* (1794) (see Fig. on p. 145]) to "The King, Councellor, Warrior, Mother & Child in the Tomb" (1805) for Blair's

---

* Something of this carnal reek survives in *Tiriel* (?1789), where Tiriel "is the king of rotten wood & of the bones of death", and where he curses his sons with "The stin*k* of your dead carcases annoying man & beast Till your white bones are bleachd with age" (ll. 76, 46–7).

    However, Blake's depictions of Edward I, in "Edward & Elinor" (1793) and in his design for Gray's "The Bard" (1797), show a vigorous though misguided hero, not a corpse.

† Gilchrist (*BR* 13–14). In the 1890s, William Blake Richmond, the son of Blake's disciple George Richmond, copied Blake's design of "The Sons of God Shouting for Joy" in the mosaics for the vault of St Paul's (*The Richmond Papers*, ed. A.M.W. Stirling [London, 1926], 378).

‡ J.T. Smith (*BR* 466). Blake may have helped to record the painting twenty-five feet long of the siege of a port discovered in 1775 in The Rose Tavern, just without Temple Bar: "A Drawing thereof was taken by Mʳ Basire, at Mʳ Gough's Expense, & Shewn to the Society [*of Antiquaries*] the 9ᵗʰ May 1776" (*BR* 423 n1).

Grave (1808) and Job's evil dream (1826). This is not an obsession with death but echoes of the highest forms of art.

Blake probably worked twelve hours a day, six days a week, on the tasks set him by Basire. However, a determined boy can always find interstices in the demands of work for his own interests, and during "the holiday hours of his apprenticeship", Blake made "a great number of historical compositions" (including "The Penance of Jane Shore", made before 1779*). "As soon as he was out of his time, he began to engrave two designs from the History of England",[19] and among the first works he advertised were "The History of England, a small book of Engravings"† and a much larger "Series of subjects ... from the History of England".[20] His ambitious line-engraving of "Edward and Elinor, a Historical Engraving", 12″ x 18½″ (1793), was probably for the larger series.

His fascination with medieval literature may be seen in his enthusiasm for Dante and Chaucer and Spenser and for Percy's *Reliques of Ancient English Poetry* (he owned the 1765 edition) and even for the pseudo-Gothic of Chatterton's Rowley poems (he owned the 1778 edition) and James Macpherson's Ossian poems whose damaged authenticity he defended defiantly: "I Believe both Macpherson & Chatterton, that what they say is Ancient Is so."[21] He wrote "An Imitation of Spencer" [*sic*] which was printed in his *Poetical Sketches* (1783), and his criticism of Chaucer's *Canterbury Pilgrims* in his *Descriptive Catalogue* (1809) was silently quoted by William Hazlitt[22] and praised by Charles Lamb as "most spirited".[23]

The forms of these ancient kings and queens haunted his visions as well. He spoke to Queen Philippa and Edward I and Edward's enemy William Wallace, he drew their portraits from the "life" as he did those of Edward III and Edward VI. The spirits of the monumental dead became a living part of his imagination.

But it was not only the sceptred English dead who absorbed his attention in these 'prentice years:

Now my lot in the Heavens is this; Milton lovd me in childhood & shewd me his face[;]
Ezra came with Isaiah the Prophet, but Shakespeare in riper years gave me his hand[;]

---

* *A Descriptive Catalogue* (1809) ¶112 says it was "done above Thirty Years ago".

  Blake's dates sometimes seem to refer to the conception or first draft of a work (such as "The Penance of Jane Shore") rather than to the date at which it was completed or printed. For instance, *Milton* and *Jerusalem* are each dated "1804" on the title page, but *Milton* is printed on paper watermarked 1808 and later and was probably first printed whole in 1811, while all copies of *Jerusalem* use paper of 1820 or later. Similarly, some copies of Blake's great colour prints dated 1795 are on paper of 1805 (see Martin Butlin, "The Physicality of William Blake: The Large Color Prints of '1795'", *Huntington Library Quarterly*, LII [1989], 1–17).

† No print is known of the smaller series, which Blake said is "now published".

Paracelsus & Behmen appeard to me, terrors appear'd in the Heavens
   above
And in Hell beneath & a mighty & awful change threatend the Ear[th.]
The American War began[.] All its dark horrors passd before my face ....

(Letter of 12 Sept 1800)

When he says "Milton ... shewd me his face" and "Ezra came with Isaiah the Prophet", he means it literally as well as figuratively. He told Crabb Robinson, "I have seen him [*Milton*] as a youth And as an old man",[24] and in *The Marriage of Heaven and Hell* (pl. 12) he teases us with a memorable fancy of when "The Prophets Isaiah and Ezekiel dined with me". The spiritual alchemists Paracelsus and Boehme "appeard to me" before he was eighteen when "The American War began" in 1776. And the worldly "terrors ... in Hell beneath" are echoed by spiritual "terrors in the Heavens". A boy of eighteen is vulnerable to the martial seductions of patriotism and the terrors of the press-gang, and some years later his brother John enlisted for a soldier.[25]

This was a formidable self-education—and it was only the beginning. Dissenting families were reading families, but few Dissenters read and observed as widely as this.

The Apprentice Poet

It was not only with drawings and engravings that Blake solaced the solitude of his holiday hours. He had been writing poems from the time he was eleven.[26] All are precocious, and some are extraordinarily accomplished. There is the predictable adolescent blood and thunder:

Beneath them roll'd, like tempests black,
   The num'rous sons of blood;
Like lions' whelps, roaring abroad,
   Seeking their nightly food.

("Gwin, King of Norway" ll. 17–20, *Poetical Sketches* p. 19)

And the new fashion for Gothic horror is inevitably visible:

The bell struck one, and shook the silent tower;
The graves give up their dead: fair Elenor
Walk'd by the castle gate, and looked in.
A hollow groan ran thro' the dreary vaults.

("Fair Elenor" ll. 1-4, *Poetical Sketches* p. 7)

As one might expect in a nation long at war, there is a deal of patriotic jingoism:

> Soldiers, prepare! Our cause is Heaven's cause[27]
> Liberty shall stand upon the cliffs of Albion,
> Casting her blue eyes over the green ocean;
> Or, tow'ring, stand upon the roaring waves,
> Stretching her mighty spear o'er distant lands;
> While, with her eagle wings, she covereth
> Fair Albion's shore, and all her families.
>
> ("Edward the Third" ll. 55–60, *Poetical Sketches* p. 55)

And even the pat morality expected in Augustan verse appears occasionally:

>   long a-gone,
> When men were first a nation grown,
> Lawless they liv'd—till wantonness
> And liberty began t'increase;
> And one man lay in another's way;
> Then laws were made to keep fair play.
>
> ("Blind-Man's Buff" ll. 65–70, *Poetical Sketches* p. 28)

Such poetry is less surprising in an engraver's apprentice than it is in the son of a Dissenter. The Enthusiasts among them believed that all dallying with temporal power was devilish, and, far from believing that "laws were made to keep fair play", they believed that Christ had come to destroy the law, sending his disciples "Against Religion & Government".[28] The characteristic act of civil power was war and as such an abomination to the faithful. Blake's sojourn in the Basire household is likely to have diluted the faith in which he grew up.

But some of the poetry is as hostile to Church and State as any Enthusiast could ask:

> When souls are torn to everlasting fire,
> And fiends of Hell rejoice upon the slain,
> O who can stand? O who hath caused this?
> O who can answer at the throne of God?
> The Kings and Nobles of the Land have done it!
> Hear it not, Heaven, thy Ministers have done it!
>
> ("Prologue" to "King Edward the Fourth" ll. 11–16, *Poetical Sketches* p. 56)

O what have Kings to answer for,
    Before that awful throne!
When thousand deaths for vengeance cry,
    And ghosts accusing groan!

          ("Gwin King of Norway" ll. 97–100, *Poetical Sketches* p. 23)

Here is a song which might well have been sung at the snug Sunday gatherings in the ale-house before the roaring fire.

One expects love-poetry from an adolescent boy, but the poems in his *Poetical Sketches* are about love rather than addressed to a lover. And their sexual suggestiveness is astonishing at a time when feminine limbs and passions were invisible and unmentionable. "Spring" is invoked to

Come o'er the eastern hills, and let our winds
Kiss thy perfumed garments; let us taste
Thy morn and evening breath; scatter thy pearls
Upon the love-sick land that mourns for thee.

O deck her forth with thy fair fingers; pour
Thy soft kisses on her bosom; and put
Thy golden crown upon her languish'd head,
Whose modest tresses were bound up for thee!

          ("To Spring" ll. 13–16, *Poetical Sketches* pp. 1–2)

And "Summer" is invited to

                     throw thy
Silk draperies off, and rush into the stream:
Our vallies love the Summer in his pride.

          ("To Summer" ll. 11–13, *Poetical Sketches* p. 2)

Combined with this sexual daring is a casualness or daring in prosody which would have left eighteenth-century readers breathless—or persuaded them in charity that these were the careless works of "untutored youth", as A.S. Mathew wrote in his preface. In an era taught to revere the brilliant regularity of Pope's heroic couplets and the majestic march of Milton's numbers, poetry like this which is neither end-stopped nor end-paused must have seemed astonishing or embarrassing. It is one thing to separate a verb from its object ("taste | Thy morn and evening breath"; "pour | Thy soft kisses"; "put | Thy golden crown") but quite another to divide an adjective from the noun it modifies ("throw thy | Silk draperies off"). And, most perplexing of all, some of the most beautiful passages depend upon such elisions, as in "To the Evening Star":

Thou fair-hair'd angel of the evening,
Now, whilst the sun rests on the mountains, light
Thy bright torch of love; thy radiant crown
Put on, and smile upon our evening bed!
Smile on our loves; and, while thou drawest the
Blue curtains of the sky, scatter thy silver dew
On every flower that shuts its sweet eyes,
In timely sleep. Let thy west wind sleep on
The lake; speak silence with thy glimmering eyes,
And wash the dusk with silver. . . .

("To the Evening Star" ll. 1–10, *Poetical Sketches* p. 5)

Had he written nothing more, Blake would deserve our remembrance for an evening star which could "speak silence with thy glimmering eyes, And wash the dusk with silver".

Mastery of the Engraver's Craft

By the time he had finished his apprenticeship, Blake was a thorough professional, confident in all the ramifications of his craft, prepared not only to engrave in any style but to teach engraving. For instance, he made Memoranda for himself about how "To Engrave on Pewter", "To Wood cut on Pewter", "To Wood cut on Copper", e.g.,

To Wood cut on Pew*ter*: lay a ground on the Plate & smoke it as for Etching. *T*hen trace your outlines and beginning with the spots of light on each object with an oval pointed needle scrape off the ground as a direction for your graver . . . .
    To Wood cut on Copper Lay a ground as for Etching, trace &ᶜ & instead of Etching the blacks Etch the whites & bite it in[.]

(Notebook p. 10)

And when he was helping with the engravings for George Cumberland's *Thoughts on Outline* (1796), Cumberland copied out

Blakes Instructions to Print Copper Plates
Warm the Plate a little and then fill it with Ink by dabbing it all over two or three times.—then wipe off all the superfluous In*k*, till the surface is clean—then with the palm of the hand <u>beneath the little finger</u> rubbed over with a little of the Ink & smoothed with whiting by rubbing it on a Ball of it. Wipe the surface of the Plate till it shines all over—then roll it

through the Press with 3 blankets above the Plate, and pastboards beneath it next the Plank—Paper may be used instead of Pastboard.[29]

It was a great day for Blake's family, and for English art, when Blake completed his apprenticeship to James Basire in August 1779. He was a fully fledged engraver, ready to practise and to train others in his craft.* Probably Basire observed the custom of his craft with a gift to the new journeyman engraver of money or of a double suit of clothes and the tools of his trade. With such a gift, the young man was trained and equipped to embark upon the ocean of business.

On 26 August 1779, after seven profitable, happy years in Basire's house at 31 Great Queen Street, Blake packed up his clothes, his books and prints and statues, his drawings, and his engraving tools and moved back to his birthplace and family at 28 Broad Street.[30] Another covering of earth was shaken off,[31] another step closer to heaven.

---

* Neither Blake nor his fellow-apprentice James Parker took up the Freedom of the City, for which they were eligible on the completion of their apprenticeships. This Freedom would have entitled them to take apprentices of their own and to set up in business within the square mile of the City, but, as each of them was working in Westminster rather than in the City of London, there may have seemed little point in doing so.

  J.T. Smith says that "Trotter, the engraver, ... received instructions from Blake" before 1780 (*BR* 466), but these instructions must have been informal advice rather than a formal apprenticeship.

CHAPTER III

1779–1787: "Delighted with Good Company"

William Blake
One who is much delighted with being in good company[.]
Born 28 Novr 1757 in London
& has died Several times Since[.][1]

"Blake be an Artist"

"The Man who never in his Mind & thoughts traveld to Heaven is No Artist."[2]

Not an artist? But Blake had been trained as an engraver. So he had, but the visions followed him into Basire's prosaic engraving shop and directed him how to go. "The spirit said to him 'Blake be an artist & nothing else. In this there is felicity[.]'"*

Blake was learning more and more explicitly that Heaven is the source of art, that the human imagination is the divine spirit, and that the road to temporal felicity lies through the creation of works of art by means of the divine spirit in the human imagination. Poetry, painting, engraving, music, sculpture, architecture: in the creation of these there is felicity.

---

* Crabb Robinson Diary of 10 Dec 1826: "His eye glistend while he spoke of the joy of devoting him-self solely to divine art." Within "divine art" he included engraving both in 1826, when he was making his Dante engravings, and in 1779.

But he still had to make his way in the world as an engraver, and he had yet to establish himself as an artist.

To consolidate his training as an artist under Henry Pars and as an engraver and artist under Basire, Blake applied in July to be a student at the Royal Academy in Somerset House in the Strand. To do so, he had to present a drawing, such as his copies of effigies in Westminster Abbey (Pl. 18) or of Joseph of Arimathea (Pl. 15), together with a testimonial from a respected artist such as his old teacher Henry Pars or his old master James Basire. His application was of course approved, for he had already been practising steadily as a student artist and then as a professional engraver for twelve years, and he was accepted to work as a Probationer in the Antique School of the Academy.

The Academy, founded with royal patronage in 1768, had quickly established itself as the primary avenue to fame and fortune for artists in Britain. Its purpose was to foster an ideal art derived from Greece and Rome suitable for the walls and cabinets of connoisseurs, rather than the mechanic, merely decorative arts appropriate to wallpaper and pottery and furniture. Its members and its patrons were gentlemen and ladies, and titles were cultivated—Royal Academicians carefully identified themselves with the suffix "R.A.", and two of the earliest Presidents of the Royal Academy, Joshua Reynolds and Thomas Lawrence, were knighted by their admiring sovereign. The Royal Academy encouraged engravers, for it was through engravings that Academicians could reach the largest and sometimes the most lucrative audience, but of course engravers were considered to be useful mechanics rather than real artists. An engraver could become an Associate of the Royal Academy but not a full Royal Academician.

The annual spring exhibitions of the Royal Academy attracted both the world of connoisseurs and the world of fashion; its library and its gallery of casts were admirable resources for lovers of classical and neo-classical art; and its free tuition and prizes for students of painting, sculpture, architecture, and engraving had a fundamental effect upon young artists. Becoming a student at the Royal Academy was the obvious step for any young Londoner aspiring to be an artist.

In October 1779, Blake and the other Royal Academy probationary students presented to George Moser, the venerable Keeper, their elaborate outlines, at least two feet high, representing an anatomical figure, with lists of the muscles and tendons.* When these probationary drawings were approved, Blake and the other six successful candidates, aged fourteen to

---

* Blake's friend John Flaxman, who was also a student at the Royal Academy, made drawings which were published after his death as *Anatomical Studies of the Bones and Muscles for the Use of Artists*, Engraved by Henry Landseer, ed. William Robertson (London: M.A. Nattali, 1833).

twenty-two, were issued on 8 October with ivory tickets which entitled them to draw in the Plaster Gallery of the Academy and to attend lectures and exhibitions for six years. Blake was admitted to study as an engraver. It would be nice to think that the students were welcomed by Joshua Reynolds, the President of the Royal Academy, on whose warranty the tickets had been issued.

The instruction at the Academy was highly organized. Students began with Plaster Models, and "Here he drew with great care, perhaps all, or certainly nearly all the noble antique figures in various views."[3] The students were required to present a drawing of a figure or a group and another, life-size, of a hand or foot.

They were then permitted to proceed to the Living Academy to sketch from nude models (Pl. 21)—and then only if they were older than twenty-one. The Living Academy models were posed from 4:00 p.m. in summer and from 6:00 p.m. in winter. The terms were 26 May to 31 August and 29 September (Michaelmas) to 9 April, with a holiday from Christmas Eve to Epiphany.[4]

Besides the regular schools of the Plaster and Living Models, there are four active Professorships in the Royal Academy, viz. of Painting, Anatomy, Architecture, and Perspective. The Professors are charged to deliver six lectures every year.... [*There is no*] provision in the Academy for instruction in Engraving ....*

Blake may have attended a few of each kind of lecture. William Hunter's lectures on anatomy were especially important to an artist whose drawings and poetry were to celebrate the Human Form Divine. Hunter may occasionally have persuaded his brother John the surgeon (Jack Tearguts, Blake's sometime neighbour in Golden Square) to demonstrate the layers and lay-out of muscles and intestines with a cadaver acquired from the resurrection men. When Blake later wrote that "a modern Man, stripped from his load of cloathing ... is like a dead corpse",[5] he was almost certainly speaking from experience.

When Blake first worked in the plaster gallery, the statues looked as the Greeks and Romans might have seen them, though of course without the paint. However, complaints were made about the explicit nakedness of the male statues, and in the spring of 1781 "an amputation of a most singular

---

* Prince Hoare, *An Inquiry into the Requisite Cultivation and Present State of the Arts of Design in England* (London: Richard Phillips, 1806), 127–8n, 125n. In 1806, the lectures on perspective "have been wholly omitted, and private tuition has been substituted", but in 1807 J.M.W. Turner was appointed Professor of Perspective.

nature [*was performed* on each cast] . . . and to each a plaister of fig-leaf [*was*] applied as a token, I suppose, of remorse". The correspondent of the *Morning Chronicle* for 5 May 1781, perhaps Blake's friend George Cumberland, expected to find next that they were clad "each in a pair of buckram drawers".*

Like students everywhere, the young artists were light-hearted, not to say disrespectful, "playing at leap frog, knocking off the hand of Michalangiolo's beautiful Fawn, spouting water, breaking the fingers of the Apollo, pelting one another with modeller's clay and crusts of bread, roasting potatoes in the stove, teizing the Keeper by imitating cats . . . ."[6] Blake tried the patience of the Keeper by challenging his most cherished ideas about art.

The young man found the emphatic neo-classicism of the Royal Academy narrow and stultifying. His own most glorious experiences of art had been with the Gothic monuments in Westminster Abbey, but the Gothic was invisible in the sculpture hall of the Academy and in most of its teachings. Blake preferred the rugged and the grand, while his teachers favoured the polished and the bland. He admired ancient frescos on church walls and painted medieval marble, and they stressed the more luscious effects of oil painting.

He relished the work of a few of the professors at the Royal Academy, such as the Professor of Ancient History Oliver Goldsmith (who died in 1774, before Blake became a student) and the Professor of Painting James Barry (elected in 1782). But with some of the most influential officers of the Academy he was at odds from the beginning:

> I was once looking over the Prints from Rafael & Michael Angel*o* in the Library of the Royal Academy[.] [*The Librarian George*] Moser came to me & said: "You should not Study these old Hard, Stiff & Dry, Unfinishd Works of Art—Stay a little & I will shew you what you should Study." He then went & took down Le Brun's & Rubens's Galleries. How did I secretly Rage. I also spoke my Mind . . . .
>
> I said to Moser, "These things that you call Finishd are not Even Begun[;] how can they then, be Finishd? The Man who does not know The Beginning never can know the End of Art[.]"
>
> (Marginalium to *The Works of Sir Joshua Reynolds, Knight* Vol. I, xlvii)

Such vigorously expressed opinions are likely to have circulated as curiosities among the officers of the Academy. Once Sir Joshua remarked to the young man,

---

* Perhaps Blake was alluding to this joke when he added transparent drawers to the naked figures of "William" and "Robert" in *Milton* pls 28 and 34 (Pl. 4).

"Well, Mr. Blake, I hear you despise our art of oil painting."
"No, Sir Joshua, I don't despise it; but I like fresco better."[7]

On another occasion, when the student brought some designs to Reynolds for advice, he was "recommended to work with less extravagance and more simplicity, and to correct his drawing. This Blake seemed to regard as an affront never to be forgotten. He was very indignant when he spoke of it."[8]

Reynolds's well-meant criticism was of course intended to show the student how to make his works more conventional and more saleable, and much of the criticism Blake was later to receive from friends and reviewers was similar in tenor. But of course Blake wished for the admiration of angels rather than of customers, and in time he came to regard such advice as a kind of conspiracy to depress divine imagination and inspired art. He said that he had "spent the Vigour of my Youth & Genius under the Opression of Sʳ Joshua & his Gang of Cunning Hired Knaves Without Employment & as much as could possibly be Without Bread".[9]

He became convinced that: "The Enquiry in England is not whether a Man has Talents & Genius, But whether he is Passive & Polite & a Virtuous Ass: & obedient to Noblemens Opinions in Art & Science. If he is; he is a Good Man: If Not he must be Starved" (Marginalium to *Reynolds*, I, 5).

He certainly knew the annual lectures of Joshua Reynolds, and he resented them with characteristic vigour. Sir Joshua's bland, assembly-line portraits of the rich and great seemed to Blake to be at the opposite extreme from the heroic art Reynolds advocated. Years later, when *The Works of Sir Joshua Reynolds, Knight, President of the Royal Academy* were published (1798), Blake annotated them in terms probably similar to those he used when he first heard them.

BLAKE:	This Man was Hired to Depress Art
REYNOLDS:	I found myself in the midst of works executed upon principles with which I was unacquainted: I felt my ignorance, and stood abashed.
BLAKE:	A Liar[!] he never was Abashed in his Life & never felt his ignorance.
REYNOLDS:	It is the florid style, which strikes at once, and captivates the eye for a time ....
BLAKE:	A Lie[!] The Florid style, such as the Venetian & the Flemish, Never Struck Me at Once nor At-All.
REYNOLDS:	[*Reynolds*] was a great generalizer ... this disposition to abstractions, to generalization and classification, is the great glory of the human mind ....
BLAKE:	To Generalize is to be an Idiot[.] To Particularize is the

Alone Distinction of Merit. General Knowledges are those Knowledges that Idiots possess.

REYNOLDS: The Students … should be taught to contend who shall have the purest and most correct outline.

BLAKE: Excellent.

REYNOLDS: … mere enthusiasm will carry you but a little way ….

BLAKE: Mere Enthusiasm is the All in All!

REYNOLDS: … enthusiastick admiration seldom promotes knowledge.

BLAKE: Enthusiastic Admiration is the first principle of Knowledge & its last.

REYNOLDS: This long laborious comparison should be the first study of the painter …. This idea of the perfect state of nature, which the Artist calls the Ideal Beauty, is the great leading principle by which works of genius are conducted.

BLAKE: Knowledge of Ideal Beauty is Not to be Acquired[.] It is Born with us[.] Innate Ideas are in Every Man[,] Born with him[;] they are truly Himself[.] The Man who says that we have No Innate Ideas must be a Fool & Knav*e*, Having No Con-Science or Innate Science ….

Man Brings All that he has or Can have Into the World with him. Man is Born Like a Garden ready Planted & Sown[.] This World is too poor to produce one Seed.

REYNOLDS: To understand literally these metaphors or ideas expressed in poetical language, seems to be equally absurd ….

BLAKE: The Ancients did not mean to Impose when they affirmd their belief in Vision & Revelation[.] Plato was in Earnest: Milton was in Earnest. They believd that God did Visit Man Really & Truly & not as Reynolds pretends.

(Marginalia [?1801–2 and ?1808–9] to Reynolds, I, title page, xv, xvii, xcviii, 16, 35, 55, 58, 157, 195)

The young man who "affirm'd his belief in Vision & Revelation and believd that God did Visit Man Really & Truly" was clearly something out of the experience of Sir Joshua Reynolds and the Royal Academy.

Blake demonstrated extraordinary precociousness in submitting a picture to the exhibition of the Royal Academy in May 1780 during his very first year as a student in the Academy schools. The drawing, which represented "The Death of Earl Goodwin" as he was struck down by divine displeasure, exhibited his fascination with the Gothic and his conviction that God visits man (Pl. 22). And not only was the drawing accepted and exhibited, but it attracted the attention of his new friend the young polymath George Cumberland (Pl. 23). Under the pseudonym "Candid", Cumberland wrote in *The Morning Chronicle and*

London Daily Advertiser for Saturday 27 May 1780 that, "though there is nothing to be said of the colouring, [*in it*] may be discovered a good design, and much character".* Such praise of his design and character must have cockered up the young man making his first attempts to impress the world of art.

From an early age, Blake distrusted oil colour as a modern and perverse invention, and he sought for a way to make the more congenial watercolours permanent and sun-proof:

> He ground and mixed his water-colours himself on a piece of statuary marble, after a method of his own, with common carpenter's glue diluted, which he had found out, as the early Italians had done before him,† to be a good binder. Joseph, the sacred carpenter, had appeared in vision and revealed *that* secret to him. The colours he used were few and simple: indigo, cobalt, gamboge, vermillion, Frank-fort black freely, ultramarine rarely, chrome not at all. These he applied with a camel's-hair brush, not with a sable, which he disliked.[10]

Blake's art was built upon a firm and determinate outline derived from Apelles in classical Greece and Raphael and Michelangelo in Renaissance Italy—and of course from his profession of engraving. But he also studied colour deeply, and some of his effects in colouring are astonishing, "beautifully prismatic", with "an unrivalled tender brilliancy", as his artist friends said.[11] Even non-professionals agreed that in finishing his own works in Illuminated Printing "He was a most splendid tinter".[12]

According to his disciple Frederick Tatham, "Blake painted on Panel or canvass covered with 3 or 4 layers of whitening & carpenters Glue; ... he used several layers of colour to produce his depths .... Washing his Picture over with glue in the manner of a Varnish, he fixed the Colours, and at last varnished with a white hard varnish of his own making."[13]

His friend J.T. Smith reported that "In this branch of the art he often acknowledged Apelles to have been his tutor, who was, he said, so much pleased with his style, that once ... [*he told Blake:*] 'You certainly possess my system of colouring....'"‡

---

* George Cumberland told his brother Richard in a letter of 6 May 1780 (British Library: Add MSS 36,492, ff. 338–41) that in the articles signed "Candid" he had taken care to praise his friends.

† J.T. Smith claimed (*BR* 472) that Blake heated his colours and that "Blake's modes of preparing his ground, and laying them over his panels for painting, mixing his colours, and manner of working, were those which he considered to have been practised by the earliest fresco-painters ... his colours he ground himself, and also united them with the same sort of glue, but in a much weaker state" and Linnell wrote (*BR* 33 n3) that Blake was pleased to find his process described in Cennino Cennini's *Trattato della Pittura*, ed. Giuseppe Tambrone (1821), a copy of which he annotated.

‡ Smith (*BR* 468); the passage continues: "I now wish you to draw my person, which has hitherto been untruly delineated." In his writings, Blake refers to "Apelles line" (comment on Malkin's son, "Florentine Ingratitude" [l. 21] in his Notebook p. 32, and his *Descriptive Catalogue* ¶110) rather than to his colouring.

One of his own formulae was for a "pure white ground" which "is brighter, and sticks faster than chalk; and it seems such a quick way of getting a showy, but really good effect".[14] Many years later, he gave a recipe for "Blake's White" to his disciple Samuel Palmer:

> Get the best whitening—powder it.
>
> Mix thoroughly with water to the consistency of cream.
>
> Strain through double muslin. Spread it out upon backs of plates, white tiles are better, kept warm over basins of water until it is pretty stiff.
>
> Have ready the best carpenters' or cabinet maker's glues made in a very clean glue pot, and mix it warm with the colour:—the art lies in adding just the right portion of glue. The TEST is, that when dry upon the thumb nail or on an earthenware palette it should have so much *and no more* glue as will defend it from being scratched off with the finger nail.
>
> This, and the cleanliness of the materials, are the only difficulties.*

The Gordon Riots

While his picture was peacefully hanging in the Royal Academy, London was seething, and then erupting, with democratic passions which threatened for a time the very fabric of society. Parliament had passed an Act in 1778 to ease the disabilities inflicted upon Roman Catholics, and in June 1780 Lord George Gordon, the President of the Protestant Association, stirred up hysterical mobs to demonstrate at and then to threaten Members of Parliament in order to enforce a repeal of the Act. Gordon's followers were carefully divided into London, Westminster, Southwark, and Scotch Divisions, they wore blue cockades, and they acted with astonishing organization and impunity.

The genii of the mob, once summoned and set loose, proved to be more than Lord George could or cared to control, and for almost a week they surged through London, burning the chapels and homes of Catholics, looting, breaking open liquor warehouses and banks and prisons, and freeing prisoners, and they "avowed their intention to destroy the Bank [*of England*], Gray's Inn, Temple, Lincoln's Inn, the Grand Arsenal at Woolwich, and Royal Palaces".†

---

* *BRS* 8–9; A.H. Palmer says that "Blake gave my father the recipe". In his *Descriptive Catalogue* ¶9, Blake claimed that before the time of Van Dyck, "all the genuine Pictures are on Plaster or Whiting grounds and none since".

† William Vincent [i.e., Thomas Holcroft], *A Plain and Succinct Narrative of the Late Riots and Disturbances in the Cities of London and Westminster ... with an Account of the Commitment of Lord George Gordon* to the Tower (London: Fielding & Walker, 1780), 31. The account is carefully derived from newspaper accounts (some of it is identical with Anon, "Anecdotes of the life of Lord George Gordon" and "Account of the Riots and Disturbances", *Westminster Magazine* [June 1780], 295–305), and the descriptions of the riots are used surprisingly carefully by Dickens in *Barnaby Rudge* (1841).

The rioters defied the civil authorities, and, when the army was finally summoned, they defied it too, and the soldiers often refused to fire upon their fellow-citizens. For six days the mob was out of control; for ordinary citizens, "Sleep and rest were out of the question", and "every man began to tremble, not only for the safety of the city, but for the constitution, for the kingdom, for property, liberty, and life, for every thing that is dear to society, or to Englishmen."[15]

Blake's radical young friend George Cumberland was a horrified witness of the riots. He stood

> near the greatest part of Sunday night [*4 June 1780*] on a wall near the Romish Chapel in Moor fields witnessing scenes wh made my heart bleed, without being able to prevent them—it was the most singular and unhappy sight in the world—the Mob encouraged by <u>Magistrates</u> and protected by <u>troops</u>—with the most <u>orderly injustice</u> destroying the property of inocent individuals—Next to L.ᵈ Gordon for whom no punishment can be too great the magistrates of this City deserve an ample share of vengeance from a basely deserted people* ... grown bold by sufferance they yesterday burnt S.ʳ G. Saville and a Chandlers who had taken one of them [*prisoner*] besides 2 schools and many private Masses—to day [*7 June*] they burnt L.ᵈ Peters Furniture Mr Hydes &c and armed with clubs to the amount as I am informed of 5000 are at this instant going to the D of Richmonds Ld Shelburns &c[;] they have broke open Newgate [*Prison*] and [*set*] the prisoners at large and at this moment it is in flames ... the soldiers its said laid down their arms to day on being ordered to fire . . ..[16]

Newgate Prison, "the strongest and most durable prison in England, that had been newly erected, and was not yet finished", was attacked partly in order to free some of the rioters who had been imprisoned there.†

No one was safe, and even Jews chalked on their doors, "THIS HOUSE IS TRUE PROTESTANT"‡ in the hope of averting the appalling and often random violence in the streets. Everyone in central London and Westminster who was not running with the mob must have been either cowering or craning for a view.

Blake too was a horrified witness of these outrages.

---

* According to [James Elmes], *London And its Environs in the Nineteenth Century* (London: Jones & Co., 1829), 36, "The lord mayor, alderman Kennett, was tried for his misconduct during these disgraceful scenes and found guilty."
† Vincent, *A Plain and Succinct Narrative*, 28, 26. Holcroft, a radical, calls the rioters "madmen and villains" and says that many "died in inebriation", for instance when they collapsed in the fires they had started in Newgate, and that "the perpetrators appeared chiefly to be boys" (29, 36, 37).
‡ Ibid., 37–8. The unstable Lord Gordon later converted to Judaism.

On the third day, Tuesday, 6th of June, "the Mass-houses" having already been demolished—one, in Blake's near neighbourhood, [*the Bavarian Embassy Chapel in*] Warwick Street, Golden Square—and various private houses also; the rioters, flushed with gin and victory, were turning their attention to grander schemes of devastation. That evening, the artist happened to be walking in a route chosen by one of the mobs at large, whose course lay [*eastward*] from Justice Hyde's house near Leicester Fields, for the destruction of which less than an hour had sufficed, through Long Acre, past the quiet house of Blake's old master, engraver Basire, in Great Queen Street, Lincoln's Inn Fields, and down Holborn, bound for Newgate [*in The City (see Horwood's map, Pl. 8)*]. Suddenly, he encountered the advancing wave of triumphant Blackguardism, and was forced (for from such a great surging mob there is no disentanglement) to go along in the very front rank, and witness the storm and burning of the fortress-like prison, and release of its three hundred inmates.[17]

Blake's anguished recollection of the scene must have been made more poignant by the subsequent legal retribution, when scores of rioters were hanged at Tyburn, many of them only boys. The vengeance of the Beast was heavy.

The images of "burning", "fire", "flames", and "rage" in his poetry and in his picture of "Fire" (1805) (Pl. 24) are likely to be related to the scenes he saw during the Gordon riots, and from them one may construct a description of the riots: "all rush together in the night in wrath and raging fire", "a mighty multitude rage furious" "in flames of red wrath burning"; "Albions mountains run with blood, the cries of war & of tumult", "Above the rest the howl was heard from Westminster louder & louder", and "Around Saint James's glow the fires"; from Westminster "Eastward & Southward & Northwar*d* are incircled with flaming fires", "In thunder smoke & sullen flames & howlings & fury & blood", "in dungeons circled with ceaseless fires"; "All is confusion, all is tumult".[18] Blake's visions of apocalypse come partly from personal experiences.

Sedition at Upnor Castle

While he was studying at the Royal Academy, Blake made friends with different kinds of young men than the artisans with whom he worked in Basire's engraving studio. These were aspiring artists, painters and sculptors, whose ambitions and radical religious and political principles were particularly congenial to the young Dissenter. His friends now included John Flaxman (Pl. 25), the earnest young sculptor, two years older than Blake, embarking on a career which was to make him Professor of Sculpture at the Royal Academy and the most distinguished monumental sculptor in

England; George Cumberland (Pl. 23), by day a clerk in an insurance office and thereafter an artist, author, and inventor, who was three years older than Blake; Thomas Stothard (Pl. 26), who had recently finished his apprenticeship as a flowered-silk pattern-draughtsman and was beginning a career which was to make him the most prolific designer of book illustrations in England—he was born two years before Blake;* and William Sharp, a seeker for radical religious and political truth who was making his reputation as one of the great line-engravers of England, and who was eight years older than Blake.[19] In succeeding years, Flaxman became Blake's "Dearest Friend"[20] and a generous recommender of Blake to potential patrons; Cumberland often praised Blake in print, learned engraving from him, corresponded with him as late as the year Blake died, and found customers for his books and prints; and Stothard fostered Blake's talent by recommending him as an engraver for the book-illustrations he designed.

Stothard sometimes organized expeditions on the River Medway, southeast of London. He and two or three friends would hire a small boat and sail for a few days of outdoor freedom, sketching the picturesque scenery as they went. It was probably during the Royal Academy school holiday in September 1780 that Stothard, Blake, and Blake's former fellow apprentice James Parker† set off gaily from the mouth of the Medway in a heavy little craft with their palettes and brushes and sketch-pads, their food and their drink, their cooking-pots and their plates and cups and utensils, their flint-and-steel for picnic-fires, their spare clothes and with their ears ringing with the cautious advice of their parents and the risible suggestions of their peers.

The ancient woods and cow-filled meadows by the side of the Medway provided the kinds of bucolic scenery recommended by some of the more modish teachers at the Royal Academy, and the river itself must have provided great excitement for these novice sailors. Not only was the tidal estuary lively with fishing vessels and colliers and barges and wherries, but upstream the young men would have sailed amongst the great battle-fleet assembled for the war with the rebellious American colonies and their impertinent French allies, from brisk little gun-boats and cutters up to the beautiful, dashing 74-gun frigates and the ponderous 100-gun ships of the line. The in-bound vessels with their crews of impressed seamen were sailing to be refitted at the greatest naval arsenal in the world at Chatham,

---

* "Trotter, the engraver, ... introduced his friend Stothard to Blake" (J.T. Smith [*BR* 466]).

† In two accounts of the incident derived indirectly from Catherine Blake (see below), the third artist is identified as "Parkes", presumably James Parker; in the one derived indirectly from Thomas Stothard, he is called "Ogleby". Another candidate is George Cumberland, who owned one of the three known copies of the print of the expedition (Fitzwilliam Museum, Cambridge), to whom Stothard wrote about 1781 to "consult about our freshwater Voyage" with Collins, Hunneman, and another (British Library Add MSS 36,198, f. 88).

which was guarded by the picturesque but largely futile sixteenth-century castle on the sharp bend of the Medway at Upnor. The city boys must have gazed with awe up the steep sides of these huge vessels at the seamen busy on deck and the top-gallant masts towering 100 feet above them, and perhaps some of the sailors not on watch were amused by the curious equipment and clumsy boat-handling of the landsmen in the little craft far below.

One day the three young painters beached their boat on the broad bend near Upnor Castle, across the river from Chatham Docks where on occasion there were as many as forty men-of-war moored together, and they were absorbed in sketching the picturesque scenery, when

> they were suddenly surprised by the appearance of some soldiers, who very unceremoniously made them prisoners, under the suspicion of their being spies for the French government; as this country was then at war with France. In vain did they plead that they were only there sketching for their own amusement; it was insisted upon that they could be doing nothing less than surveying for purposes inimical to the safety of Old England. Their provisions were brought on shore, and a tent formed for them of their sails, suspended over the boat-hook and oars, placed as uprights in the ground [see Pl. 27].[21]

They were peremptorily bustled off to be questioned by an officer, who abruptly doubted their implausible story that they were students from the Royal Academy making harmless landscape-sketches at the suggestion of their teacher—perhaps one of their sketches included a ship to give proportion and flavour to the scene. Or a sketch may have revealed the fact that there was not a single gun mounted in Upnor Castle*—if the French were possessed of this alarming information they might be tempted to repeat the exploit of the Dutch in the reign of Charles II by sailing up the Medway to attack the dockyard itself.[22]

The unworldliness of these young men, blithely making careful sketches (like that in Stothard's etching) of military fortifications of the greatest naval base in the world in time of war, almost surpasses comprehension. At least, it might appear so to naval intelligence, if that is not an oxymoron.

Because the young artists claimed the sanction of the august (or at least impressive-sounding) Royal Academy, they were not summarily haled before a magistrate, but they were put under arrest, "with a sentinel placed

---

* Samuel Ireland, *Picturesque Views on the River Medway from the Nore to the Vicinity of its Source* (London: T. & J. Egerton, 1793), 36–7, gives an account of the occasion when Ireland too was arrested (in 1791) while sketching from a little boat sheltering from the wind behind a man-of-war at Upnor. Ireland had little difficulty in persuading Commissioner Probyn at Chatham Yard of his innocence.

over them", while a messenger was sent to "certain members of the Royal Academy, to whom they appealed, to certify they were really peaceable subjects of his Majesty King George, and not spies for France".

And while they were waiting under guard for exoneration, Stothard sketched the scene of the beached boat, the makeshift sail-tent, and one other sketcher—but he tactfully omitted the sentinel. They had already had sufficient difficulty because of their indiscreet sketching of military objects.

When word was finally received from some surprised Academician (perhaps George Michael Moser, the Keeper) that the young detainees were bona fide students at the Royal Academy, their detention and sentinel were removed, and "they spent a merry hour with the commanding officer, to whom the artist [*Stothard*] remarked, that an opportunity had been given him for making a sketch he had not anticipated; while ... [*Parker*] declared that once being taken prisoner was enough for him; he would go out no more on such perilous expeditions".

For Blake, the incident must have confirmed what he had always suspected about the arbitrariness of civil and military power, about how easily such power is abused—and about how such power is an abuse in itself. How disconcerting to find that the officers of the Beast can be charming.

"Love and Harmony Combine" [23]

Blake's earliest poetry is full of rural mirth and innocent glances "Beneath the oaken tree, Where all the old villagers meet":

> I love the jocund dance,
>   The softly-breathing song,
> Where innocent eyes do glance,
>   And where lisps the maiden's tongue.

("Song", ll. 1–4, *Poetical Sketches* p. 13)

More than one poem is set in "that sweet village, where my black-ey'd maid" is "risen like the morn", and once the maid is called Kitty.* These are songs of the Surrey hills and villages from his adolescence.

Once when he was keeping company with a lively girl, he complained because she was also walking out with another young man, and she rounded on him with a flounce, saying,

"Are you a fool?"

---

* "When early morn walks forth in sober grey" (l. 7), "Fresh from the dewy hill" (l. 6), and "I love the jocund dance" (l. 18). Alan Cunningham thought that "the dark-eyed Kate of several of his lyric poems" was Catherine Boucher (*BR* 481), but this is impossible, for these poems were written before Blake was twenty, and he did not meet Catherine until he was twenty-three.

"That cured me of jealousy", said Blake[24] in telling the story with a mock-rueful face.

But there is jealousy aplenty in his poetry:

O should she e'er prove false, his limbs I'd tear,
And throw all pity on the burning air;
I'd curse bright fortune for my mixed lot,
And then I'd die in peace, and be forgot.

("Song" ll. 17–20, *Poetical Sketches* p. 17)

Perhaps the fancy-free lass of this anecdote is Polly Wood, who broke Blake's heart in the summer of 1781, when he was twenty-three years old. Blake was so profoundly affected that he fell ill, and he was sent across the river into Surrey to recover in the pretty little village of Battersea,* perhaps because his father had relations there.[25] The village was remarkable for the family seat of Pope's friend Henry St John, Viscount Bolingbroke, and for the prodigious 140-foot windmill with 80-foot sails of Hodgson, Weller, and Allaway.[26]

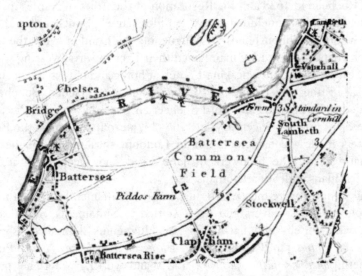

At Battersea he "lodged at the House of a market Gardener whose name was Boutcher".[27] His appearance there was electrifying, at least for William Boucher's pretty black-eyed daughter Catherine Sophia, who was then nineteen. In later years, she loved to tell the tale of this first meeting: "when

---

* Tatham (*BR* 517); Tatham was mistaken in the place (he said "Kew near Richmond", not Battersea) and in the spelling of "Boucher" but probably right in other respects, and he is the source of the similar tale by J.T. Smith (*BR* 459) and Cunningham (*BR* 481).

she first came into the Room in which Blake sat she instantly recognized
... her future partner, & was so near fainting that she left his presence until
she had recovered".[28] Clearly here was a girl who recognized affinities
instantly, as Blake did.

Catherine Boucher was the youngest of nine sisters and four brothers,[29]
the children of Mary and William Boucher. Her father's family came from
Lambeth, across the river from London, then a garden suburb where the
Archbishop of Canterbury had his palace, and her mother's family was from
Wandsworth, across the Thames and a few miles to the west of Lambeth
(see the map of Lambeth, Pl. 48). When he was married in 1738, her father
William Butcher changed the spelling of the family name to "Boucher",
perhaps reverting to an earlier spelling, and he and his wife Mary Davis
Boucher moved to Battersea, between Wandsworth and Lambeth, where he
struggled to support his multiplying family as a market-gardener.

The name "Boucher" was apparently pronounced "butcher"* rather than
"boushay". However, the spelling as "Boucher" may indicate that the name
was French in origin. If so, the family may have been part of the great waves
of French Huguenots which swept into London on the Catholic conquest
of La Rochelle in 1628 and the Revocation of the Edict of Nantes in 1685.

The Huguenots included many families named Boucher,[30] and there
were whole neighbourhoods of Huguenots in London with their own
French chapels. They long maintained their French ways, wearing wooden
shoes, eating garlic, and speaking French at home and church and a curious
English in the streets and on business—in 1702 Jacque Bouche was
recorded as living "chez my Lord Spencer en Piquedely",[31] i.e., Piccadilly.
In the early part of the century, in 1706–14, a group known as the French
Prophets made a considerable stir in London, speaking in tongues, and
associating with the followers of Jane Lead and Jacob Boehme, with
Philadelphians and Muggletonians.[32]

The refugees were mostly artisans, and the craftsmen kept together; for
example, the silk weavers and dyers settled in Spitalfields, St Giles, and
Soho, while "Felt- and hat-making by Huguenots flourished especially
[*across the Thames*] in Battersea [*where Catherine Boucher was born*], Putney,
Lambeth [*where her father was born*] and Wandsworth"[33] where her parents
were married. The transfer of these craftsmen to England sometimes had
surprising effects upon international trade:

At Caudebec in Normandy the manufacture of soft, rainproof felt hats
made from a mixture of fine vicuna wool and rabbit fur virtually ceased,

---

* Tatham, with whom Catherine Blake lived after William's death, spelled the named "Boutcher" (*BR* 517), and it was thus spelled in the notice of banns of her sister Sarah in 1788, though Sarah signed the marriage register itself as "Boucher" (see *BR* [2]).

as the hat-makers removed to Holland and England. France became an importer rather than an exporter of this kind of hat . . . . Catholic cardinals at Rome had to have their red hats made by Huguenot refugees at Wandsworth.[34]

In 1688 a Huguenot Tabernacle was established in Hog Lane,[35] where John Blake, perhaps the poet's uncle, lived in 1778–88.[36] Here, as Charles Lamb wrote, "those heroic confessors, who, flying to this country, from the wrath of Louis the Fourteenth and his dragoons, kept alive the flame of pure religion in the sheltering obscurities of Hog-lane".[37] When Hogarth drew the French Chapel in Hog Lane in 1738 (Pl. 28), the manners and costumes of the Huguenot worshippers, with clouded canes and mincing walk, were still sharply distinct from those of their English neighbours.

By the middle of the century, descendants of the refugees came to occupy important positions in the arts and crafts of London; for instance, David Garrick, the great actor-manager-playwright, was the grandson of a Huguenot, as were numbers of Basires and Bazires,[38] perhaps including Blake's master James Basire. In 1762 the Huguenot Pentecost Barker wrote: "What an alteration Time Makes!"; the offspring of "Those . . . I remember who came from France in 1685–86 . . . are more English than French, and will go to the English Church, though some few may come to us."[39] By then the Huguenot forms of worship were losing their distinctness, "Guillaume" and "Boucher" were being anglicized as "William" and "Butcher", and the old French patterns of life were being submerged in Englishness.

But the sense of a life devoted to religion and of sacrifices made for God, of the dangers to free worship and liberty posed by the Beasts of the state and the state Church, are likely to have lingered even in the assimilating families.

William Boucher was an industrious market-gardener,[40] perhaps growing not only vegetables, such as the asparagus for which the village was famous,[41] but flowers as well, for some of the Huguenots who fled first to Holland learned from the Dutch the art of raising flowers which they brought with them to England. At one point William Boucher had eighteen acres of land, few enough for supporting a large family. However, by 1763 he could not even afford to pay the parish rates on the land,[42] and thereafter the family may have been not far from indigence.

In a poor family like that of the Bouchers of Battersea with ten children, luxuries such as education and idleness were scarcely imaginable. Probably neither the parents nor the children had been to school or had learned to read and write,* and from the age of ten the children would have been expected to

---

* Catherine's sisters Sarah and Elizabeth learned at least to sign their names, for when Sarah was married in 1788, she signed her name in the marriage register, and E. Boucher signed as a witness (see *BR* [2]).

   Note that in Blake's last years, the letters written to friends and patrons to apologize for his alarming illness and weakness are written by Blake, not by Catherine.

help to support the family, by weeding in the field or finding work in the neighbourhood.* They were scarcely fit for much more than manual labour, the boys in carrying messages and the girls in domestic service. Catherine Boucher was working as a maid when she met Blake,[43] probably receiving only board and a shared bed, with Sunday afternoons as her free day.

One Sunday afternoon in the early summer of 1781, Blake found a number of sympathetic young women in the Boucher house, and he was naturally tempted to tell the tale of the hard-hearted Polly Wood. Catherine, recovered from the shock of first seeing Blake, said breathlessly that she pitied him from her heart.

"Do you pity me?" asked Blake.
"Yes, I do, most sincerely."
"Then I love you for that."
"Well, and I love you!"†

Blake instantly recognized that Catherine was "the only woman on Earth, who could have perfectly suited Him as a wife",[44] "the very woman to make him happy",[45] and, with his usual impetuosity, he asked her to marry him, and she as impetuously agreed.

Catherine had all the virtues to suit him. She had brown hair and beautiful "gleaming black eyes",[46] and "an implicit reverence" for him.[47] She was gentle and generous, she was strong and active, she was or became "an excellent cook" and "could even prepare a made dish, when need be",[48] and she "not only does all the work of the House, but she even makes the greater part of her Husbands dress".[49] She was frugal and content with the "plainest attire",[50] and she could manage money—Blake could not be bothered.

Blake was a lover of song, chiefly simple, sentimental ballads of love and death. He wrote songs from the time he was a boy—seven of the poems in *Poetical Sketches* are called merely "Song"—and he and his friends were singers. Catherine too was one who "sings delightfully",[51] and music was probably one of the things that drew Catherine and Blake together.

Most important of all, "she believed in all his visions"[52] and in his genius.

---

* No Boucher-Butcher is recorded in the Battersea Apprentice Records 1602–1900 in Wandsworth Local History Library (according to the microfilm in Westminster City Archives).

† J.T. Smith in 1828 (*BR* 459), paragraphing added. The story clearly derives from Catherine (though Smith says "from Blake") via "A friend" of Smith's, who is almost certainly Tatham; it was embroidered by Cunningham in 1830 (*BR* 481), and simplified and rehearsed by Tatham *c.* 1831 (*BR* 517–18).

In Cunningham, the simple story expands: Blake noticed Catherine "for the whiteness of her hand, the brightness of her eyes, and a slim and handsome shape, corresponding with his own notions of sylphs and naïads.... He tried how well she looked in a drawing, then how her charms became verse; and finding moreover that she had good domestic qualities, he married her."

She appears to have had the same *literal* belief in his visions as John Varley; and when he ... would tell his friends that King Alfred, or any great historical personage, had sat to him, Mrs. Blake would look at her husband with an awe-struck countenance, and then at his listener to confirm the fact. Not only was she wont to echo what he said, to talk as he talked, on religion and other matters—this may be accounted for by the fact that he had educated her; but she, too, learned to have visions;—to see processions of figures wending along the river, in broad daylight; and would give a start when they disappeared in the water.*

If the world and Blake were at odds, she always knew where the merit lay—or rather, she knew that Blake was not contaminated by the world: "*You see, Mr. Blake's skin don't dirt!*"[53]

She was, of course, illiterate, she did not speak grammatical English, she knew nothing of art or the world of ideas, of poetry and philosophy and history, and she had probably never been to London only a few miles away. But all these were faults which could be cured, and as soon as they were married Blake set to work vigorously to cure them.

It was an imprudent match, between a girl who could bring little but love and a young artisan who had yet to make his way in the world, and even Blake, who knew that "Prudence is a rich ugly old maid courted by Incapacity",[54] recognized that he would need time to win over his family— and perhaps hers—to find a place to live, and to ensure that he could really support a wife. Or perhaps it was Catherine or her father who insisted that he should do so, for prudence is a parental prerogative: "After this interview, Blake left the House ... returned to his Lodgings [*in Broad Street*], & worked incessantly that he might be able to accomplish this End at the same time resolving that he would not see her until he succeeded. This interval which she felt dolefully long was one whole year...."[55]

At home in Broad Street his family must have marvelled at the change in the morose and grumpy lad who had gone to the country to mend his broken heart. Here was Glad Day himself (see Pl. 29), joyous with love, bubbling with plans, scarcely noticing that "His marriage ... was not agreeable to his father".†

---

*   Gilchrist (*BR* 237). On 24 June 1796 Fuseli told Joseph Farington that Catherine "has imbibed some of his singularity", and in April 1812 their friend George Cumberland wrote more bluntly that "she is the maddest of the Two".

†   Cunningham (*BR* 482); his source here is not Tatham, who says that Blake obtained the "approbation & consent of his parents" (*BR* 518).

Professional Successes as an Engraver

As an apprentice, Blake had already made accomplished commercial engravings, which were of course signed by Basire as his master. These probably included some of the quarto plates in Jacob Bryant's *New System . . . of Ancient Mythology* published by Thomas Payne et al. in 1774–76, seven folio plates after his own designs for Sir Joseph Ayloff's *Account of Some Ancient Monuments in Westminster Abbey* published by the Society of Antiquaries in 1780, and sixteen folio plates for the first volume of [Richard Gough], *Sepulchral Monuments in Great Britain* which were not published by Payne until 1786. These subjects were all congenial and antiquarian.

By the time he finished his apprenticeship in August 1779, Blake had some acquaintance with the trade, with engravers and printers and booksellers, and he probably already had commissions for engravings. He knew the range of prices he might expect as a journeyman engraver: £5.5.0 for an outline engraving in quarto—this is what he received for Flaxman's *Iliad* in 1805—or for more finished plates in octavo, such as those after Stothard for *The Novelist's Magazine* in 1782–83. The payment depended upon the extent of the work required and the skill and reputation of the engraver, and it might also be affected by friendship and need; for the simple outline quarto plates for his friend George Cumberland's *Thoughts on Outline* in 1796 he received £2.2.0 apiece, and for three plates for his friend Flaxman's *Letter to The Committee for Raising the Naval Monument* in 1799 he was paid £9.0.8. Blake and his friend Parker estimated in 1804 that the quarto plates ("about 7 Inches by 5¼") for Hayley's *Life of George Romney* should cost "30 Guineas the finishd, & half the sum for the less finishd".[56] For a really ambitious and highly finished plate, such as "The Fall of Rosamund" after Stothard (see Pl. 30), he was paid £80 in 1783 by the great print-publisher Thomas Macklin.[57] In the triumphant years of English book-illustration, accomplished engravers like his acquaintance William Sharp were paid £500 or even £1,000 for a single plate.

The payment to engravers was ordinarily much more than to the designers of the same plate, despite the higher reputation of painters, for far more time was needed for engraving than for designing. Stothard ordinarily received a guinea each for his small designs, such as those for *The Novelist's Magazine*, while the engravers were paid £5 for engraving them. A highly finished quarto plate might take months to complete, and such work could not be rushed without peril. When Blake asked Parker in June 1804 about the plates for Hayley's *Life of George Romney*, Parker replied: "as they will be wanted in November I am of opinion that if Eight different Engravers are Employd, the

Eight Plates will not be done by that time".* A journeyman artisan might expect to earn one to two pounds per week, and thus two or three substantial commissions might be expected to keep an engraver in work for a year.

COMMERCIAL ENGRAVINGS 1782–83

Author	Title	Designer (Number of pl.)	Publisher	Date
		DUODECIMO		
Bonnycastle	*Introduction to Mensuration*	Stothard (1)	Johnson	1782
Anon.	*Ladies New and Polite Pocket Memorandum-Book*	Stothard (2)	Johnson	1782
Nicholson	*Introduction to Natural Philosophy*	Stothard (1)	Johnson	1782
[Ritson]	*Select Collection of English Songs*	Stothard (8)	Johnson	1782
Chaucer	*Poetical Works*	Stothard (1)	Bell	1783
		OCTAVO		
	Novelist's Magazine, Vol. VIII (Cervantes, *Don Quixote*), Vol. IX (Sterne, *Sentimental Journey*; Sarah Fielding, *David Simple*; Smollett, *Launcelot Greaves*)	Stothard (5)	Harrison	1782
Scott	*Poetical Works*	Stothard (4)	Buckland	1782
Ariosto	*Orlando Furioso*	Stothard (1)	a congery	1783
	Novelist's Magazine, Vols X–XI (Richardson, *Sir Charles Grandison*)	Stothard (3)	Harrison	1783
Henry	*Memoir of Albert de Haller*	Dunker (1)	Johnson	1783
		QUARTO		
	"Morning Amusement" "Evening Amusement"	Watteau (2)	Macklin	1782
	"The Fall of Rosamund"	Stothard (1)	Macklin	1783
	"Robin Hood & Clorinda"	Meheux (1)	Macklin	1783
		FOLIO		
Kimpton	*History of the Bible*	Stothard (1) Metz (2)	Cooke	1782

---

* Blake letter of 22 June 1804; part of the reason for the length of time is that good engravers already had commitments: "as for myself (Note Parker now speaks), I have to day turned away a Plate of 400 Guineas because I am too full of work to undertake it, & I know that all the Good Engravers are so Engaged that they will be hardly prevaild upon to undertake more than One of the Plates on so short a notice".

By these standards, Blake had been fully employed by a variety of book-sellers for his first couple of years upon the sea of business. He made a small, duodecimo plate for Enfield's very popular *Speaker* (Johnson, 1780), an octavo plate for Olivier's *Fencing Familiarized* (John Bell, 1780), five quarto plates for *The Protestant's Family Bible* (Harrison & Co, 1780–81) and five more for *The Royal Universal Family Bible* (Fielding & Walker, 1782), and a folio plate for Henry Emlyn, *A Proposition for a New Order in Architecture* (1781).[58]

With the prospect of marriage before him in the summer of 1781, he scrambled to find even more commissions. Many were from the great liberal bookseller Joseph Johnson in St Paul's Churchyard, the publisher of the timid poet William Cowper, the radical political philosopher William Godwin, the feminist Mary Wollstonecraft, the radical Tom Paine, and the scientific poet Erasmus Darwin. Most of Blake's plates (twenty-nine of thirty-five) were after the designs of his friend Thomas Stothard. The fact that the Stothard plates were for seven different publishers suggests that Stothard recommended Blake as an engraver of his designs.

Commissions from seven book- and print-sellers for thirty-four plates in 1782–83 on subjects as diverse as poetry, science, and the Bible demonstrate that Blake was regarded in the trade as a competent engraver. The separate quarto plates for Macklin were especially encouraging, for Macklin was one of the most ambitious print-sellers of the age, and for just one of Blake's plates he had paid £80, enough to support a modest artisan for a year. With such commissions in hand or in prospect, Blake could be confident that he could support a wife.

Marriage

By the middle of July 1782 Blake was back in Battersea to claim his bride, and on Tuesday 13 August he appeared at the Faculty Office for Marriage Allegations to "make Oath that the usual Place of Abode of *him this Appearer* hath been in the said Parish of *Battersea* for the Space of four weeks last past" and that he "intendeth to marry with *Catherine Butcher of the same Parish a Spinster upwards of twenty One Years of Age* ... in the *Parish Church of Battersea*". In fact, Catherine was just a few months past her twentieth birthday, and perhaps Blake had exaggerated the length of his residence in Battersea as he had Catherine's age. Or perhaps he or she didn't know her exact age.

On the same day, "the *thirteenth* Day of *August* in the *twenty second* Year of the Reign of our Sovereign Lord *George the Third* by the Grace of God of Great Britain, France, and Ireland, King, Defender of the Faith", 1782, Blake made out a Marriage Bond in which "*William Blake of the Parish of*

Battersea in the County of Surry Gentleman and John Thomas" (presumably a commercial bondsman) bound themselves in the enormous sum of £200 "to the most Reverend Father in God *Frederick* by Divine Providence, Lord Archbishop of CANTERBURY, Primate of all ENGLAND, and Metropolitan" to warrant that "[*n*]either of them [William Blake a Batchelor and Catharine Butcher a Spinster] be of any other Parish" than the ones sworn to, that there is no "lawful Let or Impediment" why they should not be married, and that the "said Marriage shall be openly solemnized in the Church or Chapel in the Licence specified between the Hours appointed in Constitutions Ecclesiastical, confirmed and according to the Form of the Book of Common-Prayer, now by law Established". Here is the language and the power of the Beast nakedly displayed.* And whereas Blake's parish was normally St James, Piccadilly, not Battersea, whereas he would not ordinarily have been considered a "*Gentleman*", and whereas Catherine was not yet twenty-one, the young couple were putting themselves dangerously in jeopardy of the law and the bondsman, of our Sovereign Lord George the Third and of the Reverend Father in God Frederick, Lord Archbishop of Canterbury.

Five days later, during the canonical hours of the morning of Sunday 18 August 1782, a cool, blustery, showery day,[59] "*William Blake* of *the* Parish *of Battersea Batchelor* and *Catherine Butcher* of *the same* Parish *Spinster* were Married" by the vicar, J. Gardnor, in St Mary's, Battersea. The church, overlooking a bend of the Thames, had been rebuilt just five years earlier on a Norman foundation, with a simple Georgian interior surrounded by a balcony and with a handsome seventeenth-century east window. The formal witnesses to the wedding were Thomas Monger, James Blake,† and Robert Munday, the parish clerk, and the marriage was affirmed in the parish register with the signature of "*William Blake*" and "*The Mark of x Catherine Butcher*", who could not read the document well enough to correct the spelling of her family name to "Boucher". Her inability to write her name was common in that time and parish; of the thirty-four persons married in 1782 in St Mary's, Battersea, fourteen signed the register with a mark.

Thus began a marriage which was to last in sunshine and in shadow for almost forty-five years: "My wife is like a flame of many colours of precious jewels."[60] Twenty years after their wedding, on 15 July 1802, William Hayley wrote that "They ... are as fond of each other, as if their Honey

* This enforced formality was established by the Marriage Act of 1754 to curb casual, informal marriages of the kind performed when Blake's mother married Thomas Armitage in 1746 and James Blake in 1751.
† James Blake is probably the poet's father rather than his brother, who might have been expected to suffix "Jun." to his name, as Blake's friend John Flaxman habitually did while his father was alive.

Moon were still shining ... they seem animated by one Soul, & that a soul of indefatigable Industry & Benevolence", and their friends regularly referred to Blake and Catherine together. They were separated for only five weeks[61] between their marriage in 1782 and Blake's death in 1827 six days before their forty-fifth wedding anniversary.

The young couple probably moved immediately into a flat in the house of Thomas Taylor* at 23 Green Street, Leicester Fields,[62] and "They live together with! a servant at a very small expence".[63] Though their rooms were humble, they had some distinguished neighbours. The great engraver William Woollett, whom Blake had met and distrusted at Basire's, lived in Green Street, and John Hunter the anatomist and Joshua Reynolds the painter were round the corner in Leicester Fields. In 1771, Reynolds's young apprentice James Northcote wrote happily that in Leicester Fields "I often hear the cock crow and have seen a hen and chickens strut as composedly through the street as they would at Plymouth",[64] and probably the descendants of those chickens were happily waking the dawn and parading the streets eleven years later when the Blakes moved into Green Street.

Catherine as a Helpmate

Catherine quickly learned to be "an invaluable Helpmate" to her husband in his work.[65] Some of her help was psychological or spiritual, for

> he fancied, that while she looked on at him, as he worked, her sitting quite still by ... [his] side, doing nothing, soothed his tempestuous mind, & he has many a time when a strong desire presented itself to overcome any difficulty in the Plates or Drawings, ... in the middle of the night risen, & requested her to get up with him & sit by his side, in which she as cheerfully acquiesced.†

Blake taught her his own crafts, so that "she draws,‡ she engraves",[66] "She prepared his colours",[67] she printed his engravings "and ever delighted in

---

* Not Thomas Taylor (1758–1835) the Platonist, who lived at 9 Manor Place, Walworth, from 1778 to 1830.

† Tatham (*BR* 526). Tatham is presumably the source of the similar story in Smith: "his application was often so incessant that in the middle of the night, he would, after thinking deeply upon a particular subject, leap from his bed and write for two hours or more" (*BR* 475).

‡ J.T. Smith said that she "produced drawings equally original, and, in some respects, interesting", but Linnell doubted that her drawings were "equally original", though he did have one which "is certainly so like one of Blake's own that it is difficult to believe it to be the production of any other mind" (*BR* 459 & n1). On the basis of contemporary inscriptions, Butlin attributes three drawings to Catherine Blake (C1–3 [*c.* 1800, *c.* 1827–31, *c.* 1830], Plates 348, 1191–2), but none of these is known to have belonged to Linnell.

the task",[68] occasionally "she coloured them with a light and neat hand",[*] and she even pulled prints commercially for his bookselling patrons. On 30 January 1803 Blake wrote proudly to his brother James: "My Wife has undertaken to Print the whole number of the plates For Cowpers Work which She does to admiration & being under my own eye the prints are as fine as the French prints & please everyone. . . . The Publishers are already indebted to My Wife Twenty Guineas for work deliverd . . .."

When they were working together in printing, Catherine would have been the clean-hand worker, laying the dampened paper on the inked plates and pulling them through the press, while Blake inked the next pair of plates to be pulled.

Blake also taught her to read and write, but there is little evidence that she did much of either. One indication of her reading was recorded in Blake's Notebook p. 88:

> South Molton Street
> Sunday Augus*t* 1807 My Wife was told by a Spirit to look for her fortune by opening by chance a book which She had in her hand[;] it was Bysshes art of Poetry. She opend the following[:]

> > I saw 'em kindle with desire
> > While with soft sighs they blew the fire[,]
> > Saw the approaches of their joy[,]
> > He growing more fierce & she less coy . . . Behn

> I was so well pleased with her Luck that I thought I would try my own . . . .

Presumably Catherine had been using Edward Bysshe's *Art of Poetry* (first printed in 1702) in order to look up something like suitable rhyme-words when the spirit interrupted her. The only drawing which can be assigned confidently to Catherine represents Agnes from *The Monk* by Matthew Gregory Lewis (1796), which implies that she had read the sensational Gothic novel—unless, of course, she had merely heard it read or heard about it.

The evidence of her writing is more sparse. She apparently signed letters of 14 September 1800 ("Catherine Blake"), of 26 October 1803 ("W. and C.

---

[*] Cunningham (*BR* 482; see also J.T. Smith 459, 460). Tatham says that "She even laboured upon his Works, . . . which from her excellent Idea of Colouring, was of no small use in the completion of his labourious designs. This she did to a much greater extent than is usually credited" (*BR* 534).

   For the kind of colouring she did, laying on a few colours per print in a simple pattern following a model Blake had made for her, see Joseph Viscomi, *Blake and the Idea of the Book* (Princeton: Princeton University Press, 1993), 133–4.

Blake"*), 11 December 1805 ("William Blake & his Wife Catherine Blake"), 1 August 1829 ("The widow of the late Wm Blake") and 4 August 1829 ("C Blake"), plus a receipt of 14 January 1808 ("for Wm Blake Catherine Blake"†). However, the letters of 1803 and 1805 are written in the first person singular in the handwriting of William Blake,‡ and that of 1800 is in the hand of William Blake and may have been composed as well as transcribed by him. The letter of 1 August 1829 is written in the third person, perhaps for rather than by Catherine, and that of 4 August 1829 is signed "C Blake" in a hand which may be different from that of the text. The only one of these signatures above suspicion is on the receipt of 1808.§

Perhaps the best evidence of Catherine's reading and writing is the gift-inscription (?4 August 1824) on a copy of a print of Blake's engraving of Robert Hawker (1 May 1820):

> M^r C Tatham
>> The humble is formed to adore;
>> the loving to associate
>>> with eternal Love
>>> C Blake

The handwriting seems to be hers, and the text, quoted from Lavater's *Aphorisms on Man* (1788), Paragraph 69, which Blake annotated, indicates that she knew Lavater's book well.

John Linnell, with whom Catherine lived in 1827–28 after Blake's death, wrote on 16 March 1831 to Frederick Tatham, with whom he was not on speaking terms and did not wish to be on writing terms, that "I will ... receive any written communication from her" (Mrs Blake). He clearly implied that he thought Catherine could write to him if she chose, though Tatham sometimes wrote in her name or on her behalf.

---

* The signatures of "W. Blake" and "C. Blake" approving the writings of Swedenborg at the first meeting of the New Jerusalem Church, 13 April 1789, are known only in the transcript in the "Minute Book of the Society for Promoting the Heavenly Doctrines of the New Jerusalem Church, Eastcheap. London. 7. May 1787. to 7. Nov. 1791" (New Church College, Woodford Green, Essex—see *BR* 35 n2).

† The receipt, with the Preston Blake Collection in Westminster Archives, is written in the fine, clerkly hand of Thomas Butts, but "Catherine Blake" is in a distinctly different hand and is not very well formed, especially the "Blake".

‡ That of 1805 concludes: "I remain Your affectionate Will Blake & his wife Catherine Blake".

§ Catherine was also thought to have been responsible for the elaborate calligraphic inscriptions on Blake's Bible designs for Butts, but such advanced skill seems to be well beyond the very modest range of writing accomplishments which can plausibly be claimed for her; see Joseph Viscomi, "Blake in the Marketplace 1852: Thomas Butts, Jr, and Other Unknown Nineteenth-Century Blake Collectors", *Blake*, XXIX (1995), 40–68.

This very sparse evidence indicates that Catherine learned to read and write, but it does not suggest that she was very good at doing either.

What she was good at was managing their finances. Blake himself "spoke of his horror of Money. Of his turning pale when money had been offerd him",[69] and he confessed that "I seldom carry money in my pockets":[70] "'Were I to love money,' he said, 'I should lose all power of original thought; desire of gain deadens the genius of man. I might roll in wealth and ride in a golden chariot, were I to listen to the voice of parsimony. My business is not to gather gold, but to make glorious shapes, expressing god-like sentiments."* His disciple Samuel Palmer said that "he worked on with serenity when there was only a shilling in the house. Once (he told me) he spent part of one of these last shillings on a camel's hair brush."[71]

When Catherine felt she had to mention that

"The money is going, Mr. Blake."
"Oh, d— the money!" he would shout; "it's always the money!"

Catherine learned to avoid these outbursts by setting

before him at dinner just what there was in the house, without any comment until, finally, the empty platter had to make its appearance: which hard fact effectually reminded him it was time to go [*from designing*] to his engraving for a while. At that, when fully embarked again, he was not unhappy; work being his natural element.[72]

Catherine knew, however, that their resources were not so depleted as the empty plate suggested, for she "always kept a guinea or sovereign for any Emergency, of which Blake never knew, even to the day of his Death. This she did for years …."[73] The only person who could manage William Blake consistently was his wife Catherine.

Blake and the Mathew Circle

About the time of his marriage, Blake was introduced to the Reverend Anthony Stephen Mathew (Pl. 31A), "of Percy Chapel, Charlotte Street,† which was

---

* Cunningham (*BR* 481); Cunningham probably embellished the words, if he did not invent them, but the sentiment is recognizably Blakean. On 30 April 1830 Linnell wrote that Blake "feared nothing so much as being rich lest he sh^d lose his Spiritual riches".

† He was, of course, a clergyman of the Church of England, but he may have been sympathetic to some kinds of Dissent, for an advertisement for a sermon preached before the Stewards of Westminster Dispensary in Mathew's Charlotte-Street Chapel was printed in the copy of Emanuel Swedenborg's *Wisdom of Angels Concerning Divine Love and Divine Wisdom* (1788) which Blake annotated.

built for him" and afternoon preacher at St Martin-in-the-Fields.* His wife Harriet Mathew (Pl. 31B) was a patroness of young artists such as the painter Edward Oram, the assistant of Philip de Loutherbourg, and of John Flaxman, who in 1784 introduced to them the eighteen-year-old painter John Thomas Smith. She fancied the new Gothic fashion fostered by Horace Walpole's innovations at Strawberry Hill and by his *Castle of Otranto* (1764), and

> Mr. Flaxman, in return for the favours he had received from the Mathew family, decorated the back parlour of their house, which was their library, with models, (I think they were in putty and sand,) of figures in niches, in the Gothic manner; and Oram painted the window in imitation of stained glass; the bookcases, tables, and chairs, were also ornamented to accord with the appearance of those of antiquity.[74]

Here was a possible patron for the art which was the first love of Blake's life and which he was slowly bringing to attention through the exhibitions at the Royal Academy.

But his introduction to Mr and Mrs Mathew proved to be an opportunity for far more than this. Harriet Mathew held cultural conversaziones in the Mathew home at 27 Rathbone Place which were "frequented by most of the literary and talented people of the day",[†] and Blake was "very much delighted with being in good Company".[75] At her salons J.T. Smith "often heard him read and sing several of his poems. He was listened to by the company with profound silence, and allowed by most of the visitors to possess original and extraordinary merit."[76]

It was particularly appropriate that Blake should *sing* his songs at Harriet Mathew's conversaziones, for she was "a great encourager of musical composers", and there were enthusiastic musicians at her gatherings.[‡] And it

---

* J.T. Smith, *A Book for a Rainy Day* (1845) (*BR* 26). Smith, who is the source for almost all the first-hand information about the Mathew circle, became an intimate friend of the Mathews' son Henry, then fifteen, with whom "in his youthful days I had many an innocent frolic". Blake was already a member of the Mathew circle when J.T. Smith met him there in 1784.

  For further details, particularly concerning Smith's mistake in calling the father (A.S. Mathew) by the name of his son (Henry Mathew), see "A.S. Mathew, Patron of Blake and Flaxman", *Notes and Queries*, CCIII (1958), 168–78, and "John Flaxman and the Mathew Clan", *Bulletin of the New York Public Library*, LXVII (1963), 443–54.

† Smith (*BR* 456). According to the anonymous memoir of Flaxman (?by his sister-in-law Maria Denman) in his *Lectures on Sculpture* (London: John Murray, 1829), xiii, his patroness "was one of the most highly-gifted and elegant women of that day; she was the intimate associate of Mrs. Montague, Mrs. Barbauld, Mrs. Chapone, Mrs. Brooke, &c." These statements may be true, but no corroboration for them has been found elsewhere. (Gilchrist echoes and embroiders this account.)

‡ Blake was probably not the only amateur singer at these gatherings, for Flaxman too "sang beautifully, having an excellent musical Voice" (Tatham [*BR* 521]), and Samuel Palmer wrote that "William Blake told me that he had heard him sing some of the ancient melodies beautifully" (*BR* 521 n3).

was not only at her conversaziones that Blake sang his songs: "Much about this time, Blake wrote many other songs, to which he also composed tunes. These he would occasionally sing to his friends; and though, according to his confession, he was entirely unacquainted with the science of music, his ear was so good, that his tunes were sometimes most singularly beautiful, and were noted down by musical professors."[77]

All his life Blake apparently composed such songs to music. Almost twenty years later, on 21 February 1802, his young friend Edward Garrard Marsh said: "I long to hear Mr Blake's devotional air . . . . His ingenuity will . . . (I doubt not) discover some method of preserving his compositions upon paper, though he is not very well versed in bars and crotchets."[78]

Poetical Sketches

The company at Harriet Mathew's salons was deeply impressed by his songs, and she

> was so extremely zealous in promoting the celebrity of Blake, that upon hearing him read some of his early efforts in poetry, she thought so well of them, as to request the Rev. Henry Mathew [*i.e.*, *A.S. Mathew*], her husband, to join Mr. Flaxman in his truly kind offer of defraying the expense of printing them; in which he not only acquiesced, but, with his usual urbanity, wrote the . . . advertisement which precedes the poems.[79]

The octavo volume of only 70 pages was very modestly produced, at a cost of perhaps £5 for, say, 50 copies,* and with little in the way of proof-reading. The title page called it merely "Poetical Sketches by W.B." (Pl. 32), with the author's identity modestly obscured by initials. The Reverend Mr Mathew's claims for the work in the preface were modest to the point of deprecation:

> The following Sketches were the production of untutored youth, commenced in his twelfth, and occasionally resumed by the author till his twentieth year [*1768–77*]; since which time, his talents having been wholly directed to the attainment of excellence in his profession, he has been deprived of the leisure requisite to such a revisal of these sheets, as might have rendered them less unfit to meet the public eye.
>
> Conscious of the irregularities and defects to be found in almost every page, his friends have still believed that they possessed a poetical

---

* Twenty are known today. The claim by Peter Ackroyd, *Blake* (1995), 86, that *Poetical Sketches* was "printed by a friend of his master Basire, and stocked by Flaxman's aunt, who owned a print shop in the Strand" is made entirely without displaying evidence but is not inherently improbable.

originality, which merited some respite from oblivion. These their opinions remain, however, to be now reproved or confirmed by a less partial
public.

Notice the discreet ambiguity of the reference to the author's devotion to
"excellence in his profession", which might lead one to conclude that he was
preparing to be a clergyman or an attorney rather than a mechanic.

It is of course impossible to believe that Blake had been so "wholly directed to
the attainment of excellence in his professions" during the six years from 1777 to
1783 that he could make no revision in his poems or correct typographical errors
in the proofs such as "greeen", "phlosophic", and "beds of dawn" for "birds of
dawn". The truth is that Blake was not much interested in such pedantry.

Indeed, he was not much interested in the volume of *Poetical Sketches*.
"The whole copy of this little work ... was given to Blake to sell to friends,
or publish, as he might think proper",[80] and he scarcely did either. The
Flaxmans and others gave away copies on his behalf, in which Blake made
perfunctory and erratic manuscript corrections, and Blake gave away a few
copies over the course of the years,* but he kept the rest by him all his life,
and when he died he still had a number of copies in unsorted, uncorrected
sheets exactly as John Flaxman and A.S. Mathew had given them to him
forty-four years before.

But others were more impressed with the *Poetical Sketches*. Flaxman sent
copies to gentlemen who might become patrons of Blake's art. One of these
(E) was inscribed "To M[r] [*William*] Long from J Flaxman", and another (F)
was a "[present *del*] from Mrs Flaxman May 15, 1784", perhaps to Isaac
Reed the Shakespeare editor. On 26 April 1784 Flaxman wrote to his new
friend the popular gentleman-poetaster William Hayley describing Blake's
book in terms strikingly similar to the account in the preface:

> I have left a <u>Pamphlet of Poems</u> with M[r] Long which he will transmit to
> Eartham [*for you*]; they are the writings of a M[r] BLAKE you have heard
> me mention, his education will plead sufficient excuse to your Liberal
> mind for the defects of his work & there are few so able to distinguish &
> set a right value on the beauties as yourself, I have beforementioned that
> M[r] Romney thinks his historical drawings rank with those of M[!] Angelo;[†]
> he is at present employed as an engraver, in which his encouragement is

---

* When *Poetical Sketches* was first printed, Blake may have given a copy (D) to his friend George
  Cumberland, but it was probably or certainly much later that copies passed "To Charles Tulk Esq[re],
  from William Blake" (C), to Samuel Palmer (G-H, R, U), Crabb Robinson (O), and John Linnell
  (T). *Poetical Sketches* was apparently never published in the sense of being offered for sale.
† Perhaps one of the designs Romney admired was Blake's apprentice engraving after Michelangelo of
  "Joseph of Arimathea Among the Rocks of Albion" (Pl. 5).

not extraordinary—M! Hawkins a Cornish Gentleman has shewn his taste & liberality in ordering Blake to make several drawings for him,* & is so convinced of his uncommon talents that he is now endeavouring to raise a subscription to send him to finish [*his*] studies in Rome[;] if this can be done at all it will be determined on before the 10th of May next at which time M! Hawkins is going out of England—his generosity is such he would bear the whole charge of Blakes travels—but he is only a younger brother, & can therefore only bear a large proportion of the expence[.]

This letter brings Blake into contexts which are truly extraordinary. Hayley's intimate friend George Romney was one of the greatest portrait-painters of the day, indeed of English history, and his comparison of Blake's historical drawings with those of Michelangelo is not only extravagant praise but was just the comparison Blake would most have relished. Up to 1784 Blake had exhibited only one historical design ("The Death of Earl Goodwin" in 1780), so Romney's comment suggests a personal familiarity with Blake and his works which we would not otherwise have suspected. Such praise from such a man could have been enormously influential.

To study in Rome was the greatest ambition of every serious European artist. Rome was the centre not merely of classical civilization but of Renaissance art, the focus of all that was taught to Historical Painters at the Royal Academy. Blake's intimate friend George Cumberland was on the verge of departure for Rome (October 1785), his friend John Flaxman was already planning for his studies in Rome (1787–94), George Romney began his studies in Rome in 1772, and Blake's later friend Henry Fuseli spent 1770–78 there. Any artist who had not worked in Rome was likely to be regarded as provincial.

The sponsorship of artistically gifted "untutored youths", as Blake was described in the preface to *Poetical Sketches*, had become a fashion in recent times. Genteel patronage of Stephen Duck the Thresher Poet in the 1750s and Ann Yearsley the Bristol Milkmaid and Robert Burns the Poet-Ploughman in the 1780s brought them a prominence and prosperity other-wise unimaginable.

The proposal of John Hawkins, who was just Blake's age, was apparently that Blake should accompany him to Rome where Hawkins would sponsor

---

* On 18 June 1783 Flaxman wrote to his wife Nancy that Mr Hawkins "at my desire has employed Blake to make him a capital drawing for whose advantage in consideration of his great talents he seems desirous to employ his utmost interest". We do not know today which Blake drawings Hawkins owned. Butlin (#152) suggests that the outlines by "J Flaxman from memory of three drawings of Blake June 1792" (reproduced in *BR* at p. 47 and as Butlin Plate 170) may have been based on the designs Blake made for Hawkins.

him. All that was needed was a little financial support from gentlemen such as William Hayley and the Reverend Anthony Stephen Mathew.

Blake must have permitted and even encouraged the enterprise. Had it succeeded, his life would have been enormously different. It is difficult to imagine the fiery antinomian republican with his barely literate wife living on gentlemanly charity in the very lair of the Pope and *dolce far niente*, of the Beast and the Whore of Babylon. But plainly Blake could imagine it, or Flaxman would scarcely have written such a letter.

No such subscription ever materialized, and Blake never went more than sixty miles from London, but he always remembered "Our good and kind friend Hawkins"[81] with affection.

This letter may be seen as the high-water mark of Blake's early promise as a poet and a painter. For a time in 1783 and 1784 he seemed to be on the threshold of social and artistic success, with blue-stocking ladies listening in silent awe to his songs and gentlemen competing to multiply his fame in verse and vision.

There was of course no review of the privately printed volume of *Poetical Sketches*, but contemporary biographers quoted the poems extensively.[82] Their comments indicated a vivid awareness of the "irregularities and defects" alluded to in the preface, and they gave a good deal more attention to the prose sketches such as "Contemplation" and "Samson" and to the dramatic fragments such as "King Edward the Third" than later critics have done. Blake's friend B.H. Malkin wrote in 1806 that in his

> specimens of blank verse ... his personifications are bold, his thoughts original, and his style of writing altogether epic in its structure. The unrestrained measure, however, ... has not unfrequently betrayed him into so wild a pursuit of fancy, as to leave harmony unregarded, and to pass the line prescribed by criticism to the career of imagination.[83]

In 1811 Crabb Robinson wrote that "there is a wildness and loftiness of imagination in certain dramatic fragments which testifies to genuine poetic feeling",[84] and in 1830 Allan Cunningham praised "King Edward the Third" for "many nervous lines and even whole passages of high merit. The structure of the verse is often defective, and the arrangement unharmonious; but before the ear is thoroughly offended it is soothed by some touch of deep melody and poetic thought."[85]

The response to the non-dramatic poems was somewhat more emphatic; Cunningham said that they were "rude sometimes and unmelodious, but full of fine thought and deep and peculiar feeling", though they will seem "harsh and dissonant" "To those who love poetry for the music of its bells",[86] and in his manuscript life of Blake of about 1831 Blake's disciple Frederick Tatham said that they are "succinct[,] original fanciful & fiery but ... more rude than refined, more clumsy than delicate".[87] Most contemporary readers of the volume probably concluded as Cunningham did that it contains "much that is weak, and something that is strong, and a great deal that is wild and mad, and all so strangely mingled that little or no meaning can be attached to it".[88]

One reason for readers' perplexity was the extraordinary range in verse form and subject: lyrics, seasons poems, dramatic sketches, created mythology, and experimental prose just one step removed from blank verse. Most of the works with original mythological subjects such as "Samson" and "Contemplation" do not go anywhere, like many of Blake's life-long mythological experiments, but a few clearly anticipate his myth of Urizen, the powerful, cold, constrictive god of Reason, as in "To Winter":

O Winter! bar thine adamantine doors:
The north is thine; there hast thou built thy dark
Deep-founded habitation. Shake not thy roofs,
Nor bend thy pillars with thine iron car.

He hears me not, but o'er the yawning deep
Rides heavy; his storms are unchain'd; sheathed
In ribbed steel; I dare not lift mine eyes;
For he hath rear'd his sceptre o'er the world.

The visual imagery is so vividly articulated that the reader sees a vision of almighty winter brooding over the frozen world, as did Blake.

And a few of the poems were as fine as anything written in the second half of the eighteenth century. In "Mad Song", the verse form is as erratic and tormented as the speaker's mind, and the frantic fear of light focuses finely his frenzied torment, like *Lear*'s Mad Tom who is a-cold:

The wild winds weep,
    And the night is a-cold;
Come hither, Sleep,
    And my griefs unfold:
But lo! the morning peeps
    Over the eastern steeps,
And the rustling birds of dawn
The earth do scorn.

Lo! to the vault
    Of paved heaven,
With sorrow fraught
    My notes are driven:

They strike the ear of night,
    Make weep the eyes of day;
They make mad the roaring winds,
And with tempests play.

Like a fiend in a cloud,
    With howling woe,
After night I do croud,
    And with night will go;
I turn my back to the east,
From whence comforts have increas'd;
For light doth seize my brain
With frantic pain.

The speaker is not Blake, but he has entered into the mind of madness with compelling fidelity.

Perhaps the finest of them all is "To the Muses", in which he played with the delicate poetical conceit of an elegy for the death of music which demonstrates by its sweetness that music is not dead:

Whether on Ida's shady brow,
    Or in the chambers of the East,
The chambers of the sun, that now
    From antient melody have ceas'd;

Whether in Heav'n ye wander fair,
    Or the green corners of the earth,
Or the blue regions of the air,
    Where the melodious winds have birth;

Whether on crystal rocks ye rove,
    Beneath the bosom of the sea
Wand'ring in many a coral grove,
    Fair nine, forsaking Poetry!

How have you left the antient love
    That bards of old enjoy'd in you!
The languid strings do scarcely move!
    The sound is forc'd, the notes are few!

He has pursued the muses through the four elements, the "chambers of the sun", the "green corners of the earth", the "blue regions of the air", and in the "bosom of the sea", and found that throughout the world they have left the "antient love". In its use of the classical muses, of the familiar trope of the singing lament for the death of song, and of the delicious dying fall of the last lines, "To the Muses" is a wonderfully eighteenth-century poem—but with a freshness and an innocent sophistication quite unlike anything else being written at the time. As Swinburne wrote 85 years later, in "To the Muses", "The Eighteenth Century died to music."[89]

"In the Moon is a Certain Island"

The Mathew salon was an island of intellect in a sea of commerce. The young musicians and painters and poets and sculptors who gathered in Rathbone Place were passionately concerned with the highest forms of the arts, with oratorios and History Painting and monumental sculpture. To Blake the artisan, this curious company with its exalted public ambitions and its petty private jealousies was unfamiliar terrain, and its denizens who apparently knew the secrets of fashion seemed to him to be at once fascinating, pathetic, and above all comic.

Some of these feelings he expressed in an odd manuscript called *An Island in the Moon* (*c.* 1784). It is something between a burlesque and a satire and a comic vignette of a self-important society in which everybody talks but nobody listens: "their tongues went in question & answer, but their thoughts were otherwise employd" (Chapter 1). It seems to be related to dramatic improvisations such as *Tea at the Haymarket* by Samuel Foote (d. 1777)[90] which were deliberately formless and unscripted so that they could be performed outside the licensed theatres. Blake called it a "piece" (Chapter 2), and it might equally well be called a farrago: "Here was great confusion & disorder" (Chapter 9).

An Island in the Moon is a satire of fashionable intellectual pretensions which clearly derives from the Mathew salon but is not quite a parody of it. Almost any form of intellectual pretension is fair game, from Chatterton* to Phebus and from chemical experiments to the fashion for balloon hats stimulated by the first manned balloon ascent in 1783. The subjects include "Pistinolog*y*, Aridology, Arograph*y*, Transmography Phizograph*y*, Hogamy Hatom*y*, & hall that", as Aradobo says (Chapter 5). The characters have quixotic names such as Quid the Cynic, Jack Tearguts, Etruscan Column the Antiquarian, and Inflammable Gass the Wind-finder, but their

---

* Compare "Chatterton never writ those poems. *A* parcel of fools, going to Bristol" (Chapter 7) with "I Believe both Macpherson & Chatterton that what they say is Ancient, Is so ... I own myself an admirer of Ossian equally with any other Poet whatever[,] Rowley & Chatterton also" (marginalia [1826] to Wordsworth, *Poems* [1815] pp. 364, 365).

actions are so familiar "that you would think you was among your friends
... the vanities are the same" (Chapter 1).

The Islanders include pious churchgoers such as Mrs Sistagatist and
Dissenters such as Mrs Nannicantipot who thinks "a person may be as good
at home" as at church (Chapter 4) and Inflammable Gass who would like
to "see the parsons all hangd" (Chapter 4), and Steelyard who "said that it
was a shameful thing that acts of parliament should be in a free state"
(Chapter 1).

The most easily identifiable individual is Jack Tearguts, a surgeon in a
charity hospital who "understands anatomy", for his name was first written
"Jack Hunter", i.e., John Hunter, the great surgeon and anatomist. Almost
equally clear is Sipsop, an apprentice to Jack Tearguts who was made quite
sick by the shrieking of "a woman having her cancer cut" (Chapter 6); he is
probably A.S. Mathew's son Henry, who was "John Hunter's favourite
pupil".*

Perhaps Henry Mathew's mother Harriet is Mrs Gimblet, for in
Flaxman's portrait of her (Pl. 31B) "the corners of her mouth seemd—I
dont know ho*w*, but very odd as if she hoped you had not an ill opinion of
her. To be sure we are all poor creatures" (Chapter 1). The extravagantly
fashionable little Jacko, whose house has twenty-six rooms and a black servant, may be little Richard Cosway the royal miniaturist (and spiritualist),
who had a huge apartment in Schomberg House and a black servant. Others
such as Suction, who is going to "knock them all up next year in the
Exhibition" and who will "hang Philosophy .... do all by your feelings",
probably include artists such as John Flaxman[†] and J.T. Smith.

Another Blake acquaintance who may have left traces in *An Island in the
Moon* is Thomas Taylor, a bank clerk a year younger than Blake who was
making a reputation for himself as a mathematician, a philosophical
enquirer, and an enthusiast for ancient wisdom, for Plato and Plotinus and
the philosophical alchemists. His enthusiasm for the Greeks was so great
that he worshipped classical statues in his back garden, and he was known
as Taylor the Pagan (Pl. 33).

Taylor gave a series of twelve lectures on Plato in Flaxman's house in
Wardour Street about 1783, and he gave another series in the Freemasons'
Tavern in Great Queen Street opposite the house of James Basire in 1784.
On 18 October 1784 George Cumberland reported that he had heard

---

[*] J.T. Smith, *A Book for a Rainy Day* (*BR* 26); for evidence that Henry Mathew may have (deliberately?) provoked the apoplectic fit which killed John Hunter, see "A.S. Mathew, Patron of Blake and
Flaxman", *Notes and Queries*, CCIII (1958), 168–78.

[†] Chapter 7. Perhaps Flaxman is Inflammable Gass who had "a place of profit that forces me to go to
church" (Chapter 4), for Flaxman collected the Watch Rates for King Square Division in May 1782
(Westminster Rate Books, A2281/106).

Mr Taylors lecture at the Free Masons Tavern … on the nature and properties of light …. He … shewed us a specimen of his lamp which was a kind of glass salver with about an ounce of Phosphorus deposited in pieces in an unctious matter, and the whole was about a span broad— it gave a pale light resembling the Moon … this he assured us had retained its light 8 Mo[*nth*]s: and next he produced a Specimen of his everlasting lamp which was a common decanter on the bottom of which was deposited some pieces [of Phosphorus] … owing [to the] excessive heat of the room, the Phosphorus took f[ire, and] in trying to extinguish it we broke his first lamp.[91]

This incident may be echoed in the *Island in the Moon* when Inflammable Gass is demonstrating experiments with a microscope and a vacuum pump and

Smack went the glass … & let out the Pestilence[.] He saw the Pestilence fly out of the bottle & cried out, while he ran out of the roo*m*:
    "Come out Come out[!] we are putrefied[!] we are corrupte*d*! our lungs are destroyd with the Flogiston."* …
    So they need not bidding go[.]

(*An Island in the Moon* Chapter 10)

Blake knew Taylor, perhaps as early as 1783, and indeed

T. Taylor gave Blake, the artist, some lessons in mathematics & got as far as the 5.th proposit^n wch proves that any two angles at the base of an isoceles triangle must be equal. Taylor was going thro the demonstration, but was interrupted by Blake, exclaiming, "ah never mind that—what's the use of going to prove it, why I see with my eyes that it is so, & do not require any proof to make it clearer."[92]

When Blake uses mathematical terminology, such as "intricate ways biquadrat*e* Trapeziums Rhombs Rhomboids Parallelogram*s*, triple & quadruple",[93] he may be reflecting his lessons with Thomas Taylor the Pagan.
    Another conversation between the two men was altogether more surreal:

"Pray, Mr. Taylor," said Blake one day, "did you ever find yourself, as it were, standing close beside the vast and luminous orb of the moon"?—
    ["]Not that I remember, Mr. Blake: did you ever?"—

---

* Phlogiston was the recently identified element of oxygen, thought to be the principle of fire, which cannot burn without it.

"Yes, frequently; and I have felt an almost irresistible desire to throw myself into it headlong." —

"I think, Mr. Blake, you had better not; for if you were to do so, you most probably would never come out of it again."[94]

This is either an anticipation by Blake or a memory by the narrator of a passage in Blake's *Marriage of Heaven and Hell* (Pl. 19) in which the narrator says: "I found myself sitting on a pleasant bank beside a river by moon light" and "flung myself ... directly into the body of the sun".

Perhaps the closest connection of the *Island in the Moon* with the conversaziones of Harriet Mathew, who was "a great encourager of musical compositions, particularly the Italians", is the fondness for singing among the Lunar Islanders—they are always bursting out singing, anything from love songs to nonsense songs and ribald songs:

"Oho" said Doctor Johnson
To Scipio Africanus
"If you dont own me a Philosopher
Ill kick your Roman Anus"

(Chapter 9)

Amid all the affectation—"Let your bounty descend to our fair ears and favour us with a fine song" (Chapter 9)—Quid bursts in impulsively: "'Hang Italian songs[.] lets have English ... English genius for ever[!] here I go'" (Chapter 9). And one of the songs he sings is "The Little Boy Lost", while Mrs Nannicantipot sings "Nurse's Song" and Obtuse Angle sings "Holy Thursday", all of which Blake later included in *Songs of Innocence*. When "Holy Thursday" is sung, "they all sat silent for a quarter of an hour" (Chapter 11), perhaps an echo of the response of Mrs Mathew's guests to Blake's songs: "He was listened to by the company with profound silence".

Already Blake was thinking of making elaborately illustrated books:

"*Then*" said he "I would have all the writing Engraved instead of Printed & at every other leaf a high finishd print[,] all in three Volumes folio,* & sell them a hundred pounds apiece. *T*hey would Print off two thousand[.]"

---

* This is significantly similar to the proposal (1797) for Young's *Night Thoughts* which was to have 150 plates designed and engraved by Blake in four slim folio volumes (*BR* 59). The plates for Young, however, were not "high finishd", the text was not engraved, and the first (and only) part was published at £1.1.0 (*BRS* 15), not £100.

"*T*hen" said she "whoever will not have them will be ignorant fools & will not deserve to live[.]"

(Last page)

Blake may have been thinking of his friend George Cumberland who was making similar experiments with printing etched texts; on 2 January 1784 Cumberland sent his brother Richard a

> specimen of my new mode of Printing—it is the amusement of an evening and is capable of Printing 2000 ... this is only etching words instead of Landscapes, but nobody has yet though[t] of the utility of it that I know of— the expense of this page is 1⁵6 without rec[k]oning time, wh was never yet worth much to authors, and the copper is worth 1/6 again when cut up.

To be sure, there was "[so]me difficulty—A work thu[s] printed can only be read with the help of a looking Glas[s] as the letters are reversed", but this could be remedied by counterproofing, printing a second copy from the first "while wet".* And of course a professional engraver would have no trouble writing backwards, though Cumberland did not know this.

Within a few years, there were a number of elaborately illustrated folio editions like this, in John Boydell's Shakspeare with 100 plates in nine folio volumes at £105 ([1791–]1802), Macklin's Poet's Gallery (1788–99) and his Bible with 65 plates in six folio volumes (1791-1800), and Robert Bowyer's edition of Hume's *History of England* with 195 plates in five folio volumes (1793–1806). But none of these had engraved text, none had anything like two thousand copies—and Boydell and Macklin were bankrupted in the attempt.†

---

*   British Library Add. MSS 36,494, ff. 231–2. For a reproduction of his poem "To the Nightingale" counterproofed so that it reads right way round (not in mirror writing), see G.E. Bentley, Jr, *A Bibliography of George Cumberland (1754–1848)* (New York & London: Garland Publishing, 1975), 50.

On 22 Jan 1819, George Cumberland wrote to his son George, "Tell <u>Blake</u> a Mr Sivewright of Edinburgh has just claimed in some Philosophical Journal of Last Month As his own invention Blake's Method—& calls it Copper Blocks I think" (*BRS* 72–3). For the difficulty in identifying John Sivewright's discovery and for similar processes described in 1820 by William Hone Lizars and Charles Pye, see *BRS* 73 n1.

† Of course, Blake expected to be paid from the profits and would not have had to pay cash for his services for:

150 designs at £20 each	£3,000
150 "high finishd" engravings at £80 each (as he was paid for a 4° plate for Macklin in 1783)	£12,000
300 engravings with text at £5 each	£1,500
Pulling 2,000 copies each of 450 plates (150 design-plates and 300 text-plates, 900,000 pulls) at 2d. per pull (French Paper copies of *Job* in 1826 cost 2.7d. each and Drawing Paper pulls 2.3d.—see *BR* 603)	£ 7,500
Distribution costs (10% of £100) to booksellers for 2,000 sets	£20,000
Royalties to author of 10% of sales	<u>£20,000</u>
	£44,000

Blake and Wedgwood

Blake had another patron of enormous promise at the time he was writing about the Mathew Salon and John Flaxman in his *Island in the Moon*. For several years Flaxman had been designing for the great pottery manufacturer Josiah Wedgwood—indeed, Wedgwood was perhaps Flaxman's chief patron at the time. In 1784 Flaxman made a series of "Drawings for Ceiling" for Wedgwood's great new house called Etruria Hall in Staffordshire, for which he was paid £4.6.6. The design represented an elaborate allegory outlined in the centre, "like paintings on the Etruscan vases", with heads of divinities in the corners. Flaxman evidently obtained the commission for his friend "Blake for painting on Ceiling Pictures". Probably Blake's copies of Flaxman's designs were on canvas which was shipped to Staffordshire, as Flaxman's sketches on paper had been. Blake's fee, £3.17.0, was paid by Wedgwood to Flaxman who gave it to Blake.[95]

Wedgwood was a generous and enlightened man, and his patronage might have led to wonderful advantages for Blake. Not only did he provide many commissions to Flaxman, but he later gave Coleridge an annuity to free him from the necessity of earning a living in the church or in Grub Street. And he gave to Flaxman for Blake £5.5.0 for "his own work",[96] which may have been another design for Etruria Hall. But nothing came of these wonderful prospects until thirty years later, when Blake received another commission, and then it was merely to engrave bedpans and teacups for the Wedgwood sales catalogues.

The Blake Family Hosiery Shop and the Parish of St James

When Blake's brother James was fifteen years old, he was apprenticed on 19 October 1768 to Gideon Boitoult of the Needlemakers' Company.[97] Boitoult, the son of a weaver of Southwark, was probably a Huguenot.

In the little hosiery shop in Broad Street, James Blake and his son James sold hats to gentlemen and stockings and caps to ladies, and most transactions must have been a matter of pence and shillings. To secure a livelihood

---

The fixed costs (ignoring ink and beer money) for three folio volumes
of 100 leaves with 50 "high finishd" engraved designs and 100 pages of
engraved text per volume would have been for 450 sheets of copper
at 7s.6d.   £168.15

625 reams of paper (300 folio leaves = 150 sheets per set for 2,000 sets,
480 sheets per ream) at £5 a ream   £3,125.00

Binding at 2s. 6d. per volume (the cost for *Job* in 1826)   £750.00
                                                                            £4,043.15

which is a substantial sum to raise for an artisan earning £50–£100 a year.

which may at times have been somewhat precarious, they needed customers on a larger scale, and the largest and most pervasive institution nearby was the Parish of St James. The St James Parish Workhouse, Infirmary, Burying Ground, and School were very near 28 Broad Street—the St James Infirmary Burying Ground was just behind it.

One of the most acute problems of all English eighteenth-century parishes was how to deal with the children of the indigent. The incidence of infant mortality among the poor was appalling—and particularly appalling in London. Some of the poor were unable or unwilling to raise their children, and every church had records of babies "Found by the Church" or "Dropped in the Lane".

This is probably the context of "Holy Thursday" in *Songs of Experience* which begins "Is this a holy thing to see" while the design depicts a woman looking down in horror at a dead baby outstretched on the cold ground.

Even when the babes were baptized and taken into the care of the parish, their prospects of life and happiness were exceedingly fragile. The mortality rate of children brought up in London workhouses, even in the Parish of St James, was 50 to 100 percent *every year*.[98]

One of the most enlightened acts of the parish, beginning in the 1760s, was to send babies from the Workhouse to wetnurses and temporary foster mothers in the country parish of Wimbledon in Surrey. The scheme was a brilliant success. The babies flourished, the mortality rate dropped dramatically, and the nurses were rewarded for their successes with the children. The children had fresh air, a village environment, and days governed by the country rhythms of nature. Perhaps Blake had actually seen them at play on Wimbledon Common when he wrote what he called "my mothers song":

When the tongues of children are heard on the green
And laughing is heard on the hill
My heart is at rest within my breast
And every thing else is still.

"Then come home my children the sun is gone down
And the dews of night arise.
Come Come leave off play & let us away
Till the morning appears in the skies."

"No No let us play for it is yet day
And we cannot go to sleep.
Besides in the Sky the little birds fly
And the meadows are coverd with Sheep."

"Well Well go & play till the light fades away
And then go home to bed."
The little ones leaped & shouted & laughd
And all the hills ecchoed.*

"They remain at Wimbledon till six or seven Years of Age",[99] when they returned to the Parish Workhouse in Poland Street (round the corner from Broad Street).

Unfortunately, in the Workhouse "Examples of Vice and Profligacy being continually before their Eyes, very little Good could be expected to arise to the Children".[100] Therefore in September 1782 a separate "Parish School of Industry" was opened for them in King Street, Golden Square, to train children seven to fourteen years old to be housemaids and appren-

---

*   *An Island in the Moon*, Chapter 11; all the punctuation is added. Significantly, the poem was called "Nurses Song" rather than "my mothers song" when it was printed in *Songs of Innocence*. Note that in summer, when "the little birds fly", the nights in England may be only six or seven hours long, so these children are being allowed to stay up playing very late.

tices, stations in life far higher than children of the poor in other parishes could expect.

This is part of the context of Holy Thursday, first celebrated in St Paul's Cathedral on Ascension Day, 2 May 1782, in which thousands of charity school children, proudly arrayed in their cherished school uniforms,* flocked to give public thanks for the charity they had received:

> Upon a holy thursday their innocent faces clean
> The children walking two & two in grey & blue & green
> Grey headed beadles walkd before with wands as white as snow
> Till into the high dome of Pauls they like thames waters flow[101]

Beginning at least as early as August 1782, at the time William Blake was married, James Blake began to sell goods in substantial quantities to dependencies of the parish of St James, Westminster. From August 1782 to June 1784, "Mr Blake Haberdasher" sold £95.9.10 worth of goods to the St James Workhouse and Schoolhouse, paid for fortnightly at the rate of £1.0.0 to £4.6.1.[102] Probably Blake's father had an exclusive agreement with the Governors and Directors of the Poor of St James Parish, the guardians of the poor, to supply hosiery and haberdashery for the Workhouse and the Schoolhouse.

However, when Blake's father died about the end of June 1784, the agreement with the parish presumably lapsed, and the supplying of haberdashery to the Parish School was taken over by Messrs Jones & Co., Haberdashers, once, on 14 October 1784, for the huge sum of £7.17.7.

After Blake's father's death, the business of "Blake & Son" at 28 Broad Street was carried on by Blake's mother Catherine Armitage Blake and by his brother James. In an attempt to regain the lost parish business, James wrote a letter to the Directors and Governors of the Poor, for consideration at their meeting on 1 April 1785:

Gentⁿ

As at this Se[a]son of the year you appoint your several Trades persons permit me to offer myself to serve you with Articles of Haberdashery for I flatter myself I am able to supply the Infirmary & School of Industry with every Article upon as low terms as any house in London & being an Inhabitant of this P[ari]sh & my family for many years hope a preference may be given me for which should I succeed shall make it my study to

---

* The children in the St James School of Industry, however, did not wear livery ([William Combe], *Microcosm of London*, III [1809], 242).

deliver for the use of the same such Articles as will bear the strictest Examination. Sh^{d} any be found not agre[e]able or otherwise not suiting shall be happy to provide such as will every way answer the use intended or exchange the Articles if not approved—

I remain Gent^{n} for Mother & Self

Broad St Golden Sq[ua]re: Your very hble Servt

Ja^{s} Blake

James Blake's application was clearly approved in principle, and from 15 April to 8 July 1785 he supplied goods for the Schoolhouse in the very substantial sum of £17.16.1, four times the average fortnightly business that his father had achieved. However, there is no further record of his relationship with the parish. Perhaps the wise guardians of the poor found some fault with his goods or his accounting, or perhaps they merely found a cheaper supplier.

The commercial standards of the Governors and Directors of the Poor in the Parish of St James were admirably high at first, and they scrupulously framed their rules and practice to avoid the possibility of persistent theft and embezzlement from the School and Workhouse and even of conflict of interest among their own members. The Governors "are prohibited from having any Benefit in any Contract or in the Service of Goods, Materials, Provisions, Necessarys for the Poor".[103]

Later, however, their political judgement might be suspected. At first the children in the school made some of their own clothing, such as shoes, and these proved to be serviceable, creating a sensible diminution of the expenses of the school. It was soon remarked that if the children could make suitable shoes for themselves, they ought to be able to make them commercially, for sale outside the school, with the profits being used to reduce the expenses of the school. From about 1786 a factory system was introduced in the school, the pretense of educating the children beyond their manual crafts was largely abandoned, and the school became a kind of workhouse for children.

This change may be alluded to in Blake's *America* (1793) (pl. 13, ll. 124–5) where "pity is become a trade, and generosity a science, That men get rich by" and in his "Holy Thursday" from *Songs of Experience* (1794) with its "Babes reduced to misery, | Fed with cold and usurous hand". The mechanics of parish charity were well known at the little haberdashery shop in Broad Street, and they may eventually have confirmed what Blake had been taught about the ways of the Beast among the children of men, even, or perhaps especially, when they claimed to be acting in charity.

John Blake, Gingerbread Baker and Soldier

About 1774, when he was fourteen, William's brother John, their parents' favourite child, was informally "apprenticed to a Gingerbread Baker".* Perhaps he was placed with Robert or Peter Blake, Bakers of Rupert Street near Golden Square, who were practising their humble craft in 1774 and 1788.[104] John "served his apprenticeship with reluctance"[105] and then, presumably about 1781, returned home to his doting parents at 28 Broad Street for a few years.

In 1784, probably shortly after his father's death, John Blake set himself up as a baker† in a small house (rated at £9) at 29 Broad Street at the corner of Broad and Marshall Streets, across from the family house at 28 Broad Street (rated at £21).[106] At the 1784 election "John Blake Marshall street Baker" came into the polling booth with his father and voted as he did, and he also voted from Marshall Street in 1788.[107] However, his charm was not enough to sell gingerbread, and he "became abandoned & miserable & literally ... sought bread at the Door of William".[108] He lost his money and his business, he could not pay the rates on his house, and, not long after the death of his mother in September 1792, he apparently ran away‡ to join the army in the English crusade against revolutionary France. "He lived a few reckless days, Enlisted as a Soldier & died".§ His charm was lost on his poet-brother, who referred to him in his letter of 22 November 1802 as "my Brother John the evil one".

Parker & Blake, Printsellers

From the cramped rooms in Green Street where William and Catherine lived, Blake carried his martial pictures of "A breach in a city, the morning after a battle" (Pl. 34) and "War unchained by an angel, Fire, Pestilence and Famine following" to the exhibition of the Royal Academy in April 1784. Perhaps his father saw them exhibited there before his death two months later.

The second picture was noticed unkindly in the *Morning Chronicle* for 27 May: "Blake in his War, Fire and Famine, outdoes most of the strange flights

---

* Tatham (*BR* 509). John Blake was not formally apprenticed for a fee to any City company, but the writs of the City companies did not run beyond the square mile of The City.

† £100 would serve to begin as a baker, according to Anon., *General Description of All Trades* (1747), 10, and J. Collyer, *The Parent's and Guardian's Directory* (1761), 57, 146. He may have begun in business with an inheritance from his father, who was buried on 4 July 1784.

‡ As the next two tenants of 29 Broad Street did (*BR* 558). And see Addenda, below.

§ Tatham (*BR* 509). He may have died abroad; at any rate, he was not buried with his parents and siblings in Bunhill Fields.

in our memory . . . 'Rending our ears asunder' . . . like *Fuseli*".[109] Blake's friend George Cumberland was no longer reviewing for the *Morning Chronicle*.

Characteristically, Blake used his images archetypally, adapting them to new situations all his life. Probably the scene in "A Breach in a City" is related to the destruction of Newgate Prison by the Gordon rioters which Blake had watched in June 1780. The broken wall in "A Breach in a City" reappears in the frontispiece to *America* (Pl. 35), with a bowed angel chained in the breach, and the woman in "A Breach in a City" grieving passionately over the corpses on the ground appears again on the title page of *America* (Pl. 36). And note that War is unchained by "an angel", as a representative of repressive temporal power. Already Blake associated the temporal powers of earth and heaven.

The elder James Blake died at the age of about 61 in the summer of 1784, and on Sunday 4 July he was buried in Bunhill Fields, the Dissenters' Burying Ground.

On his death without a will, his property would have been divided among his grieving widow Catherine and the five children. His son James Blake took over the little haberdashery shop at 28 Broad Street and responsibility for his elderly mother and his young sister Catherine Elizabeth,[110] who was then twenty and unmarried. William Blake probably inherited enough to buy "a very good . . . [*engravers' printing press*] which cost him forty pounds"[111] as well as the duty to look after young Robert Blake (then twenty-two). And John, the dissolute, charming, favourite son, may have inherited the largest portion.* The division must have been a disagreeable business, and when William Blake read in Lavater's *Aphorisms* (1788) (¶157), "Say not you know another entirely, till you have divided an inheritance with him", he marked it with two heart-felt exclamation points.

After the death of his father, Blake started a print-selling business with his old friend James Parker (Pl. 28). They took a substantial house† at 27 Broad Street, next door to Blake's natal home, where his brother James still lived with his mother Catherine and his sister Catherine Elizabeth, and across the street from his brother John's bakery shop. Blake's new home, valued in the rate books at £18, must have been almost as large as 28 Broad Street, rated at £21, but it was slightly less desirable than 28 Broad Street because it was not on a corner and therefore had half as much street frontage.

---

* Tatham (*BR* 509) says that John was "apprenticed . . . at an Enormous premium", but the fees for bakers (£5–£20) were always small compared to the £52.10 paid to apprentice William Blake as an engraver. Perhaps the enormous sum was not an apprenticeship fee but an inheritance from his father or a loan from his brothers.

† Cunningham calls it "a first floor and a shop" (*BR* 482).

Parker, seven years older than Blake, had been his fellow apprentice at Basire's. According to their friend Flaxman, Parker "is one of those Steady, persevering men, who is constantly advancing in the best pursuits of his art, he is besides, religious, mild & conscientious", an "Engraver of distinguished merit who is a punctual honest man".[112] He was so well known for "his equanimity of temper, his serenity of manners, and integrity"[113] that he became a spokesman for his fellow-engravers during the engravers' strike of 1803, and he was elected President of the Society of Engravers by 1804. At the time of his sudden death in 1805 he was a man of modest substance, with three houses, a servant, and an apprentice.[114]

He had married Anne Serjeantson on 17 August 1782,[115] the day before William Blake and Catherine Boucher were married in Battersea, and the two couples moved into 27 Broad Street with Blake's young brother Bob,[116] probably in October 1784.*

Blake had been a haunter of print-shops almost as long as he could recall, but in 1784 they were still uncommon; indeed, he could "remember when a Print shop was a rare bird in London", as he wrote in his letter of 2 July 1800.

To start a print-shop, little was needed beyond a stock of prints and plausible premises. Many print-sellers commissioned their own prints, as Macklin and Ackermann did, but this required substantial capital in order to pay the painters and the engravers and the copperplate printers.

The expense of engraving could be reduced if the print-seller himself was an engraver, and this was not uncommon; for instance, William Wynne Ryland, to whom it had been proposed to apprentice Blake, was an engraver-turned-printseller. One of the advantages of the firm of Parker & Blake in starting a print-shop, besides the fact that they already knew the profession well, was that they were both trained engravers and thus were in a position to engrave prints for their own shop without the tedious dispersal of cash to other engravers.

Yet another way to save money in a print-shop was to do the printing on the premises on one of the big rolling-presses which were peculiar to the engravers' art.† These were bulky, expensive machines, and skill in printing

---

* In a letter of 23 Oct 1804, Blake said that he had embarked upon the ocean of business "exactly twenty years" ago.

    "James Parker & Wm Blake" paid the rates at 27 Broad Street from the end of 1784 until the Christmas quarter of 1785, when Blake moved out. Parker stayed on until 1794 (*BR* 557 n1), perhaps on a ten-year lease. Parker voted Whig in the elections of 1788 and 1790 (*BR* 558 n1).

† Intaglio engravings are printed on rolling-presses under great pressure from ink in the recesses in the copper created by the burin and acid, while hand-set text is printed on flat-bed presses from ink on the surface of the type with much lighter pressure. All books with intaglio engravings and hand-set text (that is, most ambitious illustrated books down to about 1790) were printed on two different kinds of presses.

    However, in wood-engraving and in Blake's relief-etching, the images are printed from the surface, not from the recesses, and can therefore easily be printed with type-set text on an ordinary flat-bed press.

was enormously important in producing fine copies. Pulling prints was an expensive business—in 1826 pulling Drawing Paper copies of Blake's Job copperplates cost $2\frac{1}{4}$d. each, French paper copies $2\frac{3}{4}$d., and India paper copies 4d.[117] If one did the printing oneself, as Blake and Parker had been trained to do at Basire's, yet another cost could be eliminated at the mere expense of time.

Blake owned a printing press at least by 1800, when he printed Hayley's *Little Tom the Sailor* on it, and he probably acquired it as early as 1784 when he started the print-selling business with Parker. This was a major asset for the firm of Parker & Blake, an asset perhaps balanced by Parker providing a supply of prints for the firm.[118] Thereafter Blake's proofs and all copies of his works in Illuminated Printing were pulled on his own rolling-press.

The house at 27 Broad Street was probably divided into a showroom where prints could be sold, an engraving-studio for Parker and Blake with Blake's printing press in it, and living quarters for the Parkers and the Blakes. The men must have spent most of their time in the studio, while Catherine "attended to the business" in the shop.[119] "She was an excellent saleswoman, and never committed the mistake of showing too many things at one time."[120]

In April 1785 Blake carried from the print-shop in Broad Street his ambitious series of designs of "Joseph making himself known to his brethren", "Josephs Brethren bowing before him" (Pl. 37), "Joseph ordering Simeon to be bound", and "The Bard" for exhibition at the Royal Academy. All are History Paintings concerned with the heroic prophet unrecognized and dishonoured by the powers of the world but vindicated by God and posterity.

Their reception demonstrated that prophets had no more honour in Georgian London than in Biblical Egypt or thirteenth-century Wales. Blake was merely listed as a contributor to the Royal Academy exhibition in the *Morning Chronicle and Daily Advertiser* for 28 April, while the *Daily Universal Register* for 23 May remarked severely that "Gray's Bard, W. Blake, appears like some lunatic, just escaped from the incurable cell of Bedlam; in respect of his other works, we assure this designer, that grace does not consist in the sprawling of legs and arms."[121]

In the intervals of engraving and print-selling, Blake delighted in teaching his beloved brother Bob[122] the arts of painting and engraving. Probably he used the same methods he had been taught when he was an apprentice engraver under Basire and when he was a student of art at the Royal Academy: how to grind his graver and to planish a plate, how to lay in the outline and work up from the crudest details in the background to the finest details in hands and faces.

One of Robert's designs, known as The Approach of Doom, depicts a group of appalled figures gazing in horror at sight of something beyond our ken. The unseen object is probably the Great Meteor, as large as the full moon and very much brighter, which was seen on 18 August 1783.* William Blake was so impressed with Robert's design that he used it as the basis for his first experiment in Illuminated Printing (see Pl. 38).

This was a happy time for Blake, surrounded by those he loved best, and the only incident which is known to have marred their domestic happiness is an extraordinary credit to both Bob and Kate.

> One day, a dispute arose between Robert and Mrs. Blake. She, in the heat of discussion, used words to him, his brother (though a husband too) thought unwarrantable. A silent witness thus far, he could now bear it no longer, but with characteristic impetuosity—when stirred—rose and said to her: "Kneel down and beg Robert's pardon directly, or you never see my face again!" A heavy threat, uttered in tones which, from Blake, unmistakably showed it was *meant*.
>
> She, poor thing! "thought it very hard," as she would afterwards tell, to beg her brother-in-law's pardon when she was not in fault! But being a duteous, devoted wife, though by nature nowise tame or dull of spirit, she *did* kneel down and meekly murmur: "*Robert, I beg your pardon, I am in the wrong.*"
>
> "Young woman, you lie!" abruptly retorted he: "*I* am in the wrong!"[123]

Large print shops sold everything from formal portraits and landscapes and battle-scenes to caricatures and news-prints of murders and hangings. Small shops tended to be more specialized, and the firm of Parker & Blake probably carried chiefly fine prints, perhaps including the twenty proofs of plates they engraved for other publishers, the traditional perquisites of commercial engravers.[124]

Of course both James Parker and William Blake continued their ordinary work for other print-publishers while they had their shop; Blake is known to have made eleven such plates in 1784–85 and Parker at least four.[125]

But Parker & Blake had greater ambitions than this. They commissioned two designs from their friend Thomas Stothard, who was becoming the most prolific book-illustrator of the day. Stothard was an admirer of the engraving skills of both the partners in the firm of Parker & Blake. Parker was "obliged to his friend Mr Stothard for 'having so <u>often</u> recommended Mr Parker to M^r Du Roveray's notice'" as an engraver,[126] and Stothard

---

* Marilynn S. Olson & Donald W. Olson, "William Blake and August's Fiery Meteors", *Astronomical Computing* (Aug 1989), 192–4. The Great Meteor was seen on the first anniversary of the marriage of William and Catherine Blake, when Robert was twenty-one. There were splendid meteor showers, known as "The Tears of St Lawrence", in 1779, 1781, 1784, and 1789.

must have been partially responsible for the thirty-two commissions Blake received from seven different booksellers to make engravings after Stothard's designs in 1780–84.

Stothard made elegant oval designs of "Callisto" and "Zephyrus and Flora" (Pl. 39) which were engraved in stipple by Blake and "Published as the Act directs Dec.ʳ 17. 1784 by Parker & Blake No 27 Broad St Golden Square". Parker & Blake not only chose one of the most fashionable painters of the day, but Blake engraved the designs in the newly popular dotted or stipple manner, a style which obscures the clarity of the firm and determinate outlines and which he rarely used later. He is likely to have felt that he was making important concessions to Stothard and to popularity as he engraved the plates.

Not only were the design and the subject very much *à la mode*, but the printing was very elegant. "Zephyrus and Flora" and "Callisto" were delicately coloured by Parker & Blake, and the *tout ensemble* is graceful and refined.*

Stothard may in friendship have agreed to accept royalties on sales of the prints in lieu of a fee for his paintings. If so, he was probably disappointed in the result, for the prints sold but feebly. Only six copies of each design have been traced today, and the venture may have resulted in a breach between Blake the engraver and Stothard the designer. At any rate after 1784 Blake engraved no book-illustration after Stothard, and he later complained that "Stothard ... [was] such a fool as to suppose that his blundering blurs can be made out & delineated by any Engraver ... equally well with those little prints which I engraved after him ... by which he got his reputation as a draughtsman[.]"[127]

As one might expect, the little business of Parker & Blake was richer in genius than in cash, and the partners apparently ran short of credit. Because of Blake's connection with the little coterie at which he sang his songs, he was able "to benefit by Mrs. Mathew's liberality ... to continue in partnership, as a Printseller, with his fellow-pupil Parker".[128]

However, as a consequence of Blake's "unbending deportment, or what his adherents are pleased to call his manly firmness of opinion, which certainly was not at all times considered pleasing by every one, his visits [*to the Mathew salon*] were not so frequent",[129] and the firm of Parker & Blake disintegrated. There may have been difficulties in sharing the house and printshop with the Parkers; perhaps Blake "had a dispute with Parker";[130] perhaps Anne Parker fell ill;* or perhaps it was a matter simply of persist-

---

* Parker's posthumous sale by Thomas Dodd on 18–19 Feb 1807 included "Six Circles, by Blake, in colours" (#159).

ent lack of space, capital and customers.

The House in Poland Street

In the autumn of 1785 Catherine, William, and Robert Blake moved from the house and shop they shared with the Parkers at 27 Broad Street to 28 Poland Street about three streets to the north. This was the size of the house at 27 Broad Street, which was also rated at £18, but they did not need to share it with anyone else.

Probably Blake continued to sell prints from his house. At any rate, his engraving of Fuseli's "Timon and Alcibiades" bears the imprint "Published by W. Blake, Poland St. July, 28: 1790".

The street was popular with artists, poets, and folk of fashion, from Dr Charles Burney and Thomas Rowlandson to the Duke of Chandos and Percy Bysshe Shelley.† Across Oxford Road, just to the north of the end of Poland Street, there was still little "but fields, gardeners' grounds, or uncultivated suburbs".[131]

One of the amenities of the neighbourhood was the public house at 22 Poland Street, where Blake may have bought his porter. Here, according to the artist David Wilkie,

> about a dozen gentlemen meet at 2 o'clock, and have a dinner served up that only costs them 13*d*. a head, which I am sure is as cheap as any person can have such a dinner in any part of Great Britain: besides, we have the advantage of hearing all the languages of Europe talked with the greatest fluency, the place being mostly frequented by foreigners: indeed, it is a very rare thing to see an Englishman; while there are Corsicans, Italians, French, Germans, Welsh and Scotch.[132]

According to a plaque still on the wall, "In this Old King's Arms Tavern the ANCIENT ORDER OF DRUIDS was revived 28th November 1781", on Blake's

---

*   Parker's will of 1805 makes no mention of a wife, and his sister had been living with him and keeping his house for eighteen years, suggesting that Anne Parker had died by 1787.

†   Residents in Poland Street included Sir William Chambers, architect (1755–66), Dr Charles Burney, musicologist (1760–70), David Martin, engraver and publisher (1765-66), Paul Sandby, painter (1767–72), Thomas Malton, the architectural draughtsman (1772–80), Gavin Hamilton, painter (1779), the great singer the beautiful Elizabeth Billington (*c.* 1783), Thomas Busby, musical composer and contributor to the *Analytical Review* (1786 ff.), Thomas Rowlandson, caricaturist (1788–90), John Mills, stationer and news-dealer (1790–1800), Count Caumont, French refugee and distinguished bookbinder (1797–1800), Percy Bysshe Shelley, poet (1811), and, according to Fanny Burney, *Memoirs of Dr Charles Burney* (1832), I, 134, "the Duke of Chandos, Lady Augusta Bridges, the Hon. John Smith and the Miss Barrys, Sir Willoughby, and the Miss Astons".

birthday, and here Blake may have met Enthusiasts who stored his mind and myth with the Druid lore which appears in his *Milton* and *Jerusalem*.

Here in this cosmopolitan neighbourhood the Blakes lived for five years, from 1785 to 1790.

The Death of Robert Blake

Already in the winter of 1785–86, Robert Blake may have exhibited the emaciation and wracking cough characteristic of advancing consumption[133] or tuberculosis. As Bob grew weaker and more ravaged by illness, William must have grown increasingly agonized for him.* By the beginning of 1787, Robert was very ill indeed, probably terribly weak, bed-ridden, and coughing up blood. "Blake sat up for a whole fortnight with his brother Robert during his last illness",[134] and when Robert died, Blake saw his "released spirit ascend heavenward through the matter-of-fact ceiling, 'clapping its hands for joy'".[135] Bob was twenty-four years old.

After the crisis, Blake went to bed and slept for three days and nights.[136]

Because of his exhausted sleep, Catherine probably dared not or could not waken him for Robert's funeral. Blake would therefore have missed the little family group which accompanied the body of Robert Blake on 11 February 1787 to Bunhill Fields where his father had been buried two and a half years earlier.

Robert's death made a profound impression on Blake, one which he used some fifteen years later in a description of the last harvest: "Urizen rose up from his couch | On wings of tenfold joy, clapping his hands".[137] Robert's spirit stayed with Blake for the rest of his life, as a kind of reciprocal of himself (Pl. 4), and William's references to brothers and brotherhood are often freighted with the poignancy of his brother's early death, with memories of happiness and vision: "Man liveth not by Self alone but in his brother's face";[138] in heaven

... My Brother is there & My Friend & Thine
Descend & ascend with the Bread & the Wine[139]

With Angels planted in Hawthorn bowers
And God himself in the passing hours[,] ...
With my Father hovering upon the wind
And my Brother Robert just behind[.][140]

---

* The parallel of John Keats nursing his younger brother Tom through the last stages of consumption in 1818 is very strong. Keats himself died of consumption in February 1821.

The death of his brother when William was twenty-nine years old marked a period in the poet's life. It marked, as it were, the end of his intellectual apprenticeship. Had it been William who died in 1787 rather than Robert, we would remember him today as no more than a curious minor poet, a competent engraver, and a painter of more ambition than accomplishment. The triumphs are all in the future. And the triumphs for which he is best known are due to the inspiration of Robert Blake.

With the death of his brother Robert, William Blake had shaken off another covering of earth. He was another step closer to heaven.

CHAPTER IV

1787–1795: Dark Profitable Years[1]

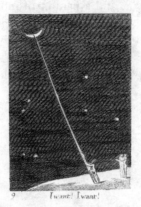

9   I want! I want!

*Thirteen years ago I lost a brother & with his spirit I converse daily &
hourly in the spirit .... I hear his advice & even now write from his
Dictate. Forgive me for ... my Enthusiasm which I wish all to partake
of Since it is to me a Source of Immortal Joy[;] even in this world by it
I am the companion of Angels.*   (Letter of 6 May 1800)

All his life Blake communed with spirits, and this communion was his
greatest joy. By it his spirit was lifted to heaven, to the companionship of
angels, and by it he regulated his life and his most practical actions.

The Road to Illumination

For years Blake, like his friend George Cumberland and others, had been
fascinated by the problems of printing and selling books without being
dependent upon conventional typesetters and booksellers. For authors and
artists whose interests were primarily in glory and beauty rather than gold
and fame, the troublesome obsession with cash exhibited by compositors
and publishers was often crippling.

Blake was a poet without a publisher and an artist without a patron, but,
unlike Cumberland, he had no private income which would enable him to
hire compositors and to publish his books at his own expense. In 1784 Blake
had written of his method of "Illuminating the Manuscript" with "all the
writing Engraved instead of Printed [*i.e., type-set*] & at every other leaf a
high finishd print",[2] and George Cumberland had published an account of
his "New Mode of Printing" with text etched instead of typeset.[3] By such
methods, the artist and the amateur author could multiply their works without the tedious intervention of compositors and publishers.

The idea of combining engraved text with design was not new; it had been done repeatedly before, for instance in *The Orthodox Communicant* (1721), for which John Sturt engraved the text with a vignette and an elaborate frame of cherubs for each page (Pl. 40).

However, both the engraving and the printing of Sturt's book were extraordinarily laborious. Such pains were economically justifiable only for a work which could be printed year after year for a secure market, such as Sturt's *Book of Common Prayer* (1717) and La Fontaine's *Fables Choisies* (6 vols, Paris, 1765–75) and William Milne's *The Penman's Repository* (1787). New and unproved work could scarcely be produced thus with any hope of secure profit. The technology was far too expensive.*

The fundamental defect of Blake's method was that engraving in intaglio and printing such "high finishd prints" would have been extremely slow, and the fundamental defect of Cumberland's New Mode was that it "can only be read with the help of a looking Glas[s], as the letters are reversed".[4]

There were two ways of simplifying these problems. The conventional mode of etching was in intaglio, in which the lines are burned with acid into the copper, and when the etching is printed on a rolling-press the paper must be forced down into the etched recesses to pick up the ink. An alternative was to etch not in intaglio but in relief, with the parts which are *not* to show burned away, leaving the designs standing high. Such etched relief designs could be printed with very light pressure on the flat-bed press used for text. Relief etching on copper was perfectly well known to engravers,[5] and the method of printing them was standard for woodblocks.

An advantage of such relief etching was that the plates could be printed rapidly and cheaply—and they could be printed on a type-press alongside type-set pages. A disadvantage was that the designs could not be "high finishd", for fine raised lines would not stand up to repeated printing. If, however, high finished designs were not essential, or if the comparatively crude designs could be enhanced by colouring or other hand-finishing, or if few copies were to be pulled, this disadvantage might be insignificant.

The ordinary method of etching was (1) to copy on paper the design (in reverse) in the size of the intended printed image, (2) to repeat the design exactly by drawing with an etching needle on a wax-covered copperplate, (3) to pour acid over the waxed plate in order to burn away the copper exposed through the wax by the etching-needle, (4) to remove the wax from the plate and take a proof to see the progress of the design, and then (5) to improve the design by further etching, engraving, and proofing.

---

* Music was printed entirely from engraved or etched plates, but here there was no alternative until economical musical types were invented. Most music texts were very brief, such as Commins's *Elegy Set to Music*, with five pages of music and a cover designed and engraved by Blake (1786).

This method, standard for copy-engraving, was less suitable for an artist-engraver creating original designs. For him, a better way to capture the nervous, vibrant lines of inspiration is to draw directly on the wax without an intervening copy—and the best method would be to draw directly on the copper. This, of course, is what engravers were trained to do.

However, the techniques of engraving, pushing a sharp instrument through copper, are so different from ordinary artistic composition, so much more cumbersome and time-consuming, that even a trained artist-engraver like Blake would feel inhibited when he took a graver in his hand. The ideal was to be able draw on copper as freely as on paper or canvas, and this was not possible in England in the eighteenth century.*

Blake had been thinking about such problems at least since 1784, and he must have talked about them with his brother Robert when he was teaching him painting and engraving in 1784–87. Blake would set his pupil tasks, such as copying a head on paper or a scene on copper, and he would show Robert how to improve them, so that in time the works became collaborations.

The crux was to be able to write or draw directly on copper—not incising the copper, not drawing lines with a pencil or brush on the copper or on wax-over-copper which were later to be cut by the graver or acid—but to make drawings which could be reproduced directly and mechanically rather than indirectly through the medium of another artist or another skill. As Blake insisted, "Engraving is drawing on Copper & Nothing Else".[6]

He brooded on the subject, and he talked to Robert and his friends about it, but the result was only the same "dull round of probabilities and possibilities".[7] Then one night, probably not long after Robert's death, his brother appeared to him and showed him the simple solution to the problem of composing directly on copper.[8]

Next morning, in great excitement Blake hurried to his studio to prepare for the great experiment, and, as soon as the shops were open, Catherine took "half a crown, all the money they had in the world, and of that laid out *1s. 10d.* on the simple materials necessary for setting in practice the new revelation".[9]

The secret was a fast-drying liquid impervious to acid, probably a variant of the ordinary engraver's stopping-out varnish, chiefly "pitch diluted with Terps",† with which the artist could write and draw directly upon the

---

* It is possible in lithography, which was invented in 1798 but did not reach England until 1803.
† Linnell (*BR* 460 n1). J.T. Smith wrote (*BR* 472–3):

> His method of eating away the plain copper, and leaving his drawn lines of his subjects and his words in stereotype, is in my mind perfectly original. Mrs. Blake is in possession of the secret, and she ought to receive something considerable for its communication, as I am quite certain it may be used to the greatest advantage both to artists and literary characters in general.

copper. The spaces round the finished words and design could then be bitten away with aquafortis in the usual way, leaving the picture and words standing in relief.

The materials Catherine Blake bought were presumably pitch, turps, and a brush with which to apply this glutinous liquid*—materials which could easily be acquired for a couple of shillings.

Note that the secret involves adapting known techniques and materials (relief etching, stopping-out varnish) to new purposes—and that the first purpose was to compose designs directly on copper, requiring only very mechanical application of acid to make them into relief plates which could be printed simply and mechanically.

One advantage of relief-etched plates was that they could be printed far more simply and rapidly than incised intaglio plates. Once the tedious business of setting up the print-shop was achieved, making the ink, dampening the paper, adjusting the press to the right pressure with blankets, the printing could be done briskly, with Blake choosing and inking a pair of plates while Catherine printed the two plates previously prepared. Sometimes two copies were pulled before the plates were re-inked. When a whole book was printed in one colour, as in Blake's early practise, they could easily print 500 pages in a week, enough to account for the sixteen copies of *Songs of Innocence* in one print-run.[10]

The first subject for the new technique was appropriately Robert Blake's design of "The Approach of Doom" (?1787) (Pl. 38).[11] In it, one can see Blake working out a variety of techniques of shading and white-line etching. Clearly he was exploring the resources of the new medium. Other experimental designs in the same medium were "Joseph of Arimathea Preaching" (1789), "Charity" (1789), and a design of a naked man being carried upwards by cherubs (1789) (*Songs* pl. a). None of them has any lettering at all. The first use of the drawing-liquid impervious to acid was for making designs directly on copper, not for making words or books. With this method there was no need for a preliminary draft—no paper copy at all.

Friendship with Fuseli

In 1787, Blake's dearest friend John Flaxman and his wife Nancy set sail for Rome, so that Flaxman could study the triumphs of sculpture there, the Laocoon, the Apollo Belvedere, Venus de Medici, the Dying Faun, and the

---

* Linnell wrote: "The most extraordinary facility seems to have been attained by Blake in writing backwards ... with a brush dipped in a glutinous liquid" (*BR* 460 n1).

Hercules Farnese. The Flaxmans were gone for seven years, and their absence must have left a chasm in the lives of the Blakes.

Blake had come to depend upon Flaxman for both professional advice and spiritual comfort.

> ... terrors appear'd in the Heavens above
> And in Hell beneath & a mighty & awful change threatend the Earth.
> The American War began. All its dark horrors passd before my face ...
> And My Angels have told me that Seeing such visions I could not
>   Subsist on the Earth
> But by my conjunction with Flaxman who knows to forgive Nervous
>   Fear.
>
> (Letter "To My Dearest Friend John Flaxman" 12 Sept 1800, punctuation added)

Probably the Blakes and Flaxmans promised to write faithfully, but mail over such a distance was very slow and dear, and few letters came through. On 21 November 1791 Nancy Flaxman asked her sister-in-law Maria Denman to persuade the Blakes to write to them in Rome, and two years later, on 20 November 1793, she was still asking for news of the Blakes.

Flaxman's absence was not all loss to Blake, however, for "When Flaxman was taken to Ital*y*, Fuseli was giv'n to me for a season".[12]

Flaxman and Fuseli (Pl. 41) were extraordinarily different men. Where Flaxman was gentle, classical, and restrained, Fuseli was rough, romantic, and passionate. Flaxman's sculptures and drawings are in quiet black and white, celebrating feminine grace and pious grief, while Fuseli's oil paintings are vibrant with colour invoking rage and madness. Each became a dominant figure in his genre; Flaxman became Professor of Sculpture at the Royal Academy and Fuseli the Keeper of the Royal Academy. Together they represented the two poles of Blake's artistic spirit.

Johann Heinrich Fussli was born in Zurich in 1741 and took holy orders there with his intimate friend Johann Caspar Lavater. When his reforming zeal made his continued presence in Zurich uncomfortable, he came to England and anglicized his name to Henry Fuseli. He was a splenetic little man, a scholar, a poet, an artist, and a wit. Blake may have learned of him first when he bought Fuseli's translation of the Abbé Winckelmann's very influential *Reflections on the Painting and Sculpture of the Greeks* (1765), while he was a student with Basire, and he may also have seen him when Fuseli lived in 1777–81 at 1 Broad Street, a few doors from Blake's family home at 28 Broad Street.

Fuseli was famous for his irascibility, which he cultivated; as Blake commented, "he is not naturally good natured but he is artificially very ill natured".[13] Blake admired Fuseli for both his character and his art:

The only Man that eer I knew
Who did not make me almost spew
Was Fuseli[;] he was both Turk & Jew
And so dear Christian Friends how do you do[?]

(Notebook p. 50)

Blake's disciple Frederick Tatham believed that "Blake was more fond of Fuseli than any other man on Earth",[14] and some contemporaries thought of Blake as "*a pupil of Fuseli*" but "*more eccentric than his master*".[15] Blake identified Fuseli with the greatest geniuses of art and literature whose works are "Drawn with a firm hand at once like Fuseli & Michael Angelo Shakespeare & Milton",[16] and he associated himself with Fuseli: great fools "never Can Rafael it Fuseli i*t*, nor Blake it".[17]

The relationship between the two men was clearly easy enough for impudence. Fuseli was famous for his strong language, and he "boasted that he could swear in nine languages".[18] Blake's young friend George Richmond used to tell of a conversation between Blake and Flaxman:

FLAXMAN: "How do you get on with Fuseli? I can't stand his foul-mouthed swearing. Does he swear at you?"
BLAKE: "He does."
FLAXMAN: "And what do you do?"
BLAKE: "What do I do? Why—I swear again! and he says astonished, '*vy, Blake, you are svaring!*' but he leaves off himself!"[19]

On another occasion, Blake showed Fuseli one of his works, and Fuseli said,

"Now some one has told you this is very fine."—
"Yes," said Blake, "the Virgin Mary appeared to me, and told me it was very fine: what can you say to that?"—
"Say!" exclaimed Fuseli, "why nothing—only her ladyship has not an immaculate taste."[20]

Blake praised Fuseli in private and in print,* and their artistic styles were strikingly similar; Stothard said on 12 January 1797 that Blake "had been misled [*by Fuseli*] to extravagance in his art". Fuseli held up Blake as a model to an errant engraver: "Let him look at the Anubis [*engraved by Blake*] in the first part of the Botanic Garden, and he will have a clue" how to do "justice

---

* Samuel Palmer wrote: "Blake *told me* about 1825 that we were one century behind the civilization which would enable us to appreciate Fuseli" (*BRS* 80), and Blake published a letter in the *Monthly Magazine* (1 July 1806) defending Fuseli: "the truth is, he is a hundred years beyond the present generation".

to my drawing".[21] Flaxman and Fuseli used to say "That a time will come when Blake's finest works will be as much sought after and treasured up in the portfolios of men of mind, as those of Michel Angelo are at present",[22] and both men used Blake's graphic ideas. Fuseli liked to say that "*Blake is d—d good to steal from!*",[23] and while he was away in Rome Flaxman signed a sheet of sketches: "J. Flaxman from memory of three drawings of Blake June 1792",* which he had last seen at least five years before. Flaxman owned a few of Blake's literary works,[24] while the only literary work by Blake which Fuseli is known to have owned is *For Children: The Gates of Paradise* (E) which he gave in 1806 to Harriet Jane Moore (aged five).

Fuseli probably persuaded his good friend Joseph Johnson, for whom Blake had worked repeatedly, to commission Blake to engrave Fuseli's designs for Lavater's *Aphorisms on Man* (1 plate, 1788), Darwin's *Botanic Garden* (1 plate in 1791, 1 more in 1795), Allen's *History of England* (4 plates, 1797), Allen's *Roman History* (4 plates, 1798), and Fuseli's own *Lectures on Painting* (1 plate, 1801). Blake was commissioned to engrave "Satan Taking His Flight Upwards from Chaos" for Fuseli's heroic project to illustrate Milton which was to be published by Joseph Johnson and James Edwards† until the project was abandoned. Most intriguing of all are the three separate plates Blake engraved after Fuseli entitled "Falsa ad Coelum" (?1790), "Satan" (?1790), and "Timon & Alcibiades" (28 July 1790), for apparently they were not published—they bear no imprint. Access to Fuseli's designs without a commission from a publisher suggests a very close relationship between Blake and Fuseli. Perhaps for a time in 1790 Blake was serving as engraver in ordinary to Fuseli.

Fuseli allowed much more latitude in interpreting his designs to Blake than he did to other engravers, and indeed his sketches for Blake seem to have been based on the premise that Blake would amplify them. Fuseli's sketch for Lavater's *Aphorisms* gives only the first Greek letter for "Know Thyself", leaving Blake to supply the rest or solicit it from Fuseli, and his

---

* *BR* 47, where the sheet is reproduced. In later years, this borrowing became a grievance to Blake: "Flaxman cannot deny that one of the very first Monuments [c. *1782*] he did I gratuitously designed for him" (Public Address, Notebook p. 53).

> To Nancy F——
> How can I help thy Husbands copying Me[?]
> Should that make difference twixt me & Thee[?]

(Notebook p. 27)

† *BR* 44, 46–7. Blake also engraved two plates after Fuseli dated 1804 for Shakespeare's *Plays* published by a congery in 1805. Fuseli may have been responsible for Blake's commission to engrave four plates for his friend Lavater's *Essays on Physiognomy* (1789–98) which Fuseli supervised and for which Johnson had a major responsibility, though neither is mentioned on the title page—see "William Blake and His Circle", *Blake*, XXX (1997), 130–1.

sensational design for the "Fertilization of Egypt" for Darwin's *Botanic Garden* does not have the bearded rain-god which Blake added. Clearly the two men shared an extraordinary artistic confidence in one another.

Through Fuseli or Johnson, Blake obtained the unbound sheets of Fuseli's translation of Lavater's *Aphorisms on Man* in 1788. He pored over the book lovingly, annotated it repeatedly, corrected Fuseli's English occasionally, and on the title page under "Lavater" he wrote "Willm. Blake" and drew a heart around the names. Aphorism ¶643 instructed the reader: "If you mean to know yourself, interline [*?i.e., underline*] such of these aphorisms as affected you agreeably in reading and set a mark to such as left a sense of uneasiness with you . . .". Blake underlined scores of aphorisms and annotated many others: "Admirable!", "Pure gold", "Bravo", "uneasy", or even "<u>False</u>". Some of the longer notes are revealing of how he understood himself: "I love laughing" (¶54), "I fear I have not many enemies" (¶151). Even more important are his comments dealing with philosophical issues, which show Blake developing ideas which were to inform his literary works, particularly the *Marriage of Heaven and Hell*.

hell is the being shut up in the possession of corporeal desires which shortly weary the man for <u>all life is holy</u>*

(¶309)

<u>love is life</u>

(¶376)

Active Evil is better than Passive Good.†

(¶409)

every genius, every hero, is a prophet [*Lavater's ¶413, underlined by Blake*]

Beauty is exuberant‡

(¶532)

every thing on earth is the word of God & in its essence is God

(¶630)

all Act is Virtue. To hinder another is not act[;] it is the contrary . . . whatever is Negative is Vice

(flyleaves)

Blake's casual citation of the Bible (¶487, 489, 533, 630), sometimes in somewhat obscure contexts such as Sodom or Uzzah and the Ark of God,

---

* Cp. "every thing that lives is Holy" (*Marriage* ¶92, *Visions* 1. 215).
† Cp. *Marriage* ¶3: "Good is the passive that obeys Reason[.] Evil is the active springing from Energy".
‡ Cp. *Marriage* pl. 10: "Exuberance is Beauty".

indicates a confident mastery of Biblical text such as one would expect of a Dissenter who had been brought up on the Bible.

Blake showed his annotated copy of Lavater's *Aphorisms* "to Fuseli; who said one could assuredly read their writer's character in *them*".[25] Blake's display of his most private thoughts to Fuseli suggests an extraordinarily confident intimacy between them.

These pithy or pretentious aphorisms of Lavater must have been in Blake's mind when he created the impudent "Proverbs of Hell" in the *Marriage of Heaven and Hell*.

Blake and the Circle of Joseph Johnson

From 1779, when he was just out of his apprenticeship, Blake had been engraving plates for the distinguished bookseller Joseph Johnson of St Paul's Churchyard. Johnson admired his skill with a graver, and "said He is capable of doing anything well";[26] "Blake is certainly capable of making an exact copy of the [*Wedgwood*] vase, I believe more so than Mr. B[*artolozzi*]",[27] despite Bartolozzi's considerably greater fame and fashionableness.

From 1779 to 1786, Johnson was one of the chief employers of Blake's graver, with sixteen plates for seven books, chiefly in duodecimo. Most of these plates are modest in ambition, such as those for Bonnycastle's *Introduction to Mensuration* (1782) and Nicholson's *Introduction to Natural Philosophy* (1782), but a few have greater aesthetic pretensions, such as the eight charming plates after Stothard for Ritson's *Select Collection of English Songs* (1783). Beginning in 1787, when Blake met Fuseli, his commissions from Johnson become increasingly ambitious.

Johnson gave Blake commissions for 90 plates in 1786–1801, including forty-four unsigned plates after Chodowiecki in duodecimo for Mary Wollstonecraft's translation of Salzmann's *Elements of Morality* (1790–91), quarto plates after Fuseli in Darwin's *Botanic Garden* (1791, 1795), many sensational quarto plates for Stedman's *Narrative of . . . the Revolted Negroes of Surinam* (1796) (Pls 44–5), and especially his plate for Fuseli's proposed Milton (1791) and his six plates *after his own designs* for Mary Wollstonecraft's *Original Stories from Real Life* (1791). As Johnson wrote to William Hayley on 4 January 1802, "Ever since I have had a connection with Mr Blake I have wished to serve him & on every occasion endeavoured to do so. I wish him to be paid for what he is now doing a fair & even liberal price . . .".[28]

Joseph Johnson (1738–1809), twenty years older than Blake, was born into a Baptist family but moved towards Unitarianism, and he had a Dissenter's sympathies with liberal social and political causes. He was a methodical, determined man, gentle and generous, and by the time Blake met him he was solidly established in his profession, though his greatest accomplishments were yet in the future. He became the chief publisher of the quiet poems of William Cowper, the scientific speculations of Dr Joseph Priestley, the radical political and philological works of John Horne Tooke, the botanical poetry of Erasmus Darwin, and the miscellaneous writings of Mary Wollstonecraft, who lived in his house for a time. He was imprisoned in 1799 by a vindictive government for selling a radical pamphlet by Gilbert Wakefield and bore his imprisonment with cheerful, genteel fortitude.

Johnson's most promising and generous actions towards Blake were, however, abortive. He agreed to publish Blake's *The French Revolution*, and even had the first book set up in type (Pl. 42). However, only page-proofs survive for the first book; the other six have disappeared entirely. The poem is a psychomachia, a war of spirits, of the spirits of freedom and privilege. Some of the noblest rhetoric in the poem defends the ancient bastions of civilization:

> Shall this marble built heaven become a clay cottage, this earth an oak
>   stool, and those mowers
> From the Atlantic mountains, mow down all this great starry harvest of
>   six thousand years?
> . . .
> Till the power and dominion is rent from the pole, sword and sceptre
>   from sun and moon
> The law and gospel from fire and air, and eternal reason and science
> From the deep and the solid, and man lay his faded head down on the rock
> Of eternity . . . .[29]

We do not know why the publication of *The French Revolution* was aborted; perhaps Blake never finished the poem; perhaps Johnson decided that the growing government hysteria about the untamed forces across the channel meant that it would be injudicious to print a work so sympathetic to the revolutionaries; certainly after 1791 events in France turned in a direction different from that Blake and the English radicals had hoped for. His view of the transformation of France from a liberal to an imperial power is expressed elsewhere in his couplet:

> When France got free Europe 'twixt Fools & Knaves
> Were Savage first to France & after: Slaves*

---

* Marginalium to Reynolds, *The Works of Sir Johua Reynolds, Knight, President of the Royal Academy* (London, 1798), p. ciii. On 12 April 1827, Blake wrote: "since the French Revolution Englishmen are all Intermeasurable One by Another[,] Certainly a happy state of Agreement to which I for One do not Agree. God keep me from the Divinity of Yes & No too[,] The Yea Nay Creeping Jesus".

Even more promising was Johnson's agreement to publish Blake's little emblem book called *For Children: The Gates of Paradise*, whose title page declares that it was "Published by W Blake N⁰ 13 Hercules Buildings Lambeth and J Johnson Sᵗ Pauls Church Yard", 1793. Customers could see

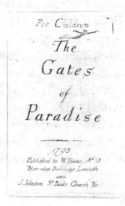

For Children, *Songs of Innocence*, and "several more of Blakes books at Johnsons in St. Pˢ. Ch. yᵈ", as Richard Twiss wrote in 1794.³⁰ However, the publicity did not do much good, for only five copies of *For Children* are known today, and perhaps not many more were sold.*

Johnson gathered round him a circle of witty, liberal friends, including many of the authors whose works he published, and he gave "plain but hospitable weekly dinners [*on Wednesdays*] at his house, No. 72, St Paul's Churchyard, in a little quaintly-shaped up-stairs room, with walls not at right angles",³¹ which was decorated with the original of Fuseli's famous painting of "The Nightmare".³² The guests included Henry Fuseli, Dr Richard Price, Dr Joseph Priestley, Thomas Christie (the editor of Johnson's *Analytical Review*), Horne Tooke, Thomas Holcroft, William Godwin, Tom Paine, and Mary Wollstonecraft.

It seems somewhat unlikely that the artisan William Blake was a member of this genteel gathering of earnest liberals,† though he was often in political sympathy with them. Gilchrist was told that

Down to his latest days Blake always avowed himself a "Liberty Boy," a faithful "Son of Liberty" .... He courageously donned ... the *bonnet rouge*—in open day, and philosophically walked the streets with the same

---

* Johnson is not known to have owned any work by Blake.
† Pace Gilchrist, who says that about 1791 "Blake was ... in the habit of meeting a remarkable coterie" at Johnson's weekly dinners (*BR* 40). Godwin's diary, the only consistent record of these gatherings, never refers unmistakably to William Blake the poet, though it does mention other Blakes (D.V. Erdman, "'Blake' Entries in Godwin's Diary", *Notes and Queries*, CXCVIII [1953], 354–6). And see Addenda, below.

on his head. He is said to have been the only one of the set who had the courage to make that public profession of faith.... When the painter heard of ... [*the Massacres in Paris of September 1792*], he tore off his white cockade, and assuredly never wore the red cap again.[33]

Blake had important connections with several of Johnson's friends. Thomas Holcroft commissioned Blake's plates for *The Wit's Magazine* (1784), and the grandfather of Thomas Christie's wife sponsored Blake's extraordinary advertisement for Moore & Company Carpet and Hosiery Manufactory in 1797–98. Joseph Johnson commissioned Blake to make designs for Mary Wollstonecraft's *Original Stories from Real Life; with Conversations, Calculated to Regulate the Affections, and Form the Mind to Truth and Goodness* (1791)—and then to make engravings of six of his own designs (Pl. 43). Of course Blake would have heard of the notorious Mary Wollstonecraft from her friends in Johnson's circle, and he may well have met her, though there is no biographical evidence that he did so.[*]

He also knew other members of the Johnson circle, including Horne Tooke, William Godwin, and Tom Paine.[34] In 1798 George Cumberland wrote to Horne Took "to recommend that neglected man of genius, and true son of Freedom Mr Blake, as your engraver" for a new edition of his *Diversions of Purleigh*.[35]

William Godwin, whose enormously influential *Enquiry Concerning Political Justice* was published in 1793, Blake "got on ill with, and liked worse".[36] Godwin is probably the person of whom Tatham was thinking when he told the story of a

free thinking Speculator, the Author of many very elaborate Philosophical Treatises, [*who*] said, that his children had not a dinner[;] Blake lent him £40[,] nearly all he had at that time by him, & had the mortification upon calling upon him on the following Sunday, to find that his Wife, who was a dressy & what is called a pretty woman, had squandered some large portion of the money, upon ... a very gorgeous dress, purchased the day following Blakes compassionate gift .... [†]

Whether or not Tatham was right in hinting that the borrower was Godwin, the story suggests that Blake was consorting with free thinking speculators,

---

* His *Visions of the Daughters of Albion* (1793) and "Mary" (Ballads MS) have often been associated with Mary Wollstonecraft, more by critical ingenuity than by fact.

† Tatham (*BR* 522); as *BR* comments (523 n1), "before 1800, Godwin did not have a wife and 'children' at the same time"; from 1800 to 1803 Blake was in Felpham; and by 1805 he was reduced, according to Cromek, to living on half a guinea a week, and it is unlikely that he then or later had £40 to lend.

that at least once, probably in the 1790s, he had substantial amounts of money to lend, and that his analysis of the speculator's physiognomy was not as acute as it had been in the case of William Wynne Ryland.

With Tom Paine, Blake's relationship was apparently much easier. He celebrated Paine as a staunch defender of political liberty in his *America* (1793), and he defended him vigorously in his marginalia to Bishop Watson's *Apology for the Bible* (1798). The government had become so exercised about the influence of Paine's *Rights of Man* (1790) that they attempted to demonize him, as hysterical governments later demonized Napoleon, Hitler, and Castro, and Paine's friends referred to him jokingly as the Demogorgon.[37]

For Paine the defender of liberty and the enemy of hypocrisy, Blake had the profoundest admiration. "Is it a greater miracle to feed five thousand men with five loaves [*as Christ did*] than to overthrow all the armies of Europe with a small pamphlet", as Paine did with *Common Sense* (1776)?[38] In his comments on Paine's dispute with the political bishop ("State trick-ster") Richard Watson, Blake concluded:

> The Perversions of Christs words & acts are attacked by Paine & also the perversions of the Bible .... Paine has not Attacked Christianity[.] Watson has defended Antichrist .... Paine is either a Devil or an Inspired man. ... It appears to me Now that Tom Paine is a better Christian than the Bishop[.] I have read this Book with attention & find that the Bishop has only hurt Paines heel while Paine has broken his head[.]
>
> (Marginalia to Watson's *Apology for the Bible*, title page verso, i, 3, 120)

Blake's notes indicate that he had already read Paine with care. The Bishop scarcely "has dared to Consider" "Paines Arguments .... One for instance which is That ... the Bible is all a State Trick thro which tho' the People at all times could see they have never ha*d* the power to throw off[.] Another Argument is that all the Commentators on the Bible are Dishonest Designing Knaves who in hopes of a good living adopt the State religion[;] this he has shewn with great force ..." (Watson, *Apology* p. 10).

Blake sides emphatically with Paine against the "Priestley Impudence"[39] of Richard Watson on political matters, but on religious issues, the ostensible subject of Watson's book, he condemns both their houses: "The Bishop never saw the Everlasting Gospel any more than Tom Paine" did.[40] According to his young friend Samuel Palmer, Blake "rebuked the profanity of Paine",[41] and his disciple Frederick Tatham wrote that "In one of their conversations, Paine said that religion was a law & a tye to all able minds. Blake on the other hand said what he was always asserting, that the religion of Jesus, was a perfect law of Liberty."[42]

Blake submerged his distrust of Paine's easy Deism in his admiration for Paine's courage and integrity as a political radical. Blake certainly associated himself with "the Paine set",* and his friends, at least, believed that he was responsible for Paine's escape from England on 12 September 1792, just steps ahead of a vengeful government: "Blake advised him immediately to fly, for he said 'if you are not now sought I am sure you soon will be'. Paine took the hint directly, & found he had just escaped in time."† Blake was probably just one of Paine's friends urging him to leave with all deliberate speed to take up his seat in the French parliament in September 1792.

The hysteria engendered by Tom Paine may on occasion have come close to Blake. The counter-revolutionary Society of Loyal Britons organized ritual protestations of loyalty all over the country, and on the night of 10 October 1793 they marched singing through the streets, threatening or even assaulting citizens who did not ostentatiously share their views, and burning effigies of Tom Paine. Blake may have seen the mob which met in Mount Row, Lambeth,[43] very near his house in Hercules Buildings (Pl. 49). Friendship with Tom Paine was dangerous to many.

Another person whom Blake met through Joseph Johnson, though scarcely a member of his set, was Captain John Gabriel Stedman. Stedman was an artist, poet, and engraver, who studied "to be singular, in as much as can be", so that he was often taken to be mad.[44] He was an extraordinary combination of contradictory qualities, from extreme sentimentality, marrying an octoroon slave, to serving the Dutch as a soldier of fortune in South America—but he closed his eyes when firing on the black rebels on the rare occasions when he actually saw them. He admired the courage and the integrity of the Negroes and owned slaves himself, with his initials tattooed on their breasts (Pl. 44). He was a keen naturalist, and no sooner did he see a new species than he shot and ate it.

While he was in Surinam, Stedman kept a journal, and he made drawings of some of the remarkable things he saw. Later he gathered these into a book entitled *Narrative, of a five years' expedition, against the Revolted Negroes of Surinam, in Guiana, on the Wild Coast of South America; from the year 1772, to 1777: elucidating the History of that Country, and describing its Productions, Viz. Quadrupedes, Birds, Fishes, Reptiles, Trees, Shrubs, Fruits, & Roots; with an account of the Indians of Guiana, & Negroes of Guinea*. The work is full

---

* Gilchrist says that, after his 1804 trial, Blake "used to declare the Government, or some high person, knowing him to have been of the Paine set, 'sent the soldier to entrap him'" (*BR* 146).

† Tatham (*BR* 531). Gilchrist dramatizes this story ("Blake laid his hands on the orator's shoulder, saying, 'You must not go home, or you are a dead man!'" [*BR* 530 n2]), but it is not clear that Gilchrist had more information about Blake's part in the affair than Tatham gives. Part of Gilchrist's information is contrary to the facts of Paine's leisurely and peaceful departure from England (*BR* 530 n2).

of fascinating detail about matters as diverse as the sexual customs of the Dutch colonists (institutionalizing temporary marriages with slave girls), how to skin a twenty-foot boa constrictor (hang it from a tree and shinny up the body with a knife), and the savagery of the Dutch slave-holders towards their slaves (hanging them alive from a hook between their ribs [see Pl. 45]).

He submitted the book to Joseph Johnson in 1791, and Johnson agreed to publish it—and to allow Stedman to keep half the subscriptions he collected.[45]

However, Johnson soon discovered the eccentricities of Stedman's character and style. Stedman's orthography was erratic—he wrote "quarl" for "quarrel" and "Bartholoz" for Bartolozzi*—his sense of cause and effect was curious, and the manuscript was as odd as its author.[46] As any sensible bookseller could see immediately, the book was crying out for an editor, and Johnson hired William Thomson, a literary man-of-all-work, to serve as male mid-wife. However, he neglected to tell the choleric Captain Stedman that he had done so. *Hinc illae lachrymae.*

Stedman's book was to be a lavishly illustrated quarto, and William Blake was engaged to make thirteen or more plates for it. As early as 1 December 1791 Stedman wrote: "About this time I re[*ceive*]ᵈ above 40 Engravings from London, Some well Some very ill . . .. I wrote to the Engraver blake to thank him twice for his excellent work but never received any answer[.]" It is interesting that Stedman was directly in touch with the engraver of his drawings, for ordinarily an engraver would deal only with the bookseller who had commissioned the work.

The plates Blake signed are dated 1 December 1792, 2 December 1793, and 1 December 1794 (though the book was not published until mid-1796), and his work on them clearly brought him in close contact with Stedman. Stedman wrote frequently to Blake,[47] though Blake rarely replied, and Stedman apparently stayed with Blake when he came up all the way from Tiverton in Devon to London. On 21 June 1794 Stedman wrote: "Call on Johnson & Blake", and on 2 June 1795 "I trip to Mᴿ & Mᴿˢ Blake".

By this time Stedman was in a rage about what had been done to his book: On 5 June he wrote: "I force Bartholozy to return my plates—and Brute Gregory to run away altogether—then take home My Spoilt M. Script and repair all plates". A few days later he "gave a blue Sugar cup to Mᴿˢ Blake . . . dined palmer—Blake—Johnsons—Rigaud—Bartholozy"—probably some of these calls were about subscriptions, for the subscription-list of Stedman's book includes "Blake (Mr. Wm), London", Thomas and William Palmer, and John Francis Rigaud, R.A.

---

* Blake writes "Bartelloze" to rhyme with "Prose" in his Public Address, Notebook p. 65.

In June 1795 Stedman

Gave oil portrait to M.ʳ Blake— ... dined at Blakes .... My book mard intirely am put to the most extreme trouble and expence .... I reconcile Johnson and cansel best part of the first volume ....

[*August 1795*] I visit Mʳ Blake for 3 days who undertakes to do busness for me when I am not in London—I leave him all my papers— ... d—n Bartholoz ... avershaw [*Louis Jeremiah Abershaw*] &c hangd [*for highway robbery on 3 August 1795*], 8—Saw a Mermaid— ... two days at blakes. ...

Septemb. ... all knaves and fools—and cruel to the excess—blake was mob'd and robbd ....

Being come home on the 18 Dec I ... Send a goose to Johnson and one to Blake .... Johnson Sends me a blur'd index—Such as the book good for nothing ....

[*In January and February 1796*] I sent [*all the preliminaries and index*] besides to London Hansard [*the printer*] ... I charged hansard not to trust the above papers with Johnson who I would now not Save from the gallows with only one of them so cruelly was I treated—and I declare him a Scound[r]ell without he gives me Satisfaction ....

[*May 1796*] Johnson, the demon of hell, again torments me by altering the dedication to the Prince of Wales &c., &c., he being a d-mn'd eternal Jacobin scoundrel.

The visionary poet and the choleric captain must have had an extraordinary friendship. On the surface there appears to be little in common between the slave-holding soldier and the slavery-hating engraver.[48]

When William Thomson revised Stedman's erratic text, Stedman was roused almost to apoplexy, but when Blake made equally extensive changes in Stedman's drawings, transforming the bloody black slaves* into classical heroes in adversity, Stedman clearly loved him for it, though he could only "d—n Bartholoz", who had made similarly extensive changes: "I force Bartholozy to return my plates ... and [*I*] repair all plates". Stedman was apparently an impulsively good man, though a bad reasoner, and Blake loved him for his good qualities.

Indeed, in some respects Blake's friendship with Stedman is like no other of which we have record. We know of no other guest who stayed in Blake's

---

* Stedman's drawings for his *Narrative* do not survive, but the descriptions in his text of the scenes depicted are a good deal more horrifying and bloody than Blake's engravings of them. And Stedman's surviving drawings of other subjects (see his *Narrative*, ed. Richard Price & Sally Price [Baltimore & London, 1988]) do not reveal an artist of the classical competence suggested by Blake's engravings after him in his *Narrative*.

house, as Stedman did repeatedly—and we know of no one else for whom Blake "undertakes to do busness for me when I am not in London". Blake was famous among his friends for his resistance to "the meer drudgery of business", for "my Abstract folly hurries me often away ... over Mountains & Valleys ... in a Land of Abstraction".[49] It must have been real friendship which induced him to take responsibility for all Stedman's papers, presumably including the manuscript of his precious book which had been so altered in print.

Not only that, but Captain Stedman's chief business at this time seems to have been war with Joseph Johnson, Blake's friend and patron. Blake's friendship with Stedman clearly put him in a very awkward position with Johnson.

Blake could scarcely please both men, and he seems to have chosen to please Stedman. It was probably in response to Blake's support for Stedman that "Mr. Johnson has, at times, written such letters to me as would have called for the sceptre of Agamemnon rather than the tongue of Ulysses".* Indeed, Blake found that after 1797 "Even Johnson & Fuseli have discarded my Graver".[50] "Corporeal Friends are Spiritual Enemies[.]"[51] Blake clearly saw Stedman as "the friend of my Spiritual Life while he seems the Enemy of my Corporeal".[52]

Stedman's enigmatic statement that "blake was mob'd and robbd" may be connected with a story Tatham told about Blake: "during his & M.rs Blakes absense [*from home*] for one day paying some friendly visit, some Thieves entered ... [his House] & carried away Plate to the Value of 60 Pounds & clothes to the amount of 40 more."†[53] One hundred pounds is a very substantial sum, almost twice the fee for Blake's seven-year apprenticeship.

If Tatham's tale is to be trusted, and Stedman's diary suggests that there may be substantial truth in it, the Blakes were more prosperous in the 1790s than the accounts of their later poverty might lead one to expect. Portable goods worth £100 are astonishing for the poet who wrote:

We eat little[,] we drink less[;]
This Earth breeds not our happiness[54]

But the Blakes did live in a style which made Stedman's gifts of an oil portrait and a blue sugar cup seem appropriate, and when they moved to Felpham they carried with them in the chaises "Sixteen heavy boxes & port-

---

*   Letter of 28 May 1804; "Johnson may be very honest and very generous, too, where his own interest is concerned; but I must say that he leaves no stone unturn'd to serve that interest, and often (I think) unfairly."
†   And see Addenda, below.

folios".[55] Even after the robbery, they were still weighted down with the world's goods. Stedman evidently knew Blake in prosperity. But prosperity is only apparent if it can be stolen.

Professional Commissions

From the middle of the 1780s, Blake devoted himself chiefly to engraving and writing rather than to drawings except for drawings for engravings such as those for Mary Wollstonecraft's *Original Stories* and Young's *Night Thoughts*. Between 1785 and 1799 he exhibited nothing at the Royal Academy.

Some of Blake's most ambitious engravings were undertaken during this period. His first commission to engrave his own design was for the cover of Thomas Commins, *An Elegy, Set to Music* (J. Fentum, 1786), but the work seems to have passed virtually unnoticed at the time, and only three copies have been traced today. He made six plates after his own designs for Mary Wollstonecraft's *Original Stories from Real Life* (J. Johnson, 1791; 1796; pirated as *Marie et Caroline*, Paris: Dentu, 1799) which were much more widely seen, though apparently they elicited no comment.

But his three designs engraved by Perry for Gottfried Bürger's very popular Gothic tale *Leonora*, translated by J.T. Stanley (William Miller, 1796), roused the critics to indignation. The reviewer for the *British Critic* for September 1796 fulminated about

the distorted, absurd, and impossible monsters, exhibited in the frontispiece to Mr. Stanley's last edition [Pl. 46]. Nor can we pass by this opportunity of execrating that detestable taste, founded on the depraved fancy of one man of genius, which substitutes deformity and extravagance for force and expression, and draws men and women without skins, with their joints all dislocated, or imaginary beings, which neither can nor ought to exist.

And the reviewer for Joseph Johnson's *Analytical Review* of November 1796 said that the painter had attempted "to exhibit to the eye the wild conceptions of the poet, but with so little success as to produce an effect perfectly ludicrous, instead of terrific".

Reviews like this prompted Blake to write some fifteen years later: "I know that all those with whom I have Contended in Art have strove not to Excell but to Starve me out by Calumny & the Arts of Trading Combination".[56]

With such a critical response, it is not surprising that thereafter most books with Blake's engravings after his own designs were commissioned chiefly by his close friends (e.g., Hayley's *Little Tom the Sailor* [1800] and Malkin's *A Father's Memoirs of His Child* [1806])* or were published by himself.

However, in the late 1780s his commissions for commercial copy-engravings were becoming more and more ambitious. The very fashionable miniature painter Richard Cosway probably persuaded his father-in-law Mr Hadfield to publish Blake's large engraving of Cosway's graceful "Venus Dissuades Adonis" (1787). Blake was hired to make four plates (May 1788 ff.) for Lavater's *Essays on Physiognomy* (John Murray et al., 1789–98), for which he was paid £39.19.6.[57] Lavater's *Physiognomy* became one of the landmarks for illustrated books of the great age of English book illustration. John Boydell, whose enormously ambitious proposal for a national illustrated edition of Shakspeare was announced in 1786, commissioned Blake to etch a folio plate (October 1788) from Hogarth's design for Gay's *Beggar's Opera* and then to finish it as an engraving for his enormous collected edition of *The Original Works of William Hogarth* (?1790 ff.). This is one of Blake's finest copy-engravings, though its size makes it unsuitable for reproduction in any work smaller than elephant folio.

The connection with Richard Cosway is particularly interesting, for Cosway was not only a very fashionable miniaturist with access to the highest social circles but a spiritualist with deep interests in alchemy and astrology, in Paracelsus, Boehme, and Swedenborg, and he had an important library of their works. And he was very well disposed toward Blake. On 27 December 1795 he wrote enthusiastically about Cumberland's

> Outline . . . of the Picture of Leonard*o*, & do not hesitate to pronounce it one of the most beautiful Compositions I ever beheld of that Great Man. . . . why do you not get Blake to make an engraving of it? I shou'd think he wou'd be delighted to undertake such a Work & it wou'd certainly <u>pay him very well</u> for whatever time & pains he may bestow upon such a Plate, as we have so <u>very few</u> of Leonardo's Works well engrav'd & the composition of this Picture is so very graceful & pleasing I am convinc'd he might put almost any Price on the Print & assure himself of a very extensive sale.

As it happened, Blake did not engrave Cumberland's Leonardo, perhaps because he was then no longer publishing copy-engravings by others and

---

* The chief exceptions are Richard Edwards's commission (?1794) for Blake's designs for Young's *Night Thoughts* (1797) and the commission (1805) to engrave his own designs for Blair's *Grave* by R.H. Cromek; Cromek seemed to be Blake's friend, but he later gave the commission for engraving Blake's designs to Louis Schiavonetti.

because he was by then fully embarked on his enormous undertaking for Young's *Night Thoughts* for Richard Edwards. But the good will shown by Cosway's suggestion is very striking, and it is possible that Cosway's friend- ship and his library were important to Blake in ways of which no direct trace survives.

Two promising commissions were from the energetic print-publisher John Raphael Smith for quarto engravings after George Morland, the cheerful inebriate and facile painter of bucolic genre scenes. The subjects for Blake's plates, "The Idle Laundress" and "The Industrious Cottager" (published 12 May 1788 at 6s. apiece), were of an obviously moralizing type not congenial to Blake, but "Few of Morland's works have had a better sale" than these two prints,[58] and, so successful were they, that "Blake's last years would have been employed ... [*in*] making a set of Morland's pig and ploughboy subjects" had it not been for the generous patronage of John Linnell.[*]

A far more congenial commission was probably that from Willey Reveley, who wrote on 18 October 1791: "M.ʳ Reveley's Compᵗˢ to Mʳ Blake[:] if he wishes to engrave any of Mʳ Pars's drawings for the Antiquities of Athens, & can do them by the end of January Mʳ Reveley will be glad to [*send*] Some to him." The commission may have come on the recommendation of Blake's old friend George Cumberland, who wrote that he "Got Blake to engrave for Athens",[59] but it might equally well have come through his old master Henry Pars, who was brother to William Pars who had copied the designs made in Athens.

Blake replied in a business-like way: "Mʳ Blakes Compᵗˢ To Mʳ Reveley[:] tho full of work he is glad to embrace the offer of engraving such beautiful things, & will do what he can by the end of January[.]"

He had not quite finished them by the end of January, for his four plates of "the Battle of the Centaurs and Lepithae" from the Temple of Theseus are dated 3 April 1792. *The Antiquities of Athens* by James Stuart & Nicholas Revett was one of the monumental works of the great age of English illus- trated-book publishing, and the enormous folio plates in Volume III (ed. Willey Reveley) (John Nichols, 1794) were greatly admired. In particular, John Flaxman wrote that Blake's prints were executed "in a very masterly manner".[60]

Even more promising was the prospectus of Robert Bowyer in January 1792 advertising a splendid edition of David Hume's famous *History of*

---

[*] W.M. Rossetti's note (Nov 1863) on the authority of Alexander Munro "as if he knew it from some authentic source" (*BR* 274). Morland made a large mural in the Fox Inn in the village of Felpham, where Blake later lived, according to a plaque on the wall of the present Fox Inn (its two predeces- sors burned down).

England with 60 huge plates and many vignettes after the first British artists. These were to be put into "the hands of the most eminent Engravers", including "W. Blake". Another Bowyer prospectus of February 1792 said that these "Gentlemen are actually engaged" for Hume, and in the catalogue of the *Exhibition of Pictures* at the Historic Gallery in May 1793 "W. Blake" was still listed among the engravers for Bowyer's Hume.[61]

Bowyer's edition of Hume's *History of England* (five folio volumes, 1793–1806), along with Boydell's national Shakspeare (nine folio volumes, 1791–1805) and Macklin's national Bible (six folio volumes, 1791-1800), all with illustrations by the best British artists engraved by the most distinguished London engravers, was to be at the centre of ambition and accomplishment of the great age of British book illustration.

Flaxman told Hayley that he might "see specimens of the best Engravers of the present time in Bowyer's History of England".[62] Success in making plates for Bowyer or Macklin or Boydell could have confirmed Blake as one of the most successful engravers of his time.

Eventually, however, Blake signed no plate for Bowyer's *History of England* or Macklin's Bible, and he made only one plate (1799) for Boydell's Shakspeare. This neglect embittered him. and on 11 December 1805 he wrote: "I was alive & in health & with the same Talents I now have all the time of Boydells Macklins Bowyers & other Great Works. I was known by them & was lookd upon by them as Incapable of Employment in those works ....." And in some disenchanted little verses in his Notebook (p. 23) he affected not to be

> angry with Macklin or Boydel or Bowyer
> Because they did not say "O what a Beau ye are"

But his exclusion from those great works clearly persuaded Blake that though he might "laugh at Fortune I am perswaded that She Alone is the Governor of Worldly Riches".[63] It was Fortune and not merit which determined worldly Riches and success.

Far more congenial was his collaboration with his old friend George Cumberland, who had recently returned from several years in Italy with his common-law wife and children and an impressive collection of prints and of theories about art. Cumberland embodied some of his theories in a book entitled THOUGHTS ON OUTLINE, SCULPTURE, AND THE SYSTEM THAT GUIDED THE ANCIENT ARTISTS IN COMPOSING THEIR FIGURES AND GROUPES: ACCOMPANIED WITH FREE REMARKS ON THE PRACTICE OF THE MODERNS, AND LIBERAL HINTS CORDIALLY INTENDED FOR THEIR ADVANTAGE. TO WHICH ARE ANNEXED TWENTY-FOUR DESIGNS OF CLASSICAL SUBJECTS INVENTED ON THE PRINCIPLES RECOMMENDED IN THE ESSAY BY GEORGE CUMBERLAND.

Cumberland himself etched sixteen of the twenty-four plates for his book, and he engaged Blake to make eight plates (dated 5 November 1794 and 1 January 1795), for which he paid him about £16.16.0 besides supplying the copperplates.[64] Blake apparently also provided the inscriptions to all the designs, for of course Cumberland, as an amateur, did not know how to write backwards, and all the inscriptions exhibit the idiosyncratic "ꞡ" with a leftward serif which Blake used at the time. Blake also instructed Cumberland in his letter of 6 December 1795 how to lay on the wax for etching, and elsewhere Cumberland wrote down Blake's directions for printing. Cumberland was particularly pleased with Blake's copies of his designs; he wrote on 17 June 1824, "Blake ... understands me, and how to keep a free and equal outline", and in the book itself he said:

> *Mr. Blake* has condescended to take upon him the laborious office of making them [*the prints*], I may say, fac-similes of my originals: a compliment, from a man of his extraordinary genius and abilities, the highest, I believe, I shall ever receive:—and I am indebted to his generous partiality for the instruction which encouraged me to execute a great part of the plates myself . . ..
>
> (pp. 47–8)

Thoughts on Outline came out in August 1796, and Cumberland gave copies to many friends, including Blake.[65] It was not until 23 December, however, that Blake replied:

> I have lately had some pricks of conscience on account of not acknowledging your friendship to me immediately on the receit of your beautiful book. . . .
>
> Go on Go on. Such works as yours Nature & Providence the Eternal Parents demand from their children[;] how few produce them in such perfection[;] how Nature smiles on the*m*; how Providence rewards them. How all your Brethren say, "The sound of his harp & his flute heard from his secret forest chears us to the labours of life, & we plow & reap forgetting our labour[.]"

And three years later Blake wrote again: "I study your outlines as usual just as if they were antiques".[66]

Thoughts on Outline sold very slowly,[67] but Cumberland was not discouraged about the importance of his ideas, and in 1829 he reprinted some of the designs, including four by Blake, in his *Outlines from the Antients*. There were few who admired Blake's talents as an engraver more than George Cumberland.

In terms of eternal fame, the most important of Blake's separately published uncoloured plates of this time were probably those he published himself: "The Accusers" (5 June 1793), "Edward and Elinor" and "Job" (both
of 18 August 1793), "Ezekiel" (27 October 1794) (Pl. 47) "Joseph of
Arimathea Preaching to the Inhabitants of Britain" (?1794), and "The Man
Sweeping the Interpreter's Parlour" (?1794). They were probably issued in
very small numbers—of "Edward and Elinor", for instance, only two copies
are known to survive—but some of them are very fine indeed. No wonder
Blake was astonished when the great illustrated-book publishers so often
ignored his talents.

"At Lambeth Beneath the Poplar Trees"[68]

In the autumn of 1790, after five years in Poland Street, the Blakes moved
to the open fields of Lambeth in Surrey, on the other side of the Thames by
way of Westminster Bridge (Pl. 48). Though just across from the Houses of
Parliament and Westminster Abbey, Lambeth was still largely rural because
much of it belonged to the Archbishopric of Canterbury. To the north there
were timberyards along the river, but most of Lambeth was still market gardens and marsh.

The area was only just being developed.* About 1770 a row of solid brick
houses called Hercules Buildings was erected in the fields on an unnamed
lane beyond Westminster Bridge Road, beside the Royal Asylum for
Female Orphans workhouse, and not far away were Bethlehem Hospital for
Lunatics, Astley's Circus and Theatre, and Lambeth Palace, the residence
of the Archbishop of Canterbury.

The Blakes rented "N.° 13 Hercules Buildings near the Asylum, Surry
Side of Westminster Bridge".† With eight or ten rooms[69] on three floors
plus a basement (Pl. 49), this was much more than just a cramped flat, or
even a few rooms above a shop. On the ground floor were two small, square,
well-proportioned rooms, and the other floors were probably similar.

In Hercules Buildings they had not merely space but unaccustomed elegance as well. There were many roomy cupboards in which Catherine could

---

* "In the beginning of the present [*eighteenth*] century, Lambeth contained 1400 houses. The present
    number, including those building or newly built, and not yet inhabited (which are about 500) is
    4250" (*Ambulator*: or, A Pocket Companion in a Tour Round London, 9th edn [London: J.
    Scatcherd, 1800], 145).
† Flaxman letter of 26 March 1800. A photograph of the house is reproduced in Thomas Wright, *The
    Life of William Blake* (Olney: Thomas Wright, 1929), I, 4. One of Blake's close neighbours in
    Lambeth may have been the engraver Abraham Cooper who, according to Flaxman's letter to Hayley
    of 1 Oct 1804, was at No 4 York Buildings, opposite the Asylum, Lambeth (MS in Pierpont Morgan
    Library).

store the silverware and china which they were accumulating. The walls were panelled to a height of three feet, and there were Georgian hob grates and marble mantelpieces.[70] Here they could entertain their growing circle of gentlemanly friends such as Thomas Butts and Captain Stedman with silver table service, the blue sugar cup Stedman gave them, and oil portraits on the wall.

The front of the house on the north was dark in winter, but it faced across the lane to open fields and the river. The stairwell led down to the back door which faced south to a long garden with a privy at the bottom among the poplar trees. Blake's studio was the back parlour, a sunny panelled room facing south over the garden. Here he composed all the Lambeth Books, from *The Book of Thel* to *Europe* and *The Book of Urizen*: "I came Into my parlour and sat down, and took my pen to write ... EUROPE".[71]

The house and garden were once a scene of terror, for here "Blake, for the only time in his life, *saw a ghost*. ... Standing one evening at his garden-door in Lambeth, and chancing to look up, he saw a horrible grim figure, 'scaly, speckled, very awful,' stalking downstairs towards him. More frightened than ever before or after, he took to his heels, and ran out of the house."*

What Blake saw coming down his stairwell in Lambeth sounds very like "The Ghost of a Flea" which he drew in 1819 (Pl. 126); certainly the flea there is a horrible grim figure, scaly, speckled, and very awful.

The Blakes had never had a garden before, and they relished it with all the delight of the house-bound city dweller. They planted a fig tree and a grape arbor,† and their friends such as the Flaxmans used to drink tea with

---

* Gilchrist (*BR* 54). Gilchrist also claims that Blake "was wont to say they [ghosts] did not appear much to imaginative men, but only to common minds, who did not see the finer spirits. A ghost was a thing seen by the gross bodily eye, a vision, by the mental." And see Addenda, below.

  J.T. Smith wrote that Blake had a vision of the Ancient of Days (Pl. 18) "at the top of his staircase" in Lambeth (*BR* 470).

† Tatham, who was born after the Blakes left Lambeth, says that the vine bore "ripe fruit ... in rich clusters" (*BR* 521), but Maria Denman, who as a girl went with her brother-in-law John Flaxman to tea with the Blakes in Hercules Buildings, said that "Blake would on no account prune this vine, having a theory it was wrong and unnatural to prune vines: and the affranchised tree consequently bore a luxuriant crop of leaves, and plenty of infinitesimal grapes which never ripened" (*BR* 521 n1).

  Richard C. Jackson (1851–1923) says that when he was "quite a boy" (*c*. 1860?), his father, who was born in 1810 and "associated with" Blake's disciples, took him to tea in the house the Blakes had occupied in Hercules Buildings. There they saw Blake's fig tree and "the luxurious vine ... nestling round the open casement", and his father told him that the vine and fig tree were a present to Blake from George Romney, the vine having been "grafted from the great vine at Versailles or Fontainbleau" (R.C. Jackson, "William Blake, An Unlooked for Discovery", *South London Observer*, 22 June 1912). Since Jackson's father was only seventeen when Blake died and cannot have seen him in Hercules Buildings, and since R.C. Jackson himself is exceedingly unreliable, it is not easy to accept—or reject—his allegations.

them in the shelter of the flourishing vines.* And in the winter of their third year, a "double-blossom peach-tree" and "a rose tree" were in "full bloom and covered with flowers" at "Hercule's [*sic*] Buildings Lambeth".[72] "My Pretty Rose Tree" (drafted in his Notebook p. 115 and etched in *Songs of Experience* in 1793), with "Such a flower as *May* never bore", and "I asked a thief to steal me a peach" (Notebook p. 114, *c*. 1793) are surely by-products of this prodigious blossoming.

They rejoiced in their space and their prosperity in Lambeth, and for a time they even kept a servant, but they soon discovered that, "as M.rs Blake declared ... the more service the more Inconvenience", so they gave her up.[73]

The spirits were good to Blake in Hercules Buildings, and in his sunny panelled study he created many of his greatest works, which bear on the title page some form of "*LAMBETH* | *Printed by William Blake*": *For Children: The Gates of Paradise* (17 May 1793), "The Accusers" (5 June 1793), "To the Public" (10 Oct 1793), *America* (1793), *Europe* (1794), *The First Book of Urizen* (1794), *The Book of Ahania* (1795), *The Book of Los* (1795), and *The Song of Los* (1795).[†] These were conceived, composed, printed, coloured, stitched, advertised, and sold in the room in Hercules Buildings, Lambeth, when "I had a whole House to range in",[74] an appropriately Herculean labour.

"Lovely Lambeth"[75] entered far more into the fabric of Blake's poetry than had any of his previous homes. It was in "Lambeths Vale Where Jerusalems foundations began",[76] and "There is a grain of Sand in Lambeth that Satan cannot find".[77]

Some passages are dense with references to Blake's neighbourhood in Lambeth, such as

> Jerusalems Inner Court, Lambeth ruin'd and given
> To the destestable Gods of Priam, to Apollo: and at the Asylum
> Given to Hercules who labour in Tirzahs Looms for bread ...
> Lambeth mourns calling Jerusalem ....

(Milton pl. 25, ll. 48–50, 54)

---

* Tatham (*BR* 521). The father of R.C. Jackson is the authority for the statement that Blake's studio was the panelled back room (Richard C. Jackson, "William Blake, An Unlooked for Discovery", *South London Observer*, 22, 29 June 1912). The panelled room, "an old vine and an old fig tree" were still visible in Hercules Buildings in 1912 (Thomas Wright, "Blake's Home, Lambeth", "D. Na. L", 4 June 1912).

    Gilchrist's silly story about the Blakes sitting naked in their Lambeth garden and inviting in friends (*BR* 53–4) was recognized as an apocryphal student tale as early as 1816—see Seymour Kirkup's reference to it in *BR* (2), 1809–10.

† *Visions of the Daughters of Albion* (1793) and *Songs of Experience* (1794) and probably *The Marriage of Heaven and Hell* (?1790) were also written and printed in Lambeth, though they bear no place on the title page.

Apollo Buildings and Apollo Gardens (recently defunct) were near Hercules Buildings, and the Royal Asylum for Female Orphans was on the site of the former Hercules Tavern.[78]

The giant figures of Blake's myth came to him in Lambeth: "Los descended to me ... trembling I stood ... in the Vale Of Lambeth; but he kissed me and wishd me health".[79] Lambeth was a splendid blessing to Blake's art.

It was also the site of drama. Two doors away lived Philip Astley, the owner of a famous circus. One day

> Blake was standing at one of his Windows, which looked into Astleys premises ... & saw a Boy hobbling along with a log to his foot such an one as is put on a Horse or Ass to prevent their straying. Blake called his Wife & asked her for what reason that log could be placed upon the boys foot: she answered that it must be for a punishment, for some inadvertency. Blakes blood boiled & his indignation surpassed his forbearance, he sallied forth, & demanded in no very quiescent terms that the Boy should be loosed & that no Englishman should be subjected to those miseries, which he thought were inexcusable even towards a Slave. After having succeeded in obtaining the Boys release in some way or other he returned home. Astley by this time having heard of Blakes interference, came to his House & demanded in an equally peremptory manner, by what authority he dare come athwart his method of jurisdiction; to which Blake replied with such warmth, that blows were very nearly the consequence. The debate lasted long, but ... they ended in mutual forgiveness & mutual respect. Astley saw that his punishment was too degrading & admired Blake for his humane sensibility & Blake desisted from wrath when Astley was pacified ....*

Blake's fiery sensibility was occasionally as plain in his actions as in his poetry.

Perhaps it was about the same time that a bystander near St Giles saw

> a wife knocked about by some husband or other violent person, in the open street ... [*and*] saw this also, that a small swift figure coming up in

---

* Tatham (*BR* 521); Tatham clearly learned the story from Catherine Blake. It is just imaginable that the boy was Abraham Cooper (1787–1868) who was employed by Astley in 1800 (*DNB*). Cooper became a battle- and animal-painter, in 1822 he was one of the recommenders of Blake to the Royal Academy charity, and in 1830 he acquired from Linnell a sketch and a letter of Blake for his autograph collection (*BR* 276, 378–9). Butlin records no Blake drawing from Cooper's collection.

full swing of passion fell with such counter violence of reckless and raging rebuke upon the poor ruffian, that he recoiled and collapsed, with ineffectual cudgel; persuaded, as the bystander was told on calling afterwards, that the very devil himself had flown upon him in defence of the woman; such Tartarean overflow of execration and objurgation had issued from the mouth of her champion. It was the fluent tongue of Blake which had proved too strong for this fellow's arm ....[80]

Blake's anger was a terrible weapon both in private and in print.

A New Heaven, a New Earth, a New Church

Like many serious Dissenters, Blake was a persistent searcher for spiritual truth. He did not expect to find it in the established Church, but it might be found almost anywhere else, not only in volumes of theological speculation but in philosophy, in literature, in hymns and in great art. Blake bought Joseph Halkett Jr's radical speculations in his *Free and Impartial Study of the Holy Scriptures recommended* (1729, 1732, 1736) and George Berkeley's *Siris: A Chain of Philosophical Reflexions* (1744) and Jacob Duché's religious *Discourses on Various Subjects* (1779) and [John & Charles Wesley], *Hymns for the Nation* (1782). All these works celebrate the supremacy of the spirit.

At the same time Blake was reading the works of the philosophical alchemists, such as Jacob Boehme, Paracelsus, and Cornelius Agrippa.[81] He probably owned *The Works of Jacob Behmen* edited by William Law (1764, 1772, 1781), whose author he believed to be "divinely inspired ... the figures in Law's transl[n] ... [*are*] very beautiful. [']Mich: Angelo co[d] not have done better' ".[82] In each of these books he was looking for evidence about the reality of the world of spirits, the essence of the universe.

Another such seeker was Blake's friend John Flaxman who had joined a reading group studying the writings of Emanuel Swedenborg.* Swedenborg declared that the Last Judgment had taken place in 1757 (the year of Blake's birth), and that the truths imparted to him by angels made it possible for the first time to understand the spiritual nature of creation. Blake was fascinated by these ideas, and about 1788 he bought copies of Swedenborg's *A Treatise Concerning Heaven and Hell, and of the Wonderful Things therein, As Heard*

---

* Another may have been Blake's brother James, who, according to Gilchrist, "would at times *talk Swedenborg*, talking of seeing Abraham and Moses" (*BR* 2).

and Seen, by the Honourable and Learned Emanuel Swedenborg (R. Hindmarsh, 1784) and of *The Wisdom of Angels, Concerning Divine Love and Divine Wisdom* (R. Hindmarsh, 1788), marking crucial passages and making notes to himself: "Mark this" (p. 204), "See N 239" (p. 196), "The Whole of the New Church is in the Active Life & not in Ceremonies at all" (p. 181). Often he presented arguments to defend Swedenborg from ignorant calumniators: What Swedenborg says contradicts what "was asserted in the society" (p. 429).

One of the most active members of this little group was Robert Hindmarsh, who was one of five readers of Swedenborg baptized "at Mr Wright's Poultry London" on 21 July 1787[83]—before there was either a Swedenborgian church or a clergyman to do so. Hindmarsh was a professional printer, and through his agency 500 copies of a circular letter were sent out on 7 December 1788 with "a general Invitation to all the Readers of the Theological Works of the Hon. *Emanuel Swedenborg*, who are desirous of rejecting, and separating themselves from the Old Church, or the present established Churches, together with all their Sectaries, through Christendom, and of fully embracing the Heavenly Doctrines of the New Jerusalem ...".[84] One of the Readers of Swedenborg who received the circular and accepted its invitation was William Blake.

As a result of this invitation, 60 to 70 readers of Swedenborg met at a public house on 13 April 1789. The meeting was conducted in a disciplined fashion, as is evident in the requirement that, before attending, all should sign a statement committing themselves theologically to a great deal: "We whose Names are hereunto subscribed, do each of us approve of the Theological Writings of Emanuel Swedenborg, believing that the Doctrines contained therein are genuine Truths, revealed from Heaven, and that the New Jerusalem Church ought to be established, distinct and separate from the Old Church." Among the names hereunto subscribed were "W. Blake" and "C. Blake".

The iron discipline of the organizers is also indicated by the fact that all thirty-two propositions put to the meeting were adopted unanimously and that these resolutions had very far reaching consequences—particularly in a nation with an established church and a great deal of intellectual ferment already stirred up by the Wesleys and by the American revolution. Some of the more striking resolutions, to which William and his wife Catherine Blake agreed, were:

4 The Old Church is dead.
7 The Old Church faith should be abolished.
13 Swedenborgians should have no connection with other churches.
17 The canon of the Bible should be Genesis, Exodus, Leviticus, Numbers,

Deuteronomy, Joshua, Judges, I–II Samuel, I–II Kings, Psalms, Isaiah, Jeremiah, Lamentations, Ezekiel, Daniel, Hosea, Joel, Amos, Obadiah, Jonah, Micah, Nahum, Habakkuk, Zephaniah, Haggai, Zechariah, Malachi; Matthew, Mark, Luke, John, Revelation; "the other Books, not having the internal Sense, are not the Word".

18 Death is only a continuation of life, and God's kingdom is one of uses.

25 The Second Coming has begun.

26 True Christianity exists only in the New Church.[85]

The effect upon Blake of Swedenborg's ideas was profound. He wrote later of "Swedenborg! strongest of me*n*, the Samson shorn by the Churches" (note the comparison of "the Churches" to the treacherous Delilah), and he condemned those who "perverted Swedenborgs Visions in Beulah & in Ulro: To destroy Jerusalem".[86] The Swedenborgian canon of the Bible, which excludes Job, Proverbs, the Song of Solomon, and about a quarter of the Protestant testaments, was reaffirmed by "the Divine Lord" in Blake's *Jerusalem*.[87] Blake's "The Divine Image", a strikingly Swedenborgian poem, may have been written for his *Songs of Innocence* (1789) in a Swedenborgian meeting-place,[88] and his design of "The Spiritual Preceptor" is based on Swedenborg's *True Christian Religion* (1781).[89]

Despite the iron discipline at the meeting, there was very soon a deep division in the New Jerusalem Church, partly over the meaning of marriage, and on further reading Blake became profoundly disillusioned with Swedenborg. He bought a copy of Swedenborg's *Wisdom of Angels Concerning the Divine Providence* (R. Hindmarsh, 1790), and he annotated it with pervasive indignation: "Cursed Folly"; "Lies & Priestcraft"; "Swedenborg is ... a Spiritual Predestinarian" (¶277 p. xix). Blake's *Marriage of Heaven and Hell* may have been started about this time to show members of the New Church that

As a new heaven is begun, ... the Eternal Hell revives. And lo! Swedenborg is the Angel sitting at the tomb; his writings are the linen clothes folded up. ...

Now hear a plain fact: Swedenborg has not written one new truth: Now hear another: he has written all the old fals[*e*]hoods. ...

Any man of mechanical talents may from the writings of Paracelsus or Jacob Behmen, produce ten thousand volumes of equal value with Swedenborg ....

(*Marriage* ¶2, 77, 80)

This mockery of Swedenborg in the voices of the Devil is not, however,

Blake's final conclusion about Swedenborg. His eventual response was not hostility but ambivalence. On 10 December 1825 he told Crabb Robinson that Swedenborg

> "was a divine teacher—he has done much & will do much good[;] he has correct.ᵈ many errors of Popery and also of Luther & Calvin["]—Yet he also said that <u>Swedenborg</u> was wrong in endeavour.ᵍ to explain to the <u>rational</u> faculty what the reason cannot comprehend[;] he should have left that ... Parts of his scheme are dangerous. His sexual religion is dangerous.

About 1797 Blake "was invited to join the Swedenborgians under [*Joseph*] Proud, but declined, notwithstanding his high opinion of Swedenborg".[90] His friends such as John Flaxman, who was a member of Proud's Hatton Garden congregation, plainly thought Blake sufficiently sympathetic to Swedenborg's ideas to make such an offer tempting.

Blake not only declined to join the New Jerusalem Church in Hatton Garden, but for the rest of his life he did not attend any church at all.[91] His participation for a time among the enthusiasts of Swedenborg's New Jerusalem Church seems to have persuaded him that even the most enlightened Church will become the vehicle for "Lies & Priestcraft".

The Illuminated Books

Thunder of Thought & flames of fierce desire[92]

A mighty Spirit leap'd from the land of Albion
... he siez'd the Trump, & blow'd the enormous blast![93]

At the same time that Blake was establishing a promising career as a professional engraver and investigating the claims of the New Jerusalem Church, he was continuing to write and to experiment with methods of etching and printing. His first works in relief etching were probably purely visual, such as "The Approach of Doom" (Pl. 38) and "Charity" of about 1788. However, relief etching was almost as applicable to text as to design, and Blake's voices were still dictating to him in "Thunder of Thought & Flames of fierce desire". His earlier manuscripts, such as "then she bore Pale desire" (?1783), "Woe cried the Muse" (?1783), and *An Island in the Moon* (?1784), had borne no illustrations, but after his adoption of relief etching virtually all his poems were accompanied by designs.

At first Blake was somewhat uncertain about the format of his books. For instance, his manuscript of *Tiriel* (?1789) has text on fifteen pages and twelve separate, highly finished designs, oriented sideways rather than vertically like the text.[94] Design and text are not physically integrated, and it would have been difficult to integrate them in print, for some of the designs have to be read in different directions, and it is not at all clear where in the text the designs should be put. Further, though it would have been easy enough to reproduce the text in relief etching, the designs, with elaborate shading and fine lines (Pl. 50), would have required a technique like intaglio line-engraving to reproduce them adequately. *Tiriel* seems to be directed towards conventional book production, or at least to a mixture of text in relief etching and designs in intaglio engraving, rather than the technique of mingled text and designs on the same plates as in all Blake's writings in relief etching.

Tiriel is the first of Blake's mythological narratives which have come to be known as Prophecies, after the titles of *America A Prophecy* (1793) and *Europe A Prophecy* (1794)—the only works to which Blake himself gave those titles.

By "Prophecy" of course Blake does not mean anything so vulgar as a prediction of the future. "Prophets in the modern sense of the word have never existed[.] Jonah was no prophet in the modern Sense for his prophecy of Nineveh failed[.] Every honest man is a Prophet ... a Prophet is a Seer not an Arbitrary Dictator" (Marginalium to Watson, *Apology for the Bible* p. 14). Blake's Prophecies are the poems or visions of seers.

Tiriel, an old, blind king, curses his sons and daughters because they will not obey his laws and wanders forth into the wilderness, led by his tormented daughter Hela. His journey ends in the garden of the mountains of Har, his father, to whom

He said, "O weak mistaken father of a lawless race[,]
Thy laws O Har & Tiriels wisdom end together in a curse[.]
Why is one law given to the lion & the patient Ox
And why men bound beneath the heavens in a reptile form[,]
A worm of sixty winters creeping on the dusky ground[?] ...
Can wisdom be put in a silver rod or love in a golden bowl[?] ...
Compelld to pray repugnant & to humble the immortal spirit
Till I am subtil as a serpent in a paradise
Consuming all both flowers & fruits insects & warbling birds
And now my paradise is falln & a drear sandy plain
Returns my thirsty hissings in a curse on thee O Har
Mistaken father of a lawless race my voice is past"[.]
                    (*Tiriel* (1789?) ll. 357–8, 360, 362–3, 370, 387–92 [see Pl. 50])

The thunder of eloquent thought is splendid, but Blake did not have a vehicle adequate to make it public.

The aphorisms which he found in Lavater were more easily adaptable to his new form of relief etching, and he experimented with two little series of philosophical statements called *All Religions Are One* (?1788) and *There is No Natural Religion* (?1788). These consist of numbered aphorisms assert-

ing the centrality of the Poetic genius and the world of spirits and the identity of all religions: "Therefore God becomes as we are, that we may be as he is."[95]

Both works are remarkably tentative: The plates are tiny, the designs rudimentary and sometimes merely decorative, and on the frontispiece to *There is No Natural Religion* Blake forgot to reverse the lettering of "The Author & Printer W Blake", so that it prints backwards. He never published either work, the order of the plates was established only in 1993,[96] and, after his first experiments with the two tractates of about 1788,* Blake did not even print them until about 1794, when they became the vehicle for his earliest experiments in colour printing. They were as little known to contemporaries as the manuscript of *Tiriel*.

Songs of Innocence

Since Blake was a boy, he had been writing songs, such as those in *Poetical Sketches* (1783) and *An Island in the Moon* (?1784), and in one copy of *Poetical Sketches* he added a series of manuscript "Songs by Shepherds". These may be the genesis of his *Songs of Innocence*, for the "Song by a Young Shepherd" (?1787) is an early version of "Laughing Song" in

---

* The date is established by a note in *The Ghost of Abel* (1822): "W Blakes Original stereotype was 1788". There is no surviving copy of the *Natural Religion* tractates printed in 1788.

Innocence. And there were already poems in *An Island in the Moon* (?1784) which could be used: "Nurses Song", "The Little Boy Lost", and "Holy Thursday". In 1789 Blake collected these and other poems into *Songs of Innocence*, and he created for it a glorious title page (Fig. on p. 17) with letters bursting into flame and foliage and with angels and pipers rejoicing on the letters themselves. Here in *Innocence* "every thing that lives is Holy".[97]

The speakers of the poems in *Songs of Innocence* are babies, children, and adults, black and white, birds, insects, and animals; none is William Blake. All speak from a sense of protection, of safety, of being in their proper places in an ordered universe. Each, whether child or adult or ant, is guided by the glow-worm, "the watchman of the night"[98] and by "God ever nigh",[99] by "angels bright Unseen . . . [*who*] pour blessing",[100] and by "Thy maker . . . [*who*] Heaven & earth to peace beguiles".[101] Each is protected by something outside himself; it is the sense of protection, rather than the reality of the protection, which brings joy and peace. These innocents do not know that there is nothing outside themselves to protect them. It is not society but vision which sustains them. In "The Chimney Sweeper", the unspeakably filthy and forlorn little boy dreams of "an Angel who had a bright key" of vision which transforms the brutal world for him: "Tho' the morning was cold, Tom was happy & warm".[102] The world is still cold and bleak, but "Tom was happy & warm" because of his vision.

The songs are about children, by children, and for children. Some, such as "The Lamb" and "Infant Joy", are in words of only one or two syllables, and the designs are simple, bold, and beautiful.*

The poems in *Songs of Innocence*, along with those in *Songs of Experience*, are the poems by which Blake was best known to his contemporaries—and to posterity. Blake printed *Songs of Innocence* for the rest of his life, he produced far more copies of it than of any of his other works in Illuminated Printing,[103] and individual poems from it were repeatedly reprinted, particularly the "Introduction", "The Divine Image", "The Chimney Sweeper", and "The Lamb".[104] Copies of *Innocence* sold at 5s. in 1793, £3.3.0 in 1818, and £5.5.0 in 1827,[105] the advancing price being due partly to much more elaborate, bold, and individual colouring in the late copies than in the light and somewhat repetitive pastel colouring of early copies.

The songs were variously appreciated even by the most percipient of Blake's admirers. Garth Wilkinson wrote that "they abound with the sweetest touches of that Pastoral life", though they exhibit, "in many cases, . . . inattention to the ordinary rules of grammar",[106] and Edward Fitzgerald concluded from his copy of *Songs of Innocence* that Blake "was quite mad:

---

* See the Figs on the title page and pp. 17, 87, 88 and Pl. 9.

but of a madness that was really the elements of great genius ill sorted: in fact a genius *with a screw loose*, as we used to say."[107] On 10 March 1811 Crabb Robinson read some of Blake's poems to William Hazlitt, and

> He was much struck with them. . . . ["]They are beautiful["], he said, "& only too deep for the vulgar[;] he has no sense of the ludicrous & as to a God a worm crawling in a privy is as worthy an obj! as any other, all being to him indifferent[.] So to Blake the Chimney Sweeper &c[.] He is ruined by vain struggles to get rid of what presses on his brain—he attempts impossibles[."]

Charles Lamb described Blake as a "mad Wordsworth",[108] and Wordsworth "consid^d B[*lake*] as hav^g the elements of poetry—a thousand times more than either Byron or Scott".[109] Wordsworth copied out poems by Blake from Malkin's account of him (1806),[110] and later he told a friend: "'I called the other day while you were out and stole a book out of your library—Blake's songs of Innocence'[.] He read and read and took it home and read and read again."[111]

Perhaps the greatest contemporary admirer of Blake's *Songs* was Samuel Taylor Coleridge, who read and commented on them with extraordinary attention.[112] He thought Blake "a man of Genius—and I apprehend, a Swedenborgian—certainly, a mystic emphatically. . . . I am in the very mire of common-place common-sense compared with Mr Blake, apo- or rather ana-calyptic Poet, and Painter!"[113] According to Crabb Robinson, "Coleridge has visited B. & I am told talks finely about him",[114] and another contemporary reported that "Blake and Coleridge, when in company, seemed like congenial beings of another sphere, breathing for a while on our earth".[115] What a treasure any account of Blake and Coleridge together would be, striking sparks of fire from one another's genius.

The Book of Thel

At the same time as he was printing *Songs of Innocence*, Blake was creating *The Book of Thel*. On the title page (Pl. 50) the shepherdess Thel observes dispassionately the courtship of plants, and in the text she laments that life seems to be without purpose:

> Ah! Thel is like a watry bo*w* and like a parting clou*d*,
> Like a reflection in a glas*s*, like shadows in the wate*r*,
> Like dreams of infants . . . .

(Thel pl. 3, ll. 8–10)

She is answered by the water lily (Part I), the cloud (Part II), and the worm "like an infant wrapped in the Lillys leaf" (Part III), who assure her that "everything that lives, Lives not alone, nor for itself".[116] Finally, in Part IV, she comes to "her own grave plot", from which she hears a "voice of sorrow breathed from the hollow pit" with a series of terrible paradoxes:

"Why cannot the Ear be closed to its own destruction? …
Why a tender curb upon the youthful burning boy!
Why a little curtain of flesh on the bed of our desire?"

The Virgin started from her seat, & with a shriek
Fled back unhinderd till she came into the vales of Har

(*Thel* pl. 8, ll. 112, 113, 121–4)

To Thel's ears, to questioning reason,* the voice from the pit is terrifying—but the last image of the book is of three naked babes riding a docile, harnessed serpent (Fig. p. 363). Though Thel is terrified, the babes are not. Thel's prying intellect cannot understand what is before her. Thel sees the world of spirits which is all round her, but she believes only in a temporal, perishing world. The intellectual text ends in terror, but the design concludes in harmony.

Blake printed and sold copies of *The Book of Thel* for the rest of his life. In 1793 the price for these eight lightly coloured plates was a modest 3s. but by 1818 it was £2.2.0, and in 1827 he was asking £3.3.0 for it.[117] Only sixteen copies have survived, and it was not until three years after Blake's death that any of it was reprinted.†

The Marriage of Heaven and Hell

While Blake was struggling with "Swedenborg! strongest of men", a source of inspiration for poem and design, and the "Cursed Folly" of Swedenborg's predestinarianism, the French Revolution broke out. Blake, like Wordsworth and Paine and many other Englishmen, saw the storming

---

* A similar progression in *For the Sexes: The Gates of Paradise* (?1825) leads through Water, Earth, and Air ("Cloudy Doubts & Reasoning Cares") to "Fire That end in endless Strife" (pls 4–7).
† Anon., "The Inventions of William Blake", *London University Magazine*, II (March 1830) (*BR* 385–6), commenting that "The title-page of this mazy dream contains a specimen of his utmost elegance in design" (Pl. 51). Garth Wilkinson wrote of *Thel* on 17 July 1839: "I *can* see some glimmer of meaning in it, and some warmth of religion and goodness; but … I should say sanity predominates in it, rather than that the work was a sane one" (C.J. Wilkinson, *James John Garth Wilkinson* [London, 1911], 30–1).

of the Bastille in Paris in apocalyptic terms as the beginning of a new and better order in Europe. He celebrated the event by etching a little two-leaf political pamphlet-poem called "A Song of Liberty" which concluded that "Empire is no more! and now the lion & wolf shall cease."[118] And then he added a Chorus to the "Song of Liberty" couched in religious terms: "Let the Priests of the Raven of dawn, no longer ... curse the sons of joy ... For every thing that lives is Holy".[119] Perhaps it was this Chorus which turned his mind again to religion and Swedenborg.

Blake combined the "Song of Liberty" with another two-leaf prose sketch mocking Swedenborg and parodying his Memorable Relations of things heard and seen in heaven with Memorable Fancies of things seen and heard in hell. "Swedenborgs writings are a recapitulation of all superficial opinions", because Swedenborg "conversed with Angels who are all religiou*s*, & conversed not with Devils who all hate religion".[120]

And then, as the idea grew upon him, he created other sections which he combined in what he called *The Marriage of Heaven and Hell* (Pl. 52). The book allows the Devil's voice to be heard eulogizing energy: "Energy is Eternal Delight"; "Exuberance is Beauty"; and "The road of excess leads to the palace of wisdom".[121] In opposition to the Devil are Angels and Heaven, representing reason, which "is call'd Satan" in the book of Job; Milton, whose Messiah is reason, "was of the Devils party without knowing it".[122]

The wisdom of the Devil is encapsulated in the proverbs of Hell which the speaker impudently collected "As I was walking among the fires of hell".[123] Some of the proverbs of Hell are manifestly modelled on Lavater's *Aphorisms*: "He who has suffered you to impose on him knows you"; "The tygers of wrath are wiser than the horses of instruction"; "The soul of sweet delight, can never be defil'd".[124]

The Marriage is mostly the Devil's man-centred wisdom: "Without Contraries is no progression"; "All deities reside in the human breast"; "God only Acts and I*s* in ... Men"; "Jesus ... acted from impuls*e*, not from rules" and broke all the ten commandments.[125] Angels aren't given many lines, and, in the Devil's narrative, they are always bested by the Devils. The work is a war of visions—or rather of the visionary devils with the unimaginative angels. In one such passage, an angel offers a view of the speaker's fate among "vast spiders" and "animals sprung from corruption", "a monstrous serpent [Leviathan] ... to the east, distant about three degrees" (the distance of Paris from London) "advancing toward us with all the fury of a spiritual existence". However, when the angel left, this "appearance was no more, but I found myself sitting on a pleasant bank beside a river by moon light and hearing a harper".[126] The speaker concludes: "we impose on one another".[127]

One of the most conspicuous features of the *Marriage* is its explicit sexual freedom. The title page shows naked couples embracing, Plate 3 depicts a nude woman giving birth to a child, and the text says: "The lust of the goat is the bounty of God. ... The nakedness of woman is the work of God."[128]

Here are challenges aplenty to morality and to Church of England orthodoxy. It is perhaps little wonder that even 70 years later Blake's pious disciple Samuel Palmer thought that some of the pages of the *Marriage* "would at once exclude the work from every drawing-room table in England",[129] that Macmillan declined to permit Gilchrist to print it in 1863—and that Swinburne joyfully created a facsimile of it in 1868.

The *Marriage* is richly illustrated, with a myriad of inter-linear designs. The twenty-seven plates were offered at 7s.6d. in Blake's prospectus "To the Public" of 1793, but it was omitted from his lists of works for sale in his letters of 9 June 1818 and 12 April 1827. He continued to sell it to select customers—only nine copies have survived. Linnell paid £2.2.0 for his copy on 30 April 1821,[130] and Blake made another for his dilettante friend Thomas Griffiths Wainewright in 1827.[131] J.T. Smith just mentioned it, but most of his early biographers were shy or ignorant of *The Marriage of Heaven and Hell*. The roaring of Rintrah in the introductory poem seems to have frightened most of Blake's contemporaries who heard it.

In early September 1792 Blake was called back across the river from Lambeth by the death of his mother at the age of 70. He must have crossed London with the little funeral cortège consisting of his wife, his brothers James and John, and his sister Catherine, to the Dissenters' Burying Ground in Bunhill Fields where Catherine had laid to rest her husband in 1784 and her son Robert in 1787. There Catherine Wright Armitage Blake was buried at 4:30 p.m. on Sunday 9 September 1792 in a grave without a headstone and probably without a service.[132]

In *Songs of Innocence* (1789) Blake had celebrated the secure joys of childhood, and in *The Marriage of Heaven and Hell* (?1790) he had defied the orthodoxies of Church and State with the flippant wisdom of the Devil. But for the decade after the death of his mother in 1792 his poems and his vision are earth-bound and lamenting, though straining to break free.

For several years after 1790, Blake's creative energies may have been chiefly directed at purely visual works. He produced a small book of engravings called *The History of England* which was finished and "Published" by October 1793,* though no copy has ever been recorded. He also began an enormously ambitious "Series of subjects from the Bible", the first of which was "Job, a Historical Engraving. Size 1 ft. 7½ in. by 1 ft. 2 in.: price 12s."[133] dated 18 August 1793 and inscribed "Job | What is Man That thou

---

* *The History of England* is known chiefly through the advertisement for it in Blake's prospectus "To the Public" (10 Oct 1793), where its description ("a small book of Engravings. Price 3s") is the same as that for *For Children: The Gates of Paradise* (1793) which is a small octavo with eighteen plates.

shouldest Try him Every Moment?". This was followed by Ezekiel, of the same dimensions, which was "nearly ready" in October 1793 but was not published for another year, on 27 October 1794 (Pl. 47). Then the Bible series was apparently abandoned.

An equally ambitious and abortive project was another series of enormous prints on the history of England, but of this only one plate is known: "Edward and Elinor, a Historical Engraving. Size 1 ft. $6\frac{1}{2}$ in. by 1 ft. price 10s.6d.",[134] dated, like "Job", 18 August 1793. The drawing had been made while he was an apprentice and the engraving begun as soon as he left Basire,[135] so it took fourteen years to complete. "Edward and Elinor" is an even rarer work than "Job" and "Ezekiel", and only one, slightly defective copy is known, used by Blake as scrap paper for his manuscript poem *Vala* pp. 87–90.

Line engravings on the enormous scale of "Job" and "Edward and Elinor" involved endless labour, and Blake clearly had difficulty in bringing them to completion—and insuperable difficulty in completing the series of subjects from the Bible and the history of England. Works composed and illustrated by himself in relief etching were far easier and quicker to accomplish—and, very surprisingly, more vendible.

Visions of the Daughters of Albion, America A Prophecy. For Children: The Gates of Paradise

Blake returned to the sexual politics with which he had flirted in *The Marriage of Heaven and Hell* and devoted a whole book to it in *Visions of the Daughters of Albion* (1793) (Pl. 53). Oothoon, "the soft soul of America" (l. 3), is raped by Bromion, whose slaves are "Stampt with my signet" (l. 21), as John Stedman's slaves had been branded with his initials (Pl. 44), and who rules by the scourge. She is scorned as a whore by her assailant Bromion and her lover Theotormon, and the poem relates her efforts to persuade them that she is pure as the plucked flower, the light-giving marygold (see Fig. on p. xxiv)—the language of flowers derives from Erasmus Darwin's *Botanic Garden* (1791) which Blake had illustrated.

Oothoon is bound not merely by the laws and customs of society against which Mary Wollstonecraft railed in her *Vindication of the Rights of Women* (1792); she is bound as well in mind-forged manacles by the way she had been taught to understand the universe and how she perceives it, by the philosophy of John Locke:

> They told me that I had five senses to inclose me up,
> And they inclos'd my infinite brain into a narrow circle ...
> Till all from life I was obliterated and erased. ...

(ll. 54–5, 57)

But these five senses do not account for what she sees, for "The Eye sees more than the Heart knows" (pl. 2):

> With what sense is it that the chicken shuns the ravenous hawk?
> With what sense does the tame pigeon measure out the expanse?
> With what sense does the bee form cells[?] . . ..
>
> (ll. 63–5)

She opposes her masculine tormentors with her sense of virgin purity:

> "I cry, Love! Love! Love! happy happy Love! free as the mountain wind!
> . . .
> Arise you little glancing wings and sing your infant joy!
> Arise and drink your bliss, for every thing that lives is holy!
>
> (ll. 191, 214–15)

Oothoon's gospel of impulsive love sounds much like the Devil's wisdom in *The Marriage of Heaven and Hell*, and, like the Devil, she finds the roots of oppression in religion, in

> The self enjoyings of self denial. Why dost thou seek religion?
> Is it because acts are not lovely, that thou seekest solitude,
> Where the horrible darkness is impressed with reflections of desire?
>
> (ll. 184–6)

But her mind-bound oppressors hear her not, and her exultant vision emancipates no one. The poem ends as it began: "The Daughters of Albion hear her woes, & eccho back her sighs" (ll. 43, 113, 218). Oothoon's sense of purity and her gospel of love leave her still enslaved with the daughters of Albion. If such visions of glory will not free the oppressed, what hope is there for them?

The eighteen plates of the *Visions of the Daughters of Albion* were lightly coloured and offered in 1793 at 7s.6d., in 1818 at £3.3.0, and in 1827 at £5.5.0.[136] Only seventeen copies have come down to us today, and no contemporary commented on the work at all.

Oothoon's proclamation of love is a social gospel with powerful political implications. The political implications are dealt with explicitly in *America: A Prophecy* (1793) (Pls 35–6). "The King of England looking westward trembles at the vision" (l. 29) of red Orc who threatens with his trumpet of fire (see Fig. on p. xxii) not merely the American colonies but the very fabric of society. Albion's Angel perceives Orc as a "Blasphemous Demon, Antichrist, hater of Dignities" with "ever-hissing jaws" (ll. 56, 98), but Orc's vision of himself on the same plate is of a boy asleep by a ram beneath spring foliage and birds (see Fig. on the half-title page, above). In turn, Orc sees Albion's wrathful prince as "A dragon form clashing his scales" (l. 15).

Orc's vision is of an apocalypse which transforms the world:

> The morning comes, the night decays, the watchmen leave their
>   stations;
> The grave is burst, the spices shed, the linen wrapped up
> . . .
> Let the slave grinding at the mill, run out into the field;
> Let him look up into the heavens & laugh in the bright air
> . . .
> . . . his chains are loose, his dungeon doors are open
> And let his wife and children return from the opressors scourge;
> They look behind at every step & believe it is a dream,
> Singing, "The Sun has left his blackness, & has found a fresher
>   morning
> . . .
> For Empire is no more, and now the Lion & Wolf shall cease."
> . . .
> For every thing that lives is holy . . . .

(ll. 37–8, 42–3, 46–51, 71)

Orc is attacking the very fundamentals of religion and society. Boston's Angel is roused to cry:

> "What God is he, writes laws of peace, & clothes him in a tempest[?]
> What pitying Angel lusts for tears, and fans himself with sighs[?]
> What crawling villain preaches abstinence & wraps himself
> In fat of lambs? no more I follow, no more obedience pay."

(ll. 126–9)

The American revolutionaries have been roused, "Shaking their mental chains" (l. 144), and the fires of Orc

>   the five gates of their law-built heaven
> . . .
> . . . consum'd, & their bolts and hinges melted
> And the fierce flames burnt round the heavens, & round the abodes of men

(ll. 222, 225–6)

The mental revolution seems to be accomplished—but the design on this triumphant concluding page shows not rejoicing and triumph but barren trees, bowed mourners, thistles, and serpents. Once again, as in *Visions of the Daughters of Albion*, the glorious vision of freedom ends in moans and sighs. The vision has not brought freedom—yet.

Blake produced seventeen copies of *America* which can be traced today, but he only coloured four of them. He asked 10s.6d. when he offered the eighteen plates for sale in 1793, but the price had advanced to £5.5.0 in 1818 and even £6.6.0 in 1827.[137]

The critics among Blake's contemporaries hardly knew what to make of *America*. Cunningham said cautiously that it was "plentifully seasoned with verse" and Crabb Robinson that it was marked by obscurity.[138] Blake's friend J.T. Smith remarked in evident perplexity that "the expressions are mystical in a very high degree", but he was more willing to evaluate the designs, some of which are "very fine".[139]

Blake's little picture-book called *For Children: The Gates of Paradise* (17 May 1793) was even more perplexing. It is plainly related to Renaissance emblem books, which combine on one page a riddling title, an enigmatic design, and a set of verses explaining in heartily moral terms the meaning of the design.

For Children is a set of eighteen very small designs, many with only a single word for title ("Water", "Earth", "Air", "Fire"). The plates have

printed numbers, so plainly the order is important, but the relationship of plate-to-plate is often perplexing, and children are unlikely to have recognized the visual context of, for instance, pl. 14 ("Does thy God O Priest take such vengeance as this?") as Ugolino and his sons and grandsons walled in to starve to death from Dante's *Divine Comedy*, or the verbal context of the frontispiece ("What is Man!") from Job vii, 17: "What is Man that thou shouldest Magnify him".*

---

* The quotation from Job appears beneath Blake's sketch for the design in his Notebook p. 68, and in his engraving for "Job" (18 Aug 1793).

In pl. 7 the figure of "Fire" is clearly that of Satan, after his fall from heaven, rousing his rebel angels with shield and spear, and the context is made somewhat clearer in the caption added to the design when it was revised in *For the Sexes: The Gates of Paradise* (?1825): "[Cloudy doubts] That end in endless strife". In the second version, Satan's eyes are closed (he is blind), serpent scales have been added to his belly (he is an hermaphrodite), and two rudimentary horns have been added. And in "The Keys of the Gates" added to *For the Sexes*, the meaning is even clearer:

> Doubt Self Jealous[,] Watry folly
> Struggling thro Earth's Melancholy[,]
> Naked in Air in Shame & Fear
> Blind in Fire with shield & spear[,]
> Two Horn'd Reasoning Cloven Fiction
> In Doubt which is Self contradiction[,]
> A dark Hermaphrodite We stood
> Rational Truth Root of Evil & Good

This seems a great deal to deduce from the single word "Fire" in *For Children*.

The series is plainly the human journey ("The Traveller hasteth in the Evening", pl. 16) from birth (Fig. on p. 29) to death as in pl. 18: "I have said to the Worm Thou art my mother & my sister". But there is no moral, as we expect from emblem books, and there is precious little explanation of the designs—until Blake revised *For Children* as *For the Sexes: The Gates of Paradise* (?1825) and added "The Keys of the Gates". *For Children* is a fascinating work but scarcely transparent.

However, Blake plainly hoped to find a commercial market for it, for he persuaded his employer Joseph Johnson to allow him to include Johnson's name on the title page:

1793
Published by W Blake Nº 13
Hercules Buildings Lambeth
and
J Johnson Sᵗ Pauls Church Yard

This is the only work in Illuminated Printing jointly published by Blake and a commercial publisher. Clearly, however, Johnson was merely selling the work, and it is unlikely that he did more than permit the work to be displayed in his shop in St Paul's Church Yard; the investment and risk were entirely Blake's.

He apparently did find a market for it, for on 13 September 1794 Richard Twiss wrote from Edmonton (just north of London) to Francis Douce: "A Lady here has just shown me . . . two curious works of Blake N° 13 Hercules Build^s Lambeth. One 'the gates of Paradise', 16 etchings [*plus frontispiece and title page*]. 24.mo the other 'Songs of Innocence' printed in colours. I Suppose the man to be mad; but he draws very well."*

But the market was a very small one indeed,† for only five copies of *For Children* have survived today. The price of 3s. in Blake's 1793 prospectus would have made it accessible "For Children" only if they had prosperous parents, and only one copy (E) is known to have been in the hands of a child: Blake's friend Henry Fuseli gave a copy to his five-year-old friend Harriet Jane Moore in 1806. Blake apparently made little attempt to find an audience for the work, for it is not listed among his other publications for sale in his letters of 9 June 1818 and 12 April 1827.

Blake's critics scarcely noticed the work, and the most extensive contemporary statement about it is Cunningham's acknowledgement that it is "not a little obscure".[140]

Blake's Notebook, Songs of Experience, *and "To the Public"*

What is the price of Experience[?] do men buy it for a song
Or wisdom for a dance in the street? No it is bought with the price
Of all that a man hath[,] his house his wife his children[.]
Wisdom is sold in the desolate market where none come to buy

(Vala p. 35, ll. 11–14)

In 1793 Blake had been printing, colouring, and selling *Songs of Innocence* for three years, and he had been composing in his brother Robert's Notebook other poems of a very different kind.‡ Some of them express the

---

* See *BR* (2). The "Lady here" may be Mrs Bliss. These are the earliest known references to *For Children* and *Songs of Innocence*.

† There is no evidence that it "became popular among the collectors of prints", as Cunningham claimed (*BR* 486).

‡ The Notebook has sketches by Robert Blake (d. 1787) and sketches and text by William Blake of *c.* 1790–94, 1801–3, 1807, 1809–12, and 1818. These include sketches of about 1790–93 used in *Marriage* (?1790), *America* (1793), *For Children* (1793), *Visions* (1793), "Job" (1793), *Europe* (1794), *Urizen* (1794), *Experience* (1794), *Song of Los* (1795), "Elohim Creating Adam" (1795), and "Satan Exulting over Eve" (*c.* 1795), some of which have quotations from Job and Ezekiel, from Chaucer (translated by Dryden), Donne's "The Progresse of the Soule", Milton's *Comus*, "Death of a Fair Infant", Sonnet XVII, and *Paradise Lost*, Shakespeare's *Hamlet* and Sonnet XV, and Spenser's *Fairie Queene*.

Devil's wisdom about the sanctity of energy, particularly sexual energy, and the association of eternity and gratified desire:

> He who bends to himself a joy
> Does the winged life destroy
> But he who kisses the joy as it flies
> Lives in eternity's sun rise[141]

> Abstinence sows sand all over
> The ruddy limbs & flourishing hair
> But desire Gratified
> Plants fruits of life & beauty there

(Notebook p. 105)

> What is it men in women do require[?]
> The lineaments of Gratified Desire[.]
> What is it women in men require[?]
> The lineaments of Gratified Desire

("The Question Answerd", Notebook p. 103)

And, more autobiographically, he wrote beside a little sketch of a man and woman sitting on the edge of a bed and taking off their stockings:

> When a Man has Married a Wife he finds out whether
> Her knees & elbows are only glued together

(Notebook p. 4)

Blake's works often celebrate the joys of freely expressed sexuality. In *The Marriage of Heaven and Hell* he hails the lust of the goat as the bounty of God, in *Visions of the Daughters of Albion* Oothoon sings of "lovely copulation bliss on bliss" (l. 201), and some of the designs of *Vala* represent copulation (e.g., pp. 40–1) and carefully emphasize genitalia (e.g., pp. 35, 44). This emphasis upon the joys of generation persisted into Blake's old age, and his designs for the apocryphal Book of Enoch (c. 1826) represent the nude daughters of men competing for the giant phalli of the sons of God.

We know a good deal about Blake's sexual ideas but very little about his sexual actions and less about those of Catherine. His verse expresses delight in "happy happy Love! free as the mountain wind!", and he told Crabb Robinson that "wives should be in common",[142] but it seems unlikely that Blake acted freely on these premises.

However, according to Gilchrist, "There *had* been stormy times . . . when both were young; discord by no means trifling . . . . But with the cause (jealousy on her side, not wholly unprovoked,) the strife had ceased also."*[143] The cause of this not-wholly-unprovoked jealousy is left discreetly untold.

Blake's theory concerning jealousy accorded with his views on love. He once told a friend, "'Do you think . . . if I came home, and discovered my wife to be unfaithful, I should be so foolish as to take it ill?' . . . 'But,' continues Blake's friend, 'I am inclined to think (despite the philosophic boast) it would have gone ill with the offenders.' "* Certainly Blake's poetry is often filled with the tumults and "torments of Love & Jealousy" (as *Vala* is sub-titled), and he wrote with rage of an apparent friend, who

> . . . when he could not act upon my wife
> Hired a Villain to bereave my Life†

But the rest is silence.

Blake drafted poems and designs for *Songs of Experience* in his Notebook, carefully constructing parallels with the poems of *Innocence*. There are poems called "Holy Thursday", "The Chimney Sweeper", and "Nurses Song" in each, and "Infant Joy" is answered by "Infant Sorrow", "The Divine Image" by "The Human Abstract", and "The Lamb" by "The Tyger". The two sets of poems illustrate "the Two Contrary States of the Human Soul".[144]

The Songs of Experience are songs of the unprotected, songs of betrayal or at least of a sense of betrayal, the laments of the victims. They are cries of honest indignation and social protest, the self-enjoyings of misery. Though invited by the bard to "Arise from out the dewy grass" and "controll The starry pole", the earth-bound lapsed souls are yet "cover'd with grey despair" and lament that they are "Chain'd in night" by "Starry Jealousy", the "Selfish father of men".[145] With self-devoted earnestness, they "build a Hell in Heavens despite".[146]

In contrast to the exuberant, graceful, singing designs of *Innocence*, the visual images of *Experience* are sparse, bleak and stark as in the title page, which shows two young people weeping over a sculptured couple on a bier as in Blake's copies of tombs in Westminster Abbey (Pls 18–19). The poems

---

* See Addenda, below.
† Gilchrist (*BR* 238). The account also says: "Mrs. Blake was a most exemplary wife, yet was so much in the habit of echoing and thinking right whatever he said that, had she been present, adds my informant, he is sure she would have innocently responded, '*Of course not!*'"
‡ "On H—ys Friendship", Notebook p. 35. The second line appears paradoxically in his adolescent Gothic poem "Fair Elenor" (ll. 67–8) in *Poetical Sketches* (1783) in which Elenor's murdered husband warns her against the accursed duke:

> He seeks thy love; who, coward, in the night,
> Hired a villain to bereave my life.

are about failures of imagination and vision; the mourning couple look down at the rigid dead sculpted in lifeless stone and do not see the dancing figures and flourishing vines around "SONGS" above them. They look down to earth rather than up to heaven. They are earth-bound, worshipping death.

The pervasive miseries of social injustice are memorably mourned in "London":

I wander thro' each charter'd street,
Near where the charter'd Thames does flow
And mark in every face I meet
Marks of weakness, marks of woe.

In every cry of every Man,
In every Infants cry of fea*r*,
In every voice; in every ba*n*,
The mind-forg'd manacles I hear[.]

How the Chimney-sweepers cry
Every blackning Church appall*s*,
And the hapless Soldiers sigh
Runs in blood down Palace walls

But most thro' midnight streets I hear
How the youthful Harlots curse
Blasts the new born Infants tear
And blights with plagues the Marriage hearse[.]

The design for "London" shows a long-bearded old man, apparently blind, being led through the bleak streets of London by a child, and when the same image was used years later in *Jerusalem* it was identified as

"London blind & age-bent begging thro the Streets".[147] The "Marks of

weakness, marks of woe" which the old man "mark[s] in every face I meet"
must be imaginary marks, for the old man is blind. The social misery which
he marks and experiences is real and pervasive, but it is not universal. The
limitation of metaphorical vision of the old man is indicated by his
blindness.

In "The Lamb" in *Songs of Innocence*, the little boy constructs a catechism for the lamb:

Dost thou know who made thee[?] . . .

He calls himself a Lamb:

He is meek & he is mild,
He became a little child:
I a child & thou a lamb,
We are called by his name.

In the poem the qualities of the creator are deduced from those of his creation; the meekness and mildness of lamb and child must echo those qualities in their creator. It is a true syllogism, but, as in most of the *Songs of
Innocence*, it is not true enough.

The same syllogism, deducing the qualities of the creator from those of
his creation, is used in "The Tyger" in *Experience*, with terrifying effect:

Tyger Tyger, burning bright,
In the forests of the night:
What immortal hand or eye
Could frame thy fearful symmetry?

In what distant deeps or skie*s*
Burnt the fire of thine eyes?
On what wings dare he aspire?
What the han*d* dare sieze the fire?

And what shoulder, & what art,
Could twist the sinews of thy heart?
And when thy heart began to beat,
What dread hand? & what dread feet?

What the hammer? what the chain,
In what furnace was thy brain?
What the anvil? what dread gras*p*
Dare its deadly terrors clasp!

When the stars threw down their spears
And water'd heaven with their tears:
Did he smile his work to see?
Did he who made the Lamb make thee?

Tyger Tyger burning bright,
In the forests of the night:
What immortal hand or ey*e*
Dare frame thy fearful symmetry?

("The Tyger", *Songs* pl. 42)

The grammar, like the logic, becomes so involved that the limbs of the creator are scarcely distinguishable from those of his terrible, bloodthirsty creation. The poem moves from physical power (who "Could frame thy fearful symmetry?") to moral daring (who "Dare frame thy fearful symmetry?"), and any answer to the question is terrifying: Yes, it is the same God who creates the meekness of the lamb and the terrors of the Tyger, or No, there are two creating Gods, one for the helpless lamb and one for the preying tyger.

But before we are overwhelmed by the terrors of the tyger and his creator, let us look at the design for "The Tyger". That is scarcely a giant, threatening predator; notice the scale of the tree behind him and the sedateness of his walk. What we see is less like an image of burning, deadly terrors, with twisted sinews and dread feet, than it is like a stuffed toy forgotten at the bottom of a tree. Blake was perfectly capable of depicting terrors, as he did in "The Great Red Dragon", "Fire", "A Breach in a City", and "The Ghost of a Flea" (Pls 5, 24, 34, 126). The image in "The Tyger" is an antidote to the terrors of the text. The poem shows the state of mind of the singer, one of "the Two Contrary States of the Human Soul", not the nature of the universe and of its creator.

The *Songs of Experience* are the complements to *Songs of Innocence*, not the answers to them. The singers of Innocence feel protected by powerful forces outside themselves, while the singers of Experience feel threatened by powerful forces they cannot control or propitiate. Neither set of singers has yet learned that the power of divinity lies not beyond us but within us.

Blake printed copies of *Songs of Experience* for the rest of his life, but almost all copies were either issued with *Songs of Innocence*, with a joint title page, or sold to collectors who already had a copy of *Innocence* with which to bind it. Few copies of *Songs of Experience*, perhaps none, were issued by themselves without an accompanying *Innocence*. Twenty-eight copies of *Experience* are known, and they were sold at prices from 5s. in 1793 to £3.3.0 in 1818 and £5.5.0 in 1827.[148]

The poems in *Experience* were admired a good deal less by contemporaries than those in *Innocence*. For instance, in 1818 Coleridge gave three poems in *Innocence* his highest praise, while none in *Experience* was so highly admired.[149] *Experience* poems were less frequently reprinted than those in *Innocence*; before 1839 only five poems from *Experience* had appeared in conventional typography, and only "The Garden of Love" and "The Tyger" were given repeatedly.[150] Crabb Robinson probably expressed a common conclusion among contemporaries when he said in 1811 that the *Songs of Experience* were "metaphysical riddles and mystical allegories" including "poetic pictures of the highest beauty and sublimity" and "poetical fancies which can scarcely be understood even by the initiated".[151]

It was "The Tyger" which drew the approbation of everyone. Malkin, who quoted it in 1806, says that it wears the "garb of grandeur", and Crabb Robinson thought it "truly inspired".[152] Charles Lamb had heard "The Tyger" in 1824 and found it "glorious", and John Linnell in 1826 heard "Crabb Robinson recite ... 'The Tiger,' before a distinguished company gathered around Mr. Aders' table".[153] Cunningham in 1830 said that "The Tyger" "has been admired for the force and vigour of its thoughts by poets of high name ... few could stamp such living images".[154] And of course today "The Tyger" may be the poem by which Blake is most widely known.

By the end of 1793, Blake had completed seven illustrated books and two very ambitious line-engravings: *Innocence* (1789), *Thel* (1789), *Marriage* (?1790), *Visions* (1793), *America* (1793), *For Children* (1793), and *Experience*,* plus "Job" (1793) and "Edward and Elinor" (1793). On 10

---

* Experience is dated "1794" on the title page, but in early copies (A–B, D) the date is invisible (if it is there), under the watercolouring, and perhaps it was added later, after the completion of the Prospectus of 10 Oct 1793 which lists *Experience*.

October 1793 he issued an etched prospectus "To the Public" offering them for sale. This is the only public advertisement he ever made, and its rarity is indicated by the facts that it has been recorded only once and that no copy has been seen since 1863.

The prospectus announces the invention of

a method of Printing both Letter-press and Engraving in a style more ornamental, uniform, and grand, than any before discovered, while it produces works at less than one fourth of the expense. . . .

The Illuminated Books are Printed in Colours, and on the most beautiful wove paper that could be procured.

No Subscriptions for the numerous great works now in hand are asked, for none are wanted; but the Author will produce his works, and offer them to sale at a fair price.

The line engravings were offered at 10s.6d. to 12s., substantial sums but little enough for large line engravings like these (c. 14″ x 19″), and the Illuminated Books were priced at 3s. to 10s.6d., significant but modest prices for illustrated books of eight to twenty-seven plates—at this time the plates were generally printed back-to-back on the same leaf. Notice that the Illuminated Books are to be mass-produced, not made individually to order,* though the mass-production was not very imposing; Blake's print-runs were probably generally less than a dozen.

What does Blake mean by Illuminated Books?

The word "Illuminated" appears only in Blake's Prospectus,[155] and only *America, Visions, Thel, Marriage, Songs of Innocence*, and *Songs of Experience* are described in the Prospectus as being "in Illuminated Printing". "The Illuminated Books are Printed in Colours" (such as green and sepia and red), whereas [*For Children:*] *The Gates of Paradise*, which is always printed simply in black, is there called merely "a small book of Engravings". Apparently, therefore, "Illuminated Printing" refers to designs and text printed on the same page "in Colours" (i.e., not in black).† Nothing is said in

---

* This is the thesis brilliantly demonstrated by Joseph Viscomi, *Blake and the Idea of the Book* (Princeton: Princeton University Press, 1993). It was only in the last ten years or so of his life that, as Blake said in his letter of 9 June 1818, "Persons wishing to have any or all of them Should Send me their Order to Print them."

† It is unlikely that "Illuminated Printing", "Printing in Colours", meant colour-printing (applying all the colours to the copperplate before printing), for, of the six works identified in the Prospectus as "in Illuminated Printing", no surviving copy of *America, Thel*, or *Innocence* was colour printed.

The few copies of *Experience* (C, F–H, T), *Marriage* (E–F), and *Visions* (F) which are colour-printed were probably printed later. *Most* copies of works created immediately after the Prospectus were colour-printed: *Europe* (1794), *Urizen* (1794), *Book of Ahania* (1795), *Book of Los* (1795), *Song of Los* (1795).

the Prospectus of hand-colouring the designs, and "Illuminated Printing" does not imply hand-colouring, though *Visions, Thel*, and *Marriage* were always hand-coloured and *America, Innocence*, and *Experience* usually are; *For Children* is never coloured.

Blake's address "To the Public" is the high-watermark of his ambition in selling his works in Illuminated Printing, the works by which he is best known in the literary world. At this time he was producing his books in very small though commercial quantities, and he hoped that he might earn significant sums from them, though he no longer talked of "Print[*ing*] off two thousand" copies "& sell[*ing*] them a hundred pounds a piece" for a three-volume folio set, as he had in *An Island in the Moon* nine years before.[156] And his other works in Illuminated Printing were produced in smaller numbers than those listed in his Prospectus.

Europe, Urizen, Song of Los, Book of Ahania, Book of Los

The Prophecies Blake wrote in 1794 and 1795 are deeply interfused with politics and with his proliferating myth. The world depicted is one of almost hopeless torment; an understanding of the origins of evil, of the cause of the mind-forged manacles, does not lead to liberation. For Blake, the 1790s are a decade of doom.

Europe A Prophecy begins with one of Blake's most famous images, "The Ancient of Days" (Pl. 54): God leans down from the sun to divide with his light-giving fingers the darkness from the light. George Cumberland appropriately inscribed his copy with a passage from *Paradise Lost*, VII, 230–6:

> In his hand, he took the Golden Compasses, prepared
> In Gods eternal store, to circumscribe
> This Universe, and all created things.
> One foot he center'd, and the other turn'd,
> Round through the vast profundity obscure,
> And said, thus far extend, thus far thy bounds[,]
> This be thy just circumference, O world![157]

According to Blake's friend J.T. Smith, "He was inspired with the splendid grandeur of this figure, by the vision which he declared hovered over his head at the top of his staircase; and he has been frequently heard to say, that it made a more powerful impression upon his mind than all he had ever been visited by".[158]

But that God-like gesture creates not a distant Eden but the serpent of

Europe, as we see on the title page which faces the frontispiece (Pl. 55). The benevolence of the Ancient of Days is nowhere visible in *Europe*.

It was

> Thought chang'd the infinite to a serpent, that which pitieth:
> To a devouring flame; and man fled from its face . . .
> Then was the serpent temple form'd, image of infinite
> Shut up in finite revolutions, and man became an Angel;
> Heaven a mighty circle turning; God a tyrant crown'd.
>
> (pl. 13, ll. 143–4, 148–50)

The poem was dictated to Blake in his parlour in Lambeth by a fairy who

> will shew you all alive
> The world, where every particle of dust breathes forth its joy.
>
> (pl. 3, ll. 18–19)

The song is about "the night of Enitharmons joy" (pl. 8, l. 90) when she sends forth her sons "That Woman, lovely Woman! may have dominion" (pl. 8, l. 92). Her sky-born emissaries sweep through the heavens blowing miraculous trumpets (Pl. 56), but the glorious trumpets broadcast not resurrection but plagues and death.

> Go! tell the human race that Womans love is Sin;
> That an Eternal life awaits the worms of sixty winters
> In an allegorical abode where existence hath never come
>
> (pl. 8, ll. 94–6)

> Enitharmon slept,
> Eighteen hundred years: Man was a Dream!
> The night of Nature . . . .
>
> (pl. 12, ll. 111–13)

> Over the doors Thou shalt not: & over the chimneys Fear is written:
> With bands of iron round their necks, fastend into the walls
> The citizens . . . .
>
> (pl. 15, ll. 191–3)

> But terrible Orc, when he beheld the morning in the east,
> Shot from the heights of Enitharmon,
> And in the vineyards of red France appear'd the light of his fury.
> . . .

Then Los arose[;] his head he reard in snaky thunders clad:
And with a cry that shook all nature to the utmost pole,
Call'd all his sons to the strife of blood.

FINIS

(*Europe* pl. 17–18, ll. 254–6, 263–5)

The poem ends with a glorious call to arms, echoing the triumphant revolution "in the vineyards of red France", but the last image is not of the
heroic sons of Los storming the barricades of tyranny but of a naked man
carrying a fainting woman and a terrified girl from the horrors of a burning
city. The best the poem offers at its conclusion is an escape from terror, not
the destruction of fear and servitude.

Europe is the same size as *America*, with which it was regularly paired,
and it probably cost what *America* did in 1793 (10s.6d.), as it did in 1818
(£5.5.0) and 1827 (£6.6.0).[159] Only nine copies, printed 1794–1821, have
survived, most of them coloured.

Those who bought *Europe* probably found the poem to be a "mysterious
and incomprehensible rhapsody ... wholly inexplicable", as J.T. Smith
did.[160] Cunningham says that, like *America*, the designs are "plentifully
sprinkled with verse".[161] For most readers the glory of *Europe* was in the
designs; Smith said that the frontispiece of "The Ancient of Days" (Pl. 54)
is "uncommonly fine ... and approaches almost to the sublimity of Raffaelle
or Michel Angelo" and pl. 12 of the angels pouring out the plague (Pl. 56)
is a "splendid composition", "perfectly admirable".[162]

Tiriel, *The Book of Thel*, and *Visions of the Daughters of Albion* are myths
of humans struggling with their fates, and *America* and *Europe* are myths of
nations struggling to shape their fates. *The First Book of Urizen* deals with
the struggles of divinity, of the eternal mind, to define itself and its universe. It is a creation myth, or rather a series of creation myths, like Genesis,
the first book of Moses.

The poem begins before time, before creation, before being:

Earth was not: nor globes of attraction[.]
The will of the Immortal expanded
Or contracted his all flexible senses.
Death was not, but eternal life sprung

(pl. 3, ll. 36–9)

Urizen is the blind law-maker, the confined creator (Pl. 57) exiled from
eternity who wishes to find or impose on everything his own reasonable
unity:

I have sought for a joy without pain,
For a solid without fluctuation

(pl. 4, ll. 54–5)

With endless energy he creates his own gospel:

Laws of peac*e*, of lov*e*, of unity;
Of pit*y*, compassio*n*, forgiveness.
Let each chuse one habitation:
His ancient infinite mansion:
One comman*d*, one jo*y*, one desire,
One curs*e*, one weight, one measure[,]
One Kin*g*, one God, one Law.

(pl. 4, ll. 78–84)

As a consequence of withdrawing himself from the eternal flux of existence, Urizen suffers fall on fall. He is confined by Los the eternal prophet:

In chains of the mind locked up,
Like fetters of ice shrinking togethe*r*,
Disorganiz'*d*, rent from Eternity.
Los beat on his fetters of iron . . . .

(pl. 10, ll. 190–3)

And now his eternal life
Like a dream was obliterated

(pl. 13, ll. 268–9)

Urizen's

     soul sicken'd! he curs'd
Both sons & daughters: for he saw
That no flesh nor spirit could keep
His iron laws one moment.

(pl. 23, ll. 443–6)

Like a spider, Urizen draws out from his sorrowing soul a web:

So twisted the cords, & so knotted
The meshes: twisted like to the human brain

And all calld i*t* The Net of Religion

(pl. 25, ll. 467–8)

The very extensive illustrations to *Urizen* contain some of Blake's most powerful images (Pl. 58), but they are images of torment and confinement. The identification of the tyranny of reason and the mental chains in which it has bound itself does not lead to freedom. The last image of the poem is of Urizen—and mankind—in chains.

Urizen, which is longer and more extensively illustrated and coloured than *America*, may have cost more than it did in 1793 (10s.6d.), but it was the same price as *America* in 1818 (£5.5.0) and 1827 (£6.6.0).[163] Blake printed copies from 1794 to about 1815, but only eight have survived, all in different plate orders and most with differing numbers of plates.

Among Blake's contemporaries, only Cunningham has left a comment on *Urizen*. The "wild verses" have "the merit or the fault of surpassing all human comprehension ... what he meant by them even his wife declared she could not tell, though she was sure they had a meaning, and a fine one ...".

With the designs, Cunningham the poet asked not so much for meaning as for force and ferocity: "it is not a little fearful to look upon; a powerful, dark, terrible, though undefined and indescribable, impression is left on the mind—and it is in no haste to be gone ...".[164]

The First Book of Urizen, which seems to many today to be one of the most succinct and powerful of Blake's mythological works, the basis for his expanding myth, apparently surpassed the comprehension of all his contemporaries, even of his wife.

One of the novelties of *Urizen* is that all copies except a late one (G, c. 1818) are colour-printed, with colours added on the copperplate. The sense of suppressed earth-forces, as of a smouldering volcano, is very powerful and is peculiarly appropriate to *Urizen*.

The Song of Los is the same folio size as *America* and *Europe* and was sometimes bound with them. This association is not coincidental, for *The Song of Los* is composed of AFRICA and ASIA, which provide a frame for *America* and *Europe*. Africa ends as "The Guardian Prince of Albion burns in his nightly tent" (pl. 4, l. 32), and the same words begin *America* (pl. 5, l. 1). And *Europe*, which concludes with Los calling "all his sons to the strife of blood" (pl. 18, l. 265), seems to be continued in Asia: "The Kings of Asia heard | The howl rise up from Europe!" (pl. 6, ll. 1-2). *The Song of Los* thus returns to the historical and social subjects of *America* and *Europe*.

The title page of *The Song of Los* (Pl. 59) announces a bleak and barren world. The reader is in the position of the aged man with his hand on a skull looking upwards at the elegant lettering of the title.

In Africa, Los, the eternal prophet, sings of how "Moses beheld on Mount Sinai forms of dark delusion", and Adam and Noah "saw Urizen give his Laws to the Nations | By the hands of the children of Los": an "abstract Law" to Pythagoras, Socrates & Plato, "A Gospel" to Jesus, "a loose Bible" to Mahomet, and "a Code of War" to Odin in the north (pl. 3, ll. 17, 8–9, 18–19, 24, 29, 30). "The human race began to wither", "Till like a dream Eternity was obliterated & erased" (pl. 3, l. 25; pl. 4, l. 35).

These laws are not codes of conduct but chains for the mind, a rational philosophy of natural cause and effect, of mundane wisdom as if it were the only wisdom:

> Thus the terrible race of Los & Enitharmon gave
> Laws & Religions to the sons of Har binding them more
> And more to Earth: closing and restraining:
> Till a Philosophy of Five Senses was complete[.]
>
> Urizen wept & gave it into the hands of Newton & Locke

(pl. 4, ll. 44–8)

In Asia, the kings were startled by the "thought-creating fires of Orc" and cried in bitterness of soul.

> "Shall not the King call for Famine from the Heath?
> Nor the Priest, for Pestilence from the fen
> To restrain! to dismay! to thin!
> The inhabitants of mountain and plain …."
>
> Orc raging in European darkness
> Arose like a pillar of fire

(pl. 4, ll. 6, 9–12; pl. 7, ll. 50–1)

and the response is an erotic apocalypse:

> The Grave shrieks with delight, & shakes
> Her hollow wom*b*, & clasps the solid stem:
> Her bosom swells with wild desire;
> And mild & glandous wine
> In rivers rush & shout & dance,
> On mountain, dale and plain.
>   The SONG of LOS is Ended

(pl. 7, ll. 59–64)

But the apocalypse is only partial, for the last words of the poem are: "Urizen Wept."

Thus, once again, despite the heroic call to arms, the poem concludes in despair and tears.

All six surviving copies of *The Song of Los* were colour-printed about 1795, and Blake did not include the poem in his lists of works for sale in 1818 and 1827. No contemporary mentions it, and even Gilchrist in 1863 does not seem to have known it.

The Book of Ahania (Pl. 60) and *The Book of Los* (Pl. 61) seem to be technological and mythological experiments. Both were conventionally etched in intaglio, not in the relief etching of the other books in Illuminated Printing. *The Book of Los* is probably etched on the backs of five copperplates for *The Book of Ahania*, for they are identical in size. Both books were colour-printed about 1795, the date on the title pages.

Both poems rework the mythological material of *The First Book of Urizen*, as if they were the second and third *Books of Urizen*. *The Book of Ahania* begins with Fuzon's rebellion against his father Urizen:

> "Shall we worship this Demon of Smok*e*,"
> Said Fuzo*n*, "this abstract non-entity[,]
> This cloudy God seated on Waters
> Now see*n*, now obscur'd; King of sorrow?"

> *(Ahania* ll. 10–14)

Fuzon wounds his father with a pillar of fire and rejoices: "'I am Go*d*,' said h*e*, 'eldest of things!'" (l. 86).

Urizen accidentally creates the tree of mystery:

> Amaz'd started Urizen! when
> He beheld himself compassed round
> And high roofed over with trees
> He arose but the stems stood so thick
> He with difficulty and great pain
> Brought his Book*s*, all but the Book
> Of iron, from the dismal shade

> (ll. 116–22)

And "On the topmost stem" of the Tree of Mystery "Urizen nail'd Fuzon's corse" (ll. 128–9).

Much of the poem is the lament of Ahania at her separation from Urizen:

> Cruel jealousy! selfish fear!
> Self-destroying: how can deligh*t*

Renew in these chains of darkness.... *

In *The Book of Los*, first Los falls into human form, and then he gives human form to Urizen.

> Los astonish'd and terrified, built
> Furnaces; he formed an Anvil[,]
> A Hammer of adamant[;] then began
> The binding of Urizen day and night

> ... till a Form
> Was complete*d*, a Human Illusion
> In darkness and deep clouds involvd.

(ll. 139–42, 174–6)

The Book of Ahania and *The Book of Los* seem to be experiments which were not repeated, and only one complete copy of each book is known. Blake did not offer them with his other works in his letters of 1818 and 1827.

No contemporary is known to have referred to them. There is no record of *The Book of Ahania* before 1861 or of *The Book of Los* before 1866.

The Great Colour Prints

While he was printing his Prophecies in 1794 and 1795, Blake experimented with methods of colouring his works. The outlines themselves were printed in shades of brown and sepia and green, and then Catherine Blake would colour each print with a few simple washes following a model Blake had made for her.†

About 1794 Blake tried adding colours to the copperplates themselves, so that all the colours could be printed at once. The process was technically intricate, for the ink had to dry so slowly that the first colour applied was still wet when the last one was added, and the last one must not be so wet that it spread more than the first colour.

The effects of this colour-printing were far darker and bolder than in the pale washes of *c*. 1790, and often they were curiously three-dimensional. The thick, sticky ink actually rose a little when the plate and paper were

---

* Ll. 233–5. This is very similar to "Earth's Answer" in *Experience*: "Cruel jealous selfish fear[!] | Can delight | Chain'd in night | The virgins of youth and morning bear?" (*Songs* pl. 31, ll. 12–15).

† Thirty years later Blake coloured individual copies much more elaborately and brilliantly, sometimes covering the whole print with watercolour.

separated, leaving a granular surface rather like lichen, a surface which is brilliantly successful in conveying the texture of rock or moss. Tatham said that they had "a sort of accidental look ... [*which*] was very enticing."[165] This tempera-like effect is extraordinarily difficult to reproduce by other methods of printing; almost all reproductions of Blake's colour-printed works are unsatisfactory.

Some of Blake's Illuminated Books such *The First Book of Urizen*, *The Book of Ahania*, *The Book of Los*, and *The Song of Los* were chiefly or entirely colour-printed, and colour-printing was used in some copies of *All Religions are One*, *Thel* (a fragment), *Europe*, *Songs*, *No Natural Religion*, and *Visions*.

So alluring was this method of colour-printing that Blake's friend the miniaturist Ozias Humphry persuaded him to print designs from some of his literary works, masking the text (which did not print very well by this method anyway), "tho to the Loss of some of the best things", as Blake commented ruefully.[166] These miscellaneous designs were collected in two groups, called the Large and the Small Book of Designs.[167] Blake's friend J.T. Smith was deeply impressed by his "great depth of knowledge in colouring" creating effects which are "most beautifully prismatic", and Richard Thomson told Smith that Humphry's books show "almost magical effects of colouring" which "almost ... resemble oil-colours".* It was probably Humphry's colour-prints about which Joseph Farington wrote in his Diary for 19 February 1796: "West, Cosway & Humphry spoke warmly in favour of the designs of Blake the Engraver, as works of extraordinary genius and imagination."†

Blake made another great series of Large Colour Prints (design-size *c.* 43cm x 53 cm) in 1795[168] which are the culmination of his work in colour printing. These consisted of (1) "Christ Appearing to the Apostles", (2) "Elohim Creating Adam" (Pl. 62), (3) "God Judging Adam", (4) "The Good and Evil Angels", (5) "Hecate", (6) "The House of Death", (7) "Lamech and his Two Wives", (8) "Naomi Entreating Ruth and Orpah to Return to the Land of Moab", (9) "Nebuchadnezzar",‡ (10) "Newton", (11) "Pity", and (12) "Satan Exulting over Eve".[169] Blake printed up to

---

* *BR* 468, 469, 472. Thomson also described Humphry's colour-printed copies of *America* (H), *Europe* (D, bound in front of the Large Book of Designs [A]), *Songs of Experience* (H), and Small Book of Designs (A), all probably acquired about 1796.

† The passage continues: "Smirke differed in opinion, from what He had seen, so do I."

‡ Samuel Palmer said in 1862 that the same design in the *Marriage* pl. 24 "gives Blake's idea of Nebuchadnezzar in the Wilderness. I have very old German translations of Cicero [*1531*] and Petrarch in which ... almost the very same figure appears. Many years had elapsed after making his own design before Blake saw the wood cut" (*BRS* 84). See Addenda, below.

three copies of each of them, and he and Catherine touched them up with watercolour.

While some of the subjects are conventional enough, the effect is often extraordinarily bizarre and powerful. "Newton", for instance, represents the great mathematician and earnest theologian crouching naked at the bottom of the sea as he traces figures in the sand, and "Elohim Creating Adam" shows the creator, with massive bronze wings, hovering in torment above Adam who is already enwrapped by the serpent. Clearly the designer of the prints had profoundly different ideas about Elohim and Newton than did his contemporaries—or ours.

Beautiful as the effects of colour-printing are, they were extremely time-consuming to achieve. It was more troublesome to colour the copperplate than to colour the print. Only two or three copies could be pulled from one colouring of the plate, and even then the duplicates often had to be extensively retouched. Blake's colour-printing is not an efficient method of multiplying designs. Only one set of the Large and Small Book of Designs was made in 1795 (thirty prints), plus a few duplicates (twenty prints), and even fewer copies were pulled of the Large Colour Prints (twenty-nine prints).[170]

Blake had difficulty in finding customers for the Large Colour Prints, and perhaps none was sold for ten years. The first known buyer is Thomas Butts, to whom Blake delivered eight of them on 5 July and 7 September 1805 for £1.1.0 each,[171] all but one of them dated "1795". However, "Nebuchadnezzar" and "Newton" are on paper watermarked J WHATMAN | 1804 and were probably printed and finished for Butts in 1805.[172] Similarly, "The House of Death", "The Good and Evil Angels", "Nebuchadnezzar", "Elohim Creating Adam", and another "Newton" were probably executed about 1805.[173]

Thirteen years later, Blake still had copies on hand when he offered the "12 Large Prints ... Printed in Colours" to Dawson Turner in his letter of 9 June 1818 at £5.5.0 apiece. Turner bought none of them, and probably Blake sold no more of the Large Colour Prints.

When Blake died, he still had at least nine of the subjects plus five duplicates, some of them still unfinished.[174] These passed to Catherine Blake and thence to Frederick Tatham. Tatham says he offered seven to an itinerant artist named James Ferguson about 1831,[175] but neither Ferguson nor any one else besides Butts is known to have bought any of Blake's greatest triumphs in colour-printing before 1843.[176]

The years from the death of Robert Blake in 1787 until the completion of Blake's great series of colour prints in 1795 were wonderfully profitable. Blake was advancing in his career with commissions for larger engravings and for some engravings after his own designs, and he was sufficiently prosperous to move to a large house in a garden suburb with a maid and with money and silver-plate to be borrowed and stolen. He became good friends with Henry Fuseli and was on the periphery of Joseph Johnson's circle of liberal wits. He invented Illuminated Printing and produced a great flowering of Illuminated Books from *Songs of Innocence and of Experience* to *The Marriage of Heaven and Hell, Thel, America*, and *Europe*. And he invented a method of colour-printing in which he produced not only many of the Illuminated Books but also his extraordinary series of large colour prints, from "Newton" to "Elohim Creating Adam". These are very extraordinary achievements.

But at the same time, these were dark years, with the death of his brother and his mother and with the perversion of the promise of the French Revolution. The establishment of the New Jerusalem Church in the glorious hope of a new age free from the fetters of ritual and state had degenerated into bickering, into "Lies & Priestcraft". Blake seems to have spent less of his effort on creating purely visual art, and he exhibited nothing at the Royal Academy during these years. The ways of the world seemed to be enmeshing him, as they did Urizen.

The vision of these years in his Illuminated Books and in his great colour prints is powerful but dark. *Thel* and *The Visions of the Daughters of Albion* end with the woes of women, and *America* and *Europe* end with the wars of Los. The *Songs of Experience* are filled with a sense of lives blasted and years wasted, of a world governed by cruelty, jealousy, terror, and secrecy. The cause of the waste and terror is often plain, in the perversion of reason and the neglect of inspiration, but the cure is neither visible nor imagined. God himself is in torments, whether seen as Urizen or as Elohim.

These years of apparent triumph were, as Blake said in his letter of 23 October 1804, dark though very profitable years. In the ways of the world, he was gaining profit and credit, but at what neglect of the spirit? Why did the genius of Oothoon and the Devil bring so little joy? Orc and Los evoke a great apocalypse of freedom, but when

The SONG of LOS Ended
Urizen Wept.

CHAPTER V

1795–1800:
The Ocean of Business [1]

Designs for Young's Night Thoughts

*A more extraordinary, original, and
sublime production of art has seldom, if
ever, been witnessed since the days of
the celebrated Mich. Agnolo.* [2]

*They were like the conceits of a
drunken fellow or a madman.
"Represent a man sitting on the moon,
and pissing the Sun out—that would be
a whim of as much merit".* [3]

The goddess "FORTUNE ALONE IS THE GOVERNOR OF WORLDLY RICHES",[4] not merit or industry.

So Blake had been taught, for the Goddess of Fortune is nearly allied to The God of This World who is Satan, and so he concluded in 1799.

But in 1795 it appeared as if genius and industry might indeed seduce the "Prince of darkness [who] is a Gentleman".[5]

For some years Blake had been dealing with James Edwards, a publisher of elaborately illustrated books and perhaps the most distinguished anti-quarian bookseller in Europe of his time. He came from a remarkable family of booksellers in Halifax which had invented styles of book-decoration that came to bear their name as Edwards of Halifax bindings, particularly with painted vellum covers and painted fore-edges. When James Edwards came from Halifax to London in 1784 at the age of twenty-eight, he established with his brother John at 102 Pall Mall a book-shop whose discrete opulence earned James the title of The Medicean Bookseller.

James Edwards and Joseph Johnson commissioned Blake to make enor-mously ambitious engravings for Fuseli's Milton in September 1791, and James Edwards, Robert Bowyer, and John Murray commissioned Blake to make engravings on a similar scale for Hume's *History of England* in June 1792. Edwards and Johnson commissioned Blake's engravings for Stedman's *Narrative ... of Surinam* on which Blake worked from 1791 to 1795. By 1795 Blake may well have had extensive dealings with James Edwards.*

James's youngest brother Richard came from Halifax to London in the autumn of 1789, when he was twenty-one. At first he probably worked at 102 Pall Mall, learning the ways of the London book-trade, but by the end of 1791 he established himself at an equally fashionable address in 142 New Bond Street. Here he produced ephemeral Church and King pamphlets and sold a modest range of books including a number jointly published with his brother James, the latter often available in elegant bindings.[6]

Most of his publications were modest in dimensions and originality, and many had a strong conformist bias. For instance, Anon., *A Review of ... the Parliament of 1784* (1792) asserts that "The Aristocracy of Great Britain ... is as much an aristocracy of talents as of rank"; [C.E. De Coetlogon], *Hints to the People of England* (1792) concludes that we have "*the best of Kings*, and the best Constitution in the World"; and Anon., *Ten Minutes Caution* (1792) warns that, if Tom Paine's system were put into practice, "the next day all the rich would be ruined ... and in a little time all the poor would be

---

* Blake speaks of calling on James Edwards in his letters of 26 Oct 1803, 27 Jan, 23 Feb, and 28 May 1804.

starved". The typography of Richard Edwards's books was of indifferent quality, and very few of them were illustrated.[*]

However, Richard Edwards was just once inspired by the great changes in the air in 1794. The standards of British typography, book design, and binding had made enormous strides in the previous three decades and now rivalled those of France and Holland and Italy. In particular, book illustration had been radically transformed by Alderman Boydell's imperial Shakspeare Gallery (1786–1805) and by his chief rivals, Macklin's Poets' Gallery (1788 ff.) and Bible (1791–1800), and Bowyer's Historic Gallery of illustrations to Hume's *History of England* (1792–1806). These great undertakings, costing tens of thousands of pounds apiece, involved most of the great English painters of the day, with commissions of up to £1,000 for a single painting; all the great line engravers in England were employed at fees of up to £800 for a single folio plate; and the best printers such as Bensley and Bulmer were commissioned. Type, ink, and printing houses were invented for the purpose. Each publisher had a fashionable gallery to which the public flocked for the annual exhibitions of specially commissioned huge paintings, and each publisher sustained public interest by issuing his works in parts over more than a decade, at a cost to subscribers of up to £105 (for Boydell's Shakspeare).

A number of illustrious illustrated folio publications grew up in the shadows of these giants, such as Boydell's Milton (3 vols, 1794–97), his edition of Farington's *History of the River Thames* (1794, 1796), and Thornton's *Flora* (1797–1807), but they were only seriously rivalled by one other British illustrated literary work. This was the edition of Young's *Night Thoughts* undertaken by the twenty-six-year-old publisher of cautious ephemera, Richard Edwards.

There was a striking incongruity both between Richard Edwards's previous publications and his public obscurity as compared to those of the titans he was challenging, and between the obscure craftsman of genius whom he commissioned to make all his designs and all his engravings, William Blake, as compared to the scores of famous Royal Academy painters and engravers employed to illustrate Bowyer's Hume, Boydell's Shakspeare, and Macklin's Bible.

William Blake was an extraordinary choice for such a Church-and-King publisher as Richard Edwards. For one thing, Blake made his living as a modest engraver of other men's designs—he was not and (as an engraver)

---

[*] The chief exception is J. Merigot, *A Select Collection of Views and Ruins in Rome and Its Vicinity. Executed from Drawings Made Upon the Spot [by Vien] in the Year 1791*, Part I (issued in fifteen numbers with 62 handsome plates March 1796–Nov 1797), but the initiative and risk were chiefly those of the engraver J. Merigot.

could not be a Royal Academician. Before the *Night Thoughts* was published in 1797, he had signed his name to only ten designs in three commercially published books.

For another thing, Blake was a political and religious radical who wore the white cap of liberty openly in the streets of London, who deplored the unimaginative singularity of "One King, one God, one Law",* and who was in fact tried for sedition in 1804. It is difficult to believe that William Blake and Richard Edwards had much in common politically, religiously, morally, or socially.

Finally, even as an engraver Blake was not widely admired or even known in 1794, though he was then thirty-seven and near the height of his power as a line-engraver. Before 1794, he had made engravings for about thirty commercial books issued by six different booksellers (eleven of the books published by Joseph Johnson), but very few were in folio size, he had received no commission for an engraving, much less for a design, for the great galleries of Boydell, Macklin, and Bowyer, and he had never been named with honour as an engraver in a review. Indeed, though he had illustrated his own works profusely, he had never made a substantial series of designs for a major literary work. It is, therefore, not easy to see what drew William Blake and Richard Edwards together.

They did, however, have a number of things in common. Both were artists and craftsmen who specialized in copying work by other men to decorate books. Blake had repeatedly been commissioned to make engravings by Joseph Johnson and his sometime-partner James Edwards, and all three men were good friends of Henry Fuseli. It is likely that Richard Edwards knew of Blake through his brother James and his brother's two friends Joseph Johnson and Henry Fuseli.

The most likely godfather of the *Night Thoughts* project is Henry Fuseli, whose huge Milton paintings Blake had been commissioned to help engrave in 1791. One of the earliest references to the *Night Thoughts* project is by Fuseli, his very high opinion of the undertaking was quoted in the 1826 catalogue of Thomas Edwards, and Blake's designs were associated with Fuseli's extravagant style by Royal Academicians.

The connection of Blake and Richard Edwards resulted in the most ambitious commercial work either ever undertook. We may be able to guess a little more confidently at the reasons why Young's *Night Thoughts* was chosen as the vehicle of their collaboration. Beyond the motives given by Edwards in his integral advertisement, we may remark that Charles

---

* *Urizen* pl. 4, 1. 84. In Blake's *Night Thoughts* designs for Richard Edwards, "*Ambition, Avarice*" are depicted with an episcopal mitre and a royal crown (#233), and "Lucifer" is shown with a papal tiara (#91).

Edwards De Coetlogon, for whom Edwards had published eight books in 1792–93, had also published an illustrated edition of Young's *Night Thoughts* (London: Chapman, 1793). It seems extremely likely that Edwards was aware of this edition and was influenced by it and by De Coetlogon to commission illustrations to it himself.

Another incentive for the project was probably Richard Edwards's acquisition of a set of first and early editions of the nine parts of *Night Thoughts* (1742–45), "the Author's own copies"[7] with "the Author's signature" on "the blank leaf".[8] The first intention may have been merely to make elaborate extra-illustrations for Richard Edwards's signed set of first editions of the separate parts of Young's *Night Thoughts*.* A little later James Edwards's good customer Richard Bull added thousands of extra-illustrations to the Macklin Bible (1792–1800) for his daughter Elizabeth,[9] and John Gray Bell added some 10,000 designs to another set of the same work.[10] Blake himself made a series of 116 watercolours in 1797 in illustration of Gray's *Poems* (1790) for his good friend John Flaxman—and the method of mounting the text leaves in larger leaves for the Gray designs is just like that used by Edwards for Young's *Night Thoughts*. It may not have been until the *Night Thoughts* watercolours were well under way that publication of the designs was thought of.

The beginning of the project was probably in late 1794.[11] Each leaf of Young's text—over 260 of them—was laid in a window cut into large leaves (*c.* 16″ x 12″) of paper watermarked 1794 | J WHATMAN for Blake's watercolours, and, probably after the watercolours were completed, these in turn were set into windows of yet larger leaves (20.5″ x 15.5″) with an ornamental ruled border round the design-leaf. The pages were consecutively numbered in brown ink, and lines to be illustrated were ticked (sometimes two per page) in the margin in pencil by Edwards (or Blake).

Blake set to work with extraordinary energy, making an average of five designs every week for over two years. "M#^{rs}# Blake has been heard to say that she never saw him except when in conversation or reading; with his hands idle".[12] This industry was not, however, without its frustrations: "*W*hile he was engraving a large Portrait of Lavater, not being able to obtain what he wanted, he threw the plate completely across the Room. Upon his relating this he was asked whether he did not injure it, to which he replied with his usual fun 'O I took good care of that'."†[13]

---

*   If an engraved edition had originally been in comtemplation, it is unlikely that the uniquely valuable author's copy would have been used as the text, with all the necessary hazards to it which that entailed from an engraver's inky fingers. Further, there would have been little point in making so many hundreds of designs, far more than could ever be published, or in elaborately colouring the ink outlines. But such colouring and such profusion were perfectly appropriate for an extra-illustrated work.

†   See Addenda, below

The spirits spoke to him he when he was engaged on all his poems and drawings. It was probably while he was brooding on Young's line "Angels should paint it [The death-bed of the just]"[14] that one such vision appeared. As Blake told Thomas Phillips when Phillips was painting his portrait in 1807 (Pl. 63),

> I was one day reading Young's Night Thoughts, and when I came to that passage which asks "who can paint an angel," I closed the book and cried, "Aye! Who can paint an angel?"
>
> A voice in the room answered, "Michael Angelo could."
>
> "And how do *you* know?", I said, looking round me, but I saw nothing save a greater light than usual.
>
> "I *know*," said the voice, "for I sat to him; I am the arch-angel Gabriel."
>
> "Oho!" I answered, "you are, are you: I must have better assurance than that of a wandering voice; you may be an evil spirit—there are such in the land."
>
> "You shall have good assurance," said the voice, "can an evil spirit do this?"
>
> I looked whence the voice came, and was then aware of a shining shape, with bright wings, who diffused much light. As I looked, the shape dilated more and more: he waved his hands; the roof of my study opened; he ascended into heaven; he stood in the sun, and beckoning to me, moved the universe. An angel of evil could not have *done that*—it was the arch-angel Gabriel.[*]

When Blake had finished the 537 huge watercolours surrounding the text on each side of the leaf,[15] two splendid separate designs were placed as frontispieces (Pl. 64), and the designs were sumptuously bound by Benedict in red morocco "extra", with the leaves gilt.

---

[*]   Allan Cunningham, *The Cabinet Gallery of Pictures* (London: 1833) (*BR* 183), all one paragraph. The anecdote begins:

> "We hear much," said Phillips, "of the grandeur of Michael Angelo; from the engravings, I should say he has been over-rated; he could not paint an angel so well as Raphael."
>
> "He has not been over-rated, Sir," said Blake, "and he could paint an angel better than Raphael."
>
> "Well, but" said the other, "you never saw any of the paintings of Michael Angelo; and perhaps speak from the opinions of others; your friends may have deceived you."
>
> "I never saw any of the paintings of Michael Angelo," replied Blake, "but I speak from the opinion of a friend who could not be mistaken."
>
> "A valuable friend truly," said Phillips, "and who may he be I pray?"
>
> "The arch-angel Gabriel, Sir," answered Blake.
>
> "A good authority surely, but you know evil spirits love to assume the looks of good ones; and this may have been done to mislead you."
>
> "Well now, Sir," said Blake, "this is really singular; such were my own suspicions; but they were soon removed—I will tell you how."

Many but not all the watercolours later engraved were marked "Engraved" or "Engraved reversed",* and two which were *not* engraved were so marked. The 1797 edition was on much larger paper than the first printings, and therefore fewer pages were needed for the text and many of the designs had to be abandoned. Further, every page of the early editions bore a watercolour, but somewhat less than half the pages of the 1797 edition bore engravings.

Of course Blake treated Young's poem seriously, but he amplified Young with his own ideas as well. *Night Thoughts* is a meditation rather than a narrative, and frequently Blake illustrates the metaphors rather than the actions, as when he illuminates the words "Oft bursts my song beyond the bounds of life" with a harper soaring through the air though his ankle is chained to the brambled earth (see Fig. on p. 161). The designs for the titles of individual Nights are often particularly compelling, as in that for Night the Third (Pl. 65), in which Narcissa with a crown of stars standing on a crescent moon is surrounded by the serpent with his tail in his mouth, the ourobouros symbolizing eternity. In Young's poem, Christ is the answer, and in Blake's designs Christ is an impressive presence, contrasting strongly with His absence from the illustrations for his own works before this time. Blake's design for "the dreadful blessing" of Christ's wounds (Pl. 66) shows His hands and feet pierced with massive nails.

All the designs are unmistakably Blakean, and some might even have appeared in his own works.[16] For instance, the illustration for "This KING OF TERRORS is the PRINCE OF PEACE" (Pl. 67) represents a venerable, bearded man, who might be taken for Blake's suffering Job or his domineering Urizen with his scroll of reason.

The earliest clear reference to the project appears in the draft of a letter of 16 March 1796 from Nancy Flaxman:

One of the Edwards has inserted the letter press Close cut of *Youngs* [*Night Thoughts*] into large Margins Making a folio Size[.] This a friend of ours is ornament^g most beautifully with designs in water colours[.] *T*he man who does it, is himself a Native Poet & sings his woodnotes whose genius soars above all rule[.] *T*will be a very lilly of the Valley or the

---

* When he was making his designs, Blake could not tell whether, when engraved, they would appear on a recto or a verso. This was a matter of some importance, for the chief parts of the design were in the bottom and wide outer margins. The designs therefore had to be reversed when a watercolour on a recto was to be printed on a verso (or vice versa).

Lines of the printed text are starred to indicate the subject of the engraving. Occasionally (e.g., on 1797, p.24) the line illustrated is on a previous page, and at least one engraving (p.41) is for a passage omitted in the 1797 edition. Several asterisked lines in 1797 are different from the lines ticked and illustrated among the watercolours.

meadows queen . . . I have some hopes it will be publishd eer I am much older. . . .*

Nancy or her husband may well have seen some of the engravings as well as the drawings by then, for twenty-two of the plates are dated 27 June 1796.

It may have been in the late spring of 1796 that Richard Edwards issued a prospectus for:

EDWARDS'S

MAGNIFICENT EDITION

OF

YOUNG'S NIGHT THOUGHTS.

EARLY in JUNE will be published, by subscription, part the first of a splendid edition of this favorite work,† elegantly printed, and illustrated with forty very spirited engravings from original drawings by *BLAKE*.

These engravings are in a perfectly new style of decoration, surrounding the text which they are designed to elucidate.

The work is printed in atlas-sized quarto, and the subscription for the whole, making four parts, with one hundred and fifty engravings, is five guineas;—one to be paid at the time of subscribing, and one on the delivery of each part.—The price will be considerably advanced to non-subscribers.

Specimens may be seen at [*Richard*] EDWARDS'S, No. 142, *New Bond-Street*; at Mr. [*James*] EDWARDS'S, *Pall-Mall*; and at the HISTORIC GALLERY [*of Robert Bowyer*], *Pall-Mall*; where subscriptions are received.[17]

At the time of the prospectus, the project was still in flux, for Part I advertised here had forty-three plates when published, not "forty". The price of £5.5.0 for 150 large engravings is extraordinarily modest, particularly when it is compared with, say, £63 for Hume's *History of England* published by Robert Bowyer at The Historic Gallery, Pall Mall, with 60 large plates (plus vignettes), at a cost to Bowyer of "not less than forty thousand pounds".[18]

---

* This transcription ignores some of the insertions and deletions of the draft; the full version may be seen in *BRS* 11. Nancy was paraphrasing Milton, *L'Allegro*, ll. 133–4: "*sweetest Shakespeare* fancies childe, | Warble[s] his native Wood-notes wild".

This letter went astray, and Nancy repeated what she could recall of it in her letter of early Nov 1797 to "Signora B—": "Blake is the artists name, '*Native Poet* he ['] &c one who has sung his wood notes wild—of a Strong & Singular Imagination[;]—he has treated his Poet most Poetically" (*BRS* 14).

† Blake had, of course, long been familiar with *Night Thoughts*, for he refers to it in his *Island in the Moon* (?1784), Chapter 8, ¶25, his illustration to Bürger's *Leonora* (1796) bears a quotation from it, and he owned a copy of the 1796 edition (*BB* 754).

One reason for the modesty of the price was the fact that the engravings were in outline only, not highly finished as in Bowyer's *History of England*, Boydell's Shakspeare, and Macklin's Bible. A more important reason was that Blake's fees as designer and engraver were exceedingly low.

The specimens to be seen at the shops of Richard Edwards, James Edwards, and Robert Bowyer were probably like the elaborate watercolour-on-vellum of The Journey of Life, a naked man with a staff.[19]

An undertaking of such ambition, by a publisher so little known and an artist of such notorious extravagance of opinion and manner, naturally was the subject of chat at the Royal Academy. Joseph Farington, that prince of gossips, recorded in his diary for 24 June 1796 what he had learned from Henry Fuseli:

> Blake has undertaken to make designs to encircle the letter press of each page of "Youngs night thoughts"[.] Edwards the Bookseller, of Bond S^r employs him, and has had the letter press of each page laid down on a large half sheet of paper. There are ab^t 900 pages.*—Blake asked 100 guineas for the whole. Edwards said He could not afford to give more than 20 guineas for which Blake agreed.—Fuseli understands that Edwards proposes to select ab^t 200 from the whole and to have that number engraved as decorations for a new edition.

Fuseli seems to refer to two commissions, the first "to make designs to encircle the letter press of each page" of Richard Edwards's copy of *Night Thoughts* and the subsequent one to engrave two hundred of them "for a new edition". The price of £21 was, as J.T. Smith said, "despicably low",[20] less than ten pence a design, but it probably did not include the copyright, which would have been the subject of a different financial agreement. And it can scarcely have included the cost of the outline engravings, for which Blake should have expected at least £5.5.0 each:[21] £225.15.0 for the forty-three engravings he finished or £787.10.0 for the 150 engravings proposed. Even if Blake expected to be repaid chiefly in glory rather than cash, the sums involved were probably substantial by his humble financial standards.†

Perhaps the agreement for financing the edition was a cooperative one, Blake to provide designs and engraved copperplates and Richard Edwards to pay for setting the text in type, for paper, printing text and then designs

---

* Blake's 543 designs are on 269 leaves.
† Blake does not seem to have nursed a gurdge against Richard Edwards, though his letters and Notebook exhibit grievances against Joseph Johnson, William Hayley, Thomas Stothard, and R.H. Cromek.

on the same leaves, labels, collation, putting the leaves in wrappers, stitching, warehousing, and advertising*—though there was precious little advertising. Such agreements were not uncommon then or later. Indeed, Richard Edwards's arrangement with the engraver Merigot for his *Select Collection of Views and Ruins in Rome and Its Vicinity* (1796–98) probably required Merigot to provide designs and engravings and Richard Edwards to pay the other expenses. If this was the arrangement for the *Night Thoughts*, then the speculator whose investment was heaviest in the book was William Blake, and his risk and eventual loss in cash and fame were probably a good deal larger than those of Richard Edwards.

Work on the engravings proceeded slowly, for "Engraving is Eternal work".[22] By the end of 1796, Edwards thought that Part I, with four of the nine nights, would be ready to be published "in a few days",[23] and he wrote for it an oddly focused

ADVERTISEMENT.

In an age like the present of literature and of taste, in which the arts, fostered by the general patronage, have attained to growth beyond the experience of former times, no apology can be necessary for offering to the publick an embellished edition of an english classick; or for giving to the great work of Young some of those advantages of dress and ornament which have lately distinguished the immortal productions of Shakspeare and of Milton.[†]

But it was not solely to increase the honours of the british press, or to add a splendid volume to the collections of the wealthy, that the editor was induced to adventure on the present undertaking. Not uninfluenced by professional, he acted also under the impulse of higher motives; and when he selected the *Night Thoughts* for the subject of his projected decoration, he wished to make the arts, in their most honourable agency, subservient to the purposes of religion; and by their allurements to solicit the attention of the great for an enforcement of religious and moral truth, which can be ineffectual only as it may not be read.

From its first appearance in the world, this poem has united the suffrages of the criticks, in the acknowledgement of its superior merit. ...

The principal charges which have been urged against this poem, and which to some degree may have affected its popularity, are the dark tints

---

* There may even have been a plan to publish one version of the edition without illustrations (neither illustrations nor Blake are mentioned on the title page). One copy was issued without illustration (*BBS* 271).

† Blake's are still the only important series of designs ever undertaken to illustrate Young's *Night Thoughts*.

of its painting; and the obscurities which occasionally occur in it to retard the progress of the reader. ....

On the immediate subject of the present edition of this valuable work the editor has only to say that he has shrunk from no expence in the preparing of it; and that to make it as worthy in every respect as possible of the public favour has been the object of his particular and solicitous attention. It has been regarded by him, indeed, not as a speculation of advantage, but as an indulgence of inclination;—as an undertaking in which fondness and partiality would not permit him to be curiously accurate in adjusting the estimate of profit and loss. If this edition, therefore, of the *Night Thoughts* be found deficient in any essential requisite to its perfection, the circumstance must be imputed to some other cause, than to the oeconomy or the negligence of the editor.

Of the merit of Mr. Blake in those designs which form not only the ornament of the page, but, in many instances, the illustration of the poem, the editor conceives it to be unnecessary to speak. To the eyes of the discerning it need not be pointed out; and while a taste for the arts of design shall continue to exist, the original conception, and the bold and masterly execution of this artist cannot be unnoticed or unadmired.

Dec. 22d. 1796.[24]

This is altogether a curious piece of puffing, built upon a foundation of self-exculpatory negatives. The book is "an indulgence of inclination" for the publisher–editor: He has "shrunk from no expence", he has not been "curiously accurate in adjusting the estimate of profit and loss", and no fault can be attributed to his "oeconomy or ... negligence". Of the unique feature of this edition, Blake's engravings, he thinks it "unnecessary to speak" other than to assert that "they cannot be unnoticed or unadmired". Even the last adjective seems to be extorted from him. His chief justifications for the edition are the religious and moral truth of Young's poem and the publisher's disinterested public spirit.

From the advertisement, one might conclude that Blake's designs were almost incidental to the enterprise. And the plausibility of his assertion that the publisher has "shrunk from no expence" may be judged in the light of the "despicably low" sum he paid for Blake's designs.

The announcement of the edition in the press stimulated gossip about it. In his diary for 12 January 1797, Joseph Farington recorded a meeting at Wright's coffee house of a committee of the Royal Academy consisting of Farington, Hoppner, Stothard, Rigaud, and Opie:

We supped together and had laughable conversation. Blakes eccentric designs were mentioned. Stothard supported his claims to Genius, but allowed He had been misled to extravagance in his art, & He knew by whom [?*Fuseli*].—Hoppner ridiculed the absurdity of his designs, and said nothing could be more easy than to produce such.—They were like the conceits of a drunken fellow or a madman. "Represent a man sitting on the moon, and pissing the Sun out—that would be a whim of as much merit."—Stothard was angry mistaking the laughter caused by Hoppners description.

As on many other occasions, Blake's attempt to represent spiritual forces in heroic dimensions was taken to be eccentric and absurd, an extravagance bordering upon madness.

Blake must have neglected other kinds of work while he was engaged upon his *Night Thoughts* designs and engravings. In 1790–93, he had made twenty-three plates a year for the booksellers, but in 1794–96 he made only five per year. These may have kept the wolf from the door—but probably Catherine Blake could see the wolf lurking round the corner.

From 1795 to 1804 Blake published nothing of his own.

Completing the plates for *Night Thoughts* seemed to take for ever. The last plates are dated 1 and 4 January, 22 March, and 1 June 1797, and the book was probably published that autumn.[25]

Then a great silence set in. Richard Edwards did not advertise the book again, he sent out no copy for review, and no review of Young's *Night Thoughts* (1797) with Blake's engravings was printed. One of the most ambitious and sensational illustrated books of that or any other time in England was ignored as if it had never been published.

And it may scarcely have been published. While Blake was labouring his last plates for *Night Thoughts*, Richard Edwards was already making arrangements to go out of business.* He attempted only half-heartedly to sell the *Night Thoughts* at all.[26] Within about six months the book was being listed by James Robson,[27] a sometime partner of his brother James Edwards, and on 1 April 1799 a patent was made out for Richard Edwards to act as Head Registrar of the Vice Admiralty Court in Minorca,[28] which had been captured from Spain in November 1798. He had probably left the shop in Bond Street and sold his stock of books by June 1798.

When Richard Edwards was disposing of his stock, he may have given Blake some copies of the *Night Thoughts*, either under the terms of their publishing agreement or as part payment for his engraving work. Twenty-

---

* After Feb 1797, he abandoned his part of Strutt's *Dress ... of England*, in Jan 1797 he suspended Merigot's *Rome* and had nothing to do with it after June 1798, and in May 1798 he withdrew from Vancouver's *Voyage* and probably from bookselling entirely.

six copies of the *Night Thoughts* were coloured* by Blake or a copyist such as Catherine Blake, some of them wonderfully beautiful. Copy Q (Pl. 64) is inscribed: "This Copy was coloured for me by Mr Blake | W.E." (perhaps William Edwards, Richard's father); copy R: "This copy col$^{\underline{rd}}$ by W. Blake"; and copy C: "W. Blake" and "as pattern".[29] One coloured copy (A) went to Blake's most important patron Thomas Butts and another (O) to Earl Spencer, who provided Richard Edwards with his sinecure in Minorca.

Blake's absorption in his *Night Thoughts* project took him out of the ordinary market for reproductive engravings, and its failure was a disaster for him. As he wrote to George Cumberland on 26 August 1799: "I live by Miracle . . . For as to Engraving in which art I cannot reproach myself with any neglect yet I am laid by in a corner as if I did not Exist & Since my Youngs Night Thoughts have been publishd Even Johnson & Fuseli have discarded my Graver."

Blake's contemporaries such as Crabb Robinson found the engravings to be of

very unequal merit; sometimes the inventions of the artist rival those of the poet, but often they are only preposterous translations of them, by reason of the unfortunate idea peculiar to Blake, that whatsoever the fancy of the spiritual eye may discern must also be as clearly penetrable to the bodily eye. So Young is literally translated, and his thought turned into a picture.[30]

On 10 March 1811 Robinson showed his copy of *Night Thoughts* to William Hazlitt, who "saw no merit in them as designs". Thomas Frognall Dibdin wrote about 1816 that "there are few books of which I love to turn over the leaves, more assiduously and carefully, than 'Young's Night Thoughts,' emblazoned by his truly original pencil",[31] and in 1824 he exclaimed:

At times, the pencil of the artist attains the sublimity of the poet: and it is amidst the wild uproar of the wintry elements—when piping winds are howling for entrance round every corner of the turretted chamber, and

---

* See *BB* 642–6, 956–7 and *BBS* 271–3. Three styles of colouring were identified in John E. Grant, Edward J. Rose, and Michael J. Tolley, *William Blake's Designs for Edward Young's NIGHT THOUGHTS*, ed. David V. Erdman (Oxford: Clarendon Press, 1980), I, 53–62, eight unnumbered reduced colour reproductions in Vol. II: Type I, with Death on the title page of Night the First in a white robe as in the watercolour (fifteen copies), Type II with a green robe (six copies), and Type III (one copy). However, this is probably simplistic, for Robert N. Essick has identified in his copy AA three distinct styles of colouring of *c.* 1800 (like Type I), *c.* 1833 (unlike Type II), and *c.* 1880 ("Blake in the Market place, 1999", *Blake*, XXXIII [2000], 103–4).

the drifted snow works its way into the window casement, however closely fastened—it is in moments LIKE THESE that I love to open that portion of the text of Young which has been embellished by the pencil of Blake.[32]

The shop catalogue of Richard's brother Thomas (1821) described them as "very spirited designs by Mr. Blake, many of them in the Style of Michael Angelo",[33] and his auction catalogue of 1826 exclaimed rapturously about

these most extraordinary and sublime conceptions of our Artist ... required the skill of a great Artist, and the poetic feeling of the original author combined. ... it may truly be averred, that a more extraordinary, original, and sublime production of art has seldom, if ever, been witnessed since the days of the celebrated *Mich. Agnolo*, whose grandeur and elevation of style it greatly resembles, and this, *alone*, if he had left no other work of merit, would be sufficient to immortalize his name, and transmit it to posterity, as that of an Artist of the very highest order. This was the late Mr. Fuseli's opinion.[34]

But none of this booksellers' hyperbole was sufficiently persuasive to sell Blake's 537 large watercolours for £300 (1821) or even £50 (1826).

According to Cunningham, "Some of those designs ... alarmed fastidious people: the serious and the pious were not prepared to admire shapes trembling in nudity round the verses of a grave divine. In the exuberance of Young there are many fine figures; but they are figures of speech only, on which art should waste none of its skill."[35]

But at least some of the serious and the pious were prepared to admire Blake's designs in a religious context. His engraving for *Night Thoughts* (1797) p. 27 was copied on the title page of *The Seraph, A Collection of Sacred Music, Suitable to Public or Private Devotion* (*c.* 1818),* and newly titled "Conscience; as a recording angel, veiled, in the act of noting down the sin of intemperance in a [*naked*] Bacchanalian". The design also illustrates there a hymn called "Conscience From Young's Night Thoughts".

The most extensive contemporary response to Blake's *Night Thoughts* engravings appeared in a dialogue by Edward Bulwer Lytton published in 1830:

---

*   The design is said to be "Drawn by the late W. Blake, Esq.ʳ R.A.", but at the time Blake was neither dead nor a member of the Royal Academy. *The Seraph* was sufficiently popular to elecit three printings.

A. Of all enthusiasts, the painter Blake seems to have been the most remarkable. With what a hearty faith he believed in his faculty of seeing spirits and conversing with the dead! And what a delightful vein of madness it was—with what exquisite verses it inspired him!

L. And what engravings! I saw a few days ago, a copy of the "Night Thoughts," which he had illustrated in a manner at once so grotesque, so sublime—now by so literal an interpretation, now by so vague and disconnected a train of invention, that the whole makes one of the most astonishing and curious productions which ever balanced between the conception of genius and the ravings of positive insanity. I remember two or three [*of his illustrations*], but they are not the most remarkable. To these two fine lines—

> "'Tis greatly wise to talk with our past hours,
> And ask them what report they bore to heaven;"

he has given the illustration of one sitting and with an earnest countenance conversing with a small shadowy shape at his knee, while other shapes, of a similar form and aspect, are seen gliding heavenward, each with a scroll in its hands [Pl. 68]. The effect is very solemn. Again the line—

> "Till death, that mighty hunter, earths them all,"

is bodied forth by a grim savage with a huge spear, cheering on fiendish and ghastly hounds, one of which has just torn down, and is griping by the throat, an unfortunate fugitive: the face of the hound is unutterably death-like.*
The verse—

> "We censure Nature for a span too short,"

obtains an illustration, literal to ridicule.—A bearded man of gigantic statu[r]e is spanning an infant with his finger and thumb [Pl. 69]. Scarcely less literal, but more impressive, is the engraving of the following:—

> "When Sense runs savage, broke from Reason's chain,
> And sings false peace till smother'd by the pall!"

You perceive a young female savage, with long locks, wandering alone, and exulting—while above, two bodiless hands extend a mighty pall, that appears about to fall upon the unconscious rejoicer [Pl. 70].

---

* In his *Vorschule der Aesthetik* (1804; 1813; 1815; 1827; 1836 . . .), Jean Paul Richter commented on a figure in the "fantastic marginal designs by Blake" (*Night Thoughts*, p. 4), "terrifying to me, which stares, bent over and shuddering, into a bush; its seeing becomes vision for me" (*BRS* 28–9).

A.   Young was fortunate. He seems almost the only poet who has had his mere metaphors illustrated and made corporeal.[36]

Even Blake's most enthusiastic admirers equated "his faculty of seeing spirits and conversing with the dead" with "a delightful vein of madness". For the unsympathetic such as Hazlitt and Hoppner, the vein of madness was scarcely "delightful". Few of them conceived of the possibility that, as the Baptist Minister John Martin said, if Blake is cracked, "his is a crack that lets in the Light".[37]

Watercolours for Gray's Poems

As early as March 1796, John and Nancy Flaxman had seen Blake's water-colours for *Night Thoughts*, which Nancy thought "most beautiful", and probably this inspired her husband to commission Blake to make a similar suite of designs from the poems of Gray as a gift for Nancy's birthday. He regularly gave her works of art for her birthday, sometimes illustrated poems created by himself, such as "The Knight of the Burning Cross" (1796) and "The Casket" (1812),[38] and sometimes by others.*

Blake's engravings for Young were finished by the summer of 1797, and in early November 1797 Nancy Flaxman wrote to "My Good Friend" "Signora B—" about Blake's designs for Young and added: "Flaxman has employ'd him to Illuminate the works of Grey for my library",[39] implying that the work was then in progress.[40]

The price was £10.10.0,[41] which at 1s.10d. per design is extraordinarily modest. However, it is at least better than the 9d. per design paid to Blake for the *Night Thoughts* drawings.

The commission was a particularly congenial one, not only because Blake loved the patron and the recipient, but because he was already an admirer and illustrator of Gray. He exhibited a watercolour for "The Bard, from Gray" at the Royal Academy in 1785, and a tempera of the same subject was shown in his own exhibition in 1809 and described in his *Descriptive Catalogue* ¶65–71.

The first step was to insert the text from *Poems by Mr. Gray* (London: J. Murray, 1790) (Pl. 71), into windows cut into 1794 | J WHATMAN paper (the same paper used for the *Night Thoughts* drawings and engravings). A red border was drawn, and then Blake added his watercolours, the pages were numbered in ink, Xs were added by the lines illustrated, and the leaves were bound. Brown

---

*   It is at least possible that Flaxman's payments of 10s.6d. For "Blakes Book" in early 1795 and 4s. for "Blake's Engravings" in Oct 1795 (*BR* 569) were for presents for Nancy's birthday. The Flaxmans owned *Poetical Sketches* (F, inscribed 1784), *Innocence* (D, about 1790), and *Innocence and Experience* (O, *Innocence* dated "April 1817", Experience acquired perhaps 1800).

fingerprints on the title page and elsewhere exemplify the "books well thumbed and dirtied by his graving hands" of which Tatham spoke.[42] Each design is titled by Blake, usually with a quotation, and on the title page verso is an invitation:

> Around the Springs of Grey my wild root weaves[;]
> Traveller repose & Dream among my leaves.
> —Will. Blake[43]

On the last page is a poem "To Mrs Ann Flaxman" which is a tactful compliment to both Nancy and John Flaxman:

> A little Flower grew in a lonely Vale[;]
> Its form was lively but its colours pale[.]
> One standing in the Porches of the Sun
> When his Meridian Glories were begun
> Leapd from the Steps of fire & on the grass
> Alighted where this little flower was[.]
> With hands divine he movd the gentle Sod
> And took the Flower up in its native Clod[.]
> Then planting it upon a Mountains brow[:]
> 'Tis your own fault if you dont flourish now[.]
>
> William Blake

Nancy had described Blake's suite of *Night Thoughts* drawings as "a very lilly of the Valley or [Mountain daisy *del*] the meadows queen",[44] and in his poem to Nancy Blake returned the compliment.

Blake's designs to Gray's *Poems* are quite different in style from those for Young's *Night Thoughts* which he had just finished. They are more light-hearted, sometimes even frivolous,* but they treat the serious poems with deep respect. The title page design (Pl. 71) shows a naked man with a harp, clearly the poet, soaring upwards on the wings of a loosely leashed giant swan, perhaps representing the illustrator. The parallel with the soaring harper in the *Night Thoughts* designs (Fig. on p. 161) is strong, but the bard for Young is earth-bound, chained down though rising. The title for the Gray illustration is "The Pindaric Genius receiving his Lyre", referring in part to "The Progress of Poesy" and "The Bard", each of which is sub-titled "A Pindaric Ode".

Some of the designs exemplify the dictum in the *Marriage of Heaven and*

---

* Design 8 for Gray's *Elegy* shows a woman tracing with her finger a tombstone inscription: "DUST THOU ART", below which is "HERE LIETH | WM BLAKE | Age 10" (*WBW* 1331n) or "103".

Hell (¶25) that: "The ancient Poets animated all sensible objects with Gods or Geniuses, calling them by the names and adorning them with the properties of woods, rivers, mountains … and whatever their enlarged & numerous senses could percieve." Thus in "The Bard", the design for "each Giant Oak & Desart Cave Sigh[s] to the Torrents awful voice beneath" shows giant personifications of Oak, Cave, and Torrent, and the one for "Ode on a Distant Prospect of Eton College" (Pl. 72) represents Father Thames looming giganticly over the oblivious bathing boys.

But as always Blake's most characteristic port is sublimity. Perhaps the noblest design among the illustrations to Gray is the one for "The Progress of Poesy" (Pl. 73), depicting Hyperion with his "glittering Shafts of war". The mighty god enthroned in the sun with calm, unimpassioned face nocks an arrow to his gigantic bow, while beneath him flaming shafts descend on the heads of the defeated. For Gray's somewhat tepid echoes of classical mythology, it is an astonishingly vibrant image.

Nancy cherished the gift and occasionally showed it to special friends, but she was reluctant to let the drawings out of her hands. In September 1805 she wrote that their friend Mr Joseph Thomas, Rector of Epsom in Surrey, who was recovering from a serious illness,

> wishes as a great favor the loan of <u>Blake's Gray</u> to amuse himself with promising that it shall not go from his chamber or be wantonly shewn to anybody[;] he wishes to make a few copies from it—to keep with his Youngs Nights Thoughts & some other works he has of Blakes[;] he wishes to collect all B— has done … respecting the Loan, I shall take [care] to consider of it[.]

But there is no evidence that she did loan it to the Rev. Mr Thomas or to anyone else, even in the cause of spreading Blake's fame and encouraging commissions for him. Perhaps if Mr Thomas had suggested that Blake should make the copies, he would have been more successful.

Blake's designs for Gray's poems were virtually unknown to his contemporaries, but they are among the most impressive achievements of his decade of marvels.

The Perils of Patronage

The designs for Young and Gray in 1794–98 were prodigious accomplishments, but they brought little in the way of golden guineas or golden opinions, and Blake did not have much other work in the profession in which he had been trained. He made three quarto plates after his own designs for

Bürger's *Leonora* (William Miller, 1796), he may have helped his friend George Cumberland with a quarto plate for Cumberland's *Attempt to Describe Hafod* (T. Egerton, 1796), he engraved eight octavo plates after Fuseli for Charles Allen's *New and Improved History of England* and his *New and Improved Roman History* (J. Johnson, 1797), another for Euler's *Elements of Algebra* (J. Johnson, 1797), and a portrait for the *Monthly Magazine* (R. Phillips & J. Johnson, 1797). Rather surprisingly, one of his most ambitious commercial plates was a folio advertisement designed and engraved by Blake for Moore & Co.'s carpets (1797), showing a palatial carpet factory scattered with royal emblems in enough detail to suggest that Blake had actually visited the factory in Chiswell Street owned by the grandfather of Thomas Holcroft's wife.

He had even less commercial engraving work in 1799–1800, though it may not have been much less profitable. His three octavo plates after his friend Flaxman for Flaxman's *Letter to the Committee for Raising the Naval Pillar or Monument* (T. Cadell Jr et al., 1799) brought him only £8.8.0 (plus 12s.8d. for the copper),[45] but for his three quarto outlines after Flaxman and Thomas Hayley for Hayley's *Essay on Sculpture* (T. Cadell Jr & W. Davies, 1800) he must have received at least £15.15.0, and for his folio plate of "Rev. John Caspar Lavater" (Johnson, 1800) he should have received a substantial sum.

Most encouraging of all was the commission to copy John Opie's design illustrating *Romeo and Juliet* for *The Dramatic Works of Shakspeare* (London: John and Josiah Boydell, print published 25 March 1799), for Alderman Boydell was the leader of the florescence of book illustration in the last two decades of the eighteenth century, and Boydell's fees for a single engraving were sometimes as high as £500 or even £1,000. Blake should have expected at least £80 for his fine plate.*

To compensate for the sparseness of commissions for engravings, Blake was finding more customers for his original art. His friend the artist Ozias Humphry showed his copies of Blake's Large and Small Books of Designs to admiring friends, and at least one of them was apparently thus persuaded to commission Blake to make another set. Dr James Curry, a young physician of Kettering near Northampton, wrote to Humphry on 15 August

---

* There was some confusion about Blake's plate. Boydell commissioned two series of engravings for Shakespeare, one merely in large folio (Blake's plate is 43 x 31 cm) for book publication and one in elephant folio (68 x 51 cm) for a *Collection of Prints . . . Illustrating the Dramatic Works of Shakspeare*. For Opie's design for *Romeo and Juliet*, an elaborate version was engraved for the elephant folio series, and a simplified version was engraved by Simon for the folio *Dramatic Works of Shakspeare*. By some accident, Blake engraved the elaborate version in the smaller size, and it was labelled "Variation", without explanation, and bound in the *Dramatic Works* after Simon's print of the simpler scene. It is possible that the confusion over the engraving of Opie's design for *Romeo and Juliet* was responsible for the fact that Blake was not asked to engrave for Boydell again.

1797: "As poor Blake will not be out of need of money, I shall beg you to pay him for me, and to take the trouble when you return to town of having a box made for the prints, & sending them by the Kettering Coach from the White Hart S.ʳ John Street Clerkenwell."[46] Blake's need of money was probably due to his neglect by the booksellers.

He probably derived some income from sales of his works in Illuminated Printing, but it is extraordinarily difficult to determine how much he earned thus. We know with some precision when Blake etched, printed, and coloured them,[47] but we rarely know when they were sold or who bought them from Blake.* The expense of them, however, was in the past, with copper and paper and etching and printing and colouring. Each copy sold from reserves would be pure profit.

Some were almost certainly given away. *America* (B) is inscribed "From the author to C. H. Tatham Oct.ʳ 7 1799". Charles Heathcote Tatham was a young architect whose work Blake admired, and "Mr. William Blake" appears in the subscription-list of Tatham's *Etchings, Representing the Best Examples of Ancient Ornamental Architectures* (1799). Twenty-five years later the two men were still on visiting terms, and Tatham's son Frederick, born in 1805, became Blake's disciple and his widow's heir.

Blake had other friends looking after his interests. George Cumberland wrote on 19 February 1798 to his friend Horne Tooke, sending him a drawing of Mercury pulling off his winged sandals and a motto from Shakespeare for a new edition of Tooke's philological *Diversions of Purleigh*, Part I (first published 1786):

> If you approve them, both the Motto and the drawing will be honoured by appearing, as you propose, with your second volume—in which case I shall take the liberty to recommend that neglected man of genius, and true son of Freedom M.ʳ Blake, as your engraver, both on account of the pleasure I know he will have in executing a work with your portrait in it, and the general moderation of his charges[.][48]

Blake's admiration for Horne Tooke and Tooke's knowledge of Blake say much about Blake's political sympathies. But neither Cumberland's motto nor his recommendation bore the hoped-for fruit.

An even more spacious opportunity seemed to present itself with Charles Townley, the great collector of Greek and Roman antiquities. Not only

---

* Date and price are intimately related, for Blake's prices escalated 1,000 percent–1,400 percent from 1793 to 1818 (e.g., *Innocence* and *Experience* sold for 5s. each in 1793 and £3.3.0 apiece in 1818), partly because of the change from Mrs Blake's very simple application of colours in early copies to Blake's elaborate and individual colouring after about 1805.

were scores of prints made of Townley's statues—Blake made one for Hayley's *Essay on Sculpture* (1800)—but Townley found engravers for his friends as well. For instance, on 23 May 1799 he wrote that his friend "M^r [*Henry*] Blundell breakfasted and deposited his book of drawings from his marbles with me that a choice may be made out of them proper to be engraved—I took him to See the progress of the plates now in hand—called on Mr Blake engraver N^r 13 Hercules Buildings, Lambeth".[49] But Blake signed none of the almost 300 plates in *Engravings and Etchings of the Principal Statues, Busts, Bass-Reliefs, Sepulchral Monuments, Cinerary Urns, &c. in the Collection of Henry Blundell, Esq. at Ince* (1809).

George Cumberland also introduced Blake to the Reverend John Trusler, the prolific author of such uplifting titles as *Luxury not Political Evil* (?1780) and *The Way to Be Rich and Respectable* (7th edition, 1796). In 1769 Trusler proposed to publish 150 sermons printed in imitation of hand-writing, so that preachers could pretend to be the composers of the sermons they delivered. For such publications he was memorably attacked as one of the "reverend parsonical banditti ... with all the chicane of sacerdotal hypocrisy".[50]

In August 1799 Blake made for him a drawing "in my best manner"[51] of "Malevolence": "A Father taking leave of his Wife & Chil*d*, Is watchd by Two Fiends incarnat*e*, with intention that when his back is turned they will murder the mother & her infant". In making the design, he had "attempted every morning for a fortnight together to follow your Dictate", but he had "been compelld by my Genius or Angel to follow where he led". "I know I begged of you to give me your Ideas & promised to build on them[;] here I counted without my host".

> And tho I call them Mine I know that they are not Mine being of the same opinion with Milton when he says That the Muse visits his Slumbers & awakes & governs his Song when Morn purples the Eas*t*,[52] & being also in the predicament of that prophet who says I cannot go beyond the command of the Lord to speak good or bad[.][53]

If Trusler approved of this "Malevolence", Blake proposed to follow it with "Benevolence", "Pride", and "Humility", with the prospect of engraving them thereafter. He must have had to bend his antinomian scruples to undertake illustrations like these of moral vices and virtues.

However, despite Blake's best manner and conventional moral matter, the reverend doctor "sent it back with a Letter full of Criticisms in which he says It accords not with his Intentions which are to Reject all Fancy from his Work". "*Your Fancy* from what I have seen of it, & I have seen variety at Mr Cumberlands seems to be in the other world or the World of Spirit*s*, which accords not with my Intention*s*, which whilst living in This World Wish to follow <u>the Nature of it</u>". As Blake commented, "I could not help Smiling at the difference between the doctrines of Dr Trusler & those of Christ."[54]

Blake replied to Trusler in a moving, eloquent, and wonderfully ill-conceived letter on 23 August 1799:

> Revd Sir
>
> I really am sorry that you are falln out with the Spiritual World Especially if I should have to answer for it ... you ought to know that What is Grand is necessarily obscure to Weak men. That which can be made Explicit to the Idiot is not worth my care. ... my figures ... are those of Michael Angelo[,] Rafael & the Antique & of the best living Models.... I know that This World Is a World of Imagination & Vision[.] I see Every thing I paint In This Worl*d*, but Every body does not see alike. To the Eyes of a Miser a Guinea is more beautiful than the Sun & a bag worn with the use of Money has more beautiful proportions than a Vine filled with Grapes. The tree which moves some to tears of joy is in the Eyes of others only a Green thing that stands in the way.... To Me This World is all One continued Vision of Fancy or Imagination ....
>
> I am happy to find a Great Majority of Fellow Mortals who can Elucidate My Visions & Particularly they have been Elucidated by Children who have taken a greater delight in contemplating my Pictures than I even hoped.

Perhaps it is not surprising that the Reverend Doctor Trusler, having been convicted of being a weak man and an idiot out of harmony with heaven, did not choose to pursue the correspondence or the commission. Blake's genius was not tact.

"Teach these Souls to Fly"

Blake was clearly a natural teacher,* and he had a surprising amount of experience in teaching his arts. He taught the crafts of engraving to his wife

---

* One of his pupils was William Seguier (1771–1843), who told George Darley "of his having been 'taught' by the celebrated William Blake—how different the master and the pupil! How different their lot! Blake earned eighteen shillings a week and immortal renown, while his scholar earned the directorship of almost all the great picture galleries" (*Athenaeum*, 18 Nov 1843 [*BR* 222]). Seguier was conservator of the royal picture galleries, first keeper of the National Gallery, and superintendant of the British Institution.

Teaching and the learned are usually treated pejoratively in Blake's writings (e.g., Urizen, "Schoolmaster of souls[,] great opposer of change" [*Vala* p.120, 1. 21), but studying and learning are not.

Catherine (1782 ff.), to his brother Robert (1784–87), and to Tommy Butts (1806–9), and he taught drawing to them and to numbers of others.

He taught by example rather than precept, and in particular he taught how to make the mind receptive to the spirit.

> I rest not from my great task!
> To open the Eternal Worlds, to open the immortal Eyes
> Of Man inwards into the Worlds of Thought; into Eternity
>
> (*Jerusalem* pl. 5, ll. 17–19)

He was fundamentally concerned not with perspective and anatomy but with harmony and inspiration. He wished to "Teach these Souls to Fly";[55] "I found them blind, I taught them how to see".[56] For Blake, at least towards the end of his life, "Prayer is the Study of Art".[57] Once his young disciple George Richmond

> related ... how he felt deserted by the power of invention. To his aston-ishment, Blake turned to his wife suddenly and said:"It is just so with us, is it not, for weeks together, when the visions forsake us? What do we do then, Kate?"
> "We kneel down and pray, Mr. Blake."[58]

Samuel Palmer remembered always the occasion when his young life was transformed by meeting Blake:

> He fixed his grey eyes upon me, and said, "Do you work with
> fear and trembling?"
> "Yes, indeed," was the reply.
> "Then," said he, "you'll do."[59]

Blake's method was to copy and praise. "To learn the Language of Art Copy for Ever is My Rule."[60] Samuel Palmer said that he showed Blake "some of my first essays in design; and the sweet encouragement he gave me (for Christ blessed little children) ... made me work harder and better that afternoon and night".[61]

Some of Blake's students were taught for love, and he acted towards them as both a gentle master and a loving father. On at least one occasion, Blake sought out his student:

> A young man passed his House daily whose avocations seemed to lead him backward & forward to some place of study, carrying a Portfolio under his Arm. He looked interesting & eager, but sickly.

After some time Blake sent Mrs Blake to call the young man in; he came & he told them, that he was studying the Arts. Blake from this took a high interest in him & gave him every instruction possible, but alas! ... the young man shortly after fell sick, & was laid upon his bed, his illness was long & his sufferings were great during which time, Mrs Blake or Blake never omitted visiting him daily & administering medicine, money, or Wine & every other requisite until death relieved their adopted of all earthly care & pain. Every attention, every parental tenderness, was exhibited by the charitable pair.[62]

He always taught for the love of his art, but he did not always do so for charity. In the 1790s,

he taught Drawing & was engaged for that purpose by some families of high rank;* which by the bye he could not have found very profitable, for after his lesson he got into conversation with his pupils, & was found so entertaining & pleasant, possessing such novel thoughts & such eccentric notions, together with such jocose hilarity & amiable demeanour, that he frequently found himself asked to stay dinner, & spend the Evening in the same interesting & lively manner, in which he had consumed the morning. Thus he stopped whole days from his work at home, but nevertheless he continued teaching, until a remarkable effort & kind flirt of fortune, brought this mode of livelihood to an inevitable close. He was recommended & nearly obtained an Appointment to teach Drawing to the Royal Family. Blake stood aghast; not indeed from any republican humours, not from any disaffection to his superiors, but because he

---

*   Gilchrist said that "Blake taught for a time in her family [Lady Bathurst it was, I think], and was admired by them. The proposal was, I believe, that he should be engaged at a regular annual salary for tuition and services such as the above [to paint a set of handscreens]; as painter in ordinary, in fact, to this noble family" (*BR* 524 n1). Lady Bathurst is probably Tryphena (1750–1807), second wife of Henry Bathurst (1714–94), Lord Chancellor, 2nd Earl Bathurst, or her daughter-in-law Georgina (d. 1841).

"Lord Bathurst" appears in a list by John Linnell (1855) of Blake's friends and patrons (*BR* 318 n2). The Bathurst estate was in Bathurst, Sussex, near Battle Abbey (*History of the Apsley and Bathurst Families*, ed. A.B. Bathurst [Cirencester: Printed by G.H. Harmer, 1903], 77), and the family pictures included many by Gainsborough, Romney, and Reynolds but none by Blake (Bathurst [ed.], *History of the Apsley and Bathurst Families*, pp. 133–6).

Blake's relationship with the family may have been in 1800–3 when he lived in Sussex; Osbert Burdett, *William Blake* (London: Macmillan, 1926), 115, claims without evidence that Blake "gave drawing lessons to Lady Bathurst's [six] children at Lavant". The present Earl Bathurst wrote to me on 10 July 1995 that he knew of no connection of his family with Blake or with Lavant, but Elizabeth Burness of Lavant tells me that the Bathurst family owned property in the village at least from 1729 to 1798, when Earl Bathurst conveyed West Lavant House to the 4th Duke of Richmond, whose sister Georgina he had married. The Richmond family seat was at Goodwood, close to Lavant, and the Duke of Richmond was the unsympathetic Justice of the Peace who presided at Blake's trial for sedition in 1804.

would have been drawn into a class of Society, superior to his previous pursuits & habits; he would have been expected to have lived in comparative respectability, not to say splendour, a mode of life, as he thought, derogatory to the simplicity of his designs & deportment. . . .

His friends ridiculed & blamed him by turns but Blake found an Excuse by resigning all his other pupils, & continued to suffice himself upon his frugality . . . .*

Probably far more of Blake's time and income were involved with teaching than we have any direct evidence for. But teaching is only art at second hand. What he most needed was a market for his own art.

The Perfect Patron: Thomas Butts

At this low ebb of his worldly prospects in 1799 Blake found the perfect patron: generous, endlessly forbearing, a family friend, a believer in Blake's genius, and, above all, willing to give Blake a free hand with his pictures and to pay him in advance. This paragon of patronage was Thomas Butts,[63] who was not a nobleman or even a rich man but an accountant in a government office, a minor civil servant—a white collar Maecenas.

Thomas and Elizabeth Cooper Butts had a big house at 9 Great Marlborough Street,† just round the corner from where Blake had lived at 28 Poland Street in 1785–90 (Pl. 7). The neighbourhood was dense with artists and their agents. Next door to the Buttses, at No 10 Great Marlborough Street, was Henry Thomas Martyn's printshop and Academy for Illustrating Natural History, and nearby were Tebaldo Monzani, music seller, Mr Thomson, print-publisher, Walter Bow, stationer, William

---

* Tatham (*BR* 523–4). Tatham's information almost certainly came from Catherine Blake, who is likely to have stressed Blake's neglect of remunerative work rather more than Blake would have done. The possibility of a royal appointment may be related to an anecdote given by Gilchrist: "Take them away! Take them away!' was the testy mandate of disquieted Royalty, on some drawings of Blake's being once shown to George the Third" (*BR* 524 n1).

   Blake certainly did not give up teaching entirely, for Tommy Butts was his pupil in 1806–9.

† 9 Great Marlborough Street is listed in the name of Mrs Butts from 1790 to 1808, when the family moved to 17 Grafton Street, Fitzroy Square (Joseph Viscomi, "A 'Green House' for Butts? New Information on Thomas Butts, His Residences, and Family", *Blake*, XXX [1996], 10–11), but Thomas Butts also had a house in Shacklewell Ward, Hackney (1786–93) and later in the green suburb of Dalston Ward, Hackney (1793–1808) (*idem*). Probably the Dalston house was used as a weekend cottage, for Blake's letters are all directed to "Mʳ Butts | Great Marlborough Street" (22 Sept, 2 Oct 1800, 11 Sept 1801, 10 Jan, 22 Nov 1802, 25 April, 16 Aug 1803—the exceptions bear no address), Butts writes from Marlborough St [Sept 1800], and the ease with which the Blakes called on the Buttses suggests that they were in relatively close proximity rather than clear across London from Lambeth to Dalston. It is not clear whether Butts kept his Blake pictures in Great Marlborough Street or in Dalston.

Bromley and C. Bestland, engravers, John Sheringham, paper stainer, and Charles Geary with his circulating library.[64]

When Thomas Butts was twenty-six, in 1783, he had been appointed Assistant Clerk in the office of the Commissary General of Musters, whose responsibility it was, *inter alia*, to warrant that soldiers receiving pay were actually alive and in uniform. He was made Joint Chief Clerk in June 1788, when his salary was £45.12.6, and by 1806 his net income had grown to over £500.* His generosity to Blake, over £400 from January 1803 to December 1810, absorbed a significant proportion of his employment income.

However, civil servants sometimes have less obvious sources of income than salary. By 1810, when the Commissary General of Musters certified that "My Chief Clerk is the sole person through whose Hands the money Transactions of this Department . . . pass", members of the family of Thomas Butts were profiting from his position of financial responsibility. His son Joseph Edward Butts joined the office in June 1799 when he was fifteen, and Thomas Butts Jr was appointed to it on 2 December 1806 when he was eighteen. The hours of work in government offices were not very extensive, but in 1809 Thomas Butts certified that J.E. Butts had done 1,140 hours of overtime work (or about five hours per weekday) and that T. Butts Jr had performed 1,163 hours of over-time.† Further, Joseph Edward Butts rented rooms in the office of the Commissary General of Musters, and, when the War Secretary complained, the scandal was covered up by the Commissary General of Musters.

When Thomas Butts died in 1845, he was a prosperous man, with shares in coal mines and railroads and extensive property holdings. Some of this wealth certainly came from inheritance, but some probably derived from the perquisites of high office.‡

Thomas Butts was not the only capitalist in the family. Betsy Butts had a boarding school for girls,§ a ladies' seminary, at 9 Great Marlborough

---

* Most of the facts about his professional career derive from "Thomas Butts, White Collar Maecenas", *PMLA*, LXXI (1956), 1052–66. Note that the 1788 salary (£45.12.6) does not include fees and that the 1806 figure (£746.3.1) includes both fees and £200 or more which Butts had to pay to the other Joint Chief Clerk who had retired with gout but continued to receive his salary.

† No other person in the office was paid for overtime. There were complaints about such overtime, and no more was claimed after 1810.

   Note that Blake's letters were directed to the Butts home in Marlborough Street rather than to the office of the Commissary General of Musters, where Butts would not have had to pay postage on them.

‡ Through the influence of Thomas Butts, James Blake, probably the poet's brother recently retired from the family hosiery shop (1812), was employed in the office of the Commissary General of Musters in 1814–16.

§ An impressive argument that *The Book of Thel* (1789) concerns the "green-sickness" characteristic of boarding-school girls, fostered by conduct-books stressing modesty and restraint, is made in Hisao Ishizuka, "Thel's 'Complaint': A Medical Reading of Blake's *The Book of Thel*", *Eibungaku Kenkyu Nihon Eibungakkai: Studies in English Literature, The English Literary Society of Japan*, LXXIII (1997), 245–63.

Street, and the rates for the building were paid in her name. By 1801 there were eighteen girls living there,* and perhaps other girls came in by the day. The young ladies would have been taught history and geography, manners and morals, a fine script and a neat stitch, with extras such as French and dancing, art or even mathematics.

Perhaps Blake taught at the school for young ladies at 9 Great Marlborough Street—indeed, his first acquaintance with Betsy and Thomas Butts may have been through the school. If so, his relationship with the Butts family may have begun with Betsy Butts, the mistress of the school. When Blake writes to Butts of "those things [*in art*] which a Boarding School Miss can comprehend in a fortnight",[65] he may well be referring to what he himself taught in Mrs Butts's boarding school for young ladies. And when he addressed his poem "The Phoenix | to Mrs Butts", he described "Mrs Butts's Bird" in a context appropriate for a school or a nursery

> Where little Children sport & play
> And they strok'd it with their hands
> All their cooe's it understands....[66]

Blake's relationship with Betsy Butts was strong and affectionate, though of course his business and correspondence were with Thomas Butts. On most of the occasions when we know Blake made social calls on the Buttses (on 12 May, 13 and 16 September 1800), it was, according to their son Tommy, in order to have breakfast or tea "with mama". At Felpham, the Blakes "dedicated a Chamber to her Service ... [*with*] a fine view of the Sea",[67] and Blake sent poems to her ("The Phoenix" and "To Mrs Butts" in his letter of 2 October 1800). It is at least possible that Betsy Butts was as much Blake's friend and patron as her husband.

In the miniature portrait Blake painted of Thomas Butts (1801) (Pl. 74A), we see a slim gentleman of about forty, dressed carefully in a white stock and a coat with a gold epaulet on his right shoulder as if an officer's uniform. He is wearing a short white wig and holding a little book in his right hand,

---

* The Census return for Westminster of 1801 records the twenty-two occupants of the house: nineteen females and three males (?Thomas Butts and their sons Tommy and Joseph Edward) (see "The Daughters of Albion and the Butts Household", *Blake*, XVIII [1984], 116). Of these twenty-two residents, three were "Persons chiefly employed in Trades, Manufactures, or Handicrafts", which must have included Elizabeth, Thomas Butts, and his son Joseph Edward.

    No 9 Great Marlborough Street is identified as a School in the commercial sections of *Holden's Triennial Directory* for 1805–7 and the 1808 supplement, according to Viscomi, "A 'Green House' for Butts?", *Blake*, XXX [1996], 11). The eighteen females who lived there apart from Mrs Butts but were not employed must have been students. Teachers, cooks, and 'tweenies probably came in daily rather than living at 9 Great Marlborough Street.

and his expression is somewhat prim. Except for his elegance, he is what we might expect of a careful accountant who required his protégé to sign receipts for the monies given him. Blake tended to be careless about money, but his chief patron was not.

Blake's portrait miniature of Mrs Butts (Pl. 74B) eight years later depicts a plump, determined woman of about fifty in a fashionably *décolleté* dress, with her hair piled high, and holding (rather awkwardly) a fan in her right hand. There is little in either portrait to indicate the qualities of character which inspired such devotion in Blake or such admiration of his art.

Catherine and William Blake were on intimate social terms with Betsy and Thomas Butts, exchanging visits, joking, giving presents. The Buttses came to the Blakes on Tuesdays,[68] and when the Blakes went to the Buttses they were served from a George III teapot and stand and a George III silver mug.[69] The gatherings at the Butts house were family affairs, at which twelve-year-old Tommy Butts was present,* and Betsy probably brought her needlework, which was sufficiently admired in the Butts family to be kept for a century and a half.[70] Catherine made a painting of "Agnes" from *The Monk* (1796) by M.G. Lewis which she gave to Betsy Butts,[71] and Blake may have given Butts the elaborate mahogany cabinet in which Butts and his son Tommy kept engraving tools when Blake taught them engraving—in 1910 it still had plates by Butts and Blake in a secret drawer.[72]

The correspondence between Butts and Blake after the Blakes had moved to Felpham sometimes flirts with social and theological impropriety. On 22 September 1800 Blake began his letter with "Dear Friend of My Angels" and Butts replied:

> Marlborough Street
>
> Dear Sir
>
> I cannot immediately determine whether or no I am dignified by the Title you have graciously conferred on me—you cannot but recollect the difficulties that have unceasingly arisen to prevent my discerning clearly whether your Angels are black white or grey and that on the whole I have rather inclined to the former opinion and considered you more immediately under the protection of the black-guard[;] however at any rate I

---

* In his diary Tommy wrote: Tuesday 13 May 1800: "Mr. and Mrs. Blake and Mr. T. Jones drank tea with mama"; Wednesday 10 Sept: "Mr. and Mrs. Blake, his brother, and Mr. [*Thomas*] Birch [*surgeon of St Thomas's Hospital*] came to tea"; Saturday 13 Sept: "Mr. Blake breakfasted with Mama"; and Tuesday 16 Sept 1800: "Mr. Blake breakfasted with mama". Tommy seems to have regarded the Blakes as honorary aunts and uncles, and on Monday 14 Aug 1809, when he was twenty, he wrote to his mother: "This morning I breakfasted with George before I went to South Molton Street; you wished me to do so while you and my Father are out of Town. Mr. and Mrs. Blake are very well, they say I am browner and tallker;—they intend shortly to pay the promised visit at Epsom."

should thank you for an introduction to his Highness[']s Court, that when refused admittance into other Mansions I may not be received as a stranger in His.

... Your good Wife will permit & I hope may benefit from the Embraces of Neptune but she will presently distinguish betwixt the warmth of his Embraces & yours, & court the former with caution[.] I suppose you do not admit of a third in that concern or I would offer her mine even at this distance[.] Allow me before I draw a Veil over this interesting Subject to lament the frailty of the fairest Sex for who alass! of us my good Friend could have thought that

So Virtuous a Woman would ever have fled
From Hercules' Buildings to Neptunes Bed[?]

... *E*xcuse me, as you have been accustomed from friendship to do, but certain opinions imbibed from reading, nourishd by indulgence, and rivitted by a confined Conversation, and which have been equally prejudicial to your Interest & Happiness, will now I trust, disperse as a Daybreak Vapour, and you will henceforth become a Member of that Community of which you are at present ... but a Sign to mark the residence of dim incredulity, haggard suspicion, & bloated philosophy—*W*hatever can be effected by sterling Sense[,] by opinions which harmonize society & beautify creation, will, in future be exemplified in you & the time I trust is not distant and that because I truly regard you when you will be a more valorous Champion of Revelation & Humiliation than any of those who now wield the Sword of the Spirit ....
... when you die
... may your faithful Spirit upward bear
Your gentle Souls to him whose care
Is ever sure and ever nigh
Those who on Providence rely ....

The argument that "your Interest" has been harmed by "certain opinions" and the wish that Blake may hereafter become a "Champion of Revelation & Humiliation" suggest a political and religious conventionality[*] surprising in a man who admired Blake and was loved by him.

---

[*] It has repeatedly been alleged that Butts and Blake were drawn together by their interest in Swedenborgianism (Mary Butts, *The Crystal Cabinet* [London, 1937], 16; J. Bronowski, *William Blake, 1757–1827: A Man Without a Mask* [London, 1943], 62; D.V. Erdman, *Blake Prophet Against Empire* [Princeton: Princeton University Press, 1954], 268, 356), but no evidence is offered, and none of the charities to which Thomas Butts left bequests is Swedenborgian. His reference in this letter to "the opinion of the Archbishop of Canterbury" suggests that he was a conventional member of the established church.

Blake's reply, on 2 October, meekly accepted Butts's evaluation:

Friend of Religion & Order

   I thank you for … your reprehension of follies by me fosterd. Your prediction will I hope be fulfilled in m*e*, & in future I am the determined advocate of Religion & Humility the two bands of Society.

And with his letter to Butts he included his extraordinary "first Vision of Light" (see Chapter VI).

Butts must indeed have been a dear friend for Blake to honour him with a share in this world-transforming vision.

Blake also sent a poem "To Mrs Butts":

Wife of the Friend of those I most revere,
Recieve this tribute from a Harp sincere[.]
Go on in Virtuous Seed sowing on Mold
Of Human Vegetation & Behold
Your Harvest Springing to Eternal life
Parent of Youthful Minds & happy Wife

His celebration of Betsy Butts as mother and teacher is in an altogether more terrestrial and conventional mould (a "tribute from a Harp sincere") than the exaltation in his poem to Thomas Butts of the earth-transforming "jewels of Light" which "Appeard as One Man". But even in the poem to Betsy Butts there are the references to "those I most revere" and to "Human Vegetation" which reveal the visionary in the protégé.

A year later, on 11 September 1801, Blake lamented that "I am still so much your debtor & you so much my Credit-er …. I thank you again & again for your generous forbearance of which I have need", a generosity of forbearance which distinguished Butts from almost all Blake's other patrons.

And in the new year, on 10 January 1802, he wrote:

what you tell me about your sight afflicted me not a little …. it is a part of our duty to God & man to take due care of his Gifts & tho we ought not think <u>more</u> highly of ourselves, yet we ought to think <u>As</u> highly of ourselves as immortals ought to think ….

   Your approbation of my pictures is a Multitude to Me …. Your kind offer of pecuniary assistance I can only thank you for at present because I have enough to serve my present purpose here. … Patience! if Great things do not turn out it is because such things depend on the Spiritual & not on the Natural World …. whatever becomes of my labours I would rather that they should be preservd in your Green House (not as you mistakenly call it dung hill) than in the cold gallery of fashion.—The Sun may yet shine & then they will be brought into open air[.]

But you have so generously & openly desired that I will divide my griefs with you that I cannot hide what is now become my duty to explain— ... The Thing I have most at Heart! more than life or all that seems to make life comfortable witho*u*t, Is the Interest of True Religion & Science & whenever any thing appears to affect that Intere*st* (Especially if I myself omit any duty to my Station as a Soldier of Christ) It gives me the greatest of torments, I am not ashamed afraid or averse to tell You what Ought to be Told[,] That I am under the direction of Messengers from Heaven Daily & Nightly .... if we fear to do the dictates of our Angels & tremble at the Tasks set before us, if we refuse to do Spiritual Act*s*, because of Natural Fears or Natural Desires! Who can describe the dismal torments of such a state!—I too well remember the Threats I heard! "If you who are organized by Divine Providence for Spiritual communio*n*, Refuse & bury your Talent in the Earth even tho you Should want Natural Brea*d*, Sorrow & Desperation pursues you thro life! & after death shame & confusion of face to eternity—Every one in Eternity will leave you[,] aghast at the Man who was crownd with glory & honour by his brethren & betrayd their cause to their enemies. You will be calld the base Judas who betrayd his Friend!"—Such words would make any Stout man tremble & how then could I be at ease? But I am now no longer in That State & now go on again with my Task Fearless ....

Blake's commissions from Butts were on an heroic scale. On 26 August 1799, Blake wrote to Cumberland: "I am Painting small Pictures from the Bible .... My Work pleases my employer & I have an order for Fifty small Pictures at One Guinea each which is Something better than mere copying from another artist. But above all I feel myself happy & contented let what will come ...."[*]

The exaltation produced by such a commission and such subjects must have been extraordinary. Blake had already made designs from the Bible in his great colour prints of 1795 (see "Elohim Creating Adam", Pl. 62),[†] but

---

* Notice that the letter does not specify the sex of "my employer", which allows the possibility that it was Betsy Butts rather than Thomas. Eventually Blake made 135 temperas and watercolours for the Buttses.

  Blake's tempera for "The last supper[:] Verily I say unto you, that one of you shall betray me", which was exhibited at the Royal Academy in May 1799, may be the earliest picture by Blake which Butts acquired.

† In July and Sept 1805, Blake delivered to Butts (at £1.1.0 each) his colour-prints of "Good and Evil Angels", "The House of Death', "God Judging Adam", "Lamech and His Two Wives", "Nebuchadnezzar", "Newton", "God Creating Adam", and "Christ Appearing" (Butlin #289, 294, 297, 301, 306, 320, 323, 325), according to his account of 3 March 1806 (*BR* 572–3), and Butts later acquired the colour-prints of "Satan Exulting over Eve", "Pity", and "Hecate" (Butlin #291, 310, 316).

he had never had a commission for finished separate pictures on such a scale before.

With such a congenial order, Blake set to work with his characteristic industry. For these designs, he adapted the traditional method of fresco painting; according to his friend J.T. Smith,

> His ground was a mixture of whiting and carpenter's glue [*rather than egg*], which he passed several times in thin coatings: his colours he ground himself, and also united them with the same sort of glue, but in a much weaker state. He would, in the course of painting a picture, pass a very thin transparent wash of glue-water over the whole of the parts he had worked upon, and then proceed with his finishing.*

In this medium, he painted some fifty pictures from the Bible for Butts, most of them 15″ x 10½″. Many of the subjects are traditional, such as "Moses Placed in the Ark of Bulrushes" and "The Flight into Egypt", but some are unusual, such as "'Christ the Mediator': Christ Pleading before the Father for St. Mary Magdalene", and several do not derive from any Biblical text, such as "The Christ Child Asleep on the Cross" and "The Virgin Hushing the Young Baptist, Who Approaches the Sleeping Infant Jesus". But they omit a few favourite Biblical subjects such as David slaying Goliath.

The texts for illustration may often have been selected by Butts, for in his letter of 22 November 1802 Blake asks "what Subject you choose to be painted". But the treatment of the text was of course Blake's.

The subjects range through the Old and New Testaments, but most come from Genesis, Exodus, Matthew, Mark, Luke, and John. One each of the temperas of 1799–1800 is based on Esther, Job, Susannah, and Corinthians. The subjects, such as "Job and His Daughters", are familiar enough, but these books, plus Ruth and Acts which Blake later illustrated in watercolour for Butts, were not among the canon of the Bible accepted by Blake and other Swedenborgians at the first meeting to establish the New Church in April 1789 (see pp. 127–8, above). Evidently Butts was happy to

---

* J.T. Smith (*BR* 472). Smith continues:

> This process I have tried, and find, by using my mixtures warm, that I can produce the same texture as possessed in Blake's pictures.... Blake preferred mixing his colours with carpenter's glue, to gum, on account of the latter cracking in the sun, and becoming humid in moist weather. The glue-mixture stands the sun, and change of atmosphere has no effect upon it.

> However, Blake's temperas have often darkened, and some, of which there are verbal records, may have been destroyed because they were so much damaged.

have illustrations not only from the entire Protestant Bible but from the Apocrypha such as Susannah as well.

The designs are heartily Protestant, but they eschew some of the more extreme political subjects, such as one for Psalm ix, 16: "The wicked is snared in the worke of his own hands" representing Guy Fawkes.* Few of the designs represent priests. But they do include "The King of Babylon in Hell" (*c*. 1805), with the King wearing a Papal tiara, and the colour-print of "Satan Exulting Over Eve" (Pl. 6) seems to show Satan copulating with Eve, which must have been a surprise to most Bible readers.

Butts liked a few of the temperas so well that Blake made second versions for him, for example "The Christ Child Asleep upon a Wooden Cross Laid upon the Ground" (both *c*. 1799–1800).[73] Perhaps the variant version was to decorate Mrs Butts's school, perhaps even for teaching morality and art.

Blake seized the few Biblical opportunities to depict the naked human form divine. "Lot and His Daughters" (*c*. 1799) shows Lot's two diaphanously draped daughters removing the napkin which conceals their drunken father's nakedness, and "Bathsheba at the Bath" (*c*. 1799) shows the nakedness not only of Bathsheba but of another woman and of two half-grown children as they are watched by David from a great distance. While some of Blake's Bible temperas may have been hung in Mrs Butts's school, the full frontal nudity of Lot and Bathsheba was surely reserved for more mature eyes.

The financial arrangement for these pictures was that Butts advanced sums to Blake and Blake repaid him with paintings, drawings, and prints. At first the records may have been kept somewhat informally, but, with Blake's rooted indifference about money,† they probably soon became confused. From 1803 Butts made out careful receipts to be signed by Blake normally in the form: "Receiv'd of Mr Butts five Pounds 5/. on further account | William Blake".[74] In September 1800, there was "Balance [*of £14.10.8*] due from me [*Blake*] previous to my going to Felpham",[75] and on 16 August 1803 Blake sent "7 Drawings" to Butts which he thought "about balances our account". In the years for which detailed records survive, January 1803–December 1810, Butts paid Blake £401.4.10 (including £12.19.0 "By

---

* *The History of ye Old & New Testament in Cutts* ([London]: Iohn Williams, 1671), a series of engravings often bound with conventional Bibles, e.g., *The Holy Bible* (London: John Bill & Christopher Barker, 1680) (Bible Society in Cambridge University Library). Note also the design for II Samuel xxii, 44: "Thou hast delivered me from the strivings of my people" called "King Charles the II his Returne".

† Blake did keep an "account Book in which I have regularly written down Every Sum I have recievd from you", as he told Hayley on 28 Dec 1804, but the book has not survived, and Blake only refers to it because he had forgotten "the Twelve Guineas which you Lent Me".

Coals"*) or £50 a year. This was probably the bulk of Blake's income for these years, enough to provide him with security and independence.

Blake had completed twenty-nine pictures for Butts when he went to Felpham in 1800, including the miracle of "The loaves and fishes" exhibited at the Royal Academy in May, and he took with him orders for twenty-one more.[76] Over the next five years he completed the order Butts gave him in 1799 for temperas from scenes in the Bible and went on to an even larger series of Biblical watercolours, some of them of astonishing power and originality (see "Jacob's Dream" [*c.* 1805], Pl. 130; "Christ Baptising" [1805], Pl. 3; and "The Great Red Dragon and the Beast from the Sea" [1803], Pl. 5). Many of these bore on the mounts elaborate Biblical inscriptions in an unidentified hand, perhaps by one of Butts's sons Joseph Edward or Tommy.[77]

Even when Blake is dealing with conventional subjects, such as the Crucifixion, his focus is spiritual and original. "The Soldiers Casting Lots for Christ's Garments" (1800) (Pl. 76) is dominated by a giant cross, but it is seen from the back, with only Christ's arms visible, while in the foreground Roman soldiers are dicing—the contrast between the material world and the spiritual could scarcely be more stark.

The designs increasingly focus upon the apocalyptic visions of the Bible. "Ezekiel's Wheels" (*c.* 1803–5) (Pl. 77) depicts Ezekiel's tremendous vision of The Living Creatures or Zoon (Blake called them Zoas) who convey the spirit of God and who more and more absorb Blake's own growing myth. "God Blessing the Seventh Day" (*c.* 1805) (Pl. 78) shows only God and nothing of what he is blessing—and it seems to show a sevenfold God.

After about 1803 there are terrifying scenes from Revelation of the Beast and the Whore, such as "The Great Red Dragon and the Beast from the Sea" (1803–5) (Pl. 5), "The Great Red Dragon and the Woman Clothed with the Sun" (one of *c.* 1803–5 and one of 1805), "The Number of the Beast is 666" (*c.* 1805), and "The Whore of Babylon" (1809) (Pl. 75). The design for Revelation x, 1–2: "And the Angel which I Saw Lifted up his Hand to Heaven" (*c.* 1805) (Pl. 79) epitomizes the majesty of Blake's man-centred universe in an heroic nude for whom earth, sea, temporal power, and the temporal spectator are merely the context of spiritual might.

Butts did not confine his commissions to Biblical designs, for in 1805 he bought most of Blake's great colour-prints invented in 1795 and his apoca-

---

* Receipt of 3 March 1806 (*BR* 573).

   The coal may have been supplied by Daniel Fearon (b. 1772), Coal Merchant, who in 1802 had married Diana Butts, perhaps the sister (Ann, b. 1769) of Blake's patron (Viscomi, "A 'Green House' for Butts?", *Blake*, XXX [1996], 7, 11). John G Fear[o]n was a witness at the second marriage (15 June 1826) of Blake's patron Thomas Butts to the widow Elizabeth Delauney (Joseph Viscomi, "William Blake's 'The Phoenix | to Mrs Butts' Redux", *Blake*, XXIX [1995], 12–15).

lyptic series of "Pestilence", "Fire" (Pl. 24), "War", and "Famine" of 1805.[78]

Blake developed his Butts watercolours of "Job and His Daughters" (*c.* 1799–1800) and "Job Confessing His Presumption to God Who Answers Him from the Whirlwind" (1803–5) into his great series of nineteen Job watercolours (1805–6).

Later Blake made whole suites of watercolours for Butts based upon *Paradise Lost* (12 designs, 1807?), *Comus* (8 designs, 1815?), "On the Morning of Christ's Nativity" (6 designs, 1815?),* *L'Allegro* (6 designs, 1816–20), and *Il Penseroso* (6 designs, 1816–20). As late as 1826 Butts may have bought Blake's tempera of "The Body of Abel Found by Adam and Eve". Butts was a devoted patron to Blake to the very end of Blake's life.

He fostered Blake's art in ways besides purchasing it. In 1822 he permitted Blake to copy three of his *Paradise Lost* designs for John Linnell, and in 1821 he let him copy his Job watercolours for the suite of engravings Linnell commissioned. In gratitude, Blake would probably have given him a set of the prints, but Butts insisted on paying for them, "his own decision quite in Character", as Blake said.[79]

Butts also bought Blake's poetry, including *Thel*, *Songs of Innocence and of Experience*, *Milton*, and *Jerusalem*.† These purchases included virtually all the books Blake printed after 1799 when Butts first became his patron. However, Blake did not sell him most of his earlier books,[80] and the support Butts provided to Blake was primarily for his pictures.

In the annals of honourable patronage, few men have been responsible for evoking so many great works of art as Thomas Butts. Without his enlightened generosity, most of Blake's great Bible illustrations might never have seen the light of day, and Blake would almost certainly have been reduced perilously close to abject poverty.

---

* Blake's watercolours for *Paradise Lost* (1808), *Comus* (1815), and "On the Morning of Christ's Hativity" (*c.* 1815) were copied from those he had made for the Rev. Joseph Thomas (1807, 1801, 1809).

† Butts owned *Poetical Sketches* (1783) (copy B), *Thel* (1789) (L), *America* (1793) (F), *Visions* (B), *Europe* (1794) (C plus pl. 1), *Songs of Innocence and of Experience* (1794) (E), *Song of Los* (1795) (B), Young's *Night Thoughts* (1797) (coloured copy A), "A Descriptive Catalogue" advertisement (1809) (A), *Descriptive Catalogue* (1809) (O), *Milton* (1804–?10) (A), "Blake's Chaucer: An Original Engraving" (1810) (B), *Jerusalem* (1804–?20) (I), *On Homer's Poetry* (?1821) (A), and *The Ghost of Abel* (1822) (A).

  However, some of these works were acquired by Butts long after they were composed, for *Songs* was bought on 9 Sept 1806, the *Descriptive Catalogue* and its advertisement were bound in or after 1820, and *America* and *Europe* were bought after Blake's death at the Cumberland sale in 1835.

The Threat of Politics

Blake sympathized with Tom Paine and George Cumberland and the young William Wordsworth and all those who deplored the Church and King politics of Pitt's Tory administration. However, he abominated Pitt's politics not merely because they were politically wrong but because they were political. At the high tide of British radicalism, before it was stemmed and diverted by the notorious Two Acts of 1795, Blake may have been surrounded by political activists and government informers, but his own struggles were all in the mind. He was never a joiner or a builder of street barricades. His most active campaigning was against the entire race of politicians and governors, and he waged his campaigns chiefly in the margins of the books he was reading.

When he acquired the elegant little edition of Bacon's *Essays* published by James Edwards in 1798, he wrote beside Bacon's worldly wisdom, "the Wisdom of this World is Foolishness with God". When Bacon deplored the "discords, and quarrels, and factions" which are "a sign the reverence of government is lost", Blake exclaimed indignantly: "When the Reverence of Government is Lost it is better than when it is found". He said that "The Prince of darkness . . . is a Lord Chancellor", like Bacon. And he concluded: "Bacon supposes that the dragon Beast & Harlot are worthy of a Place in the New Jerusalem[.] Excellent Traveller Go on & be damnd".[81]

Even more telling and intemperate were his jagged exclamations in the margins of *An Apology for the Bible, in a Series of Letters, Addressed to Thomas Paine* by Bishop Watson (1798). The political or at least popular pretensions of the pamphlet were indicated by its price of "One Shilling, or Fifty Copies for Two Pounds", clearly designed to be put in the hands of as many readers as possible.

Blake's comments on Watson's work were headed by the unequivocal assertions:

> To defend the Bible in this year 1798 would cost a man his life
> The Beast & the Whore rule without control . . . .
> I have been commanded from Hell not to print this as it is what our Enemies wish[.][82]

He identified the author as a "State trickster" writing with "Priestly Impudence" and "Serpentine Dissimulation", "an Inquisitor" with a "cloven foot". "The laws of the Jews . . . were what Christ pronounced them[,] The Abomination that maketh desolate, i.e. State Religion, which is the Source of all Cruelty". Blake "attribute[s] the English Crusade against France . . . to State Religion".[83]

To these dissimulations of State Religion, Blake opposes the voice of God: "Conscience in those that have it is unequivocal, it is the Voice of God"; "God does & always did converse with honest Men"; "the Holy Ghost . . . in Paine strives with Christendom as in Christ he strove with the Jews". For Blake, the struggles of Paine and the Bishop over the moral precepts of the Bible are perverse irrelevancies: "The Gospel is Forgiveness of Sins & has No Moral Precepts[;] these belong to Plato & Seneca & Nero". For those who understand the natures of State Religion and of inspiration, "henceforth every man may converse with God & be a King & Priest in his own house".[84]

Blake's judgment of the vindictiveness of the government was, alas! but too accurate. His friend and patron Joseph Johnson, who had showed his political discretion by declining to publish Blake's *French Revolution* (1791) and Tom Paine's *Rights of Man* (1791), was arrested and imprisoned in 1799 for selling an outspoken political pamphlet, and Benjamin Flower was imprisoned for six months in 1799 for publishing reflections upon the Bishop of Llandaff.* In 1798, to defend conscience and the Voice of God against the tricksters of State Religion was likely to cost a man his liberty if not his life.

Vala *and the Shattered Paradise*

Blake's creative activities from 1795 to 1800 were prodigious, with the great series of colour-prints, almost 800 large drawings,[85] and sixty-nine engravings, most of them in folio for *Night Thoughts*. But his most extraordinary achievement of these prodigious years was his great Prophecy called *VALA or The Death and Judgement of the Eternal Man: A DREAM of Nine Nights*† (see Pl. 80).

Blake began the poem while he was working on his *Night Thoughts* drawings and engravings. Like Young's poem, Vala is organized in nine nights, and the fair copy is on very large leaves of J WHATMAN | 1794 paper which Blake was given for his *Night Thoughts* drawings. Indeed, The Four Zoas is largely written on proofs of the *Night Thoughts* engravings. And like

---

* Benjamin Flower's daughter Sarah Flower Adams refers casually to Blake in *The Monthly Repository* (1835)—see *BR* (2).

† *Vala* is the first title of the poem; later, perhaps about 1807, Blake retitled it *The Four Zoas*: The torments of Love & Jealousy in The Death and Judgement of Albion the Eternal Man. It is convenient to distinguish between the first version of perhaps 1796–1802 as *Vala* and the later version (see Chapter VI) as *The Four Zoas*.

   The only full-size reproduction is in *Vala* or *The Four Zoas: A Facsimile of the Manuscript, a Transcript of the Poem, and a Study of its Growth and Significance*, ed. G.E. Bentley, Jr (Oxford: Clarendon Press, 1963).

the *Night Thoughts*, *Vala* is illustrated with enormous designs which surround the text.

Vala was conceived on a scale far more ambitious than any of Blake's previous Prophecies. *Europe* had 265 lines, and *Urizen* had 517, but *Vala* had some 2,000 lines, and, when it was revised as *The Four Zoas*, it grew to over 4,000 lines. While the copperplates of *America* and *Europe*, the largest of Blake's early works, are about 23 x 17 cm, the leaves of Vala are more than three times as large (*c.* 41 x 32 cm). And while the earlier Prophecies were probably completed in about a twelve-month—Blake came to believe that "No Work of Art, can take longer than a Year"*—*Vala* and *The Four Zoas* was probably composed, illustrated, revised, and recopied for over ten years, from about 1796 to about 1807.

In the process of growth and revision, the character of the poem changed profoundly. At first it was concerned with intellectual judgement and spiritual despair. It was revised to celebrate a glorious Christian renovation. What began as an intellectual psychomachia, a war of spirits, was brought down to earth with a web of references to Druid and Christian history and with superimposed place names from Britain and the Holy Land.

Blake probably drafted the poem and perhaps some of its designs in a notebook, now lost. By the time he had finished his work on the *Night Thoughts* engravings, he was ready to copy out the title in a flourishing hand and sign it "by William Blake 1797" (Pl. 80). He transcribed the poem in an elegant, spacious copperplate hand on the spacious, elegant leaves of WHATMAN paper, beginning:

> This is the Dirge of Eno which shook the heavens with wrath
> And thus beginneth the Book of Vala which Whosoever reads
> If with his Intellect he comprehend the terrible Sentence
> The heavens shall quak*e*, the earth shall move & shudder & the
>   mountains
> With all their woods, the streams & valleys: wail in dismal fear
>
> (*Vala* Night the First p. 1)

The mythological context is that of *The First Book of Urizen*. However, in *Urizen* the world is created and divided through the binary struggles of

---

* "Blake's Chaucer: The Canterbury Pilgrims" (1809). The passage continues: "it may be worked backwards and forwards without end, and last a Man's whole Life; but he will, at length, only be forced to bring it back to what it was, and it will be worse than it was at the end of the first Twelve Months". And in his Public Address (1810–11) (Notebook p. 44) he wrote: "Let a Man who has made a drawing go on & on & he will produce a Picture or Painting but if he chooses to leave off before he has spoild it he will do a Better Thing".

Urizen and Los, while in *Vala* the myth reaches its final development with four giant figures, and it is explicitly situated in the human psyche.

> Four Mighty Ones are in every Man: a Perfect Unity
> Cannot Exis*t*, but from the Universal Brotherhood of Eden
> The Universal Man . . . .
> Los was the fourth immortal starry one[86]

To the struggles for dominion of Los and Urizen are added two other Giant Figures, Tharmas and Luvah, and in the final form of the poem they are called *The Four Zoas*.* In *Jerusalem*, "the Four Zoa's . . . are the Four Eternal Senses of Man".[87] When united in Eternity, the Zoas probably looked like the four-headed, winged living creatures (Zoon) of Ezekiel's Vision (Pl. 77), but in their fallen state, in the designs to *Vala*, their form is that of giant men.

The designs often represent voluptuous nude women, sometimes in erotic contexts. Two female dragons are on p. 26, one with the vulva carefully emphasized, and a naked woman on p. 44 has her belly overdrawn with what seem to be Gothic church buildings. There are partially erased designs† which seem to represent coupling on pp. 39–41, and on p. 27 a voluptuous nude woman rises from the loins of a skeletal old man (Pl. 81). The designs even more than the words are concerned with the powers of women, and the text is loud with the wars of love and jealousy.

In part *Vala* is a continuation of Enitharmon's enchantment in *Europe* "That Woman, lovely Woman! may have dominion":[88]

> Arise you little glancing wings & sing your infant joy[!]
> Arise & drink your bliss
> For every thing that lives is holy[;] for the source of life
> Descends to be a weeping babe[;]
> For the Earthworm renews the moisture of the sandy plain
>
> (*Vala*, Night the Second, p. 34, ll. 77–81)

But the emphasis is upon the constrictions of creation rather than freedom from them.

---

* In *The Four Zoas*, the word "Zoas" is used only in the title page, but it appears repeatedly in *Milton* and *Jerusalem*. The Zoas are clearly associated with The Living Creatures of Ezekiel's Vision: "They are the Four Zoas that stood around the Throne Divine", "the Four Zoas of Albio*n*, the Four Living Creature*s*, the Cherubim of Albion" (*Jerusalem* pl. 59, 1, 13, pl. 63, ll. 2–3).

† It is not clear who erased the designs—Blake or Linnell, in whose family the manuscript was from about 1825 to 1918, or Gilchrist or W.M. Rossetti or E.J. Ellis or W.B. Yeats to whom the family showed it.

The tygers of wrath called the horses of instruction from their
     mangers[.]
They unloos'd them & put on the harness of gold & silver & ivory[.]
In human forms distinct they stood round Urizen prince of light
Petrifying all the Human Imagination into rock & sand ...
Albion gave his loud death groan[,] the Atlantic Mountains trembled

                         (Night the Second p. 25, ll. 3–6, 9)

The created universe is but a cage and chain for humanity:

Thus were the stars of heaven created like a golden chain
To bind the Body of Man to heaven from falling into the Abyss

                         (Night the Second p. 33, ll. 16–17.)

Some of the most eloquent poetry of *Vala* is a lament for the ills of
experience:

What is the price of Experience[?] do men buy it for a song
Or wisdom for a dance in the street? No it is bought with the price
Of all that a man hath[,] his house his wife his children[.]
Wisdom is sold in the desolate market where none come to buy
And in the witherd field where the farmer plows for bread in
     vain. ...
It is an easy thing to laugh at the wrathful elements[,]
To hear the dog howl at the wintry door, the ox in the slaughter house
     moan[,]
To see a god on every wind & a blessing on every blast ...
Thus could I sing & thus rejoice, but it is not so with me

                  (Night the Second p. 35, ll. 11–15, p. 36, ll. 3–5, 13)

In *Vala*, as far as Blake copied it out in his fine Copperplate Hand and
revised and extended it in his modified Copperplate Hand (that is, on pp.
1–18, 23–42), there is scarcely more promise of escape from this world of
experience than there is in *Visions of the Daughters of Albion* of 1793 or
Europe of 1794. The poem provides a profound analysis of man's limitations
but no hint of escape from the prison—no suggestion that it is conceiving
of the world as a prison that makes it a prison, that the key to the Gates of
Paradise is in the mind.

Blake worked and reworked the poem, and in each revision it seemed to
become more promising and less coherent. Eventually he ceased to make
changes or even additions in his fine copperplate hands, and he continued
them in the ordinary hand in which he wrote his letters. His confidence that

the work was complete or completable seems to have diminished. It was not until he received a new inspiration for it that *Vala* was transformed from a myth of the torments of love and jealousy into an affirmation of escape and salvation in Christ (see Chapter VI).

On 2 July 1800, Blake wrote to his friend George Cumberland:

> I begin to Emerge from a deep pit of Melancholy, Melancholy without any real reason for *it*, a disease which God keep you from & all good men. . . . I have been too little among friends which I fear they will not Excuse & I know not how to apologize . . . [*to*] the few friends I have dared to visit in my stupid Melancholy.

Despite the magnificent hopes with which the decade began, with the New Jerusalem Church and the French Revolution, and despite his splendid accomplishments then in art and in poetry, the 1790s seem have been a decade of despair for Blake, absorbed by "Death Despair & Everlasting brooding Melancholy".[89] It was not until much later, in the revised Night the Seventh of *Vala*, that Blake could write:

> Lift up thy blue eyes Vala & put on thy sapphire shoes[;]
> O Melancholy Magdalen behold the morning breaks

> (Night the Seventh b p. 93, ll. 1–2)

CHAPTER VI

1800–1804: Sweet Felpham and Rex vs Blake

O God protect me from my friends,
that they have not power over me[.]
Thou hast giv'n me power to protect myself
from my bitterest enemies.[1]

Corporeal Friends Are Spiritual Enemies[2]

Blake had many corporeal friends, friends like George Cumberland and John Flaxman and Henry Fuseli and Thomas Butts, who helped him to find commissions and who looked out for his worldly interests. He was, as he said to Cumberland, "very much obliged by your kind ardour in my cause" and "obliged to you & to all who do so".[3] He addressed Butts as "Friend of My Angels" and Flaxman as "Sculptor of Eternity" and "My Dearest Friend".[4]

However, his corporeal interests and his spiritual concerns were often at odds. His well-wishers told him that he should concentrate upon the drudgery of business, upon copy-engraving, if necessary even at the cost of neglecting his visions and the pictures and poems they inspired, and Blake found this unimaginable.

The problem was to find a patron who sympathized with his spiritual concerns and who would let him follow his genius in his own way. Only slowly did Blake learn that corporeal friends may be spiritual enemies and that he had sometimes been too trusting in giving to others his friendship and his fate.

John Flaxman introduced Blake to his friend and patron William Hayley in 1784, in the hope that Hayley might assist in sending Blake to study in Rome. Nothing came of this proposal, but in succeeding years Blake, Flaxman, and Hayley became intimately involved with one another.

William Hayley was a gentleman and a man of property, the squire of his Sussex village of Eartham, a political liberal,* and a popular poet. His social standing was immensely higher than that of the mechanic William Blake and the artist-craftsman John Flaxman, though he generously waived such class distinctions. His letters to the engraver and the sculptor are addressed to "My Dear Blake" and "My very dear Flaxman",[5] while Blake and Flaxman saluted Hayley as "Dear Sir".† The social distance between Blake and Hayley was something both men wished to ignore but could not.

Patronage of William Hayley

Hayley was a genuinely good and generous man, as he proved in sustaining the poet William Cowper in his madness and the artist George Romney in his depression. As Robert Southey wrote: "Everything about that man was good except his poetry."[6] Blake's friend John Flaxman, William Cowper's young cousin Johnny Johnson, the son of Hayley's friend the composer John Marsh, and many others came to depend upon Hayley as a kind of beloved and benevolent uncle. There can be little doubt that Hayley meant well and did well—but, in an avuncular fashion, he also knew what was best for his friends. For the poor, like the Widow Spicer whose sailor son drowned at sea, and for the helpless, like William Cowper, he was usually right, finding money and moral support for them.

He was a learned man, fluent in French, Spanish, and Italian, Hebrew, Latin, and Greek, well-connected, and independent. When Alderman Boydell needed a biography for his massive illustrated edition of Milton, he chose William Hayley to write it. Hayley was deeply sympathetic to Milton,

---

* The cautious Tory Joseph Farington described him as "a violent republican" (*The Diary of Joseph Farington*, ed. Kenneth Garlick & Angus Macintyre [New Haven & London: Yale University Press, 1978], II, 288–9 [6 Jan 1796]).

† Most of Blake's letters to Hayley begin "Dear Sir", and Flaxman's letter to Hayley about Blake of 1784 begins "Sir" (*BR* 27).

  Equals addressed each other by surname: "Dear Flaxman" (19 Oct 1801), "Dear Cumberland" (23 Dec 1796), "Dear Blake" (Cumberland, 18 Dec 1808) or "My Dear Blake" (Flaxman, 31 July, 7 Oct 1801).

  In this context, it is striking that Blake usually addressed his patron the artist John Linnell as "Dear Sir" and Linnell's wife as "Dear Madam".

and his biography proved immensely influential throughout the nineteenth century. Indeed, Boydell and John Nicols his printer found Hayley indiscreetly sympathetic to Milton, and they required that Milton's manifest republicanism should be softened or omitted in Hayley's life when it was printed in 1794. The emasculation of his hero did not please Hayley, who was so indignant that he secured from Boydell permission to publish the full biography in 1796 with Hayley's and Milton's republican sympathies brazenly displayed. The independence of Hayley's character and the liberality of his politics fluttered the dovecotes of his county friends such as the Earl of Egremont at Petworth and the Duke of Richmond at Goodwood.

Hayley indulged himself with harmless affectations, such as fostering a poetry society in his village,[7] riding his horse under "an extensive covered way" in inclement weather,[8] and describing himself as the Bard of Sussex and the Hermit of Eartham—his fifteen-year-old son addressed him as "My very dear Bard" and "Dearest of Prophets".[9]

His marriage was an unhappy one, but his felicity was restored when Miss Betts, a housemaid at Eartham, bore him a son in 1780. Hayley gave the boy his own name, had him christened Thomas Alphonso Hayley, took him into his house, and rested his tenderest hopes upon his infant son.

When Tom was fourteen he was apprenticed to John Flaxman.* Flaxman took Tom into his own house and became a second father to him (Pl. 82). Tom wrote to his father: "The Flaxmans I like more & more he is such a man he cannot be praised too much for any of his qualities & Mrs Flaxman is so good to me as is also the immortal painter".[10]

Flaxman was responsible for far more than teaching Tom the art of sculpture. He took him to church, saw that he read his Bible,† and taught him the classical languages. On 10 March 1795 Tom told his father that "we have begun to talk Latin",[11] and on 29 May 1797 he reported: "I have begun to read Hesiod through to Mr Flaxman we began with his works & days".[12]

---

* Tom's indenture was for the conventional seven years from 1 Feb 1795, at £40 per annum for the first three and a half years and free thereafter (Flaxman's letter to Hayley, 25 Sept 1796 [Trinity College, Cambridge]). Flaxman had only recently returned from Italy, and this arrangement secured him an income while he was re-establishing himself in London.

   Tom explained that there was some urgency to formalize his apprenticeship, "that I may be secure without any expence from the Supplementary Militias to which I am at present liable" (Tom to his father, 19 Dec 1796 [West Sussex Record Office, #50]). During the invasion scare that winter, "I hear that part of the coast is or is to be laid under martial Law if it extends to Sussex I shall be obliged if I am with you to serve my country in person" (West Sussex Record Office, 20 Feb 1797 [#63]).

† Flaxman wrote to Johnny Johnson, 26 March 1823 (collection of Mary Catherine Barham Johnson):

   concerning the religion of Thomas Hayley I think it may be considered as habitual and practical, he attended Church regularly, read his Bible, obeyed the Commandments, believed that every good gift was from God and that our everlasting state must depend upon the good or evil actions done in the body, in a word he was a worthy youth ....

He played "on Mrs Flaxmans Piano forte",[13] and he went visiting with his master: "Calld on Mr Stothard & Mr Romney with Mr Flaxman".[14]

He was probably well known to all the Flaxmans' friends, including the Blakes who lived across the river in Lambeth. In June 1796 he told his father: "I have not yet seen anything of Blake or his drawing[.] I have written this on Saturday eve. that I may if possible take a walk to his house tomorrow morning. . . . You know it is a great distance from us."[15] It is even possible that Blake taught Tom drawing or etching.[16]

Flaxman was genuinely impressed with the boy's promise, and Tom boasted to his father: "I have begun modelling [in clay] and made such a performance Mr Flaxman says he did not execute for 4 years after his first attempt".[17] Many years later Flaxman wrote that Tom was "possessed of sufficient ability to give promise that he might have done something considerable in his profession if he had lived longer".[18] The boy's father, of course, thought that Tom would become the "English Michael Angelo".[19]

Plates for Hayley's Essay on Sculpture

Hayley composed a poetical *Essay on Sculpture:* In a Series of Epistles to John Flaxman, which was partly a celebration of his Tom and of Tom's master. Blake was engaged to engrave its three plates, including "The Death of Demosthenes" designed by Tom and a portrait of "Thomas Hayley, the Disciple of John Flaxman, from a Medallion" by Flaxman (Pl. 83A). Hayley felt an increasing sense of urgency about these plates, for by 1799 Tom had developed a debilitating disease which confined him to a wheelchair and left him racked with pain though uncomplaining.

On 18 February 1800 Blake sent Hayley a proof of Demosthenes which "has been approved by Mr. Flaxman", and Hayley told friends that Blake "has done the outline of dear Toms Demosthenes delightfully";[20] "the sight of it has been a real Gratification to his [*Tom's*] affectionate Spirit— . . . I yet hope the dear departing angel will see his own engraved portrait arrive before his own departure". *

Hayley wrote to Flaxman about the delay in receiving the proof, and Flaxman was as puzzled as Hayley:

It is equally Surprizing & unaccountable that you have had no farther news of the Engravings, for Mr Howard finished a beautiful drawing

---

* Hayley to Samuel Rose, 25 Feb 1800; on 14 March Hayley wrote to Rose: "My beloved Cripple is sinking gradually in all probability ... no news yet of the <u>Medallion</u>—I hope He will yet see it engraved".

from the Medallion of my Friend Thomas I think four weeks ago, since which time it has been in the hands of M.ʳ Blake & the copper plate from it is most likely done by this time . . . .[21]

It was not until 1 April that Blake could "With all possible expedition . . . send you a proof of . . . your & our Much Beloveds Countenance".

The print to which Hayley and Tom had looked forward so eagerly was, however, a "most mortifying disappointment", as Hayley told Rose the next day,

for mortifying you will allow it to be when I tell you the portrait instead of representing the dear juvenile pleasant Face of yr Friend exhibits a heavy sullen sulky Head which I can never present to the public Eye as the Image of a Being so tenderly & so justly beloved. I believe I must have a fresh outline & a mere outline instead of it . . . .

I rode to consult the dear cripple on this unfortunate Head of Himself & He agrees with me that the drawing is all wrong[.]

Notice that the fault is with the drawing by Howard, not the engraving by Blake.

Blake was asked to retouch the plate, which he did (Pl. 83A), returning a new proof very rapidly, and on 17 April Hayley sent him a long list of minutely detailed suggestions for improving the revised version:

My Dear Blake,

You are very good to take such pains to produce a Resemblance of our dear disabled artist—you have improved yr first plate a little, & I believe with a little more alteration it may be more like than the second outline.

. . . would it not give a little younger appearance to shorten the space between the nose & the upper lip a little more . . . [*and*] making the Dot at the corner of the mouth a little deeper . . . .

I have to thank Heaven (as I do with my whole Heart) for having been able to <u>gratify this dear departing angel</u> with a sight of his <u>own</u> <u>Portrait united</u> to the <u>completion</u> of a <u>long</u>, & <u>severely interrupted work</u>; which <u>He</u> most tenderly pressed me to <u>complete</u> & which nothing I believe but <u>his wishes</u> could have enabled my wounded spirit to pursue under the Heart-rending affliction of seeing a child so justly beloved <u>perishing by slow Tortures</u>. His Life may probably not last many days . . . .

Tom died on Friday 2 May 1800, and Blake hurried to send Hayley his revised proof of "the Shadow of the departed Angel" with a poignant letter of condolence: "I know that our deceased friends are more really with us than when they were apparent to our mortal part. . . . The Ruins of Time builds Mansions in Eternity."[22]

Escape from the Pit of Melancholy

In the summer of 1800, Blake sank into "a Deep pit of Melancholy, Melancholy without any real reason for it",[23] in which London seemed a dark dungeon bound in mind-forged manacles or a "terrible disart".[24] His well-meaning friends such as Joseph Johnson and Henry Fuseli urged him to be businesslike and prompt with his commercial engravings. As Blake lamented, "I find on all hands great objections to my doing any thing but the meer drudgery of business & intimations that if I do not confine myself to this I shall not live[.] This has always pursud me."[25]

This of course was intolerable, for

I cannot live without doing my duty to lay up treasures in heaven . . . . The Thing I have most at Heart! more than life or all that seems to make life comfortable without Is the Interest of True Religion & Science . . . . But if we fear to do the dictates of our Angels . . . if we refuse to do Spiritual Acts, because of Natural Fears or Natural Desires! Who can describe the dismal torments of such a state!—I too well remember the Threats I heard!—"If you who are organized by Divine Providence for Spiritual communion, Refuse & bury your Talent in the Earth even tho you Should want Natural Bread, Sorrow & Desperation pursues you thro life! & after death shame & confusion of face to eternity. Every one in Eternity will leave you[,] aghast at the Man who was crownd with glory & honour by his brethren & betrayd their cause to their enemies."[26]

He was rescued from the dungeon of London by William Hayley, who loved Blake for his simplicity of character and his religious fervour, for his unworldliness and his vulnerability. Hayley plainly thought that he could help Blake's worldly fortunes and calm his spiritual agitation as he had those of his pious, vulnerable, suicidal friend William Cowper.

Visit to Felpham

In early July, Blake made the day-long trip from London to work with

Hayley in the little seaside village of Felpham in Sussex* (Pl. 84). Hayley had a number of tasks for him, one of which was an engraving of Tom. With his usual benignity and complaisance, Hayley wrote a poem to encourage the engraver:

M[*arine*] T[*urret*] July 12

Sonnet

Blake whose pure thoughts the patient Graver guide
Kindly attentive to affection's Prayer
Let willing art exert her fondest Care
Well to portray in Nature's blooming pride
a youth as dear to both as ever died
For in his morn of Life, a morn how fair,
In his expanding Talents rich & rare
all that announced perfection they descried.

Laborious artist of a liberal Heart
atone for Errors of a skillful Hand
That failed the due Resemblance to impart
To that dear Form which prompts my tear to start.
As truth herself let his new portrait stand
Correctly beautiful & mildly grand!†

For Hayley, Blake is "patient", "Kindly attentive", liberal-hearted, and "Laborious" but subservient to the "perfection" of the "expanding Talents" of his dead son. From a grieving father, this is understandable, but from a patron it is ominous.

Hayley also gave Blake an especially precious copy of his *Triumphs of Temper* inscribed with a poem:

Accept, my gentle visionary, Blake,
    Whose thoughts are fanciful and kindly mild;

---

* On 5 July 1800, Flaxman sent with Blake a letter and gifts to Hayley, and on 16 July Hayley wrote to Flaxman that "our good enthusiastic Friend Blake will (in his Zeal to render the Portraits of our beloved scholar [*Tom*] more worthy of Him) extend the time of his Residence in the south a little longer than we at first proposed".

This is the first time Blake is known to have travelled outside the London area, aside from his sailing expedition on the Medway in 1780.

Flaxman's pronunciation of the name of the village is indicated by his spelling of it as "Felfham" (letter to Blake of 31 July 1801).

† *BR* 68, all punctuation added.

Notice that "the Errors of a skillful Hand" are those of Henry Howard the creator of the drawing, not of Blake the engraver.

Accept, and fondly keep for friendship's sake,
  This favor'd vision, my poetic child.

Rich in more grace than fancy ever won,
  To thy most tender mind this book will be,
For it belong'd to my departed son;
  So from an angel it descends to thee.

W.H.

July, 1800*

The bonds of burgeoning affection between Blake and Hayley must have been very strong.

Hayley was a vigorous author with many projects in hand which required illustrations,[†] and he invited Blake to move to Felpham so that they could work side by side. Blake found the invitation alluring—"My fingers Emit sparks of fire with Expectation of my future labours"[‡]—but as usual he was moved more by affection than by interest. He accepted the invitation because he had fallen in love with Felpham and with an enchanting little thatched cottage at the edge of the village facing across an open field to the sea (Fig. on p. 202). He described to Cumberland his

happy alteration ... I have taken a Cottage at Felpham on the Sea Shore of Sussex between Arundel & Chichester. Mr Hayley the Poet is ₐsoon to beₐ my neighbour[;] he is now my frien*d*; to him I owe the happy suggestio*n*, for it was on a visit to him that I fell in love with my Cottage. I have now better prospects than ever[.] The little I want will be easily supplied[;] he has given me a twelvemonths work already, & there is a great deal more in prospect[.] I call myself now Independent. I can be Poet

***

* Smith (*BR* 463). The copy of *Triumphs of Temper* (1799) which Blake kept all his life and which Catherine inherited has not been traced today. On 5 July 1800 Nancy Flaxman asked Hayley "for a Pocket volume from the dear Boy's Library", and on 16 July Hayley sent her "such a little Book as she desires ... by the Favor of Blake".

† Blake's "patient Graver" was working on a copy of Romney's "exquisite portrait" of Tom which Hayley "could not bear to send away" for an engraver to copy it (Hayley letter of 22 July 1800) and on "the two engraved portraits of Him [*Tom*] more faithful ... than the miserably unjust Medallion in the Essay on Sculpture" which were to be printed in November with Hayley's memoir of his son (Hayley, 13 Sept 1800). However, Hayley's "Memoirs of Thomas Alphonso Hayley, the Young Sculptor" were not printed until 1823 in Hayley's autobiography, where they bore no plate, and neither Blake engraving is known.

On this Felpham visit, Blake also made "a small drawing" after Tom's life-size self-portrait (Hayley, 22 July), and he "improv'd, in a Copy of considerable size, the Miltonic design" of Romney (Hayley, 16 July), which has not survived.

‡ Letter of 16 Sept 1800. About 1801, Coleridge wrote: "I have myself once seen ... flashing silver Light proceed from the tips of my fingers" (*Collected Letters of Samuel Taylor Coleridge*, ed. E.L. Griggs [Oxford, 1959], IV, 731).

Painter & Musician* as the Inspiration comes. ... *We* lie on a Pleasant shore[;] it is within a mile of Bognor to which our Fashionables resort[.] My Cottage faces the South about a Quarter of a Mile from the Sea, only corn fields between.† ... it is certainly the sweetest country upon the face of the Earth. ...

... Rending the manacles of Londons Dungeon dark
I have rent the black net & escap'd. See My Cottage at Felpham in joy
Beams over the sea a bright light over France, but the Web & the Veil I
    have left
Behind me at London resists every beam of light; hanging from heaven
    to Earth
Dropping with human gore. Lo! I have left it! I have torn it from my
    limbs[.]
I shake my wings ready to take my flight![27]

On this visit to Felpham, Blake may have stayed at The Fox Inn,‡ whose landlord, Mr Grinder, was the proprietor of the cottage by the sea. Blake was so enchanted by the cottage that he agreed immediately with Mr Grinder to rent it for £20 a year,§ from mid-September.

He joined Hayley on his ride across the fields to drink "a dish of Coffee" with "the Lady of Lavant", Harriet Poole,** in her "peerless Villa".††

---

*   Though we know that Blake composed music for his own songs, this is the only place where he describes himself as a musician.

†   The cornfield was common land, though most of the land in the neighbourhood belonged to the Duke of Richmond.

‡   Since Blake's time, the Fox has been twice rebuilt after fires, the first of which destroyed a ship (perhaps the *Fox*) painted on the wall by the profligate George Morland (d. 1804) in payment of a pub debt (according to a plaque on the wall).
      Reproductions of The Fox Inn and of Hayley's Turret House may be seen in Thomas Wright, *Life of William Blake* (Olney, 1929).

§   The rent is given by Smith (*BR* 461). On 22 July Hayley wrote that Blake has "taken a cottage".
      The landlord may be the George Grinder who was a witness (signing with an X) at the marriage of Thomas Harrad and Elizabeth Challen on 22 May 1793 (typescript *Copy of all the Marriages, Baptisms & Burials 1557–1812 in the Parish Registers* [of St Mary's, Felpham], transcribed by W.H. Challen [British Library: 09915 t 9]).

**   Letter of 27 Nov 1805. Hayley "seiz[d] a pen, while the Coffee is coming to the table" to reply to Johnny Johnson's letter "that has met me this instant in the apartment of our benevolent Paulina, at Lavant" (18 Nov 1801).
      Blake refers to "the Good Genii that Surround Miss Pooles Villa" in his letter of 16 Sept 1800, on the eve of his departure from London.

††   Johnny Johnson, 17 March 1801; Blake refers to it as "the Villa of Lavant blessed & blessing" (27 Jan 1804).
      "Miss Pooles House at Lavant [*was*] built" in 1797 but she apparently did not move in until 1798, according to John Marsh's Diary, XXII, 172 (Huntington Library). The Villa, now known as Robson's Orchard, is on the mid-Lavant road to Chichester; according to an Abstract of Deed dated 13 April 1870 (generously sent to me by Mr Christopher Butcher, the present owner), it included "a Chaise House and Stable".

Lavant was on the post-road from London via Midhurst to Chichester, and Hayley rode there on Tuesday and Friday mornings[28] to get his mail as soon as possible. Soon it became, as Hayley said, Blake's "constant custom to attend me to the House" of Paulina,[29] and Blake in turn became devoted to "our Good Paulina whose Kindness to Me shall recieve recompence in the Presence of Jesus".[30] He remembered with gratitude "when she first mounted me on my beloved Bruno",[31] the horse Tom used to ride, and he once thought of moving to "Lavan*t*, & in or near the road to London for the sake of convenience".[32] Harriet Poole became one of Blake's most loyal friends in Sussex.

On his return to London, Blake described the white thatched cottage to Catherine in great excitement: three rooms and a kitchen on the ground floor* and three bedrooms on the upper floor with "a very fine view of the Sea";† a narrow flintstone-walled garden of "10 yards square"[33] where one could grow vegetables and flowers; rural peace and village neighbours such as Catherine had known in the garden-village of Battersea; and above all independence, free from the encumbrances and dirt of London, freedom to see visions, dream dreams, and speak parables.

Catherine was caught up in Blake's vision "like a flame of many colours of precious jewels",[34] and she used Blake's language to describe it:

Away to Sweet Felpham for Heaven is there[;]
The Ladder of Angels descends thro the air[;]
On the Turret its spiral does softly descend[,]
Thro the village then winds[,] at My Cot it does end . . . .

The Bread of sweet Thought & the Wine of Delight
Feeds the Village of Felpham by day & by night . . . .[35]

Blake's worldly prospects under Hayley's benevolent protection seemed wonderfully promising, and his friends such as "Mr Butts rejoiced aloud, deeming his . . . fortune made".‡

---

* Gilchrist (1863), I, 156–7, describes "A thatched wooden verandah, which runs the whole length of the [*south front of the*] house" and "latticed windows" which are not depicted in the design of "Blakes Cottage at Felpham" in *Milton* pl. 36 and which no longer exist in 1997. The building was probably erected in the seventeenth century.

† Letter of 22 Sept 1800. Gilchrist (*BR* 561–2) says: "Often, in after years, Blake would speak with enthusiasm of the shifting lights on the sea he had watched from these windows." My wife and I have repeatedly admired this sea-view at dawn as the guest of Heather Howell, the generous owner of Blake's Cottage today. Alas, there are now post-World War II bungalows between Blake's Cottage and the sea.

‡ Gilchrist (*BR* 71). Flaxman too was "highly pleased with the exertion of Your [*Hayley's*] usual Benevolence", but he warned that "if he [*Blake*] places any dependence on painting large pictures, for which he is not qualified, either by habit or study, he will be miserably decieved" (19 Aug 1800).

Move to Felpham

On his return to London, Blake began preparations for moving from his Lambeth house, but he was also at work for his friends. In response to Blake's letter of 2 July about his "Deep pit of Melancholy", George Cumberland sent him copies of his *Anecdotes of the Life of Julio Bonasoni* (1793) with "A Plan for the Improvement of the Arts in England" by the formation of National Galleries, and his *Captive of the Castle of Sennaar* (1798), a Utopian novel which Cumberland had suppressed for fear that its radical social, sexual, and political views would attract unwelcome attention from the government. Cumberland also probably reported that he had tried in vain to find customers for Blake's books, perhaps he ordered some of them for himself,* and he asked Blake to help propagate his proposal for National Galleries.

Blake responded on 1 September with characteristic enthusiasm to all these initiatives:

> To have obtained your friendship is better than to have sold ten thousand books ....
>
> Your Vision of the Happy Sophis† I have devour. O most delicious book[,] how canst thou Expect any thing but Envy in Londons accursed walls. You have my dear friend given me a task which I have endeavourd to fulfill[.] I have given a sketch of your Proposal to the Editor of the Monthly Magazine‡ desiring that he will give it to the Public[;] hope he will do so. I have shewn your Bonasoni to Mr Hawkins§ my friend ....

In anticipation of leaving London perhaps for ever, William and Catherine made a round of calls on their friends,[36] urging them to visit Felpham. They intended to leave on Tuesday the 16th, but, as Blake told Hayley that day, "My Dear & too careful & over joyous Woman has Exhausted her strength to such a degree with expectation & gladness added to labour in our removal that I fear it will be Thursday before we can get away from this—City."

---

* Cumberland owned *America* (F), *Europe* (C), *Song of Los* (D), and *Visions* (B), all bound together, plus *Thel* (A), *For Children* (C), and *Songs* (F), with the last of which Blake's recently discovered letter of thanks was apparently kept.

† Sophis is a utopian community in remotest Africa which retains most of the virtues of classical Greece but with liberated women and without war or slaves; for details of surviving copies and of its unpublished sequel, an alternative, primitive Christian Utopia, see *The Captive of the Castle of Sennaar*, ed. G.E. Bentley, Jr (Montreal, Kingston, London, Buffalo: McGill-Queen's University Press, 1991).

‡ Richard Phillips. Blake's letter (signed "A.B.") was not printed in the *Monthly Magazine* for August 1800–January 1801.

§ John Hawkins, the Cornish gentleman who in 1784 tried to raise a subscription to send Blake to study in Rome (*BR* 27–8). On 11 Aug 1800, Hayley wrote to Hawkins that Blake "thought one Circumstance would increase his Felicity ... seeing you also settled in Sussex".

They finally left* in the cool, clear dawn of Thursday 18 September: Blake, his wife Catherine Sophia, his sister Catherine Elizabeth, and "Sixteen heavy boxes & portfolios full of prints".[37] The luggage included all their worldly goods: Blake's library; his notebooks, sketches, manuscripts such as *An Island in the Moon*, *Tiriel*, and *Vala*; watercolours; the proof copy of *The French Revolution* and the remaining copies of *Poetical Sketches* (at least fifteen); his copperplates and copies of his works in Illuminated Printing; blank paper; boxes of gravers, etching needles, wax, varnish, turpentine, and ink; and the crates for his printing press; not to mention clothing, cooking and eating utensils, and furnishings. All this exhausted the packers and filled the chaises.

They "traveld thro a most beautiful country on a most glorious day"; "All was Chearfulness & Good Humour on the Road".

However, they did not arrive at their cottage until almost midnight, "owing to the necessary shifting of our Luggage from one Chaise to another for we had Seven Different Chaises & as many different drivers". By the time Blake and the two Catherines had moved all their dunnage into the cottage and collapsed into their beds,† they must have been exhausted.

Next morning, they explored the cottage with its "thatched roof of rusted gold" and discovered it to be all Blake had promised and more:

> our Cottage ... is more beautiful than I thought i*t*, & more convenient. It is a perfect Model for Cottages & I think for Palaces of Magnificence[,] only Enlarging not altering its proportions & adding ornaments & not principals. Nothing can be more Grand than its Simplicity & Usefulness. Simple without Intricacy it seems to be the Spontaneous Effusion of Humanity congenial to the wants of Man. No other formed House can ever please me so well nor shall I ever be perswaded I believe that it can be improved either in Beauty or Use.[38]

When the Catherines explored Felpham, they found a few score houses and a few hundred people,[39] a public house (prop. Mr Grinder), a smithy (William Stone, blacksmith), a mill (prop. Mr Cosens), and the Norman church of St Mary (rector, Combe Miller) with its checkered flintstone tower and its ring of four ancient bells which could be heard all over the village.[40]

It was a real farm village, with farm beasts in the streets, farm labourers

---

* The coach from London to Chichester left from the Bolt-in-Ton, Fleet Street, and Golden Cross, Charing Cross, on Tuesdays, Thursdays, and Saturdays ([Alexander Hay], *Chichester Guide* [?1804], 35), and Blake said that from Chichester "the Coach goes three times a week to London" (letter of 11 Sept 1801).

† Blake and Catherine shared a double-bed, even in sickness, for Hayley had once "the pain of seeing both confined to their Bed" (singular) (15 July 1802).

in the pub, and farm harvest from the rich fields all around them that autumn. In the field near their cottage and the sea, "Lambs bleat to the sea-fowls cry".[41] On market days they might overhear a discontented drover in the lane muttering to St Anthony,

You can pook and you can shove,
But a Sussex pig he wun't be druv.[42]

The Blakes loved it all.

Felpham is a sweet place for Study, because it is more Spiritual than London[.] Heaven opens here on all sides her Golden Gates; her windows are not obstructed by vapours[.] Voices of Celestial inhabitants are more distinctly heard & their forms more distinctly seen ....

The Villagers of Felpham are not meer Rustics[,] they are polite & modest.* Meat is cheaper than in London, but the sweet air & the voices of winds trees & birds & the odours of the happy ground makes it a dwelling for immortals.

Chichester is a very handsom[e] City Seven miles from us[;] we can get most Conveniences there. ... what we have seen [*in the Country*] is Most Beautiful, & the People are Genuine Saxons[,] handsomer than the people about London.[†]

The great magnate of the neighbourhood was the Duke of Richmond,[‡] who owned much of the land in and around Felpham and whose great estate at Goodwood was on the route from Felpham to Lavant. Other substantial gentlemen with land abutting Felpham on the route to Chichester were William Brereton,[§] Justice of the Peace, whose estate was at Nytimber,

---

* "*A*ll orders and descriptions of people in this favored spot [*Felpham*] are remarkable for the amenity and cheerfulness of their manners and for civility and hospitality" ([Richard Dally], *The Bognor, Arundel and Littlehampton Guide* [Chichester: Printed by William Mason, 1828], 55).

† Letters of 21, 22 Sept, 2 Oct 1800. In 1804, Chichester (pop. 3,752) still had its stone wall and the city gate on the Eastern (Felpham) side. There were markets on Wednesday and Saturday which were especially notable for oysters and lobsters ([Alexander Hay], *The Chichester Guide, and Directory* [Chichester: J. Seagrave (?1804)], 31, 34).

‡ General Charles Lennox (1735–1806), K.G., 3rd Duke of Richmond, Lord Lieutenant of Sussex (1763), Minister Plenipotentiary (1765), Secretary of State (1766–67), Master-General of Ordnance and member of cabinet (1782–95), vigorous advocate (1782) and later bitter opponent of parliamentary reform and universal suffrage.

§ William Brereton (1757–1820) had been at Eton, St John's College (Cambridge), and Lincoln's Inn. He came from a military family; his grandfather had been Lieutenant-Colonel in the Horse Guards; his father, Colonel Cholmondley Brereton, was killed in battle in 1760; and his uncle, Lieutenant Francis Brereton, of the Guards, was killed at Fontenoy in 1745.

   Much of my information about Sussex gentlemen and Justices of the Peace originates from correspondence in 1979 with Professor Roussel Sargent of Horsham, Sussex.

Pagham; John Peachey,* J.P., of Rumboldswyke and North Bersted; and John Quantock,† J.P., with property at Midhurst and South Mundham (Pl. 84). All these men later became important in Blake's life and his myth.[43]

Blake would have met their labourers and their tenant-farmers, and he was soon known in the neighbourhood as a sympathetic friend. When war and blockade caused agricultural distress, Blake's sympathies were with the poor, who were "compell[ed] to live upon a Crust of bread",[44] and with the farmer in "the witherd field [who] ... plows for bread in vain".[45] Jerusalem's "Villages die of the Famine", and "Sussex shuts up her villages".[46]

> One Mite wrung from the Labrers hands
> Shall buy & sell the Misers Lands
>
> ("Auguries of Innocence" ll. 81–2 [Ballads MS p. 17])

Indeed Blake looked forward to the day when "The poor Smite their opressors[,] they awake up to the harvest",‡ and he may have expressed such opinions to his new friends. Certainly he believed that "the peaceable Villagers have always been forward in expressing their kindness for us", and three years later, when Blake was in trouble, it "struck a consternation thro all the Villages round" Felpham.[47]

Best of all for Blake at Felpham,

> Work will go on here with God speed.—A roller & two harrows lie before my window.§ I met a plow on my first going out at my gate the first morning after my arrival & the Plowboy said to the Plowman, "Father, The Gate is Open."—I have begun to Work & find that I can work with greater pleasure than ever.
>
> I am more famed in Heaven for my works than I could well concieve[.]

---

* John Peachey (1752–1830) had been a student of New College (Oxford) and barrister of the Middle Temple.

† John Quantock (1742–1820) had been Captain in the Queen's Bays (Second Regiment of the Dragoon Guards) but sold his commission about 1782. He was a Major of the Sussex Volunteers, Deputy-Lieutenant of Sussex in 1803, and Mayor of Chichester in 1807. His son Matthew Heather Quantock (1783–1812), who drowned while skating, was buried in Chichester Cathedral with a monument by John Flaxman portraying John Quantock and his wife Mary mourning and with an epitaph by William Hayley.

‡ *Vala* p. 117, l. 19.

> the Opressors of Albion in every City & Village
> ... mock at the Labourers Limbs! they mock at his starvd children[;]
> They buy his Daughters that they may have power to sell his Sons
>
> (*Jerusalem* pl. 30, ll. 27–9)

§ "*My* window" must have overlooked the road beside the cottage, indicating that Blake's study and printing-room was the first room on the west side.

In my Brain are studies & Chambers filld with books & pictures of old
which I wrote & painted in ages of Eternity, before my mortal life ....[48]

Visions of Felpham

In Felpham nature opened her beauties to him with a minuteness unheard
in his poetry before. "Immediately the Lark mounted with a loud trill from
Felphams Vale".[49]

> He leads the Choir of Day! trill, trill, trill, trill,
> Mounting upon the wings of light into the Great Expans*e*,
> Reechoing against the lovely blue & shining heavenly Shell:
> His little throat labours with inspiration; every feather
> On throat & breast & wings vibrates with the effluence Divine
>   (*Milton* pl. 31, ll. 30–4)

Even the humblest creatures draw his sympathy and love:

> The Spider sits in his labourd Web, eager watching for the Fly[;]
> Presently comes a famishd Bird & takes away the Spider[;]
> His Web is left all desolate, that his little anxious heart
> So careful wove: & spread it out with sighs and weariness
>   (*Vala* p. 18, ll. 4–7)

The first great gift of Felpham to Blake was to open his eyes to new kinds
of natural beauty.

Two days after they had settled the sticks and feathers of their nest, Blake
wrote to Butts that "My Wife & Sister are ... courting Neptune for an
Embrace",[50] and when he had finished his letter, he probably followed them
down the narrow lane called Straight to the lonely pebbled shore.* There,
as he looked over the dancing sea, he had what he described to Butts as "My
first Vision of Light":

> Over Sea over Land
> My Eyes did Expand

---

* The beach at Felpham, "one of the loneliest spots on the coast", is the site of the crime in Dorothy
Sayers, "The Unsolved Puzzle of the Man with No Face" in her *Lord Peter*, ed. James Sandoe (New
York: Flare Books, 1972), 212–14. The Sussex coast has long been receding and the peninsula of
"Selsey ... submitted to be devour By the waves", but his "Emanation rose above The flood, and
was nam'd Chichester" (*Jerusalem* pl. 40, ll. 48–50) when, in 1075, the Bishopric of Selsey was trans-
ferred to Chichester because of erosion of the coast.

Into regions of air
Away from all Care[,]
Into regions of fire
Remote from Desire
. . ..
In particles bright
The jewels of Light
Distinct shone & clear—
Amazd & in fear
I each particle gazed
Astonishd Amazed
For each was a Man
Human formd. Swift I ran
For they beckond to me
Remote by the Sea
Saying: "Each grain of Sand
Every Stone on the Land
Each rock & each hill
Each fountain & rill
Each herb & each tree
Mountain hill Earth & Sea
Cloud Meteor & Star
Are Men Seen Afar"
. . ..
My Eyes more & more
Like a Sea without shore
Continue Expanding
The Heavens commanding
Till the Jewels of Light[,]
Heavenly Men beaming bright[,]
Appeard as One Man
Who Complacent began
My limbs to infold
In his beams of bright gold
. . ..
Such the Vision to me
Appear'd on the Sea*

---

* Letter of 2 Oct 1800. This vision of the Heavenly Man who infolded Blake's limbs "In his beams of bright gold" is strikingly similar to his vision of Los, "a terrible flaming Sun": "I became One Man with him" (*Milton* pl. 20, ll. 6, 12).

Blake's work was indeed well begun.

This was their first experience of sea and sand and shore, and they delighted in courting Neptune for an embrace in fair weather and in hearing the surf roaring in the distance in storm while they were snug in their cottage. The shore world was wonderful to them in discoveries natural and spiritual: "A Piece of Sea Weed serves for a Barometer[;] it gets wet & dry as the weather gets so".[51]

> To see a World in a Grain of Sand
> And a Heaven in a Wild Flower[,]
> Hold Infinity in the palm of your hand
> And Eternity in an hour
>
> ("Auguries of Innocence" ll. 1–4 [Ballads MS p. 13])

It was not only natural beauties that Blake saw transformed at Felpham. Near Felpham were "trees & fields full of Fairy elves",[52] and once, he said, when

> I was walking alone in my garden, there was great stillness among the branches and flowers and more than common sweetness in the air; I heard a low and pleasant sound, and I knew not whence it came. At last I saw the broad leaf of a flower move, and underneath I saw a procession of creatures of the size and colour of green and gray grasshoppers, bearing a body laid out on a rose leaf, which they buried with songs, and then disappeared. It was a fairy funeral.*

These funeral fairies seem to be from rural folklore.[53] Later, however, Blake calls fairies "elemental beings", the spirits "of the Four Elements", "rulers of the vegetable world", and "Fairies of Albion afterwards Gods of the Heathen".[54]

Blake's sister stayed in Felpham for a week to help them move in, and she came again briefly about the same time next year,[55] when Blake walked from Felpham, past Goodwood House of the Duke of Richmond, to meet her in Lavant.[56] The brevity of her visits was doubtless because the two Catherine Blakes did not get on with each other:

---

* Cunningham (*BR* 489). The account begins somewhat implausibly: "'Did you ever see a fairy's funeral, madam?' he once said to a lady, who happened to sit by him in company. 'Never, sir!' was the answer. 'I have,' said Blake, 'but not before last night.'" The only times Blake had a garden of his own were in Lambeth (1790–1800) and Felpham (1800–3), but the times he dined out on such stories were in the 1820s. The story probably came from John Varley, Blake's credulous admirer of 1818–27, who gave "much curious information" to Cunningham in 1829 (*BR* 375), but "last night" may be an embroidery by Cunningham.

Fairies and elves appear occasionally in Blake's poetry, but never in terms as conventional, not to say darling, as in Cunningham's anecdote.

Must my Wife live in my Sister's bane,
Or my Sister survive on my Loves pain?[57]

The walk to Lavant was entrancing,

With Angels planted in Hawthorn bowers
And God himself in the passing hours

and Blake saw on the wind his father and his brother Robert and "my Brother John the evil one". But he also saw terrors.

... before my way
A frowning Thistle implores my stay.
What to others a trifle appears
Fills me full of smiles or tears;
For double the vision my Eyes do see,
And a double vision is always with me.
With my inward Eye 'tis an old Man grey;
With my outward, a Thistle across my way.

The Old Man tells him that

Los the terrible thus hath sworn,
"Because thou backward dost return
Poverty Envy old age & fear
Shall bring thy Wife upon a bier"
. . . .
I struck the Thistle with my foot
And broke him up from his delving root
. . . .
Then Los appeard in all his power:
In the Sun he appeard descending before
My face in fierce flames[;] in my double sight
Twas outward a Sun: inward Los in his might
. . . .
"We eat little[,] we drink less;"
"This Earth breeds not our happiness."
"Another Sun feeds our life's streams,"
"We are not warmed with thy beams;"
"Thou measurest not the Time to me"
"Nor yet the Space that I do see;"
"My Mind is not with thy light arrayd."
"Thy terrors shall not make me afraid."

When I had my Defiance given,
The Sun stood trembling in heaven
. . . .
Los flamd in my path & the Sun was hot
With the bows of my Mind & the Arrows of Thought—
My bow string fierce with Ardour breathes,
My arrows glow in their golden sheaves;
My brothers & father march before;
The heavens drop with human gore.

Now I a fourfold vision see
And a fourfold vision is given to me;
Tis fourfold in my supreme delight
And three fold in soft Beulahs night
And twofold Always. May God us keep
From Single vision & Newton's sleep![58]

Surrounded by the fourfold vision, Blake is protected from the mortal terrors of "Poverty Envy old age & fear". He struggled with the terrors and transformed them.

Work with Hayley

To Blake's delight, on their arrival "Mr Hayley recievd us with his usual brotherly affection, [*and*] I have begun to work."[59] The first new work to which Hayley set Blake was doubtless the broadsheet ballad of *Little Tom the Sailor* which Hayley wrote on 22 September in order to relieve the necessities of the children of the Widow Spicer of Folkestone. Blake was pressed into service to etch the text in relief (as in Illuminated Printing) with head- and tail-pieces after his own designs (Pl. 85) and to print it—and perhaps Blake was expected to give his labour and genius as charitably as Hayley had. Copies of the ballad, dated 5 October, were printed somewhat sporadically; as late as 26 November Catherine Blake was still pulling copies, some in black and some in colour.*

Blake moved his paraphernalia of engraving—copper, wax, gravers,

---

* Letter of 26 Nov 1800. A copy printed in sepia and strikingly hand-coloured is in a private collection (*BBS* 224).

  Blake's printing press was probably set up in his cottage in the first room one entered from the road. Notice that Catherine is printing in the cottage while Blake is engraving and drawing in Hayley's Turret House.

burins, acid, paper, grinding tools—to the study of Hayley's Turret House in the centre of Felpham, and there he went every day and all day to make drawings and engravings for Hayley's works—Hayley repeatedly refers in his letters to the "amiable artist now working by my side on the plates".*

> And Felpham Billy rode out every morn
> Horseback with [*Blake*] over the fields of corn†

Hayley on his horse Hidalgo and Blake on Bruno.

In such intimate association, Hayley's benevolence and Blake's enthusiasm had to be finely tuned to make the relationship work. And at first it plainly worked very well indeed.

Hayley commissioned Blake to decorate his library with oval heads of European literary worthies from Homer to Cowper.‡ The likenesses were traditional ones, but the background details were invented by Blake. As the project evolved, Hayley managed to focus it more and more upon his dead son; five of the portraits were after drawings by Tom, and Blake's copy of Tom's self-portrait (Pl. 83B) occupied a place of honour among these literary titans on Hayley's library walls.

Blake plunged into the work with characteristic energy. On 26 November 1800 he said that he had been "Absorbed by the poets Milton, Homer, Camoens, Ercilla, Ariosto, and Spenser, whose physiognomies have been my delightful study". The growing burden of work Hayley was finding for him prevented him from continuing at such a rate, but by 11 September 1801 he was confident that "Mr Hayleys Library . . . is still unfinishd but is in a finishing way & looks well". Hayley was manifestly pleased with the Heads of the Poets (as they are somewhat inaccurately called), and it may have been these likenesses which suggested to Hayley that he should encourage Blake, as he had Romney, to focus upon portrait-painting.

---

* Letter of 25 July 1801. On 1 Oct 1801, Hayley said that "the warmhearted indefatigable Blake works daily by my side"; on 22 Nov 1801 he spoke of the "artist who works constantly in my study"; and on 16 May 1802 he said that Blake "is at this moment by my side, representing on Copper . . .". On the other hand, Hayley remembered "calling at the cottage in Felpham . . . [*and*] finding Blake grinding away, graver in hand" (see *BR* [2] under August 1802).

† "And his legs", ll. 21–2, Notebook p. 22; Blake calls himself "Death" in the savage poem. Blake must have done a good deal of riding while he was at Felpham, for Lavant, to which he and Hayley went regularly, was eleven miles away. His horse Bruno would have been stabled at Hayley's stable.

‡ The portraits represent (1) Cowper, (2) Spenser, (3) Chaucer, (4) Cicero, (5) Voltaire, (6) Shakespeare, (7) Dryden, (8) Milton, (9) Tasso, (10) Camoens, (11) Ercilla, (12) Pope, (13) Otway, (14) Dante, (15) Demosthenes, (16) Homer, (17) Klopstock, and (18) Thomas Hayley. Chaucer, Milton, Otway, Dante, Klopstock and Tom Hayley replaced Cowley, Sappho, Euripides, Ariosto, Horace, and Gibbon in an earlier version of the plan (*BR* 69–70). The finished portraits, now in the City Art Gallery, Manchester, are reproduced in Butlin pl. 436–53.

Commissions for the Reverend Joseph Thomas

Blake had commissions from patrons besides Hayley. On 31 July 1801 Flaxman wrote to Blake care of Hayley:

> The Revd Joseph Thomas of Epsom desires You will at Your leisure, make a few Sketches of ... any Size you please from Milton's Comus for Five Guineas, he also desires You will make two designs in bister or Indian Ink, from Shakespeare's Troylus & Cressida, Coriolanus, either of the 3 plays of Henry 6th, Richard the 3^d or Henry the 8th, each design for one play for which he will give a Guinea each . . ..
>
> [*Nancy and I*] are pleased with the reciprocal affection of the Bards . . ..*

These were commissions to be relished, particularly that for Milton. Not only had "Milton lovd me in childhood & shewd me his face",[60] but Hayley was an authority on Milton, and his library was rich in Miltoniana. Blake's own *Milton A Poem* was written during these Felpham years, and it must have been profoundly influenced by his renewed study of Milton generated by Mr Thomas's commission for designs to *Comus*.

However, it took a little time for Blake to get to them. Eleven weeks later he thanked Flaxman for recommending "Mr Thomas your friend ... [*who*] has been at Felpham & did me the favor to call on me. I have promisd to send my Designs for Comus when I have done them directed to you".[61]

Thomas was dazzled by Blake's designs—in 1805 Nancy Flaxman said that "he wishes to collect all B—has done"†—and eventually Blake made for him eight illustrations for *Comus* (1801) (Pl. 86), six for Shakespeare (*Richard III* [*c.* 1806], *Julius Caesar* [1806], *Hamlet* [1806], *As You Like It* [1806], *Henry VIII* [1809], and *Henry VIII* Part I [1809]), twelve for *Paradise Lost* (1807), six for Milton's "Ode on the Morning of Christ's Nativity" (1809) (Pl. 87), plus *Songs of Innocence and of Experience* (Q). At a

---

* Flaxman specifies the size of the Shakespeare designs (12″ x 8½″) so that they would fit into Mr Thomas's copy of the Second Folio (1632), now in the British Museum Print Room.

   On 7 Oct 1801 Flaxman wrote: "the little commissions I troubled you with in my last are such as one friend offers unwillingly to another on account of the Scanty recompence ... when they are done let me have them & I will take care to get the money for you".

   Joseph Thomas (1765–1811) was the Rector of Epsom. "William Blake, Esq." subscribed to Thomas's *Religious Emblems* (1809), as did Flaxman, who had made a monument for Thomas's father-in-law John Parkhurst in 1797. Facts about Joseph Thomas are set out in Leslie Parris, "William Blake's Mr. Thomas", *Times Literary Supplement*, 5 Dec 1968, 1390.

† Letter of Sept 1805; "I have a little commission to give to Blake for him". Thomas also bought copies of Young's *Night Thoughts* (1797) and Blair's *Grave* (1808) with Blake's designs.

guinea per design plus £10.10.0 for the *Songs*,[62] this comes to £44.2.0, perhaps half a year's income.

Such commissions for original art, rather than for copy-engraving, were delicious to Blake, but they divided his loyalties and his energies—some of the Thomas commissions were not completed until eight years later. Already he was behind-hand with his commissions from Thomas Butts, and Hayley was impatient for him to finish the portraits for his library and the engravings for his life of Cowper.

Must the duties of life each other cross?
Must every joy be dung & dross?
Must my dear Butts feel cold neglect
Because I give Hayley his due respect?[63]

Hayley thought of Blake as an indefatigable worker[64] and as "the kind enthusiastic engraver at my side",[65] but he had far less regard for Blake as an original artist. For the sake of Blake's prosperity and the progress of the Cowper biography, Hayley wished Blake to confine his energies to copy-engraving and to Hayley's interests. As Blake wrote a few months after the commission from Joseph Thomas: "I find on all hands great objections to my doing any thing but the meer drudgery of business & intimations that if I do not confine myself to this I shall not live."*

Miniature Portraits

Hayley felt that as Blake had left London "for the sake of settling near me . . . it seems to be a duty incumbent on me to use every liberal method, in my power, to obtain for his industrious ingenuity, the notice and favour of my Countrymen".[66] He therefore undertook to find suitable work for Blake among his friends in Sussex, and "I have taught Him to paint in miniature & in Truth He has improved his excellent versatile Talents very much in this retired scene, where He has constant access to several very fine works of art by my Friend Romney, & by that very wonderful young artist, my dear departed child!"†

---

* Letter of 10 Jan 1802. On 11 Sept 1801 Blake promised to send Butts some drawings soon, but it was apparently not until 22 Nov 1802 that he sent the first two pictures; on 6 July 1803 he sent another and reported that he had seven more "in great forwardness", and only on 16 Aug 1803 did he send the last drawings, which "I believe about balances our account" from 1799.

† Hayley letter of 25 Feb 1801. Blake is known to have made miniatures of Thomas Butts (Pl. 92A), Betsy Butts (1809) (Pl. 92B), and their son Tommy (1809), of William Hayley (1801) (*BR* [2], 9 May 1801), of Johnny Johnson (Pl. 89), of Mrs Hayley (*BR* 80), and of Cowper after Romney (*BR* 79), and he almost certainly made others for Hayley's acquaintances in Sussex which have disappeared as that of Johnny Johnson did for many years. In particular, Blake was encouraged to imitate the style of Hayley's friend the miniaturist Jeremiah Meyers (1735–89) (*BRS* 15).

At first Blake was enthusiastic: "My present employments are in Miniature Painting[.] Miniature is become a Goddess in my Eyes & my Friends in Sussex say that I Excell in the pursuit. I have a great many orders & they Multiply."[67]

He was identified in the neighbourhood as a Miniature Painter,[68] and the recognition and commissions which his portraits brought him must have been agreeable.

Blake laboured for two years on his miniature of Butts.[69] When the portrait was completed (Pl. 74A), the result did not please him, for, as he wrote on 22 November 1802, "If you have not nature before you for Every Touch you cannot Paint Portrait." He was determined to make "a good likeness" of Butts, and by 6 July 1803 he was confident that "I am become a likeness taker & succeed admirably well. *B*ut this is not to be atchievd without the original sitting before you for Every tou*c*h, all likenesses from memory being necessarily very very defective".

Part of his study may have been to make a likeness of himself (Pl. 88), carefully copying his own features* in the mirror but of course reversing right and left. The portrait is of a man in early middle age with a high forehead, hair receding from a widow's peak, and compelling eyes. Indeed, the eyes dominate the picture; here is Power. They make clear why those who met Blake felt a force in him which was either inspiration or madness. They make it easy to see why, for Blake, the world is a world of vision:

> What immortal hand or eye
> Could frame thy fearful symmetry?

But miniature likenesses are far removed from visionary art.[70] In time Blake became impatient with miniature:

> When H—y finds out what you cannot do
> That is the very thing he[']ll set you to
>
> (Notebook p. 35)

though he did not entirely abandon the practice. Miniature finishing in the illuminated books and in fresco was one thing, miniature portraits quite another.

Hayley's Biography of William Cowper

Hayley was an irrepressible memorializer, and the deaths of friends sent

---

* The artist, subject, and date of the portrait are not clearly established.

him straight to his desk to commemorate them in sonnet or in epitaph.[*] When Tom died, Hayley determined to write a book about him, and when his dear friend William Cowper died in the spring of 1800 he was equally determined to foster a fitting biography of him.

With Tom, all the papers and facts were in his own possession, but with Cowper the situation was far more intricate. The biography should of course include Cowper's letters, which Blake called "Perhaps or rather Certainly the very best letters that ever were published",[71] and Cowper's papers and the Cowper family interest were controlled by Cowper's redoubtable cousin Lady Hesketh, who "almost adord her Cousin the poet & thought him all perfection".[72] Lady Hesketh was determined that no hint should appear in print of Cowper's manifest madness, partly because she was afraid that this would confirm rumours of his affiliation to the Methodists.[73] No biography of value could be written without her help, and no honest biography could be written with it.

Hayley proposed that Lady Hesketh should write the biography and that he should provide engravings for it (22 July 1800). Lady Hesketh was not willing to appear so publicly in print, and she thought that she could control the biography by controlling Hayley's access to Cowper's papers. She therefore gave permission for Hayley to write the biography, and, so long as she trusted Hayley's discretion, she provided Cowper papers for the life.

Hayley therefore had to spend much of his biographical energy in supplication and cajoling, tasks at which he was very good. On 25 February 1801 he wrote to Lady Hesketh:

> pray, my dear Lady, have you the little picture of his Mother.—I think the Life should contain an engraving of that Portrait, as well as of her Son, & I have an excellent enthusiastic Creature, a Friend of Flaxman, under my own Eye residing in this village; He is by profession an Engraver . . . . I intend that this very amiable Man shall execute, under my own Inspection, all the plates for the Work; & I am persuaded He will produce a Head of Cowper, that will surprise & delight you; & assuredly it will be executed <u>con amore</u>, as he idolizes the Poet, & will have as fine a portrait to work from, as ever pencil produced.

To demonstrate the qualities of the painting and of the engraver, and to test

---

[*]   "Hayley wrote epitaphs upon his dearest friends before their eyes were well closed—a sort of poetical carrion crow!" (Caroline Bowles to Robert Southey, *The Correspondence of Robert Southey with Caroline Bowles*, ed. Edward Dowden [London & Dublin, 1881], II, 64), and he confessed that "I have been a great Scribbler of Epitaphs in the last month" (18 Nov 1801).

Lady Hesketh's compliability, Hayley had Blake make a miniature of Romney's crayon portrait of Cowper (Pl. 89) which he sent to her.

This was a tactical mistake, for she responded to its hints of Cowper's madness with

> a degree of horror, which I shall not recover from in haste! ... I think it dreadful! Shocking! and ... I intreat you on my Knees not to suffer so horrible a representation of our angelic friend to ... disfigure a work I long so much to see .... I cannot bear to have it in my possession nor wou'd I for worlds, shew it to any one.... [*I intreat*] that you will not be so cruel as to multiply this fatal resemblance, by having the picture engrav'd[!][74]

Hayley replied suavely and disingenuously: "you may be confident that I shall endeavour not to wound yr affectionate Feelings on this Subject—The experiment I have already made has convinced me that no Engraving from the work of Romney would satisfy yr Imagination".[75]

Blake's work on the engraving after Romney went on steadily, but Hayley thought it prudent to pray for his success in a poem addressed to his dead son:

> My Angel Artist in the skies[,]
>   Thou mayst inspirit & controul
> a Failing Brother's Hand & Eyes
>   or temper his eccentric Soul.
>
> Now to the feeling Blake attend[,]
>   His Copies of dear Cowper view
> And make his Portraits of our Friend
>   Perfect in Truth as Thou art true[.][76]

Friendship with Johnny Johnson

Hayley was assiduous in introducing the feeling Blake to his wide acquaintance, both to gentry and aristocrats in the neighbourhood and to literary friends through his very extensive correspondence.* The most amiable and

---

* The literary correspondents to whom he introduced Blake include John Carr (traveller), Daniel Parker Coke (politician), Charlotte Collins, Samuel Greatheed, Lady Hesketh (Cowper's cousin), Johnny Johnson (Cowper's cousin), Samuel Rose (solicitor), Charlotte Smith (poet and novelist), and Joseph Cooper Walker (Irish antiquarian). Among the most important of the local gentry to

enthusiastic among his correspondents was the young divinity student Johnny Johnson, Cowper's cousin, whom Hayley was consulting about his life of Cowper. Blake described Johnny as being, like himself, "a happy Abstract, known by all his Friends as the most innocent forgetter of his own Interests",[77] and Johnny sent fond, frivolous greetings to Blake in many of his letters to Hayley: "Remember me most kindly to our dear friend Blake, and the Duck to whom he is a Drake!"* Indeed, Johnny made an appointment to call on Thomas Butts, presumably to see his collection of Blake's drawings, but forgot to go.[78]

Blake also made a portrait miniature of Johnny when he visited Felpham in January 1802, representing the earnest cleric rather than the "innocent forgetter of his own Interests" (Pl. 90), and he painted for him pictures of Cowper's "Olney Bridge", of "Winter", and of "Evening". Johnny was a good though careless friend to Blake.

Friendship with the Composer John Marsh and his Son the Poet Edward Garrard Marsh

A more substantial friend was the Chichester attorney John Marsh, whose energies were chiefly expended in composing and fostering music and in superintending his extensive estates. He had a very large house in Chichester,† where he entertained Sussex friends and travelling musicians, and he frequently visited his good friend Miss Poole in Lavant. On 22 October 1800,

---

whom Hayley introduced Blake are John Marsh and his poetical son Edward Garrard Marsh (b. 1783) and Harriet Poole; the local aristocrats comprehended Earl Bathurst (Lavant), the Earl of Egremont (Petworth), the Countess of Portarlington (sister of the Earl of Bute), and the Duke of Richmond (Goodwood House). Through Hayley Blake also met R. Dally (solicitor), William Guy (physician), William Metcalfe (Hayley's servant), William Meyer (artist), Joseph Seagrave (printer), and Mr Waller (carver).

    Charlotte Collins proposed to Hayley that Blake should engrave the drawing by her neighbour Mr Spilsbury of Mrs Poyntz's prize bull, but nothing came of the proposal to unite the interests of "these Knights of the Brush, & the Burin" (28 June 1802).

*   Letter of 17 March 1801. Johnny sends greetings to Blake in his letters to Hayley of 17 March, 17 June, 13 Aug, 13, 21 Oct, 2 Nov 1801, 30 Jan, 17 Feb, 23, 31 March, 10 April, 20 May, 11 June, 7, 22 July, 3 Dec 1802, 21 April, 22 Sept 1803, 6, 13, 27 Jan 1804, and Hayley sent Blake's greetings to Johnny in letters of 19 Nov 1800 (*BR* [2]), 3 Sept, 1, 25 Oct, 18 Nov 1801, 18 Jan, 3 Feb, 11 March, 16 May, 6, 28–9 June, 6 Aug 1802.

    Johnny's mature opinion of Blake was that he was "a pupil of Fuseli, but tho' a worthy creature, more eccentric than his master" (14 June 1822; see *BR* [2]).

†   In Jan 1802 he was taxed for forty-nine windows but managed to get the total reduced to forty-four (the Journal of John Marsh [Huntington Library], XXIII, 70–1). In 1802 his "Clear Income" after taxes, etc., was £1,058.3.0 (Vol. XXII, 148–9). He had moved from Canterbury to Chichester in 1787 (XXII, 162).

Wishing to introduce [*his 17-year-old son*] Ed.ᵈ to M.ʳ Hayley, I . . . drove him to Felpham where after having some coffee with M.ʳ H: we went with him . . . to M.ʳ Blake's an Engraver M.ʳ H. had lately brought down from London & settled in a Cottage at Felpham, in order to prepare some ornamental Engravings, Vignettes &.ᶜ for his Works. Here M.ʳ Hayley gave me a Ballad he had written, called yᵉ little Sailor Boy which M.ʳ Blake had engraved & ornamented with a small Plate at yᵉ top & bottom, which Ballad as we drove home I began setting to music . . . .*

Marsh clearly liked Blake and may have heard Blake "say how much he preferred a cat to a dog as a companion because she was so much more quiet in her expression of attachment".[79] Eighteen months later, when "our white Cat produced 4 white Kittens", "we saved [one] for M.ʳ Blake of Felpham, (M.ʳ Hayley's Friend)".[80] It is agreeable to picture Blake, sitting quietly for once, with a white kitten playing with its tail on his lap, or even perhaps, like the Pythagorean in *An Island in the Moon* (¶3, 1), "talking of virtuous cats".

Marsh's son Edward Garrard became a steadfast friend of Hayley, despite the difference in their ages, and they often exchanged poetry in their letters. When the young man came home to Chichester between his terms at Wadham College, Oxford, he frequently walked out to dine with Hayley at Felpham, sometimes staying the night. On these visits he saw Blake working with Hayley, and he plainly came to know him well, even adopting his very words. On 8 February 1802 he wrote to Hayley about his composition "written for the most part, while I was walking homeward from the land of inspiration, or (to use the words of the poetical sculptor) 'from Felpham, mild village'".† "The land of inspiration" and "Felpham, mild village" are indeed Blake-like phrases, and Edward Marsh's use of them demonstrates considerable intimacy with Blake.

Hayley, Edward Marsh, and Blake all composed songs for music, and two weeks later Edward Marsh wrote to Hayley: "I long to hear M.ʳ Blake's devotional air, though (I fear) I should have been very aukward in the attempt to give notes to his music. His ingenuity will however (I doubt not) discover some method of preserving his compositions upon paper, though he is not very well versed in bars and crochets".[81] But alas! no music by Blake is known to have survived.

---

* *BR* (2). Edward Garrard Marsh had already won a prize for verse at Mr Richardson's school in 1800 (The Journal of John Marsh, XXI, 55). The voluminous musical publications of John Marsh apparently do not include his setting of Hayley's *Little Tom the Sailor*.

† *BRS* 18. In his letter of 21 Feb 1802, he corrected himself: "I have some idea I mistitled [our friend *Blake*] in my last a poetical sculptor instead of a poetical engraver".

    Years later, on 14 Oct 1806 E.G. Marsh refers to "M.ʳ Blake's sentiment . . . that every Englishman ought to be a judge of painting" (*BRS* 44), but on 9 Jan 1810 wrote to Hayley: "you never made a happier exchange than when you employed her [*Caroline Watson*] instead of Blake" in the new prints for Cowper (*BRS* 60).

Blake plainly reciprocated Edward Marsh's admiration, and in his letter to Hayley of 27 January 1804 he wrote:

God bless & preserve You ... & with you my much admired & respected Edward the Bard of Oxford whose verses still sound upon my Ear like the distant approach of things mighty & magnificent[,] like the sound of harps which I hear before the Suns rising[,] like the remembrance of Felphams waves & of the Glorious & far beaming Turret, like the Villa of Lavant[,] blessed & blessing ....*

The charm of the verses may have been partly in the manner in which they were delivered, for the young man's poetry in his letters seems to a twenty-first-century eye even more stereotyped than Hayley's.[†]

Learning Greek and Hebrew with Hayley

Blake spent with Hayley not only hours of labour but hours of recreation also. Hayley was a linguistic virtuoso, and, when he discovered that Blake had no Greek and was eager to learn it, he began teaching him. On 8 November 1801 he told Johnny Johnson, who was editing the second edition of Cowper's translation of Homer: "Blake & I read every Evening that Copy of the Iliad, which yr namesake of St pauls [*Joseph Johnson*] was so good as to send me, comparing it with the 1st Edition & with the Greek as we proceed". And three months later, he wrote: "Here is instantaneously a Title page for Thee, & a Greek motto, which I & <u>Blake</u> who is just become a <u>Grecian</u> & literally learning the Language consider as a <u>happy Hit</u>!"[82]

A year later Blake was still diligently studying. On 30 January 1803 he wrote to his brother:

I go on Merrily with my Greek[‡] & Lati*n*; am very sorry that I did not begin to learn languages early in life as I find it very Eas*y*; am now

---

* It is difficult to believe that Marsh is also "Oxford, immortal Bard!" who spoke "the words of God" "with eloquence" over Albion in *Jerusalem* pl. 46, ll. 7–8.

† E.G. Marsh letter to Hayley, 6 Nov 1802:

> Postscript
> You'll let the Meyers and Mr Blake
> My kind remembrances partake[.]

‡ There are Greek inscriptions in *Vala* p. 3 (from the New Testament), *Jerusalem* pl. 4, Laocoon, his engraving for Lavater's *Aphorisms* (1788), and his marginalia to Thornton's translation of *The Lord's Prayer* p. 1. For arguments for and against Blake's responsibility for the learned annotations and translation of Sophocles, see Michael Phillips, "William Blake and the Sophocles Manuscript Notebook" and G. E. Bentley, Jr, "William Blake and the Sophocles Enigma", *Blake*, XXXI (1997), 44–71.

learning my Hebre*w*: [*Hebrew for aleph beth gimmel.*]* I read Greek as flu-
ently as an Oxford scholar & the Testament is my chief master[;]† astonishing indeed is the English Translation[,] it is almost word for word & if
the Hebrew Bible is as well translated which I do not doubt it is we need not
doubt of its having been translated as well as written by the Holy Ghost[.]

Blake's discovery of his gift for languages may have had enormous consequences. His credulous disciple Frederick Tatham claimed that he "had a
most consummate knowledge of all the great writers in all languages.... I
have possessed books well thumbed and dirtied by his graving hands, in
Latin, Greek, Hebrew, French, and Italian".‡

It may have been about this time, and with Hayley's assistance, that Blake
learned French; in later years he "would declare that he learnt French, sufficient to read it, in a few weeks".[83] On 26–7 March 1802 Hayley "read
Klopstock [*from German*] into English to Blake", and on 9 May E.G. Marsh
wrote to Hayley: "I may perhaps expect to hear you read it [*i.e., translate
Klopstock at sight*], as the good M.[r] Blake has heard you read French
authors".§ It may have been sight-translations like these that Blake refers to
in his letter of 22 November 1802:

Remembring the Verses that Hayley sung
When my heart knockd against the root of my tongue

Blake as a Critic of Hayley's Verses

Hayley also consulted Blake about verses for monumental inscriptions. In
one he wished that his wife's "deep nervous Woes, of wondrous Weight"
would be recompensed by

all, that from blameless sufferings below
Mortality can hope, or Angels Know![84]

---

* There are Hebrew inscriptions on Blake's *Night Thoughts* drawing 438 (1796) and engraving p. 63
(1797), *Milton* pl. 15, e, his Enoch lithograph (1807), Laocoon, and *Job* pl. 1, 3.
† The Oxford scholar he had in mind may well have been Edward Garrard Marsh. Flaxman had taught
Tommy Butts by having him read the New Testament in Greek.
‡ *BR* 41 n4. In his Life of Blake, Tatham wrote: "he had read almost every thing in whatsoever lan-
guage, which language he always taught himself.... among the Volumes bequeathed by M.[rs] Blake to
the Author of this Sketch, the most thumbed from use are his Bible & those books in other lan-
guages" (*BR* 526–7). Samuel Palmer agreed that "W.B. *was* mad about languages" (1 Sept 1862,
BRS 10).
§ *BRS* 20. Blake's ribald view of Klopstock may be seen in his Notebook poem "When Klopstock
England defied" (Notebook p. 5). Klopstock is represented among the portraits Blake made for
Hayley's library.

Another was for Cowper's devoted friend Mary Unwin, who

> Endur'd affliction's desolating Hail,
> And watch'd a Poet thro' Misfortune's vale . . . .

If it pleases you my dear Johnny, as I hope it may from the applause it has receiv'd from the accomplish'd Lady of Lavant, from our good enthusiastic Blake, & two or three more very delicate Critics, let us have it inscribed . . . .[85]

Blake came to find his role as a delicate critic of Hayley's poetry wonderfully trying.

Hayley had many errands around the county, and Blake often rode with him. On 4 November 1801, they happened to go to Hayley's former residence, "the great house at Eartham", where they had what Hayley called "the mournful Gratification of attending . . . the few last Hours" of his "chearful & affectionate" old servant William Metcalf "(near 80)"; "providence conducted his dissolution in a manner most merciful to his own Feelings & those of his affectionate Master".[86] Blake's design for "The Death of the Good Old Man" (1805) (Pl. 91) may well be based on this experience.

In the intervals of work on his engravings for Hayley and his portraits for Hayley's library, Blake was given incidental commissions for gifts to Hayley's friends. Hayley sent to Mrs Romney copies by Blake of two Romney self-portraits,* and he asked Blake to copy his changing designs for Cowper's monument.[87] Blake must have felt at times degraded from Hayley's engraver-in-ordinary to his personal copy machine. It would be agreeable but probably illusory to think that for these professional services Blake received professional cash rewards.

The Blakes continued to rejoice in their little thatched house: "We are very Happy sitting by a wood fire in our Cottage[,] the wind singing above our roof & the sea roaring at a distance".[88] In the intervals of work, they played word games and told riddles: "he calls her A Love lie Girl" and "an Ell taken from London is Undone".[89]

"*B*ut if sickness comes all is unpleasant".[90] Blake became "persuaded . . . that the air [*of Felpham*] tho warm is unhealthy". "My Wife has had Agues & Rheumatisms almost ever since she has been here",† and Hayley said that

---

* 19 May 1801 (*BRS* 15). Romney's admiration for Blake may be seen in his acquisition (probably from Blake about 1795) of *America* (A), *Urizen* (B), *Visions* (F), and perhaps *Europe* (A) and *Marriage* (D)—they appeared in the posthumous sale of his son's possessions at Christie's on 9 May 1834 (*BBS* pp. 285–6).

† Letter of 30 Jan 1803. There are repeated references to the ill-health of the Blakes, particularly Catherine (e.g., Blake's letter of 10 Jan 1802 and Hayley's letter of 16 May 1802).

On their return to London, Catherine Blake's rheumatism was cured by "Mr. Birch's Electrical Magic" (18 Dec 1804). The surgeon John Birch was a family friend whom Blake invited to Felpham on 11 Sept 1801.

"poor Mrs Blake has suffer'd most severely from Rheumatism".[91] The charming cottage with which he had fallen in love proved to be a cause of suffering to them both.

Changing Relationship with Hayley

Blake's attitude towards his friend Hayley was also changing. When they arrived in the village, "Mr Hayley recieved us with his usual brotherly affection", and twenty months later he assured Butts that still "Mr Hayley acts like a Prince. I am at complete Ease ... Felpham in particular is the sweetest spot on Earth".[92] Hayley was equally persuaded of Blake's happiness in the village,[93] and as late as 22 November 1801 he told Lady Hesketh that "our respective Labours never clash".

But though Blake's labours did not clash with Hayley's, Hayley's labours, or at least his priorities, seemed increasingly to clash with those of his protégé. Blake was often "so full of work that I have had no time to go on with the Ballads" or his own writings and designs, and his head was often "full of botheration about various projected works" of Hayley's.[94]

Blake was discovering that corporeal friends may be spiritual enemies, and he was more and more torn between Hayley's daily insistence that Blake should confine himself to engraving and the imperatives of his creative genius.[95] On 10 January 1802 he confided to Butts:

My unhappiness has arisen from a source which if explord too narrowly, might hurt my pecuniary circumstance$s$. As my dependence is on Engraving at present & particularly on the Engravings I have in hand for Mr H. ....

[*We are*] determin'd not to remain another winter here but to return to London.

I hear a voice you cannot hear that says I must not stay
I see a hand you cannot see that beckons me away

Naked we came here[,] naked of Natural things & naked we shall retur$n$; but while clothd with the Divine Mercy we are richly clothd in Spiritual & suffer all the rest gladly ....

He had reluctantly and finally concluded

That I can alone carry on my visionary studies in London unannoyd & that I may converse with my friends in Eternit$y$, See Visions, Dream Dreams & prophecy & speak Parables unobserv'd & at liberty from the Doubts of other Mortal*s*—perhaps Doubts proceeding from Kindness, but Doubts are always pernicious Especially when we Doubt our Friends ....[96]

He still believed that Hayley "will do ultimately all that both he & I wish", but he was soon "determind to be no longer Pesterd with his Genteel Ignorance & Polite Disapprobation".[97] He came to see Hayley as a Pharisee and a Pick Thank:

To H—
Thy Friendship oft has made my heart to ake[;]
Do be my Enemy for Friendships sake

To forgive Enemies H. does pretend
Who never in his Life forgave a friend

(Notebook pp. 37, 34)

Indeed, Hayley seems to have been partly the model for Satan in Blake's *Milton* which Blake was creating amidst Hayley's well-meant commercial importunities:

> ... You know Satans mildness and his self-imposition,
> Seeming a brother, being a tyran*t*, even thinking himself a brother
> While he is murdering the just ....

(Milton pl. 5, ll. 23–5)

Despite the indignation expressed in his <u>Notebook</u> and letters, Blake was discreet in his dealings with Hayley—when he complained of Hayley to his brother, he asked him "to keep it a secret & to burn this letter because it speaks so plain".* Hayley's casual references to Blake in his letters became less frequent—after a four-month hiatus, Johnny Johnson wrote to him, "is our dear Blake <u>dead</u>? You are as silent about him as the <u>grave</u>"[98]—and he learned to treat Blake with "the utmost caution",[99] but he continued to defend Blake's interests vigorously. He recommended Blake to the Countess of Portarlington and her "powerful friends" as "an artist of great original powers and of uncommon Merit in his Inventions in wch Line he is perhaps unequal'd among the B[*ritish*] Artists .... M^r B ... & his wife ... have passed their lives together with so scanty an Income as scarcely to have afford[*ed*] them the means of subsistence—".[100]

And he wrote to Lady Hesketh on 15 July 1802:

---

* Letter of 30 Jan 1803. "Palamabron fear'd to be angry lest Satan should accuse him of Ingratitude" (*Milton* pl. 5, ll. 13–14).

I know I shall interest your Heart & Soul in <u>his Favour</u>, when I tell you, that He resembles our beloved Bard [*Cowper*] in the Tenderness of his Heart, & in the perilous powers of an Imagination utterly unfit to take due Care of Himself—with admirable Faculties, his sensibility is so <u>dangerously acute</u>, that the common rough Treatment which true genius often receives from <u>ordinary Minds</u> in the commerce of the World, might not only wound Him <u>more than it should do</u>, but really reduce Him to the Incapacity of an Ideot . . . but in all he does, however wild or hasty, a penetrating eye will discover true Genius . . . he often reminds me [*of Cowper*] by little Touches of <u>nervous Infirmity</u>, when his mind is darkend with any unpleasant apprehension.

This earnest and well-meant defence of the fragility of Blake's sensibility and the danger that common treatment by *ordinary Minds* might "reduce Him to the Incapacity of an Ideot" makes it easy to sympathize with Palamabron-Blake's prayer in *Milton*:

> O God protect me from my friend*s*, that they have not power over
>   me[.]
> Thou hast giv'n me power to protect myself from my bitterest enemies.
>
> <div align="right">(<i>Milton</i> pl. 7, ll. 5–6)</div>

The delicate and (on Blake's side) somewhat intermittent and precarious friendship between Blake and Hayley continued but in an altered form. On July 1803 Blake wrote that "I have brought down his affected Loftiness & he begins to think I have some Geni*us*, as if Genius & Assurance were the same thing". But Hayley's loyalty to Blake persisted even in the most trying circumstances, and Blake continued to serve Hayley energetically long after he had left Hayley's direct patronage in Felpham.

Study of Art

When Blake was refocusing his life in Felpham, he "recollected all my scattered thoughts on Art & resumed my primitive & original ways of Execution in both painting & engravin*g*, which in the confusion of London I had very much lost & obliterated from my mind".[101]

I have now given two years to the intense study of those parts of the art which relate to light & shade & colour & am Convincd that either my understanding is incapable of comprehending the beauties of Colouring or the Pictures which I painted for you Are Equal in Every part of the Art

& superior in One to any thing that has been done since the age of Rafael.
... There is nothing in the Art which our Painters d*o*, that I can confess
myself ignorant of[.] I also Know & Understand & can assuredly affirm
that the works I have done for You are Equal to Carrache or Rafael (and
I am now Seven years older than Rafael was when he died) ... or Else I
am Blind Stupid Ignorant and Incapable ...*

One of his methods of study was to read the lectures of Sir Joshua
Reynolds, which he quoted in his letter of 22 November 1802 and annotated
extensively:

There is no End to the Follies of this Man
    This is All Self-Contradictory: Truth & Fals[*e*]hood Jumbled
Together
    Without Minute Neatness of Executi*o*n The Sublime cannot Exist!
Grandeur of Ideas is founded on Precision of Ideas
    To My Eye Rubens's Colouring is most Contemptible[.] His Shadows
are of a Filthy Brown somewhat of the Colour of Excrement[;] these are
filld with tints & messes of yellow & red[.] His lights are all Colours of
the Rainbow laid on Indiscriminate[*ly*] & broken one into another.
    Taste & Genius are Not Teachable or Acquirable but are born with
us[;] Reynolds says the Contrary

             (Marginalia to Reynolds, *Works* pp. 63, 15, 52, 135, 198)

Hayley's Designs to A Series of Ballads

Perhaps in response to Blake's impatience with mere copy-engraving,
Hayley "chanced to compose" at the end of 1801 a series of ballads founded
on anecdotes relating to animals in order to amuse Blake. "They succeeded
perfectly as an amusement to my Friend; and led him to execute a few rapid
sketches" illustrating the ballads. These so impressed a small private circle
that Hayley and Blake decided to increase the number of ballads and to
print them with three engravings each in fifteen monthly numbers at 2s.6d.
each, in order to exhibit Blake's talents "for original design, and delicate
engraving".[102]
Blake was to be the publisher, and all the profits were to be his. He
arranged for paper to be sent down directly from a stationer in London[103]

---

* Letter of 22 Nov 1802 (alpha). These radical theories of art, exalting Raphael and Michelangelo and
scorning Titian and Rembrandt, are displayed at greater length and with more hyperbole in his
Descriptive Catalogue (1809).

and for Hayley's friend Joseph Seagrave of Chichester to print the text while Blake "& his excellent Wife (a true Helpmate!) pass the plates thro' a rolling press in their own cottage together".[104] Hayley presumptuously proposed that his correspondents should become ballad mongers among their friends,* which would save Blake the 16⅔ percent bookseller's commission.

Hayley busily sent copies to his friends such as John Flaxman, Johnny Johnson, and Lady Hesketh, and he was probably responsible for sending review copies to the *Sussex Chronicle* and the *European Magazine*.†

The first responses were cheerful. Flaxman placed five subscriptions for the series, Charlotte Collins sold seven copies of "The Elephant" (the first ballad), Johnny Johnson's cousin thought "The Elephant" "interesting and novel in the extreme", and Flaxman wrote that "the Etchings have Spirit & Sentiment".[105] Hayley exulted that "Blake & his Elephant are marching triumphantly on the road of prosperity ... elated by the applause of Flaxman—Bravo!"[106]

However, this triumph was premature. Samuel Greatheed in Newport Pagnell could find not a single customer for the first ballad, and Lady Hesketh in Bath secured no more than half a dozen, though she had written to her Cowper relations "that I shall expect to see all their Names, and to have all their Interest exerted towards the work".[107]

Even worse, she reported that "some among the very few now here, who have any pretensions to Taste", such as Lord and Lady Harcourt, Lord Spencer, the Bishop of Worcester, and Princess Elizabeth, "find many defects in your friends engravings".[108] Lady Hesketh herself complained that "the faces of his babies are not young, and this I cannot pardon!"[109] (Pl. 92).

Worst of all, she told her young kinsman Johnny Johnson, "by the Sketches he [*Blake*] has given in these Ballads, People of Taste do not think him at all worthy to engrave designs for the life of Cowper".[110] She may have been in Blake's mind when he wrote: "The Enquiry in England is not whether a Man has Talents & Genius, But whether he is Passive & Polite & a Virtuous Ass: & obedient to Noblemens Opinions in Art & Science. If he is; he is a Good Man: If Not he must be Starved".[111]

The labour of designing and engraving four plates per month, printing them, collating them with the text, and putting the ballads in sugar-paper

---

* Note that Lady Hesketh promptly circumvented this intention by having her own bookseller in Bath obtain and distribute to her subscribers all the ballads after the first (letter of 3 July 1802).

† The *Sussex Chronicle* for 2 June 1802 said that the first ballad "will give Rank to our County and City for producing that which in its Poetry, Typography, and skill of the *Burin*, will claim competition with some of the proudest efforts of the Metropolis", and the *European Magazine* for Aug 1802 said that the artist "has executed his share of the undertaking much to his credit" (*BRS* 21, 22).

wrappers of course interfered with Blake's work for Hayley. Production of new copies and of new ballads slowed down, and, after the appearance of "The Elephant" (1 June), "The Eagle" (1 July), "The Lion" (5 August), and "The Dog" (9 September 1802), there was a long pause. Four months later, Blake told his brother: "I have had no time to go on with the Ballads", but they "are likely to be Profitable for we have Sold all that we have had time to print. Evans the Bookseller in Pallmall says they go off very well".[112]

But in the autumn of 1803 his principal London agent "Mr. Evans ... gives small hopes of our ballads; he says he has sold but fifteen numbers at the most, and that going on would be a certain loss of almost all the expenses."[113]

Blake paid £30 to Seagrave* for printing perhaps 250 copies of each of the first four ballads. At half a crown per ballad, Blake needed to sell 240 copies to recoup his expenses (ignoring postage and the $\frac{1}{6}$ commission for copies which went through the hands of booksellers). It is plain that he did not sell anything like so many copies, and his adventure with the *Designs to A Series of Ballads* clearly left him out of pocket—even ignoring payment for printing and collating the plates and putting the ballads in covers, labours performed by Catherine and William Blake. Of course there was nothing left for the designer and engraver of the plates.

Blake was able to balance his books as a publisher only by borrowing £12.12.0 from Hayley to pay Seagrave's bill for the ballads.[114]

Plates for Hayley's Cowper

Hayley's chief labour, indeed almost his obsession, was his biography of William Cowper, and Blake's professional relationship with Hayley depended largely upon the plates he was engraving for it. The most sensitive of these plates was Romney's portrait of Cowper (Pl. 89). Hayley and Blake were determined that the print should be a faithful likeness of the crayon portrait, and Lady Hesketh was equally determined that it should suppress the portrait's hints of Cowper's madness.

Hayley sent a proof of the Romney portrait for Flaxman's opinion, and

---

* On 28 Dec 1804 Blake thanked Hayley for "the Twelve Guineas which you Lent Me when I made up 30 Pounds to pay our Worthy Seagrave in part of his Account". Presumably the "part" of Seagrave's account was the £12.12.0 rather than the £30. Hayley said Blake had "paid a Bill of 30£ for paper" (letter of 3 April 1803) which I take to represent payment to Seagrave for paper and printing of the *Designs*.

  When Blake wrote on 11 Dec 1805 that he should "be able to Settle with him [*Seagrave*] Soon what is between us", he was presumably referring to his indebtedness not for the *Designs* (1802) but for the *Ballads* (1805), for which the publisher Richard Phillips "will go equal shares with me in the expence and the profits, and ... Seagrave is to be the printer" (letter of 22 Jan 1805).

he replied most satisfactorily: "In the Engraving of Cowper I think my friend Blake has kept the spirit of the likeness most perfectly".[115] And to encourage Lady Hesketh that he was doing everything possible to ensure the faithfulness of the engraving, Hayley sent her a poem:

> Good Angels guide the Graver's Hand
>   With perfect skill to trace
> Those Looks, that could the Heart command,
>   The Light of Cowper's Face!
>
> Shew Character, surpass'd by none!
>   Wit, modest as a child!
> and spirits like a vernal Sun,
>   Tho penetrating, mild!
>
> So shall his portrait with regard,
>   And with his Verse contend;
> Displaying all, that made the Bard
>   Affections' favorite Friend![116]

He tried to elicit Lady Hesketh's sympathy for Blake by comparing him to Cowper:

> if it were possible to Keep his too apprehensive Spirit for a Length of Time unruffled, He would produce Works of the pencil, almost as excellent & original, as those works of the pen, which flowed from the dear poet .... I endeavour to be as kind as I can to [*the Blakes*] ... & indeed I consider it as a point of devotion to the two departed Angels (Cowper & Tom!) to be so, for I am confident I could gratify their Spirits in nothing so much, as in befriending two wonderful Beings, whom they both, were they still on Earth, & possest of Health, would peculiarly delight to befriend.[117]

But Lady Hesketh was proof against such analogies, and in her reply she could not "help lamenting the resemblance which you imagine Subsists between your friend and Him who will ever live in our remembrance!"[118]

Blake too felt an intimate sympathy with Cowper. In his poem on "William Cowper Esq[re]", he concluded:

> You see him spend his Soul in Prophecy[,]
> Do you believe it a Confounded lie
> Till some Bookseller & the Public Fame
> Proves there is truth in his extravagant claim

For tis atrocious in a Friend you love
To tell you any thing that he cant prove
And tis most wicked in a Christian Nation
For any Man to pretend to Inspiration.

(Notebook p. 52)

And in response to Spurzheim's suggestion that Methodism is a "fertile cause of insanity", Blake wrote: "Cowper came to me and said, 'Oh! that I were insane, always. . . . Oh! that in the bosom of God I was hid. You retain health, and yet are mad as any of us all—over us all—mad as a refuge from unbelief—from Bacon, Newton, and Locke'" (Marginalium to Spurzheim, *Observations on . . . Insanity* (1817) pp. 153–4).

Blake clearly loved Cowper the prophet, spending his soul in prophecy. This was dangerous ground for those who loved Cowper for his modest wit and mild spirits. Hayley told Lady Hesketh:

> my Friend the anxious, enthusiastic Engraver says, that all the Demons, who tormented our dear Cowper when living, are now labouring to impede the publication of his life.—To which I reply that it may be so, but if it is, I am confident my two dear Angels the Bard [*Cowper*] & the Sculptor [*Tom*] will assist us in our Conflict with the powers of darkness, & enable us to triumph over all their Machinations.*

When the biography finally appeared in the last days of 1802, Hayley despatched copies to his most sympathetic correspondents, and Lady Hesketh responded with astonishing docility: "I must tell you that I admire Romneys head of all things! now it is Softened[;] of the engraving I pretend not to Judge, but I like it."[119]

This was far better than either Blake or Hayley could have hoped, non-committal though it is about the quality of the engraving. Blake wrote to his brother in exultation:

> My Heads of Cowper for M^r H's life of Cowper have pleasd his Relations exceedingly & in Particular Lady Hesketh & Lord Cowper[;] to please Lady H was a doubtful chance who almost adord her Cousin the poet &

---

* Hayley letter of 20 Dec 1802. Hayley apparently wrote something similar to E.G. Marsh, who replied on 3 Feb 1802: "I am sorry to hear" that the first two volumes of Cowper are not yet published; "Blake's idea diverted me. But though I wish even a double portion of Cowper's spirit both to his biographer and his engraver, I hope they will have no concern with his dæmons" (*BRS* 23).

thought him all perfection & she writes that she is quite satisfied with the portraits & charmed by the great Head in particular tho she never could bear the original Picture[.][120]

It was not only the engravings which were honourable and profitable, for "My Wife has undertaken to Print the whole number of the Plates for Cowpers work which She does to admiration & being under my own eye the prints are as fine as the French prints & please every one. . . . The Publishers are already indebted to My Wife Twenty Guineas for work deliverd. . .".*

Hayley's life of Cowper was profitable and honourable for both Hayley and the Blakes.

Blake's Plan to Become a Commercial Publisher

Blake was enormously impressed by Hayley's commercial success as an author,[†] and he believed that he could imitate this success himself. In January 1803, he told his brother:

I am only sorry that I did not know the methods of publishing years ago & this is one of the numerous benefits I have obtain by coming here for I should never have known the nature of Publication unless I had known H & his connexions & his method of managing. It would now be folly not to venture publishing.

He was persuaded that

The Profits arising from Publications are immense & I now have it in my power to commence publication with many very formidable works, which I have finishd & ready[.] A Book price half a guinea may be got out at the Expense of Ten pounds & its almost certain profits are 500 G. . . . I am now Engraving Six little plates for a work of Mr H's[‡] for which I am to have 10 Guineas each & the certain profits of that work are a fortune such

---

* Letter of 30 Jan 1803. The Blakes printed twelve proof sets of the two plates for Vol. III of *Cowper*, but Blake then had to "send the Plates to [*Joseph*] Johnson who wants them to set the Printer to work upon" instead of Catherine Blake (Blake's letter of 31 March 1804).

† Rumour had it, at least in 1813 when Alexander Stephens published his *Memoir of John Horne Tooke* (I, 498n), "that Mr. Hayley obtained the almost incredible sum of eleven thousand pounds by the life of Cowper alone!"

‡ Hayley's *Triumphs of Temper* (1803) has six plates by Blake dated 1 May 1803 after designs by Flaxman's sister-in-law Maria Denman.

as would make me independent supposing that I could substantiate such a one of my own & I mean to try many[.]

He had therefore decided to "come to London in the Spring to commence Publisher . . . . I know that the Public are my friends & love my works & will embrace them whenever they see them. My only Difficulty is to produce fast enough".*

Blake's estimate of the profits arising from publication are, of course, absurd. A book whose production costs were £10 and whose sale price was 10s.6d would have to sell 1,019 copies in order to make a profit of £525—and, at commercial printing rates,† the "Book" would have only five quarto pages.

For the prospective publisher, there were other formidable problems as well, such as the need for capital and the jealousy of other publishers. Nine months later, when Blake was endeavouring to persuade R.H. Evans to be his co-publisher in a new octavo edition of Hayley's *Ballads*, he concluded ruefully: "as far as I can judge of the nature of publication, no chance is left to one out of the trade".[121]

Therefore Blake did not become a commercial publisher, though he did continue to plan books in conventional typography. Five years later he told his friend George Cumberland: "I have Myself begun to print an account of my various Inventions in Art for which I have procured a Publisher",[122] and in the advertisement of his 1809 exhibition he announced "a Work on Art, now in the Press" which would include "the whole Process" of his redis-covery of the lost art of Fresco painting. This may be what he described in his *Descriptive Catalogue* (¶9) of 1809 as "another work on Painting" inquir-ing whether Rubens or Van Dyke was the villain responsible for bringing "oil Painting into general opinion and practice".

However, this "Work on Art" never appeared, and the only book which Blake himself had printed in conventional typography was his *Descriptive Catalogue* (1809)—and this was published only in the sense that his brother sold copies of it to those who came to see Blake's exhibition of frescos in his haberdashery shop. Blake never published a work by anyone else, and the

---

* Letter of 30 Jan 1803. In *Jerusalem* pl. 3, Blake wrote that his works had "reciev'd the highest reward possible; the love and friendship of those with whom to be connected is to be blessed"—but then he deleted the words "love", "friendship", and "blessed".

† The fine printer Thomas Bensley estimated on 10 Oct 1800 that the cost of printing 1,000 copies of a book (including paper, printing, and hot-pressing) would be £15.15.0 per text-sheet of four quarto pages (MS in the Huntington Library). Counting the cost of paper alone at £5 per ream of 500 sheets, £10 would pay for 1,000 copies of "A Book" of only eight quarto pages. In his letter of 18 Dec 1808, Cumberland suggested that Blake could describe his artistic inventions in "a little work" of "about 6 Pages [*selling*] for a guinea".

For more realistic cost-estimates for printing a book, see *BR* (2) under June 1805.

only form in which he published his own works was in Illuminated Printing and in intaglio engraving.

In 1803 Blake was "full of work . . . & my prospects of more & more work continually are certain".[123] These prospects were probably for (1) retouching his four quarto plates for a new edition of Hayley's *Cowper*; (2) engraving new plates for an octavo edition of Cowper; (3) designing and engraving quarto plates for Cowper's translation of Milton's Latin and Italian poems;[*] (4) engraving the twelve quarto plates for Hayley's life of Romney; (5) engraving thirty more quarto plates for Hayley's *Designs to A Series of Ballads*; and (6) engraving six octavo plates for Hayley's *Triumphs of Temper*. Blake understood that these commissions had been promised to him, but eventually he made only one plate for Hayley's *Romney* (1809)[†] and six for Hayley's *Triumphs of Temper* (1803). Hayley's support for Blake dwindled calamitously after Blake left Felpham.

An Immense Number of Verses

Every day in the study of the Turret House, Hayley and Blake worked industriously side by side. Absorbed in his work, each left the other to his own arcana. Blake had brought up to the house his copperplates and graving tools, his acid and wax, his pens and his brushes, and sometimes he worked on his own poems and etchings rather than on Hayley's. All the etchings he made in Felpham were made in Hayley's study, for he could not afford to keep duplicate sets of all his professional tools in the cottage.

Though Blake was full of the world's work for Hayley, he was also listening to the spirits and writing from their dictation:

none can know the Spiritual Acts of my three years' Slumber on the banks of the Ocean unless he has seen them in the Spirit or unless he should read My Long Poem descriptive of those Acts for I have in these three years composed an immense number of verses on One Grand

---

* Cowper's translations of Milton's Latin and Italian poems were proposed as part of Milton's poetical works in 1791 (*BR* 44) with plates after Fuseli by Blake, *inter alia*, but the project was abandoned. Hayley refers to Blake's engravings for the translation in letters of 6 Aug 1802 and 15 Jan 1803, and Blake wrote that it was to be "ornamented with Engravings from Designs from Romney, Flaxman & Y^r hble Servt & to be Engravd also by the last mentioned" (6 July 1803); "this work will be very profitable to me" (30 Jan 1803). It was published as Milton's *Latin and Italian Poems*, tr. William Cowper, ed. John Johnson (Joseph Johnson, 1808) with no plate by Blake.

† Blake's published plate in Hayley's *Romney* (1809) is for "The Shipwreck", but he referred frequently in his letters (7, 26 Oct, 13 Dec 1803, 27 Jan, 23 Feb, 16 March, 4 May, 22 June, 28 Sept, 23 Oct, 18, 28 Dec 1804) to his progress on his engraving of the portrait of Romney, which did not appear in Hayley's book and is otherwise unknown.

Theme Similar to Homers Iliad or Miltons Paradise Lost the Persons & Machinery intirely new to the Inhabitants of Earth (some of the Persons Excepted)[.] I have written this Poem from immediate Dictation twelve or sometimes twenty or thirty lines at a time without Premeditation & even against my Will. The Time it has taken in writing was thus renderd Non Existen*t*, & an immense Poem Exists which seems to be the Labour of a long Life all producd without Labour or Study. I mention this to shew you what I think the Grand Reason of my being brought down here[.]*

This poem is

a Sublime Allegory which is now perfectly completed into a grand Poem[.] I may praise it since I dare not pretend to be any other than the Secretary[;] the Authors are in Eternity[.] I consider it as the Grandest Poem that this World Contains[.] Allegory addressd to the Intellectual powers while it is altogether hidden from the Corporeal Understanding is My Definition of the Most Sublime Poetr*y*; it is also somewhat in the same manner defind by Plato. This Poem shall by Divine Assistance be progressively Printed & Ornamented with Prints & given to the Public. But of this work I take care to say little to Mr H. since he is as much averse to my poetry as he is to a Chapter in the Bible[.] He knows that I have writ it for I have shewn it to him, & he has read Part by his own desire & has looked with sufficient contempt to inhance my opinion of it.[124]

This "immense number of verses" written in 1800–3 may have included both *Milton* and *Jerusalem*, whose title pages are dated 1804† (Pls 93, 110). *Milton* in particular describes "the Spiritual Acts of my three years' Slumber on the banks of the Ocean".

Blake was always an early riser, wakened perhaps by "the sound of harps

---

* Letter of 25 April 1803.

> My Vegetated portion was hurried from Lambeths shades[,]
> He [*Los*] set me down in Felphams Vale & prepard a beautiful
> Cottage for me that in three years I might write all these Visions
> To display Natures cruel holiness: the deceits of Natural Religion[.]
>
> (*Milton* pl. 36, ll. 22–5)

† It cannot be *Vala*, which is dated 1797 on its title page. *Milton* was continued after Blake returned to London, for it refers to his trials (Oct 1803 and Feb 1804) and to South Molton Street (*Milton* pl. a, l. 21), where he moved in the autumn of 1803. On 11 Dec 1805, Blake wrote: "It will not be long before I shall be able to present the full history of my Spiritual Sufferings to the Dwellers upon Eart*h*, & of the Spiritual Victories obtaind for me by my Friends". *Milton* was probably finished about 1811 and *Jerusalem* about 1820.

which I hear before the Suns rising",[125] and he lit the fire and put on the kettle before his Catherine was awake. One stormy morning just before dawn, when the surf was thundering on the shore across the field, as Blake walked in his garden at Felpham in the gloaming, he was overwhelmed by a series of visions which are at the heart of *Milton*.

The first was of Ololon, "a Virgin of twelve years", who met the lark as she descended at dawn:

> as the
> Flash of lightning but more quick the virgin in my Garden
> Before my Cottage stood . . ..
>
> > (*Milton* pl. 36, ll. 17–20; see Fig. on p. 202.)

Unsurprised and unafraid, Blake asked her:

> "What is thy message to thy friend: What am I now to do[?]
> Is it again to plunge into deeper affliction? behold me
> Ready to obey, but pity thou my Shadow of Delight[.]
> Enter my Cottag*e*, comfort her, for she is sick with fatigue[.]"
>
> > (*Milton* pl. 36, ll. 29–32)

Ololon is seeking Milton, for she is his "Sixfold Emanation" representing his three wives and his three daughters.[126]

The second vision is of Milton himself:

> Miltons shadow fell
> Precipitant loud thundring into the Sea of Time & Space.
>
> Then first I saw him in the Zenith as a falling star
> Descending perpendicular, swift as the swallow or swift:
> And on my left foot falling on the tarsus, enterd there. . . .* [Pl. 4]
>
> [Milton] Descended down a Paved work of all kinds of precious stones
> Out from the eastern sky; descending down into my Cottage
> Garden: clothed in blac*k*, severe & silent he descended.[127]
>
> I beheld Milton with astonishment & in him beheld
> The monstrous Churches of Beulah, the Gods of Ulro dark . . ..
>
> > (*Milton* pl. 37, ll. 15–16)

---

* *Milton* pl. 14, ll. 45–50. Notice that in *Milton* the visions are not described in the order in which they occurred. Blake's vision clearly echoes that of Paul of Tarsus (Acts xxii, 6).

The third vision of that fateful morning is of Los in the rising sun. As Blake bent down and

> bound my sandals
> On: to walk forward thro' Eternity, Los descended to me:
> And Los behind me stood; a terrible flaming Sun: just close
> Behind my back: I turned round in terror, and behold,
> Los stood in that fierce glowing fire; & he also stoop'd down
> And bound my sandals on in Udan-Adan; trembling I stood
> ... but he kissed me and wishd me health,
> And I became One Man with him arising in my strength:
> Twas too late now to recede. Los had enterd into my soul:
> His terrors now possesd me whole!* [Pl. 94]

At the same time,

> The Spectre of Satan stood upon the roaring sea ...
> Gorgeous & beautiful ...
>
> I also stood in Satans bosom & beheld its desolations:
> A ruind Man: a ruind building of God not made with hands
>
> (*Milton* pl. 39, ll. 9, 12, 15–16)

The visions end in an apocalypse:

> Jesus wept & walked forth
> From Felphams Vale clothed in Clouds of bloo*d* to enter into
> Albions Bosom, the bosom of death[,] & the Four surrounded him
> In the column of Fire in Felphams Vale; then to their mouths the Four
> Applied their Four Trumpets & them sounded to the Four winds[.]
>
> Terror struck in the Vale I stood at that immortal sound[.]
> My bones trembled. I fell outstretchd upon the path
> A moment, & my Soul returnd into its mortal state
> To Resurrection & Judgment in the Vegetable Body
> And my sweet Shadow of Delight stood trembling by my side[.]
>
> Immediately the Lark mounted with a loud trill from Felphams Vale
>
> (*Milton* pl. 44, ll. 19–29)

---

* *Milton* pl. 20, ll. 4–9, 11–14; ll. 10–11 strangely specify that Blake was "standing in the Vale Of Lambeth", though the scene is that with Ololon and Milton in Blake's garden in Felpham.

These three visions, framed by the mounting lark, are the central acts of the poem. *Milton* describes how

> Milton ... walkd about in Eternity
> One hundred year*s*, pondring the intricate ways of Providence
> Unhappy tho in heav'n— he obey'd, he murmur'd no*t*, he was silent
> Viewing his Sixfold Emanation scatter'd thro' the deep
> In torment!
>
> (*Milton* pl. 3, ll. 16–20)

He determines "To go into the deep her to redeem & himself perish",[128] and he "took off the robe of the promise, & ungirded himself from the oath of God. And Milton said: 'I go to Eternal Death!'"[129] (Pl. 95). This is an unexampled act, "that one of the holy dead should willing return".[130]

> I come to Self Annihilation[.]
> Such are the Laws of Eternity that each shall mutually
> Annihilate himself for others good, as I for thee[.]
>
> (*Milton* pl. 39, ll. 34–6)

In *Milton*, these relatively straightforward visions are overlaid with an intricate symbolism combining Biblical and British places which often seems arbitrary and opaque to the Corporeal Understanding:

> Rahab & Noa*h* dwell on Windsors heights[.]
> Where once the Cherubs of Jerusalem spread to Lambeths Vale
> Milcahs Pillars shine from Harrow to Hampstead ....
>
> (*Milton* pl. 35, ll. 9–11)

But the same symbolism seems to speak directly to the Intellectual Powers in the great Jerusalem lyric which has become one of the best known and best loved songs in English:

> And did those feet in ancient tim*e*
> Walk upon Englands mountains green:
> And was the holy Lamb of Go*d*
> On Englands pleasant pastures seen!
>
> And did the Countenance Divin*e*
> Shine forth upon our clouded hills?
> And was Jerusalem builded here,
> Among these dark Satanic Mills?

Bring me my Bow of burning gold:
Bring me my Arrows of Desire:
Bring me my Spear: O clouds unfold:
Bring me my Chariot of Fire!

I will not cease from Mental Fight,
Nor shall my Sword sleep in my hand:
Till we have built Jerusalem,
In Englands green & pleasant Land.

(*Milton* pl. 2)

Blake's sword did not sleep in his hand as he was building Jerusalem's green and pleasant land in Felpham.

As well as creating *Milton*, Blake was working on revisions of *Vala*. Now, however, he no longer wrote *Vala* in the beautiful copperplate hands with which he had begun (pp. 1–18, 23–42); his continuations were in the ordinary hand in which he wrote his letters. The rest of the poem was written on proofs of his engravings for Young's *Night Thoughts* which he had brought from London, so that he could now make his designs for *Vala* only on every second page. The revisions of *Vala* were on a scale considerably less ambitious and imposing than the first version.

These revisions to *Vala* may have been made when Blake was asserting his independence from Hayley in the spring of 1802. In printing his plates for Hayley's *Designs to a Series of Ballads* in May 1802, he used proofs of his *Night Thoughts* engravings as backing-sheets, so that the pressure of the press would be just right. On the back of one of these *Night Thoughts* proofs there was accidentally left an offset from the text and an indentation from the engraving from *Ballads* p. 9. And on this proof Blake later wrote *Vala* p. 48.

The new text of *Vala* adapts the myth in *The Book of Urizen*,* and it continues the themes of imprisonment and helplessness expressed in Nights the First to the Third.

He could not take their fetters off for they grew from the soul
Nor could he quench the fires for they flamd out from the heart
Nor could he calm the Elements because himself was Subject

(*Vala*, p. 71, ll. 1–3)

---

* A passage of forty lines in *Urizen* (pls 10–11, 13) is repeated in *Vala* (pp. 54–5) and in *Milton* (pl. b). Blake started to alter "Night" into "Book" (end of Night the Fourth and beginning and end of Night the Fifth, pp. 56, 57, 66) but then cancelled his changes.

   The text of *Vala* written about 1802–3 is for Nights the Fourth to the Seventh[a] (pp. 43–84, 112, which were stitched together separately from pp. 1–18, 23–42) plus revisions of Nights the First to the Third (pp. 1–42).

It is eloquent about the arts of social control:

> If you would make the poor live with temper[,]
> With pomp give every crust of bread you give[;] with gracious cunning
> Magnify small gifts[;] reduce the man to want a gift & then give with
>   pomp[.]
> Say he smiles if you hear him sigh[;] If pale say he is ruddy[.]
> Preach temperance[:] say he is overgorgd & drowns his wit
> In strong drink tho you know that bread & water are all
> He can afford[.] Flatter his wife[,] pity his children till we can
> Reduce all to our will as spaniels are taught with art[.]
>
> (*Vala* p. 80, ll. 14–21)

But there is no respite offered from the relentless rounds of oppression and resentment.

Nemesis Slouches Towards Felpham

When Blake moved to Felpham in 1800, the village seemed a haven of peace from the turbulence of London and the threat of war.

But war and turbulence were not far away. In nearby Chichester, companies of Loyal Volunteers paraded once a month, and Hayley and his friend John Marsh were writing patriotic songs.

Despite their martial appearance, however, many of these volunteers were notably reluctant, in part because of

> an Idea that was gone abroad & had been industriously propagated viz.[t] that the several Volunteer Corps were the cause of keeping up the high price of Provisions, by inducing the Shopkeepers &c. to charge what they pleas'd in the confidence of being protected from ye effects of Riots &[c] by the Volunteers.[131]

The officers of the Loyal Volunteers had a difficult time keeping their companies embodied, and they were not always successful.

When the Peace of Amiens was proclaimed in 1801, Blake rejoiced in apocalyptic terms:

> Peace opens the way to greater [Works] still[.] The Kingdoms of this World are now become the Kingdoms of God & his Christ & we shall reign with him for ever & ever [*Revelation xi, 15*]. The Reign of Literature & the Arts Commences[.] Blessed are those who are found studious of Literature & Humane & polite accomplishments. Such have their lamps burning & such shall shine as the stars . . . .

Now I hope to see the Great Works of Ar*t*, as they are so near to Felpham[,] Paris being scarce further off than London. But I hope that France & England will henceforth be as One Country and their Arts One ....[132]

Artists longed to see the treasures in the Louvre looted by Napoleon from his conquered kingdoms and to meet the great French artists such as Jacques Louis David. Blake may well have hoped to visit Paris during the peace, as did the Royal Academicians John Flaxman, Henry Fuseli, and Joseph Farington.

After a year of peace, while Britain and France regrouped their forces, war was declared once more, and the Volunteer Corps was reconstituted; on 16 August 1803 General Charles Lennox, the Duke of Richmond, appointed Blake's neighbour John Quantock, M.P., as a field officer in the new corps, and on 27 September 1803 he appointed Blake's friend John Marsh as commander of the first company.[133]

Meanwhile in Cornwall, military nemesis was on the march towards peaceful Felpham. Napoleon mustered his flat boats along innumerable creeks and estuaries of France, waiting for a strong east wind to blow away the blockading English fleet and to carry the invasion flotilla across the Channel. In response, troops of the regular British army were hurriedly assembled on the threatened coast of England, in Sussex and in Kent.

In May 1803 the First Regiment of Royal Dragoons (cavalry so-called because they were armed with the short, large-bore musket called a dragon) marched from Truro in Cornwall to Dorchester in Devon, and in the early summer of 1803 they marched to Chichester, where they were quartered until February 1804.[134]

Sound the War trumpet terrific[,] Souls clad in attractive steel[!]
Sound the shrill fife[,] serpents of war! I hear the northern drum.
Awake, I hear the flappings of the folding banners[.]
The dragons of the North put on their armour[;]
Upon the Eastern sea direct they take their course[.]
The glittring of their horses trappings stains the vault of night

(*Vala* p. 91, ll. 24–9)

And a troop of the First Regiment of Dragoons (the Royals) commanded by Brevet-Major George Hulton* was quartered at The Fox Inn in Felpham.

---

* The career of the gallant, "efficient and popular" Hulton is summarized in C.T. Atkinson, *History of the First Regiment of Dragoons 1661–1934* (Glasgow: Printed for the Regiment by ... The University Press, Glasgow, [?1935]), 255, 492: Cornet (1794), Lieutenant (1795), Captain-Lieutenant (10 April 1800), Captain (10 May 1800), Brevet Major (March 1803). Presumably he paid the £700 to which the cost of a cornetcy was reduced in order to assist recruiting (p. 237). About the time Hulton obtained his cornetcy, Blake was paid £21 for his 537 designs for Young's *Night Thoughts*.

Royal Dragoons in Felpham

One may imagine the turmoil caused by the invasion of seventy-five jack-booted heavy dragoons on their prancing black chargers (Pl. 96) in a farming village with some 80 houses. The streets were thronged with cavalry, the public rooms of The Fox were crowded with uniformed men, the price of feed for horses and food for men increased with this sudden demand, orders were barked in the quiet streets, housewives locked up their fat hens and their nubile daughters, dashing military regalia outshone the quiet work-wear of farm labourers and shopping housewives, brazen trumpets frightened mooing cattle in the village lanes, and the even tenor of village life was disrupted from pub to field, from public highway to private garden:

> they scent the odor of War in the Valley of Vision[.]
> All Love is lost! terror succeeds & Hatred instead of Love
> And stern demands of Right & Duty instead of Liberty
>
> (*Jerusalem* pl. 22, ll. 9–11)

Among Major Hulton's troop in Felpham were two friends who entered Blake's life abruptly. John Schofield,* a fustian-cutter, had taken the King's shilling and enlisted in the First Regiment of Royal Dragoons at Sarum in Wiltshire on 19 March 1793. He was promoted to corporal on 18 December 1794 and to sergeant on 3 September 1797. He managed to hold this rank for sixteen months, but on 30 December 1798 he was reduced to private for drunkenness, and he remained at that rank for the rest of his service.†

---

* His name is spelled "Scholfield", "Schofield", "Schoffield", and "Scholefield" in the War Office documents (Paul Miner "Visions in the Darksom air: Aspects of Blake's Biblical Symbolism", in *William Blake*: Essays for S. Foster Damon, ed. Alvin H. Rosenfeld [Providence: Brown University Press, 1969] 465), and "Scolfield" in the trial documents sworn to in the presence of his lieutenant (*BR* 128, 129, 131 n2, 134 & n1) but also "Scofield" (p. 124, 125 n1) and "Scholfield" (p. 125, 144). The variety of the spelling of his name may suggest that Schofield was illiterate.

  Blake gives "Scholfield" ("Blake's Memorandum"), "Scofield" (*Milton* pl. 17, l. 59; *Jerusalem* pl. 5, l. 27; pl. 7, l. 47; pl. 11, l. 21; pl. 19, l. 19; pl. 43, l. 50; pl. 60, l. 14), "Schofield" (*Jerusalem* pl. 7, l. 25), "Scofeld" (*Jerusalem* pl. 43, l. 51), "Skofield" (*Jerusalem* pl. 17, l. 59; pl. 22, l. 3; pl. 58, l. 30; pl. 68, l. 1), and "Skofeld" (*Jerusalem* pl. 8, l. 41; pl. 15, l. 2; pl. 32, l. 11; pl. 36, l. 17; pl. 67, l. 22; pl. 71, l. 38; pl. 90, l. 40).

† Miner, "Visions in the Darksom air", pp. 465–6. Schofield served in the Peninsular War in Portugal from September 1809 until November 1811 and died at Canterbury on 31 Jan 1812. (It is probably just coincidence that in *Jerusalem* pl. 17, l. 59 Los asks: "Go thou to Skofield: ask him if he is Bath or if he is Canterbury".) The fact that "He says he was degraded on account of drunkenness" derives from Samuel Rose on the basis of evidence from Schofield (*BR* 142) rather than from the War Office records. It required some ingenuity to get drunk on a private's income of 2s. a day, of which 9d. was for the horse (Atkinson, *History*, 239), but British soldiers are notoriously ingenious.

  Schofield was born in Manchester (War Office MS 25/1392, cited in Miner, "Visions in the Darksom air", p. 466); the name is particularly common in Yorkshire.

  The Regiment moved to East Anglia in April 1804 (Atkinson, *History*, 242).

One of his companions was John Cock, who had served in the Berkshire Fencibles (a militia unit) until he enlisted as a private in the Royal Dragoons on 21 March 1800.* As the Giants of Albion lament in *Jerusalem*, "Scofield & Kox are let loose upon my Saxons!"[135]

In the summer of 1803, Blake was on edge because of the strain of his relationship with his patron, and he had to exert heroic self-restraint in the face of Hayley's genteel disapprobation of his poems and designs. "*Every* one in This Country [*is*] astonishd at my Patience & Forbearance of Injuries upon Injuries".[136] Blake was wounded by criticism not only of his private character—his "nervous Infirmity" and his "dangerously acute" sensibility—but also of his engravings. On 7 August Hayley told Flaxman that "the Ladies … find Fault with the Engravings" Blake had made after Flaxman's sister Maria for Hayley's *Triumphs of Temper* (1803), and "The Engravings of Cowper have been also heavily censur'd". One can understand therefore what Flaxman called "Blake's irritability".[137]

In the circumstances, the presence of swaggering soldiers in the village must have been to Blake a sign that the Beast was verily among them, in their lanes and in their houses. And when he found one in his garden, that must have seemed to him the last straw.

Incident in the Garden

On Friday 12 August, a still, windless day, Blake was "making Verses"[138] in the thatched cottage, perhaps "Auguries of Innocence":

> He who shall train the Horse to War
> Shall never pass the Polar Bar . . . .
> The Soldier armd with Sword & Gun†
> Palsied strikes the Summers Sun . . . .
>
> Nought can deform the Human Race
> Like to the Armours iron brace
> ("Auguries of Innocence" ll. 41–2, 77–8, 99–100 from the Ballads MS)

As he was concentrating on making the verse come right, he was startled to

---

* Miner, "Visions in the Darksom air", 466. His name was spelled "Cook" when he enlisted. He was discharged in Ireland on 24 Sept 1808.

   Blake spells the name "Kock" (*Jerusalem* pl. 32, l. 11) and "Kox" (*Jerusalem* pl. 5, l. 27; pl. 7, ll. 23, 48; pl. 8, l. 41; pl. 19, l. 19; pl. 36, l. 17; pl. 43, l. 51; pl. 71, l. 42).

† Blake rarely refers to "the murdering gun" (*Jerusalem* pl. 9, l. 6), but he drew attention in apocalyptic terms to similarities between his own "Albion Rose" (*c.* 1804) and a print of a youth used as a target in Ezekiel Baker, *Thirty-Three Years Practise and Observation with Rifle Guns* (1813)—see *BR* (2) under 1813.

hear voices in his little garden.* He knew that William, the ostler at The Fox Inn, was at work there, but he could not imagine who was talking to William. When he heard "something that I thought insulting",[139] he came out to find Private Schofield casually "leaning against the garden wall"[140] while William went on with his work.

Schofield had come to tell William "that he could not do the job of work he was to do, for he was order'd to march to Chichester",[141] and William "invited [*him into the garden*] as an assistant".[142] However, Blake did not know

> that he was so invited. I desired him as politely as was possible to go out of the Garden,[143] he made me an impertinent answer[.] I insisted on his leaving the Garden[;] he refused[.] I still persisted in desiring his depar-ture[;] he threatend to knock out my Eyes with many abominable impre-cations & with some contempt for my Person[;] it affronted my foolish Pride[.] I therefore took him by the Elbows & pushed him before me till I had got him out [*of the garden*].[144]

> I am certain that if I had not turned the Soldier out of my Garden I never should have been free from his Impertinence & Intrusion.[145]

High words were exchanged, doubtless with mutual condemnation, reflections upon ancestry and occupation, and threats for the future; the sol-dier damned the Blakes and threatened to knock their eyes out,[146] and Blake may have damned the soldier and his comrades and their profession. But William the ostler, who could not have been far away in the little garden and was probably hovering anxiously near the disputants, "heard me Say nothing of ... Sedition".† Indeed, "Mr. Cosens, owner of the Mill at

---

* The official evidence about the incident in the garden consists of the "Information and Complaint of John Schofield", the bonds of Blake, Privates Schofield and Cock, and Lieutenant Hulton, the True Bills concerning sedition and assault found by the Quarter Sessions jury in Oct 1803, the verdict of the jury at the second trial of 11 Jan 1804, "The Speech of Counsellor Rose In Defence of Blake the Artist", and the discharges of Blake, Hayley, and Seagrave from their bonds (*BR* 122–34, 140–4, *BRS* 24–5, 28).

  The unofficial evidence consists chiefly of Blake's letter of 16 Aug 1803, "Blake's Memorandum in Refutation of the Information and Complaint of John Scholfield", Hayley's autobiography (*BR* 144–5), John Marsh's autobiography for 11 Jan 1804 (*BR* (2)), the *Sussex Weekly Advertiser* report of 16 Jan 1804, and Hayley's letter of 5 Feb 1804.

  In this account of what happened in Felpham on 12 Aug 1803, I have quoted Blake and Rose his counsellor as if what they alleged were true, and I have presumed that Blake was innocent of utter-ing sedition then. This was, after all, the conclusion of the jury in 1804 who had more facts than I have and who might have been encouraged to convict in a situation of government-fostered war-hysteria. Of course Blake and his wife may have been, and indeed probably were, guilty of sedition on other occasions.

† Blake's "Memorandum", confirmed in Rose's "Speech": "The Ostler ... will prove to you ... that he heard no such expressions uttered by Mr Blake".

  Perhaps Schofield said something like, "Sir, I am a soldier of the King, and I am here upon His Majesty's business, to defend the realm from French invaders", and Blake may have replied, "Damn you and damn your business; you have no business in my garden. Get out before I throw you out."

Felpham, [*who*] was passing by in the Road ... Says we certainly were not quarrelling."[147]

When Blake had pushed Schofield out of the garden,

> I intended to have left hi*m*, but he turning about put himself into a Posture of Defiance threatening & swearing at me. I perhaps foolishly & perhaps not, stepped out at the Gate & putting aside his blows took him again by the Elbows & keeping his back to me pushed him forwards down the road about fifty yards[,] he all the while endeavouring to turn round & strike me & raging & cursing which drew out several neighbours. *A*t length when I had got him to where he was Quarterd [*fifty yards away*], which was very quickly don*e*, we were met at the Gate by [*Mr Grinder*] the Master of the Hous*e*, The Fox Inn, (who is the proprietor of my Cottage) & his wife & Daughter, & the Mans Comrade [*John Cock*] & several other people[.]*

Uproar at The Fox

Naturally Private Schofield, who was in Felpham to defend his country by force from Napoleon's ever-triumphant armies, was humiliated when paraded before the gaping villagers by a little man like Blake without being able to retaliate except at the top of his voice. It was one thing to be insulted in a private garden at the edge of the village and quite another to be exhibited as a gesticulating fool before his own quarters and comrades and a good part of the village.

Those present in the street before The Fox included Mr Cosens of the mill, Mr Grinder (the landlord of The Fox) and his wife and daughter, Blake's neighbour Mrs Haynes (the wife of the miller's servant) and her daughter, Hayley's gardener (?Mr Hosier), and Schofield's comrade Private Cock, and not far away were William (Blake's gardener and the ostler at The Fox), and an old man named Jones who was giving his custom to the tap-room of The Fox. All of them knew Blake, and all were capable of comparing what they knew of his peaceableness in the past with the turbulence of strange drunken soldiers at present.

Schofield was beside himself with humiliation and frustration, raging and incoherent,† and he appeared to be intoxicated; Hayley's gardener said to

---

* Letter of 16 Aug 1803. According to Rose's Speech, the landlord's wife "Mrs Grinder separated them".

† His incoherence is demonstrated by the wonderfully confused "Information and Complaint of John Scofield". Presumably Schofield was sober when he made his deposition before the Justice of the Peace.

Private Cock, "Is your Comrade drunk?"* Private Cock shared his comrade's indignation and joined Schofield in vilifying Blake. The uproar
threatened to spread through the troop and the village until "My Landlord
compelld the Soldiers to go in doors [*into the stable*] after many abusive
threats against me & my wife".[148]

Schofield's Revenge

In the stable, Schofield and Cock conferred urgently and decided that what
Blake had said was seditious, or that it could be made to sound seditious.†
Having settled what they would do, Schofield and Cock "came together into
the Tap-room, [*and*] threatened to knock [*the ostler*] William's Eyes out ...
because W—— refused to go with him to Chichester, and Swear against
me. William Said that he would not take a false Oath, for that he heard me
Say nothing of the Kind (i.e. Sedition)[.] Mrs. Grinder then reproved the
Soldier for threatening William ...".[149]

Next day "Mr. Hosier heard him Say that he would be revenged, and
would have me hanged if he could."[150] Schofield told "Mrs. Grinder [*wife
of the landlord of The Fox*], that it would be right to have my House
Searched, as I might have plans of the Country which I intended to Send to
the Enemy; he called me a Military Painter; I suppose mistaking the Words
Miniature Painter, which he might have heard me called."[151]

Over the weekend of 13 and 14 August, Schofield and Cock organized
their evidence and presented it to their captain, who sent them to "Esquire
Hayley to hear what he had to say"[152] about his protégé. Hayley of course
had not been present at the fracas, but his emphatic statements about the
peaceableness of Blake's character[153] did not deter the two soldiers. On
Monday the 15th they went before Blake's neighbour John Quantock, the
Justice of the Peace, and made a wonderfully confused deposition alleging
that Blake had spoken seditiously.

The heart of the charge was that both in the garden and in the road Blake
had "Damned the King of England—his Country and his Subjects—[*and
said*] that his soldiers were all bound for Slaves & all the poor people in general". For good measure, Schofield added that Blake said he "wo^d certainly

---

* Blake's Memorandum. The supposition of drunkenness is particularly plausible at the door of a
  public house concerning a man who had already been convicted of being drunk while on duty.
      Blake inscribed a drinking vessel called a rummer with an indifferent couplet about "immoral
  drink" (a sentiment he does not exhibit elsewhere) and signed it "BLAKE IN ANGUISH FELPHAM
  AUGUST 1803" (see the reproduction and text in *BBS* 70–1).
† Blake said that "This method of Revenge was Planned between them after they had got together into
  the Stable" (letter of 16 Aug 1803).

begin to cut throats" to aid the French when Napoleon landed and that Catherine said: "altho she was but a Woman she wo.^d fight as long as she had a Drop of Blood in her ... for Buonaparte".* However, Schofield's quarrel was not really with Catherine, and she was not charged with sedition.

These were serious charges, and, at a time when invasion was threatened and nerves on edge, they were very dangerous. If convicted of sedition, Blake would not have been drawn and quartered, as he would have been if convicted of treason, but he could have been imprisoned and fined.

The Magistrates and the Military

And his judges and the Government were allied to the military. Next day, 16 August, Blake's neighbour John Quantock, the Justice of the Peace who had recorded Schofield's deposition, was made a field officer of the corps of Loyal Volunteers by the Duke of Richmond, the greatest man in the vicinity. Indeed, "the Lawyer who wrote down the Accusations told me [*Blake*] in private [*that they*] are compelld by the Military to suffer a prosecution to be enterd into† altho they must known & it is manifest that the whole is a Fabricated Perjury."[154]

The military was concerned not only by the threat of Napoleon's invasion barges but also by the deplorable attitude of the public to the troops stationed on them, and by the instability of the Loyal Volunteers. A typical incident occurred about a fortnight later:

> our Volunteers all met the Duke of Richmond at the Townhall at 4 in the afternoon concerning a proposal then made by his Grace for the Volunteers instead of having Cloth for Regimentals equal to that of Serjeants in ye Militia &c. that had been promised them on their enrolling to accept the comon ordinary clothing of privates, to induce them to agree to which, a great coat was offer'd in addition; but this being

---

* Schofield's "Information and Complaint". Such bloodthirsty sentiments and actions are quite out of character with what we know of the Blakes. They might deplore kings and armies—"war is energy Enslavd" (*Vala* p. 120, l. 42)—but they scarcely offered to cut throats.

† I am told by my friend David Worrall that it was common practice for local magistrates to ask the Home Office to fund the prosecution in cases of sedition and to forward the evidence to demonstrate the plausibility of the case. Dr Worrall has not found such evidence in the relevant Home Office files, but at the very least the Chichester bench of magistrates plainly found the evidence of Blake's sedition plausible. Many of the Justices of the Peace were officers in the Loyal Volunteers and had an interest in making an example to quell the unruly citizenry.

scouted, & a great clamour rising against the proposal, ... the whole Battallion refused & seceeded, except about 20. or 30 ....*

The discontent was kept alive by handbills posted throughout the town, to the great amusement of the townsmen.

But it was no laughing matter to William Blake.

On the morning of Tuesday 16 August, Blake was required to appear before John Quantock, J.P., and post a bond of £100 (more than a year's income) as surety for his appearance at the next Quarter Sessions in October. And he had to find two others, his patron William Hayley and his printer Joseph Seagrave, to put up £50 each to guarantee his presence.[155] Blake probably had to borrow money from Hayley for his bond, for he certainly did not have £100 lying about in his cottage on a Monday morning.

On the same day, Privates Schofield and Cock each had to post £50 bonds for their appearance to give evidence at the trial, lest they slip or be shipped away, and Major George Hulton posted a bond for £50 to warrant his appearance then to prefer the indictment.

Blake's Defence

The crux of Blake's defence was that a charge of sedition could not be sustained on the allegation of one witness. The seditious words were said to have been spoken in the garden, where those present were Blake, his wife, Private Schofield, and Blake's gardener. Blake and the gardener affirmed that no seditious words had been spoken there—Catherine's evidence was never summoned in court (she was not there) or cited by others—and Schofield's word alone was not sufficient.

To remedy this defect, Private Cock (but apparently not Private Schofield) swore that Blake had uttered sedition in front of the inn stable. Blake carefully canvassed the evidence of every person there; "I have all the Persons who were present at the Stable Door ... to Say that I did not utter Such Words." And "If we prove the Comrade perjured who swore that he heard me D—n the K—g, I believe the whole Charge falls to the Ground."[156]

---

* John Marsh's Autobiography (Huntington Library) for Oct 1803 (the day is obscure). The passage continues: "so at length seem'd to end our Chichester volunteering, as the Duke gave no other option than accepting yᵉ proposed alteration or withdrawing from yᵉ Corps". The corps was actually "disbanded" but was reformed later.

According to the *Sussex Weekly Advertiser* for 2 Jan 1804 (as reported to me by Professor Roussel Sargent), the subscribers to the clothing fund for the Chichester Volunteers included [William] Brereton (£52.10), Major [John] Quantock (£10.10.0), and Richard Dally; Brereton and Quantock were Justices of the Peace at Blake's 1804 trial, and Dally was his solicitor then.

It was plain to the villagers of Felpham, as it was to Blake, that "If such a Perjury as this can take effect, any Villain in future may come & drag me and my Wife out of our Home, & beat us in the Garden, or use us as he pleases, or is able, & afterwards go and Swear our Lives away."[157]

His neighbours expressed their sympathy to Blake and their fear of the military:

> it has struck a consternation thro all the Villages round. Every Man is now afraid of speaking to or looking at a Soldier, for the peaceable Villagers have always been forward in expressing their kindness for us . . . .. Every one here is my Evidence for Peace & Good Neighbourhood & yet such is the present state of things this foolish accusation must be tried in Public.[158]

But of course it was not the peaceable villagers who decided whether the accusation was sufficiently plausible to warrant a prosecution. This decision was made by the gentlemen on the bench of magistrates. And many of the Justices of the Peace were not only sympathetic to the military, who were protecting their property and their prices, but were officers in the military themselves.

Blake was in anguish about "my perilous adventure", and his wife was "much terrified", but he did not lose his "conviction that all is come from the spiritual World for Good & not for Evil".[159]

Blake scrambled for information to defend himself; he talked to all the witnesses of the excitement in the garden and at the stable door, and he wrote to Thomas Butts in the hope that Butts could "learn something about the Man" Schofield in the office of the Commissary General of Musters.[160]

Return to London

Meanwhile Blake had to get on with the ordinary business of winding up his affairs in Felpham. He sent Butts seven drawings on 16 August, which "I believe about balances our account" for the monies Butts had advanced him before the Blakes left London. And on 18 September, just three years from when they had moved to Felpham, he and Catherine packed up all their worldly goods once more, and trundled back to London.[161]

On his return, Blake found London remarkably changed. "Art in London flourishes",[162] "The shops in London improve; everything is elegant, clean, and neat; the streets are widened where they were narrow; even Snow Hill is become almost level and is a very handsome street, and the narrow part of the Strand near St. Clement's is widened and become very elegant."[163]

Until Blake's fate was decided at the Michaelmas Quarter Sessions in October, it may have seemed scarcely worth while to find their own London lodgings, and they stayed "at his Brothers a Stocking Shop—Broad Street Carnaby Market",[164] where William and Catherine Sophia Blake shared the house with James and Catherine Elizabeth Blake.

The Trial at Petworth

The Michaelmas Quarter Sessions were held on Tuesday 4 October at Petworth, the seat of the Earl of Egremont. Blake came down to Petworth by himself—there is no evidence that he was accompanied by Catherine or by a lawyer, though Hayley was there.[165] Blake must have been fairly hopeful that the trial would prove to be a mere formality and that it would be manifest to the jury that "the whole accusation is a wilful Perjury".[166]

The case of Rex vs Blake was tried before some of the most substantial gentlemen of the county as Justices of the Peace, including Charles Lennox Duke of Richmond, George Obrien Earl of Egremont, Lieutenant-General John Whyte, Nathaniel Tredcroft, John Peachey, and William Brereton.[167] Several of them were probably like Nathaniel Tredcroft, who was "a very active magistrate", the "perfect type of an old Sussex Squire ... [*who*] always wore powder in his hair and his dress was a blue tail-coat with gilt buttons, buff waistcoat, and drab cloth trousers, with either top boots or gaiters".[168] And of course the soldiers were in their dress uniforms of red and gold jackets, white leather breeches, black hats with plumes, and gleaming jack-boots. Blake must have seemed out of place in such surroundings, in his plain black coat and hat, far from his friends in Felpham and perhaps supported by little more than his own testimony.

The Justices and jurors were plainly prepared to make examples of those defying the military, for at this Michaelmas Quarter Sessions "A bill of indictment was ... found against ten men at Little-Hampton, for creating a riot and rescuing a man from the custody of a pressgang".[169]

Blake seems to have felt that his neighbours John Peachey and William Brereton were particularly biased against him, for they, along with Privates Schofield and Cock who made the accusation, Major Hulton who preferred the indictment, and John Quantock, J.P., who recorded the complaint and bonds, appear repeatedly in *Jerusalem* as "terrible sons" of Albion, "Raging against their human natures".[170]

It must have been a terrible shock to Blake when "The Jurors for our Lord the King upon their Oath present[*ed*]" that he was "a Wicked Seditious and Evil disposed person" who had attempted "with force and arms" to "encourage and incite as far as in him lay the Enemies of our said

Lord the King to invade this Realm" and that he had said "Damn the King and his Country; his Subjects and all you Soldiers are sold for Slaves". Even more astonishing, the jury concluded that he "did beat, wound, and ill treat [*John Schofield*], so that his Life was greatly despaired of". None of this charge of bearing arms and wounding Schofield "so that his Life was greatly despaired of" had appeared in Schofield's "Information and Complaint", and the latter part about desperate wounding is merely a matter of form which appears in the printed part of an "Assault" charge.

Whatever the truth as to whether Blake said "Damn the King", it is inconceivable from everything else we know of Blake's life that he "incite[*d*] as far as in him lay the Enemies of . . . the King to invade this Realm" or that he wounded Private Schofield "so that his life was greatly despaired of". These parts of the True Bill are plausibly supported neither by Schofield's Complaint nor by other evidence, and they are plainly a travesty of the truth.

Blake was required to plead to the charge, and he declared that he was Not Guilty.* He was then asked whether he was ready to be tried immediately or wished to put off (to traverse) his case until the next Quarter Sessions, to be held at Chichester in January 1804. Blake of course chose to postpone the decision, and he, Hayley, and Seagrave were bound for the same bonds as previously for the security of Blake's appearance at Chichester.

On his return to London, Blake wrote to Hayley to thank him for his "generous & tender solicitude about your devoted rebel" and to say that he had found his "wife in very poor health". But though his worldly prospects were discouraging, his resilient spirit still rejoiced:

> Every Engraver turns away work that he cannot execute from his super-abundant Employmen*t*, yet no one brings work to me[.] I am content that it shall be So as long as God pleases . . . . I laugh & sing for if on Earth neglected I am in heaven a Prince among Princes, & even on Earth beloved by the Good as a Good Man . . . as Man liveth not by bread alone I shall live altho I should want bread—nothing is necessary to me but to do my Duty & to rejoice in the exceeding joy that is always poured out on my Spirit . . . .[171]

This is an extraordinary letter for a man who had just been judged by a jury of his peers to be "a Wicked Seditious and Evil disposed person" and was awaiting his trial before a bench of hostile magistrates.

---

* Had he pleaded Guilty, a rare occurrence in eighteenth–century rural courts, the case would have been tried immediately.

Move to South Molton Street

During the autumn, the Blakes moved to 17 South Molton Street,* in the Parish of St George. South Molton Street is a short street running north at an oblique angle into Oxford Street, about a mile northwest from Blake's birthplace in Golden Square (see the map of Westminster, Pl. 8).

Here they took a small flat up one flight of stairs.[172] They were cramped into a very small space "in their one apartment ... the Bed on one side and a picture of Alfred and the Danes on the wall"[173]—and somehow they made space for the bulky printing press and all the gear of engraving and printing.[174] They lived in this small flat, usually in cheerful obscurity, for the next eighteen years.

Their new neighbourhood had none of the spaciousness and isolation of their beloved thatched cottage at Felpham—no tree, no garden, no open field, no sheep in the lanes—but two streets away to the east was Hanover Square, about four streets northeast was Cavendish Square, and the same distance to the south was Berkeley Square, where there were at least reminders of the green of the countryside. And on South Molton Street itself were individuals and businesses which provided metropolitan advantages inaccessible in a village: artists, friends of friends, and a jobbing printer.†

For Blake, the area was especially notable for its proximity to Tyburn, where criminals had been executed. "Calvarys foot Where the Victims were preparing for Sacrifice" was "Between South Molton Street & Stratford Place", near "Tyburns Brook where Victims howl & cry".[175] When he moved to South Molton Street, Blake felt that he was a victim preparing for sacrifice.

In the modest obscurity of 17 South Molton Street, Blake later painted some of his greatest works, including his designs for Job, Blair's *Grave*, the

---

* Gilchrist says that "Blake writes from South Molton Street" in his letter of 26 Oct 1803 (which has since disappeared), and Flaxman says Blake "lives at N.º 17 South Molton Street, Oxford Street opposite Stratford Place" in his letter of 25 Dec 1803. The first surviving Blake letter dated from South Molton Street is that of 27 Jan 1804.

　The rates at 17 South Molton Street were paid by Mark Martin, presumably his landlord (*BR* 563). Linnell says that "upon his Landlord leaving off business & retiring to France", Blake moved to Fountain Court, though Martin continued to pay the rates for some time thereafter (*BR* 395, 563).

† The artist Edward Bird was at No. 29 (1818); George Cumberland's friends Townley and Dayley (the cousin of the Bristol artist John Eagles) were at No. 61 (1813) and No. 51 (1814) (*BR* 563, 232); and the firm of [Ann] Watts & [Edward] Bridgewater at [31] Southmolton-street printed the advertisements for Blake's *Descriptive Catalogue* (1809) and "Blake's Chaucer: The Canterbury Pilgrims" (1809), while Watts & Co, Southmolton St, printed his "Exhibition of Paintings in Fresco" (1809)—they did not print the *Descriptive Catalogue* (1809) or "Blake's Chaucer: An Original Engraving" (1810).

　Their fellow-lodgers at 17 South Molton Street included "the young & very amiable Mʳˢ Enoch" (letter of 14 Jan 1804) and, according to Gilchrist, a French woman (*BR* 563).

Bible, Milton, and Virgil, and he wrote there at least parts of *The Four Zoas*, *Milton*, and *Jerusalem*: "I write in South Molton Stree*t* what I both see and hear".[176] *Jerusalem* was "Printed by W Blake S^th Molton S^t", as well as *Milton* and new copies of most of his earlier works in Illuminated Printing.

All autumn Blake was busy with tasks for Hayley's life, as well as engravings after Fuseli for Shakespeare; "business comes in & I shall be at ease if this infernal business of the soldier can be got over".[177]

"This Infernal Business of the Soldier"

Of course this infernal business of the soldier hung over everything. Blake's friends rallied to his defence. Hayley volunteered to serve as a character witness, a crucial consideration in a village matter, and he arranged for his friend Samuel Rose to serve as Blake's attorney. Johnny Johnson anxiously sent his wishes for "Success to the Rose Amen",[178] and Flaxman wished for "A happy release from his afflictions to poor Blake":

> I have no doubt from what I have heard of the Soldier's character and the merits of the case that the bill will at least be thrown out by the Court as groundless & vexatious—Blake's irritability as well as the Association & arrangement of his ideas do not seem likely to be Soothed or more advantageously disposed by any power inferior to That by which man is originally endowed with his faculties ....[179]

On the other hand, Lady Hesketh told Hayley that "Mr Blake . . . appeard to me much to blame, even upon his own representation of the matter, but if I may give credit to some reports which reachd me at that time, M.^r B: was more <u>Seriously</u> to blame than you were at all aware of ...."[180] Even two years after the trial, she lamented Hayley's intimacy with one "whom, for y^r sake, I ever <u>tremble</u> to think of, and whom certainly I will <u>not name</u>", and to Johnny she wrote: "My hair stands on end to think that Hayley & Blake are as dear friends as ever! He talks of him as if he was an Angel! . . . I don't doubt he will poison him in his Turret or set fire to all his papers, & poor Hayley will consume in his own Fires."[181]

Blake tardily commissioned the Chichester solicitor Richard Dally to act on his behalf in collecting information,[182] but his chief character witness was almost disabled when, as Hayley said, "a new stout & tall Horse fell suddenly in his Canter & had I not luckily had on a new strong Hat my skull would have been smashed".[183] Hayley cheerfully told "his intimate medical Friend Mr Guy", "you must patch me up very speedily, for living or dying, I must make a public appearance within a few days at the Trial of our Friend Blake".[184]

The military tension of the time is indicated in a letter from Blake's friend Joseph Johnson: "The French are daily expected in immense force, the weather will decide perhaps whether they land or not, should they do so the carnage must be dreadful—we are not unprepared having 400,000 men in arms."[185]

When Blake returned to Sussex for his trial at the Chichester Quarter Sessions, he may have stayed with Harriet Poole at her villa in Lavant. The trial was to be held on Tuesday 10 January 1804 in the gaunt old Guildhall which had once been the chapel of the convent of Grey Friars,* and it may have been at this time that Blake wrote "The Grey Monk":

"Seditious Monk" they sound afar
"In vain condemning Glorious War
And in thy Cell thou shalt ever dwell[.]
Rise War & bind him in his Cell[.]"
. . . .

When Satan first the black bow bent
And the Moral Law from the Gospel rent
He forg'd the Law into a Sword
And spilld the blood of Mercys Lord
. . . .

But vain the sword & vain the Bow[.]
They never can work wars overthrow[!]
The Hermits prayer & the widows tear
Alone can free the world from fear
. . . .

For the tear is an intellectual thing
And a Sigh is the Sword of an Angel King
And the bitter groan of the Martyrs woe
Is an arrow from the Almighties bow.[186]

The Trial at Chichester

The trial was attended by Blake, his advocate Samuel Rose, his chief char-

---

* The chapel was 82′ x 32′ x 42′ high (Richard Dally, *The Chichester Guide* [Chichester: P. Binstead, 1831], 19), but "by no means elegant", and in it were "erect[ed] galleries for the grand and petit-juries" (Alexander Hay, *The History of Chichester* [Chichester: J. Seagrave; London: Longman and Co., 1804], 389–90).

acter witness William Hayley, and by his friend John Marsh and his wife. According to Marsh, on 10 January,

M.ʳ Hayley who meant to be examined as to his character & to speak in his favor, came over to breakfast & spend the day with us, during yᵉ greatest part of which we all attended yᵉ Hall, but yᵉ Trial did not come on. In the evening therefore after tea (at which we were joined by Mʳ Rose the Advocate employed by M.ʳ Hayley for his protegée) M.ʳ Hayley returned to Felpham in preference to sleeping from home & return'd the next morning, when he and I again attended yᵉ Hall about 4. when at length yᵉ cause came on & lasted till after 5 ....[187]

Most of the magistrates, who included the Duke of Richmond, John Peachey, and John Quantock,[188] had already heard Blake's first trial at the Quarter Sessions in Petworth in October, and Blake thought once again that they did not seem very sympathetic.

The prosecutor stressed "the atrocity and malignity of the charge" against Blake,[189] and Rose in his speech defending Blake agreed "that such an offence is incapable of extenuation". His task was not to palliate the offence but "to shew that my client is not guilty of the words imputed to him". This was a difficult task, as the Petworth jury had already brought in a True Bill on the subject.

He stressed the traditionally peaceful character of artists, the dubious characters or even "malignity" of his accusers, and the internal inconsistencies of the accusations:

I am instructed to say, that Mʳ Blake is as loyal a subject as any man in this court:—that he feels as much indignation at the idea of exposing to contempt or injury the sacred person of his sovereign as any man ....

The Ostler is allowed to have been in the Garden, he was in a situation to hear all that passed—& he will prove to you by & bye that he heard no such expressions uttered by Mʳ Blake ....

[*At the stable door,*] Mʳˢ Grinder [*who*] separated them ... was as near to Blake as Cock was ... & heard no such words....

Apparently before Rose had called any witness, "in the midst of his defence a sudden illness siez'd Him, & altho' he maintained his station, He ended his Speech with apparent Infirmity".[190]

Blake listened to the evidence with a "flashing eye",[191] and, doubtless to the scandal of the bench of magistrates, "in the middle of the trial, when the soldier invented something to support his case, ... [*Blake*] called out

'*False!*' with characteristic vehemence, and in a tone which electrified the whole court and carried conviction with it."*

Despite Rose's incapacity, "After a very long and patient hearing he [*Blake*] was by the Jury acquitted, which so gratified the auditory, that the court was, in defiance of all decency, thrown into an uproar by their noisy exultations."†

It was not only the plebeian audience in court which rejoiced at a verdict which freed a peaceable and amiable man and helped to free them from fear of the military, for

> The exultation of Hayley was great; & the greater because He had observed, with concern & Indignation, that the chairman of the Sessions, the old Duke of Richmond was bitterly prejudiced against Blake; & had made some unwarrantable observations in the course of the trial, that might have excited prejudice in the Jury.—
>
> *A*s soon therefore as their verdict was given, Hayley approached the duke, & said "I congratulate your Grace, that after having been wearied with the condemnation of sorry Vagrants, you have at last had the gratification of seeing an honest man honorably delivered from an infamous persecution. Mr Blake is a pacific, industrious, & deserving artist."—
>
> The duke replied rather impolitely—"I Know nothing of Him."
>
> ["]True, my Lord,["] rejoined the Poet, ["]your Grace can Know nothing of Him; & I have therefore given you this information: I wish your Grace a good Night."—
>
> It was late in the Evening, & Hayley was eager to present the delivered artist to their very Kind & anxious Friend the Lady of Lavant ....[192]

The relief for Blake must have been enormous, and he met a suitably joyous response with Harriet Poole. On 12 January he stayed with her in Lavant, returning on the 13th to his anxious wife in London.‡

---

* Gilchrist (*BR* 146); this is what "Mrs Blake used afterward to tell", but, as she was not at the trial, her information must have come from Blake. Marsh speaks of "the Soldiers (who were examined separately) not agreeing in their evidence & failing to make good their accusation". At the time of Blake's trial, a prisoner could not give evidence on his own behalf. And see Addenda, below.

† *Sussex Weekly Advertiser*, 16 Jan 1804. Blake's friend and surety Joseph Seagrave was the founder, printer, and publisher of the journal, and perhaps its editor and author of this news report.

  The court summary of the verdict said that "the said William Blake is not Guilty of the Sedition aforesaid" and "not Guilty of the Assualt [*sic*] aforesaid" (*BR* 140).

  According to Marsh, Blake's trial lasted from "about 4 ... till after 5"—Hayley had time to chat with the Duke of Richmond and be back at Marsh's house for dinner "at 1/2 past 5". If this 90-minute hearing was thought to be "long and patient", the attention given to sorry vagrants must have been remarkably brief.

‡ Marsh says on Wednesday 11 Jan that Blake returned "by the next day's coach to London". However, the coaches left Chichester for London on Monday, Wednesday, and Friday mornings, and therefore the next coach was on Friday 13 Jan. Blake says that his letter of the morning of Saturday 14 Jan 1804 was written "immediately on my arrival" though after "I have seen Flaxman".

There he found that

My poor wife has been near the Gate of Death as was supposed by our kind & attentive fellow inhabitan*t*, the young & very amiable M*rs* Eno*ch*, who gave my wife all the attention that a daughter could pay to a mother but my arrival has dispelld the formidable malady .... [*My*] heart & soul are more & more drawn towards you [*Hayley*] & Felpham & its kind inhabitants .... Gratitude is Heaven itself[;] there could be no heaven without Gratitude[.][193]

It is no wonder that Catherine was terrified by the implications of Blake's absence. She had expected that the trial would take place on Tuesday the 10th and that Blake, if acquitted, would return on Wednesday the 11th. When Thursday passed without him, she must have assumed that he had been convicted.

Blake's gratitude to Hayley after his trial was deep and was expressed not only in his letters but in the endless errands he ran for Hayley in London among picture dealers and booksellers and friends. For instance, soon after his return to London from the trial, Blake copied the inscription on Hayley's "noble present to M*r* Rose", and Rose told his father-in-law that he had been "magnificently remunerated by Hayley" for "my Defense of Blake".[194]

But in time the well of his gratitude to Hayley was drained dry. At first he wrote doggerel about him in his Notebook, such as that

> On H——the Pick thank
> I write the Rascal Thanks til he & I
> With Thanks & Compliments are quite drawn dry

> (Notebook p. 41)

But as he brooded over his wrongs, he persuaded himself that Hayley had been somehow allied with Schofield and Cock and Quantock. In *Jerusalem*, the character named "Hyle", who seems to represent Hayley, is associated with Skofeld, Kox, Kwantok, Peachey, Brereton, and Hutton.[195] And in his Notebook doggerel Blake wrote "On H——s Friendship":

> when he could not act upon my wife
> [*He*] Hired a Villain to bereave my Life*

---

* Notebook p. 35, ll. 5–6. In "Fair Eleanor" from *Poetical Sketches* (p. 10), the ghost of Eleanor's lover bids her to "beware the cursed duke ... who, coward, in the night, Hired a villain to bereave my life".

Gilchrist says that Blake "used to declare the Government, or some high person, knowing him to have been of the Paine set, 'sent a soldier to entrap him'" (*BR* 146), a declaration which Gilchrist, most subsequent scholars, and I dismiss as paranoid.

The Toils of Friendship

Thus Blake's "three years slumber on the banks of the Ocean"[196] in lovely Felpham ended in turmoil and anguish. Friends who had seemed to be generous and loving proved to be bitterest enemies in the spirit—and then, when tested, proved to be loyal and steadfast friends after all. The toils of the world and the duties of the spirit proved yet again to be irreconcilable. The Blakes had withdrawn from the community of the great world in London to work in the little world of Felpham under the protection of one man and his friends. As Blake's worldly fortunes became more and more completely tied to the interest of William Hayley, his spiritual independence diminished. And as he tried to break free from his dependence upon William Hayley, he seemed to endanger his worldly fortunes. Loyalty to the world seemed treason to the spirit.

And on the eve of his departure from Felpham, the world intervened in his life in the most brutal fashion. As he was writing verses in his cottage, the soldier invaded his garden; the Beast was at the very door. Blake was "a slave bound in a mill among beasts".[197]

Blake's escape from the perils of the Beast and the courts of justice was due not to his truth and integrity but to the loyalty and support of his Felpham patron from which he was just divorcing himself. Without the legal defence of his attorney Samuel Rose and the character witness of his patron William Hayley, Blake's trial at Chichester might well have had the same result as the trial at Petworth: Guilty of Sedition. Loyalty to the duties of the spirit seemed to be sedition to the world.

The little community of Felpham had not proved the refuge for which the Blakes had hoped. The retreat to London was a retreat to a community of two.

CHAPTER VII

1804–1810: "Drunk with Intellectual Vision"

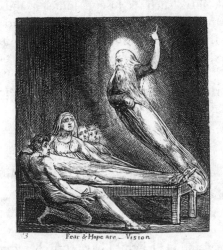

³ Fear & Hope are — Vision

*"I am really drunk with intellectual vision whenever I take
a pen or graver into my hand"*[1]

"A City of Assassinations"

The chartered streets of London were a far cry from the sheep-filled lanes
of Felpham:

> It is very Extraordinary that London in so few years from a City of meer
> Necessaries or at l[e]ast a commerce of the lowest order of luxuries should
> have become a City of Elegance in some degree …. There are now I
> believe as many Booksellers as there are Butchers & as many Printshops
> as of any other trade[.] We remember when a Print Shop was a rare bird
> in London ….[2]

When he first returned to London, Blake found that "no one brings work
to me", so "I suppose I must go a Courting which I shall do awkwardly".[3]
He tramped through the crowded streets doing endless chores for Hayley—
talking to booksellers such as Richard Phillips and picture dealers such as
William Saunders, locating Romney's pictures and patrons, sending Hayley

new prints and books, serving as Hayley's agent with publishers*—and before he had finished one set of chores Hayley gave him more. His letters are filled with fruitless industry, with the toils of the world's empty work.

Even when engraving "business comes in" and, later, when he found "every thing promising, Work in Abundance",[4] it was often a sordid business. "I am not apt to believe literally what booksellers say", even the most distinguished booksellers such as Joseph Johnson and Richard Phillips. Indeed he found that "in London every calumny and falsehood utter'd against another of the same trade is thought fair play. Engravers, Painters, Statuaries, Printers, Poets, we are not in a field of battle but in a City of Assassinations."†

The freedom for which he had longed in London seemed as distant as it had in Felpham.

"O Glory! and O Delight!"

Then suddenly, in October 1804, he was freed from the toils of the Beast and the Whore, from the dominance of his dark devil,

> For now! O Glory! and O Delight! I have entirely reduced that spectrous Fiend to his station, whose annoyance has been the ruin of my labours for the last passed twenty years of my life. ... Nebuchadnezzar had seven times passed over him; I have had twenty; thank God I was not altogether a beast as he was; but I was a slave bound in a mill among beasts and devils; these beasts and these devils are now, together with myself, become children of light and liberty, and my feet and my wife's feet are free from fetters. ... Suddenly, on the day after visiting the Truchsessian Gallery of pictures,‡ I was again enlightened with the light I enjoyed in

---

* In particular, Blake was Hayley's confidential agent in the proposal by the bookseller Richard Phillips (which "I hope [*you*] will adopt & embrace") that Hayley should become the editor or *éminence grise* of a review which "may be calld a Defence of Literature" (letter of 7 April 1804). Blake was also the intermediary in the negotiations for Phillips to become the publisher of Hayley's poems (letters of 19, 22 Jan, 22 March 1805). For further details of the negotiations, and especially Hayley's insistence that Seagrave should be his printer, see *BR* 156–60. Phillips said that "Poor Blake ... has been sadly tortured by these untoward circumstances" (5 March 1805).

† Letter of 28 May 1804. Hayley quotes Blake's phrase about "a City of [*character*] Assassinations" in his letter to Flaxman of 18 June 1804, and Flaxman replied on 2 Aug that the term was not relevant to him: "this was only a poetic *jeu d'esprit* which neither did nor intended harm". The context of Blake's letter is far less frivolous than Flaxman suggests.

‡ The *Catalogue of the Truchsessian Picture Gallery, now exhibiting in the New Road, opposite Portland Place* (1803) described about 1,000 pictures. The context is explored in Morton D. Paley, "The Truchsessian Gallery Revisited", *Studies in Romanticism*, XVI (1977), 165–77. We cannot be sure whether the Truchsessian Gallery was the cause or the occasion for Blake's renewed vision.

my youth, and which has for exactly twenty years been closed from me as by a door and by window-shutters.* ... he is become my servant who domineered over me, he is even as a brother who was my enemy. Dear Sir, excuse my enthusiasm or rather madness, for I am really drunk with intellectual vision whenever I take a pencil or graver into my hand, even as I used to be in my youth, and as I have not been for twenty dark, but very profitable years.[5]

Blake was once again a Child of Light—but the intervals between the bursts of illumination were not so great as he imagined when he began "to Emerge from a deep pit of Melancholy".† In one of the memorable fancies of the *Marriage of Heaven and Hell* (1790), an angel shows the narrator "a burning city", a black sun, and "terrific shapes of animals sprung from corruption" which are "Devils, and are called Powers of the air", but, when the angel leaves, the speaker is left with a harper singing by moonlight.[6] "My first Vision of Light" on the shore at Felpham is in Blake's letter of 2 October 1800, and his fourfold vision of Los in the sun is in that of 22 November 1802. In *Milton*, Ololon descends like "the Flash of lightning" into his garden at Felpham; the shadow of Milton fell like a falling star in his cottage garden; Blake "became One Man with" Los in the sun; and "Jesus ... walked forth From Felphams Vale".[7] Blake's illuminations were intermittent but dazzling.

"War Within my Members"

The ruinous deep pits of "Melancholy without any real reason for it", "a Disease",[8] followed by the glory and delight of illumination, suggest melancholia, a mild form of what was later called manic-depression.‡ His mood-swings, his unpredictability even to closest acquaintances, and his sudden anger at earnest friends working for his worldly welfare, all suggest an unstable personality and help to explain why friends like Hayley spoke of his "<u>dangerously acute</u>" sensibility, of his "Imagination utterly unfit to take

---

* The "exactly twenty years" may begin when Blake and Parker set up their print shop at 27 Broad Street in the autumn (?Oct) of 1784 (*BR* 557–8).

† Letter of 2 July 1800. Blake's sudden vision "on the day after visiting the Truchsessian Gallery" is often regarded as the great turning point of his life, a renewal of his faith in Christ, and a commitment to creative art (watercolour drawings) rather than reproductive art (engravings after other artists). None of these changes is as abrupt as his apocalyptic letter suggests.

‡ Fred Dortort, *The Dialectic of Vision*: A Contrary Reading of William Blake's *Jerusalem* (Barrytown [N.Y.]: Station Hill Arts, 1998), 13, argues that the "two totally contradictory sets of meanings" in *Jerusalem* may originate in "an internal conflict ... [*in Blake's own*] personality".

due Care of Himself", and of the need to "Keep his too apprehensive Spirit for a Length of Time <u>unruffled</u>".[9]

Before this, Blake had written of his struggles with what he called "this Spirit of Abstraction":

> I labour incessantly & accomplish not one half of what I intend because my Abstract folly hurries me often away while I am at work, carrying me over Mountains & Valleys which are not Real ... This I endeavour to prevent & with my whole might chain my feet to the world of Duty & Reality, but in vain! ... I so far from being bound down take the world with me in my flights & often it seems lighter than a ball of wool rolled by the wind ... who shall deliver me from this Spirit of Abstraction & Improvidence?[10]

The struggle between imagination and reason is vivid here.

Blake's writings are punctuated with "Desperation" and "Desolation", with "Death despair & everlasting brooding melancholy".[11] They suggest at least an acquaintance with the phenomenon of melancholia. In *The French Revolution*, the Governor of the Bastille is "sudden seiz'd with howlings, despair, and black night"; in *Songs of Experience*, Love "builds a Heaven in Hells despair"; and *For the Sexes* depicts a tormented man "Struggling thro Earths Melancholy".[12]

For Blake, melancholy is associated with "Reasoning Doubt Despair & Death", with "Doubts & fears unform'd & wretched & melancholy".[13]

> He who shall teach the Child to Doubt
> The rotting Grave shall neer get out
> . . . .
> He who replies to words of Doubt
> Doth put the Light of Knowledge out
> . . . .
> He who Doubts from what he sees
> Will neer Believe do what you Please[.]
> If the Sun & Moon should doubt
> Theyd immediately Go out ...
>
> ("Auguries of Innocence" ll. 87–8, 95–6, 107–10, Ballads Manuscript pp. 17–18)

Reasoning leads to doubt and despair, and "Doubts are always pernicious".[14] "Doubt ... is Self contradiction"; it is embodied by "this Satan, this Body of Doubt that Seems but Is Not".[15]

The contraries to Doubt and Despair are Faith and Hope, which seem to represent the two sides of Blake's genius, his two dæmons: "Fear & Hope are—Vision."[16] In *Vala*, Tharmas speaks of "all my Demons of Despair & hope".[17] Hope and Despair, like Innocence and Experience, are "the two Contrary States of the Human Soul", "Where the impressions of Despair & Hope for ever vegetate".[18]

The binary character of Blake's myth before about 1802, the struggle for dominance between the imaginative Los and the reasonable Urizen, may be an echo of the struggle Blake felt within himself; it may be a method of understanding and representing the Two Contrary States of his own soul.[*]

Long after October 1804, when Blake subdued the "fiend" who had long "domineered over me", he was still struggling with his dæmons of despair and hope: "Tuesday Jan[ry.] 20, 1807 Between Two & Seven in the Evening—Despair"; "23 May 1810 found the Word Golden".[19]

Blake believed that "Every mans leading propensity ought to be calld ... his good Angel",[†] what Socrates called his Dæmon,[‡] and he said that he had "been compelld by my Genius or Angel to follow where he led".[20]

However, "Man is a twofold being, one part capable of evil & the other capable of good",[§] and one part could dominate the other. Occasionally, "this Angel ... is now become a devil"—though "my Devil ... is a good naturd Devil after all"—and alternatively "these devils are now ... become children of light and liberty".[21] These are parts of, divisions within, the soul. In *Vala*, Orc speaks of "my divided Spirit", and The Eternal Man laments "the war within my members".[22]

Blake suffered such a war within his members, and his friend Thomas Butts reminded him: "you cannot but recollect the difficulties that have unceasingly arisen to prevent my discerning clearly whether your Angels are black white or grey".[23] Blake wrote in 1804: "I have indeed fought thro a Hell of terrors & horrors (which none could know but mysel*f*) in a divided Existence now no longer divide*d*, nor at war with myself[,] I shall travel on in the strength of the Lord God as Poor Pilgrim says".[24]

Blake was sometimes bewildered by the alternation between his dæmons, between his periods of accomplishment and those of frustration: "at certain

---

[*]   After 1802 the pattern becomes fourfold—"Now I a fourfold vision see" (letter of 22 Nov 1802 [beta])—with the addition of the Zoas Tharmas and Luvah, and eventually Los is identified with Christ.

[†]   Marginalium to Lavater, *Aphorisms*, fly-leaf. Sometimes Blake calls his spirits "angels" and sometimes "devils" or "fiends"; Butts calls them "Guardians" and "faithful spirits" (letter of Sept 1800), and Blake speaks of the "guardians" of his cottage (letter of 26 Nov 1800).

[‡]   In 1825, Crabb Robinson described Blake's "Socratic countenance" and quoted him as saying: "I was Socrates ... [*or*] A sort of brother" (*BR* 309, 310).

[§]   Marginalium to Lavater's *Aphorisms*, 164. He told Crabb Robinson: "Every man has a Devil in him" (18 Feb 1826).

periods a blaze of reputation arises round me in which I am considerd as one distinguishd by some mental perfection but the flame soon dies again & I am left stupefied and astonishd[.] O that I could live as others do in a regular succession of Employment ... ".[25]

He spoke of his spirits to his friends, and the spirits spoke to him: "I too well remember the Threats I heard [*from my* Angels] ... 'if you ... bury your Talent in the Earth ... Sorrow & Desperation pursues you thro life!'"[26] Failure to exercise his artistic genius would lead to melancholia and despair.

To his friends, "when he said *my visions* it was in the ordinary unemphatic tone in which we speak of trivial matters that every one understands & cares nothing about—In the same tone he said—repeatedly the 'Spirit told me'"[27] and his friends understood the context. He addressed Hayley as the "Leader of My Angels", Flaxman as the "Sculptor of Eternity", and Butts as "Friend of My Angels",[28] and they smiled at his enthusiasm.

But when he used the same kind of terminology about his enemies in a public context, the public was bewildered: "The spirit of Titian was particularly active, in raising doubts concerning the possibility of executing without a model, and when once he had raised the doubt, it became easy for him to snatch away the vision time after time.... Rubens is a most outrageous demon ... Correggio is a soft and effeminate and consequently a most cruel demon ...."[29] The display of such attitudes in print was thought by his contemporaries, and ours, to indicate madness.

For Blake, the joy of creation was intoxicating; he was "drunk with the Spirit", with "the wine of Eternity", the "wine of Los".[30] The fruits of this divine intoxication may have included manuscript poems in his Notebook and the Ballads Manuscript, and it certainly may be seen in his work on *Vala, Milton,* and *Jerusalem* and in his drawings. But the chief difference visible in his works of about this time is the incorporation of Christianity into his myth, the identification of Los the imagination with Christ, and the dominance of Los–Christ in his myth.

Work for Hayley

At Christmas time in 1804 in London, as Blake and Catherine were thinking of Hayley, and

Remembering our happy Christmas at lovely Felpham, our spirits seem still to hover round our sweet cottage and round the beautiful Turret. I have said <u>seem</u>, but am persuaded that distance is nothing but a phantasy. We are often sitting by our cottage fire, and often we think we hear your voice calling at the gate.[31]

But the joy of the season was muted by the death of "my Generous Advocate" Samuel Rose, who had fallen ill at the trial in Chichester while delivering his speech in defence of Blake. Ten days later Blake wrote: "Farewell Sweet Rose thou hast got before me into the Celestial City. I also have but a few more Mountains to pas*s*, for I hear the bells ring & the trumpets sound to welcome thy arrival among Cowper's Glorified Band of Spirits of Just Man made Perfect ...."[32]

Blake's errands for Hayley in London rarely produced cash or engraving commissions for him. At the same time Hayley was canvassing for other engravers for the new octavo edition of his life of Cowper and for his biography of Romney,* engraving commissions which Blake had expected or hoped to have. Flaxman was reluctantly persuaded to advise Hayley about engravers,† and indeed Hayley "confided the execution of the plate ... to your kind care".[33] Flaxman was in a very awkward position between friendship for Blake and loyalty to Hayley.

Flaxman said that some of the engravings of Hayley's new protégée Caroline Watson were "miserably executed".[34] He gave advice about the tardiness of William Sharp, and he recommended Blake's old partner James Parker and the young Yorkshire engraver Robert Hartley Cromek.[35] However, Lady Hesketh told Hayley that she was "<u>ardent</u> in my wishes that the ingenious Catherine [*i.e., Caroline Watson*] shou'd have the Glory of embellishing your Work", and indeed she had written to tell her that the commission was hers.‡ In the event, plates for the new octavo edition of Cowper and for the new quarto biography of Romney on which Blake had counted were engraved by Caroline Watson.

---

* Hayley was distressed by Blake's prices and by his delays in finishing plates and in delivering prints—see Blake's letters of 12, 16, 21, 31 March 1804; in his letter of 1 April 1804, Hayley writes of his "consternation" that Blake's proofs have not arrived in time to be delivered with the copies of Cowper to be sent to special friends.

† Letters of 1 May, 8, 16 June, 7 Nov 1804, 14 Nov 1805. Flaxman's belief in Blake as an engraver is indicated by his recommendation that Blake should make three of the outlines of his designs for *The Iliad* (1805), for which Blake was paid £15.15.0 (according to the Longman records [*BR* 571] and Flaxman's letters of 1 May 1804 and 11 March 1808). On 19 Aug 1814 he described "M͞r Blake [*as*] the best engraver of outlines".

‡ Letter of 14 Nov 1804. E.G. Marsh wrote to Hayley on 9 Jan 1810: "Caroline Watson's engravings [*in* your life of Romney] are beautiful in the extreme; and you never made a happier exchange than when you employed her instead of Blake" (*BRS* 60), but Johnny Johnson said that they had both "failed just as much, in their Engravings of Romney's fine head of Cowper" (13 Nov 1824 [*BRS* 80]), and he said that her engraving of the portrait of Anne Bodham "has by no means the character of the Original tho͟ʰ better than Blake's" (14 June 1822 *BR*[2]).

Blake faced the change bravely: "The idea of Seeing an Engraving of Cowper by the hand of Caroline Watson is I assure you a pleasing one to me[;] it will be highly gratifying to see another Copy by another hand & not only gratifying but Improving, which is better".[36] And a week later John Carr wrote to Hayley: "I yesterday called upon M.ʳ Blake ... with respect to Caroline Watson's engraving, he observed that his feelings were not wounded, & that he was completely satisfied with your wishes."[37] But he must have felt betrayed, particularly when he found that more than half the engravings for Romney were to go to her, leaving him with only one.

Publishing Hayley's Ballads *(1805)*

Perhaps in part to make up for Blake's natural disappointment in losing these lucrative commissions, Hayley proposed that his new publisher Richard Phillips should print a new edition of his *Ballads* in octavo with new engravings by Blake and that the expenses and profits of the edition should be shared equally between the bookseller and the engraver.* Phillips agreed on 11 February 1805 to Hayley's "Scheme of benevolence", and Blake told Hayley that he was "Truly proud ... to be in possession of this beautiful little estate".[38]

However, Blake seems not to have considered that in this partnership he was making himself liable for very substantial costs, most of which he could not control, and that he would have to lay out large sums of cash in addition to making his designs and engravings before he could expect any return. There were to be five plates "as highly finishd as I can do them ... the Price 20 Guineas each[,] half to be paid by P——" as part of the cost-sharing agreement; "of these five I am making little high finishd Pictures the Size the Engravings are to be".[39] Blake must have worked at the engravings very industriously, for the five finished plates are dated 18 June 1805, just three months later.

When the book was published, one copy was sent to Blake's Chichester friend "Mr. Weller, with grateful Remembranc[e] from William Blake", and another was sent by Hayley to Lady Hesketh as "a <u>respectful offering</u> of <u>gratitude</u> to <u>you</u> from a very *industrious* tho not very <u>prosperous</u> artist—

---

* Hayley had always anticipated an octavo edition with plates designed and engraved by Blake (see his letter of 3 April 1803); what is new is the proposal for profit-sharing. Hayley also specified that "I shall only expect to receive 30 Copies to present to my particular Friends, reserving also the right to reprint them in a collection of my Works" (28 Feb 1805). At 6s. per copy, thirty copies have a market value of £9.

smile on his gratitude, tho you will frown on some productions of his pencil, particularly <u>the last</u>, which He thinks his <u>best</u>!"[40] She replied: "I confess I think with you that the Horse is a little extra! to say nothing of the extreme composure of the Lady" (Pl. 97).[41]

The reviews of the volume were scarcely encouraging. Even a friendly one suggested that "The plates ... mark the genius, if not the taste" of Blake,[42] while some were savage. Robert Southey, the master of the un-gentle craft of reviewing, said (anonymously) that Hayley's volume

> is so incomparably absurd that no merit within his reach could have amused us half so much. ... The poet has had the singular good fortune to meet with a painter capable of doing full justice to his conceptions; and, in fact ... we know not whether most to admire the genius of Mr. William Blake or of Mr. William Hayley.[43]

Blake's last references to the *Ballads* of 1805 are despondent. On 27 November 1805 he told Hayley: "I cannot give you any Account of our Ballads for I have heard nothing of Phillips this Age", and on 11 December he lamented that "our Beautiful Affectionate Ballads" have been "mockd & despised".

On the publication in June 1805 of William Hayley's *Ballads* (1805), Blake became liable for his share (*c.* £23) of the publication-costs,[44] and though he expected to receive half the proceeds from the sales, these were slow in coming in and probably never equalled his investment in cash and kind.

To pay his debt to Phillips, Blake may have had to borrow substantial sums of money, and the sacrifices he had to make to repay his debt may well have reduced him to living on a pittance. In October 1805, according to R.H. Cromek, "you and Mrs. Blake were reduced so low as to be obliged to live on half-a-guinea a week!"[45]

Less than thirty months after the *Ballads* were published, Thomas Bensley's warehouse was destroyed by fire on 5 November 1807,[46] and unsold, unbound sheets of Hayley's *Ballads* (1805) and its copperplates which he had printed were almost certainly lost then.

Meanwhile, Phillips had secured a valuable author in William Hayley, he had not had to advance the cost of the designs and engravings for the *Ballads*, and all the copies sold in his own shop would have brought him 1s.9d. each, a profit not subject to division with Blake.

Blake may well have felt that he had been used as a pawn between two powerful players. The sorry result of Blake's venture with Hayley's *Ballads* was due to the book's lack of popularity and to the disastrous fire at Bensley's warehouse in 1807, but the fair prospects which Blake had painted for himself when the venture was first mooted in 1805 were always illusory. The venture served a useful purpose for Richard Phillips, but no substantial profit was ever likely for either of the sharers until a second edition was published. Blake felt as if he was with shrewd, calculating businessmen rather than with friends:

P—— loved me not as he lovd his Friends
For he lovd them for gain to serve his Ends[.]
He loved me and for no Gain at all
But to rejoice & triumph in my fall

(Notebook p. 34)

Designs for Blair's Grave *(1805)*

In the summer of 1805, a plausible Yorkshire engraver named Robert Hartley Cromek embarked upon a new career as a picture publisher, and the first person he approached was the obscure William Blake.

Cromek lived at No. 64 Newman Street, just north of Oxford Street, amidst a nest of successful artists,* and he was plainly a likable, enlightened man (Pl. 98). His protégé Allan Cunningham said, "I loved the man much; he had a good taste, both in Poetry and Painting, and his heart was warm and kind: I have missed him much."[47] Flaxman claimed that "M.ʳ Cromek is a man of independent Spirit & is very handsomely employed as he well deserves",[48] and his fellow-engraver John Pye remembered him as "a shrewd, clear-headed North Country man. He was nominally an Engraver; but his tastes and sympathies lay in another direction.... He appeared to me to be very intelligent, and always inclined to use his pen, when he could find occasions for so doing."[49]

Cromek spoke the language of enlightened art, though he spoke it in a marked Yorkshire accent; in Blake's poems, at any rate, he says "Mennywouver" for "manoeuvre", "Jenous" for "genius", and "Jenny Suck awa" for "je ne sais quoi".[50] He wrote to the poet James Montgomery,

Milton says it [fame] is the approbation of "Fit audience tho' few". ... No Age every [*sic*] produced many great Minds & few Ages have pro-

---

* His neighbours in Newman Street included Thomas Banks, R.A. and Henry Howard, R.A. (No. 5), Benjamin West, P.R.A. (No. 14), George Dawe, R.A. (No. 22), Henry James Richter, President of the Associated [watercolour] Artists (No. 26), Thomas Stothard, R.A. (No. 28), Cornelius Varley, founder of the Watercolour Society (No. 42), John Bacon, R.A. (d. 1799) and Joseph Bacon (No. 68).
    Newman Street is close to Poland Street where Blake lived in 1785–90 (see Pl. 8 for Horwood's map of Westminster).

duced any—As there can be but few Men of Genius so, I grant, to be one of them, is to be, as far as relates to this World, unhappy, unfortunate; the Mock & scorn of Men; always in strife & contention against the World & the World against him; but, as far as relates to another World, to be one of these is to be Blessed! He is a Pilgrim & stranger upon Earth, travelling into a far distant Land, led by Hope & sometimes by Despair but—surrounded by Angels & protected by ye immediate Divine presence he is the light of the World. therefore Reverence thyself, O Man of Genius!—

There exists in this Country a vast, formidable Party with the Edinburgh Reviewers at their Head who contemn, & to the utmost of their power spread abroad their contempt for <u>Poets & Poetry</u>, & of all the Works of Fancy & Imagination[,] denying & blaspheming every power of the Mind except reasoning & thence demonstrating their Design to depress true Art & Science & to set up false Art & science in their stead— The false art & the true Art are the Tares & Wheat—the encouragement which Men of Genius receive from Men of the World is the same encouragement as the Wheat receives from the Tares: they <u>must</u> grow together 'till the time of Harvest—[51]

These sentiments—the exaltation of the man of genius scorned by the world, a stranger and pilgrim on earth surrounded by angels, false and true art mingled like the Wheat and the Tares until the Last Harvest—they sound wonderfully like William Blake, and one may imagine what a responsive chord they would have struck in his breast.

When Cromek was collecting unpublished poems by Burns, he wrote of him in terms extraordinarily similar to those Hayley used of Cowper:

So great is my Zeal that I often think the spirit of Burns would be <u>soothed</u> if it were permitted to hover over me, & regard my ardent & heartfelt Occupation. . . . my veneration for his Memory will induce me to suppress every thing hostile to his Character & to the feelings of his better Days—[52]

But some who knew Cromek came to very different conclusions. George Cumberland, Jr, who lived with his brother Sydney at the Cromeks in 1808, wrote to his father that "It is very unpleasant at Mrs Cromek's . . . they take great liberty's with me, my home & abroad amusements & Study's are frustrated by their selfish dispositions, <u>true Yorkshire</u>."*

* Letter of 20 Dec 1808 (*BR* 209 n2). Cumberland sent drawings and messages to Blake via his sons at the Cromeks (1 Dec 1808), and in 1808 he "Settled with Mrs Cromac for 1 fortnight board—2.2.—" (British Library Add MSS 36,591 I, f. 404). Allan Cunningham lived with the Cromeks for eight months in 1810.

Allan Cunningham's son remarked that "Cromek had rather lax ideas about *meum et tuum*". Cromek wrote to Allan Cunningham, "I envy you the sight of Lady Nithsdale's letter—pray steal it, at all events, mark its date and compare it with the printed copy".[53] And Cunningham told his son of an occasion when the gentle and tolerant

Sir Walter Scott was talking to him of some of the chief curiosities he possessed at Abbotsford—"I had once—I am sorry to say once—an original letter from Ben Jonson to Drummond of Hawthornden, all in Ben's own beautiful handwriting—I never heard of another." My father mentioned one he had seen in London in Cromek's hands. Scott used some strong expression, and added, "the last person I showed the letter to was Cromek, and I have never seen it since".[54]

In the acknowledgements in the edition of Blair's *Grave* (1808) with designs by Blake, Cromek neglected to mention the author of the designs, and in his *Remains of Nithsdale and Galloway Song* (1810) he neglected to mention that they had been chiefly collected, and indeed composed, by his young friend Allan Cunningham. As Walter Scott remarked, "Cromek is a perfect Brain-sucker living upon the labours of others".[55]

Cromek's character is seen perhaps most clearly in a remark he made to James Montgomery: "I value your Remarks on the <u>Reliques</u> [*of Burns*] infinitely more, because <u>they</u> come home, more immediately, to my business & bosom."[56]

Cromek was a friend of John Flaxman, of George Cumberland, and of Thomas Stothard. Blake and Cromek had engraved plates for some of the same books, and indeed about this time Blake designed and engraved the frontispiece of B.H. Malkin's *A Father's Memoirs of His Child* (Pl. 99) which Cromek re-engraved for the published work in 1806 (Pl. 100). Cromek's version is considerably more conventional than Blake's, the child being led heavenward by an angel is significantly more darling, but this scarcely seems to explain why Blake's responsibility for the engraving was suppressed and Cromek's name inserted by itself.

In the early autumn of 1805, as Blake told Hayley, "my Friend Cromek"

came to me desiring to have some of my Designs. *H*e namd his Price & wishd me to Produce him Illustrations of The Grave A Poem by Robert Blair. *I*n consequence of this I produced about twenty Designs which pleasd so well that he with the same liberality with which he set me about the drawings, has now set me to Engrave them. He means to Publish them by Subscription with the Poem . . ..*

Flaxman gives more details in a letter of 18 October:

M.ʳ Cromak has employed Blake to make a set of 40 drawings from Blair's poem of the Grave 20 of which he proposes [*to*] have engraved by the Designer and to publish them with the hope of rendering Service to the Artist, several members of the Royal academy have been highly-pleased with the specimens and mean to encourage the work, I have seen several compositions, the most Striking are, The Gambols of Ghosts according with their affections previous to the final Judgment—A widow embracing the turf which covers her husband's grave—Wicked Strong man dying [Pl. 111]—the good old man's Soul recieved by Angels—†

Flaxman's report that Cromek gave the commission "with the hope of rendering Service to the Artist" agrees with what Cromek claimed himself. He later wrote that he had done so "to create and establish a reputation for you [*Blake*]".[57] But a desire to serve the artist by establishing his reputation is not incompatible with making money for both artist and sponsor. Cromek clearly hoped to foster the fortunes of both artist and publisher by his enterprise—and he was very enterprising.

Apparently Blake made forty drawings for Blair's *Grave*, from which Cromek chose twenty. For these twenty he paid "the insignificant sum of one guinea each".[58] The price-per-design was the same as Butts paid Blake for his Biblical watercolours, but Cromek's £21 payment was not only for the twenty drawings but for the right to publish them as well.

Blake must have worked very rapidly indeed if he made forty drawings and twenty finished, engravable designs in just two months. On 14 November, Flaxman wrote to Hayley:

on the Subject of Engravers you will be glad to hear that Blake has his hands full of work for a considerable time to come and if he will only

---

*   Letter to Hayley of 27 Nov 1805: "our Progress . . . is but of about two Months Date". In his Prospectus of Nov 1805, Cromek speaks of his "private Friendship" for Blake. Blair's *Grave* was Cromek's first publication of an edition (Anon. [?Allan Cunningham], "Biographical Sketch of Robert Hartley Cromek", Robert Blair, *The Grave* [London: R. Ackermann, 1813] [*BR* 167]). According to J.T. Smith, Cromek gave Blake the commission with "the promise, and indeed . . . the express agreement, that Blake should be employed to engrave them" (*BR* 464).

†   According to *The Antijacobin Review* (Nov 1808), some drawings, "which though submitted to public inspection at the Royal Academy, have not yet been subjected to the operation of the *Burin*".

condescend to give that attention to his worldly concerns which every one does that prefers living to Starving, he is now in a way to do well[.]

In October, Flaxman understood that Cromek proposed for Blake to engrave all twenty designs, and as late as 27 November Blake understood that he was to engrave "about twenty Designs". For them he should have expected to be paid £31.10.0 each, or £15.15.0 if less finished, as he was for his somewhat smaller plates for Hayley's lives of Cowper and Romney.[59] At this rate, he might expect £315–£630 for engraving the twenty plates for Blair's *Grave*. With such handsome expectations from the engravings, Blake might well accept a modest payment for the designs themselves.

One of Cromek's first actions with Blake's finished designs was to take them to the Royal Academy to solicit support for the undertaking. A very impressive number of Academicians were willing to lend him their names publicly, including the President, Benjamin West, and Blake's friends Richard Cosway, John Flaxman, Henry Fuseli, and Thomas Stothard,[60] and Cromek named them prominently in his prospectuses. This was an exceedingly promising beginning.

Elated by such solid backing, Cromek printed a Prospectus in November so that he could begin to solicit subscriptions to the work. This advertised

A NEW AND ELEGANT EDITION OF BLAIR'S GRAVE, ILLUSTRATED WITH FIFTEEN PRINTS* FROM DESIGNS INVENTED AND TO BE ENGRAVED BY *WILLIAM BLAKE;* WITH A PREFACE CONTAINING AN EXPLANATION OF THE ARTIST'S VIEW IN THE DESIGNS, AND A CRITIQUE ON THE POEM.

The Work has been honoured with the Subscriptions and Patronage of the following Gentlemen [*members of the Royal Academy*] . . . .

The Preface will be contributed by BENJAMIN HEATH MALKIN, Esq. M.A. F.S.A.†

The Proprietor of the present Work, diffident of his own Judgment in general, and more particularly in a Case, where private Friendship and personal Interests might be suspected of undue Influence, was afraid to venture on ushering this Prospectus into the World, merely on his own Opinion. That he might know how far he was warranted in calling the Attention of the Connoisseurs to what he himself imagined to be a high and original Effort of Genius, he submitted the Series of Drawings to

---

*   The Prospectus lists the 15 "SUBJECTS PROPOSED TO BE ENGRAVED", including "The Widow embracing her Husband's Grave" (reproduced at *BR* 166), "Death pursuing the Soul through the Avenues of Life" (collection of Robert N. Essick), and "Friendship" which were not engraved.

†   Cromek's edition of *The Grave* (1808) has no preface and nothing signed by Malkin.
    Malkin's "Explanation of the Artist's View in the Designs" to Blair's *Grave* promised here probably became the essay "Of the Designs" in the 1808 *Grave*.

Mr. WEST, and Mr. FUSELI, whose Character and Authority in the highest Department of the Art are unquestionable. The latter Gentleman has favoured the Proprietor with some Observations from his elegant and classical Pen, with Permission to make them public: they are decisive in their Testimony, and as they preclude the Possibility of any additional Remarks, they are here subjoined ....

"... The Author's Invention ... and the Execution of the Artist, equally claim Approbation, sometimes excite our Wonder, and not seldom our Fears, when we see him play on the very Verge of legitimate Invention; but Wildness so picturesque in itself, so often redeemed by Taste, Simplicity, and Elegance, what Child of Fancy, what Artist would wish to discharge? The Groups and single Figures on their own Basis, abstracted from the general Composition, and considered without Attention to the Plan, frequently exhibit those genuine and unaffected Attitudes, those simple Graces which Nature and the Heart alone can dictate, and only an Eye inspired by both, discover.* Every Class of Artists, in every Stage of their Progress or Attainments, from the Student to the finished Master, and from the Contriver of Ornament, to the Painter of History, will find here Materials of Art and Hints of Improvement!"

. . .

The original Drawings, and a Specimen of the Stile of Engraving, may be seen at the Proprietor's, Mr. CROMEK, 23, Warren Street, Fitzroy Square, London, where also the Names of SUBSCRIBERS will be received.†

This is extraordinarily emphatic praise from Blake's friend Fuseli,‡ though Blake might have been surprised to find that the vocabulary is that of sensibility rather than sublimity.

---

*   This claim may be the stimulus for the assertion in the description "Of the Designs" in the *Grave* (1808) that "These Designs, detached from the Work they embellish, form of themselves a most interesting Poem". Note that Fuseli was discussing the twenty watercolours shown at the Royal Academy in the autumn of 1805, not the twelve engravings made from them in 1806.

†   *BRS* 30–3 (with reproductions).

    Fuseli's evaluation in this Prospectus is reprinted from standing type in the second Blair Prospectus of Nov 1805 and, with trifling changes, chiefly in capitalization, in Blair's *Grave* (1808), xii–xiv, and a flyer of ?July 1808 reprints the paragraph quoted here about Blake. The unsigned reviews in *The Examiner*, 7 Aug 1808 [by Robert Hunt] and in *The Antijacobin*, Nov 1808 responded with incredulity to Fuseli's claims for Blake's designs.

    Fuseli's friend John Knowles said in his *Life and Writings of Henry Fuseli* (1831) that Blake "distributed" this first Nov 1805 Prospectus (*BR* 168 n1), but he is unlikely to have done so more actively than in suggesting to Cromek possible patrons of the undertaking, as he did in his letter of 27 Nov 1805.

‡   Blake helped to repay his debt to Fuseli by writing to the *Monthly Magazine* in June 1806 defending Fuseli's "Count Ugolino" in the Royal Academy exhibition from an attack on it in *Bell's Weekly Messenger*, though "Such an artist as Fuseli is invulnerable, he needs not my defence." Blake depicts Dante's Ugolino in *For Children* pl. 14, *Marriage* pl. 16, his portrait of Dante for Hayley's library, and in a late tempera.

On 27 November, Blake wrote to Hayley about "the Spirited Exertions of my Friend Cromek" who had "set me to Engrave" "about twenty Designs" for Blair's *Grave*. "He means to Publish them by Subscription with the Poem as you will see in the Prospectus which he sends you in the same Pacquet with the Letter."* The advantage of publishing by subscription was that it permitted the speculator to receive a substantial part of his returns before he had committed himself to the costs of paper and printing.

Apparently Blake had not yet seen the first Prospectus when he wrote his letter, for he would scarcely have spoken of engraving twenty designs if he had known that the Prospectus called for only "FIFTEEN PRINTS . . . ENGRAVED BY *WILLIAM BLAKE*".

Two weeks later, Blake still felt confident of his prospects when he wrote on 11 December to Hayley thanking him "for the kind Reception you have given my New Projected Work. It bids fair to Set me above the difficulties I have hitherto encounterd."†

He might have felt betrayed had he known that Cromek's letter to Hayley enclosing Blake's letter and the Prospectus said that Blake's "work has too much mind and too little of the hand in it to be generally understood".‡ This was an ominous opinion in a publisher intending to reach a wide audience.

Perhaps Cromek too had had a shock. The Prospectus sent to Hayley said that "a Specimen of the Stile of Engraving, may be seen" at Cromek's house. Almost certainly Cromek had not seen this engraved Specimen when he wrote the advertisement. Indeed, Blake may have delivered the promised specimen to Cromek when he brought the letter to be sent to Hayley.

The specimen Blake brought to Cromek is probably the design of "DEATHS DOOR" boldly engraved in white-line on a black background (Pl. 101). This unconventional technique would have dismayed a bookseller who was aiming for popularity or at least for extensive sales and who had been anticipating something like Blake's engraving of Cowper after Romney for Hayley's biography (Pl. 89) or perhaps his simpler engravings for Young's *Night Thoughts* (Pl. 64–70). Cromek must have said to himself,

---

* As part of his Spirited Exertions, "Cromek, engraver, called [*on the artist Joseph Farington*] and brought designs by <u>Blake</u> to illustrate 'Blair's grave' " (30 Nov 1805).
† The "kind Reception" probably consisted of promises to find subscribers, such as Hayley's friends William Guy, Miss Harriet Poole, W.S. Poyntz, Joseph Seagrave, and Richard Vernon Sadleir. The omission of Thomas Butts and George Cumberland from the Blair subscription list may be due, as Cromek wrote on 14 Aug 1808, to "the d—d carelessness of my Printer" who omitted Cumberland's name from the list. "Your Name has also some influence, & consequently the affair is to the last degree unlucky."
‡ Letter of 27? Nov 1805 (see *BR* [2]. It is possible that the untraced Prospectus sent to Hayley had been emended like the one sent "With Mr Cromek's respects" to "Mr Tomlinson" so that the phrase "AND TO BE ENGRAVED BY *WILLIAM BLAKE*" was replaced by "and to be engraved by L. Schiavonetti" (*BRS* 33 n2).

"This will never do"[61] and set out immediately to find a more compliant engraver.*

The man he turned to was Luigi Schiavonetti, friend and follower of the fashionable Francesco Bartolozzi. Schiavonetti agreed promptly to accept this very large and profitable commission, and between 27 November, when Blake wrote his letter to Hayley, and the end of the month Cromek issued another Prospectus for Blair's *Grave*. This Prospectus was almost identical to the previous one—indeed, it was printed from standing type, including the date of "Nov. 1805"—but it incorporated some crucial changes. There were now to be not "FIFTEEN PRINTS" but "TWELVE VERY SPIRITED ENGRAVINGS", they were to be engraved not "BY *WILLIAM BLAKE*" but "BY *LOUIS SCHIAVONETTI*", and patrons were no longer invited to inspect "a Specimen of the Stile of Engraving" at Cromek's house,[62] because the only engraving Cromek had in hand was by Blake, not Schiavonetti.

When Blake discovered that the engraving commission expressly promised to him had been given to Schiavonetti, his Notebook erupted with little pustules of coruscating verse:

Cr— loves artists as he loves his Meat[;]
He loves the Art but tis the Art to cheat

A petty Sneaking Knave I knew
O Mʳ Cr—— how do ye do[?]

(Notebook p. 29)

Flaxman may have seen Blake's white-line engraving of "Death's Door", for on 1 December he wrote to Hayley:

Blake is going on gallantly with his drawings from the Grave, which are patronized by a formidable list of R.A's and other distinguished persons—I mentioned before that he has good employment besides, but still I very much fear his abstracted habits are so much at variance with the usual modes of human life, that he will not derive all the advantage to be wished from the present favourable appearances[.]

---

* Thomas Stothard's son wrote that "Cromek found, and explained to my father that he [*Blake*] had etched one of the subjects [*for Blair's GRAVE*], but so indifferently and so carelessly ... that he employed Schrovenetti [*i.e.*, Schiavonetti] to engrave them" instead (Robert T. Stothard, "Stothard and Blake", *Athenaeum* [1886] [*BR* 172]).

  Cunningham said that Blake made "an experiment or two" in engraving designs for Blair's *Grave* (*BR* 490), but, as all his other information about Cromek and Blake's *Grave* designs comes from J.T. Smith, it seems likely that this is merely Cunningham's characteristic embroidery of his source. There is no other evidence that Blake engraved a second plate for Blair's *Grave*.

Flaxman may well have suggested to Blake that he might make more effort to accommodate himself to Cromek's attempts to sell his designs, a suggestion Blake would not have taken kindly. Indeed, this may have been the beginning of a breach between the two old friends. On 17 December Flaxman wrote to Hayley:

> When You have occasion to write to Mʳ Blake pray inquire if he has sufficient time to spare from his present undertaking to engrave, my drawings of Hero & Leander, & the orphan family, if he has not I shall look out for another engraver. I would rather this question should be proposed by you then me because I would not have either his good nature or convenience strained to work after my designs[.][63]

And two and a half years later, Flaxman told Hayley, "at present I have no intercourse with Mʳ Blake".*

Schiavonetti must have begun his engravings of Blake's designs for Blair's *Grave* with great vigour, probably beginning with the one for "Death's Door". A proof for this, dated as early as 1 February 1806 (Pl. 102), is a mirror image of Blake's (Pl. 101): white for black, right for left, regular, deft, and smooth for bold, varied, and powerful (notice the techniques of lines used for shading). It is also much larger than Blake's (17.5 x 29.7 cm vs 11.7 x 18.6 cm); the scale of engraving-size has increased while Cromek decreased the number of engravings.

Blake's plate of "Death's Door" might well have appeared to the public, as it did to Stothard's son, to have been "etched ... so indifferently and so carelessly" that Cromek did well to suppress it.[64] But Schiavonetti's etchings moved the reviewers to exclamatory ecstasy for the "unrivalled graver of L. SCHIAVONETTI": "Rich dotted lines in the half tints, just direction and playfulness of line throughout, diversified touch, and vigorous drawing, rank ... [*them*] among the best Engravings ... in any country."† And

---

* Letter of 4 May 1808. As early as his return from Felpham, Blake felt neglected by Flaxman: On 23 Feb 1804 he wrote to Hayley: "Flaxman ... is so busy that I believe I shall never see him again but when I call on him for he has never yet since my return to London had the time or grace to call on me". The relations between Flaxman and Blake may have been strained, but they were not broken, for on 22 Nov 1806 Flaxman paid £1.1.0 for "Blake's drawing", presumably the "singularly grand drawing of the Last Judgment, by Blake", which appeared in his sale at Christie's, 1 July 1828, Lot 61 (*BR* 575).

† Robert Hunt's review in *The Examiner* (7 Aug 1808) is glowing about Schiavonetti, acerbic about Blake; the comment refers specifically to the frontispiece. The hostile *Antijacobin Review* (Nov 1808) said that the engravings "are executed with much spirit and truth" and are "highly commendable", and Rees's *Cyclopaedia* (1811?) spoke of their "fine feeling, and a congenial, unstudied simplicity of style" (*BRS* 64).

   Blake wrote that "The Modern Chalcographic Connoisseurs & Amateurs admire only the work of the journeyman Picking out of whites & blacks in what is called Tints" (Public Address, Notebook p. 63).

   The delay in publishing the *Grave* from the autumn of 1805 until the summer of 1808 may have been due in part to the time needed to finish the engravings; on 17 April 1807 Cromek wrote that only "One half of Blake's Work is completed" (*BRS* 46), and as late as 21 July 1807 Schiavonetti said that he had not quite "completed the last judgment" (*BRS* 53).

Cromek thought, or at least advertised, that they were "exquisitely finished".[65]

Had Blake made the engravings, the cost might have been modest.
Schiavonetti's fees, on the other hand, were certainly substantial. For his
thirteen plates, he is likely to have been paid over £500; for "The Last
Judgment" alone he asked £63 because of "the quantity of work that there
is".[66]

Malkin's Memoirs *(1806)*

When Blake's friendship with Cromek was betrayed, fortunately he could
turn to more loyal and disinterested supporters.

In the autumn of 1805, Blake met Benjamin Heath Malkin of Hackney.*
The context may have been Blake's designs for Blair's *Grave*, for which
"Benj. Heath Malkin, Esq., M.A., F.S.A., Hackney", was a subscriber.
Malkin had seen and admired the drawings and Fuseli's praise of them,[67]
and indeed, he agreed to write a preface to the edition.[68]

Malkin was still mourning the death of his prodigious son Thomas
Williams Malkin, who had died in 1802 at the age of six. He had published
a memoir of his son in *The Monthly Magazine* (Nov 1802), but he wished to
do more. He therefore expanded the 1802 memoir, and for it he commissioned Blake to design and engrave a frontispiece of the dead boy being
taken to heaven (Pls 99–100) and an estimate of the artistic talents of the
little boy. Blake praised his son's art for displaying "a firm, determinate outline" and for "that greatest of blessings, a strong imagination".

In a letter of 4 January 1806 to Thomas Johnes which serves as a preface
to *A Father's Memoirs of His Child*, Malkin travelled "a little out of the
record, for the purpose of descanting on [*William Blake's*] merit, which
ought to be more conspicuous, and which must have become so long since,
but for opinions and habits of an eccentric kind".[69]

Malkin's biographical information could have come only from Blake
himself, with its accounts of what Blake "thinks himself authorized to
pronounce",[70] particularly about his early life. It is a systematic narrative,
not merely anecdotal, with many wonderful details, such as the auction-
eer who "knocked down to him a cheap lot [*of prints*], with friendly precipitation". While Malkin is deeply sympathetic, he remarks how Blake's

---

* Blake may have met Malkin (1769–1842) through Butts, who had a house in Hackney in 1786–1808
  or through George Cumberland, who was a friend of Malkin's friend Thomas Johnes. Malkin was
  later the distinguished Headmaster of King Edward's School, Bury St Edmunds (1809–28), and he
  was remembered with affection by a number of his pupils who became Cambridge Apostles.

"peculiar notions", especially his "Enthusiastic and high flown notions on
... religion", began to interrupt his career; with the public, he had a
reputation "as an engraver, who might do tolerably well, if he was not
mad".[71]

Malkin treats Blake's poetry very seriously, comparing it to works from
Ben Jonson, Revelation, Milton, and Shakespeare.[72] Of course, he quotes
only the lyrical poetry. Blake must have shown him his own copies of
Poetical Sketches and *Songs of Innocence and of Experience*, and Malkin gave
a copy of *Songs of Innocence* to Thomas Johnes in 1805.*

This is the first substantial account of Blake, and indeed it exceeds the
bulk of everything which had previously been printed about him. Malkin's
transcripts from *Poetical Sketches, Songs of Innocence*, and *Songs of
Experience* made these works available to a far wider audience than Blake
had reached,† and the reviews of Malkin's book provided the first published
comments (besides Malkin's) on Blake as a poet.

Malkin's admiration of Blake's poems was not confirmed by the reviews
of his book. *The Literary Journal* (July 1806) said that in his poetry "Mr.
Blake has successfully heightened the 'modern nonsense'"; *The British
Critic* (Sept 1806) concluded that Blake as a poet seems to be "chiefly
inspired by ... divine Nonsensia"; *The Monthly Review* (Oct 1806) asked,
"if Watts seldom rose above the level of a mere versifier [*as Malkin had written*], in what class must we place Mr. Blake, who is certainly very inferior to
Dr. Watts?"; and *The Monthly Magazine* (Jan 1807) concluded that "The
poetry of Mr. Blake ... does not rise above mediocrity; as an artist he appears
to more advantage". Only the *Annual Review* (Jan 1807) found praise for
him, though in double negatives: Blake's "poems are certainly not devoid of

---

*   *Innocence* (P) is inscribed "the gift of M͟r͟ Malkin 1805" and bears the crest of Thomas Johnes (*BB*
409).
    The only work with designs by Blake in Evans's catalogues of *the Valuable Library of Benjamin
Heath Malkin* (22, 24–8 March 1828) and *the Collection of Engravings of Benjamin Heath Malkin* (31
March 1828) is Blair's *Grave* (1808), Lot 237 in the former sale, though Malkin owned a number of
books with Blake's engravings after the designs of other artists.

†   Malkin printed "How sweet I roam'd" and "Song [I love the jocund dance]" from *Poetical
Sketches*, "Laughing Song", "Holy Thursday", and "The Divine Image" from *Innocence*, and
"The Tyger" from *Experience*, and several of these were reprinted from Malkin in the *Literary
Journal* (July 1806), *Annual Review* (1807), Anon., *Perambulations in London*, ed. Priscilla
Wakefield (1809, 1814), Jane and Ann Taylor, *City Scenes* (1818–45), and *Dawn of Light* (April
1825) (*BR* 622, 623, *BBS* 156–7, *BRS* 83). William and Dorothy Wordsworth copied from Malkin
all these save "How sweet I roam'd" and "The Divine Image" in a notebook of 1800–8 (*BR* 430
n1).
    A thousand copies were printed for Malkin (it was a frankly vanity publication), Malkin himself
gave away forty-seven copies—he may have given several to Blake, for Blake sold one to Thomas
Butts (*BR* 574)—and 450 copies were pulped in 1811 (*BB* 595).
    Note that Blake's *Poetical Sketches* was apparently not published in the sense of being offered for
sale.

merit".[73] Once again, an attempt to bring Blake into popularity as a poet had failed.

Despite this failure, Blake and Malkin remained such good friends that in 1812 Malkin edited *The Prologue and Characters of Chaucer's Pilgrims*,[74] to praise Blake's plate of Chaucer's pilgrims.

The appearance of Malkin's biographical account of Blake in his *Memoirs of His Child* may have been another result of Cromek's betrayal of Blake, for it was probably first intended for the preface of Cromek's edition of Blair's *Grave* with Blake's illustrations. Only the admiration of Malkin and his ingenuity in linking the prodigious qualities of Blake to those of his six-year-old-son made it possible for the public to see Blake even in this abbreviated form.

Brilliant Patronage of Thomas Butts

The friend upon whom Blake depended most confidently was, of course, his generous, steady patron Thomas Butts. From Butts he had a stream of commissions,* probably worth enough to support the very modest needs of William and Catherine: £35.2.0 in 1805, £49.8.4 in 1806, £87.12.6 in 1807, £56.15.0 in 1808, £83 in 1809, and £94.10.0 in 1810.[†] Among the most important designs Blake made for Butts at this time were the nineteen for the Book of Job (1805–6) and the twelve for *Paradise Lost* (1808) adapted from the smaller set of Joseph Thomas (1807).

The *Paradise Lost* designs which Blake made for Thomas Butts in 1808 are among his greatest visual accomplishments. Some of the most dazzling of them are "Satan Calling Up His Legions", "The Rout of the Rebel Angels", "Raphael Warning Adam and Eve", and "The Temptation and Fall of Eve" (Pls 103–6). In each of them, Blake has represented power and grace in scenes of supernatural tension and in a manner demonstrating that he has understood Milton profoundly and extended Milton's meanings in characteristically Blakean ways.

---

* See "Jacob's Dream" (Pl. 130), "Christ Baptising" (1805) (Pl. 3), "The Great Red Dragon and the Beast from the Sea" (1803–5) (Pl. 5), "Fire" (1805) (Pl. 23), Elizabeth Butts (1809) (Pl. 72B), "The Whore of Babylon" (1809) (Pl. 74), "Ezekiel's Wheels" (1803-5) (Pl. 76), "God Blessing the Seventh Day" (1805) (Pl. 77), and "Vision of the Last Judgment" (1807) (Pl. 104), all of which were owned by Butts.

† *BR* 570–8. The receipts, mostly merely "on further account", do not mention Butts's copies of *Thel* (L), *Jerusalem* (I), *Milton* (A), *Poetical Sketches* (B), the coloured *Night Thoughts* (A), or the designs for Job and *Paradise Lost*, so Butts may have made further payments to Blake for them, unless, like his copies of *America* (F), *Europe* (C), and *Songs of Los* (B), they were acquired after Blake's death.

The surviving receipts end in 1810, but the commissions did not, for from 1811 to 1820 Blake painted at least thirty-three more pictures for Butts,[75] including some of his most ambitious works: "Allegory of the Spiritual Condition of Man" (1811?), "Epitome of Hervey's 'Meditations Among the Tombs'" (?1820), and the illustrations for *Comus* (1815?), "On the Morning of Christ's Nativity" (1815?), *L'Allegro*, and *Il Penseroso* (*c.* 1816).

Perhaps equally welcome to Blake was the commission from Butts for "teaching your Son [*Tommy*] at 25 Guineas per Annum", beginning on Christmas day 1805.[76] Tommy's friend Seymour Kirkup said that Butts "placed his son with him as a pupil to learn engraving that he might possess a manuel art to serve him as a reso[*u*]rce in case of any misfortune such as losing his situation."[77] Eight engravings signed "T Butts" and "TB" survive as indications of what Tommy learned, and there was a family tradition that "the father seems to have profited far more by these lessons [*with Blake*] than the son did".[78] Blake did more than supply the technique and the inspiration for these lessons; he also provided the copperplates, one of which is on the back of *America* pl. a.[79] The most ambitious of the Butts engravings, called "Christ Trampling on Satan", is carefully based on a drawing by Blake and may well have some engraved touches by Blake as well.

These lessons kept Blake in very close touch with the Butts family. On 14 August 1809 Tommy wrote to his mother who was on holiday in Epsom, "This morning I ... went to South Molton Street; you wished me to do so while you and my Father are out of Town. Mr. and Mrs. Blake are very well, they say I am browner and taller;—they intend shortly to pay the promised visit at Epsom."

During these difficult years for Blake, Thomas Butts provided far more of his income than all other known sources combined. He also helped to maintain Blake's emotional equilibrium in years when the public seemed to have deserted him. A very large proportion of Blake's finished drawings are due to the enlightened liberality of one patron of genius: Thomas Butts, the white collar Maecenas.

Blake was, of course, making commercial engravings at the same time: An octavo plate after Flaxman for Prince Hoare's *Academic Correspondence* (1804); two more after Fuseli for Shakspeare's *Plays* (1804); three quarto plates after Flaxman for *The Iliad* (1805); a quarto plate after Romney in 1805 for Hayley's *Life of George Romney* (1809); and an octavo plate after Sir Joshua Reynolds for Prince Hoare's *Inquiry into the ... Arts of Design in England* (1806)—in addition, of course, to the five octavo plates after his own designs for Hayley's *Ballads* (1805) and the quarto plate after his own design for Malkin's *Memoirs* (1806). For most of these commissions, he was probably indebted to his friends. And after 1806 he made no commercial book engravings for eight years,* until Longman commissioned him to copy Flaxman's designs for Hesiod in 1814–17. After Cromek took from Blake the commission for engraving his own designs for Blair's *Grave*, Blake largely abandoned for many years the craft in which he was trained and by which he had previously earned the chief part of his income.

Cromek's Puffing of Blair's Grave

Meanwhile, Cromek, who had committed himself to large payments to Schiavonetti for engraving Blake's designs, was assiduously soliciting subscriptions for *The Grave*, each with a one-guinea deposit. He made what Blake called "expensive advertizing boasts"[80] for it, he got friends such as Hayley and Fuseli to write for him,† and he travelled extensively, to Birmingham and Manchester and Wakefield and Edinburgh. Wherever he went, he placed puffs in the local newspapers,[81] and he carried with him for exhibition Blake's drawings and "Specimens of the Style of Engraving".‡ These travels were, of course, expensive, but they were also successful. He reported: "I got 72 subscribers to <u>The Grave</u> at Manchester in less than 3 Weeks",[82] and altogether he found over 578 subscribers for 688 copies. Before he printed a single copy of Blair's *Grave* in 1808, he had received over £700 in subscriptions for it. By 1809 Blake calculated that Cromek had "received fourteen hundred guineas and more from the profits of his [*Blake's*] designs".[83]

Cromek's plans for the work were remarkably variable. In November 1805 he advertised fifteen plates engraved by Blake after his own designs and then twelve plates engraved by Schiavonetti. In the same prospectuses, he advertised a preface, which he did not print, but he did print a description "Of the Designs" which he did not advertise. He announced in 1806 that the work would be printed by the distinguished London printer

---

* Chaucer's *Prologue* (1811) with two plates after Blake's own designs was clearly published in order to advertise Blake's large plate for the Canterbury Pilgrims rather than in the expectation of making money.

† Cromek managed to get his paid advertisements repeated word for word as editorial opinions, for instance, in the *Birmingham Gazette*: "We have never experienced greater satisfaction than in announcing to our readers ... specimens [*of illustrations for Blair which*] ... may ... be ranked amongst the most vigorous and classical productions of the present age" (*BRS* 43).

‡ *Birmingham Gazette* and *Birmingham Commercial Herald* for 28 July 1806. The earliest dated Schiavonetti proofs are dated 1 Feb 1806 ("Death's Door") and 1 June 1806 ("Christ Descending"). The drawings were shown at the Royal Academy by Oct 1805 (Flaxman's letter of 18 Oct 1805), in Birmingham (*Birmingham Gazette* and *Birmingham Commercial Herald* for 28 July 1806), and Manchester (Cowdray's *Manchester Gazette* for 7 Nov 1807).

Thomas Bensley,[84] then in May 1807 he said that it would be printed in Edinburgh in James "Ballantyne's best manner",[85] and finally he proclaimed that it "is printing in the most elegant Style, by BENSLEY".[86] In 1807 he decided to add a facsimile page from Blair's manuscript,[87] and then in 1808 he substituted for this a frontispiece portrait of Blake painted by Thomas Phillips.[88] In April 1807 Blake wrote a dedication to the Queen, which Cromek printed, but he declined to pay for Blake's vignette to accompany the dedication. And Blake's twelve designs were arranged in five different orders in advertisements and in print.[89]

One of Cromek's greatest coups was the frontispiece-portrait of Blake painted by Thomas Phillips, a young man who had become an Associate of the Royal Academy only in 1804. Phillips was becoming fashionable in a field densely populated by great portrait-painters; in 1806 he had made a portrait of the Prince of Wales, and in 1814 he made two very successful portraits of the notorious Lord Byron.

Why Phillips undertook to mingle Blake with his fashionable sitters is unknown.* Perhaps he and Blake were friends; Blake gave him a copy of *Songs of Innocence and of Experience*,[90] and Phillips subscribed to the edition of *The Grave* with Blake's designs.† And Phillips may have been responsible for the commission to Blake to engrave Phillips's portrait of Earl Spencer in 1813.

In April 1807[91] Blake was posing in Phillips's painting-room at 8 George Street in very uncharacteristic surroundings. He wore an unfamiliar starched shirt, a stock, an elegant coat, and a gold watch-fob, perhaps all of them painting-props from Phillips's studio like the bench on which he sat (Pl. 63). The props are unfamiliar except for the pencil in his hand, but the rapt expression in his eyes is perfectly characteristic.

The expression was elicited by Phillips when he got Blake to tell of a visit from the Archangel Gabriel. Blake's visitor proved his *bona fides* by open-

---

* According to William Carey, *Critical Description and Analytical Review of "Death on the Pale Horse", Painted by Benjamin West, P.R.A.* (31 Dec 1817), Phillips painted Blake's portrait "for CROMEK", but this may mean no more than that Cromek had it engraved for *The Grave* (1808).

† "T. Phillips, Esq., R.A." (Phillips had become a full member of the Royal Academy in 1808) appears in the subscription list for *The Grave*, implying that he had subscribed for it. However, his copy of *The Grave* (1808) was inscribed to "T. Phillips, Esq., R.A. from his greatly obliged servt R.H. Cromek, July 15th 1808" (*BRS* 59), implying that it was a gift from Cromek. Similarly, when, on 14 Aug 1808, Cromek sent George Cumberland the copy of *The Grave* which "you had ye goodness to subscribe for", he said that he was presenting the book "as an acknowledgement, at least, of the many kindnesses, I received from you & your good family when in Bristol", as if the work which Cumberland had paid to subscribe for were a gift from Cromek. Probably Phillips too had paid for the copy which Cromek inscribed as if it were a gift.

ing the roof of Blake's study: "he ascended into heaven; he stood in the sun, and beckoning to me, moved the universe."[92]

This rapt expression "has rendered his portrait one of the finest of the English school".[93] When the painting was exhibited at the Royal Academy in May 1807, within a few weeks of its completion, it was recognized as a masterpiece.

Perhaps as a token of his admiration for Blake and for Blake's designs illustrating *The Grave*, Phillips gave the portrait to Cromek,[*] and Cromek commissioned Schiavonetti to engrave it as a frontispiece to his edition of *The Grave*. When *The Grave* was published, the frontispiece was uniformly praised without reservation, even by those who thought its subject mad and dangerous. *The Examiner* (7 Aug 1808) said it was "among the best Engravings of Portraits in any country"; *The Antijacobin Review* (Nov 1808) asserted that it "would alone confer a lasting fame on Schiavonetti"; and the *Monthly Magazine* (1 Dec 1808) concluded that it was "to the utmost degree creditable to Schiavonetti". Perhaps the most curious example of the pervasive popularity of Phillips's portrait of Blake is its appearance on a set of silver buttons commemorating the fiftieth anniversary of the accession of George III.[†] The only aspect of *The Grave* on which all critics agreed was the distinction of Phillips's portrait of Blake and Schiavonetti's engraving of it.

Chaucer's Canterbury Pilgrims[‡]

The commissions for the designs and engravings by Blake and Thomas Stothard are the subjects of considerable confusion and ill temper.

---

[*] The *Antijacobin Review* (Nov 1808) said that "The portrait itself ... [*was*] presented to Mr. Cromek" by Phillips. In his advertisement of 1808, Cromek thanked Phillips for the portrait (*BR* 192), in the same way that he thanked Schiavonetti for his engravings, but he did not say that Phillips had given the portrait to him.

[†] See *BR* (2). No plausible explanation has been found for this association of the obscure William Blake with these powerful public figures, except for the distinction of Phillips's portrait of him.

Blake was also in the public eye in the portrait of him by W. Fraser exhibited at the Royal Academy in May 1809 (*BRS* 59), and G. Harlow made a portrait of "William Blake—drawn from life" which belonged to Fuseli (*BR* 222 n3).

[‡] The origins of the designs by Blake and Stothard are vexed points in their biographies. For recent efforts to sort the grain from the chaff, the Wheat from the Tares, see especially (**1**) Dennis Read, "The Rival *Canterbury Pilgrims* of Blake and Cromek: Herculean Figures in the Carpet", *Modern Philology*, LXXXVI (1988), 171–90: "the idea to paint an illustration of the Canterbury pilgrims and make an engraving of the painting originated with Cromek, not Blake". He argues that the Miller in Blake's Canterbury Pilgrims design and Satan, "The Miller of Eternity" (*Milton* pl. b, l. 42), represent Cromek; (**2**) Aileen Ward, "Canterbury Revisited: The Blake–Cromek Controversy", *Blake*, XXII (1988–89), 80–92: "Blake's version of the affair is ... probably a gradual reconfiguration of the events", showing that he "seems to have been driven to the edge of sanity" about 1809; (**3**) G.E. Bentley, Jr, "'They take great liberty's': Blake Reconfigured by Cromek and Modern Critics—The Arguments from Silence", *Studies in Romanticism*, XXX (1991), 657–84: "Blake deserves a Scottish verdict of Not Proved" (p. 684).

Essentially there are three versions of what happened: Cromek, Blake and Stothard's. They cannot all be true. Was someone lying or simply mistaken?

Cromek's Story

In the autumn of 1806, when he was thirty-six years old, Robert Hartley Cromek journeyed back to Wakefield in his native Yorkshire, and there he was married on 24 October to Mrs Elizabeth Change, the daughter of his mother's brother Samuel Hartley,[94] a prosperous corn-factor.

On his return to London from this journey,[*] he was under the necessity of passing a few hours in Halifax to wait for a further conveyance. To while away the time, he resorted to books, his usual amusement, and picked up in a bookseller's shop a copy of Chaucer. On perusing the CANTERBURY TALES, he was so struck with the picturesque description of the pilgrims, that he conceived the idea of embodying the whole procession in a picture. On his return to town, he immediately suggested the design to Mr. Stothard, who seized the idea with a spirit and feeling entirely correspondent to those of his young friend, and undertook to execute it for him … Mr. Cromek … made the most diligent researches into all records, whether written or pictorial, which characterized the age of Chaucer, and brought the result of them to Mr. Stothard.[†]

---

[*]   Manuscript "Memorials of the life of R.H. Cromek", Collected and edited by his son [T.H. Cromek] dated 27 July 1865 (in the possession of Mr Wilfred Warrington), silently quotes the obituary in *The Grave* (1813) and adds the crucial detail that this journey was made "about the time of his marriage". This and much other information about Cromek was brought to my attention by Professor Dennis Read.

    The obituary from *The Grave* (1813) specifies that the journey from which Cromek was returning was *after* the publication of Blair's *Grave* (July 1808), but this is irreconcilable with many other known details; for instance, a prospectus for Cromek's Canterbury Pilgrims is dated Feb 1807. Cromek's son is far more likely to be correct, even though he was only a small child when his father died. Presumably his information came from his mother, who must have been with Robert Cromek on the trip back to London.

[†]   Anon., "Biographical Sketch of Robert Hartley Cromek", in Robert Blair, *The Grave* (London: R. Ackermann, &c., 1813), xlviii. The author is probably Allan Cunningham, who had lived for a time with the Cromeks in London. The obituary repeatedly quotes a Poetical Friend of Cromek, identified in a footnote as "Mr. Allan Cunningham, who, in the grand though obscure capacity of a Scottish peasant, a title which he so proudly owns, has given the brightest proof that genius may grow from the very elements which threaten its existence" (p. l). It also praises *The Remains of Nithsdale Song* (much of which was composed by Cunningham and passed off as traditional ballads): "Never was there a work published more interesting, more sentimental, and at the same time more chastely whimsical than this" (p. l).

    The bookshop in Halifax may be that of Thomas Edwards, the brother of Richard Edwards who commissioned Blake's *Night Thoughts* engravings.

Pl. 1. Parish Church of St James, Piccadilly, designed by Sir Christopher Wren (1684), where William Blake was christened in 1757.

Pl. 2. Baptismal font in St James, Piccadilly, designed by Grinling Gibbons, in which William Blake and his siblings were christened.

Pl. 3. "Christ Baptising" (watercolour, 1805, 31.9 x 38.4 cm, Butlin #485), with the Holy Ghost descending upon Christ as he baptizes a babe in his arms from a carved marble font before a young couple with two kneeling children (like the Blake family in 1757), watched by elders (sponsors?) on the right and by other parents with babes yet to be christened on the left.

(*facing page*) Pl. 4A and B. *Milton* (B) pls 29 and 33 (coloured relief etchings, 1804[-?11], 16.0 x 11.2 cm and 14.0 x 10.8 cm) showing "WILLIAM" and "ROBERT" receiving the inspiration of Milton as a star falling on their feet. The design for "WILLIAM" is repeated in Blake's twentieth design for Job in which Satan (above the falling ploughman) is seen destroying Job's son.

Pl. 5. "The Great Red Dragon and the Beast from the Sea: 'And Power was given him over all Kindreds, and Tongues, and Nations'" (watercolour, *c.* 1803–5, 40.1 x 35.6 cm, Butlin #521) by Blake from Revelation xiii, 1–2 showing the monstrous power of civil and religious authority.

Pl. 6. "Satan Exulting Over Eve" (colourprint, *c.* 1795, 42.5 x 53.2 cm, Butlin #292) showing the Serpent apparently coupling with Eve. For a similar coupling, see "The Temptation and Fall of Eve" (Pl. 106).

Pl. 7. 28 Broad Street, Golden Square, St James Parish, where Blake was born in 1757 and where he saw God's head at the window when he was three years old. Here his father and brother had a hosiery and haberdashery shop from 1752 to 1812, displaying goods in the shop-windows in Broad Street (now called Broadwick Street), to the right and in Marshall Street, and here Blake held his private exhibition of pictures in 1809-10. Notice the windows in Marshall Street which were bricked up because of Pitt's window tax. The building was torn down after 1959 and replaced by an unfortunate edifice called Blake Buildings.

Pl. 8. The Parish of St James, Westminster (bordered on the north by Oxford Street, on the south by the Thames), a quarter of sheet B2 (53 x 59.5 cm) (22 June 1792) of the thirty-two engraved sheets making up R. Horwood's *Plan of the Cities of London and Westminster, the Borough of Southwark, and Parts adjoining Shewing every house* (London: R. Horwood, 1792-99). It shows (a) 5 Glasshouse Street, where James Blake lived 1744-53; (b) St George's Chapel, Hanover Square, where Catherine Wright was married to Thomas Armitage in 1746 and to James Blake in 1752; (c) 28 Broad Street, the haberdashery shop above which James and Catherine Blake brought up their family; (d) St James's Church, Piccadilly, where the Blake children were christened 1753-64; (e) 27 Broad Street where Blake and Parker had their print shop 1784-85; (f) 29 Broad Street where Blake's brother John lived 1784-93; (g) 28 Poland Street where Blake and Catherine lived 1785-90; (h) corner of Broad and Poland Streets, where Blake's friend Henry Fuseli lived 1777-81; and (i) 10 Great Marlborough Street where Blake's patron Thomas Butts lived.

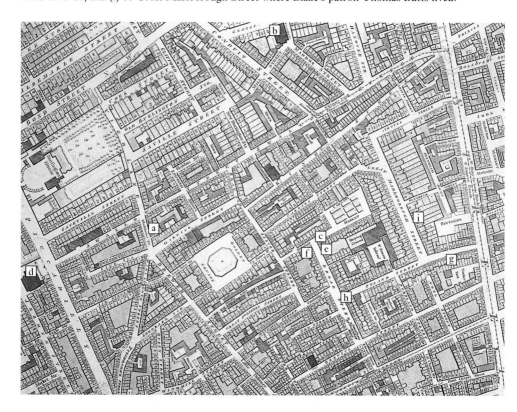

Pl. 9. "A Cradle Song" (electrotype of relief etching, 11.3 x 7.2 cm, 1789)
from *Songs of Innocence* (*Songs* pl. 16).

Electrotype copies were made of sixteen plates from *Songs of Innocence and of Experience* for Gilchrist's *Life of William Blake, "Pictor Ignotus"* (1863), and then the original copperplates were lost. Electrotypes (now in the Fitzwilliam Museum) were made from the Gilchrist plates, and later the Gilchrist electrotypes were destroyed. However, as the process of electrotyping is mechanical, the surface is a faithful copy, and prints could be made from it indistinguishable from those printed by Catherine and William Blake. The copperplate, of course, shows the image and text reversed.

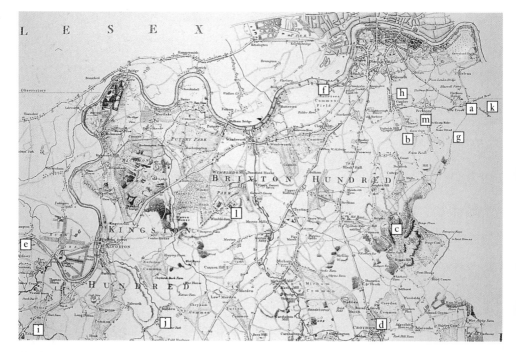

Pl. 10. *Map of the County of Surrey, From a Survey made in the Years 1789 and 1790 ... By Joseph Lindley and William Crosley ...* Engraved by H. Baker (London: Lindley & Crosley, 13 April 1793), a four-sheet map, each part 55.7 x 42 cm, but the section reproduced here (most of the second sheet) is only 40 x 27 cm. Gilchrist describes "a favourite day's ramble ... [*south-east*] to [a] Blackheath, or south-west, over [b] Dulwich and [c] Norwood hills, through the antique rustic town of [d] Croydon, ... to the fertile verdant meads of [e] Walton-upon-Thames; much of the way by lane and footpath". Such very long walks probably also included many of the nearby places mentioned in *Milton* and *Jerusalem*: [f] Battersea, [g] Brockley Hills, [h] Camberwell, [i] Esher, [j] Malden, [k] Shooter's Hill, and [l] Wimbledon, as well as [m] Peckham Rye, where Blake saw a tree filled with angels.

Pl. 11. William Wynne Ryland (oval stipple engraving by D. P. Pariset after P. Falconet, 1768), fashionable stipple-engraver and artist, whose face made the fourteen-year-old Blake think in 1772 that "he will live to be hanged", as he was in 1783. It would not be surprising if Blake had seen this print, for it was sold by the French painter Peter Falconet at his shop in Broad Street, Carnaby Market, very close to where the Blakes lived.

Pl. 12. Blake's master "James Basire Born Oct.[r] 6 1720; Died Sept.[r] 1802", antiquarian line-engraver, frontispiece in John Nichols, *Literary Anecdotes of the Eighteenth Century ...* IX (London: Printed for the Author, 1815).

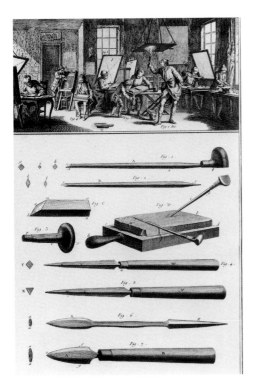

(*above left*) Pl. 13 *Recueil de Planches sur les Sciences, les Arts libéraux, et les Arts méchaniques, avec leur Explications*, V (Paris: Briasson, David, le Breton, 1767) (for Diderot & D'Alembert's *Encyclopédie*), Gravure pl. 1: Fig. 1, waxing the plate; Fig 1 Bis, a flambeau smoking the plate, which is hung from the ceiling because it is too large to hold in one hand; Fig 2 (at the left), pouring l'eau fort over the etched plate; Fig. 3 (in the middle), engraving — "g" is the picture he is copying; Fig. 4, biting with acid; Fig. 5, pouring off the acid; Fig. 6 (at the left), engraving with a burin — the copperplate is on a cushion; Fig. 7 (at bottom right), pounding out mistakes. D is an oilstone.

Pl. 14 *Recueil de Planches sur les Sciences, les Arts libéraux, et les Arts méchaniques, avec leur Explications*, VII (Paris: Briasson, David, le Breton, 1769) (for Diderot & D'Alembert's *Encyclopédie*), Imprimerie en taille douce pl. 1. The scene represents: Fig. a: Inking the plate over a fire; Fig. b: Wiping the surface of the intaglio plate with the heel of the hand, leaving ink only in the etched recesses; Fig. 1: The huge wooden press; Fig. 2: Heaving on the great bars to force the flat bed bearing the inked plate with the paper on top between the rollers; and Fig. 3: The printer's table with prints on it. Note the prints drying on the line stretched near the ceiling and the absence of artificial light.

Very few changes in printing intaglio plates were made between 1645, when an earlier form of this design was printed in Abraham Bosse, *Traicté des manières de graveur en taille doux*, and 1772 when Blake began his apprenticeship as an engraver.

Pl. 15 "Joseph of Arimathea Among The Rocks of Albion Engraved by W. Blake 1773 from an old Italian Drawing[.] This is One of the Gothic Artists who Built the Cathedrals in what we call the Dark Ages Wandering about in sheep skins & goat skins of whom the World was not worthy[;] such were the Christians in all Ages[.] Michael Angelo Pinxit" (F) (line engraving, State 2, *c*. 1810, 25.6 x 14 cm), Blake's apprentice engraving (1773) as emended. The transmutation of the subject, from the Roman Centurion at "The Crucifixion of St Peter" in Michelangelo's fresco, to Christ's disciple as a suffering artist in England was characteristic of Blake's work all his life.

Pl. 16 Oliver Goldsmith, poet, novelist, Grub-street hack, etching by J. Bretherton. As a boy Blake thought Goldsmith's head "finely marked", though contemporaries like Boswell thought it "coarse and vulgar".

Pl. 17 James Parker (pencil sketch by John Flaxman, *c.* 1795), Blake's fellow-apprentice, with whom he quarrelled (1773) and future partner in a print-shop (1784–85). His short hair would enable him to wear a wig.

Pl. 18. Monument of Aymer de Valence (d. 1296) in Westminster Abbey (*c.* 1776, Butlin #28)—Blake's apprentice drawing for [Richard Gough], *Sepulchral Monuments of Great Britain*, I (1786).

Pl. 19. Monument of Aymer de Valence in Westminster Abbey, showing the difficulty young Blake must have had in drawing from the top of the monument.

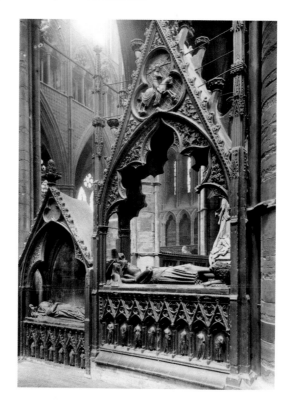

Pl. 20. "The Sons of God Shouting for Joy" (line engraving, 1826, 16.6 x 10.8 cm) for Blake's
Illustrations to the Book of Job, pl. "14", a design which he thought he could have repeated for the great
west window of Westminster Abbey and which was copied in the 1890s by William Blake Richmond in
the mosaic for the vault in St Paul's Cathedral.

In the watercolour Blake made of this design for Butts (1805-6), there are only four sons of God; in the
engraving, Blake made the number seem indeterminate or infinite by adding arms in each margin.

Pl. 21. A nude academic model (black chalk, *c*. 1780, 47.9 x 37 cm, Butlin #71) with his right hand resting on a support omitted by the artist, drawn by Blake probably when he was a student at the Royal Academy. Students were not allowed to draw from the Living Academy until they were twenty-one. Sir Geoffrey Keynes guessed that the subject is Robert Blake, who was eighteen in 1780.

Pl. 22. "Death of Earl Goodwin" (pen and watercolour, *c*. 1779, 18.1 x 12.7 cm, Butlin #60), the first picture Blake exhibited at the Royal Academy (1780). The picture shows Earl Goodwin at dinner with Edward the Confessor (11 April 1053) when he prayed God to choke him "if I had any hand in the death of that Prince" (the King's Brother Alfred), whereupon "a morsel ... choked him immediately, to the great astonishment of the Standers-by".

George Cumberland praised in print the picture's design and character.

Pl. 23. "George Cumberland", stipple engraving (15.8 x 17.9 cm) by T. Woolnoth after a miniature by Nathan Branwhite (of Bristol), which served as the frontispiece of Cumberland's *Essay on the Utility of Collecting the Best Works of the Ancient Engravers of the Italian School ...* (1827). Cumberland was Blake's friend from about 1780 until Blake's death in 1827.

The style is very similar to Phillips's portrait of Blake (Pl. 63). Each man leans on his right elbow, with a pencil in his right hand (to indicate that he is an artist), and each is wearing a dark, heavy-collared coat and a white stock, with a watch-chain on his waistcoat. Cumberland is more florid and somewhat more heavy-set, with scarcely kempt hair. He seems to be sketching in an oblong sketchbook.

Pl. 24. "Fire" (watercolour, *c.* 1805, 31.7 x 42.8 cm, Butlin #194), probably derived in part from scenes Blake saw during the Gordon Riots of June 1780.

Pl. 25. John Flaxman (self-portrait, *c.* 1784), the ambitious young sculptor and Blake's patient, faithful, life–long friend. The hand shown appears to be his right hand, but of course it is his left hand, seen in a mirror.

Pl. 26. Thomas Stothard, pencil sketch by John Flaxman (17.8 x 14 cm). Stothard was an extraordinarily prolific book-illustrator whose designs Blake engraved and who was Blake's friend from about 1780 until the great breach over the Canterbury Pilgrims design about 1807.

Pl. 27. The picnic arrest at Upnor Castle (etching, ?1780), designed by Thomas Stothard and etched by Stothard (according to his son Alfred) or, less plausibly, by Blake (according to Catherine Blake). Note the sketching artist, the hat of an absent artist—and the omission of the sentinel guarding them.

Pl. 28 William Hogarth's "Noon" (line engraving, 50.3 x 40.6, 1738) from "The Four Times of Day" showing the French Chapel in Hog Lane. In both their gilded refinement and their black-hooded simplicity, the congregation leaving the church at 12:30 after Sunday service contrasts strongly with their English neighbours.

Pl. 29. "Glad Day" (B) (colour print, 1795, 20.1 x 27.2 cm), a design made originally in 1780.

Pl. 30. "The Fall of Rosamund" (line engraving, 1783, circle 15.35 cm in diameter) designed by Stothard and engraved by Blake, for which Macklin paid Blake £80.

Pl. 31A. "A S Mathew" (sketch, *c.* 1784) by John Flaxman. Mathew was Blake's patron and the author of the deprecatory preface to his *Poetical Sketches* (1783).

Pl. 31A. "Harriet Mathew", the wife of A. S. Mathew (pencil sketch, c. 1784) by John Flaxman. At her cultural conversaziones about 1783 Blake used to sing his songs.

"The corners of her mouth seem'd—I don't know how, but very odd as if she hoped you had not an ill opinion of her".

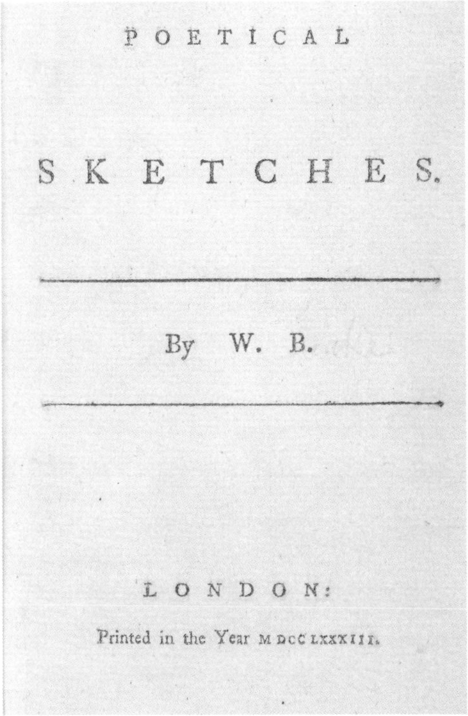

POETICAL

SKETCHES.

———————————

By W. B.

———————————

LONDON:

Printed in the Year M DCC LXXXIII.

Pl. 32. *Poetical Sketches* (1783) (S), title page (13.9 x 22.3 cm). Notice that the author is identified only by his initials and that neither bookseller nor printer is named. The work was circulated privately, not published.

The style of the title page is severely classical, the style of Blake's sponsor A.S. Mathew, though the poems are exuberantly Gothic and Romantic.

Pl. 33. Thomas Taylor the Pagan (oil by Sir Thomas Lawrence, ?1812, *c.* 3' x 4'), banker's clerk, mathematician, and Platonist, who taught Blake some Euclid and may figure in his *Island in the Moon* (?1784). In the portrait, a folio volume of "PLATO" lies beside Taylor, and in the background is a view of the Acropolis to identify Taylor as the translator of Plato (1804).

Pl. 34. "A Breach in a City the Morning after a Battle" (watercolour, *c.* 1790–95, 29.7 x 46.3 cm, Butler #189), a version of Blake's lost Royal Academy exhibition picture (1784). The scene is probably influenced by the storming of Newgate Prison by the Gordon Rioters which Blake saw in June 1780. The broken wall and the woman mourning over the slain are repeated in his *America* (1793) (Pls 35-6), and a figure similar to the defeated angel is in "Satan Calling Up His Legions" for *Paradise Lost* (Pl. 103).

Pl. 35. *America* pl. 1 (frontispiece, relief etching, 1793, 23.4 x 16.9 cm) (M), with the broken wall, now occupied by a manacled angel, probably repeated from his "A Breach in a City" (1784) (Pl. 34).

Pl. 36. *America* pl. 2 (title page, relief etching, 1793, 23.5 x 16.7 cm) (M), with the woman mourning over the slain adapted from "A Breach in a City" (1784) (Pl. 34).

Pl. 37. "Josephs Brethren Bowing before Him" (watercolour, *c*. 1785, 40.3 x 56.2 cm, Butlin #155) exhibited at the Royal Academy in 1785.

Pl. 38. "The Approach of Doom" (relief
etching, 29.7 x 20.9 cm, ?1787), drawn by
Robert Blake in his Notebook and then etched
by William Blake; later it was cut down to
form pls 12–13, 20, 27 of the *Marriage*.

Pl. 39. "Zephyrus and Flora" (stipple
engraving, 17 December 1784, oval 17.4 x 23.5
cm, Second State) engraved after Thomas
Stothard by William Blake for the firm of
Parker & Blake, 27 Broad Street, Golden
Square, indicating the popular style aimed at
by the firm of Parker & Blake, with a classical
subject treated sentimentally and reproduced
in stipple.

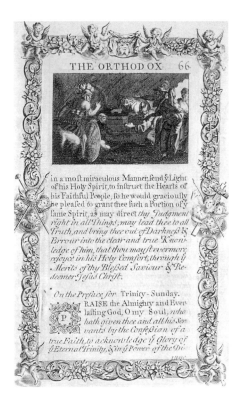

Pl. 41 "Henry Fuseli" (miniature, 1825) (5.4 x 4.2 cm), made by Moses Haughton to be given as a memorial of Fuseli's death in 1825, in a gem-studded golden case inscribed "Henry Fuseli | April 16 1825 | Noi siam vermi | Nati a formar l'angelica farfalla" (from Dante). Fuseli was Blake's admired friend from 1787 until his death.

The miniature is a copy [by Moses Houghton] of Houghton's original exhibited at the Royal Academy in 1803 and engraved by Moses Houghton in 1808 and by R.W. Sievier in 1820. Leigh Hunt called it "an admirable likeness ... in this state of dignified extravagance ... looking ready to pounce".

This is one of two copies presented to the family of Fuseli's friend James Carrick Moore; on the death in 1904 of his daughter Julia they passed to George Heath (descendant of the family of engravers), from whom they went in 1926 to his son Philip Heath; Philip Heath presented the inferior miniature in 1947 to the Ashmolean Museum, Oxford, and the superior one passed on his death in 1976 to his son John Heath, who sold it in 1991 to E.B. Bentley for G.E. Bentley, Jr.

(*facing page*) Pl. 40. *The Orthodox Communicant* (London: Engraven by J. Sturt & Sold by R. Ware and J. Tinney, [1721]), pp. 66-7.

The engraving and the printing of the work must have been extraordinarily laborious and expensive—the engraving was said to be on silver. Four framing-plates of cherubs were printed separately from the 91 plates of text-plus-vignette, and each page thus had to be printed twice (once for the frame and once for the text). Notice how the catchword on p. 66 ("vine") overlaps with the frame, indicating that it was printed twice.

An octavo sheet of letterpress with sixteen pages would have been printed twice, once on the recto and once on the verso. However, a sheet of Sturt's octavo *Orthodox Communicant* would have been printed at least eight times (with all four frames at once) or, more probably, thirty-two times, page by page. (The same frame is used on pp. 76-7, 80, which would have been impossible if they had been printed as a set.)

When Blake wrote in *An Island in the Moon* of making a book with "all the writing Engraved instead of Printed [*i.e.*, *type-set*], & at every other leaf a high-finish'd print", he was probably thinking of a work like Sturt's, though on a much larger scale.

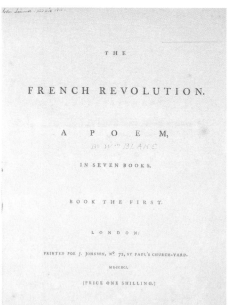

Pl. 42. *The French Revolution* (London: Joseph Johnson, 1791) (title page, 29.6 x 22.2 cm). Note that Blake's name is omitted from the printed lettering. According to the Advertisement, "The remaining [*six*] Books of this Poem are finished, and will be published in their Order", but only the first book survives, in this proof copy.

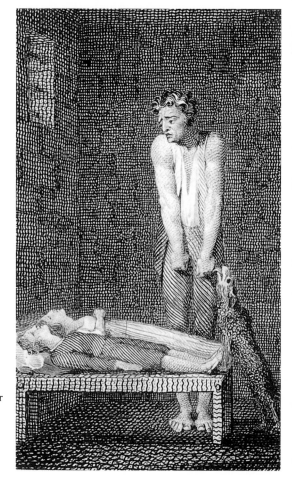

Pl. 43. Mary Wollstonecraft's *Original Stories from Real Life* (1791) at p. 24 (line engraving, 15.7 x 9.2 cm), designed and engraved by Blake. Blake has transmuted her sentimental moralizing into monumental terms. He repeated the motif on the title page of his own *Songs of Experience* (1794) (Fig. on p. 145) with mourners over the dead.

Pl. 44. "Family of Negro Slaves from Loango" (line engraving, 1792, 18.1 x 13.4 cm), designed by John Gabriel Stedman and engraved by Blake for Stedman's *Narrative*, II (1796). Note the initials "J.G.S." on the man's breast and the possible connection with Blake's *Visions of the Daughters of Albion* (1793), pl. 4: "Stampt with my signet are the swarthy children of the sun".

Pl. 45. "A Negro hung alive by the Ribs to a Gallows" (line engraving, 1792, 18.0 x 13.2 cm) designed by Stedman and engraved by Blake for Stedman's *Narrative*, I (1796). Blake has almost certainly simplified and classicized Stedman's lost design.

Stedman deplored such cruelty to slaves and believed that Negroes were better off as slaves in the Americas than as free men in Africa.

Pl. 46 Frontispiece designed by Blake and engraved by Perry for Bürger's *Leonora* (line engraving, 1796, 20.1 x 16.6 cm). Reviewers found the design "ludicrous", with "men and women without skins" (i.e., naked?) and "imaginary beings, which neither can nor ought to exist". Blake was repeatedly criticized for depicting spirits and "imaginary beings", because such spirits "ought not to exist", whereas Blake thought that the world was primarily spiritual.

Pl. 47 "Ezekiel: I take away from thee the Desire of thine Eyes, Ezekiel xxiv C 16" (line engraving, 46.4 x 50.4 cm, 27 October 1794, Second State [after 1803, perhaps as late as 1818]), one of Blake's most impressive line engravings, published by himself.

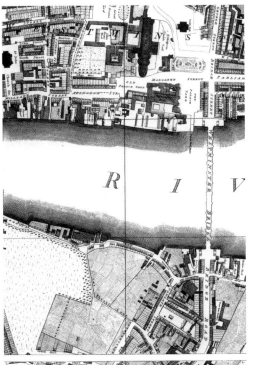

Pl. 48 Westminster, the Thames, and Lambeth, parts of sheets C3 and D3 (24 May 1799) of R. Horwood's *Plan of the Cities of London and Westminster* (1792-99). The Houses of Parliament and Westminster Abbey are on one side of Westminster Bridge and on the other 13 Hercules Buildings where Blake lived in 1790-1800, The Asylum (for female orphans, a workhouse), timber yards along the river, and market gardens. Lambeth Palace, the residence of the Archbishop of Canterbury, is just off the map down river.

Pl. 49 The north front of 13 Hercules Buildings, Lambeth (then called 23 Hercules Road) (sketch by Frederick Adcock). The round plaque over the door probably records that Blake lived here from 1790 to 1800. The row of twelve chimney-pots suggests that there was a fireplace in each room. The tiled roof and large mullioned windows distinguish the Blakes' house from the less ambitious adjoining one to the right.

Hercules Buildings was torn down between 1928 and 1931 and replaced by an unfortunate edifice called Blake Buildings.

Pl. 50 "Tiriel Dead Before Hela" (watercolour, 17.8 x 27.1 cm, ?1789, Butlin #198), illustration for *Tiriel*. Note that the fine detail and shading of the design make it unsuitable for reproduction in the simple black-and-white tones of relief etching, the method by which Blake produced most of his subsequent prophecies.

Pl. 51 *The Book of Thel* (L) pl. 2 (title page, coloured relief etching, 15.5 x 10.7 cm, 1789) The shepherdess Thel with her crook, at the left, observes a naked man flying from a blossom to embrace a clothed woman. Above them, the letters of the title burgeon in flame-plants, men, and angels, and over all arches a vine-clad willow. Thel is learning the sexual facts of life from the plants, as in Erasmus Darwin's "The Loves of the Plants" (1789), Part II of his *Botanic Garden*.

Pl. 52 *The Marriage of Heaven and Hell* (B) pl. 1 (title page, relief etching, 15.2 x 10.3 cm, ?1790). Note: no author is identified—but of course many works were printed without the author's name; there is no date—and consequently Blake could not assert his copyright in the work; and there is no indication of printer or publisher—though these were required by law.

Above "HEAVEN" the scene is barren, but around "HELL" it is fecund (cp. *The Book of Thel* title page [Pl. 51]). When the couple at bottom were sketched, the design was entitled: "Is all joy forbidden" (*WBW* 1323).

Pl. 53 *Visions of the Daughters of Albion* (E) pl. 2 (title page, coloured relief etching, 16.3 x 12.9 cm, 1793). The Virgin Oothoon dances "Over the waves ... in wing'd exulting swift delight", while above her is a tormented god in flames (Theotormon), and girls of mild silver and of furious gold sport in the rainbow beside them. The Visions seem to be of both torment and joy.

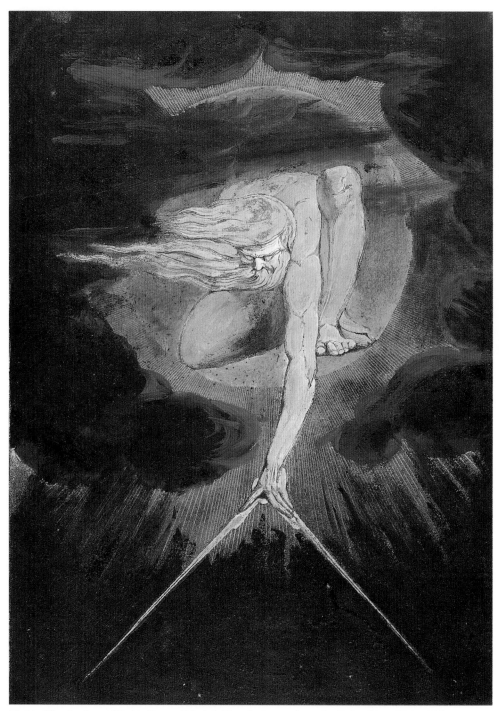

Pl. 54. The Ancient of Days, *Europe* (L) pl. 1 (frontispiece, coloured relief etching, 23.4 x 16.9 cm, 1794). The sketch for it in Blake's Notebook, p. 96, bears a motto from the poem, pl. 5, l. 52: "Who shall bind the Infinite". Blake coloured another copy of this print on his death-bed.

This is probably the most widely-known image by Blake. J.T. Smith called it "mighty and grand", approaching "the sublimity of Raffaelle or Michel Angelo".

A related design may be seen in "The Rout of the Rebel Angels" (1808) for *Paradise Lost*, with Christ kneeling in the sun (Pl. 104).

Pl. 55 *Europe* (L) pl. 2 (title page, coloured relief etching, 23.9 x 17.3 cm, 1794). The serpent seems to be the creation of the Ancient of Days which faces him.

Pl. 56 *Europe* (L) pl. 12 (coloured relief etching, 23.4 x 16.6 cm, 1794). George Cumberland identified the subject in his copy as "Mildews blighting ears of Corn", while the text says the Angels are broadcasting "plagues". The "S" shape of the grain is very like that in "The Divine Image", reversed (see the title page of *The Stranger*).

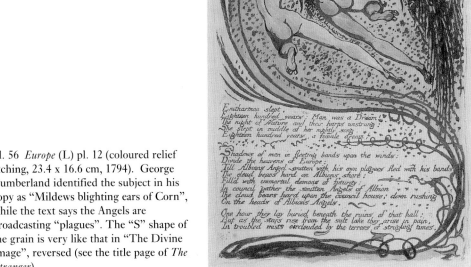

Pl. 57 *The First Book of Urizen* (G), pl. 1 (title page, watercoloured relief etching, 14.9 x 10.3 cm, 1794). Before carved stones like tombs or tablets of the law, blind Urizen copies with a quill in either hand "The secrets of dark contemplation" from a book of hieroglyphs onto surfaces he cannot see. One copy is inscribed:

"Which is the Way"
"The Right or the Left"

Pl. 58 *The First Book of Urizen* (G) pl. 22 (watercoloured relief etching, 15.6 x 10.1 cm, 1794). Urizen in torment, self-manacled at wrists and ankles, suffers for his magnificent obsession, though his head still emits divine light. One copy is inscribed:

"Frozen doors to mock"
"The Wor*l*d, while they within torments uplock"

Pl. 59 *Song of Los* (E) pl. 2 (title page, colour-printed relief etching, 24.3 x 17.2 cm, 1795). Perhaps the scene represents "Adam, a mouldering skeleton ... bleach'd on the garden of Eden: And Noah as white as snow On the mountains of Ararat".

Pl. 60 *The Book of Ahania* (A) pl. 2 (title page, colour-printed intaglio etching, 13.6 x 9.8 cm, 1795).

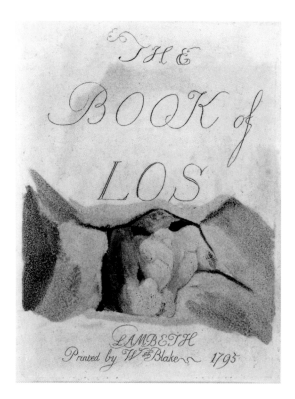

Pl. 61 *The Book of Los* pl. 2 (A) (title page, colour–printed intaglio etching, 13.5 x 9.8 cm, 1795).

Pl. 62 "Elohim Creating Adam" (colour print, 51.5 x 57.5 cm, 1795, Butlin #289). Both Adam and his creator are in torment.

Pl. 63 Portrait of Blake by Thomas Phillips (1807) engraved by Luigi Schiavonetti as the frontispiece to Blair's *Grave* (1808). During the sitting, Blake told the story of Michelangelo and the Archangel Gabriel. Phillips "marvelled much at this wild story; but he caught from Blake's looks, as he related it, that rapt poetic expression which has rendered his portrait one of the finest of the English school."

The pencil in Blake's right hand indicates (truly) that he is an artist, the designer of the illustrations for Blair's *Grave*; the frilled shirt and elegant chair suggest (falsely) that he is a gentleman. The chair was a studio prop, and perhaps the shirt and ill-fitting coat were as well.

Seymour Kirkup wrote that Blake "had an abstracted look as if he did not see what he was looking at. The fault of the portrait in B's Grave is that he seems too tall— That is only owing to the hands & arms being badly sketched, too large for the face".

Pl. 64 Young's *Night Thoughts* (1797), p. 65 (title page for Night IV, line engraving, 39.7 x 33.0 cm): "The Christian Triumph", showing Christ, naked and in glory, breaking from the rocky tomb, while two winged angels bow before him.

The watercolour for the design was the frontispiece for the whole series of 537 designs, and the Night IV title page had a quite different design (Butlin #330 110). Sketches for it were used in *Vala* pp. 16, 58, 116, and a proof of the engraving was used for *Vala* p. 114. Note that all these *Night Thoughts* reproductions are greatly reduced in size here.

Pl. 65 Young's *Night Thoughts* (1797) p. 43 (title page for Night III, line engraving, 41 x 32.7 cm), showing Narcissa surrounded by the ourobouros, the serpent with his tail in his mouth. The design on the verso of the watercolour for this engraving shows the serpent completely encoiling a terrified figure in chains (Butlin #330 79), and the line "Nature revolves" is illustrated by the ourobouros (Butlin #330 257).

Pl. 66 Young's *Night Thoughts* (1797) p. 73 (line engraving, 39.7 x 31.5 cm), showing "the dreadful blessing" of Christ's stigmata. This engraving gave Blake particular trouble; it went through at least four different states, the first showing Christ's head in profile and the rest with His head turned partly toward us, as here. In the watercolour (Butlin #330 121), Christ faces to the left.

Pl. 67 Young's *Night Thoughts* (1797) p. 63 (line engraving, 41.3 x 32.6 cm), illustrating the line "This KING OF TERRORS is the PRINCE OF PEACE". In the watercolour (Butlin #330 108), the scroll inscription is meaningless—and sideways—and the line starred is "*Death*, the great Counsellor, who Man inspires With every nobler Thought".

When making his engraving, Blake did not know that the text (the last in Night III) would end half-way down the page, so he could not use that space for his own design.

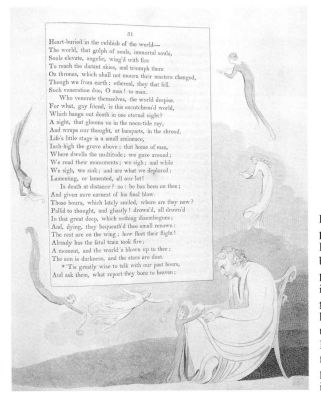

Pl. 68 Young's *Night Thoughts* (1797) p. 31 (line engraving, 40.4 x 32.1 cm). Flights of hours, male and female, bring scrolls bearing reports of "our past hours" to the wise man, illustrating the asterisked lines "'Tis greatly wise to talk with our past hours, And ask them, what report they bore to heaven". As Bulwer Lytton commented: "Young was fortunate. He seems almost the only poet who has had his mere metaphors illustrated and made corporeal."

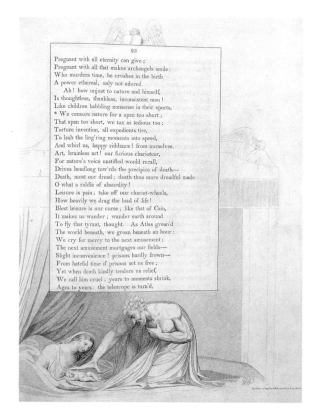

Pl. 69 Young's *Night Thoughts* (1797) p. 23 (line engraving, 39.4 x 33.0 cm). A father measures with his hand-span the minute dimensions of his infant, illustrating the metaphor, "We censure nature for a span too short". Above the bed and the text, angels guard the fragile life.

Blake's plates for Young are signed with "WB" beneath "inv & sc" (invented and engraved) which he used on no other engravings, though he did use it on some watercolours (see Pl. 79).

Pl. 70 Young's *Night Thoughts* (1797) p. 46 (line engraving, 40.8 x 32.3 cm), illustrating Young's line: "sense runs savage broke from reason's chain". Blake shows a voluptuous nude young woman with a broken manacle on her right ankle dancing gloriously, while above her Death's sable pall is about to envelop her. Blake seems to glorify the escape from reason. In the watercolour (Butlin #330 81), her calf-length hair is quite indiscrete. Cunningham wrote that "the serious and the pious" readers were "alarmed ... [*by*] shapes trembling in nudity round the verses of a grave divine".

The young woman is adapted from Venus Anadyomene, which Blake had Tommy Butts copy when he was learning to engrave; Tommy's Venus is almost exactly as discrete as the engraving in *Night Thoughts*.

Pl. 71 "The Pindaric Genius recieving his Lyre" (watercolour, 1797, 16 x 9 cm, Butlin #335.1) for the title page of Gray's *Poems* (1790). The swan is being ridden with a very loose rein.

Pl. 72 Father Thames (watercolour, 1797, 16 x 9 cm, Butlin #335-16) for Gray's "Ode on a distant prospect of Eton College", representing, according to Blake's inscription, the lines

Say Father Thames for thou hast seen
Full many a sprightly race

with Windsor Castle in the background. The design exemplifies what Blake wrote in *The Marriage of Heaven and Hell*: "The ancient Poets animated all sensible objects with Gods or Geniuses, calling them by the names and adorning them with the properties of woods, rivers, mountains".

86 THE PROGRESS OF POESY.
O'er her warm cheek, and riſing boſom, move
The bloom of young deſire, and purple light
of Love.
II. 1.
Man's feeble race what ills await!
Labour, and Penury, the racks of Pain,
Diſeaſe, and Sorrow's weeping train,
And Death, ſad refuge from the ſtorms of Fate!
The fond complaint, my ſong, diſprove,
And juſtify the laws of Jove.
Say, has he given in vain the heav'nly Muſe?
Night, and all her ſickly dews,
Her ſpectres wan, and birds of boding cry,
He gives to range the dreary ſky:
Till down the eaſtern cliffs afar
Hyperion's march they ſpy, and glitt'ring
ſhafts of war.
II. 2.

Pl. 73 Hyperion (watercolour, 1797, 16 x 9 cm, Butlin #335.46) for Gray's "Progress of Poesy", which represents, according to Blake's inscription, the phrase "Hyperions march they spy & glittering Shafts of war". Hyperion exhibits the same kind of ambiguity as Blake's Ancient of Days (*Europe* pl. 1) (Pl. 54), another commanding god enforcing his power from the sun.

Pl. 74A Miniature portrait on ivory (1801) of Thomas Butts (aged forty-one) (oval 8.4 x 6.3 cm, Butlin #376), the "attempt at your likeness" which Blake said in his letter of 11 September 1801 he had transmitted from Felpham to Mrs Butts "by my Sisters hands". Butts seems to have a military uniform with an epaulet, though he is not known to have had military rank. The miniature is framed with plaited and coiled hair, presumably that of the sitter. Apparently Mrs Butts expressed some reservation about the fidelity of the portrait, for on 6 July 1803 Blake wrote to Butts: "I am determind that M*rs* Butts shall have a good likeness of You ... but this is not to be atchievd without the original sitting before you for Every touc*h*, all likenesses from memory being necessarily very very defective".

Pl. 74B Portrait miniature on ivory (1809) of Betsy Butts (aged about 50) (oval 8.7 x 6.6 cm, Butlin #377), signed "1809 W Blake pinx", eight years later than the miniature of her husband.

  There is a disconcerting but slight and probably coincidental similarity between the portrait of Betsy Butts and "The Whore of Babylon" painted for Thomas Butts in the same year (see Pl. 75), each showing a somewhat plump woman of a certain age with a narrow mouth and a hint of a double-chin.

Pl. 75 "The Whore of Babylon" (watercolour, 1809, 27 x 22.8 cm, Butlin #523), derived from Revelation xvii, 1-4: "the great whore" is "arrayed in purple and scarlet-colour, and decked with gold and precious stones and pearls, having a golden cup in her hand full of abominations", "the wine of her fornication"; she is "sit[*ting*] upon a scarlet-coloured beast, ... having seven heads and ten horns".

  The Whore is directing wine-bearing and trumpeting spirits from her Cup of Abominations to incite the iron-clad warriors who are being devoured by the Beast.

  The facial resemblance of The Whore and Betsy Butts (see Pl. 74B), for whose husband Blake painted this picture, must be coincidental.

Pl. 76 "The Soldiers Casting Lots for Christ's Garments" (watercolour, 1800, 44 x 33.5 cm, Butlin #495), in Blake's exhibition (1809). Notice the Gothic buildings in the background. The contrast is very strong between the earth-bound soldiers looking eagerly downwards and the mourners in the background looking upwards at Christ.

Pl. 77 "Ezekiel's Wheels" (watercolour, c. 1803-5, 39.5 x 29.5 cm, Butlin #468). Ezekiel, the astonished dreamer at the bottom of the design, is overwhelmed by his stupendous vision of a fiery whirlwind out of which came "four living creatures" (zoon in Greek) in "the likeness of a man", "And every one had four faces, and ... four wings", "their wings were full of eyes"; "over their heads was the likeness of a throne ... and upon the likeness of the throne was the likeness as the appearance of a man". "This was the appearance of the likeness of the glory of the Lord. And when I saw it, I fell upon my face" (Ezekiel i).

Blake does not show the Living Creatures with "the sole of a calf's foot" or the faces of a man, a lion, an ox, and an eagle.

Pl. 78 "God Blessing the Seventh Day" (watercolour, *c.* 1805, 42 x 35.5 cm, Butlin #434). The biblical text, Genesis ii, 2–3, says merely that "on the seventh day God ended his work [*of creation*] ... And God blessed the seventh day". Blake's design shows nothing of God's creation. Instead, we see only God in a light-giving tear-drop shape surrounded by six winged figures; perhaps together they represent the seven Kabalistic sephiroth of the manifested deity. Certainly there is little in the Mosaic text to warrant the depiction of God in multiplicity as he rests from his six-fold work.

Pl. 79 "And the Angel which I Saw Lifted up his Hand to Heaven" (watercolour, *c.* 1805, 39.3 x 26.2 cm, Butlin #518) shows, at the bottom, John writing his scroll and above him the "mighty angel ... clothed with a cloud ... and his face was as it were the sun, and his feet as pillars of fire: And he had in his hand a little book open; and he set his right foot upon the sea, and his left foot on the earth" (Revelation x, 1-2). (Blake omits the "rainbow ... upon his head".) Behind him, in his cloud-cloak, are seven venerable riders, perhaps the "seven kings" who comprise the Beast which "shall make war with the Lamb" (Revelation xvii, 10, 14). The design both literally depicts the text and majestically rises above it. It is signed in the bottom right corner ("WB" under "inv") in the style first used for his *Night Thoughts* engravings (see Pl. 69).

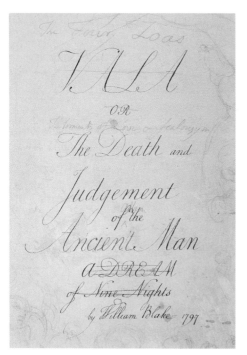

Pl. 80 *Vala* (?1796-1807), p. 1 (pen and ink, 39.7 x 31.3 cm), much reduced in size here. The title "VALA" was altered to "The Four Zoas", "Eternal Man" was changed to "Ancient Man", and "A Dream of Nine Nights" was deleted.

The faint pencil design seems to represent the Last Judgement, with a naked trumpeter plunging down the top right margin towards figures emerging from the earth below the title.

Pl. 81 *Vala* (?1796-1807), p. 27 (pen and ink, 41.2 x 32.4 cm), showing Blake's large, elegant copperplate hand in which he began transcribing his poem, with about sixteen lines-to-a-page on pp. 1-14, 17-18, 23-30.

The design below the text of a bearded skeletal man with a cloven hoof for a hand and with a voluptuous nude woman rising from his loins may represent Luvah "Reasoning from the loins" (p. 28, l. 2).

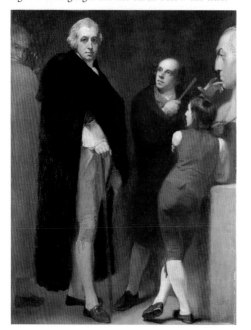

Pl. 82 Oil painting by George Romney of John Flaxman (*second from right*) modelling a massive bust of William Hayley (the tall figure), watched by Hayley's natural son Thomas Alphonso Hayley (*at the right*) who was apprenticed as a sculptor to Flaxman, with a glimpse of Romney (*at the extreme left*). Hayley is posing as a gentleman, with cloak, knee breeches, and walking stick, rather than as an author.

Pl. 83A Thomas Hayley (engraving by Blake, April 1800) after a copy by Henry Howard of the medallion by Flaxman for Hayley's *Essay on Sculpture* (1800) (line engraving, 16.1 x 22.4 cm). In April 1800 Tom was dying of an incurable spinal disease, and his father was desperately anxious "to <u>gratify this dear departing angel</u> with a sight of his <u>own Portrait</u>". Hayley was mortified by the first proof because Howard's "drawing is all wrong", but he was mollified by Blake's efforts to improve it.

Pl. 83B Blake's portrait of Tom Hayley (Autumn 1800, 41 x 50.3 cm, Butlin #343.18) which was included among the worthies of European literature such as Milton, Ariosto, and Homer in Hayley's Library at the Turret House in Felpham. The drawing was intended in part to compensate for the defects in the drawing for Blake's engraving of Tom (Pl. 83A).

Pl. 84 Ordinance Survey Map of South-Western Sussex, 1" to the mile (1813) showing Felpham (a) seven miles south-east of Chichester (b). Blake's cottage is at the southern corner of Felpham, The Fox Inn is on the inner corner of the adjacent cross-roads, and Hayley's Turret House is in the centre of the village. Much of the land in the neighbourhood was owned by the Duke of Richmond, whose estate at Goodwood (c) is just east of Lavant (d). The road to Lavant eleven miles to the north-west of Felpham goes through Chichester, but Hayley and Blake rode there "horseback ... over the fields of corn". In 1801, Felpham had eighty-two houses and 536 inhabitants.

   Notice the number of Barracks close to Felpham, at Little Hampton (e) to the east and at S. Bersted (f), Allwick (g), and Selsea (h) to the west.

Pl. 85 Hayley's broadside ballad *Little Tom the Sailor*, Printed for & Sold by the Widow Spicer of Folkstone for the Benefit of her Orphans October 5 1800 (head- and tail-pieces, relief etchings, 16 x 11 cm and 3.5 x 12 cm). This is the first use of Blake's technique of relief etching for a commercial work by another author. Catherine Blake printed copies in brown and sepia, but very few have survived.

Pl. 86 "Comus with his Revellers" (watercolour, *c.* 1801, 21.8 x 18.1 cm, Butlin #527.1): the Virgin lady frightened by Comus and his animal-headed sensual revellers, one of a suite of eight watercolours from *Comus*, made for the Rev Mr Joseph Thomas. When Blake repeated the series for Thomas Butts (*c.* 1815, Butlin #528 1), he gave Comus a goblet as well as a wand and omitted the Attendant Spirit in the sky.

 Hayley apparently felt that Blake's work for others such as Joseph Thomas interfered with his engravings for Hayley's works.

Pl. 87 "The Annunciation to the Shepherds" (1809) from Milton's "On the Morning of Christ's Nativity", ll. 8–12 (watercolour, 25.5 x 19.3 cm; Butlin #538 2) for Joseph Thomas. In the smaller, later version for Butts (Butlin #542.2), the figures in the sun are naked and younger, and two pyramids or tents have been added in the middle distance.

In "God Blessing the Seventh Day" (c. 1805) (Pl. 78), God is surrounded by a sun made of angels, and in "When the Morning Stars Sang Together" for Job (Pl. 20) are similar rejoicing angels with crossed arms.

Pl. 88 Self-portrait(?) of Blake(?) (pencil and grey wash heightened with white, 23.6 x 20.4 cm, *c.* 1803 [watermarked "G PINE 1802"], not in Butlin). This strange portrait, which showed up suddenly in 1974, surely represents William Blake. Comparing it with the Phillips portrait (1807) (Pl. 63), the high-collared coat with its odd lapels, the white stock, the domed forehead, piercing eyes, arched eyebrows, and hair receding from a peak are very similar, though the Phillips portrait shows a rounder chin, wider mouth, and greyer hair. Flaxman's full face portrait inscribed on the verso "Wm Blake 1804" (frontispiece of *Blake Records*) is quite similar to the portrait here in costume and hair peak (with a little less hair), but is significantly older and more solid. The most striking and disconcerting parallel is in Blake's Visionary Head (*c.* 1820) (Pl. 125) which Linnell inscribed "Imagination of a Man who[m] Mr Blake has rec[d] instruction in Painting &c from", in which the mouth and right eyebrow are extraordinarily similar. Perhaps the portrait here should be called "The Spiritual Form of William Blake".

The portrait was probably made by Blake when working on his portrait-miniatures about 1803. Notice the oval shape of the picture, traditional for miniatures (see Pls 74A-B, 90). The eyes, which to the self-portraitist are most conspicuous, are awesomely compelling. This is a portrait of Blake as he saw himself "not with but through the eye".

Pl. 89 "WILLIAM COWPER ... *From a Portrait in Crayons Drawn from the Life by Romney in 1792 Engravd by W Blake 1802*" from William Hayley, *The Life, and Posthumous Writings, of William Cowper, Esqr.* (1803), Vol. I frontispiece (line engraving, 18.4 x 14.3 cm). The hint of madness in the portrait inspired Cowper's cousin Lady Hesketh with "horror .... I think it <u>dreadful! Shocking!</u> and ... I intreat you on my Knees not to suffer so horrible a representation of our angelic friend to be presented to the publick". She was "<u>determin'd— absolutely determind!</u>" that it should not be published in Hayley's life. To the great relief of Blake and Hayley, when the book was published she said that she "admire[*d*] Romneys head of all things!"

Pl. 90 The Reverend Johnny Johnson, William Cowper's cousin (miniature by Blake, oval 9.0 x 7.8 cm, January 1802, Butlin #347) showing him leaning on a book and with an imaginary Gothic church in the background representing his ambition to become a canon in a cathedral. The miniature stayed in the Johnson family, but its connection with William Blake was forgotten until my wife and I identified it in 1955.

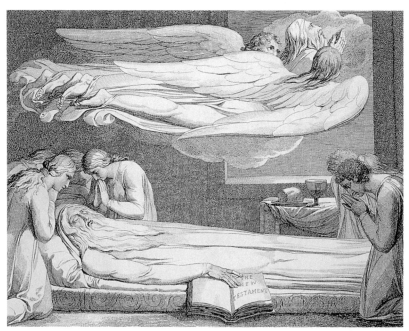

Pl. 91 "The Death of The Good Old Man ... Sure the last end Of the good Man is peace! How calm His exit!" (1805) (etching, 27.7 x 24 cm, by Luigi Schiavonetti after Blake's design, 1806) for Robert Blair, *The Grave* (1808). The Good Old Man may in part represent Hayley's old servant William Metcalfe, whose death on 27 October 1801 at the age of almost eighty Blake and Hayley happened to witness. Two of the mourners at the foot of the bed might then allude to Blake and Hayley.

Pl. 92 "The Eagle" (Blake's etching of his own design, 16.1 x 11.4 cm), for the second Ballad of Hayley's *Designs to A Series of Ballads* (July 1802). The Ballads were intended to enrich Blake and to advertise his talents as designer and engraver, but they failed in all respects; they lost money for Blake, and they lost him subsequent commissions, e.g., for Hayley's *Romney* (1809). Lady Hesketh complained on 10 July 1802 that "yr ingenious friend pays little Respect to the 'Human Face Divine' for certainly the Countenance of his women and Children are ... less than pleasing"; the child in "The Eagle" is "without any of those Infantine Graces which few babies are without, and which are to me so delightful".

Pl. 93 *Milton A Poem* in 12 Books (B), pl. 1 (title page, coloured relief etching, 16.9 x 11.3 cm, 1804). The divided state of Milton, seen naked from the back amidst clouds and flames, is illustrated by his divided name and by the text written in three different directions.

Blake's friend Thomas Griffiths Wainewright commented in perplexity: "The title says in 12 books! My copy [*?B*] has but 3! yet 'Finis' is on the last page! How many should there be?" The first numeral in "12 Books" is quite clearly etched, but each of the four surviving copies has only two books (not three), and the "12" was altered to "2" in two copies.

The motto, "To Justify the Ways of God to Men", is appropriately taken from *Paradise Lost*, I, 26.

Pl. 94 *Milton* (B) pl. 21 (coloured relief etching, 16.0 x 11.1 cm, 1804[-?11]): As Blake kneels in his garden at Felpham to bind on his sandals, Los appears behind him in the sun, and Blake turns in terror towards him.

Pl. 95 *Milton* (B) pl. 13 (coloured relief etching, 16.0 x 11.1 cm, 1804[-11?]), a splendid illustration of Milton, standing before a rising sun, as he "took off the robe of the promise, & ungirded himself from the oath of God".

Pl. 96 A mounted officer of the Royal Dragoons from *The British Military Library*, II (1809). Their uniform was a red coat, white leather breaches, black jack-boots, and a black hat with feathers, and their weapons were a carbine with a 26" barrel, plus (depending upon rank, &c) pistols, swords, and bayonets. An officer's jacket alone cost £10. The horses were a uniform black, and from 1799 their tails were docked, as here.

Brevet Major George Hulton was probably accoutred like this when he preferred the charges of sedition and assault at Blake's trials in 1803 and 1804.

Pl. 97 "The Horse" (line engraving by and after Blake, 14.8 x 9.0 cm) for Hayley's *Ballads* (1805). This copy, the only one known to have been coloured, probably by Blake, is similar to Blake's separate tempera of "The horse" (Butlin #366) in the striking auburn hair of the mother and her blue dress and cap, though the blue is stronger in the engraving than in the tempera.

The stallion has thrown his rider and frightened the little girl but not her mother, and he "stood before her fondly tame".

Hayley thought that Lady Hesketh "will frown on some productions of his pencil, particularly the last, which He thinks his best!", and she replied: "I confess that I think with you that the Horse is a little extra! to say nothing of the extreme composure of the Lady". Dante Gabriel Rossetti claimed that the horse was "absolutely snuffling with propriety". But the moment depicted is one of stasis, not of drama.

Pl. 98 Robert Hartley Cromek (1770-1812) (sketch, *c.* 1805, by Blake's friend Thomas Stothard), probably made about the time of Cromek's commissions for Blake's illustrations to Blair's *Grave* (1805) and Chaucer's *Canterbury Tales* (1806). Cromek's look of youthful eagerness is very engaging, while his low forehead and prominent nose are in strong contrast to those of Blake (see Pls 63 [portrait by Phillips] and 88 [self-portrait]).

The sitter is not identified on the sketch, but the subject is unmistakably the same as in Flaxman's portrait-sketch labeled "Mr Cromeck" (*sic*) (reproduced in *BR* at p. 168). The touselled head in each sketch indicates that Cromek customarily wore his hair unkempt and unpowdered.

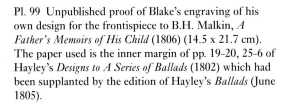

Pl. 99 Unpublished proof of Blake's engraving of his own design for the frontispiece to B.H. Malkin, *A Father's Memoirs of His Child* (1806) (14.5 x 21.7 cm). The paper used is the inner margin of pp. 19-20, 25-6 of Hayley's *Designs to A Series of Ballads* (1802) which had been supplanted by the edition of Hayley's *Ballads* (June 1805).

Pl. 100 Published frontispiece (14.5 x 21.7 cm) of Master T.W. Malkin, engraved by Blake and altered by R.H. Cromek for B.H. Malkin's *A Father's Memoirs of His Child* (1806). Cromek has made the design a good deal more conventional, adjusted the background shading with a uniform series of parallel lines instead of varied and with streaks of light, retouched the clouds and rays of light, made the face of the boy being led heavenwards fatuously darling, and made the central portrait bolder with shading.

For Cromek to work on another man's engraving may have been somewhat unusual, for his fellow engraver John Pye said: "I affirm as my belief that he <u>never engraved anything</u> that he could get done by assistants", and there is other evidence that Cromek put his name to work chiefly done by others. The motive for the change from Blake to Cromek in Malkin's frontispiece is not known. Certainly Malkin admired Blake deeply and said so in the introduction to his book.

Pl. 101 "DEATHS DOOR" (white-line engraving, 18.6 x 11.7 cm [Nov 1805]) by Blake after his own design for Blair's *Grave* (1808). According to the description "Of the Designs" in Blair's *Grave*, it represents "The Door opening, that seems to make utter darkness visible; age, on crutches, hurried by a tempest into it. Above is the renovated man seated in light and glory."

One preparatory drawing for "Death's Door" (Butlin #632) suggests that the old man and the risen youth are bas reliefs on a pyramidal funeral monument with extensive but illegible inscriptions on the base. The engraving technique (probably the one Blake described in his Notebook p. 10: "To Wood cut on Copper") seems peculiarly appropriate to a representation of Death's Door.

Blake had used the design of the old man in his Notebook p. 71, *For Children: The Gates of Paradise* (1793) pl. 17 ("Death's Door") and *America* (1793) pl. 14, and he had used the risen man in *Marriage* (1790) pl. 21 and *America* (1793) pl. 8.

Pl. 102 "Death's Door" (intaglio etching, 29.7 x 17.5 cm, "*London Published by R H Cromek Feby 1st 1806*") by Luigi Schiavonetti after Blake's design for Blair's *Grave*. This is the earliest dated proof of Schiavonetti's engravings for Blair's *Grave*. It differs from Blake's engraving of the same subject (Pl. 101) in being considerably larger, reversed, and particularly in being conventional intaglio etching with black lines on a white background, rather than Blake's experimental white lines on a black background.

The design of "Death's Door" was reproduced on Whitman's tomb.

Pl. 103 "Satan Calling Up His Legions" (1808) (watercolour, 51.8 x 39.3 cm, Butlin #536 1), one of a suite of twelve watercolours from *Paradise Lost*, I, 300–34, made for Thomas Butts, repeated from the much smaller set (*c.* 25 x 21 cm) painted in 1807 for the Rev Mr Joseph Thomas. Blake had previously made "An experiment Picture" of the same subject (a tempera, 1795–1800, Butlin #661) for his 1809 exhibition and copied in his tempera for the Countess of Egremont (*c.* 1800–5, Butlin #662), which show Satan on a pinnacle and multitudes of fallen followers below him.

  In this design, Satan's shield and spear are behind him, ready for use, and the manacled figure crouching in the bottom right is related to the manacled, defeated angel in the frontispiece to *America* (see Pl. 35).

Pl. 104 "The Rout of the Rebel Angels" (watercolour, 49.1 x 38.2 cm, 1808, Butlin #536 7) from *Paradise Lost*, VI, 835-66, for Thomas Butts. In the version of the design for Joseph Thomas (Butlin #529 7), Christ kneels on his right knee in the sun and directs his fearful force downwards, in a pose disconcertingly like that of The Ancient of Days, the frontispiece of *Europe* (Pl. 54). This version for Butts is slightly less disconcerting because Christ has both knees on the ground. In each design, the sun is surrounded by six angelic figures, suggesting that together they represent the seven Sephiroth of the created world (see Pl. 78). The number and attitudes of the falling figures have been altered in the second (Butts) version of the design, but, in each, two of the damned still form parentheses round the central figure.

Pl. 105 "Raphael Warning Adam and Eve" (watercolour, 49.7 x 39.7 cm, 1808, Butlin #536 6) from *Paradise Lost*, V, 377-85, 443-50, 512-28, for Thomas Butts. The design of the scene for Joseph Thomas (Butlin #529 6: *Paradise Lost*, V, 451 ff., VII, 40-59) has been fundamentally re-conceived. The earlier design, in pale blues and greys, shows a figure with a halo standing between penitent Adam and weeping Eve, wearing sparse fig-leaves and both standing, while a crowned figure rains down arrows and a serpent-girt female (Sin) pours out vials of poison. The Butts scene, in tones of rich, pale brown, depicts an earlier moment: Adam and Eve are not yet fig-leaf clad or penitent, Raphael has gorgeous wings and a crown, an arching arbour of lilies frames the design, and, in the distant background, the serpent wreathes through the forbidden tree. On a rustic table behind Eve are heaped the vegetable riches of Paradise, and behind wander the beasts before the fall, elephant, ostrich, lions and cattle.

Pl. 106 "The Temptation and Fall of Eve" (watercolour, 49.7 x 38.7 cm, 1808, Butlin #536.9) from *Paradise Lost*, IX, 780-4, for Thomas Butts. The serpent coiled round Eve's loins offers her the apple in his mouth, in a kind of kiss, while Eve supports his head. The version for Joseph Thomas (1807) (Butlin #529 9) is essentially similar, but here the lightning goes past or through Adam's hands, and the tree seems to be made of woven thorn-vines.

In "Satan Exulting over Eve" (Pl. 6), the serpent is wrapped around Eve's loins, while in "Satan Watching the Endearments of Eve" (Butlin #529 5: *Paradise Lost*, IV, 325-35), the serpent is wrapped round the loins of Satan, and Eve's loins are exposed.

Pl. 107 Thomas Stothard, "The Pilgrimage to Canterbury" (etched proof by Louis Schiavonetti dated Nov 1809, 26.7 x 94 cm). R.H. Cromek gave the commission for the engraving first to William Bromley, then to Louis Schiavonetti (d. 1810), and then to Louis Schiavonetti's brother Nicolo (d. 1813). After Cromek's death in 1812 the engraving was continued by James Heath and Worthington, and it was finally published 1 Oct 1817. According to the Prospectus for Stothard's design in Blair's *Grave* (1808), "The costume of each person is correct with an antiquarian exactness" and "The Scene ... is laid in that part of the road to Canterbury which commands a view of the Dulwich Hills", but, as Blake remarks in his *Descriptive Catalogue* (1809), this "was not the way to Canterbury" from Southwark. Apparently they are going west rather than east. Among Stothard's procession, according to the Prospectus, is a "*Goldsmith*", "a character that Chaucer has not", as Blake points out in the *Descriptive Catalogue*.

Pl. 108 "Chaucer's Canterbury Pilgrims" (line engraving designed, engraved and probably coloured by Blake, 35.7 x 97 cm) (London: William Blake, 8 Oct 1810), Third State. Riding eastward towards the sunrise from the courtyard of the Tabarde Inn in Southwark (across the river from London), the pilgrims are carefully discriminated in their physiognomies, costumes and steeds, as described by Blake in his account of the drawing in his *Descriptive Catalogue* (1809). Near the end of the procession, the Wife of Bath (very like the Whore of Babylon [Pl. 75]) is perilously seated sideways (not sidesaddle, like the Lady Abbess), Chaucer rides next-to-last, Henry Baillie our host is gesticulating in the middle of the procession, and the ploughman, between the Host and the Wife of Bath and wearing a wide-brimmed hat, looks remarkably like William Blake.

In his Notebook p. 117, Blake wrote that he had "minutely labourd" "every Character & every Expression, every Lineament of Head Hand & Foot, every particular of dress or Costume, ... every Horse is appropriate to his Rider".

Pl. 109 William Blake, "The Vision of the Last Judgment" (pen and watercolour over pencil, 1808, 51 x 39.5 cm, 1808, Butlin #642), painted for the Countess of Egremont. Blake used many of these teeming images in other designs.

Blake made watercolours of the Last Judgement for Thomas Butts (1806; 1807; 1809; Butlin #639, 641, 645), for John Flaxman (1806, Butlin #640 [now lost]), for the Countess of Egremont (1808, Butlin #642), unsold (1809, Butlin #643-4), plus an unfinished tempera (1810-27, Butlin #648) for the Royal Academy exhibition of 1828, and his design for "The Day of Judgment" (1805) for Blair's *Grave* (1808). George Cumberland Jr said of the Royal Academy design in 1815: "he has been labouring at it till it is nearly as black as your Hat—the only lights are those of a Hellish Purple".

Pl. 110 *Jerusalem* (A) pl. 2 (title page) (relief etching, 22.5 x 16.2 cm). "Jerusalem is named Liberty Among the Sons of Albion" (*Jerusalem* pl. 26, l.54).

Pl. 111 "Death of the Strong Wicked Man" (Blake's design [1805] engraved by Louis Schiavonetti [1806], 28.1 x 24.1 cm) for Blair's *Grave* (1808), with the soul of the dying man rushing through the window, while his "daughter hides her face with horror ... and his frantic wife rushes forward, as if resolved to share his fate". Flaxman and Crabb Robinson thought it was one of "the most Striking" or "one of his best drawings" for *The Grave*, but the *Anti-Jacobin Review* was "shocked at the outrage done to nature and probability", and Robinson said that "giving bodily form to spiritual beings" as here was "most offensive".

In a notebook of 1811, Francis Douce wrote of designs like this one:

> Blake's figures are as if, like Procrustes' men, they had been stretched on a bed of iron; as if one person had laid hold on the head and another on the legs, & pulled them longer. Nor are some of the figures by Stothard, Flaxman & Fuseli exempt from this fault.

Pl. 112 "Gods and Titans" struggling, from John Flaxman, *Compositions from the Works Days and Theogony of Hesiod* (1817) pl. 34 (25.4 x 22.8 cm), engraved by Blake. Jove (i.e., Zeus) drives from heaven the serpentine lesser deities, in a scene distinctly similar to Blake's design of "The Rout of the Rebel Angels" (1808) for *Paradise Lost* (see Pl. 104).

The unshaded outlines are in stipple, rows of tiny dots, perhaps imitating the pencil of the design, though Blake had represented Flaxman's *Iliad* (1805) with sharp, continuous lines.

Pl. 113 "Mirth" (stipple engraving, 17.5 x 13.8 cm, *c.* 1820), for *L'Allegro*, ll. 13, 25-8, 31-6, is a fairly faithful copy of Blake's watercolour (16.1 x 12.1 cm, Butlin #543 1) for Thomas Butts (*c.* 1816)

In the Second State (*c.* 1820), Blake burnished the plate extensively, converted it into a dramatic line engraving, and inscribed it "SPORT that wrinkled CARE derides" (the figures to the left of the head of Mirth), "LAUGHTER holding both his sides" (the figure to the right), and, very lightly at the bottom, "Solomon says Vanity of Vanities all is Vanity [*Ecclesiastes i, 2*] & what can be Foolisher than this".

Pl. 114 "The Sun at his Eastern Gate" (watercolour, for *L'Allegro*, ll. 57-68, 16 x 12.2 cm, *c*. 1816, Butlin #543 3), one of a suite of six designs for *L'Allegro* made for Thomas Butts. In *L'Allegro*, "the Great Sun begins his state Robed in Flames & amber Light", and, according to Blake's description of his design, "beneath in small Figures [*is*] Milton walking by Elms on Hillocks green The Plowma*n*, The Milkmaid the Mower whetting his Scyth*e*, & the Shepherd & his Lass under a Hawthorne in the dale".

A watercolour of a similarly noble youth with a sceptre surrounded by tiny floating figures represents "Satan in his Original Glory: 'Thou Wast Perfect Till Iniquity Was Found in Thee'" (*c*. 1805: Butlin #469).

Pl. 115 "Melancholy" (watercolour, 16.2 x 12.2 cm, *c*. 1816, Butlin #543 7), one of a suite of six illustrations for *Il Penseroso*, ll. 31-4, 37-9, 45-54, 56-60, made for Thomas Butts. Melancholy, a diaphonously-draped Pensive Nun, with "looks commencing with the Skies", walks beneath "The Cherub Contemplation" with "golden Wing Guiding the Fiery wheeled Throne" "While Cynthia checks her dragon yoke".

Pl. 116 "Christ Ministered to by Angels" (watercolour, *c.* 1816, 16.4 x 13.6 cm, Butlin #544 11), one of a suite of twelve watercolours for *Paradise Regained*, IV, 581-5 made apparently as an unsuccessful speculation. Floating angels beneath Christ offer him a basket of bread and a rummer of wine.

Pl. 117 "Mʳˢ Geo Stephen" (oil sketch, 17 x 29 cm, 1821 inscribed "J Linnell" in ink at the bottom and with the subject's name in pencil), presumably painted in preparation for the oil portrait on panel (25.4 x 10.3 cm) which Linnell painted for £15.15 (1821) and exhibited at the Royal Academy (1822). Linnell also painted portraits of George Stephen (1827, exhibited at the Royal Academy in 1829), and a miniature (1829). In August 1824, Stephen paid (via Linnell) "to Mʳ Blake for C. Pilgrims [£]1 1", and on 1 July 1833 Linnell went "To Mʳ Geo Stephen Coleman St to meet Miss Blake @ Administering to her Brothers Effects".

Pl. 118A John Linnell, sketch by Blake (35.7 x 23.8 cm, 1825, Butlin #688), inscribed by Linnell: "at Hampstead Drawn by Mr Blake from the life 1825. intended as The Portrait of J. Linnell".

Pl. 118B John Varley haranguing Blake, sketch by John Linnell (11.0 x 17.6 cm, Sept 1821), inscribed "Mr Blake Mr Varley" and "J L Sept 1821". In his Autobiography, Linnell wrote: "I have a sketch of the two men as they were seen one night in my parlour [*in Cirencester Place*] near midnight, Blake sitting in the most attentive attitude listening to Varley who is holding forth vehemently with his hand raised. The two attitudes are highly characteristic of the men for Blake by the side of Varley appeard decidedly the most sane of the two."

Varley carefully inscribed Blake's portrait of him (Butlin #689): "J. Varley Born august 17. 1778 18$\frac{m}{5}$ [Sagittarius] ascending".

Pl. 119 Visionary Head of (?) Edward III (24.2 x 20.5 cm, *c.* 1819, Butlin #735). During Blake's sanguinary conversation with him, the king, displeased, "bends the battlement of his brow upon you".

Pl. 120 Visionary Head of "The Spirit of Voltaire" (23.8 x 16.3 cm, *c.* 1819-20, Butlin #749). Blake made a portrait of Voltaire for Hayley's library (1800), he quoted Voltaire in his marginalia to Reynolds, *Works* (1798), and part of "The Everlasting Gospel" (?1826) "was Spoke by My Spectre to Voltaire Bacon &c".

Pl. 121 Visionary Heads of William Wallace and Edward I (19.8 x 26.9 cm, Oct 1819, Butlin #734). The Scottish patriot and his mortal enemy Edward I appeared to Blake one after the other and permitted their portraits to be taken.

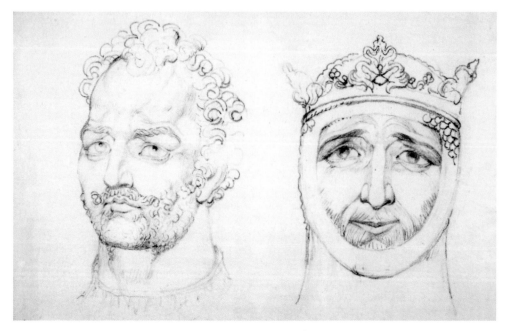

Pl. 122 Visionary Head of "Owen Glendower" (25.4 x 20.3 cm, *c.* 1819) p. 59 of The Larger Blake-Varley Sketchbook. Glendower (?1359-1416), who called himself the Prince of Wales, rebelled against Henry IV to liberate the Welsh. The sense of supercilious power in the face is very impressive.

Pl. 123 Visionary Head of "The Great Earl of Warwick Brother [*i.e., cousin*] to Edward the 4th" (25.4 x 20.3 cm, *c.* 1819) p. 38 of The Larger Blake-Varley Sketchbook. Richard Neville (1428-71), the Kingmaker, was effectively ruler during the early years of Edward IV and arbiter of England.

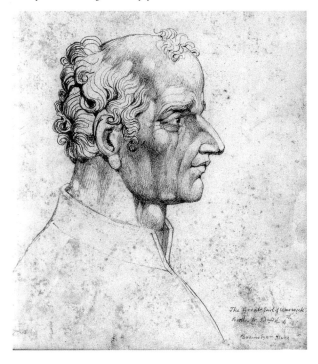

Pl. 124 Visionary Head of "Colonel Blood who attempted to Steal the Crown" (25.4 x 20.3 cm, *c.* 1819), p. 39 of The Larger Blake-Varley Sketchbook. Thomas Blood (?1618-80) was an adventurer who was rewarded with estates in Ireland for his support of Parliament. At the Restoration of King Charles in 1660, he was dispossessed. In 1663, he plotted to surprise Dublin Castle and capture the Lord Lieutenant, but he and his confederates were betrayed. Blood escaped, but the others were hanged.

  In 1671, Blood and three confederates carrying rapiers in canes talked their way into the Tower of London, tied up the Keeper of the Regalia, and had got out with the Crown, the Globe, and the Sceptre before they were accidentally discovered and caught. Blood refused to confess except to the King himself in a private audience. As a result, his forfeited Irish estates were restored, and Blood became a favourite of the King.

  Blood's jaunty bravado seems wonderfully credible in Blake's Visionary Head.

Pl. 125 Visionary Head: "The Portrait of a Man who instructed Mʳ Blake in Painting &c. in his Dreams" (26 x 20.6 cm, *c.* 1819, Butlin #755), a replica, perhaps by Linnell, imitating even the individual hairs of Blake's original (Butlin #753). The minutely-depicted shape of the skull is probably influenced by the newly-modish study of phrenology. The portrait bears a disconcerting resemblance to Blake's self-portrait of sixteen years previously (Pl. 88).

Pl. 126 Visionary Head of The Ghost of a Flea (15.3 x 17.9 cm, *c.* 1819, Butlin #692 98). Blake also sketched the Flea full-length in the Small (Butlin #692 94) and Large Blake–Varley Sketchbooks (the latter design lost) and painted him in tempera (Butlin #750). He may have seen the magnified head of a flea engraved for Robert Hooke, *Micrographia, or some Physiological Descriptions of Minute Bodies made by Magnifying Glasses* (1665). The flea also may be in part a reminiscence of the ghost Blake saw twenty years before stalking down his staircase at Lambeth, "a horrible grim figure, 'scaly, speckled, very awful'".

Pl. 127 Four relief-etched scenes for Thornton's edition of Virgil's *Pastorals* (1821) (15.0 x 7.4 cm) invented and engraved by Blake. The young shepherds are clad in transparent tights; when the same designs were transformed into wood-cuts, the clothing was altered to frocks (see Figs on pp. 389, 391).

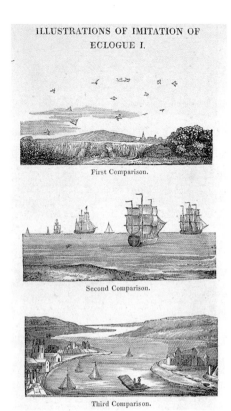

First Comparison.

Second Comparison.

Third Comparison.

Pl. 128 Three woodcuts for Thornton's edition of
Virgil's *Pastorals* (1821) (7.4 x 15.0 cm) designed by
Blake and copied by an anonymous engraver to show
how Blake's own unconventional blocks "ought to be"
made. The prints are light, open, and mechanical,
virtually unrecognizable as designs by Blake or as
illustrations for Virgil with those eighteenth-century
ships.

Blake's blocks had four designs on them. However, in
order to insert the type-set text (e.g., "First
Comparison" here), they had to be cut apart.

Pl. 129 "So the Lord blessed the latter
end of Job", line engraving for
Illustrations for The Book of Job pl. "21"
(*c.* 21.9 x 17.1 cm, 1826), showing Job
restored to prosperity, surrounded by his
daughters with musical instruments in
their hands. In the very similar first
design of the series the musical
instruments are hung on the tree. (Job
with his harp is like the harper in "The
Voice of the Ancient Bard", *Songs* pl. 54.)

According to Gilchrist, "To friends who
remember Blake in Fountain Court,
those calm patriarchal figures of Job and
his wife in the artist's own designs, still
recall the two, as they used to sit together
in that humble room".

Pl. 130. "Jacob's Dream" (watercolour, *c.* 1805, 39.8 x 30.6 cm, Butlin #438), exhibited by Blake at the Royal Academy (1808) and in his own private exhibition (1809).

Pl. 131 "Dante Adoring Christ" (watercolour, 52.7 x 37.2 cm, *c.* 1824–27, Butlin #812 90), one of what Samuel Palmer called "the sublimest design[*s*] from his (not superior) Dante", *Paradiso* Canto XIV. Notice that Dante worships without the intervention of Beatrice (the Church).

A similar design of a devotee worshiping Jesus is in *Jerusalem* (1804[–?20]) pl. 77, and others are among his Bunyan designs (?1824) and in "The Archangel Michael Foretelling the Crucifixion" for *Paradise Lost*, XII (1807; 1808; 1822) (Butlin #829 14, 529 11; 536 11; 537 3).

Pl. 132 The Circle of the Lovers (or Lustful) (line engraving, *c.* 1824–27, 35.4 x 27.9 cm), the first of Blake's seven unfinished plates for Dante's *Inferno*: "and like a corse fell to the ground" (Canto V, l. 137).

Pl. 133 "Laocoon" (line engraving, 27.6 x 22.8 cm, *c.* 1826), adapted by Blake from his engraving (1 Oct 1815) of the cast (in the Royal Academy) of the statue (in the Vatican) for Flaxman's article on "Sculpture" in Rees's *Cyclopaedia* (July 1816). The original statue depicts the Trojan priest and his two sons attacked by two great sea-serpents for offending Apollo (or Athena) during the Trojan Wars. For Blake they represent Jehovah and his two sons Satan and Adam, on the premise that "The Gods of Priam [*Troy*] are the Cherubim of Moses", and the serpents represent "Evil" and "Good". In this engraving, Blake has restored hands, arms and serpent heads missing from the cast.

When Blake was making his drawing among the students in the Royal Academy, he sat on a low stool close to the cast with his glasses on upsidedown, and this eccentricity persuaded the students that Blake was mad. However, Seymour Kirkup asked him the reason for wearing his glasses thus, and, when

Kirkup understood that it was so that Blake would not have to crane his head back so far to see the top of the statue through them, "we laughed at the young criticisers".

Pl. 134 A Daughter of Men between two Watchers (pencil drawing, 52.6 x 37 cm, *c.* 1826, Butlin #827 1) illustrating *The Book of Enoch*, tr. Richard Laurence (1821). The Watchers' "parts of shame resembled horses" and give off light, and the Daughter of Men, whose hand seems to be turning into claws, reaches towards one phallus and stares in fascination at the other.

The Watchers, Sons of God, Angels of Heaven, have been "led astray ... without resistance"; they told the women the secrets of heaven and begot on them monstrous offspring 500' high, and God punished them by burying them beneath the earth.

Pl. 135 Portrait sketch by Blake of Catherine Blake (pencil, 28.6 x 22.1 cm, *c.* 1805, Butlin #683), drawn on a leaf of Hayley's *Designs to A Series of Ballads* (1802)—notice the show-through of the text. The sketch shows the traces of beauty in poverty remarked by Blake's friends.

Pl. 136 Frederick Tatham, portrait from memory by George Richmond (pen and brown ink, March 1829, 10.2 x 8.9 cm), inscribed "March—1829—Paris" and "Recollection of Fred[k] Tatham". Tatham and Richmond were both "Antients"; Richmond became a very successful portrait-painter, and Tatham cared for Blake's widow and burned his manuscripts.

Cromek himself said:

I always wished to see a picture of Chaucer's pilgrims on the road, travelling in company together, when they determined to beguile the way by
telling stories. But I was quite aware, that the great objection to such a
picture would be the monotonous uniformity of a procession .... I felt
convinced that, in the hands of Stothard, the subject was one capable of
being made a great deal of without the faults that were apprehended
having anything to do with it.[95]

Cromek commissioned Stothard to paint a picture of Chaucer's
Canterbury Pilgrims. When Cromek subsequently exhibited Stothard's
design, it proved to be the most popular picture Stothard ever painted, and
by May 1807 three thousand visitors[96] had paid 1s. apiece to see it.

By February 1807 Cromek had commissioned William Bromley to
engrave the picture,[97] and then, probably in the summer of 1807, he substituted Luigi Schiavonetti;* when Luigi Schiavonetti died in 1810 with the
plate still unfinished,† first Francis Engleheart and then Luigi
Schiavonetti's brother Niccolo were commissioned in his place; when
Cromek died in March 1812 and Niccolo in 1813, Cromek's widow commissioned James Heath and his studio to complete it. Elizabeth Cromek, left
largely unprovided-for at Cromek's death, was able to finance the engraving
of Stothard's print only by selling the plates of Blair's *Grave* to Ackermann
for £120.‡ The engraving of Stothard's Canterbury Pilgrims was finally finished and copies of the print delivered to subscribers in 1817, ten years after
the engraving was begun (Pl. 107) and almost exactly eight years after
Blake's plate of the same subject was published.

The subscriptions for the print were substantial; "it had altogether the
most extensive sale of anything of the kind published within the last

---

* As late as Aug 1807, Cromek was still advertising Bromley as the engraver for Stothard's picture (*The
  Artist*, 1 Aug 1807). Presumably Luigi Schiavonetti could not begin to work vigorously upon
  Stothard's Canterbury Pilgrims plate until he had finished the engravings for Blair's *Grave*, and this
  was not until at least the summer of 1807—Schiavonetti said that the "Last Judgment" for Blair was
  "nearly completed" in July, and on 17 April 1807 Cromek said of *The Grave*, "I shall not be able to
  publish it 'till the next Winter" (*BRS* 45).
† George Cumberland Jr wrote in Nov 1809 that Schiavonetti's "etching of Mr. Stothard Pilgrims ...
  is finished", and an etched proof in the collection of Robert N. Essick is signed by Schiavonetti and
  dated 20 Nov 1809 in the imprint (Pl. 106). But this was only the first (or, counting Bromley, perhaps the second) step in the completed engraving.
‡ Undated letter of *c*. 1812 (*BRS* 70). On 3 Feb 1813, Elizabeth Cromek's neighbour Ralph Rylance
  wrote: "Mrs C. ... had assigned over the Chaucer engraving [*of the Canterbury Pilgrims*] to her father
  who is to defray the further expenses and reimburse himself 'out of the first & readiest' as Burns
  says" (*BRS* 71). About 1812 Stothard said that to complete the engraving, "The sum the engraver
  requests is three hundred and thirty guineas ...; for this, he promises to complete it in fifteen
  months, from the time he begins it" (Mrs Bray, *Stothard* [1851], 141–2).

hundred years" (1750–1850), and by 1851 "few houses, where the master has a library, or has any pretensions to a love or knowledge of the fine arts, are without the print, framed and hung in a conspicuous place".*

Stothard's Story

Stothard's account of the commission varies somewhat from Cromek's. He apparently told Allan Cunningham:

> Mr. Cromek had given the commission for painting the subject of the Canterbury Pilgrims. There had been no previous conversation on the subject, though it must long have occupied the thoughts of the projector, for, on the matter being first mentioned to Mr. Stothard, and before he gave answer to the proposal, he took from his folio a sketch of the subject, shewing that it had been long contemplated and only wanted the sanction of a commission to set him to work.†

In this version of the story, Cromek stimulates Stothard to renew a project he had begun long before, Cromek perhaps supplying the format as well as the commission.

Stothard's picture was well known to his friends while he was painting it. John Flaxman's wife Nancy wrote "a Valentine" on 14 February (1807) to Mrs J. Clarke and her husband the Revd Mr F. Clarke:

> Another new work about to be made public, is a picture by Stothard painted after the Manner of an old Illumination, the subject is from Chaucer the Pilgrims of the Tabard Inn setting forth toward Canterbury,

---

* Mrs Bray, *Stothard*, 140, 130–1.
  According to Joseph Farington, on 17 Feb 1818 (*The Diary of Joseph Farington*, ed. Kathryn Cave, XV [New Haven & London: Yale University Press, 1984], 5169):

  > Landseer ... spoke of the Print from *Stothard's "Chaucer Pilgrims"* from which an Engraving begun by *Schiavonetti* & finished after His death by *Heath* having had 200 proofs taken off & abt. 500 other impressions, the Plate had been worked upon by *Worthington*, an Engraver, formerly pupil to Bromley, the Engraver, witht. Heath's knowledge who says He has spoiled the plate. Worthington had the care of it for Mrs. Cromek, the Proprietor. There were 700 Subscribers to the plate.

† Anon. [?Allan Cunningham], "On the Genius of Stothard", *Arnold's Magazine* (1834), 436. Perhaps the "sketch of the subject" was the one Stothard inscribed "The first drawing of the Canterbury Pilgrims—made for Ritson", referring to the print of it in *The English Anthology*, ed. Joseph Ritson (1793–94), III, at p. 1 (the drawing and the print after it are reproduced in Andrew Moore's catalogue of the exhibition 2 Oct–28 Nov 1993 at Norwich Castle Museum, *William Blake: Chaucer's Canterbury Pilgrims* [Norwich: Norfolk Museums Service, 1993]).

preceeded by the Millar playing on his bagpipes & marshal'd by the Host—they are passing the Dulwich hills—he has group'd them judiciously, taken great care of the costume, & given much individual Character to the personages—It is likely to become a very great favorite with the Public—The print will be nearly 3 feet long by 12 inches high & is generally intended for a frieze over the low chimney pieces of the dining parlors—[98]

Notice that Nancy Flaxman mentions neither Cromek nor Blake.

According to J.T. Smith, who was a friend of both Blake and Stothard,

During the time Stothard was painting the picture, Blake called to see it, and appeared so delighted with it, that Stothard, sincerely wishing to please an old friend with whom he had lived so cordially for many years, and from whose works he always most liberally declared he had received much pleasure and edification, expressed a wish to introduce his portrait as one of the party, as a mark of esteem.[*]

Blake might have called to see his friend Stothard's picture in the winter of 1806–07 as John and Nancy Flaxman did.

In a letter of 1813, Stothard wrote

When I undertook to paint the picture of the Canterbury Pilgrims, the price agreed was sixty pounds: the degree of finish was left to me at the conclusion of it. In the progress of the work, the subject and design appearing more important—worthy of more attention than either of us at first apprehended, Mr. Cromek, himself made the following proposition: That, if I on my part would give one months' additional attention to the picture, over and above what was at first agreed, he would make the sum one hundred pounds. This additional forty was to be paid as soon as he could collect from his subscribers. This he did not do, excusing himself on the score of the expense he was at in the advertising, &c., &c. He sold the picture to Mr. Hart Davis for three hundred pounds, or guineas.[†] He

---

[*] J.T. Smith (*BR* 465–6). None of the figures in Stothard's print seems much like Blake, but, even if Stothard did intend to introduce Blake's portrait, he may have changed his mind when Blake became so indignant about his picture.

  The intimacy of Blake's friendship with Stothard is indicated by the fact that Stothard owned not only *The Book of Thel* (E) but the notebook of Blake's dearly beloved brother Robert (*BB* 656).

[†] Note that by May 1807 Cromek should have received £150 from 3,000 visitors to the exhibition of Stothard's picture, and more poured in steadily; £1,050 for 200 proof copies sold at £5.5.0 each (ad in *The Grave* [1808]; £6.6.0 in the Feb 1807 ad) plus £1,575 for 500 ordinary copies at £3.3.0 plus £300 for the painting would have brought in £3,075 by 1818. There were also the substantial profits from the sales of Blair's *Grave*. And *still* Stothard was not paid the £40 promised him.

then in like manner excused himself as he had done before; and as I received his plea of his success with the public with indulgence, and as the plate was in progress towards completion, deferred my demand till publication. This I have done in his alleged difficulties.[99]

Clearly Stothard was suspicious of Cromek's "alleged difficulties" about money.

Blake's Story

Blake's friend John Thomas Smith carefully reported both sides of the story. According to him, while Blake was working on his designs for Blair's *Grave,*

> Cromek had asked Blake what work he had in mind to execute next. The unsuspecting artist not only told him, but without the least reserve showed him the designs sketched out for a fresco picture; the subject Chaucer's "Pilgrimage to Canterbury;"* with which Mr. Cromek appeared highly delighted. Shortly after this, Blake discovered that Stothard ... had been employed to paint a picture, not only of the same subject, but in some instances similar to the fresco sketch which he had shown to Mr. Cromek.[100]

In his research for his picture, Blake went to Southwark to see the Tabarde Inn from which Chaucer's pilgrims set out; "This Inn is still extant under the name of the Talbot, and the Landlord, Robert Bristow, Esq. of Broxmore near Rumsey, has continued a board over the gateway, inscribed 'This is the Inn from which Sir Jeffery Chaucer and his Pilgrims set out for Canterbury.' "[101] He took pains to make the painting chronologically accurate: "the Costume is correct according to authentic monuments".[102]

According to the contemporary witness of Crabb Robinson, "It was after

---

* Blake said that the Canterbury Pilgrims "was painted in self-defence against the insolent and envious imputation of unfitness for finished and scientific art; and this imputation, [*was*] most artfully and industriously endeavoured to be propagated among the public by ignorant hirelings" (*Descriptive Catalogue* [1809] ¶48). This is consistent with a date of 1806, when Blake learned that Cromek had taken from him the commission for engraving the Blair designs. The conception of the Canterbury Pilgrims design is said by the anonymous editor of *The Prologue and Characters of Chaucer's Pilgrims* (1812) to have been due "To the genius and fancy of that celebrated Artist, Mr. Blake" (*BR* 230).

the friends of Blake had circulated a subscription paper for an engraving of his <u>Canterbury</u> Pilgrim's [*in 1806*] that *Stodart* was made a party to an engraving of a painting of the same subject by himself".* But Stothard probably did not know that Blake had made a design of the same subject and dimensions until Blake's anger told him so.

One of the peculiarities of both Blake's picture and Stothard's is their shape (Pls 107–8), designed to go over a mantelpiece: Blake's tempera is $53\frac{15}{16}''$ x $18\frac{3}{8}''$, and his print is 3′ 1″ x 1′.[103] By an interesting coincidence, Stothard's print is the same size as Blake's.[104] Certainly the shape was appropriate to a procession of horsemen, and it may have been confirmed by Lord Elgin's frieze of marble horsemen from the Parthenon which was unpacked in London in 1807.† But it is curious that two pictures of such an unusual subject should be almost identical in shape and size.

There were a number of illustrated editions of Chaucer available in 1806, many of them with plates showing mounted riders.[105] In all these books, the plates are higher than they are wide, and none of them shows the entire procession. What Stothard and Blake added to Chaucer iconography was the entire procession of pilgrims in a design far wider than it was high, Blake's pilgrims riding to the right and Stothard's pilgrims riding to the left.

Both Stothard and Blake had made drawings for Chaucer before Cromek approached them. Stothard had designed fifteen plates for Bell's Chaucer (1783), and he made a design of Chaucer's mounted pilgrims for *The English Anthology*, ed. Joseph Ritson (1793-94). Blake engraved one of Stothard's designs for Bell's Chaucer (1783), he used a quotation from Chaucer on a design for *For Children* (1793)[106] in his Notebook, and in his head of Chaucer for Hayley's Library (1800) Blake included two mounted pilgrims taken from Urry's edition of Chaucer (1721). Both Stothard and Blake had clearly been thinking of illustrating Chaucer before 1806.

* Crabb Robinson's Reminiscences (1852) (*BR* 538); there is no parallel to this passage in his diary. Gilchrist rephrased Crabb Robinson's statement and added the date: "a subscription paper for an engraving of *The Canterbury Pilgrims* had been circulated by Blake's friends . . . in 1806" (*BR* 179). No such subscription paper of 1806 is known to survive, but Crabb Robinson is a very reliable witness.

† Duncan Macmillan believes that Blake's picture "clearly derives from the . . . Panathenaic procession" (review of David Bindman, *Catalogue of the Blake Collection of the Fitzwilliam Museum Cambridge* [1970] in *Blake Newsletter*, V [1971–72], 205–6, endorsed by Butlin 653). However, as both Stothard's and Blake's pictures were well advanced by the end of 1806, long before Lord Elgin's crates were opened, the resemblances in the original conception of their pictures to the friezes from the Parthenon must be coincidental—unless, of course, they modified them after 1806 to conform to the Parthenon friezes. Barron Field wrote about 1830 that in Stothard's picture "the horses are all barbs, from the Elgin Marbles" (*BR* [2] under 1830). Alternatively, they might have been based on the engravings from the Parthenon made by Blake for Stuart & Revett's *Antiquities of Athens* (1794).

Blake's later friend John Linnell provided a correction to J.T. Smith's account with

> particulars which Mr Blake affirmed to me & which certainly explain his version of the case—Cromec according to Blake employed or engaged him to finish the frescoes as he called it of the Canterbury Pilgrims for him for 20 Guineas with the understanding that the remuneration for the whole would be made adequate by the price to be paid to Blake for the Engraving which Blake stipulated he should execute,* but as Cromec secretly negociated with Bromley to engrave this subject from Blakes Drawing which he tried to obtain from Blake without paying more than the 20 Gs but Blake who had some good reason to suspect Cromec refused to let him have it & Blake supposed that Cromec then went to Stothard and commissioned him to paint his Canterbury pilgrims of the size & character that it had been arranged by Blake to engrave his Drawing & when he heard that Mr Stothard had begun a picture for Cromec of the same subject & size he immediately set about the engraving his own Drawing ...
>
> Stothard['s] account of the affair may be to a great extent veracious as far as he is concerned because when Cromec went to him to commission him to paint the subject having been disappointed in the trick he attempted with Blake he of course said nothing to Stothard about Blakes design though he must have suggested the size and treatment as they are so much alike in these respects.[107]

Linnell's account adds to the story the price agreed to by Cromek for Blake's design (£21), the understanding that a generous fee for the engraving would compensate for the slightness of the price of the drawing, and the claim that William Bromley had been secretly commissioned by Cromek to engrave Blake's plate.

As Cromek had paid Blake a modest price for his drawings for Blair's *Grave*, agreed and advertised that Blake would engrave them and then suddenly, and apparently without telling Blake, shifted the engraving commission to another engraver, it is easy to see why Blake, and most subsequent critics, concluded that Cromek had done the same thing with the Canterbury Pilgrims. The fact that Cromek's first advertisement for Stothard's

---

* Blake should have expected at least £200, for Luigi Schiavonetti agreed to engrave Stothard's picture of the Canterbury Pilgrims of the same size as Blake's for £881, and when he died in 1810 he had "earned only £275" (A.C. Coxhead, *Thomas Stothard, R.A.* [London: A.H. Bullen, 1906], 13). After Cromek had (presumably) paid Luigi and Niccolo Schiavonetti for what they had done to Stothard's plate, there was still work estimated at £346.10.0 to be done on it, according to Stothard's letter of 1813 (*ut supra*).

Canterbury Pilgrims of February 1807 names Bromley as the engraver makes more plausible Linnell's claim that Bromley had first been engaged to engrave Blake's Canterbury Pilgrims design as well. The only difference in the two situations is that in the second instance Cromek took from Blake the commissions not only for the engravings but for the design as well.

Until late April 1807 Blake was still contributing to Cromek's edition of *The Grave*, sitting to Thomas Phillips for the portrait which was later engraved for Blair's *Grave*, and offering Cromek a drawing to be engraved with his dedication of his *Grave* designs to the Queen. It may have been only then that he discovered Cromek's duplicity in hiring Bromley to engrave first Blake's design from the Canterbury Pilgrims and then Stothard's.*

Blake and Linnell plainly believed that Cromek had acted dishonestly, or at least that he had indulged in sharp business practices. Cromek's version of the affair requires us to believe that Blake had indulged in the kind of sharp business practice, in copying the conception, dimensions, and organization of Stothard's design for the Canterbury Pilgrims, which Cromek had manifestly practised with respect to Blake's *Grave* designs and elsewhere. In weighing the contradictory claims to business probity of William Blake and of Robert Hartley Cromek, the evidence is very heavily upon the side of William Blake.

Blake had at least learned something from his first dealings with Cromek, for he declined to part with his Chaucer design until he had a commitment from Cromek, presumably in cash, that he would make the engraving from it.

In this crisis, as in so many others, Thomas Butts once again proved to be Blake's knight in shining armour, for he purchased Blake's tempera of the Canterbury Pilgrims—though he may not have done so until some years later.[108]

The evidence that has survived from consistently credible witnesses indicates that Cromek went to Blake in the late autumn of 1806 with a proposal for a picture of Chaucer's Canterbury Pilgrims and discovered that Blake was already happily embarked on such a subject. Cromek offered to buy it for £21 and to commission Blake to engrave it, but Blake declined to part with his design until he had a more binding commission for the engraving than Cromek had given him for his Blair designs.

Cromek then went to Stothard with a similar proposal, apparently even specifying the dimensions and the treatment of the design, and Stothard too showed him drawings on the subject, perhaps those he had been

---

* Alternatively, he might have learned of Cromek's duplicity in the winter of 1807, from gossip—"Tuesday, Jan^ry 20, 1807 between Two & Seven in the Evening—Despair" (Notebook p. 10)—or from Cromek's Chaucer prospectus of February 1807.

commissioned to make for Chaucer editions of 1783 and 1793. Stothard embraced Cromek's proposal with enthusiasm and accepted his commission for £60. Cromek then commissioned William Bromley to engrave Stothard's design when it was finished and proceeded to advertise the picture and print vigorously. By February 1807 the painting was finished,[109] on exhibition,[110] and attracting thousands.

When Blake discovered not only that he had been betrayed by his recent nemesis Cromek but that his old friend Stothard had made a design of the same subject, style, and dimensions as his own which Cromek was publishing, he erupted in fury.

Anger & wrath my bosom rends[;]
I thought them the Errors of friends
But all my limbs with warmth glow[;]
I find them the Errors of the foe

(Notebook p. 23)

When Blake read in Cromek's Prospectus of February 1807 that "The Proprietor of this undertaking finds it difficult to express his own and the general sense of Mr Stothard's qualifications, without violating that admirable Artist's known reserve and modesty of nature", he wrote in his Notebook:

On S
You say reserve & modesty he has
Whose heart is iron[,] his head wood & his face brass[,]
The Fox the Owl the Beetle & the Bat
By sweet reserve & modesty get Fat

(Notebook p. 36)

And he wrote a long poem in which "Bob Screwmuch" is Robert Hartley Cromek, "Stewhard" is Stothard, and "Stewhards soul ... he [*Screwmuch*] buckled to his Back",[111] like Christian with his burden in *Pilgrim's Progress*.

On 17 April 1807, Cromek wrote to the poet James Montgomery an indulgent letter which mentions Blake's eccentricity but says nothing of violent accusations against Cromek:

That "wild & wonderful genius" is still in Fairy Land; still believing that what has been called <u>Delusion</u> is the only <u>Reality</u>! What has been called Fancy & Imagination the Eternal World! & that this World is the only Cheat, Imagination the <u>only Truth</u>! . . .

[*20 April 1807*]

   Since I wrote the above Blake's Drawings for "The Grave" have been presented to the Queen & Princess at Windsor—I received a Letter from Miss Planta, stating Her Majesty's wish that Mʳ Blake would dedicate the Work to Her—This circumstance has so much pleased Blake that he has already produced a <u>Design</u> for the Dedication & a poetic Address to the queen marked with his usual Characteristics—Sublimity, Simplicity, Elegance and Pathos, his wildness <u>of course</u>. I shall transcribe the Lines— I have only to request that you will not suffer them to be copied—

            To the Queen
The Door of Death is made of Gold
That Mortal Eyes cannot behold;
But when the Mortal Eyes are clos'd,
And cold, and pale, the Limbs repos'd,
The Soul awakes, and wondr'ing, sees
In her mild Hand the golden Keys:
The Grave is Heavn's golden Gate,
And rich, and poor, around it wait;
O Shepherdess of England's Fold
Behold this Gate of Pearl and Gold.

To dedicate to England's Queen
The Visions that my Soul has seen,
And by Her kind permission, bring
What I have borne on solemn Wing
From the vast Regions of The Grave,
Before Her Throne my Wings I wave,
Bowing before my Sovereign's Feet[:]
"The Grave produc'd these Blossoms sweet"
"In mild repose from Earthly strife",
"The Blossoms of Eternal Life".
            Your Majesty's devoted Subject and Servant
            William Blake[112]

Blake wrote to Cromek offering his design for the dedication for £4.4.0 and criticizing Stothard's picture of the Canterbury Pilgrims. Cromek replied:

                              64, *Newman Street*
                              May, 1807

Mr. Blake,—Sir, I recᵈ, not withᵗ great surprise, your letter, demanding 4 guineas for the *sketched vignette*, dedⁿ to the Queen. I have returned the drawing w^h this note, and I will briefly state my reasons for so doing. In the first place I do not think it merits the price you affix to it, *under any circumstances*. In the next place I never had the remotest suspicion that you c^d for a moment entertain the idea of writing *me* to supply money to create an honour in w^h I cannot possibly participate. The Queen allowed *you*, not *me*, to dedicate the work to *her!* The honour w^d have been yours exclus^y, but that you might not be deprived of any advantage likely to contribute to your reputation, I was willing to pay Mr. Schiavonetti *ten* guineas for etching a plate from the drawing in question.

Another reason for returning the sketch is that *I can do without it*, having already engaged to give a greater number of etchings than the price of the book will warrant; and I neither have nor ever had any encouragement from *you* to place you before the public in a more favourable point of view than that which I have already chosen. You charge me w^h *imposing upon you.* Upon my honour I have no recollection of anything of the kind. If the world and I were to settle accounts tomorrow, I do assure you the balance w^d be considerably in my favour. In this respect "*I am more sinned against than sinning.*" But, if I cannot recollect any instances wherein I have imposed upon *you*, several present themselves in w^h I have imposed upon *myself.* Take two or three that press upon me.

When I first called on you I found you without reputation; I *imposed* on myself the labour, and an Herculean one it has been, to create and establish a reputation for you. I say the labour was Herculean, because I had not only the public to contend with, but I had to battle with a man who had predetermined not to be served. What public reputation you have, the reputation of eccentricity excepted, I have acquired for you, and I can honestly and conscientiously assert that if you had laboured thro' life for yourself as zealously and as earnestly as I have done for you your reputation as an artist w^d not only have been enviable but it would have placed you on an eminence that w^d have put it out of the power of an individual, as obscure as myself, either to add to it or take from it. *I also imposed on myself* when I believed what you so often have told me, that your works were equal, nay superior, to a Raphael or to a Michael Angelo! Unfortunately for me as a publisher the public awoke me from this state of stupor, this mental delusion. That public is willing to give you credit for what real talent is to be found in your productions, *and for no more.*

I have imposed on myself yet more grossly in believing you to be one altogether abstracted from this world, holding converse w^h the world of spirits!—simple, unoffending a combination of the *serpent* and the *dove.* I really blush when I reflect how I have been cheated in this respect. The most effectual way of benefiting a designer whose aim is general patronage is to bring his designs before the public through the medium of engraving. Your drawings have had the *good fortune* to be engraved by one of the first artists in Europe, and the specimens already shown have already produced you orders that I verily believe you otherwise w^d not have rec^d. Herein I have been gratified, for I was determined to bring you food as well as reputation, tho' from your late conduct I have some reason to embrace your wild opinion, that to manage genius, and to cause it to produce good things, it is absolutely necessary to starve it;* indeed this opinion is considerably heightened by the recollection that your best work, the illustrations of "The Grave," was produced when you and Mrs. Blake were reduced so low as to be obliged to live on half-a-guinea a week!

Before I conclude this letter, it will be necessary to remark, when I gave you the order for the drawings for the poem of "The Grave," I paid you for them more than I could then afford, more in proportion than you were in the habit of receiving, and what you were perfectly satisfied with, though I must do you the justice to confess much less than I think is their real value. Perhaps you have friends and admirers who can appreciate their merit and worth as much as I do. I am decidedly of opinion that the 12 for "The Grave" should sell at least for 60 guineas. If you can meet with any gentleman who will give you this sum for them, I will deliver them into his hands on the publication of the poem. I will deduct the 20 guineas I have paid you from that sum, and the remainder 40 d^o shall be at your disposal.

I will not detain you more than one minute. Why sh^d you so *furiously rage* at the success of the little picture of "The Pilgrimage"? 3,000 people have now *seen it and have approved of it*. Believe me, yours is *"the voice of one crying in the wilderness!"*

You say the subject is *low*, and *contemptibly treated*. For his excellent mode of treating the subject the poet has been admired for the last 400 years! The poor painter has not yet the advantage of antiquity on his side, therefore w^h some people an apology may be necessary for him. ...

I remain, sir

Your real friend and well-wisher,

R.H. Cromek†

Cromek's debonair impudence is stunning. Much of what he says is either *suggestio falsi* or *suppressio veri*. The dedication of Blair's *Grave* to the Queen, whose name heads the subscription list, would of course have

---

* Blake believed exactly the opposite.

† Letter of May 1807, "a duplicate of the original", lent by Cromek's son Thomas to Allan Cunningham in 1833 and not returned (John Bell, "Blake and Cromek", *Spectator*, No. 1,836 [4 Nov 1882], 1411); it has not been traced since it was lent by Allan's son Peter for publication in *The Gentleman's Magazine* in 1852. When Crabb Robinson saw it in *The Gentleman's Magazine*, he said that it had been written "in order to convict B. of selfishness—It cannot possibly be substantially true" (*BR* 548).

increased subscriptions and Cromek's profits.* The price of the book had not been changed, but the number of engravings had been reduced from twenty to fifteen to twelve. Cromek paid Blake exactly what he was in the habit of receiving, £1.1.0 a design. It is Stothard's treatment of the subject which Blake thought low, not Chaucer's.

Perhaps most strikingly, if Blake had sold Cromek twenty drawings for £21 and Cromek returned to him "the 12 for 'The Grave'" for £21, Cromek would have had eight Blake drawings for nothing, as well as the copyright in the *Grave* designs. Of course Cromek offers to return the drawings only "on the publication of the poem".

It was Cromek who sent Blake like a prophet "*crying in the wilderness*". Blake's commissions declined after this time, rather than increasing as Cromek alleged. As Cromek said in his letter to James Montgomery, this is "the encouragement which Men of Genius receive from Men of the World ... the same encouragement as the Wheat receives from the Tares".

Publication of The Grave

Cromek was collecting subscriptions for *The Grave* and Stothard's Canterbury Pilgrims at the same time, and both were highly successful. "The Grave is going on very well", he wrote (17 November 1807); "It has been a very lucrative ... Speculation" (2 July 1808).[113]

In June and July Cromek sent out copies to subscribers,† and the effect on some of them, such as the Edinburgh artist John Scott, was sensational:

> the breath of the spirit blown through the judgment trump on the title-page seemed to have roused him as well as the skeleton there represented. The parting of soul and body after the latter is laid on the bier; the meeting of a family in heaven—indeed nearly every one of the prints he looked upon as almost sacred, and we [*his children*] all followed him in this ....[114]

And the critic William Paulet Carey praised every aspect of Blake's plates:

> They abound in images of domestic gentleness and pathos; in varied grace, and unadorned elegance of form. Their primitive simplicity of disposition and character, is united with bold and successful novelty, and a

---

* In March 1807, Hoppner secured permission for Cromek to dedicate the print of Stothard's Canterbury Pilgrims to the Prince of Wales (*BRS* 44 n1), and Cromek advertised the dedication in his Prospectuses, for instance, the one printed with Blair's *Grave* (1808).

† Cromek also sent Blake "2 Copies, but he has not had the common politeness to thank me for them" (14 Aug 1808).

devotional grandeur of conception. . . . there is not an image capable of exciting disgust, or offence in the whole. . . . his style is uniformly chaste. His energy is devoid of extravagance or distortion . . . .*

For others, the sensation caused by Blake's *Grave* designs was of a different nature. Cromek's correspondent James Montgomery sold his subscription copy because "several of the plates were hardly of such a nature as to render the book proper to lie on a parlour table for general inspection". And the conspicuously unclothed "celestial messenger" on the title page, "seen in an almost perpendicular position, head downwards, and with his trumpet close to the ear of a corpse which is just beginning to revive", exemplifies such "solemn absurdity" that it "afforded Montgomery a very amusing topic of conversation".†

Unfortunately for Blake, most of the reviews admired Schiavonetti's "unrivalled graver" but deplored Blake's designs. In *The Examiner* for 7 August 1808, Leigh Hunt's brother Robert praised Schiavonetti's "Rich dotted lines in the half tints, . . . playfulness of line . . . diversified touch" and "masterly execution", but the "visionary" Blake's drawings and the "frantic" Fuseli's defence of them outrage probability and show "The utter impossibility of representing the *Spirit* to the eye". "In fine, there is much to admire, but more to censure in these prints. . . . nearly all the allegory is not only far fetched but absurd".‡

Blake answered the attack in his *Descriptive Catalogue* (¶68) next year:

---

* William Carey, *Description and Analytical Review of "Death on the Pale Horse", Painted by Benjamin West, P.R.A.* (London, 1817; reprinted Philadelphia 1836; ¶2–5 reprinted in *Repository of Arts and Letters, Fashions, Manufactures, &c* [1818]) (*BR* 246), and some phrases (e.g., "devotional grandeur of conception") were repeated in Carey's *Desultory Exposition of an Anti-British System of Incendiary Publication, &c* (1819) (*BR* 624–5). According to *The Literary Gazette* (Nov 1827), "Few persons of taste are unacquainted with the designs by Blake . . . of Blair's Grave".

    In Dec 1820, Blake was one of forty-six artists who allowed their names to be printed in a testimonial stating that "Mr. Wm. Carey . . . is eminently qualified . . . to discharge the duties of Keeper" of an art collection.

† *BR* 194. Robert Hunt censured the "most indecent attitudes" of figures in "The Day of Judgment" and "The meeting of a Family in Heaven" (*BR* 196–7), and when the "The Skeleton Re-Animated" (the title page) and "The Day of Judgment" were re-engraved in reduced size for the edition of 1847, the genitals of the naked gentlemen were covered, and "The meeting of a Family in Heaven" was omitted entirely, presumably because of the provocative embraces of flimsily clad couples.

‡ R[obert] H[unt], "Blake's Edition of Blair's Grave", *Examiner*, 7 Aug 1808. The attack on Blake and Fuseli seems to be part of a campaign in *The Examiner* against "the Folly and Danger of Methodism", a folly which is demonstrated in any manifestation of a belief in the spiritual. Three weeks later, Leigh Hunt included Blake in a list of "The Ancient and Redoubtable Institution of Quacks" (28 Aug 1808) and *The Antijacobin Review* for Nov 1808 said Cromek's advertisement smacked of "quackery".

    [John Landseer], "The Italian School of Engraving" (1811?), Rees's *Cyclopaedia* (1819), praises at length Schiavonetti's etchings for Blair's *Grave* as "works of great merit, and . . . lasting reputation" (*BRS* 64).

The connoisseurs and artists who have made objections to Mr. B.'s mode of representing spirits with real bodies, would do well to consider that the Venus, the Minerva, the Jupiter, the Apollo, which they admire in Greek statues, are all of them representations of spiritual existences of God's immortal, to the mortal perishing organ of sight; and yet they are embodied and organized in solid marble. Mr. B. requires the same latitude and all is well.

The very long review in *The Antijacobin Review* for November 1808 was even more savage. In the "Death of the Strong Wicked Man" (Pl. 111), "the mind is shocked at the outrage done to nature and probability" by the "perfectly *corporeal* representation of the 'masculine Soul' of the dying man". These "absurd effusions", which offer "violence to true taste", are "the offspring of a morbid fancy; and we think, that this attempt 'to connect the visible with the invisible world, by a familiar and domestic atmosphere,' has totally failed".

Perhaps the unkindest cut of all was the conclusion:

The dedication ... to the Queen, written by Mr. Blake, is one of the most abortive attempts to form a wreath of poetical flowers that we have ever seen. Should he again essay to climb the Parnassian heights, his friends would do well to restrain his wanderings by the strait waistcoat. Whatever licence we may allow him as a painter, to tolerate him as a poet would be insufferable.

Blake almost certainly saw this issue of *The Antijacobin Review*, but he may well have remained ignorant of the wonderfully emphatic account of his designs in *The Scots Magazine*, perhaps written by the artist Robert Scott:

We do not recollect to have any where seen so much genius united with so much eccentricity. The author shews throughout a turn of mind altogether his own. A solemn and mystic character, a habit of mind continually dwelling upon the abodes of death and the invisible world, an intimate familiarity with those ideas, which, to common minds, appear the most distant and visionary, appear to fit him peculiarly for the singular task he has here undertaken; and have enabled him to produce a work, altogether *unique*, and possessing high claims to admiration. The strength of the expression, and the lively representation of the different attitudes, have perhaps seldom been equalled.

There is just one circumstance ... which we cannot quite go along with; this is the representation of the soul in a bodily form. Such an idea we think is greatly too bold ....

Upon the whole, we think this is a work which can be contemplated by no artist, or man of taste, without extreme interest.[115]

It is wonderfully unfortunate for Blake that public blame was so readily visible in influential London journals while public praise was so remote from him. The chief victim of such reviews was Blake, for Cromek already had his subscriptions in hand when the reviews appeared; they could scarcely affect sales of *The Grave*.

The last and briefest of the reviews of *The Grave* appeared in *The Monthly Magazine* for 1 December 1808:

The series of engravings ... forms one of the most singular works ever published in England. In respect to the executive merits of the designs, there is considerable correctness and knowledge of form in the drawing of the various figures; the grouping is frequently pleasing, and the composition well arranged; some of them have even an air of ancient art, which would not have disgraced the Roman school. In the *ideal* part ... which is supposed to connect them with the poem, there is a wildness of fancy and eccentricity, that leaves the poet at a very considerable distance. Some are, perhaps, exceptionable ....

The author of these designs is an engraver of no mean talents in his art, and is said to receive the conceptions of them from "Visions bright," which, like the Muse of Milton—

"Visit his slumbers nightly, or when morn
Purples the East."*

Blake's designs for Blair's *Grave* earned him £21 and betrayal from Cromek and scorn in the most outspoken contemporary reviews.

The Afterlife of *The Grave*

But they were the works by which he was best known for the rest of the nineteenth century. Over 700 folio copies were distributed to subscribers,†

---

* Blake quotes the same two lines from *Paradise Lost*, VII, 29–30 in his letter to Dr Trusler of 16 Aug 1799. The author of the review had very good information.
† The "List of Subscribers" details 688 copies, and Cromek lamented the omission of some of the names in his letter of 14 Aug 1808.

and Cromek also sold an unknown number of copies of the quarto edition, also of 1808.

When Cromek died in March 1812, he left most of his property to his impecunious sister, hoping that his wife would be supported by her prosperous Yorkshire father. She, poor thing, had to make do with Cromek's copyrights and pictures. Her neighbour Ralph Rylance wrote on 30 December 1812 that "Mrs Cromek, the widow, is selling her late husbands books and prints", and five weeks later he wrote that she was offering "Blake's original Designs for Blair's Grave with other curious Drawings of his, valued at thirty Pounds and likely to sell for a great deal more if ever the man should die. ... These Sir are now on sale, and I suppose Mrs C. is urgent for the disposal of them ...."*

Stothard wrote, with a fine orthographical heterodoxy, that "Mʳˢ Cromack has (with a view to Shivonetty [*Niccolo Schiavonetti*] proceeding on [it (*the engraving of Stothard's Canterbury Pilgrims design*) imme]diately) sold blayrs grave for one hundred & twenty pound" to Rudolph Ackermann.[116] Ackermann published Blake's plates in 1813 with Blair's *Grave* in folio (the plates redated 1 March 1813) and again in 1826 with the Spanish refugee poet Jose Joaquin de Mora's *Meditaciones poeticas* composed "solamento como illustraciones de las estampas": "solely as illustrations of the engravings"[117] (the plates re-lettered "*Pub. por R. Ackermann, Londres, y en Megico*"). Blair's *Grave* with Blake's designs was published again [in 1870 by John Camden Hotten] with an 1813 imprint of Ackermann (the inscriptions re-lettered as in 1813 though with fragments of the Spanish still visible), and the plates were printed yet again in 1926. Blake's designs were re-engraved about a quarter of the original size by A.L. Dick and published with Blair's poem in New York in 1847, 1858, and 1879.

Virtually every later nineteenth century account of Blake praises his designs for Blair's *Grave*. They kept Blake's name and genius alive, while more often than not Cromek's name was recorded with contumely.

Poetical Recreations

Blake commemorated some of his sense of outrage in poetical squibs in his Notebook, but at the same time he was creating some of his most wonderful poetry, celebrating the triumph of faith over doubt.

---

* Ralph Rylance to William Roscoe, 30 Dec 1812, 3 Feb 1813 (*BRS* 70, 71). Roscoe did not buy the Blair drawings, and the only other record of them (before they were rediscovered in 2001) was in the auction (in Edinburgh by C.B. Tait) of the property of the late Thomas Sivwright of Meggetland, 1–19 Feb 1836, Lot 1835.

In the Ballads Manuscript he wrote:

> Auguries of Innocence
> To see a World in a Grain of Sand
> And a Heaven in a Wild Flower[,]
> Hold Infinity in the palm of your hand
> And Eternity in an hour
> . . .
> He who mocks the Infant's Faith
> Shall be mock'd in Age & Death.
> He who shall teach the Child to Doubt
> The rotting Grave shall neer get out[.]
> . . .
> The Questioner who sits so sly
> Shall never Know how to Reply[.]
> He who replies to words of Doubt
> Doth put the Light of Knowledge out.
> . . .
> A Riddle or the Crickets Cry
> Is to Doubt a fit Reply
> . . .
> He who Doubts from what he sees
> Will neer Believe do what you Please[.]
> If the Sun & Moon should doubt
> Theyd immediately Go out
> . . .
> We are led to Believe a Lie
> When we see not Thro the Eye
> . . .
> God Appears & God is Light
> To those poor Souls who dwell in Night
> But does a Human Form Display
> To those who Dwell in Realms of day
>
> ("Auguries of Innocence", ll. 1–4, 85–6, 93–4, 103–4, 107–10, 125–6, 129–32)

In all his trials, Blake never ceased to see the Human Form of God.

Blake was also working on the last revisions of *Vala*. He changed the title:

FIRST VERSION, *c.* 1797   SECOND VERSION, *c.* 1807

VALA   The Four Zoas
or   The torments of Love & Jealousy in
The Death and   The death and
Judgment   Judgment
of the   of Albion the
Eternal Man   Ancient Man*

The Zoas, which appear for the first time here, are

> four Wonders of the Almighty ...
> Fourfold each in the other reflected[;] they are named Life's in
>   Eternity[,]
> Four Starry Universes going forward from Eternity to Eternity
>
> (*Vala* p. 123, ll. 36, 38–9)

He revised the whole of the poem, scrapped and rewrote the old versions of Nights the Eighth to the Ninth, and then rewrote Night the Eighth once more. The additions to the earlier Nights include Hebrew and Christian symbolism[118] for the first time, with an inscription on p. 3 using the Greek he began learning in 1802, and then the Biblical place names are often replaced by others from Britain.[119]

In vision, Los sees the Lamb of God coming to "Give his vegetated body ... To be cut off & separated that the Spiritual body may be Reveald".[120] His vision is opposed by Urizen in the Synagogue of Satan: "Thus was the Lamb of God condemnd to Death[.] | They naild him upon the tree of Mystery weeping over him".[121]

The Synagogue of Satan decides "To burn Mystery with fire" and from her ashes reform Mystery as "Deism And Natural Religion as of old so now anew began Babylon again in Infancy Calld Natural Religion", "For God put it into their heart to fulfill all his will".[122]

> Terrified at Non Existence[,]
> For such they deemd the death of the body[,] Los his vegetable hands
> Outstretchd[;] his right hand branching out in fibrous Strength
> Siezd the Su*n*; His left hand like dark roots coverd the Moon
> And tore them down cracking the heavens across from immense to
>   immense[.]

---

* *Vala* p. 1 (Pl. 79). This may have been one of the last changes Blake made in the poem, and he did not alter the text to conform to it; for instance, the word "Zoa" is not used again in the poem (though it reappears in *Milton* and *Jerusalem*), and the Nights are still called "Vala". In the text he changed "Eternal Man" to "Albion"—but not beyond p. 56.

Then fell the fires of Eternity with loud & shrill
Sound of Loud Trumpet thundering along from heaven to heaven
A mighty sound articulate "Awake ye dead & come
To Judgement from the four winds[!] Awake & come away[!]"
Folding like scrolls of the Enormous volume of Heaven & Earth
With thunderous noise & dreadful shakings racking to & fro[,]
The heavens are shaken & the Earth removed from its place
. . .
And all the while the trumpet sounds[,] from the clotted gore & from
   the hollow den
Start forth the trembling millions into flames of mental fire
Bathing their limbs in the bright visions of Eternity[.]
. . .
                                                   This night
Before the mornings dawn the Eagle called the Vulture[,]
The Raven calld the hawk[,] I heard them from my forests black[,]
Saying "Let us go up for soon I smell upon the wind
A terror coming from the South." The Eagle & Hawk fled away
At dawn & Eer the sun arose the raven & Vulture followd[.]
. . .
       rivn link from link the bursting Universe explodes[.]
All things reversd flew from their centers[;] rattling bones
To bones Join, shaking convulsd the shivering clay breathes . . .
                (*Vala* p. 117, ll. 5–16; p. 118, ll. 17–20, 33–8; p. 122, ll. 26–8)

The poem ends:

                    Urthona rises from the ruinous walls
In all his ancient strength to form the golden armour of science
For intellectual War[.] The war of swords departed now[,]
The dark Religions are departed & sweet Science reigns[.]
                                      (*Vala* p. 139, ll. 7–10)

As Northrop Frye writes, "There is nothing like the colossal explosion of creative power in the Ninth Night of *The Four Zoas* anywhere else in English poetry."[123]

But Blake never etched *Vala* or *The Four Zoas*, and eventually he simply gave the beautiful manuscript to John Linnell. Instead he incorporated large sections of *The Four Zoas* into *Jerusalem*.[124]

The Evolution of *Jerusalem*

Jerusalem matured over many years, from at least 1804, the date on the title page (Pl. 110), until 1820, when the first complete copy was printed. It begins with a reference to "my three years slumber on the banks of the Ocean" (1800–3) and concludes with an apocalypse of "The Four Living Creatures[,] Chariots of Humanity Divine".[125]

The poem is about "the passage through | Eternal Death! and of the awaking to Eternal Life".[126] Its purpose is

> to open the immortal Eyes
> Of Man inwards into the Worlds of thought; into the Eternity
> Ever expanding in the Bosom of God, the Human Imagination
>
> (*Jerusalem* pl. 5, ll. 18–20)

"*Ev'ry* morn ... at sun-rise ... I see the Saviour ... dictating the words of this mild song".[127] "When this Verse was ... dictated to me", Blake scorned blank verse[128] and chose instead the septenaries he had used in *America* and *Europe*. Apparently the dictation of the spirits consisted of ideas and images for which Blake chose the form of words. "Every word and every letter is studied and put into its fit place".[129]

Like *Milton*, *Jerusalem* is extensively involved with Blake's own life, but whereas *Milton* reflected events in his spiritual life, in visions of Milton and Ololon and Los, *Jerusalem* incorporates very substantial elements from his temporal life, particularly his trials for sedition in 1803 and 1804 and the attacks upon his pictures and his sanity in *The Examiner* in September 1809. It adds many new characters to his myth:

> I write … of the terrors of Entuthon:
> Of Hand & Hyle & Coban, of Kwantok, Peache*y*, Brereto*n*, Slayd & Hutton
>
> (*Jerusalem* pl. 5, ll. 24–5)

Here are the soldiers who accused him of sedition in August 1803, Privates John Schofield and John Cock and Lieutenant George Hulton, and the magistrates who found him guilty in October 1803, William Brereton, John Peachey, and John Quantock; they appear throughout *Jerusalem* among the twelve Sons of Albion.

On most of the same plates is found another Son of Albion called Hand, who derives his name from the pointing hand identifying editorial contributions in *The Examiner*:

> The Examiner whose very name is Hunt
> Calld Death a madman trembling for the affront
>
> (Notebook p. 22, ll. 15–16)

The very name of *The Examiner* is Hunt because it was edited by Leigh Hunt and printed by John Hunt, and the art criticisms were written by Robert Hunt. The three Hunt brothers are equated with Anytus the tanner, Melitus the poet, and Lycon the orator, the accusers of Socrates.* Three-headed Hand is depicted on pl. 50, "Three brains in contradictory council brooding

incessantly" (*Jerusalem* pl. 70, l. 5). These Sons of Albion, such as "Skofield's Nimrod the mighty Huntsman Jehovah",[130] are in perverse alliance against inspiration, the Holy Ghost.

Blake laboured on *Jerusalem* over many years. In the summer of 1807, George Cumberland said that "Blake has eng.d 60 Plates of a new Prophecy!",†

---

* In his Public Address (*c*. 1811) Blake "hopes that his Friends Anytus Melitus & Lycon" understand that "the Poison of Calumny" cannot persuade "the English Public" that his Canterbury Pilgrims was "Painted by a Madman" (Notebook p. 86). Hand's "indignant self-righteousness" and "scorn of others … Freeze round him the bars of steel" (*Jerusalem* pl. 7, ll. 75, 71, 72), apparently alluding to Hunt's imprisonment in 1813–15 for an attack in *The Examiner* upon the Prince Regent.

† Blake pulled some proofs in 1807.

and in 1809 Blake described it in his *Descriptive Catalogue* (¶75) as a "voluminous" work containing "the ancient history of Britain, and the world of Satan
and of Adam" which he "will, if God please, publish". On 24 July 1811 he
showed it to Robert Southey, but it was "not ready for sale" then.[131] In 1812
"Detached Specimens" were shown at the exhibition of the Associated
Painters in Water Colours, and Blake was probably still at work on it in April
1815 when he told George Cumberland Jr that "his time is now intirely taken
up with Etching & Engraving". *Jerusalem* probably did not achieve its full
hundred plates until 1820, when Blake printed the first complete copies and
when a puff for it appeared in the *London Magazine*.[132]

The poem is based upon the premise that "every thing is conducted by
Spirits"; "God is within & without! he is even in the depths of Hell!"[133]

Jerusalem embodies a revisionist history: "Britain [*was*] the Primitive Seat
of the Patriarchal Religion", and the "Inhabitants of Earth [are united] in
One Religion, The Religion of Jesus ... the Everlasting Gospel".*

> London walkd in every Nation mutual in love & harmony[.]
> Albion coverd the whole Eart*h*, England encompassd the Nations
>
> (*Jerusalem* pl. 24, ll. 43–4)

It is also a new Gospel: "This is the Covenant Of Jehovah: If you Forgive
one-anothe*r*, so shall Jehovah Forgive You That He Himself may Dwell
among You".[134]

It is also a Gospel of art: "I know of no other Christianity and of no other
Gospel than the liberty both of body & mind to exercise the Divine Arts of
Imagination"; "Imagination is the real & eternal World of Which this
Vegetable Universe is but a faint shadow".[135]

> Go, tell them that the Worship of God, is honouring his gifts
> In other men: & loving the greatest men bes*t*, each according
> To his Genius: which is the Holy Ghost in Man; there is no other
> Go*d* than that God who is the intellectual fountain of Humanity
>
> (*Jerusalem* pl. 91, ll. 7–10)

The messiah of this Gospel is Los, the Spectre of Urthona, who "kept the
Divine Vision in time of trouble".[136]

The triumph of this Gospel ushers in the apocalypse:

> And now the time returns again:
>   Our souls exult & Londons tower*s*

---

* *Jerusalem* pl. 27, ¶1. The Kabbalistic "tradition that Man anciently containd in his mighty limbs all
things in Heaven and Earth" was "recieved [*by the Jews*] from the Druids" (*Jerusalem* pl. 27, ¶4).

Recieve the Lamb of God to dwell
  In Englands green & pleasant bowers.

(Jerusalem pl. 77, ll. 9–12)

The poem concludes with

All Human Forms identified[,] even Tree Metal Earth & Stone: all
Human Forms identified, living[,] going forth & returning wearied
Into the Planetary lives of Years Months Days & Hours[;] reposing
And then Awaking into his Bosom in the Life of Immortality

And I heard the Name of their Emanations[:] they are named Jerusalem

(Jerusalem pl. 99, ll. 1–5)

Blake coloured only one complete copy of *Jerusalem*, which he valued at
£21,[137] and he sold only one copy, on the day before he died.[138]

After his death, Tatham was assiduous in showing the coloured copy of
Jerusalem to others. J.T. Smith (1828) quoted from it; *London University
Magazine* (1830) alluded to it; Allan Cunningham (1830) said it was
"exclusively wild"; "The crowning defect is obscurity", though "many of
the figures" in copy E are "worthy of Michael Angelo"; and Tatham (?1831)
spoke of "thrilling lines" from it.[139]

Jerusalem is Blake's most ambitious and most daunting work. Like Los,
Blake felt that he must

  Create a System or be enslav'd by another Mans[.]
I will not Reason & Compare: my business is to Create

(Jerusalem pl. 10, ll. 20–1)

But *Jerusalem* was a Gospel and an apocalypse invisible to his contemporaries.

Patronage of Lord Egremont

One of the most munificent patrons of Blake's time was the Earl of Egremont,
whose county seat at Petworth was not far east of Felpham. He had been one of
the magistrates at Blake's trial at Petworth (October 1803), and he was certainly
friendly to Blake, for, after Blake's death, he called on Catherine Blake "and,
recalling Blake's Felpham days, said regretfully, 'Why did he leave me?' "*

---

* Gilchrist (*BR* 363). The Earl is not known to have owned any work from this period, but after Blake's
death he bought *Job* for £6.6.0 and "The Faerie Queene" (*c.* 1825) (Butlin #811), though he declined
the Dante drawings (*BR* 600, 363, 409).

Perhaps Lord Egremont is the

nobleman [*who*] once sent him some oil of walnuts he had had expressed purposely for an artistic experiment. Blake tasted it, and went on tasting, till he had drunk the whole. When his lordship called to ask how the experiment prospered, the artist had to confess what had become of the ingredients. It was ever after a standing joke against him.[140]

Blake had painted "Satan Calling Up His Legions" (?1800–5) for the Earl's wife, who lived in London, and for her he made his extraordinary "Vision of the Last Judgment" (1808)* (Pl. 109), echoing and extending "The Day of Judgment" for *The Grave*. For the picture he wrote her a poem similar to the dedication to his *Grave* designs:

> The Caverns of the Grave Ive seen
> And these I shewd to Englands Queen
> But now the Caves of Hell I view[:]
> Who shall I dare to shew them to[?]
> . . .
> Egremonts Countess can Controll
> The flames of Hell that round me roll[.]
> If she refuse I still go on
> Till the Heavens & Earth are gone
> Still admired by Noble minds[,]
> Followd by Envy on the winds[.]
> Reengravd Time after Time[,]
> Ever in their Youthful prime
> My designs unchangd remain[.]
> Time may rage but rage in vain
> For above Times troubled Fountains
> On the Great Atlantic Mountains
> In my Golden House on high
> There they Shine Eternally

(Notebook p. 87)

And for his friend the miniaturist Ozias Humphry he wrote in January 1808 a long description of "The Design of The Last Judgment, which I have completed by your recommendation for The Countess of Egremont".

---

* Butlin #642, 662. At the same time, Blake was exhibiting "Jacob's Dream" (Genesis xxviii, 12) (see Pl. 130) and "Christ in the Sepulchre, guarded by Angels" at the Royal Academy in May 1808.

The design itself is a mighty mustering of human figures, of which Humphry said:

> a Subject so vast, & multitudinous was never perhaps, more happily concievd.—
>
> The Size of this drawing is but small not exceeding twenty Inches by fifteen or Sixteen (I guess) but then the grandeur of its conception, the Importance of its subject, and the sublimely multitudinous masses, & groups, wch it exhibits . . .. In brief, It is one of the most interesting performan.^{ces} I ever saw; & is, in many respects superior to the last Judgment of Michael Angelo and to give due credit & effect to it, would require a Tablet, not less than the Floor of Westminster Hall.[141]

Here is praise of which Blake could well be proud.

In his letter to Humphry, Blake explains his design in wonderful detail. At the top, is "Christ seated on the Throne of Judgment". "The whole upper part of the Design is a view of Heaven opened". The heads of infants in the glory behind Christ represent "Eternal Creation flowing from The Divine Humanity in Jesus". Around Christ are the "Four Living Creatures [*Zoas*] filled with Eyes, attended by seven Angels with Seven Vials of the Wrath of God". Above "Christ appears the Tabernacle with its Veil opened" and "the Cross in place of the Ark". On Christ's right is Baptism, "On his left is the Lords Supper; the two introducers into Eternal Life".

On the right is "the Resurrection of the Just; the left ... is appropriated to the Resurrection & Fall of the Wicked". At Christ's feet kneel Adam and Eve, and behind them are Abraham and Moses. Beneath Moses falls "Satan wound round by the Serpent". Beside the trumpeting angels in the centre, "The Book of Death is opend on Clouds by two Angels"; at the top left two angels hold open "The Book of Life". The woman standing on the moon and crowned with stars by the trumpeter represents "the Christian Church".

Beneath Christ

> the Earth is convuls'd with the labours of the Resurrection; In the caverns of the Earth is the Dragon with seven heads and ten horns, Chained by two Angels & above his Cavern on the Earths Surface, is the Harlot also siezed & bound by two Angels . . ..
>
> Such is the Design which you my Dear Sir have been the cause of my producing & which; but for you might have slept till the Last Judgment.[142]

Readers and viewers of Blake's works would give a great deal to have such explanations for others of his drawings and writings.

This picture of "The Last Judgment" made for the Countess of Egremont may be the subject of Crabb Robinson's anecdote about Blake and the Archangel Gabriel:

> once when he was carrying home a picture which he had done for a lady of rank, and was wanting to rest in an inn, the angel Gabriel touched him on the shoulder and said, Blake, wherefore art thou here? Go to, thou shouldst not be tired. He arose and went on unwearied.[*]

Blake clearly believed that the Archangel Gabriel had a special care of him.

Selling Blake's Print of the Canterbury Pilgrims

Blake observed that the success of Blair's *Grave* was achieved by Cromek's energetic puffery, and he attempted to use some of Cromek's methods. He published two prospectuses of his print, one called "Blake's Chaucer: The Canterbury Pilgrims" (15 May 1809) and the other "Blake's Chaucer: An Original Engraving" (1810). These he sent to his friends—Francis Douce had a copy of the first and Thomas Butts of the second—but he was not very successful at it, and only four copies have been located today.

He also sent copies of the prospectuses to printsellers. One of these, Robert Bowyer, sent a copy of Blake's prospectus to the great Earl Spencer, commenting that "W:B: has already a very fine Etching & he has reason to believe it will be one of the finest Engravings which has been seen in this country for some Years."[143] This was a remarkably disinterested act, since subscriptions were to be sent to Blake's brother's house at 28 Broad Street, and Bowyer could therefore have received no profit from his recommendation.

In the Prospectuses Blake insisted upon his role as artist and engraver:

THE Designer Proposes to Engrave, in a correct and finished Line manner of engraving, similar to those original Copper plates of ALBERT

---

[*] Crabb Robinson, *Vaterländisches Museum* (*BR* 452). The anecdote was told to Robinson by a friend (Flaxman?) who had it from Blake.

> This very conviction of supernatural suggestion makes him deaf to the voice of the connoisseur, since to any reproach directed against his works he makes answer, why it cannot in the nature of things be a failure. "I know that it is as it should be, since it adequately reproduces what I saw in a vision and must therefore be beautiful."

It is not clear whether this is the conclusion of Blake's friend who told the story or of Robinson himself.

DURER, LUCAS, HISBEN, ALDEGRAVE and the old original Engravers, who were great Masters in Painting and Designing, whose method, alone, can delineate Character ...

The Artist engages to deliver it, finished, in One Year from September next.—No Work of Art, can take longer than a Year: it may be worked backwards and forwards without end, and last a Man's whole Life; but he will, at length, only be forced to bring it back to what it was .... The Value of the Artist's Year is the Criterion of Society: and as it is valued, so does Society flourish or decay.[*]

He described the Canterbury Pilgrims at length in the *Descriptive Catalogue*, stressing the eternal qualities of Chaucer's poem:

The characters of Chaucer's Pilgrims are the characters which compose all ages and nations: as one age falls, another rises, different to mortal sight, but to immortals only the same; for we see the same characters repeated again and again, in animals, vegetables, minerals, and in men; nothing new occurs in identical existence; Accident ever varies, Substance can never suffer change nor decay.

Of Chaucer's characters, as described in his Canterbury Tales, some of the names or titles are altered by time, but the characters themselves for ever remain unaltered[†] .... Names alter, things never alter. I have known multitudes of those who would have been monks in the age of monkery, who in this deistical age are deists. As Newton numbered the stars, and as Linneus numbered the plants, so Chaucer numbered the classes of men.[‡]

Blake also described "my rival's prospectus" in terms which mingle shrewd criticism and unworthy railing:

---

[*] "Blake's Chaucer: The Canterbury Pilgrims" (1809) ¶1, 3. The prospectus was printed by Watts & Bridgewater, Blake's near neighbours in South Molton Street. The subscription price was £4.4.0 (reduced in 1810 to £3.3.0, the price for the print of Stothard's design), and subscriptions were received at 28 Broad Street both in 1809, when the painting was on exhibition there, and in 1810, after the exhibition had closed. It is curious that Blake did not offer proof copies.

Blake's insistence upon completing the engraving in a year is partly related to the fact that the etching of Stothard's plate was begun in the summer of 1807, was still not finished two years later when Blake wrote his first prospectus, and indeed the print was not published until October 1817, more than ten years after it was begun.

[†] This phrase is adapted by the editor of *The Prologue and Characters of Chaucer's Pilgrims* (1812) (*BR* 230).

[‡] *Descriptive Catalogue* ¶16–17. Hazlitt echoed this in his *Lectures on the English Poets* (1818): "Chaucer, it has been said, numbered the classes of men, as Linnaeus numbered the plants. Most of them remain to this day: others that are obsolete, and may well be dispensed with, still live in his description of them".

he has jumbled his dumb dollies together, and is praised by his equals for it . . . .

All is misconceived, and its mis-execution is equal to its misconception. . . . I have been scorned long enough by these fellows, who owe to me all that they have; it shall be so no longer.

I found them blind, I taught them how to see;
And, now, they know me not nor yet themselves.

(Descriptive Catalogue ¶52, 58, 64)

Such passionate resentment prompted acquaintances such as Thomas Frognall Dibdin to conclude that

When Blake entered the arena with *Stothard*, as a rival in depicting the *Dramatis Personae* of Chaucer's Canterbury Tales, he seems to have absolutely lost his wits; his pencil was as inferior to the former, as his burin was to that of *Cromek* [*i.e., Schiavonetti*], who engraved Stothard's immortal picture.[144]

Blake also drafted a work to be entitled

Chaucers Canterbury Pilgrims
Being a Complete Index of Human Characters as
they appear Age after Age

and he even devised a proclamation of it:

This Day is Publishd Advertizements to Blakes Canterbury Pilgrims from Chaucer, Containing Anecdotes of Artists. Price 6[d145]

Much of the draft of this "Public Address" is devoted to attacking the members and motives of the Chalcographic Society, whose secretary was Robert Hartley Cromek. In February 1810 the society had announced through *The Examiner* a grandiose plan to subsidize engraving in England in the persons of the members of the Chalcographic Society. Blake denounces, often in notably intemperate language, the motives of these "Monopolizing Traders"[146] and their pretentious attempts to "improve" the art of engraving by meretricious means.

When John Landseer attacked the society in a pamphlet, Cromek supposed on 20 August 1810 that he would be deputed by the Society to reply. However, shortly thereafter, according to William Carey, "incurable jealousies and dissensions broke out . . . [*among the*] professional members [*i.e., the engravers*] . . . and the society was dissolved".[147] The dissolution of the Chalcographic Society dissolved one of the chief focuses of Blake's Public Address, and the work was never published.

An unnamed friend of Blake, perhaps B.H. Malkin, produced a little edition of *The Prologue and Characters of Chaucer's Pilgrims* ... Intended to Illustrate a Particular Design of Mr. William Blake, Which Is Engraved by Himself (1812) which may be seen at Colnaghi's, Mr [James] Blake's, 28 Broad Street,* and at the Publisher's, Mr Harris. The Editor says: "I have selected the Prologue and the Characters, that the heads, as represented by Mr. Blake, may be compared with the lineaments drawn by Chaucer".[148] And for the work Blake made two engravings, the first one representing seven of the pilgrims themselves. But *The Prologue and Characters of Chaucer's Pilgrims* too is an uncommon work, and only a handful of copies have been traced today. It cannot have brought Blake many new subscribers.

Blake also exhibited his Chaucer tempera in 1812 at the Water Colour Society, but the only published response to it was ambivalent. According to *The Lady's Monthly Museum* (June 1812), it "is a picture of mongrel excellence" with "a repulsive appearance". "That it is the work of genius, no one will deny; it possesses all the truth, the costume, and the manners of the times; and the artist is perhaps worthy of the highest commendation for his industry, research, and correctness", but it exemplifies an "imitation of the arts in their degraded state", and the reviewer preferred Stothard's version.[149]

On the other hand, *The Gentleman's Magazine* (Sept 1812) said that Blake's Canterbury Pilgrims are "well-painted".[150] And Charles Lamb said: "His pictures, one in particular the Canterbury Pilgrims (far above Stothard's) have great merit, but hard, dry, yet with grace. He has written a Catalogue of them, with a most spirited criticism on Chaucer, but mystical and full of Vision."[151]

The Canterbury Pilgrims is one of Blake's finest plates and one of his most popular, though nothing like on the scale of popularity of Stothard's.†

But at least the costs of the print were low.‡ The first two copies sold at

---

* James Blake moved from 28 Broad Street by the end of 1812.

† Five states of Blake's Canterbury Pilgrims have been distinguished, the first with 1 surviving copy, the second with 2, the third with 23, the fourth (*c.* 1820–23) with 3, and the fifth with 26, many of them posthumous, plus 142 recorded but not traced (R.N. Essick, *The Separate Plates of William Blake* [Princeton: Princeton University Press, 1983], 60–89). One copy was coloured by Blake but not sold before his death.

‡ If the cost per square centimetre of the copper for Blake's Chaucer (94.8 x 30.5 cm or 2,891.4 cm²) was the same as for Flaxman's *Hesiod* (1814–17) (plates *c.* 35 x 25 cm or 875 cm² at 7s. 4d. each [*BB* 558]), the price would have been about £1.4.2½.

The paper had to be three to four times the size of that for Flaxman's *Iliad* (1805) and Hesiod (1817) which cost £4.8.0 and £4.0.0 per ream (*BB* 561, 558). The cost for the Canterbury Pilgrims paper might have been about £14.14.0 per ream, making 7d. per sheet and 3½d. per pull. (Ruthven Todd, "A Tentative Note on the Economics of The Canterbury Pilgrims", *Blake*, XI [1977], 30–1, estimates that paper 101.6 x 126.2 cm would have cost 6d. per pull.)

£3.3.0* may have paid all expenses, and thereafter each copy sold at this price should have brought them more than £3.0.0. For forty copies, they might have received over £100.

Of course this ignores what the Blakes might have expected for designing, engraving, and printing. They would not have expected what the fashionable Stothard received for his painting of the same scene in the same size (£60) or what his engravers had for their labours (£881), but they might reasonably have hoped for a quarter to a half of this (£220–£440). What they received was certainly far less even than fair professional wages, not to mention the profit a speculator might hope for on his investment. But they certainly made a profit.

Blake as a Publisher

In the dark days when Cromek and Stothard seemed to Blake to have betrayed him, he still had loyal friends and admirers like Ozias Humphry and George Cumberland who found commissions for him.

Blake had been experimenting with the new technique of lithography, which had been invented in the 1790s, brought to England in 1800, and patented. The patent-holders were eager to demonstrate that their method of drawing directly on stone for printing offers wonderful advantages to creative artists, and to exhibit the capacities of their process they published a collection of prints by well-known painters.[152] They rented out stones and printed from them, and Blake took advantage of this about 1807 to make a lithographic print of "Enoch" inscribed, also in Hebrew, "And Enoch walked with God" (Genesis v, 24). His lithographic techniques differed from those advocated by the proprietors, and George Cumberland wrote down on a copy of "Enoch":

If the Blakes did the printing the cash cost for labour would have been nil. Blake's *Milton* was probably printed in 1811, so we know that Blake was using his press then.

For twenty-five copies of Blake's Canterbury Pilgrims, the total out-of-pocket expenses might have been £1.4.2½ for copper plus 7s. 3½d. for paper (25 x 3½d.)—total: £1.11.6. (Todd estimates about £4.4.0.)

The costs of producing a few copies of each of the two Prospectuses for the Canterbury Pilgrims may have been no more than £2.0.0.

* The few contemporary sale-records of the Canterbury Pilgrims (*BR* 362, 605, 592, 594, 597) indicate that they were rarely sold at the advertised price of £3.3.0.

Aug 1826	Mr & Mrs Aders	£2. 2.0
Sept 1827	John Linnell	£1.19.0[?]
Sept 1827	Mr Flowers, India	£2.12.6
Jan 1828	Crabb Robinson, 2 copies each at	£2.12.6
Jan 1828	Barron Field	£2.12.6
March 1835	Samuel Boddington, "a proof"	£3. 3.0

William Blake's directions for making lithographs

White Lyas—is the Block[;] draw with Ink composed of Asphaltum dis-solved in dry Linseed Oil—add fine venetian Tripoli & Rotten Stone Powder. Let it dry. *W*hen dry saturate the stone with water and Dab it with the broad Dabber and cover it very thinly with best Printers Ink—and Print as a block—of Blake.*

Plainly Cumberland thought that Blake's method, which is related to his technique of Illuminated Printing, might be valuable to himself and perhaps to other artists, and, years later, Cumberland's son used lithography to reproduce his father's *Scenes Chiefly Italian* (1821).

On 18 December 1808, Cumberland wrote to his old friend:

Dear Blake,

A gentleman of my acquaintance to whom I was shewing your incom-parable etchings last night, was so charmed with them, that he requested me to get him a compleat Set of all you have published in the way of <u>Books</u> coloured as mine are;†—at the same time he wishes to know what will be the price of as many as you can spare him, if all are not to be had, being willing to wait your own time in order to have them as those of mine are.

With respect to the money I will take care that it shall be reced and sent to you through my Son as fast as they are procured.

Cumberland secured an immediate answer next day by directing his son to "take the above to Mr Blake and get him to answer it <u>directly</u> on the Sheet of Paper on which you write your answer".

Dear Cumberland

I am very much obliged by your kind ardour in my cause & should immediately Engage in reviewing my former pursuits of printing if I had not now so long been turned out of the old channel into a new one that it is impossible for me to return to it without destroying my present course[.] New Vanities or rather new pleasures occupy my thoughts[.]

---

* *BRS* 55. The limestone called lias, which comes from near Bath, was said by C. Hullmandel, *The Art of Drawing on Stone* [1824], 2, to be "too soft and porous" for printing, as compared with the German Kellheim stone. "Tripoli" or "Rotten Stone" is a fine earth used as a powder for polishing metal. The unusual characteristics of these directions are discussed in Robert N. Essick, *The Separate Plates of William Blake* (Princeton: Princeton University Press, 1983), 56–7, which is the source of my infor-mation about the context of "Enoch".

† Cumberland had watercoloured copies of *Thel* (A) and *Visions* (B) and colour-printed copies of *Europe* (C), *Song of Los* (D), and *Songs* (F), as well as uncoloured copies of *America* (F) and *For Children: The Gates of Paradise* (C). It is not clear, therefore, whether "<u>Books</u> coloured as mine are" would be watercoloured or colour-printed.

New profits seem to arise before me so tempting that I have already involved myself in engagements that preclude all possibility of promising any thing.

Thus, even with a firm order in hand, Blake declined to return to his old channel of printing and colouring his own books. Indeed, between 1804 and 1818, he may have printed only six copies of works in Illuminated Printing, all but one in 1811.*

His new vanities and pleasures may have included his intention, of which he had talked to Cumberland in the summer of 1807, "to publish his new method [*of etching*] through means of stopping lights". Next spring Cumberland made himself a memorandum, that "Blakes new mode of Stopping lights [*is*] to be published in Nicholson", that is, in William Nicholson's *Journal of Natural Philosophy, Chemistry, and the Arts*. In his letter of 18 December 1808 Cumberland continued:

You talked also of publishing your new method of engraving—send it to me and I will do my best to prepare it for the Press.— Perhaps when done you might with a few specimens of Plates make a little work for sub-scribers of it ... selling about 6 Pages for a guinea to non Subscribers—

To this Blake replied:

I have Myself begun to print an account of my various Inventions in Art for which I have procured a Publisher & am determind to pursue the plan of publishing what I may get printed without disarranging my time which in future must alone be devoted to Designing & Painting ....

No trace survives of such a separately published "account of my various Inventions in Art".†

---

* In 1802, Blake seems to have printed *Innocence* (O, R/Y) and the *Innocence* in the combined *Songs* (P) plus *Experience* (P–Q); in 1804 he printed *Innocence* (P–Q) and the *Innocence* with the combined *Songs* (Q); in 1807 he apparently pulled *Jerusalem* proofs plus *America* (M); and in 1811 he printed *Innocence* (S) plus the *Innocence* with *Songs* (S) and *Milton* (A–C) (Joseph Viscomi, *Blake and the Idea of the Book* [1993], 377–9).

If Blake received what he asked for them in his letter of 9 June 1818, he would have had £5.5.0 for *America*, £31.10.0 for three copies of *Milton*, and £6.6.0 for two copies of *Innocence*. But probably he was paid a good deal less than this.

Notice that Blake's letter implies that he has not a single copy in stock with which to supply Cumberland's friend.

† In the advertisement of his exhibition (15 May 1809), ¶9, Blake wrote that "The Art [*of fresco painting*] has been lost: I have recovered it. How this was done, will be told, together with the whole Process, in a Work on Art, now in the Press", and in his *Descriptive Catalogue* (1809) ¶9 he said that in "another work on Painting" he would tell how he had recovered the lost art of Fresco painting and who was "guilty of this villa[i]ny" of first bringing "oil Painting into general opinion and practice". Perhaps the accounts of engraving and of fresco painting were to appear in the same work.

Blake's Exhibition and Descriptive Catalogue *(1809)*

Disappointed in his attempt to reach the public through Cromek with his own engravings of his designs for Blair's *Grave* and for Chaucer's Canterbury Pilgrims, Blake determined to hold a retrospective exhibition of his own works. He could not, he felt, count on public institutions any more, for "my Designs, being all in Water-colours, (that is in Fresco) are regularly refused to be exhibited by the *Royal Academy*, and the *British Institution* has, this year, followed its example".* If his pictures were to be exhibited, he had to exhibit them himself.

He could not afford to rent fashionable rooms and risk the losses incurred by his friend Henry Fuseli for his Milton Gallery in 1798 and 1799, and there was not enough space to hold the exhibition in his cramped flat in South Molton Street. He therefore arranged for his pictures to be seen in his brother's haberdashery shop in Broad Street, as Cromek had shown Stothard's Canterbury Pilgrims painting in his house near Stothard's in Newman Street. Blake's "paintings filled several rooms of an ordinary dwelling house",† and the visitors to Blake's exhibition might also become customers for his brother James.

It was, of course, unusual to hold an exhibition in a shop, but it was not unknown in elegant premises in the Strand or Oxford Street. However, Golden Square had never been a thoroughfare, and in 1809 the neighbourhood was no longer as Blake remembered it from his childhood. In the 60 years since Blake's mother had first made it her home, the area had been subsiding from gentility into mournful bohemianism, becoming a region of tobacco smoke and public song. Aristocrats and patrons were finding more spacious and elegant squares farther west, and probably by 1809 the neighbourhood was already what it became by about 1825:

---

* "Exhibition of Paintings in Fresco" ¶10. This statement is curious on two accounts. In the first place, though the works in Blake's exhibition were indeed "all in Water-colours", only #1–10 (Butlin #649, 651, 653, 655, 657–661, 663) are "in Fresco" or tempera (on a prepared surface which absorbs colour), while #11–16 are ordinary watercolours (Butlin #69, 438, 456, 495, 500, 664). And in the second place, Blake had exhibited his ordinary watercolours of "Jacob's Dream" and "Christ in the sepulchre, guarded by angels" at the Royal Academy as recently as 1808 (#438, 500), and both of them were also in his own exhibition (*Descriptive Catalogue* #13–14) as examples of what "the *Royal Academy* and the *British Institution* ... have excluded". Perhaps he meant that the Royal Academy and the British Institution "regularly refused" his temperas. (His temperas of Chaucer, Pitt, and Nelson, #1–3 of the 1809 catalogue, were shown in the 1812 exhibition of the Associated Painters in Water-Colours.) Or perhaps, at the time when the "Exhibition of Paintings in Fresco" advertisement was written, Blake had not yet decided to include the watercolours (#10–16) in the exhibition.

† Crabb Robinson, Reminiscences (1852) (*BR* 537). Robinson says that the exhibition was "at a Hosiers" shop, but it is possible that James Blake was then no longer in business as a hosier. Even if he was, the pictures may have been exhibited in the living quarters rather than in the shop itself.

Although few members of the graver professions live about Golden Square, it is not exactly in anybody's way to or from anywhere. It is one of the squares that have been; a quarter of the town that has gone down in the world, and taken to letting lodgings. Many of its first and second floors are let furnished to single gentlemen, and it takes boarders besides. It is a great resort of foreigners. The dark-complexioned men who wear large rings, and heavy watch-guards, and bushy whiskers, and who congregate under the Opera Colonnade, and about the box-office in the season, between four and five in the afternoon, when Mr. Saqvin gives away the orders,—all live in Golden Square, or within a street of it. Two or three violins and a wind instrument from the Opera band reside within its precincts. Its boarding-houses are musical, and the notes of pianos and harps float in the evening time round the head of the mournful statue, the guardian genius of a little wilderness of shrubs, in the center of the square. On a summer's night, windows are thrown open, and groups of swarthy moustachio'd men are seen by the passer-by lounging at the casements, and smoking fearfully. Sounds of gruff voices practising vocal music invade the evening's silence, and the fumes of choice tobacco scent the air. There, snuff and cigars, and German pipes and flutes, and violins, and violoncellos, divide the supremacy between them. It is the region of song and smoke. Street bands are on their mettle in Golden Square; and itinerant glee-singers quaver involuntarily as they raise their voices within its boundaries.[153]

The decline of his natal neighbourhood entered deeply into Blake's mind and myth:

The Corner of Broad Street weeps; Poland Street languishes
To Great Queen Street & Lincolns Inn all is distress & woe.[154]

"The Ancient Britons"

He assembled sixteen pictures for his exhibition and sale,* some painted as long ago as 1793. Most of the pictures were of modest dimensions, 10″ x 12″ or less, but one of them, "The Ancient Britons" was bigger than all the rest put together, 14′ x 10′, the largest picture Blake ever made, with "Figures full as large as Life".[155] It was so large that it could only be moved

* The prices must have been on the pictures themselves, for they do not appear in the catalogue.

conveniently when rolled up, very few private walls could accommodate it, and only a collector with a very large house could think of buying it.

"The Ancient Britons" was a subject over which Blake had long brooded,[156] though his picture did not take its final form until he talked to William Owen Pughe about Welsh antiquities. After 1806, when the impecunious William Owen inherited some property and added Pughe to his name, he commissioned Blake to paint "The Ancient Britons". Owen Pughe had published *The Cambrian Biography, or History of Celebrated Men Among the Ancient Britons* (1803), and it was therefore very appropriate that he should commission Blake's great painting of "The Ancient Britons".

Blake's description of the picture begins with a translation of Welsh triads, which Robert Southey thought was "supplied to him no doubt by that good simple-hearted, Welsh-headed man, William Owen, whose memory is the great storehouse of all Cymric tradition and lore of every kind".[157] Southey said Owen Pughe "found everything which he wished to find in the Bardic system, and there he found Blake's notions, and thus Blake and his wife were persuaded that his dreams were old patriarchal truths, long forgotten, and now re-revealed. They told me this".*

As the picture disappeared early in the nineteenth century, all we know of it are contemporary descriptions. According to Blake's account of it in his *Descriptive Catalogue*, "The Ancient Britons" represents "the last Battle of King Arthur" in the fifth century A.D., when all the Britons were "overwhelmed by brutal arms" except for "the most Beautiful, the most Strong, and the most Ugly", "The three general classes of men" who "remain for ever unsubdued, age after age"; "these three marched through the field unsubdued, as Gods, and the Sun of Britain set".†

The Beautiful Man has the "form and features that are capable of being the receptacles of intellect". The Ugly Man, who "represents the human reason", approaches

to the beast in features and form, his forehead small, without frontals; his

---

* Robert Southey, 8 May 1830. Southey said that Owen Pughe "found our Blake after the death of Joanna Southcote" (1814), but the date should be before 1811, when Blake was finishing "The Ancient Britons" for Owen Pughe and when Southey made his only visit to the Blakes in July. Southey continues: "I, who well knew the muddy nature of Owen's head, knew what his opinion upon such a subject was worth. I came away from the visit with so sad a feeling that I never repeated it."

   No other work by Blake is known to have belonged to Owen Pughe.

† *Descriptive Catalogue* ¶73, 72. The "Exhibition of Paintings" ¶1 describes the picture as showing "Three Ancient Britons overthrowing the Army of armed Romans", but the account in the *Descriptive Catalogue* makes it clear rather that they were the only Britons *not* overthrown by the Romans.

   Blake thought that "The Ancient Britons" was the most important of his pictures, and he listed it first in the advertisement for his exhibition.

jaw large; his nose high on the ridge, and narrow; his chest and the stamina of his make, comparatively little, and his joints and his extremities large; his eyes with scarce any whites, narrow and cunning, and every thing tending toward what is truly Ugly; the incapability of intellect.

The Strong Man is "a receptacle of Wisdom, a sublime energizer .... Strength consists in accumulation of power to the principal seat ... strength is compactness, not extent nor bulk".[158]

The naked warriors exhibit "The flush of health in flesh, exposed to the open air, nourished by the spirits of forests and floods ... in Mr. B.'s Britons, the blood is seen to circulate in their limbs".*

Each of

The Roman soldiers rolled together in a heap before them ... shew[s] a different character, and a different expression of fear, or revenge, or envy, or blank horror, or amazement, or devout wonder and unresisting awe.

The dead and the dying, Britons naked, mingled with armed Romans, strew the field beneath. Among these, the last of the Bards ... is seen falling, outstretched among the dead and the dying; singing to his harp in the pains of death.

Distant among the mountains, are Druid Temples, similar to Stone Henge. The Sun sets behind the mountains, bloody with the day of battle.†

The picture excited hyperbole in praise and blame from the few who saw it. Tommy Butts's friend the young art student Seymour Kirkup called it "his masterpiece".[159]

In texture it was rather mealy (as we call it) & it was too red, The sun seemed setting in blood. It was not Greek in character, though the figures reminded one of Hercules, Apollo & Pan—They were naked Britons— ... There is more power of drawing in it than in any of his works that I have known, even in Blair's Grave.[160]

---

* *Descriptive Catalogue* ¶87. On 25 Jan 1866 Seymour Kirkup wrote that Blake's "Britons went naked—I am not sure if he gave them a sort of bathing-drawers, to make them dacent—I think there were, made of small scales—" (*BR* [2]). In *Vaterländisches Museum* (1811), Crabb Robinson says that "his naked forms are almost crimson", and in his Reminiscences he said that the colouring of flesh was "very like that of the red Indians" (*BR* 436, 450; 538).

† *Descriptive Catalogue* ¶84–6. On 25 Jan 1866 Seymour Kirkup said that the light in the picture did *not* come from the sun (*BR* [2]).

"It is perfectly original, & as good [as] if not better than ... the great antiques".[161]

And Crabb Robinson wrote in *Vaterländisches Museum* (1811) that "His greatest and most perfect work is entitled 'The Ancient Britons.' It is founded on that strange survival of Welsh bardic lore which Owen gives ...."[162]

Other critics fulfilled Flaxman's warning that if Blake "places any dependence on painting large pictures, for which he is not qualified, either by habit or study, he will be miserably decieved".[163] Robert Southey said that "The Ancient Britons ... was one of his worst pictures,—which is saying much",[164] and Robert Hunt wrote in *The Examiner* (17 Sept 1809) that "This picture is a complete caricature ... the colouring of the flesh is exactly like hung beef".

"The Ancient Britons" was not quite finished when it was exhibited in 1809, or at any rate Blake was still adding finishing touches to it two years later, for on 16 January 1811 Owen Pughe wrote in his diary: "Mrs W. Blake came to ask about the painting of the 3 escapees from Camlan that her husband was doing for me ...."[165] When the great picture was finally delivered, Owen Pughe presumably took it to his estate at Nantglyn, near Denbigh, Wales, and it has never been recorded since.

Other Exhibition Pictures

The first pictures in the catalogue,* the ones whose subject-matter was most likely to seize public attention, were "The spiritual form of Nelson guiding Leviathan" and "The spiritual form of Pitt, guiding Behemoth ... [and] directing the storms of war",† representing the powers of the Beast by sea and by land. Admiral Horatio, Viscount Nelson had died heroically on the

---

* Besides "The Spiritual Form of Nelson" (I, *c*. 1805–9, Butlin #649), "The Spiritual Form of Pitt" (II, 1805? Butlin #651), "The Canterbury Pilgrims" (III, 1808? Butlin #653), and "The Ancient Britons" (V, 1809? Butlin #657, now lost), the pictures in Blake's 1809 exhibition were "The Bard, from Gray" (IV, 1809, Butlin #655), "A Subject from Shakspeare" ("The Horse of Intellect leaping from the cliffs of Memory")(VI, *c*. 1795? Butlin #658), "The Goats" (VII, 1809? Butlin #659, now lost), "The Spiritual Preceptor" (VIII, 1809? Butlin #660, now lost), "Satan calling up his Legions" (IX, *c*. 1795–1800, Butlin #661), "The Bramins" (X, 1809? Butlin #663, now lost), "The Body of Abel found by Adam and Eve" (XI, c. 1805–9, Butlin #664), "Soldiers casting lots for Christ's Garments" (XII, 1800, Butlin #495) (Pl. 75), "Jacob's Ladder" (XIII, *c*. 1805, Butlin #438) (see frontispiece), "Angels hovering over the body of Jesus in the Sepulchre" (XIV, c. 1805, Butlin #500), "Ruth" (XV, 1803, Butlin #456), and "The Penance of Jane Shore" (XVI, *c*. 1793, Butlin #69).

† Blake's opinion of military heroes is indicated by his reference to "War & its horrors & its Heroic Villains" (marginalium [1798] to Bacon's *Essays* p. 32). About 1809, Blake also drew "The Spiritual Form of Napoleon" (Butlin #652) (not in *The Descriptive Catalogue* and now untraced), and in a letter of 28 May 1804 he wrote: "as the French now adore Buonaparte and the English our poor George; so the Americans will consider Washington as their god. ... In the meantime I have the happiness of seeing the Divine countenance in such men as Cowper and Milton more distinctly than in any prince or hero".

deck of his flagship at the Battle of Trafalgar in 1805, the former Prime Minister William Pitt had died in 1806, and the public and the art world were scrambling to commemorate them.* But few artists described their tributes to these patriots as

> compositions of a mythological cast, similar to those Apotheoses of Persian, Hindoo, and Egyptian Antiquity, which are still preserved on rude monuments, being copies from some stupendous originals now lost .... The Artist having been taken in vision into the ancient republics, monarchies, and patriarchates of Asia, has seen those wonderful originals called in the Sacred Scriptures the Cherubim, which were sculptured and painted on walls of Temples, Towers, Cities, Palaces, and erected in the highly cultivated states of Egypt, Moab, Edom, Aram, among the Rivers of Paradise, being originals from which the Greeks and Hetrurians copied Hercules Farnese, Venus of Medicis, Apollo Belvidere, and all the grand works of ancient art.[166]

In his *Descriptive Catalogue* (¶4) "Mr. B. appeals to the Public", but the public was bewildered by his immediate appeal to paintings from visions of "Moab, Edom, Aram, among the Rivers of Paradise". J.T. Smith wrote of Blake's "allegorical ... pictures which the present writer, although he has seen them, dares not describe", and the reviewer in *The Lady's Monthly Museum* (1812) said of Pitt and Nelson: "we dare say they may be very fine; but they are also too sublime for our comprehension; we must therefore deprecate the mercy of the lovers of the Fuselian and the Angelesque".[167]

The public was also bemused by polemics against oil painting (as opposed to watercolours) and colourists and Stothard and the demonization of misguided colourists: Blake condemns Rubens as "a most outrageous demon", Correggio as "a most cruel demon", and "that infernal machine called Chiaro Oscura, in the hands of Venetian and Flemish Demons".[168] Those readers paying attention noticed that Blake seemed to use "demon" as a synonym for "villain", as in the reference to the "villainy of ... [*those*] who first brought oil Painting into general opinion and practice".[169] But most concluded, from Blake's outraged theological treatment of these normally neutral artistic issues, that the author was mad. And certainly it was ill-judged to use such terms without establishing a context and to assume that his

---

* In his *Descriptive Catalogue* ¶11, Blake wrote:

> The Artist wishes it was now the fashion to make such monuments [pictures, and ... basso relievos, and ... statues one hundred feet in height], and then he should not doubt of having a national commission to execute these two Pictures on a scale that is suitable to the grandeur of the nation ... in high finished fresco ....

readers had read Cromek's prospectus for Stothard's Canterbury Pilgrims.

A common response was probably that of Crabb Robinson: "In this Catalogue Blake writes of himself in the most outrageous language—Says 'This Artist defies all competition in colouring'—That none can beat him, for none can beat the Holy Ghost ...".[170]

Blake also presents a new version of British history:

> The British Antiquities are now in the Artist's hands; all his visionary contemplations, relating to his own country and its ancient glory, when it was as it again shall be, the source of learning and inspiration. ...
>
> Adam was a Druid, and Noah; also Abraham was called to succeed the Druidical age, which began to turn allegoric and mental signification into corporeal command, whereby human sacrifice would have depopulated the earth. All these things are written in Eden. The artist is an inhabitant of that happy country. ...
>
> The antiquities of every Nation under Heaven, is no less sacred than that of the Jews. They are the same thing as Jacob Bryant, and all anti-quaries have proved. ... All had originally one language, and one religion, this was the religion of Jesus, the everlasting Gospel. Antiquity preaches the Gospel of Jesus.
>
> (Descriptive Catalogue ¶74, 77)

All this has a context which was asserted by Jacob Bryant and other spec-ulative mythologists, but it was a context unfamiliar to most picture-lovers and picture-critics. Blake had seriously misjudged the art-loving public, while Cromek had successfully exploited it.

Blake intended his exhibition to open on 15 May 1809[171] and to "*close ... the 29th of September* 1809",[172] but it clearly stayed open much longer than that. As late as 11 June 1810 Crabb Robinson took Charles Lamb and his sister to see it. The price of entrance to the exhibition was 1s., just what it cost to see the far larger and more fashionable Royal Academy exhibition, and the *Descriptive Catalogue* cost 2s.6d. and included admission to the exhibition. In preparing his catalogue, Blake forgot to include the address of the exhibition itself, and he had to add it by hand to copies sold at the door.

Perhaps fifty to a hundred copies were printed, but only twenty-one are recorded today.* But despite its rarity, the *Descriptive Catalogue* was for many years the best known literary work which Blake published. It is described and

---

* Of the twenty-one recorded copies, only eleven are corrected; presumably the others were not sold and stayed with Blake until his death.

quoted by all his early biographers,[173] and it is implicit in most of the arguments concerning his madness.

Responses to the Exhibition and the Descriptive Catalogue

On 14 October 1809, George Cumberland Jr commented neutrally that "the Book is a great curiosity. He [*h*]as given Stothard a compleat set down", and on 13 November his father replied more frankly: "Blakes Cat. is truly original—part vanity part madness—part very good sense . . . did he sell many Pictures?"*

On 23 April 1810 Crabb Robinson went to the exhibition, paid for four copies of the *Descriptive Catalogue*, and "bargained that I should be at liberty to go again—'Free! As long as you live' said the brother—astonished at such a liberality, which he had never experienced before nor I dare say did afterwards—Lamb was delighted with the Catalogue . . . ."[174]

In 1811 Crabb Robinson said that the *Descriptive Catalogue* is "a veritable folio of fragmentary utterances on art and religion, without plan or arrangement . . . [*But*] even amid these aberrations gleams of reason and intelligence shine out".[175] J.T. Smith in 1828 said that is "perhaps the most curious of its kind ever written", and Cunningham in 1830 asserted that it contained "matter . . . utterly wild and mad".[176]

The only review of Blake's exhibition and catalogue was by Robert Hunt, who had savaged Blake's designs for Blair's *Grave* in *The Examiner* of August 1808. In the issue for 17 September 1809 he wrote anonymously of "Mr. Blake's Exhibition":

> If beside the stupid and mad-brained political project of their rulers, the sane part of the people of England resquired [*sic*] fresh proof of the alarming increase of the effects of insanity, they will be too well convinced from its having lately spread into the hitherto sober region of Art.† . . . *When*

---

* The answer to Cumberland's question must be "Some but not all". Nos I, III, XII–XV (Butlin #649, 653, 495, 438, 500, 456) were acquired, probably about 1810, by Thomas Butts (according to surviving receipts, Butts paid Blake £177.10.0 "on further account" from 7 April 1809 to 18 Dec 1810), and No. V (#657) by William Owen Pughe. However, some of the rest may have lingered on Blake's hands for ten years and more. No. XI (#664) was acquired by John Linnell, who met Blake in 1818, and Nos IV, IX (#651, 655, 661) by Samuel Palmer, who met Blake about 1824. Butlin (p. 472) is probably wrong when he says that "No works appear to have been sold" from the exhibition.

For Cumberland's marginalia to his copy of the *Descriptive Catalogue*, see *BR* (2) under Nov 1809.

† Fuseli is said to be "on the verge of insanity" and his paintings often represent "furious and distorted beings of an extravagant imagination". Blake may have been thinking of this slur when he wrote in his Notebook (p. 25):

> To H[*unt*]
> You think Fuseli is not a Great Painter[.] Im Glad[;]
> This is one of the best compliments he ever had[.]

the ebullitions of a distempered brain are mistaken for the sallies of genius by those whose works have exhibited the soundest thinking in art, the malady has indeed attained a pernicious height, and it becomes a duty to endeavour to arrest its progress. Such is the case with the productions and admirers of WILLIAM BLAKE, an unfortunate lunatic, whose personal inoffensiveness secures him from confinement, and, consequently, of whom no public notice would have been taken, if he was not forced on the notice and animadversion of the EXAMINER, in having been held up to public admiration by many esteemed amateurs and professors as a genius in some respect original and legitimate. The praises which these gentlemen bestowed last year on this unfortunate man's illustrations of *Blair's Grave*, have, in feeding his vanity, stimulated him to publish his madness more largely, and thus again exposed him, if not to the derision, at least to the pity of the public. ... Thus encouraged, the poor man fancies himself a great master, and has painted a few wretched pictures, some of which are unintelligible allegory, others an attempt at sober character by caricature representation, and the whole "blotted and blurred," and very badly drawn. These he calls an Exhibition, of which he has published a Catalogue, or rather a farrago of nonsense, unintelligibleness, and egregious vanity, the wild effusions of a distempered brain.... That insanity should elevate itself to this fancied importance, is the usual effect of the unfortunate malady; but that men of taste, in their sober senses, should mistake its meaning and distorted conceptions for the flashes of genius, is indeed a phenomenon.*

Blake's Retreat from the Public

Such attacks by what Blake called "The Cunning sures & the aim at yours"[177] were probably responsible for his retreat from publicity. In the address "To the Public" in *Jerusalem*, where he had written of "the love and friendship of those with whom to be connecte*d* is to be blessed" and begged: "Dear Reade*r*, forgive what you do not approv*e*, & love me for this energetic exertion of my talent", he later went back and erased the words "love", "friendship", "blessed", "forgive", and "love".[178] He no longer felt that he could trust the public. In his Public Address in his Notebook, he wrote:

---

* In his Public Address (Notebook p. 52), Blake said that

> The manner in which my Character both as an artist & a Man has been blasted ... may be seen particularly in a Sunday Paper cal[*l*]d the Examiner Published in Beaufort Buildings (We all know that Editors of Newspapers trouble their heads very little about art & science & that they are always paid for wh[at] they put [in] up[on] these ungracious subjects)[.]

The Painter hopes that his Friends Anytus Melitus & Lycon [*the accusers of Socrates*] will percieve that they are not now in Ancient Greece & tho they can use the Poison of Calumny the English Public will be convincd that such a Picture as this Could never be Painted by a Madman or by one in a State of Outrageous manners as these Bad Men both Print & Publish by all the means in their Power.*

"Blakes apology for his Catalogue" claims that

Poor Schiavonetti died of the Cromek
A thing thats tied about the Examiners neck
*W*ho cries all art is fraud & Genius a trick
And Blake is an unfortunate Lunatic

(Public Address, [Notebook p. 62])

In *Jerusalem* pl. 93, he pointedly associated his three accusers with Anytus, Melitus, and Lycon, the accusers of Socrates (see Fig. on p. 313). And in a violent doggerel poem about his enemies he associated Hunt, who had bitterly attacked him, with Prince Hoare, who had merely praised his enemy:

The Examiner whose very name is Hunt
Calld Death a Madman trembling for the affront
Like trembling Hare sits on his weakly paper
On which he usd to dance & sport & caper

(Notebook p. 22)

For ten years after the fiasco of his exhibition, Blake retreated from the public, though he continued to labour at his *Jerusalem*. It was not until after 1818 when he attracted a little coterie of young artists, some of them scarcely more than boys, that Blake committed himself to publishing and public engraving once more. Through them he achieved not prosperity but serenity, and because of them he created his greatest triumphs in line engraving, *The Illustrations of the Book of Job* and the illustrations to Dante's *Inferno*. Until then, Robert Hunt and the Cunning sures had almost silenced him.

---

* Public Address (Notebook p. 86). Crabb Robinson said (10 Dec 1825) that Blake had "a Socratic countenance", and when he asked Blake, "What resemblance do you suppose is there between your Spirit & the Spirit of Socrates", Blake replied: "'The same as between our countenances[.']—He paused & added—['']I was Socrates.['] And then, as if correcting himself: [']A sort of brother—I must have had conversations with him—So I had with Jesus Christ—I have an obscure recollection of having been with both of them'".

CHAPTER VIII

1810–1818: "I Am Hid"

Fuseli Indignant almost hid himself—I am hid[1]

"BLAKE IS A WILD ENTHUSIAST, ISN'T HE?"
Ever loyal to his friend, the sculptor [John Flaxman] drew him-
self up, half offended, saying, "Some think me an enthusiast."[2]

In the nine years from 1810 to 1818, Blake was largely hidden from the world, so much so that some wondered if he was still alive. Certainly he was in obscurity, but he was not idle.

He was making new friends who have left important records of him, friends such as the young art student Seymour Kirkup, the mysterious author who signed himself "Juninus", the journalist and attorney Henry Crabb Robinson, the hopeful young aristocrat Charles Henry Bellenden Ker, the Swedenborgian Charles Augustus Tulk, Robert Southey, about to be appointed Poet Laureate, Sir Thomas Lawrence, about to be elected President of the Royal Academy, and the poet, lecturer, and opium-addict Samuel Taylor Coleridge. After 1815 Blake resumed work with his graver, making plates for Flaxman's *Hesiod* (1816-17), Rees's *Cyclopaedia* (1815–19), and Wedgwood's Catalogue of Earthenware and Porcelain (1815–16). About 1816 he made an extraordinary series of illustrations for Milton's poetry, and in 1818 he began again to make copies of his works in Illuminated Printing.

Seymour Kirkup on the Nature of Blake's Visions

Blake's reputation for wildness and obscure enthusiasm was alarming or intriguing to most of those who heard of him and to many who knew him but slightly. In 1810 Tommy Butts introduced Blake to his friend the young art-student Seymour Kirkup, and Kirkup was fascinated and at first bewildered by Blake.[3]

At the time, Kirkup did not believe in the existence of spirits, and consequently he doubted the sanity of Blake who not only believed in them but saw them and talked to them; Kirkup thought that Blake's belief was honest but deluded. "He was the more a child of nature and of the kindest (as I experienced) & most sincere".

> I knew Blake well, and liked him, and respected him, for he was one of the honestest and most upright, and most sincere men I ever knew. ... There never was an honester man than he, or one who lived in a finer poverty,—poor but strictly simple in his habits ... [4]

> I was a partisan of the colourists, his opponents,* & thought him mad†—as I always treated him with respect & did not presume to contradict him he was very kind & communicative to me—& so I believe he was to every body except Schiavonetti.[5]

> Blake was an honest man, and I always thought so—but his sanity seemed doubtful because he could only give his word for the truth of his visions. There were no other proofs, and what was so incredible required the most perfect proofs ....[6]

> I never suspected him of imposture. His manner was too honest for that. He was very kind to me, though very positive in his opinion, with which I never agreed. His excellent old wife was a sincere believer in all his visions. She told me seriously one day, "I have very little of Mr. Blake's company; he is always in Paradise."[7]

Blake talked freely about the spirits who visited him, though, according to Kirkup, he "would waive the question of his spiritual life, if the subject seemed at all incomprehensible or offensive to the friend with him".[8] Kirkup was troubled by Blake's talk of spirits and visions:

> Poor Blake had no proof of the truth, so they said he was mad or a

---

* Kirkup says he was a partisan of the English "school of colourists for which Blake always reproached me" (letter of 12 Nov 1868 to Swinburne [*BR* (2) under 1809–10]).

† "I thought him mad. I do not think so now" (Kirkup to Lord Houghton, 25 March 1870 [*BR* 221]).

humbug. I never believed the latter. I always tho! him honest, but he had no witnesses.[9]

    I had no <u>proof</u>, nor had any body, not even either of the Butts's. The great defect in Blake & Swedenborg was that there was no testimony—only their word—not enough in what is so incredible as the super-natural—I therefore thought Blake mad & neglected him—[10]

However, fifty years later Kirkup was persuaded by his own repeated experiences of the reality of the spirit-world, and he therefore re-evaluated what he remembered of Blake:

> As a psychological study Blake's visions were unsupported by any testi-mony, as much as Swedenborg's—were they waking dreams?—are dreams madness? I have studied them . . .. I had only to guard against <u>two</u> things, <u>hallucination</u> & <u>trick</u>, which I did with the most jealous incredulity, & 12 year's experience has only confirmed the existence of Spirits—. . . I have seen but 4 times . . . but I have seen innumerable <u>apports</u> & other phenomena which make me believe all the rest possible, tho' not certain—& so of Blake's & Swedenborg's prodigies—[11]

It was only thirty years and more after Blake's death that Kirkup came to believe Blake was not deluded and that the spirits he spoke of had a reality beyond Blake's imagination.

The Journalist and the Visionary: Crabb Robinson and William Blake

Another enquirer who was fascinated by Blake's wildness and Enthusiasm was Henry Crabb Robinson. Robinson had recently returned from Spain as the war correspondent of *The Times*. He was or became the good friend of Samuel Taylor Coleridge, William Wordsworth, Charles Lamb, William Hazlitt, and Robert Southey, and in his diaries he recorded in extraordinary detail conversations with them and with hundreds of others. Crabb Robinson's papers are one of the richest archives for information about Romantic poets and their time. From them we derive some of the most vivid vignettes which have survived about William Blake.

Crabb Robinson was a matter-of-fact journalist, later an attorney, while Blake was a matter-of-vision artist. The gulf between them was bridged by Robinson's powerful curiosity and later, when he met Blake in 1825, by respect and good will on both sides.

Robinson recalled that

On my being acquainted with Flaxman I found ... that Fl: thought highly of him and tho' he did not venture to extol him as a genuine Seer—Yet he did not join in the ordinary derision of him as a madman— Without having seen him, Yet I had already conceived a high opinion of him And thought he would furnish matter for a paper interesting to Germans*—And therefore when Fred: Perthes the patriotic publisher at Hamburg wrote to me in 1810 requesting me to give him an article for his Patriotische Annalen I thought I cd do no better than send him a paper on Blake ....†

He was aware of the objection to "recording the ravings of insanity in which it may be said there can be found no principle ... and from which therefore nothing can be learned", but this, he thought, does not apply to Blake's form of "Monomania".[12]

Robinson therefore began to call on persons who could give him information about Blake. The first of these was William Upcott, the under-librarian of the London Institution, who had inherited some important Blake books on the death on 9 March 1810 of his father the miniaturist Ozias Humphry: *Songs of Innocence and of Experience* (H), and the Small Book of Designs, plus *America* (H) bound with *Europe* (D) and the Large Book of Designs. Upcott, like his father, was a good friend to Blake,‡ and he very readily showed his Blakes and talked about them when Robinson called on him on 19 April 1810.

The day after calling on Upcott, Robinson also called on Elizabeth Iremonger, whom he described as "a Unitarian ... a sort of free-thinker— She kept good company And I owed her much by introduc^g me to some of my genteelest friends". She was collecting what she called "*Livres Choisies*" in the 1790s, and she wrote of herself: "Quiet & Retirement, Rural Simplicity & neatness ... Books to my Taste, & a Friend to my Heart— these are requisite ingredients to my System of Happiness &, possessing these, I have not a Wish for more." Robinson spent the morning transcribing Blake poems from Miss Iremonger's copies.§

---

*   Robinson had studied at Jena in 1802–5.

†   Crabb Robinson Reminiscences (1852) (*BR* 537). In his Diary, he wrote of "the insane poet painter & engraver Blake": "Dr Malkin having, in the memoirs of his Son given an account of this extraordinary genius with Specimens of his poems I resolved out of these to compose a paper" (*BR* 223).

‡   Upcott allowed Crabb Robinson to transcribe his copies of *America* (H) and *Europe* (D) (*BR* 446–7), Upcott probably provided the facts for the Blake account in [John Watkins & Frederick Shoberl], *A Biographical Dictionary of the Living Authors of Great Britain and Ireland* (London: Henry Colburn, 1816) and for the obituary in the *Gentleman's Magazine* (Oct 1827) see "Ozias Humphry, William Upcott, and William Blake", *Humanities Association Review*, XXVI (1975), 116–22.

§   *BR* 224–5. Robinson went back to Mrs Iremonger's on 7 May; all together he copied poems from *Poetical Sketches*, *Songs of Innocence*, *Songs of Experience*, *America*, *Europe*, the proposal for an "Exhibition of Paintings in Fresco", and the dedication to Blair's *Grave*, probably mostly from the collections of Upcott and Miss Iremonger (*BR* 224 n3, *BRS* 60–1), and he quoted most of them in his essay on Blake.

On 23 April, with the commission from Dr Perthes still in mind:

> In order to enable me to write this paper, ... I went to see an exhibition
> of Blake's Original paintings at a Hosier's in Carnaby Market[,] Blake's
> brother[.] These paintings filled several rooms of an ordinary dwelling
> house And for the Sight a half crown was demanded of the Visitor for
> which he had also a Catalogue— This catalogue ... is a very curious
> exposure of the state of the artists mind—I wished to send it to Germany
> and to give a copy to Lamb & others—So I took four ....[13]

Robinson went back to Blake's exhibition with Charles Lamb and his
sister on 11 June, and it may have been Robinson who persuaded Robert
Southey to see the exhibition as well.[14] On 25 June 1810 Robinson said that
he had had a very interesting conversation with Josiah Conder and Jane
Taylor about Blake, and Jane Taylor was sufficiently interested to include
"Holy Thursday" from *Songs of Innocence* in her *City Scenes* (1818).*

Robinson's essay on Blake for *Vaterländisches Museum* (1810) is based
chiefly upon Malkin's account of Blake and Blake's own works. In his
Reminiscences, Robinson said that the essay "has nothing in it of the least
value",[15] but it has a few facts not in Malkin and valuable judgments about
Blake, indicating what it was that convinced an intelligent, sympathetic contemporary that Blake was mad.

Robinson's title is "William Blake, Artist, Poet, and Religious Mystic",
but his intended audience is not the critic or the theologian but "the psy-
chologist". He takes his motto from Shakespeare: "The lunatic, the lover,
and the poet | Are of imagination all compact", and he identifies Blake as of
the "race of ecstatics, mystics, seers of visions, and dreamers of dreams", as
one exemplifying the "union of genius and madness in single remarkable
minds", as one who combines "great mental powers" with "claims to supernatural gifts". It is Blake's "religious convictions ... [*which have*] brought
on him the credit of being an absolute lunatic"; "this belief of our artist's in
the intercourse which ... he enjoys with the spiritual world has more than
anything else injured his reputation".[16]

Robinson exemplifies Blake's madness from the *Descriptive Catalogue* and
the exhibition and his genius from *Poetical Sketches* and *Songs of Innocence
and of Experience*.

In Blake's art, the madness consists "in giving bodily form to spiritual

---

* Jane Taylor says that the ceremony is "well described" in Blake's poem (*BR* 254). There were
editions of *City Scenes* in 1818 (3), 1823, 1828, and 1845. Jane Taylor's source may have been Priscilla
Wakefield, *Perambulations in London and Its Environs* (1809, 1814), which also prints the innocent
"Holy Thursday".

beings", as in the "Death of the Strong Wicked Man" (Pl. 114) and "The Reunion of the Soul & the Body".[17] Some of the pictures, such as the Spiritual Forms of Nelson and Pitt, are so mysterious that "the present writer ... dares not describe" them.[18]

But "amid these aberrations gleams of reason and intelligence shine out",[19] particularly in lyrics such as "To the Muses" which exhibit "wildness and loftiness of imagination". The *Songs of Innocence and of Experience* "deserve the highest praise and the gravest censure", exhibiting "poetical pictures of the highest beauty and sublimity" and poems "which can scarcely be understood even by the initiated".[20] Robinson quotes the "Introduction" and "Holy Thursday" from *Innocence* and "The Garden of Love" and "The Tyger" from *Experience* as examples of the highest beauty and passages from *America* and *Europe* to exemplify "mysterious and incomprehensible rhapsody", works so obscure that Robinson cannot "decide whether it is intended to be in prose or verse".*

And Robinson concludes: "perhaps ... as an artist Blake will never produce consummate and immortal work, as a poet flawless poems", but he is "a man in whom all the elements of greatness are unquestionably to be found, even though those elements are disproportionately mingled".[21]

Crabb Robinson's essay on Blake in *Vaterländisches Museum* exemplifies the difficulties felt by a man of remarkable sympathy for poetry and poets in accepting Blake's art and poetry on his own terms. Few of Blake's contemporaries even attempted to do so, and "while professional connoisseurs know nothing of him, his very well-wishers cannot forbear betraying their compassion, even while they show their admiration."[22]

Robinson was eager to talk about Blake, and at a literary "Breakfast with [*William*] Rough" on 27 January 1811 they "Conversed on Blake, Coleridge &c & Landor the author of Gebir".

Six weeks later, on 10 March 1811, Robinson showed off his newly purchased edition of Young's *Night Thoughts* (1797) with Blake's plates:

had a call from Turner & from W. Hazlitt. I shewed W.H. Blake's Young. He saw no merit in them as designs[.] I read him some of the Poems— He was much struck with them & expressed himself with his usual strength & singularity[.] ["]They are beautiful,["] he said, ["]& only too deep for the vulgar[;] he has no sense of the ludicrous & as to a

---

* Crabb Robinson, *Vaterländisches Museum* (*BR* 454). On 11 Nov 1863, Crabb Robinson wrote of *America*: "When I attempted to read it some years since I thought it Sheer Madness" (see *BR* [2]).

His descriptions of the *Songs* and *Night Thoughts* (*BR* 443, 441) are largely repeated in Friedrich Adolph Ebert, *Allgemeines Bibliographisches Lexikon* (Leipzig: F.A. Brockhaus, 1821, 1830), I, 199; II, 1097 (tr. Arthur Browne, *A General Bibliographical Dictionary* [Oxford, 1837], I, 196; IV, 2018 [*BR* 270, 375–6]).

God a worm crawling in a privy is as worthy an obj.! as any other, all being to him indifferent[.] So to Blake the Chimney Sweeper &c[.] He is ruined by vain struggles to get rid of what presses on his brain—he attempts impossibles—["] I added—["]he is like a man who lifts a burthen too heavy for him; he bears it an instant, it then falls on & crushes him[."]*

Had Blake been present, and in an explanatory mode, he might have remarked that "every thing that lives is holy!" or that "every thing on earth ... in its essence is God" or even:

Let the Human Organs be kept in their perfect Integrity
At will Contracting into Worms or expanding into Gods ....[23]

Or, more wisely, he might have kept silent, content with what is beautiful and too deep for the vulgar, content to have been ruined for the vulgar while exalted in the spirit.

Four months later, on 24 July 1811, Robinson

Returned late to C. Lamb's[.] Found a very large party there—Southey had been with Blake & admired both his designs & his poetic talents; At the same time that he held him for a decided madman. Blake, he says, spoke of his visions with the diffidence that is usual with such people And did not seem to expect that he sho.d be believed. he showed S. a perfectly mad poem called Jerusalem—Oxford Street is in Jerusalem.

If Southey had been a little more patient, he might have remarked that Oxford Street is not in Jerusalem the city; rather, the woman named Jerusalem sees "a Gate of Precious stones and gold ... Bending across the road of Oxford Street".[24]

Many years later, Southey wrote to Caroline Bowles: "Much as he is to be admired, he was at that time [*1811*] so evidently insane, that the predominant feeling in conversing with him, or even looking at him, could only be sorrow and compassion. ... And there are always crazy people enough in the world to feed and foster such craziness as his."[†]

Crabb Robinson was clearly fascinated by Blake, and he talked of him to a surprising range of friends. On the morning of Sunday 24 May 1812, he

---

* Hazlitt described Blake as "a profound mystic" (*The Plain Speaker* [1826]), but his use of the term "mystic" was latitudinous, applying also to Flaxman, Varley, and Cosway (*BR* 332).
† Southey letter of 8 May 1830: "I have nothing of Blake's but his designs for Blair's *Grave*, which were published with the poem. His still stranger designs for his own compositions in verse [?*JERUSALEM*] were not ready for sale when I saw him, nor did I ever hear that they were so."

walked across the fields to Hampstead Heath with Wordsworth, and Wordsworth remarked "that there is insanity in Lord B[*yron*]'s family and that he believes Lord B to be somewhat cracked— I read W. some of Blake's poems[;] he was pleased with Some of them and consid^d B as hav^g the elements of poetry—a thousand times more than either Byron or Scott . . .".

Wordsworth was indeed impressed by the poems, for he said to a friend: "'I called the other day while you were out and stole a book out of your library—Blake's songs of Innocence'[.] He read and read and took it home and read and read again."[25] On 12 January 1813 Robinson said that after Coleridge's lecture, he talked to Thomas Barnes (the editor of *The Times*) and Barron Field about "Blake's poems of whom they knew nothing before", and three days later he called on C. Aikin "with Blake's Young".

After this, Crabb Robinson, or at least his Diary, neglected Blake almost entirely for thirteen years, until December 1825 when he met him for the first time in surprising circumstances.

Blake clearly interested Crabb Robinson more for his eccentricity than for his designs or his verses. Blake was, as Seymour Kirkup wrote, "a psychological study", and Crabb Robinson and all his friends seem to have been confident that, as Southey said, Blake was "evidently insane", "a decided madman", suffering from "vapours" or even self-delusion. Blake's pictures and his poems exhibited splendid possibilities, but all were vitiated by madness. The uniform testimony as to Blake's madness from these great writers and critics, from Lamb and Hazlitt and Southey and Wordsworth and Crabb Robinson himself, should make Blake's readers two hundred years later wonder whether Blake's contemporaries were not right, whether Blake was, at least in these years 1810–18, suffering from delusions.

But none of these great men knew Blake personally—only Southey had actually met him, and that but once—and none knew his works better than superficially. Of course a superficial verdict of madness does not preclude a profound verdict of madness. But readers two centuries later may still reflect that they have far more evidence about Blake than Lamb and Hazlitt and Wordsworth and Crabb Robinson did in 1810–13; they may reserve the right to judge for themselves on more extensive evidence, though with less genius than Crabb Robinson's friends had.

And whatever the verdict as to Blake's madness, posterity has clearly concluded that Blake's works are far more interesting than his eccentricity. As Blake wrote: "It is very true what you [*English engravers*] have said for these thirty two Years[.] I am Mad or Else you are So[;] both of us cannot be in our right Senses[.] Posterity will judge by our Works".[26]

Blake himself distinguished between the "sanity" of rational doubt and the "madness" of profound religious belief. To the argument that "religion often leads to insanity", he responded with a vision: "Cowper came to me and said, 'Oh! that I were insane, always. . . . Oh! that in the bosom of God I was hid ... as a refuge from unbelief.' "[27] To the worldly, those who believe in vision and God seem to be insane. To the truly religious, faith is a refuge in the bosom of God from unbelief.

Other Admirers

In his growing isolation, Blake may have had more admirers than he realized. A generous critic in the *Repository of Arts* who signed himself Juninus wrote in 1810 that Blake's designs

> from Blair's *Grave*, lately engraved, are excellent studies for a young artist. Blake has lately received much deserved commendation from Fuseli. Perhaps, this engraver has more genius than any one in his profession in this country. If he would study the ornamental requisites more, he would probably attain much higher celebrity than he has already acquired.[28]

Juninus later showed remarkably intimate knowledge of Blake in a dialogue about prints between a teacher Miss K and her pupil Miss Eve. They begin with "The Fall of Rosamund" engraved by Blake for Macklin twenty-seven years before, in 1783 (Pl. 30). Miss K explains that

> "The same engraver executed a large print in the stroke manner from Hogarth [*in 1790*]. It represents a scene in the *Beggar's Opera* . . . .
>
> "This artist seems to have relinquished engraving, and to have cultivated the higher department of designing and painting with great success. His works shew that he must have studied the antique with considerable attention."
>
> *Miss Eve.*—"If those ingenious men, the engravers, were to ask this man of genius why he abandoned his profession, he might with truth answer to most of those by whom it is followed, in the words of the poet:
>
> > 'I hear a voice you cannot hear,
> >   'That says I must not stay:
> > 'I see a hand you cannot see,
> >   'That beckons me away.' "[29]

Blake's cultivation of "the higher department of designing and painting" was known chiefly to the few who saw his 1809 exhibition. Even more striking, Juninus and Miss K seem to have known Blake's private determination of 19 December 1808 that "my time … in future must alone be devoted to Designing & Painting".

Miss Eve was yet more intimately familiar with his ways, for she quotes the same lines from Thomas Tickell's "Lucy and Colin" that Blake did in his letter to Butts of 10 January 1802. Juninus and his creatures were good friends indeed to Blake.

Another of Blake's admirers was Charles Henry Bellenden Ker, a young man with a light purse, expensive tastes, and great though illusory expectations. His father John Bellenden Ker was carrying on a lawsuit to gain the title and enormous entailed estate of his second cousin William 7th Baron Bellenden and 4th Duke of Roxborough.

On 20 August 1810, Charles Ker wrote to George Cumberland: "Blake's Grave— What a very fine work it i*s*, and how much justice Schiavonetti has done it[*; it is*] with! excepti[*on*] the best thing of the sort which has appear[*ed*] this Century. I wish I were rich enough to buy it: but <u>alas!</u> I am the very Picture of Poverty …."

Ker's picturesque poverty had not, however, prevented him from ordering two pictures from Blake, depending upon a happy result of his father's lawsuit to enable him to pay for them. It was probably later in August 1810 that he wrote again to Cumberland:

> I meant to have spoken today to you about Blake but I was in such a state I forgot it—Near 3 Y.! ag*o*, When I went to him—I said ["]M.! Blake we (meaning my father) are so near getting the Roxburgh Cause that at your leisure you shall make me 2 Drawings and when Ive got it I will pay you for them["]— well the other Day after having some time before written to him—he sent me home the 2 Drawings 20 G[*UINEA*]*S*[.] Now I was I assure you thunderstruck as you as well as he must know that in my present circumstances it is ludicrous to fancy I can or am able to pay 20 Gs. for 2 Drawings not Knowing Where in the World [*to*] get any money. Nor do I at all conceive I am obliged to pay for them— now he desired in his note that the money was paid in a fortnight or part of it—intimating that he should take hostile Mode[*?*] if it was not— now if he thinks proper to pursue the latter he is welcome and I wish you to call on him and shew him this and also that he may be informed of the grounds on which I meant to resist the payment[*;*] first as to the time when they were ordered which in his letter to me he admits was even then 2 years ago—therefore at that time I was not of age—next a young gentleman who can prove the terms on which they were ordered— these will be the grounds on which I shall rest if he insists on immediate payment and you can tell him my Attorney … is Mr Davis 20. Essex Street Strand—but of course the moment either by any success of my father &.! I am enabled I shall pay him. You will act as you think best[.]

I trouble you with this as from some peculiar misfortunes I am not able to attend to any thing[.]*

Ker plainly felt that he had some obligation to Blake, for he wrote again to Cumberland on 27 August:

Blake—I wrote at last to propose 15Gs. no— then to pay the price any mutual friend or friends sh^d put on them— no— then I proposed to pay 10! first & 10! afterw.^{ds} no— and then he arrested me—and then defended the action and now perhaps [*his?*] obstinacy will never get a shilling of the 20 L [*he ori*]ginally intended to defraud me of . . . .

Having been an over-trusting creditor with Cromek, and perhaps observing what had happened to Stothard when he agreed to postpone his payment from Cromek, Blake seems to have become remarkably firm and hardheaded with this young sprig of the aristocracy. At the very least, he knew that the cousin of a duke would have a very different conception of "the very Picture of Poverty" from that of a struggling artist with few hopes except from heaven.

No trace of this arrest and law-suit has been found, and Blake may merely have flourished a lawyer at Ker. But, whatever his method, it was successful.

Blake seems to have raised his price for the two drawings from twenty guineas to thirty guineas, perhaps because the money was long overdue.

Cumberland apparently took Blake's part in this tedious quarrel, and when Ker wrote again to Cumberland, he was distinctly grumpy. He said that he had called on Stothard with a commission from Lord Digby, and

I think it right to tell you this as you recommended me, and you may fancy, that as I disputed with your friend Blake I may with Stothard[.] But Blake is more knave than fool and made me pay 30 Guineas for 2 Drawings which on my word were never orderd and which are as [*word illeg*] as they are infamously done: You are very shabby not to come near me— I learnt from Stothard you were in town but I take it I am out of favour . . . .[30]

The claim that the "2 Drawings . . . were never orderd" is more than a little disingenuous in the light of Ker's own statement in the letter quoted

---

* Ker to Cumberland, n.d. (*BR* 227–8). If *DNB* is correct in guessing that Ker was born in 1785, the commission would have been made before 1806 when he came of age. Ker's Blake drawings have not been identified.

previously that Blake "shall make me 2 Drawings" and that "of course the moment ... I am enabled I shall pay him". Perhaps his judgment that the drawings "are infamously done" is also a reflection of his *amour propre* rather than of truth.

Cromek too accused Blake of being wily and worldly while pretending to innocence and ignorance; "I really blush when I reflect how I have been cheated in this respect".[31] In each case, the wiliness and knavery seem to have been in the accuser.

After the failure of his exhibition in 1809–10, Blake's pictures appeared only once more on public display. In 1812 four of his works were shown in the spring exhibition in Bond Street of the Associated Painters in Water Colours: "Sir Jeoffrey Chaucer and Twenty-seven Pilgrims leaving the Tabarde Inn", "The Spiritual Form of Pitt guiding Behemoth", "The Spiritual Form of Nelson guiding Leviathan", and "Detached Specimens of an original illuminated Poem, entitled '*Jerusalem the Emanation of the Giant Albion*'".[32] The first three had been the first three pictures in his own exhibition, and the last probably consisted of pls 25, 32, 41, and 47 from his still-unfinished Prophecy.*

These were pictures which Blake plainly hoped might have an immediate public appeal. However, the only known review of them in *The Lady's Monthly Museum* in June 1812 exhibited more perplexity than approval: "*Sir Geoffrey Chaucer and the Pilgrims*, by BLAKE, is a picture of mongrel excellence, ... an imitation of the arts in their degraded state", and "the pictures ... [*of Pitt and Nelson*] are too sublime for our comprehension".[33]

And, to add insult to injury, "the landlord siezed the contents of the gallery in distraint of rent".[34] Presumably Blake's pictures had to be negotiated out of the landlord's hands by Blake or perhaps by the kind friend who had lent them—Butts later owned Chaucer and Nelson and perhaps already did so by 1812.

As Blake sank deeper into obscurity, a few faithful old friends continued to look out for his interests and to learn from him. George Cumberland called on Blake during his spring visit to London, on 12 April 1813, and reported in his notebook that he "Saw Blake who recommended Pewter to Scratch on with the Print— He is Doing Ld Spencer". Perhaps the advice was similar to Blake's memorandum in his own Notebook (p. 10) about 1807: "To Wood cut on Pewter". "Ld Spencer" must be the fine portrait of

---

*   If Butts, who acquired Nelson and Chaucer, owned them as early as 1812, he must have been the lender to the 1812 exhibition. (Earlier Butts had certainly offered Blake such a favour, for on 10 Jan 1802 Blake thanked Butts for "Your Obliging proposal of Exhibiting my two Pictures".) The owners of Pitt and the *Jerusalem* plates in 1812 is not known.

"The Right Honourable Earl Spencer" signed "T[*homas*] Phillips R A. pinx" and "W Blake. sculp".

The following spring, on 3 June 1814, Cumberland again called on Blake and found him "still poor still Dirty ... passed even^g with Stothard Newman St—still more dirty than Blake yet full of Genius".

John Flaxman too continued to look out for Blake's interests. When John Bischoff wrote to him about an engraving after Flaxman's monument for the history of Leeds by Dr T.H. Whitaker, Flaxman replied on 19 August:

> If the Revd Doctor should be satisfied with an <u>outline</u> of the Monument, such as those published of Homer's Iliad & Odyssey, as well as some in Cowper's translations of Milton's Latin poems, which is now a favorite style of decoration in books, I can make the outline myself & will request the Editor's acceptance of it—the engraving including the Copper plate will cost 6 Guineas if done by Mr Blake the best engraver of outlines—*

Notice that Flaxman is giving the design and copyright in it for nothing. However, even with the lure of the modest price and "the best engraver of outlines", the proposal came to nothing.

In his diary for 30 January 1815, Crabb Robinson reported that he went to see Flaxman and found him

> very chatty & pleasant[.] He related some curious anecdotes of [*William*] <u>Sharpe</u> the Engraver who seems the ready dupe of any & every religious fanatic & impostor who offers himself. ... Sh: tho' deceived by [*Richard*] Brothers became a warm partisan of Joanna Southcoat [*after June 1795*]— He endeavoured to make a convert of Blake the engraver,† but as Fl: judiciously observed, such men as Blake are not fond of playing the second fiddle— Hence Blake himself a seer of visions & a dreamer of dreams wo^d not do homage to a rival claimant of the privilege of prophecy— Blake lately told Fl: that he had had a violent dispute with the Angels on some subject and had driven them away. [*James*] *Barry* partook much of this strange insanity. ... excessive pride equally denoted Blake & Barry—

---

* The book was T.H. Whitaker, *Loides and Elmete* (1816), with no Blake plate.

† In 1802, Joanna Southcott announced that she would bring forth Shiloh, and in 1813 she revealed that she was pregnant by the Holy Ghost. In the next year she died of the dropsy. Blake's little poem "On the Virginity of the Virgin Mary & Johanna Southcott" (Notebook p. 6) does not suggest belief in these claims.

Perhaps the "violent dispute with the Angels" is related to his internal quarrel between the doubt of reason and the hope of faith.

One of Blake's new patrons was Charles Augustus Tulk, an enthusiastic Swedenborgian and a friend of John and Nancy Flaxman. Tulk's daughter believed that Blake and his wife "were rescued from destitution by Mr. C.A. Tulk".[35] He bought from Blake *Poetical Sketches* (C), *Songs of Innocence and of Experience* (J), and several Blake drawings based on Swedenborg's Memorable Relations (now untraced), "one of them of a female Angel instructing a number of children in the spiritual world".*

This drawing may be the one referred to by Nancy Flaxman in her letter to her husband of July 1816:

> tell me ... how Hesiod goes on, I have had some discourse with our Friend [*?Tulk*] about Blakes book & the little drawings—It is true he did not give him anything for he thought It would be wrong so to do after what pass'd between them, for as I understand B— was very violent[,] Indeed beyond all credence only that he has served you his best friend the same trick [*some*] time back as you must well remember—but he bought a drawing of him, I have nothing to say in this affair[.] It is too tickilish, only I know what has happened both to yourself & me, & other people are not oblig'd to put up with B s odd humours—but let that pass[.]

Such quarrels sound like those of a man standing on his dignity when the world has left him little else to stand on.

Probably unbeknownst to Blake, his literary fame was growing. In 1816 he was included in *A Biographical Dictionary of the Living Authors of Great Britain and Ireland* as "an eccentric but very ingenious artist ... principally the engraver and publisher of his own designs", which include *For Children: The Gates of Paradise, Songs of Experience* [but not *Songs of Innocence*], *America, Europe*, and the *Descriptive Catalogue*.[†] This is the first time after Malkin's biography (1806) that he was considered in print primarily as an author.

Young artists were particularly drawn to Blake. A young man who admired Blake at the time was an engraver named William Ensom, who

---

* Caroline Tulk Gordon (*BR* 250). Tulk may also have owned *No Natural Religion* (M), *All Religions are One* pl. 1, and two drawings (Butlin #151, 257). About 1843, C.A. Tulk printed twelve copies of *Songs of Innocence and of Experience* with spaces where the owner could copy Blake's designs (*BB* 436).

† [J. Watkins & F. Shoberl], *A Biographical Dictionary of the Living Authors of Great Britain and Ireland* (1816) (*BR* 244). The compilers knew enough about Blake to specify that he had lived in Hercules Buildings, Lambeth, and in Felpham. The strange bibliography is repeated in Watt's *Bibliotheca Britannica* (1819) and in the *Gentleman's Magazine* obituary of Blake (1827) (*BR* 259, 356).

received a silver medal for a pen and ink head of William Blake at the anniversary dinner of the Society for the Encouragement of Arts, Manufactures, and Commerce in the Freemason's Tavern on 30 May 1815.[*]

The ambitious Liverpool sculptor John Gibson paused in London in 1817 on his way to study in Rome, with letters of introduction to Flaxman, Fuseli, and others.

> I also presented myself without a note of introduction to Mr. Blake, after showing him my designs, he gave me much credit for the invention which they displayed; he showed me his cartoons [*i.e., watercolours*], and complained sadly of the want of feeling in England for high art, and his wife joined in with him and she was very bitter upon the subject.[36]

Apparently Catherine Blake took a very full part in such calls.

Though the rich rarely bought Blake's books, they sometimes saw him in society. In 1818, the royal diarist Lady Charlotte Bury recorded a dinner party given by Lady Caroline Lamb, Byron's sometime mistress and *bête noire*. Lady Charlotte sat next to the debonair and fashionable Sir Thomas Lawrence:

> There was another eccentric little artist, by name Blake; not a regular professional painter, but one of those persons who follow the art for its own sweet sake, and derive their happiness from its pursuit. He appeared to me full of beautiful imaginations and genius; but how far the execution of his designs is equal to the conceptions of his mental visions, I know not, never having seen them. *Main d'oeuvre* is frequently wanting where the mind is most powerful. Mr. Blake appears unlearned in all that concerns this world, and from what he said, I should fear he was one of those whose feelings are far superior to his situation in life. He looks care-worn and subdued; but his countenance radiated as he spoke of his favourite pursuit, and he appeared gratified by talking to a person who comprehended his feelings. I can easily imagine that he seldom meets with any one who enters into his views; for they are peculiar, and exalted above the common level of received opinions. I could not help contrasting this humble artist with the great and powerful Sir Thomas Lawrence, and thinking that the one was fully if not more worthy of the distinction and the fame to which the other has attained, but from which *he* is far removed. Mr. Blake, however, though he may have as much right, from talent and merit, to the advantages of which Sir Thomas is possessed, evidently lacks that worldly

---

[*]   William Ensom may be the person who inscribed a copy of Young's *Night Thoughts* (1797) (Q): "This Copy was colour'd for me by Mr. Blake. | W.E." (*BR* 238–9).

wisdom and that grace of manner which make a man gain an eminence in his profession, and succeed in society. Every word he uttered spoke the perfect simplicity of his mind, and his total ignorance of all worldly matters. He told me that Lady C—— L——had been very kind to him. "Ah!" said he, "there is a deal of kindness in that lady." I agreed with him, and though it was impossible not to laugh at the strange manner in which she had arranged this party, I could not help admiring the goodness of heart and discrimination of talent which had made her patronise this unknown artist. Sir T. Lawrence looked at me several times whilst I was talking with Mr. B., and I saw his lips curl with a sneer, as if he despised me for conversing with so insignificant a person. It was very evident that Sir Thomas did not like the company he found himself in, though he was too well-bred and too prudent to hazard a remark upon the subject.[37]

Blake was well aware of his humble status in the art-world. " 'They pity me,' he would say of Lawrence and other prosperous artists, who condescended to visit him; 'but 'tis they are the just objects of pity: I possess my visions and peace. They have bartered their birthright for a mess of pottage.' "[38]

Whatever Sir Thomas Lawrence thought of Blake's social position, he admired his pictures, for later he bought a number of them. He knew of Blake from the admired engraving Blake had made of his portrait of Cowper for Hayley's life of Cowper (1803), and in 1805 he had publicly praised Blake's designs for Blair's *Grave*.[39] Much later Sir Thomas bought Blake's "The Dream of Queen Katharine" and "The Wise and Foolish Virgins" for the generous price of £15.15.0 apiece;[40] the latter was said to be "Sir Thomas's favourite drawing, and he commonly kept it on his table in his studio as a study".* And in April 1826, Lawrence paid £10.10.0 for a proof copy of Blake's *Job* engravings priced at £5.5.0.[41] This may have been the gift from Lawrence, made when Blake was "in great pecuniary distress", which "had relieved his distresses, and made him and his wife's heart leap for joy", as he told a friend "with tears of joy and gratitude in his eyes."† Sir Thomas Lawrence was a good friend to Blake's art.

Samuel Taylor Coleridge was certainly deeply impressed by Blake.

---

* John Poynder, who bought it at Lawrence's sale in 1830 for £8.15.0 (*BR* 400). The dealer Joseph Hogarth wrote about 1877 that Lawrence paid Blake £26.5.0 each for "The Wise and Foolish Virgins" and "Shadrach and his Companions Coming from the Fiery Furnace" (*BR* 468 n3). Neither the latter drawing nor Hogarth's authority is known. Linnell offered Blake's *Paradise Regained* designs in Feb 1827, but Lawrence did not buy them (*BRS* 108).

† William Etty, letter of 25 March 1830 (*BRS* 97), dating the incident "a year or two ago" (i.e., after Blake's death) and identifying the friend merely as one "who lives near Charing Cross". The generosity of Sir Thomas Lawrence was well known, but the munificence of the gift which Etty attributes to him (£100 in "bills") is hard to believe in view of Catherine Blake's poverty when Blake died. The multiplication of a generous £10.10.0 payment to a £100 gift is a fault not unknown to the raconteur and the purveyor of gossip.

"Charles Augustus Tulk took Coleridge to see Blake's picture of 'The Last Judgement' and ... the author of *Christabel* poured forth concerning it a flood of eloquent commentary and enlargement."* It may have been Tulk who wrote: "Blake and Coleridge, when in company, seemed like congenial beings of another sphere, breathing for a while on our earth; which may easily be perceived from the similarity of thought pervading their works."[42]

Tulk lent Coleridge his copy of *Songs of Innocence and of Experience* (J), and on Friday 6 February 1818 Coleridge wrote to Henry Francis Cary:

I have this morning been reading a strange publication—viz. Poems with very wild and interesting pictures, as the swathing, etched (I suppose) but it is said—printed and painted by the Author, W. Blake. He is a man of Genius—and I apprehend, a Swedenborgian—certainly, a mystic emphatically. You perhaps smile at my calling another Poet, a Mystic; but verily I am in the very mire of common-place common-sense compared with Mr Blake, apo- or rather ana-calyptic Poet, and Painter!

Next day he wrote to Tulk about the *Songs*:

I begin with my Dyspathies that I may forget them: and have uninterrupted space for Loves and Sympathies. Title page and the following emblem [*frontispiece to INNOCENCE*] contain all the faults of the Drawings with as few beauties, as could be in the compositions of a man

* J. Spilling (1887), probably quoting a letter from Garth Wilkinson (*BRS* 86). Crabb Robinson said in a letter of 19 Feb 1826: "Coleridge has visited B. & I am told talks finely about him."

who was capable of such faults + such beauties— The faults—despotism in symbols, amounting in the Title page to the . . . [*Greek for "odium"*], and occasionally, irregular unmodified Lines of the Inanimate, sometimes as the effect of rigidity and sometimes of exossation—like a wet tendon. So likewise the ambiguity of the Drapery. Is it a garment—or the body incised and scored out?—The <u>Limpness</u> (= the effect of Vinegar on an egg) in the upper of the two prostrate figures on the Title page, and the <u>eye</u>-likeness of the twig posteriorly on the second,—and the strait line down the waist-coat of pinky goldbeater's skin in the next drawing, with the I don't know whatness of the countenance, as if the mouth had been formed by the habit of placing the tongue, not contemptuously, but stupidly, between the lower gums and the lower jaw—these are the only <u>repulsive</u> faults I have noticed. The figure, however, of the second leaf (abstracted from the <u>expression</u> of the countenance given it by something about the mouth and the interspace from the lower lip to the chin) is such as only a Master learned in his art could produce.

He evaluated the poems as they are arranged in Tulk's copy J with symbols indicating "It gave me great pleasure",* "still greater",† "and greater still",‡ "in the highest degree",§ and "in the lowest".**

Two poems puzzled him particularly. The evaluation for "A Dream" is merely "?", and of "The Little Vagabond" he wrote to his Swedenborgian friend:

Tho' I cannot approve altogether of this last poem and have been inclined

---

* *Innocence:* "The Shepherd", "Spring" ("last stanza" "still greater"), "Nurse's Song" (Fig. on p. 88), "The Ecchoing Green" (Fig. on p. 87) ("the figures" "gave me great pleasure", "and of the second leaf" "still greater"), "A Cradle Song" (Pl. 9), "On Anothers Sorrow", "The Little Boy Lost" ("the drawing" "still greater" pleasure), and "The Little Boy Found"; *Experience:* "Introduction", "Infant Sorrow", "The Clod and the Pebble", "The Fly", "Holy Thursday", "The Little Girl Lost" and ". . . Found" ("the ornaments most exquisite!"), "To Tirzah" ("it gave me great pleasure" "and yet" "in the lowest"), "The Poison Tree" ("it gave me great pleasure" "and yet" "in the lowest"), "London" (Fig. on p. 146), and "The Sick Rose".

† *Innocence:* "Laughing Song" and "The Lamb"; *Experience:* "Earth's Answer", "The Garden of Love", "The Tyger" (Fig. on p. 147) ("I am perplexed—and have no opinion"), and "A Little Boy Lost".

‡ *Innocence:* "Holy Thursday", "Infant Joy" (Fig. on p. 1) ("N.b. for the 3 last lines [Thou dost smile. I I sing the while I Sweet joy befall thee] I should wish—'When wilt thou smile,['] or—[']O smile, o smile! I'll sing the while.[']—For a Babe two days old does not, cannot <u>smile</u>—and innocence and the very truth of Nature must go together. Infancy is too holy a thing to be ornamented"), "The School Boy"(Fig. on p. 16).

§ *Innocence:* "The Divine Image" (Fig. on title page), "The Little Black Boy" ("Yea" "in the highest degree" plus "in the highest degree"), "Night".

** *Songs of Innocence:* "The Blossom", "The Voice of the Ancient Bard", and "The Chimney Sweeper"; *Songs of Experience:* "My Pretty Rose Tree", "Ah! Sun Flower", "The Lily" (three poems on one plate), "Nurse's Song", "The Chimney Sweeper", and "A Little Girl Lost" ("I would have had it omitted—not for the want of innocence in the poem, but for the too probable want of it in many readers").

to think that the error, which is most <u>likely</u> to beset the Scholars of Em. Sw is that of utterly demerging the tremendous incompatibilities with an evil will that arise out of the essential Holiness of the abysmal Aseity in the Love of the eternal <u>Person</u>—and thus giving temptation to <u>weak</u> minds to sink this Love itself into <u>good nature</u>—yet I still disapprove the mood of mind in this wild poem so much less than I do the servile, blind-worm, wrap-rascal Scurfcoat of FEAR of the *modern Saints* (whose whole Being is a Lie, to themselves as well as to their Brethren) that I should laugh with good conscience in watching a Saint of the new stamp, one of the Fixt Stars of our eleemosynary Advertisements, groaning in wind-pipe! and with the whites of his Eyes upraised, at the <u>audacity</u> of this Poem!— Anything rather than <u>this</u> degradation of Humanity ["with which how can we utter 'Our Father'"], and therein of the incarnate Divinity!—*

Coleridge's sympathies and dyspathies differ strikingly from those of the twentieth century—and from those of his contemporaries. All the poems which pleased him best were from *Songs of Innocence*, and his final judgment of "The Tyger", which overwhelmed the best of his contemporaries and ours, was: "I am perplexed—and have no opinion".

This last was the common judgment on Blake by those who had not dismissed him as a wild Enthusiast or madman. Coleridge differs from them in taking Blake's poetry and art with real seriousness and with exalting joy. In Blake's darkest days, the praise of such men as Coleridge must have done much to mitigate his odd humours and to show that there were some in England who had deep feeling for high art.

Engravings for Flaxman's Hesiod (1814–1817)

Flaxman was more successful in helping Blake with another commission. While in Rome, Flaxman had begun a series of designs for the Greek poet Hesiod, as a companion to his suites of outline engravings-without-text for *The Iliad* (1793), *The Odyssey* (1793), Dante (1793), and Aeschylus (1795). Blake already knew the series well, for not only had they become famous all over Europe, but he had engraved three supplementary designs for *The Iliad* in 1805 for £5.5.0 per plate.

Flaxman interested the firm of Longman in the series and in 1814 Longman commissioned Blake to make all thirty-seven plates for Hesiod, also at £5.5.0 apiece. For Blake, this was an enormous commission, second

---

* Coleridge omits "The Human Abstract".

in extent only to his forty-three plates for Young's *Night Thoughts* (1797) and probably more profitable. The £194.5.0 for Hesiod is the largest sum he is known to have received for a single set of designs or engravings.

The arrangement was for Blake to buy the copper, engrave Flaxman's designs, pull his own proofs on his press at home, and bring them into Longman. When the proofs were approved, Blake was paid, and a writing-engraver named Jeffreys added the inscriptions.

For the first season, Blake worked very vigorously on the Hesiod engravings, producing almost a finished plate per week. He brought in twelve proofs from 22 September to 30 December 1814 and was paid £63 for his labour and £5.9.7$\frac{1}{2}$ for the copper.[43] He also kept a set of proofs for himself. He pulled the working proofs on both sides of the leaf and on scraps of paper he had frugally preserved, such as proofs for earlier commercial work and for his own works in Illuminated Printing.[44]

After this first burst of accomplishment in the autumn of 1814, Blake's work on *Hesiod* slowed down considerably. In the next year he brought in only nine plates. And the last sixteen plates took another year, 4 January 1816-23 January 1817. The plates bear imprints dated as late as 1 January 1817, but they cannot have been published even then, for Blake turned in his last plates three weeks after this.

The work had been going on for seventeen months before Flaxman and Longman signed a contract for the publication of the *Hesiod* designs, Flaxman providing the drawings and Longman agreeing "to be at the expense of engraving the same".[45] Longman also arranged for the advertising, and through a perverse proof-reading error the engraver was identified as "J. Blake",[46] a mistake which persuaded at least one author that the Hesiod plates had been made by John Blake, William's brother.[47]

Like all Flaxman's published series of illustrations, *Hesiod* had a curious history. The original edition sold very slowly; 200 copies were printed in 1817, and in 1838 there were still eighteen left.[48] However, the *Hesiod* designs very rapidly achieved a European reputation. There were continental editions copying Blake's engravings published in Rome by Beniamino del Vecchio (n.d.); in Paris by Bance & Bénard (engraved by Mme Soyer, 1821), by P. Feillet (1823), and by Reveil (with *Œuvres de Flaxman*, 1836, 1847); in Florence by Luigi Piazzini (1826); and Blake's original plates were reprinted in London by Bell & Daldy (1870). For most of the nineteenth century, the place where Blake's work was most readily visible on the continent was in his engravings for Flaxman's *Hesiod* (1817).

Flaxman's designs were in the starkest outline, almost entirely without shading or depth, delineating the static figures appropriate to his profession as a sculptor. Even the most powerful of them, such as "Gods and Titans" (Pl. 112), seem to represent the potentiality for action rather than the act itself, the bow-string drawn but not yet loosed, the lightning-javelins poised but still unflung. The sense of imminent force is powerful but diffused; Blake may well have felt that these were fine designs but that he could have done them better.*

Blake on the Fringes of Politics

In his young manhood, Blake had worn the cap of liberty, and he had been on the outskirts of the dangerously liberal circle of Joseph Johnson and of the incendiary mob that stormed Newgate Prison in 1780. But though he deplored the ways of the Beast, he had never taken part in political events, had not even voted.

On at least two occasions, however, he may be seen commenting on the great political events of the moment. On 21 April 1815, George Cumberland's sons George and Sydney went to see Blake, and young George reported to his father:

> We call upon Blake yesterday evening[,] found him & his wife drinking Tea, durtyer than ever[;] however he received us well & shewed his large drawing in Water Colors of the last Judgment[.] *H*e has been labouring at it till it is nearly as black as your Hat—the only lights are those of a <u>Hellish Purple</u>—† *H*is time is now intirely taken up with Etching‡ & Engraving—upon which subject I shall ask his advice if I do not shortly Succeed more to my wishes— I have made some pretty things but not worth send[*ing*] you—Blake says he is fearful they will make too great a Man of Napoleon and enable him to come to this country— M^{rs} B says that if this Country does go to War our K—g ought to loose his head—

---

* Gilchrist says that Flaxman's "kind office" in securing him the *Hesiod* commission "Blake did not take quite in good part. He would so far rather have been recommended as a designer! ... They are sweet and graceful compositions, harmonious and contenting so far as they go, but deficient in *force*, as Blake himself thought Flaxman to have always been" (*BR* 233). These conclusions are probable, but I know no direct evidence for them and suspect that Gilchrist is here putting plausible words in Blake's mouth.

† Butlin #648 (?1810–27, untraced since 1847), 17′ high, described by J.T. Smith, *Nollekens* (*BR* 467–8) as having "upwards of one thousand figures" in "exquisite finishing"; Blake asked £26.5.0 for it, but Tatham still had it in 1846 or 1847. Tatham inscribed a tracing of it "The original picture was six feet long and about five wide, and was very much spoiled and darkened by overwork; and is one of those alluded to in his Catalogue as being spoiled by ... 'blotting and blurring demons'" (*BR* 235 n4). Evidently Blake should have taken his own advice: "Let a Man who has made a drawing go on & on & he will produce a Picture or Painting but if he chooses to leave off before he has spoild it he will do a Better Thing" (Public Address, Notebook p. 44). According to Gilchrist, Blake "was wont to affirm: 'First thoughts are best in art, second thoughts in other matters'" (*BR* 236).

    R.C. Jackson said that his father saw Blake's "Last Judgment" in Fountain Court where Blake lived after 1821 (*BR* 235 n4).

‡ "Etching" must refer to Blake's etchings for *Hesiod*. According to Gilchrist, "He despised etching needles", and it is true that he worked chiefly or even "wholly with the graver in latter years" (*BR* 234).

To his son's letter, George Cumberland replied laconically: "You have a free estimate of Blake—& his devilish Works— he is a little Cracked, but very honest—as to his wife she is maddest of the Two— He will tell you any thing he knows".

Five years later, with the death of "An old, mad, blind, despised, and dying king",[49] radical dissent focused on the portly and dissolute Prince Regent who was about to be crowned as George IV. The heir of George III had had a succession of mistresses, in 1785 he secretly married one of them (Mrs Maria Anne Fitzherbert), and in 1795 he publicly married Princess Caroline of Brunswick-Wolfenbüttel. Princess Caroline was soon deserted, and thereafter for several years she lived abroad.

On learning of the death of George III, Princess Caroline returned to England for the coronation, to the delight of radicals and sentimentalists and to the deep dismay of her husband. On 6 June 1820 Cumberland called on Blake "and read the Courier to him about Queens arrival". Crowds cheered her in the streets, and pamphleteers and caricaturists rejoiced in print. This German princess became a symbol of suffering from arbitrary power, the darling of English democrats and republicans.

One of the ways to plague the Prince Regent was to publicize his infidelities. Another of his mistresses was Mrs Harriet Quentin, often referred to as "Mrs Q". The radical print-seller Isaac Barrow commissioned Blake to engrave a portrait by H. Villiers of the pretty Mrs Q, and his print was published on 1 June 1820, at the height of the agitation concerning Caroline's attempts (vain, as it turned out) to attend the coronation and assume her title as Queen.* Blake was thus on the fringe of a sensational event and acting as the agent of a notoriously radical print-seller.

New Artistic Work: Watercolours for Milton, Engravings for Rees and Wedgwood

Blake's long delay in completing his huge *Hesiod* commission after such an energetic beginning in the autumn of 1814 may have been due to his work on illustrations for Milton's minor poetry. These drawings included 6 for "On the Morning of Christ's Nativity" and 6 for *Comus* (both sets adapted

---

* See David Worrall, "The Mob and 'Mrs. Q': William Blake, William Benbow and the Context of Regency Radicalism", pp. 169–84 in *Blake, Politics, and History*, ed. Jackie DiSalvo, G.A. Rosso, & Christopher Z. Hobson (New York and London: Garland Publishing, 1998). "Mrs Q" was one of the most popular of Blake's prints; fifteen copies have been traced, and forty-three others are recorded.

    Another connection of Blake with political radicals of the time is his drawing of two visionary heads (Butlin #763A) on the back of an engraved "View of the Building in Cato Street, where the Conspirators were discovered and arrested on the Evening of the 23rd Feby 1820" (published by J. Brown, 1820).

from those of Joseph Thomas, *c*. 1815), 6 for *L'Allegro* (*c*. 1816), 6 for *Il Penseroso* (*c*. 1816), and 12 for *Paradise Regained* (*c*. 1816). For *Comus, L'Allegro*, and *Il Penseroso* Blake wrote out descriptions of the designs. Blake may have made the designs on his own initiative without a commission.

These Milton illustrations were a kind of work which Blake could not resist. He called on the famous bibliographer Thomas Frognall Dibdin to talk about them, and Dibdin recalled:

I soon found the amiable but illusory Blake far beyond my ken or sight. In an instant he was in his "third heaven"—flapped by the wings of seraphs, such as his own genius only could shape, and his own pencil embody. The immediate subject of our discussion—and for which indeed he professed to have in some measure visited me—was, "the minor poems of Milton." Never were such "dreamings" poured forth as were poured forth by my original visitor . . . .

"What think you, Mr. Blake, of Fuseli's Lycidas—asleep, beneath the opening eyelids of the morn?"

"I don't remember it."

"Pray see it, and examine it carefully. It seems to me to be the pencil of poetry employed to give intelligence and expression to the pen of the poet" . . . .

I learnt afterwards that my Visitor had seen it—but thought it "too tame"—tameness from Fuseli!

I told Mr. Blake that our common friend, Mr. Masquerier, had induced me to purchase his "*Songs of Innocence*," and that I had no disposition to "repent my bargain." This extraordinary man sometimes— but in good sooth very rarely—reached the sublime; but the sublime and the grotesque seemed, somehow or the other, to be for ever amalgamated in his imagination; and the choice or result was necessarily doubtful. Yet there are few books of which I love to turn over the leaves, more assiduously and carefully, than "Young's Night Thoughts," emblazoned by his truly original pencil.[50]

The new Milton designs exhibited all Blake's old exuberance. In *L'Allegro*, the designs for "Mirth" and "The Sun at his Easter Gate" (Pls 114–15) show Mirth and the Sun in very similar poses surrounded by rejoicing figures, though Mirth is dancing for joy, and the sun is seen in solemn majesty. Blake began an engraving of "Mirth" (Pl. 113), full of intoxicating energy, and he may have thought of engraving the rest of the designs for *L'Allegro* as well, and for Milton's other poems. However, the project got no further than this one plate, and only two copies of it are known.

The design for "Melancholy" for *L'Allegro* (Pl. 115) embodies measured harmony, with two figures on each side of her, one more at each shoulder, and above her head "Contemplation" with his fiery throne.

The scene of "Christ Ministered to by Angels" for *Paradise Regained* (Pl. 116) is similarly symmetrical. Christ's gesture does not make it clear whether he will accept or reject the bread and the wine offered to him. The twelve designs for *Paradise Regained* are the same number as Blake had made in illustration of *Paradise Lost*, though *Paradise Regained* is a far shorter poem.

The drawings for "On the Morning of Christ's Nativity", *Comus*, *L'Allegro*, and *Il Penseroso* found a purchaser in the faithful Thomas Butts, but it was not for many years that anyone showed an interest in *Paradise Regained*. Finally, John Linnell bought them for £10 in the autumn of 1825, and, doubtless for Blake's benefit, he offered them to Francis Chantrey for £20 and to Sir Thomas Lawrence in February 1827 for £50,[51] alas in vain. And Linnell paid the artist's ultimate accolade to Blake's *Paradise Regained* designs by making a wonderful set of copies of them.*

Yet another interruption to Blake's work on Flaxman's *Hesiod* drawings was also probably arranged by Flaxman. For many years, Flaxman had made designs for the great pottery manufacturer Josiah Wedgwood, and he had been responsible for the copies Blake made of his designs for the ceiling of Wedgwood's house in Staffordshire in 1784. About 1815 "Mr Flaxman introduced Blake to Mr Wedgwood" and persuaded him to employ Blake to engrave for the firm's catalogues "The Designs of the Pottery [*which*] were made by Mr. Flaxman".[52] Wedgwood would send to Blake the soup terrine or bedpan to be represented, and Blake would draw it and send the drawing to Wedgwood, who would despatch another piece of pottery. When all the drawings were completed, Wedgwood directed how they should be arranged on the copperplates.[53]

Blake worked on the Wedgwood drawings all autumn,[54] and in the new year he began his engravings. Eventually he engraved 189 pieces of earthenware and porcelain on eighteen copperplates and was paid £30 for his work on 11 November 1816, a very modest fee.[55]

Another commission Blake received through Flaxman was for Abraham Rees's *Cyclopaedia*, which began publication in January 1802 and was finally completed in August 1820. Flaxman had written the anonymous articles on Basso Relievo and Sculpture[56] published in 1804 and 1816,

---

* Six of the designs came to light again in 1994 and were acquired by Professor Robert N. Essick; see Essick, "Blake in the Marketplace, 1994", *Blake*, XXXVIII (1995).

and in 1815 Blake was commissioned to make seven plates for them. Among the earliest were representations of "Hercules Farnese" (Sculpture pl. II) and "Venus de Medicis", "Apollo Belvedere", and "Laocoon" (Sculpture pl. III).* Blake owned plaster casts of all these save "Laocoon" and he may have made his drawings for Rees partly from them.

For the Laocoon, he went to the Royal Academy to copy from the full-size, restored cast of the original in the Vatican. There he found a crowd of students already working in the sculpture gallery. Blake sat down quietly among them, at the foot of the statue, and set to work. Blake's later disciple Frederick Tatham liked to tell about the occasion: "When M.ʳ B. was drawing this his old friend Fuseli came in & said 'Why Mr. Blake you a student[!] you might teach us'".[57] And he extended the story somewhat for Gilchrist: "'What! you here, *Meesther Blake?*' said Keeper Fuseli; 'we ought to come and learn of you, not you of us!' Blake took his place with the students, and exulted over his work, says Mr. Tatham, like a young disciple; meeting his old friend Fuseli's congratulations and kind remarks with cheerful, simple joy."[58]

One of the students copying there, Seymour Kirkup, wrote of the occasion over fifty years later:

I remember his coming to the Academy to draw the Laocoon. I was there & saw him sitting on a low stool close under the cast. The students came to me & said, ["]look at Blake, he has got his spectacles up side down & he says they were made on purpose to be worn so. Is he—not— mad?["] I saw directly that he had to look so high above him that reversing the spectacles assisted him, as it raised them, the convexity resting upon his nose—he said it was better so than a double concave as they sometimes are—& we laughed at the young criticisers ....[59]

In all, Blake made seven plates for Rees's *Cyclopaedia* in 1815–19, with a duplicate of one of them. For the first of these, on "Aug 19 [*1815*] M.ʳ Blake was [*paid*]—for a plate of Sculpture [£]10 10".[60] If he were paid at the same

---

* Blake's plates (1815–19) were for Armour pl. IV–V, Basso Relievo pl. IV, Gem Engraving pl. XVIII, Sculpture pls I–IV; Blake engraved two different but almost identical plates for Gem Engraving (*BBS* 246).

 He also made drawings for "An Egyptian Hieroglyphical Sphinx" and "Jupiter with the thunder and trident, a Greek gem of the oldest style" (engraved anonymously for Basso Relievo pl. I), and for "Hercules and Apollo contending for the Tripod from the Villa Albani" (Basso Relievo pl. II, engraved by William Bond) (*BBS* 246).

 "Hercules Farnese" (Sculpture pl. II) is the model for Giant Despair in his "Christian and Hopeful Escaping from Doubting Castle" for Bunyan's *Pilgrim's Progress* (*c.* 1824), and Venus (Sculpture pl. III) is the model for Cambel in *Jerusalem* pl. 81.

generous rates for his other drawings and engravings for Rees, he would have received £73.10.0 for his work for Longman, the equivalent of a year or more of work.

The task was the merest copy-engraving, of course, but it made Blake's skill as an outline-engraver visible to a wide audience, for Longman printed 6,250 copies each of the sections with Blake's prints.

Resumption of Book Printing

Blake also attracted the attention of the Yarmouth banker and autograph collector Dawson Turner. Turner wrote to William Upcott about buying "a copy of the 1st edition of Blake's Blair's Grave",[61] and, when Upcott told him about the Blake books he had inherited from his father Ozias Humphry, Turner wrote directly to Blake himself. On 9 June 1818, Blake replied to him with

a List of the different Works you have done me the honour to enquire after—unprofitable enough to me tho Expensive to the Buyer[.] Those I printed for Mr Humphry [*the Large and Small Books of Designs*] are a selection from the different Books of Such as could be Printed without the Writings tho to the Loss of some of the best things For they when Printed perfect accompany Poetical Personifications & Acts without which Poems they never could have been Executed[.]

		£.s.d
America	18 Prints folio	5.5.0
Europe	17 do folio	5.5.0
Visions &c	8 do folio	3.3.0
Thel	6 do Quarto	2.2.0
Songs of Innocence	28 do. Octavo	3.3.0
Songs of Experience	26 do Octavo	3.3.0
Urizen	28 Prints Quarto	3.3.0
Milton	50 do Quarto	10.10.0
12 Large Prints[,] Size of Each about 2 feet by 1 & ½ Historical & Poetical[,] Printed in Colours	Each	5.5.5

These last 12 Prints are unaccompanied by any writing[.]

The few I have Printed & Sold are sufficient to have gained me great reputation as an Artist which was the chief thing Intended But I have never been able to produce a Sufficient number for a general Sale by means of a regular Publisher[.] It is therefore necessary to me that any Person wishing to have any or all of them Should Send me their Order to Print them on the above terms & I will take care that they shall be done at least as well as any I have yet Produced[.]*

This letter indicates another great change. Seven years before, a commission for "a compleat Set of all you have published in the way of *Books*" Blake had declined because "my time . . . in future must alone be devoted to Designing & Painting".

However, by the summer of 1818, Blake's commissions for Flaxman's *Hesiod* (1814–17), Wedgwood's *Catalogue* (1815–16), and Rees's *Cyclopaedia* (1815–18) were substantially complete, and he was in financial difficulty again. John Linnell said that when he met Blake that summer, he had "scarcely enough employment to live by".[62]

Blake's only other new engraving commission since 1813 was from a miniaturist named Charles Borckhardt for engraving his conventional and self-consciously darling designs of "The Child of Nature" and "The Child of Art". These plates are of substantial size (38.1 x 24.8 and ? x 27.9 cm), and Blake might therefore have expected a significant sum for his stipple-and-line engravings of them. If, however, the production was a shared enterprise, with payment based upon sales, the rewards may have been very small; only three prints on two pieces of paper have been traced for "The Child of Nature", and "The Child of Art" has survived only in traces of the framing-line and imprint visible in a mezzotint engraved on top of it by someone else.[63]

Stimulated perhaps by Dawson Turner's enquiry about his books, Blake now returned to his old channel of making new copies of his works in Illuminated Printing. This was easier for him because he had already had to set up his printing studio to pull proofs of his engravings for Flaxman's *Hesiod*, for Rees's *Cyclopaedia*, and for Wedgwood. About 1818 he produced *Thel* (N–O), *Marriage* (G), *Visions* (N–P), *Songs* (T–U), *Urizen* (G), and *Milton* (D) using the same RUSE & TURNERS | 1815 paper printed in shades of orange and orangish-red ink, with hand-coloured designs, red ink borders and plate-numbers.† The fact that he printed two and three

---

* The list omits *For Children* because it is not coloured, and *Book of Ahania* and *Book of Los*, probably because only one copy of each had been printed. The omission of *Marriage* is more curious, because Blake printed copy G in 1818. Dawson Turner did not buy any of these books.

    Blake had apparently printed *Songs of Innocence* (S) and the *Innocence* copy of *Songs* (S) plus *Milton* (A–C) in about 1811.

† Joseph Viscomi, *Blake and the Idea of the Book* (1993), 330; Viscomi is the authority for dating all the copies of Blake's works in Illuminated Printing discussed here. Blake also printed two copies of "The Chaining of Orc" (1812) derived from a design in *Vala* p. 62.

    Note that in 1818 Blake was prepared to sell (from stock?) his twelve Large Historical & Poetical engravings of 1795, but no copy from as late as this is known.

copies of some titles at the same time demonstrates that he was printing for stock, on speculation, rather than on commission; *Visions* (O), for instance, was not sold until after December 1825.

Several of the copies printed in 1818 may, however, have been finished for individual customers. *Milton* (D) was bound with *Thel* (O) and "*exquisitely finished in colours by Blake himself* . . . expressly for his principal patron Mr [*James*] Vine of the Isle of Wight".[64]

Blake's prices had increased enormously since he printed his 1793 Prospectus; in 1818 he was asking eight to fourteen times the earlier prices. *Songs of Innocence*, for instance, went from 5s. in 1793 to £3.3.0 in 1818, and *America* from 10s.6d. to £5.5.0. The new prices could be justified in part by the very elaborate colouring which Blake invested in them. Indeed, some of the colouring in the later copies is so dense and extensive, covering even the text-areas, as to make them difficult to read, though exquisite to see.

The consequence of the substantial prices was that only wealthy or devoted customers were likely to be tempted by them. After all, there were probably whole months in which Blake did not earn as much as £5.5.0, the price of *America* in 1818, not to mention the £10.10.0 he asked then for *Milton*.

During the years of his neglect by the public, Blake was still supported by a few friends. Though he had lost the patronage of William Hayley, and his friend Joseph Johnson the bookseller had died in 1809, and the public ignored or mocked his 1809 exhibition of pictures and its *Descriptive Catalogue*, Blake still had admirers such as Seymour Kirkup and Crabb Robinson and Samuel Taylor Coleridge.

The difficulty was that these new friends were not patrons. For a time Blake gave up printing his own works (1811–18), he laid aside his graver (1805-15), and he wrote no new poems (1807?–25?). And when he did resume his graver in 1815, it was chiefly for fairly humble copy-work such as for Rees's *Cyclopaedia* and Wedgwood's porcelain catalogue. None of these new engraving commissions was for his own designs.

In these dark years, Blake was justified in feeling that "I am hid". What he had lost were patrons.

What he found were friends.

CHAPTER IX

1818–1827: The Ancients and the Interpreter

I hear a voice you cannot hear that says I must not stay
I see a hand you cannot see that beckons me away[1]

The Inspiration of Youth

"May God make this world to you, my child, as beautiful as it has been to me."[2]

In the summer of 1818 Blake met a new friend, and through this new friend his life began to change profoundly. The change was not so much in his material circumstances as in his confidence that he was admired and cherished. Thereafter he was the centre of a tiny but expanding circle of young admirers who called themselves, in mockery of their extreme youth, "The Ancients" and Blake's humble walk-up flat "The House of the Interpreter". They found in Blake a serenity and an inspiration which transformed their lives, and they in turn transformed his.

After the years of struggle with the ways of the Beast, of fashion, and of prosperity, Blake was now content to accept his lot in the world. Rather than envying the successful, as he had done in his youth, he came to perceive that they had missed God's main chance. In short, as a contemporary wrote: "he was a living commentary on Jeremy Taylor's beautiful chapter on Contentedness".[3]

Once at a party he met a very beautiful little girl, "nursed in all the elegancies and luxury of wealth". When she was

> presented to Blake, he looked at her very kindly for a long while without
> speaking, and then stroking her head and long ringlets said "May God
> make this world to you, my child, as beautiful as it has been to me". She
> thought it strange at the time, she said, that such a poor old man, dressed
> in such shabby clothes, could imagine the world had ever been so beautiful
> to him as it must be to her ... but in after years she understood well enough
> what he meant ....[4]

This shining serenity in poverty made a profound impression on his new friends.

During these years, Blake was deep in obscurity. That indefatigable art-enthusiast William Paulet Carey wrote of Blake in 1817: "I never had the good fortune to see him; and so entire is the uncertainty, in which he is involved, that after many inquiries, I meet with some in doubt whether he is still in existence ... his professional encouragement has been very limited, compared with his powers."[5]

And on 15 May 1824 Charles Lamb wrote to James Montgomery:

> Blake is a real name, I assure you, and a most extraordinary man, if he be
> still living. He is the Robert Blake, whose wild designs accompany a splen-
> did folio edition of the Night Thoughts.... . He paints in water colours,
> marvellous strange pictures, visions of his brain which he asserts that he
> has seen. They have great merit. He has <u>seen</u> the old welch bards on
> Snowdon—he has seen the Beautifullest, the Strongest, & the Ugliest
> Man, left alone from the Massacre of the Britons by the Romans, & has
> painted them from memory (I have seen his paintings) and asserts them
> to be as good as the figures of Raphael & Angelo, but not better, as they
> had precisely the same retro-visions & prophetic visions with himself. ...
> His Pictures, one in particular the Canterbury Pilgrims (far above
> Stothard's)[,] have great merit, but hard, dry, yet with grace. He has writ-
> ten a Catalogue of them, with a most spirited criticism on Chaucer, but
> mystical and full of Vision. His poems have been sold hitherto only in
> Manuscript. I never read them, but a friend at my desire procured
> the Sweep Song. There is one to a Tiger, which I have heard recited,[*]
> beginning

---

[*] The reciter was probably Crabb Robinson; Linnell vividly remembered "hearing Crabb Robinson recite Blake's poem, 'The Tiger,' before a distinguished company gathered around Mr. Aders's table. It was a most impressive performance" (A.T. Story, *Life of John Linnell* [1892] [*BR* 286]).

Tiger Tiger burning bright
Thro' the deserts of the night—

which is glorious. But alas! I have not the Book, for the man is flown, whither I know not, to Hades or a Mad House—but I must look on him as one of the most extraordinary persons of the age.*

John Linnell,
Bringer of Honour to the Prophet and Profit with the Honour

The first of Blake's new, much younger friends, was John Linnell, a landscape and portrait painter and engraver of growing distinction.

Linnell was a man remarkably like Blake in many ways. He was just Blake's height, 5′ 5″, and, like Blake, he went his own way when the ways of the world did not please him. He never went to school, and in 1804, when he was twelve years old, he lived as a pupil with the artist John Varley at 15 Broad Street, Golden Square, a few doors down from 28 Broad Street where William and Catherine stayed the previous autumn with Blake's brother James.

Like Blake, Linnell was profoundly a Dissenter, and he spoke the language of Enthusiasm: "The mind that rejects the true Prophet ... generally follows the Beast also for the Beast & False-Prophet are always found together."†

Like Blake, he lived for his art—he spoke of "my first love of poetical Landscape which I lived to paint—the portraits I painted to live"[6] (Pl. 117).

There were, however, two great differences between Linnell and Blake. First, Linnell was successful in pleasing prosperous patrons and in managing the ways of the world.‡ He adopted "the simplest & shortest methods of

---

* Lamb's information about Blake apparently comes chiefly from Crabb Robinson and from Blake's *Descriptive Catalogue* which Robinson had given him.
  The context was Lamb's contribution of Blake's "The Chimney Sweeper" from *Innocence* to *The Chimney-Sweeper's Friend, and Climbing-Boy's Album*, ed. James Montgomery (1824)—"Blake's are the flower of the set". The account of Montgomery's book in *The Eclectic Review* (June 1824) did not know "how to characterize the song given from Blake's 'Songs of Innocence'. It is wild and strange, like the singing of a 'maid in Bedlam in the spring;' but it is the madness of genius" (*BRS* 80).

† Quoted from f. 13ʳ of the fragmentary "Autobiography of John Linnell" (in the collection of his descendant John S. Linnell), written in the 1850s with later insertions of 1863–64. Many of the facts untraced above derive from this manuscript. John Linnell's father James was, in 1830, a frame-maker in Hart Street (*BR* 393 n3).
  For a time Linnell attended the Baptist services of John Martin, and later he was drawn to the Quakers, but his way was always his own, as his fellow-worshippers let him know.

‡ Linnell exhibited almost 1,300 pictures in 1807–81 (David Linnell, *Blake, Palmer, Linnell and Co.: The Life of John Linnell* [(Lewes), Sussex: The Book Guild, 1994], 355–406); Blake exhibited seventeen pictures in 1780–1812, plus his own private exhibition of sixteen pictures in 1809.

business, to pay ready money & give no credit", and by the time he was twenty-five he had amassed £530 in Bank Securities, enough to justify him in getting married.[7]

The other great difference was that Linnell did not see visions.

At the end of the summer of 1817, Linnell withdrew £50 from his funded property, and

> I went Sep.[r] 15. to Scotland to be married. My determination to be married there in order to avoid the degrading & as I consider it blasphemous character of the church ceremony was the chief thing which had delayed my marrying so long for at that time the journey to Scotland was the only escape from the clerical imposition ... that priestly usurpation .... I ... became convinced that such a step was necessary to satisfy my conscience ....[*]

The journey from London to Edinburgh took almost seven days, and he and his fiancée rode much of the way on the outside of the coach, in fair weather and in foul, in sunshine, in moonshine, in wind and in rain.

Even after they reached Edinburgh,

> I was pressed by some dissenters to adopt their semi-clerical plan but I said I had come all the way from London to testify against the usurpation of a civil act by clergy of any sort. Marriage belonged properly to the law & the magistracy & as it was proved to be thoroughly legal and binding to declare yourselves married persons before a magistrate I would only do this & no other plan w.[d] I adopt. So this was done accordingly on the 24.th [8]

Clearly Linnell was a man of extraordinary integrity.

He was also a man with a mischievous sense of humour. In 1809 a gentleman offered through an intermediary to buy a painting by the twenty-one-year-old artist if he would agree to cut off a strip four inches wide on each side of it and rather more at the top. Linnell replied: "'pray does the gentleman wish to have the outside pieces or the inside['], for I doubted which would be worth most".[9]

Linnell was a gifted teacher of art, and among his pupils was George Cumberland, Jr. In June 1818, young George wrote to his father "I have

---

* Linnell, Autobiography, p. 51. It is characteristic of Linnell that he describes in detail his motives of conscience, the costs of the journey, and the itinerary, while he scarcely mentions his fiancée (on the trip north) and his bride (on the trip south), and he speaks resolutely in the first person singular: "I went ... to Scotland to be married", "I consider it blasphemous". Linnell was a thoughtful and a generous man, as his treatment of Blake demonstrates, but his manner in person and in his Autobiography often gave the erroneous impression that he was hard, grasping, and egotistical.

introduced him [*Linnell*] to Blake[,] they like one another much and Linnel[*l*] has promised to get him some work".*

Linnell was engraving his portrait of the Baptist minister James Upton, and he commissioned Blake to lay in the outlines. On 23 June he bought "a Copper Plate from Mr Pontifex for to engrave Mr Uptons Portrait on", and next day he went "to Mr Blake (Evening) deliverd to Mr Blake the Picture of Mr Upton & the Copper Plate—to begin the engraving".†

As Linnell commented years later, this work was very welcome, Blake

having scarcely enough employment to live by at the prices he could obtain[;] everything in Art was at a low ebb then . ... I soon encountered Blake's peculiarities and [*was*] somewhat taken aback by the boldness of some of his assertions[.] I never saw anything the least like madness for I never opposed him spitefully as many did but being really anxious to fathom if possible the amount of truth which might be in his most startling assertions I generally met with a sufficiently rational explanation in the most really friendly & conciliatory tone [Pl. 128]. Even when John Varley to whom I had introduced Blake & who readily devoured all the marvellous in Blakes most extravagant utterances [Pl. 118B][,] even to Varley Blake would occasionally explain unasked how he beleived that both Varley & I could see the same visions as he saw making it evident to me that Blake claimed the possession of some powers only in a greater degree that all men possessed and which they undervalued in themselves & lost through love of sordid pursuits—pride, vanity, & the unrighteous mammon[.][10]

Linnell promptly became an important force in Blake's professional and social life. He multiplied Blake's social contacts, he made Blake a part of his young and growing family, he introduced him to patrons, took him to exhibitions and plays, gave Blake engraving work, commissioned Blake's wonderful engravings for Job and Dante, and refined Blake's engraving techniques. The florescence of Blake's art and serenity in the last years of his life is largely due to John Linnell.

---

* Linnell lived then at 38 Rathbone Place, "and here I first became acquainted with William Blake", "but at the End of 1818, I took a House No 6, Cirencester place Fitzroy Square" (Linnell Autobiography ff. 105, 104) (see Horwood's Map of Westminster, Pl. 8).

† Linnell's Journal (*BRS* 102).

Linnell carefully took Blake's receipts "For Laying in the Engraving of Mr Uptons portrait" on 12 Aug (£2), 11 Sept (£5), 9 Nov (£5), and 31 Dec 1818 (£3.15.0) (*BR* 580, 581). This total of £15.15.0 indicates that Blake did extensive work on Linnell's Upton plate, for he was paid only £5.5.0 each for his finished outline engravings for Flaxman's *Iliad* (1805) and *Hesiod* (1814–17).

The copperplate-maker Pontifex paid Linnell £12.12.0 for his painting and £52.10.0 for his engraving of Upton (*BRS* 122). Linnell worked on the engraving of Upton from 18 Sept 1818 to 3 June 1819 (*BRS* 103), and the print was "Published July 1st 1819 by R Pontifex" (*BRS* 103).

On Friday 10 July Linnell "went with Mr Blake to Lord Suffolks to see pictures | to [*Pall Mall to*] see Leonard Da Vinci's Last Supper", and on 21 August they went together to the print-dealer Colnaghi.[11] Three days later "M^r & Mrs Blake [*came*] to Tea", and on 9, 11 and 18-19 September Linnell went to Mr Blake in the evening, the last two times with John Varley.[12] On 12 September 1818 "Mr Blake Brought a proof of Mr Upton's Plate | left the Plate & named 15£ as the | Price of what was already done by him— | —Mr Varley—& Mr Constable stay'd with Blake".[13]

On one such occasion, John Constable showed Blake one of his sketch books, and Blake "said of a beautiful drawing of an avenue of fir trees on Hampstead Heath, 'Why, this is not drawing, but *inspiration*;' and Constable replied, 'I never knew it before; I meant it for drawing.'"[14]

Had Blake thought it to be merely a drawing of fir trees, he would not have been interested in it.

John Varley and the Visionary Heads

Blake's friends and his work had always associated him with the art and science of physiognomy. Artists, like actors, had to be able to represent character through the face, and drawing-manuals showed stock expressions for rage, envy, longing, and fear. When Blake's admired Lavater wrote in his *Aphorisms* (¶124), "Who has a daring eye, tells downright truths and downright lies", Blake underlined it and wrote beside it "*most True*". Lavater's intimate friend Fuseli was an ardent physiognomist, and it was probably Fuseli who arranged for Blake to make engravings for Lavater's *Essays on Physiognomy*. There was an enormous vogue for physiognomy, and many, like William Cowper in 1790, were "very much of Lavater's opinion, and persuaded that faces are as legible as books".[15]

The vogue became, if not more scientific, at least more systematic when it was taken up by J.G. Spurzheim in his *Physiognomical System*. John Linnell bought a copy of Spurzheim's *Deranged Manifestations of the Mind, or Insanity* when it was published in 1817,[16] and Blake made notes from it. Blake was learned in physiognomy,* and to explain why he was a "Liberty Boy" he "would jokingly urge in self-defence that the shape of his forehead made him a republican. 'I can't help being one,' he would assure Tory

---

* The first life-mask made by James S. Deville the phrenologist (1 Aug 1823) was "of Blake's head as representative of the imaginative faculty" (George Richmond [*BR* 278]). Richmond comments on the bust's uncharacteristic "look of severity" and says that "Mrs. Blake did not like the mask [*or* Phillips's portrait] . . . but Blake's friends liked the mask."

friends, "any more than you can help being a Tory: your forehead is larger above; mine, on the contrary, over the eyes.' "[17]

Another believer in physiognomy was Linnell's former teacher John Varley, who was a prolific landscape artist, debtor, and astrologer. In religion he was a sceptic, but he was a profound believer in the stars.

Varley was a great bear of a man, alarmingly strong, and alarmingly hopeful of all his worldly prospects. He was repeatedly arrested for debt and as repeatedly rebounded with undiminished ebullience; he used to say, "all these troubles are necessary to me .... If it were not for my troubles I should burst with joy!"[18]

When Linnell introduced Varley to Blake, Varley was fascinated by Blake's accounts of his visions, and he became convinced that the visions were connected with the spirit world of astrology. Indeed, he wrote *A Treatise on Zodiacal Physiognomy* (1828), and he illustrated it with plates after Blake's Visionary Heads.

Varley is the source, if he is not the author, of the account of Blake's horoscope in the astrological journal called *Urania* in 1825:

> he seems to have some curious intercourse with the invisible world; and, according to his own account (in which he is certainly, to all appearance, perfectly sincere), he is continually surrounded by the spirits of the deceased of all ages, nations, and countries. He has, as he affirms, held actual conversations with Michael Angelo, Raphael, Milton, Dryden, and the worthies of antiquity. He has now by him a long poem nearly finished, which he affirms was recited to him by the spirit of Milton;* and the mystical drawings of this gentleman are no less curious and worthy of notice, by all those whose minds soar above the cloggings of this terrestrial element ....
>
> ... we have been in company with this gentleman several times, and have frequently been not only delighted with his conversation, but also been filled with feelings of wonder at his extraordinary faculties; which, whatever some may say to the contrary, are by no means tinctured with superstition, as he certainly believes what he promulgates. ... it is probable, that the extraordinary faculties and eccentricities of ideas which this gentleman possesses, are the effects of the MOON in CANCER in the twelfth house (both sign and house being mystical), in trine to HERSCHELL from the mystical sign PISCES, from the house of science, and from the mundane trine to SATURN in the scientific sign of AQUARIUS, which latter planet

---

* This may be a garbled account of *Milton*, though that poem is not said to be "recited ... by the spirit of Milton", and copies had been printed and sold by 1811.

is in square to MERCURY in SCORPIO, and in quintile to the SUN and JUPITER, in the mystical sign of SAGGITTARIUS. The square of MARS and MERCURY, from fixed signs, also, has a remarkable tendency to sharpen the intellects, and lay the foundation of extraordinary ideas.

Linnell, however, had no patience with astrology, and he was persuaded that Blake saw no connection between his visions and the stars. He wrote that

Varley could make no way with Blake towards inducing him to regard Astrology with favour [Pl. 118B]. Blake w.ᵈ say ["]your fortunate nativity I count the worst[;] you reckon that to be born in August & have the notice & patronage of Kings to be the best of all where as the lives of the Apostles & Martyrs of whom it is said the world was not worthy w.ᵈ be counted by you as the worst & their nativities those of men born to be hanged.["] Varley believed in the reality of Blakes visions more than even Blake himself—that is in a more literal & positive sense that did not admit of the explanations by which Blake reconciled his assertions with known truth. . . . It was Varley who excited Blake to see or fancy the portraits of historical personages—as Edward & Wallace, David, Solomon, the man who built the pyramids,* &c. &c. most of which I have. I painted in oil the heads of King Edward & W.ᵐ Wallace for Varley from these drawings in black lead pencil [*by*] Blake, also the Ghost of a Flea.†

But though Blake may not have believed in the influence of the stars, some of his sitters did. "Hotspur said . . . we should have had the Battle had it not been for those cursd Stars[.] Hotspur Said he was indignant to have been killd through the Stars Influence by such a Person as Prince Henry who was so much his inferior."[19]

According to Blake's disciple Frederick Tatham,

He always asserted that he had the power of bringing his Imagination

---

* According to Anon. [probably John A. Heraud], "Blake's Poetry", *Monthly Magazine* (1839) (*BRS* 75),

> "Call up, and paint the Founder of the Pyramids," said some one to the artist-visionary.
> "There he is," replied Blake, "a stately man, in purple robes, with a book full of golden leaves on which he sketches his designs."

Blake's surviving design of The Man Who Built the Pyramids is a pencil sketch (Butlin #692 103 with colour notes), as is the replica by Linnell (Butlin #752). This vision of the "Founder of the Pyramids" is echoed in Heraud's *The Judgment of the Flood* (1834) (*BRS* 75 n3).

† Linnell, Autobiography (*BR* 263–4). In *Jerusalem* pl. 91, ll. 36–7, "Los reads the Stars of Albion: the Spectre reads the Voids Between the Stars".

When Blake writes of "my Evil Star" in his letter of 27 Jan 1804, he seems to mean little more than bad luck.

before his minds Eye, so completely organized, & so perfectly formed & Evident, that he persisted, that while he copied the vision (as he called it) upon his plate or canvas, he could not Err; & that error & defect could only arise from the departure or inaccurate delineation of this unsubstantial scene. He said that he was the companion of spirits, who taught, rebuked, argued, & advised, with all the familiarity of personal intercourse. What appears more odd still was the power he contended he had, of calling up any personage of past days, to delineate their forms & features, & to converse upon the topic most incidental to the days of their own existence . . . .*

In the autumn of 1819, Blake began to record for Varley the visions which he saw late at night. Sometimes he drew these Visionary Heads almost nightly, as Varley's inscriptions on them indicate:

14 Oct 1819: "R.^d Coeur de Lion. Drawn from his spectre", "Born 1156. Died april 6. 1199 [astrological symbols for Pisces, Capricorn] 10.h [Libra] at Birth", "W Blake fecit Octr 14 1819 at 14 Past 12-Midnight"
18 Oct 1819: "The Man who built the Pyramids drawn by William Blake", "Octr 18. 1819. 15 Degrees of [Cancer] Cancer ascending"
22 Oct [1819?]: "22.^d octr", sketches of a devil and a man in armour
27 Oct 1819: "Cassibelane" and "Cassibelane the British Chief" "By Blake Octr. 27 1819 11 P M"
29 Oct 1819: "the Empress Maud said rose water was in the vessel under the table octr. 29 friday. 11 PM. 1819. & said there were closets which contained all the conveniences for the bedchamber"; "Can you think I can endure to be considered as a vapour arising from your food[?] I will leave you if you doubt I am of no greater importance than a Butterfly"; "Spiritual communication to mr Blake"; "Empress Maud not very tall"
30 Oct 1819: "Wat Tyler by Wm Blake, from his Spectre, as in the act of striking the Tax Gatherer on the head. Drawn Octr 30. 1819. 1h AM"†

---

* Tatham (*BR* 518–19). This simplistic statement is echoed by Gilchrist (*BR* 260): "In sober daylight, criticisms were hazarded by the profane on the character or drawing of these or any of his visions. 'Oh, it's all right!' Blake would calmly reply; 'it *must* be right: I saw it so.'"
We may take as mere foolish hyperbole the account of T.F. Dibdin, *The Library Companion* (1824) (*BR* 289): "he is at times shaking hands with Homer, or playing the pastoral pipe with Virgil".

† Butlin #729, 752, 692 99, Larger Blake-Varley Sketchbook ff. 81, 83, Butlin #692 23 and 692 5, 737. (Christie's catalogue for 21 March 1989 reproduced *The Larger Blake–Varley Sketchbook*, which was discovered after the publication of Butlin [1981].)
The inscriptions on the Visionary Heads are chiefly by Varley, sometimes by Linnell on counterproofs. The Visionary Heads, mostly undated, were probably made chiefly in 1819–20; for instance, the heads of William Wallace and Edward I bear no date, but Linnell copied them in oil for Varley on 23, 26 Oct and 1 Nov 1819 (*BRS* 104).

These midnight seances attracted the attention of many who otherwise would have ignored Blake, and a surprising number of lurid accounts were published about them — accounts which may, however, be substantially true. At least they are fairly consistent both with each other and with the inscriptions on the Visionary Heads themselves.

Much of the information about these Visionary Heads derives from John Varley, though usually he is not named. According to Allan Cunningham, Varley told him:

"I know much about Blake—I was his companion for nine years. I have sat beside him from ten at night till three in the morning, sometimes slumbering and sometimes waking, but Blake never slept; he sat with a pencil and paper drawing portraits of those whom I most desired to see. I will show you, Sir, some of these works."

He took out a large book filled with drawings, opened it, and continued, "Observe the poetic fervour of that face—it is Pindar as he stood a conqueror in the Olympic games. And this lovely creature is Corinna, who conquered in poetry in the same place. That lady is Lais, the courtesan— with the impudence which is part of her profession, she stept in between Blake and Corinna, and he was obliged to paint her to get her away.

"There! that is a face of a different stamp—can you conjecture who he is?"

"Some scoundrel, I should think, Sir."

"There now—that is a strong proof of the accuracy of Blake—he is a scoundrel indeed! The very individual task-master whom Moses slew in Egypt.

"And who is this now—only imagine who this is?"

"Other than a good one, I doubt, Sir."

"You are right, it is a fiend—he resembles, and this is remarkable, two men who shall be nameless; one is a great lawyer, and the other—I wish I durst name him—he is a suborner of false witnesses."

"This other head now?—this speaks for itself—it is the head of Herod; how like an eminent officer in the army!"*

Some at least were made later:

Aug 1820: "old Parr when young Viz 40", "Aug 1820 W. Blake fect."
18 Sept 1820: "Pindar drawn by Blake Septr 18.1820" and "Lais The Courtesan"
After 1821: "The Egyptian Task Master slain by Moses", "Seen in a Vision by Wᵐ Blake & Drawn while the Same remained Before him, My Self J. Varley being Present, in the Front room first floor No. 3 Fountain Court near Exeter Change" where Blake lived 1821-27
1825: "Head of Achilles drawn by Willm Blake at my request. 1825" (Butlin #748, 711, 696A, 707).

*   Cunningham ¶38 (*BR* 497), divided here into several paragraphs. Cunningham also says that "The most propitious time for those 'angel-visits' was from nine at night till five in the morning" (*BR* 496).

One anonymous author wrote:

I have been present on these occasions. One night, while we were engaged in criticizing his own extravagant, yet occasionally sublime illustrations of the book of Job, engraved by himself [*1825*], he suddenly exclaimed, "Good God! here's Edward the Third!" [Pl. 119]

"Where?"

"On the other side of the table; *you* can't see him, but I do; it's his first visit."

"How do you know him?"

"My spirit knows him—how I cannot tell."

"How does he look?"

"Stern, calm, implacable; yet still happy. I have hitherto seen his profile only, he now turns his pale face towards me. What rude grandeur in those lineaments!"

"Can you ask him a question?"

"Of course I can; we have been talking all this time, not with our tongues, but with some more subtle, some undefined, some telegraphic organ; we look and we are understood. Language to spirits is useless."

"Tell him that you should like to know what he thinks of the butcheries of which he was guilty while in the flesh."

"I have, while you have been speaking."

"What says his majesty?"

"Briefly this: that what you and I call *carnage* is a trifle unworthy of a notice; that destroying five thousand men is doing them no real injury; that, their important parts being immortal, it is merely removing them from one state of existence to another; that mortality is a frail tenement, of which the sooner they get quit the better, and that he who helps them out of it is entitled to their gratitude. For, what is being hewn down to the chine to be compared with the felicity of getting released from a dreary and frail frame?"

"His doctrines are detestable, and I abhor them."

"He bends the battlement of his brow upon you; and if you say another word, will vanish. Be quiet, while I take a sketch of him."[20]

According to another eye-witness account,

One of the less plausible dialogues invented by Cunningham ¶41 (*BR* 499) is attributed to a

friend, on whose veracity I have the fullest dependence, [*who*] called one evening on Blake, and found him sitting with a pencil and a panel, drawing a portrait with all the seeming anxiety of a man who is conscious that he has got a fastidious sitter; he looked and drew, and drew and looked, yet no living soul was visible.

"Disturb me not," said he, in a whisper, "I have one sitting to me."

"Sitting to you!" exclaimed his astonished visitor, "where is he, and what is he?—I see no one."

"But I see him, Sir," answered Blake haughtily, "there he is, his name is Lot—you may read of him in the Scripture. *He* is sitting for his portrait."

Butlin records no Visionary Head of Lot.

he related to us ... That the first time he saw King Saul, he was clad in armour. That his helmet was of a form and structure unlike any that he had seen before, though he had been in the armories of all nations since the flood. Moreover, that King Saul stood in that position which offered only a view in part of the said helmet, and that he could not *decently* go round to view the whole.

Thus the sketch of the helmet,—for artists have a rule not to touch at home upon that which they have sketched abroad ... this rule, Mr. Blake invariably maintained ....

"Some months after" (the first sitting,) said Mr. Blake, "King Saul appeared to me again (when he took a second sitting,) and then I had an opportunity of seeing the other part of the helmet."

We saw the said helmet when completed, and, in sober truth can assert, that the helmet and the armour are most extraordinary!*

One of his midnight portraits was of "The Spirit of Voltaire" (Pl. 120). According to Crabb Robinson,

"I have had,["] he said ["]much intercourse with Voltaire—And he said to me 'I blasphemed the Son of Man And it shall be forgiven me—but they' (the enemies of Voltaire) [']blasphemed the Holy Ghost in me, and it shall not be forgiven to them[' ".]

I asked him in what language Voltaire spoke—His answer was injenious and gave no encouragement to cross questioning[.] "To my Sensations it was English[.] It was like the touch of a musical Key—he touched it probably French, but to my ear it became English[."]†

One of the fullest and most impressionistic accounts was given by Jane Porter, a correspondent of the Flaxmans and a friend of Crabb Robinson. Her novel called *The Scottish Chiefs* (1810) dealt with Edward I and his great rival the Scottish patriot William Wallace. A few years later, she said, her friend John Varley (whom she did not name) told her that Blake

was often in the habit of speaking ... with a force of language, and indig-

---

* Anon., "William Blake" [obituary], *Literary Chronicle* (1 Sept 1827). The only known portrait of Saul (Butlin #696 [Plate 910]) shows no helmet. An analogous design is inscribed by Linnell: "King Edward the first as he now exists in the other world, according to his appearance to Mr Blake; he here has his scull enlarged like a crown" (Butlin #735 [Plate 947]).

† Crabb Robinson, Reminiscences for 18 Feb 1826 (1852) (*BR* 547). By this time, Blake was apparently no longer drawing the Visionary Heads, for "I also enquired as I had before about the form of the persons who appeared to him And Asked Why he did not <u>draw</u> them,—[']It is not worth while[,'] he said, [']Besides there are so many that the labour would be too great—And there would be no use in it' ".

nation at the fact, as if the noble victim [Wallace]'s death had been only an event of yesterday.

In one of my friend's calls on the young painter, he found him in an almost breathless ecstacy, which he explained to him, by telling him that he had just achieved two sketches—one of Sir William Wallace, the other of his enemy, Edward the First!—Both chiefs having actually appeared to him successively, and had successively stood, at his earnest request, to allow him to make a hasty sketch of their forms [Pl. 121].

... the painter told my friend, that having turned to dip his pencil for a further touch, when he looked up again, the vision was gone! ... [*Blake explained:*] "He was sitting, meditating, as he had often done, on the heroic actions and hard fate of the Scottish hero, when, like a flash of lightning, a noble form stood before him; which he instantly knew, by a something within himself, to be Sir William Wallace. He felt it was a spiritual appearance; which might vanish away as instantly as it came; and, transported at the sight, he besought the hero to remain a few moments till he might sketch him. ... with his accustomed courtesy, he smiled on the young painter;—and the sketch was outlined, with a tint or two besides. But, while eagerly proceeding, the artist bent his head once too often, to replenish his pencil; and turning again, to pursue the whole contour, the spirit of the "stalworth knight" had withdrawn from his mortal ken. But (Blake proceeded to say,) it had not left a Vacancy! Edward the First stood in its place; armed from head to foot, in a close and superb suit of mail; but with the visor of his helmet opened.

The artist, it appears, had as little difficulty in recognising the royal hero; as, when his heart, as well as his eyes, bowing before the august figure just departed, told him it was the Caledonian patriot he beheld. His English loyalty, however, made him rise before the royal apparition. Nevertheless, he saluted the monarch with the same earnest privilege of enthusiastic genius, which had dictated the request to the Scottish chief; and he asked the stern-looking, but majestic warrior-king of England, to allow him to make a corresponding sketch. This too, was accorded. And he had arrived at about the same point, as in the former portrait, when the British hero also disappeared;—and Blake was left—not so disappointed at not having accomplished all he wished, as enraptured at having been permitted to behold two such extraordinary characters; and to have thus far, identified their personal presence to himself; and to the world, to all posterity!*

---

* Jane Porter, *Scottish Chiefs* (1841) (*BR* 261–3). Her description differs in important ways from the sketch which survives (Butlin #734). In her account there are two coloured paintings on canvas which Varley "showed ... to me", not one pencil sketch on paper; Wallace has "blue eyes", "golden

Allan Cunningham also embroiders the story a little, as usual:

> so docile were his spiritual sitters, that they appeared at the wish of his friends. Sometimes, however, the shape which he desired to draw was long in appearing, and he sat with his pencil and paper ready and his eyes idly roaming in vacancy; all at once the vision came upon him, and he began to work like one possesst.
>
> He was requested to draw the likeness of Sir William Wallace—the eyes of Blake sparkled, for he admired heroes.
>
> "William Wallace!" he exclaimed, "I see him now—there, there, how noble he looks—reach me my things!"
>
> Having drawn for some time, with the same care of hand and steadiness of eye, as if a living sitter had been before him, Blake stopt suddenly, and said, "I cannot finish him—Edward the First has stept in between him and me."
>
> "That's lucky," said his friend, "for I want the portrait of Edward too."
>
> Blake took another sheet of paper, and sketched the features of Plantagenet; upon which his majesty politely vanished, and the artist finished the head of Wallace.[21]

Many of the Visionary Heads are fascinating studies of character. Among the most striking are Owen Glendower (Pl. 122), the Earl of Warwick (Pl. 123), and Colonel Blood (Pl. 124). The first two are famous fifteenth-century warriors, king-makers and earth-shakers, but the third is an adventurer of the time of Blake's grandfather, a bravo who sauntered out of the Tower of London with the royal regalia in 1671 and then talked his way out of a noose and into the king's favour.

Blake's visitants were strongly marked characters whose destinies might seem to have been written in the stars. Many of them were notorious criminals, such as "Catherine Hayes Burnt for the Murder of her Husband" (1726), "Mother Brownrigg" (hanged 1767), and "Miss Blandy who poisoned her father" (hanged 1752).[22] Perhaps they were chosen by Varley in

---

tinted hair", and a "breastplate of plain workmanship, half covered by his plaid broached, on the shoulder", none of which is visible in the sketch; and Edward I wears a crown over chain mail but has no helmet-and-visor. (Further, Blake was not "young" but 53 when *The Scottish Chiefs* was first published in 1810.) Either there are two lost oils of Edward I and Wallace, or Jane Porter has indulged in culpable novelist's license. Or she may be describing Linnell's oil copy (Oct 1819), not the original sketches.

According to J. Sartain, *The Reminiscences of a Very Old Man 1808–1897* (1899), the painted portrait which Varley showed him was inscribed: "William Wallace appeared and stayed long enough for me to paint this portrait of him, when King Edward the First took his place and I painted him also. He promised to come again and bring his wife and children. W. Blake" (*BR* 260–1). However, this inscription is not otherwise known.

the hope that their phrenological features would correspond to their known characters.

Some of the individuals represented were famous but anonymous, such as "The Egyptian Task master who was killd & Buried by Moses", "The Man who built the Pyramids", and "a Man who instructed M.ʳ Blake in Painting in his Dreams &c."[23] (Pl. 125).

It was not only the heroes of the past who appeared to Blake.

"For many years," said he, "I longed to see Satan—I never could believe that he was the vulgar fiend which our legends represent him—I imagined him a classic spirit, such as he appeared to him of Uz [*i.e., Job*], with some of his original splendour about him.

At last I saw him. I was going up stairs in the dark, when suddenly a light came streaming amongst my feet, I turned round, and there he was looking fiercely at me through the iron grating of my staircase window. I called for my things—Katherine thought the fit of song was on me, and brought me pen and ink—

I said, [']hush!—never mind—this will do[']—as he appeared so I drew him—there he is."

Upon this, Blake took out a piece of paper with a grated window sketched on it, while through the bars glared the most frightful phantom that ever man imagined. Its eyes were large and like live coals—its teeth as long as those of a harrow, and the claws seemed such as might appear in the distempered dream of a clerk in the Herald's office.

"It is the gothic fiends of our legends,["] said Blake—["]the true devil—all else are apocryphal."*

The most sensational of these visions represented the Ghost of a Flea. John Varley said:

As I was anxious to make the most correct investigation in my power, of the truth of these visions, on hearing of this spiritual apparition of a Flea, I asked him if he could draw for me the resemblance of what he saw: he instantly said, "I see him now before me." I therefore gave him paper and a pencil, with which he drew the portrait [Pl. 126]. . . .

I felt convinced by his mode of proceeding, that he had a real image before him, for he left off, and began on another part of the paper, to make

---

* Cunningham ¶40 (*BR* 498), paragraphing added. The drawing of Satan has not been traced since 1830 (Butlin #694).

   J.T. Smith says Blake saw the Ancient of Days which he depicted in the frontispiece to *Europe* (Pl. 53) "at the top of his staircase" (*BR* 470).

a separate drawing of the mouth of the Flea, which the spirit having opened, he was prevented from proceeding with the first sketch, till he had closed it.[*]

During the time occupied in completing the drawing, the Flea told him that all fleas were inhabited by the souls of such men, as were by nature bloodthirsty to excess, and were therefore providentially confined to the size and form of insects; otherwise, were he himself for instance the size of a horse, he would depopulate a great portion of the country. He added, that if in attempting to leap from one island to another,[†] he should fall into the sea, he could swim, and should not be lost.

This spirit afterwards appeared to Blake, and afforded him a view of his whole figure. . . .[‡]

An anonymous author said that

The flea communicated to Mr. Blake what passed, as related to himself, at the *Creation*. "It was first intended," said he (the flea) "to make me as big as a bullock; but then when it was considered from my construction, so armed—and so powerful withal, that in proportion to my bulk, (mischievous as I now am) that I should have been a too mighty destroyer; it was determined to make me—no bigger than I am."[24]

And Allan Cunningham added more details and embroidery. According to his anonymous friend,

I called on him one evening, and found Blake more than usually excited. He told me he had seen a wonderful thing—the ghost of a flea! "And did you make a drawing of him?" I inquired. "No, indeed," said he, "I wish I had, but I shall if he appears again!" He looked earnestly into a corner of the room, and then said, "here he is— reach me my things—I shall keep my eye on him. There he comes! his eager

---

[*] Gilchrist may have had no more evidence than this when he wrote that sometimes, "in the midst of his portrait, he would suddenly leave off, and, in his ordinary quiet tones and with the same matter-of-fact air another might say 'It rains,' would remark, 'I can't go on,—it is gone! I must wait till it returns;' or, 'It has moved. The mouth is gone;' or, 'he frowns; he is displeased with my portrait of him'" (*BR* 260).

[†] According to J.T. Smith (1828), Blake said of "This personification, which he denominated a Cupper, or Blood-sucker", "were that lively little fellow the size of an elephant, he was quite sure, from the calculations he had made of his wonderful strength, that he could bound from Dover to Calais in one leap" (*BR* 467).

[‡] John Varley, *Zodiacal Physiognomy* (1828) (*BR* 372–3, paragraphing added); it is also quoted in a review [?by W.P. Carey], *Literary Gazette* (27 Dec 1828). Varley explained that "This spirit [*which*] visited his imagination" "agrees in countenance with one class of people under Gemini." *Zodiacal Physiognomy* contains an engraving of the Flea.

tongue whisking out of his mouth, a cup in his hand to hold blood, and covered with a scaly skin of gold and green;"—as he described him so he drew him.*

Blake's Sanity and the Visionary Heads

Naturally many who heard that Blake drew pictures of the famous and infamous dead and had conversations with his invisible visitants concluded that he must be mad. And any lingering suspension of disbelief was likely to be banished when they learned that some of the visitants were not long-dead men and women but heretofore unimagined beings, such as Gemini and Cancer and the Ghost of a Flea. So plain was Blake's madness to some that they assumed he must have been confined in a madhouse.†

After 1820, most accounts of Blake refer to his Visionary Heads either as evidence of his madness or as something to be explained away[25]—perhaps as a joke on Varley. Scarcely anyone allows for the possibility that Blake drew what he really saw and that what he saw was really there, an extraordinary or spiritual phenomenon.

From Blake's earliest appearances in public, his pictures and poems were characterized as the work of a madman. A review of the 1785 Royal Academy exhibition said that his "Bard ... appears like some lunatic, just escaped from the incurable cell of Bedlam"; in 1797 the artist John Hoppner asserted that Blake's designs "were like the conceits of a drunken fellow or a madman"; and in 1826 Southey praised his design of "The Reunion of the Soul and the Body" for Blair's *Grave* in curiously ambivalent terms: "the highest genius alone could have conceived it, and only madness have dared to attempt the execution".‡

---

* Cunningham ¶39 (*BR* 498), paragraphing and quotation marks added.

  According to Walter Thornbury, *British Artists from Hogarth to Turner* (1861), Blake "drew his 'Demon Flea' " "At the house of the father [*Samuel Leigh*] of my old friend Leigh, the artist" (James Matthews Leigh [1808–60]), where "Blake was a frequent visitor, as was Varley" (*BR* 264). It was "by the desire of Mʳ Leigh" that Blake inscribed William Upcott's autograph album on 16 Jan 1826, and "Mʳ Leigh Bookseller", Strand, subscribed for Blake's *Job* on 10 Jan and 29 April 1826 (*BR* 587, 591).

† According to Anon., "Hôpital des fous à Londres", *Revue Britannique* (July 1833), in Bedlam, the author interviewed Jonathan Martin (the York Minster incendiary) and William Blake, "un homme grand et pâle .... Il conversait avec Michel-Ange, il causait avec Moïse, il dinait avec Sémerimas", he was drawing there in Bedlam the Ghost of a Flea (*BR* 299 n1). The essay is plagiarized and embroidered from Anon., "Bits of Biography, No. 1: Blake, the Vision Seer, and Martin, the York Minster Incendiary", *Monthly Magazine* (March 1833).

‡ *BRS* 8; *BR* 58, 326. The testimony about Blake's madness among contemporaries who did not know him is close to unanimous: T.F. Dibdin (?Spring 1816): "absolutely lost his wits"; *Literary Gazette* (Oct 1828): "madness"; *Gentleman's Magazine* (Feb 1830): "an amiable enthusiast, on the wrong side of the line of demarcation as it respected his sanity"; *Monthly Review* (March 1830): "extraordinary lunatic"; *Fraser's Magazine* (March 1830): "Blake's brain became fevered: he mistook the dreams of fancy for reality"; *Edinburgh Review* (April 1834): "able but, alas! insane"; Walter Cooper Dendy, *The Philosophy of Mystery* (1841): "Blake was a visionary, and thought his fancies real—he was mad" (*BR* 244; 370; 379; 626; 380, 391; 489 n1).

Often the grounds for the conclusion that Blake's art is mad were that he represented the spiritual world in forms disconcertingly like those of the material, tangible world. In damning Blake's *Grave* designs, Robert Hunt assumed "The utter impossibility of representing the *Spirit* to the eye" and concluded that Blake is "an unfortunate lunatic, whose personal inoffensiveness secures him from confinement".[26]

Similarly, the unconventionality or wildness of Blake's poetry was regularly taken to indicate madness, even by the best judges, Blake's poetical peers. Wordsworth said of *Songs of Innocence and of Experience*: "There is no doubt this poor man was mad, but there is something in the madness of this man which interests me more than the Sanity of Lord Byron & Walter Scott".[27] "Lamb used to call him a 'mad Wordsworth'", and Walter Savage Landor wished that Blake and Wordsworth "could have divided his madness between them".[28] Robert Southey, the Poet Laureate, "held him for a decided madman ... he showed S. a perfectly mad poem called Jerusalem", and William Beckford said that "The Tyger" "seems to have [*been*] stolen ... from the walls of Bedlam".*

Most of these men had not met Blake, and they drew their conclusions from his works rather than his person. However, even men who knew him well concluded, as Fuseli did, that "Blake has something of madness ab! him".[29] According to Crabb Robinson, Flaxman "did not join in the ordinary derision of him as a madman",[30] but he did speak of "Blake's irritability", and he said: "I very much fear his abstracted habits are ... much at variance with the usual modes of human life".[31] William Hayley wrote of the "perilous powers of ... [*Blake's*] Imagination", his "nervous Irritation", and his "sensibility ... so <u>dangerously acute</u>", that he "has <u>often appeared to me on the verge of Insanity</u>".[32] Blake's intimate friend George Cumberland said that "Blakes Cat. is truly original—part vanity part madness—part very good sense".†

Some of the most telling evidence comes from Crabb Robinson, a careful observer and a responsible reporter. Before he met Blake, Robinson described him in 1811 as "insane", exhibiting "the union of genius and

---

* Crabb Robinson Diary for 24 July 1811 (*BR* 229); Beckford MS note on "The Tyger" in Malkin (*BR* 431 n1). The *Antijacobin Review* (Nov 1808) said of Blake's Dedication to Blair's *Grave*: "Should he again essay to climb the Parnassian heights, his friends would do well to restrain his wanderings by the strait waistcoat"; according The *Eclectic Review* (June 1824), Blake's "The Chimney Sweeper" from *Innocence* "is wild and strange, like the singing of a 'maid in Bedlam in the spring,' but it is the madness of genius" (*BRS* 80); Edward Bulwer Lytton wrote in the *New Monthly Magazine* (Dec 1830): "what a delightful vein of madness it was—with what exquisite verses it inspired him!"; and Cunningham (1830) wrote that in *Poetical Sketches* "There is ... a great deal that is wild and mad, and all so strangely mingled" (*BR* 480).

† Cumberland letter (13 Nov 1809). He also wrote in Nov 1809: "They say Blake was mad: If so Shakespeare & Milton were so too" (*BR* [2] under 1809–10).

madness".[33] When he met Blake in 1825, Robinson did not change his mind, writing of him as a "Madman", and of his "mad doctrines", his "interesting insanities".* It is "his religious convictions [*which*] had brought on him the credit of being an absolute lunatic", the "half crazy crotchets abo! the two worlds".[34]

There seems to have been a change in Blake by 1820. His intimate friends John Flaxman and William Hayley had written of "Blake's irritability" (2 Jan 1804), his "nervous Irritation" (3 Aug 1805), his "little Touches of nervous Infirmity" (15 July 1802), "on the verge of Insanity" (3 Aug 1805), like the mad William Cowper. Southey concluded from his visit to Blake in 1812 that "You could not have delighted in him—his madness was too evident, too fearful. It gave his eyes an expression such as you would expect to see in one who was possessed".[35]

However, those who met Blake after 1820 were struck by his serenity. Crabb Robinson, who met him in 1825, said that "he had an air of inspiration—But not such, as without a previous acquaintance with him, or attending to *what* he said, would suggest the notion that he was insane. There was nothing *wild* about his look."[36]

The young men who met Blake through Linnell not only did not think him mad; they thought him singularly sane. Samuel Palmer wrote: "I remember William Blake, in the quiet consistency of his daily life, as one of the sanest, if not the most thoroughly sane man I have ever known."† According to John Linnell, "I never in all my conversations with him c^d for a moment feel there was the least justice in calling him insane—he could always explain his paradoxes satisfactorily when he pleased but to many he spoke so that 'hearing they might not hear'".[37] Edward Calvert told Gilchrist, "I saw nothing but sanity ... saw nothing mad in his conduct, actions, or character". Francis Oliver Finch was sure that "He was not mad, but perverse and wilful; he reasoned correctly from arbitrary, and often false premises." John Varley's brother Cornelius asserted that "There was nothing mad about him", and "James Ward, who had often met Blake in society and talked with him, would never hear him called mad."‡

---

* Crabb Robinson, Diary for 10 Dec 1825, 18 Feb 1826; when Robinson met Samuel Palmer in Wales in 1836, he "soon satisfied him that in calling B insane I was not repeating the commonplace declamation against him" (*BR* 363).

† Samuel Palmer, "Fictions Concerning William Blake", *Athenaeum*, No. 2498 (11 Sept 1875), 348–9. In a letter of 5 Feb 1881, he said that Blake was "*of all men whom I ever knew*, the most *practically sane, steady, frugal* and *industrious*" (*The Letters of Samuel Palmer*, ed. Raymond Lister [Oxford: Clarendon Press, 1974], 1061).

‡ Gilchrist (*BR* 268). Seymour Kirkup, who knew Blake in 1810–16, said on 24 Feb 1870: "I used to think him mad then, but I think now he was quite sound" (*BR* 221 n4), and Henry Francis Cary "abandoned, after he came to know him, the notion he had taken up of his 'madness'" (Gilchrist [*BR* 233 n1]).

Blake viewed the world from the vantage point of Enthusiasm; he believed that the world is moved by spirits, and he saw and spoke to these spiritual realities. As he commented on Swedenborg, "Who shall dare to say . . . that all elevation . . . is Enthusiasm & Madness"?[38] To those who identified enthusiasm with madness, Blake said, "I am Mad or Else you are So[;] both of us cannot be in our right Senses."[39] According to James Ward, "Blake himself would sometimes . . . [*say*] that 'there are probably men shut up as mad in Bedlam, who are not so: that possibly the madmen outside have shut up the sane people'."[40]

Blake as Linnell's Protégé

Linnell was assiduous in introducing Blake to men of taste who might be of use to him. He took Blake to see the collector Edward Denny and the successful miniaturist Anthony Stewart on 17 June 1819, "to see Harlowes copy of Transfiguration" on 20 August, to William Hookham Carpenter the bookseller and print-connoisseur on the 21st, and later that day he took James Holmes the miniaturist "to Mr Blake Evening".

In 1819, Linnell began acquiring poems by Blake. His first recorded purchase was £1.19.6 "for Songs of Innocence & Experience One Copy" on 27 August 1819,[41] followed by 14s. "for 2^d n°. of Jerusalem" on 31 December 1819, plus 15s. more for "Bal of Jerusalem" fourteen months later, on 4 February 1821.[42] He bought "A copy of his Marriage of Heav. & Hell" for £2.2.0 on 30 April 1821 and "A Book of Europe & America (not fin^d.)" for £1 on 8 August 1821.[43] These are modest prices, much less than Blake asked from others — his price-list of 1818 included *America* and *Europe* at £5.5.0 each and *Songs* at £6.6.0*—but then in these years most of the sales Blake had were found for him by Linnell. It was appropriate that Blake should charge Linnell the price of friendship rather than of commerce.

In time Linnell's library contained perhaps the most extraordinary collection of Blake's books ever formed.† Some of these works he bought on straight

---

* Letter of 9 June 1818. On 20 July 1827, George Cumberland wrote: "for Blake I have spared no pains but have no success. They seem to think his prices above their reach, yet they seemed very anxious to have his works" (*BRS* 87).

† Linnell owned "The Accusers" (C), *All Religions are One* (A), *America* (O), *Descriptive Catalogue* (K [bought 25 Aug 1831 from Mrs Blake for 2s. 6d.]), *Europe* (K), *Urizen* pl. 21, *For the Sexes* (A–B, K), *The French Revolution* (unique proof copy), *Ghost of Abel* (B), *Jerusalem* (C) plus pl. 51, *Marriage* (H, L–M), "Mirth" (A), *On Homer* (B), *Poetical Sketches* (D [received 1866] and T [bought 25 Aug 1831 from Mrs Blake for 2s. 6d.]), *Songs* (R [bought 1819] and AA [bought in 1835]), *There is No Natural Religion* pl. a2, and *Vala* (unique MS)—plus drawings such as those for Job, Dante, and the Visionary Heads, letters, receipts, and books owned by Blake (e.g., Chapman's Homer). *America* (O), *Europe* (K), *Jerusalem* (C), and *Songs* (R) were uniformly bound in white vellum about 1824.
    It is slightly surprising that Linnell did not own *Thel, Milton, Song of Los, Urizen*, or *Visions of the Daughters of Albion*; it is less surprising that he did not own *Ahania* or *The Book of Los* which survive in unique copies probably printed *c.* 1795, long before Linnell met Blake.

commission, such as the splendid drawings illustrating Job and Dante; some he was given by Blake, such as the unique copies of *The French Revolution* and *Vala*; a few he bought after Blake's death from his widow, probably at least in part in charity; and some he acquired long after Blake's death.

During the years he knew Blake, Linnell kept a journal which is remarkable for its conciseness: 8 September 1818, "Hannah born"; 7 November 1823, "second Son Born $\frac{1}{2}$ past 8 morning". In the journal he recorded many of the visits he made to or with Blake:

Linnell's Record of Blake in his Journal[44]

1820

24 April	Went with Blake to [The Society of Painters in Oil and Water Colours] exhibition at Spring Gardens, where we met the Duke of Argyll
8 May	Went with Blake to Mr Wyatt and to Lady Ford to see her pictures
11 May	Went with Blake and Varley to Mr Denny for tea
9 Oct	Went with Blake to Dr Thornton

1821

3 Feb	Dr Thornton came to dinner and we went to Blake
9 Feb	Blake came in the evening
8 March	Went with Blake to the British Gallery, and Blake dined with me
27 March	Went with Blake to Drury Lane Theatre [to see Sheridan's *Pizarro*]
30 April	Went with Blake to the water colour exhibition
7 May	Went with Blake to Somerset House exhibition [of the Royal Academy]
20 May	Went with Blake to Hampstead
8 June	Went with Blake to Drury Lane Theatre [to see the opera *Dirce or The Fatal Urn*]
26 Aug	Went with Blake to Mr Woodburn in Hendon
8 Sept	"Traced outlines from Mr Blakes Designs from Job all day— I Mr Blake & Mr Read with me all day"
10 Sept	"Traced outlines from Mr Blakes drawings of Job—all day I Mr Blake finishing the outlines—all day.... I Mr Blake took home the drawings of Job"
11 Sept	"Mr Blake brought a Drawing of Cain & Abel"
12 Sept	"Began a Copy of Cain & Abel"
14 Sept	Continued with the copy of Cain & Abel
27 Oct	Blake came in the evening

| 11 Nov | Sunday: Blake dined with us |
| 9 Dec | Sunday: Blake dined with us |

1822

14 April	Sunday: Blake and Varley dined with us
8 May	Went with Blake to Mr Vine
9 May	"Mr Blake began copies from his Drawings from Miltons P.L. [*Paradise Lost*]"
13 July	Went with Blake to Sir Thomas Lawrence

1823

17 April	Went with Blake to the British Museum to see Prints
24 April	Went with Blake to the British Museum
5 May	Went with Blake to the Royal Academy Exhibition
25 June	Went with Blake to the British Gallery "&c."

1824

| 14 May | Went to Mr Vine, Mr James, and Blake |
| 4 Aug | Varley, C.H. Tatham and his Son [Frederick], and Blake dined with us at Hampstead |

1825

28 Jan	Called on Blake &c [and paid him £10]
4 March	Went with Blake "to Dixon's proving Job"
5 March	Went with Blake "to Lahee's proving Job"
9 March	Called on Blake and others
8 April	Called on Blake "&c" [and paid him £3.10.0]
3 May	Went with Blake to the [Royal Academy] exhibition
6 Aug	Went with Blake to Mrs Aders, 11 Euston Square
7 Nov	Called on Blake
10 Dec	Dined at Mr Aders with Blake and H.C. Robinson

1826

17 May	Called on Blake
12 July	Called on Blake
13 July	Called on Blake, Dr Young, "&c"

1827

9 Jan	Called on Blake and gave him £5
7 Feb	Called on Blake to speak to him about living [with us] at Cirencester Place
8 Feb	Left with Sir Thomas Lawrence Blake's *Paradise Regained* drawings, price £50
17 April	Went with Blake to Mr Ottley
15 May	Called on Blake "&c"
11 July	Went to Somerset House and Blake
17 July	Went to Blake "&c"
3 Aug	Called on Blake

10 Aug	Called on Blake; "not expected to live"
12 Aug	"Mr Blake died"
13 Aug	Went to see Mrs Blake and B. Palmer "@ Mr Blake's Funeral"
14 Aug	Went "to Sir Thos Lawrence @ Mrs Blake"
16 Aug	Sent a copy of *Jerusalem* to Ottley
18 Aug	Went to Mrs Blake

Linnell's laconic journal only hints at events, and it ignores Blake on many occasions when the two men were together. For instance, Linnell's journal for Thursday 2 November 1821 records merely that he went to see *Œdipus*, and his cash account book adds that he paid to Dr Thornton 4s. for a ticket to a box for *Œdipus*.[45] However, he wrote then in a letter that "Mr Varley, Mr Blake & myself were much entertained Thursday Evening last by witnessing a representation of Oedipus in the West London Theatre as it much exceeded our expectations as to the effect of the Play & the performance of the Actors.[46] Their expectations may have been very different from what they in fact saw. The play had been advertised as "the *Œdipus Tyrannus* of Sophocles ... 'being its first appearance these 2440 years' ",[47] i.e., since 619 B.C., 123 years before the birth of Sophocles. However, they saw what the indignant *Times* reviewer called "a cut-down edition of the bombastic yet powerful tragedy [*1678*] of [*Nathaniel*] Lee and [*John*] Dryden upon the same subject".*

It is chiefly from Linnell's taciturn Journal that we learn of Blake's surprisingly extensive experience in seeing plays. We might have expected Blake to share the Dissenter's scorn for the kind of "fop" who "Saunters about the Playhouses[,] who Eats & drinks for business not for need".[48] But in fact, Blake's adolescent "King Edward the Third", "King Edward the Fourth", and "King John" from *Poetical Sketches* (1783) and his more mature *Island in the Moon* (?1787) are theatrical and perhaps even designed for performance, and he illustrated numerous plays such as Shakespeare's *Macbeth* and *Romeo and Juliet*, and Milton's *Comus* and Gay's *Beggar's Opera* and Sophocles' *Philoctetes*.†

And he spoke of the stage and actors with an easy familiarity which suggests first-hand knowledge. On 22 March 1805 he sent Hayley gossip about the theatrical sensation William Henry West Betty: "The Town is Mad.

---

*   *The Times* (2 Nov 1821) (*BRS* 78).

   See Michael Phillips, "William Blake and the Sophocles Manuscript Notebook" and G.E. Bentley, Jr, "William Blake and the Sophocles Enigma", *Blake*, XXXI (1997), 44–9, 65–71 for arguments that William Blake the poet was, or more probably was not, the author of a translation of Sophocles' *Ajax*.

†   Blake made engravings after Hogarth for *The Beggar's Opera* (1788) and after John Opie for *Romeo and Juliet* in Boydell's *Shakspeare* (1803) plus drawings for *Comus* (1801), Shakespeare (1806, 1809), and Sophocles, *Philoctetes* (1812) (Butlin #527, 547, 676).

Young Roscius like all Prodigies is the talk of Every Body. ... I have no curiosity to see him as I well know what is within the compass of a boy of 14, & as to Real Acting it is like Historical Painting[,] No Boy's Work."

But only from Linnell's Journal do we learn when he went to the theatre and what he saw.

Many of the calls Linnell made with Blake were probably to introduce him to potential patrons, some of whom were already buyers of Linnell's own art. When Blake went with Linnell on 10 July 1818 "to Lord Suffolks to see Pictures" and to Pall Mall "to see Leonard Da Vinci's Last Supper", he may have gone on with him to Mr James Vine, to whom Linnell delivered a picture.[3]* Eventually Vine bought at least five book by Blake: *Thel* (O) bound with *Milton* (D), *Jerusalem* (J, posthumous), *Songs* (V), all similarly bound in half russia, and a proof copy of *The Book of Job*. These were important sales for Blake, at £2.2.0 for *Thel*, £6.6.0 for *Songs*, £10.10.0 for *Milton*, and £5.5.0 for *Job*.†

Similarly, on 17 June 1819 Linnell took Blake to call on one of his own patrons, a dreamy young man named Edward Denny, and Denny took tea with Blake, Varley, and Linnell on 11 May 1820.‡ In the autumn of 1821 Denny wrote to Linnell about the "drawings" which "Mr. Blake ... is making for me",[49] and six years later Denny wrote to Blake asking for a copy of the edition of Blair's *Grave* (1808) which Blake had illustrated and which Denny thought "one of the most beautiful and interesting things I have seen of your's".[50] Denny also bought a copy of *Job*, "<u>a great work</u>" of "exquisite beauty & marvellous grandeur", "truly sublime".[51] Such patronage must have been wonderfully welcome to Blake in these hard years.

The most remarkable of the new friends to whom Linnell introduced Blake was Thomas Griffiths Wainewright, gentleman-pupil of Fuseli, dilettante, essayist, and painter. Charles Lamb said that "kind light hearted

---

* *BRS* 102. Vine lived at "Corner Brunswick Square [*and*] Grenvill Street" according to Linnell's Account Book (*BRS* 275 n2), and he was at Grenville Street, Brunswick Square, London, when on 18 June 1837 he made codicil to his will (PRO: Prob 1111882 13204), but he was buried on 16 July 1837 in the Baptist church of St John, Niton, Isle of Wight, near his daughter Augusta, who was born in 1821 at Puckster Close, Puckster, Isle of Wight, implying that in 1821 the Vines were resident there.

† The prices of *Thel*, *Songs*, and *Milton* are given in Blake's letter of 9 June 1818 and of *Job* in Linnell's account book (*BR* 590).

   Blake wrote directions for "The Order in which the Songs of Innocence & of Experience ought to be paged & placed", perhaps to direct Catherine how to arrange Vine's copy (the only copy in this order), suggesting that they had no other copy in stock to use as a model (Joseph Viscomi, *Blake and the Idea of the Book* [1993], 335–6). However, after this time, the Blakes arranged most copies of the *Songs* in a different but uniform order.

‡ *BRS* 103, 104. From Aug to Nov 1821, Linnell painted portraits of Edward Denny (reproduced in *Blake*, XXI [1987–88], 104) and five members of Denny's family for £162.5.0 (*BRS* 76, 103 n1). In 1821 Denny lived at King's End House, Worcester, but by 1826 he was in Barbourne House, Worcester.

Wainwright" "was a genius of the Lond. Mag."[52] Blake probably admired his essays as he did his paintings—he said that Wainewright's picture of "The Milk Maid's Song" was "very fine"[53]—and in return Wainewright praised Blake sententiously in private and frivolously in print. In 1827 Wainewright told Linnell that Blake's "fate is a national disgrace; while his pious content is a national example",[54] and in *The London Magazine* for September 1820 he wrote:

> Dear, respected, and respectable Editor!
> ... my exertions to procure crack-contributors have been nearly as zealously unremitting as your own. ... my learned friend Dr. Tobias Ruddicombe,* M.D. is, at my earnest entreaty, casting a tremendous piece of ordnance,—*an eighty-eight pounder!*† which he proposes to fire off in your next. It is an account of an ancient, newly discovered, illuminated manuscript, which has to name "Jerusalem the Emanation of the Giant Albion!!!" It contains a good deal anent one "*Los*," who, it appears, is now, and hath been from the creation, the *sole* and fourfold dominator of the celebrated city of *Golgonooza*! The doctor assures me that the redemption of mankind hangs on the universal diffusion of the doctrines broached in this M.S.[55]

Wainewright was "In great impatience to devour the treasure of his great mind".[56] He did not buy a copy of *Jerusalem*, which was first printed in 1819-20, but in 1826 he bought a copy of *Milton* and a proof copy of *Job* (£5.5.0),[57] and in 1827 he commissioned coloured copies of *The Marriage of Heaven and Hell* and of *Songs of Innocence and of Experience*.‡ For the last, at least, the payment was munificent; in his letter of 12 April 1827, Blake wrote: "I am now Printing a Set of Songs of Innocence & Experience for a Friend at Ten Guineas which I cannot do under Six Months consistent with my other Work." At this rate, Wainewright probably paid £6.6.0 for the *Marriage*, £10.0.0 for *Milton*,[58] plus £10.10.0 for the *Songs*. This total of £27.6.0 must have been very welcome to the impecunious Blakes. When Blake died, E.F. Wainewright wrote to Linnell: "We shall indeed <u>deeply</u> sympathise with you on the loss of so great an artist, and I fear Mʳ Wˢ regrets will be most poignant that he did not enjoy once again the pleasure of an hour with him".[59]

---

* Blake's pseudonym here may derive from his crisp yellow hair which, in his youth, "stood up like a curling flame", according to Tatham (*BR* 518).

† Canon were defined by the weight of the ball they threw. Thirty-two pounders were sometimes used for harbour-defences. The recoil of an 88-pounder would have destroyed any ship then afloat.

‡ The commission is mentioned in Wainewright's letter to Linnell of Feb 1827 (*BR* [2]). Wainewright apparently owned *Descriptive Catalogue* (F), *Marriage* (I), *Milton* (B), *Songs* (X), Job (1826), Blair's *Grave* (1813), Malkin (1806) (*BBS* 127 n160), and the Riddle MS (*BB* 339 n2).

Wainewright was a sincere admirer and a generous patron of Blake. But Blake's skill in physiognomy was not sufficiently acute to tell him that the gay, the frolic Wainewright was paying him in 1826 with money derived from a forgery and that he would later poison several of his relatives in order to get their insurance.*

Another Blake collector of the time was the author Isaac D'Israeli. In 1819 he was trying to acquire "a copy of Blake's Young"[60] (i.e., *Night Thoughts* [1797]), and in 1824 his friend T.F. Dibdin said that D'Israeli "possesses the largest collection of any individual of the very extraordinary drawings [*i.e., prints*] of Mr. Blake; and he loves his classical friend to disport with them".† These may have represented a significant income to Blake.

Blake's Virgil *Woodcuts*

Linnell also helped Blake to find work as a commercial book-illustrator. By the autumn of 1818, he had introduced Blake to Dr Robert John Thornton,[61] the Linnells' loyal family physician,‡ and both Blake and Linnell were commissioned to make illustrations for Thornton's edition of *The Pastorals of Virgil, with a Course of English Reading, Adapted for Schools*; in which all the Proper Facilities are Given, Enabling Youth to Acquire the Latin Language, in the Shortest Period of Time, Illustrated by 230 Engravings.§

Dr Thornton was a somewhat surprising patron, for Blake came to believe—and may have believed in 1820—that Thornton was "one of the learned that mouth", like the learned Caiphas, Pilate and Herod, in contrast

---

* Wainewright was tardily convicted of the 1826 forgery and deported to Tasmania in 1837.

† T.F. Dibdin, *The Library Companion* (9 Aug 1824). By 1835, Isaac D'Israeli said he had 160 of Blake's designs (*BR* 244–5), and eventually he and his son Benjamin Disraeli owned "The Accusers" (H), *America* (A) and pl. d, *Book of Thel* (F), *Europe* (A), *First Book of Urizen* (B), "Joseph of Arimathea Preaching" (F), *Marriage* (D), *Song of Los* (B), *Songs* (A), and *Visions* (F). Some of these, such as *America* (A), *Urizen* (B), and *Visions* (F), were probably acquired after Blake's death, at the Romney sale in 1834. (Butlin records no Blake drawings from the D'Israeli collections.) For the difficulties in identifying what D'Israeli owned in 1824, see *BR* [2] (under 1819).

   Benjamin Disraeli wrote in 1862 that his "father was not acquainted with Mr Blake" (*BRS* 74). However, though D'Israeli may not have known Blake, he certainly knew George Cumberland, who sent him a copy of his *Captive of the Castle of Sennaar* (1798) (Australian National University) before he suppressed it.

‡ R.J. Thornton made a "Certificate" "that Mʳ Linnell is a patient of mine for imbecility or Weakness of Limbs for which he is incapable of serving in the Militia" (Ivimy MSS).

§ This is the title of the Third Edition (1821), though "Youth" is spelled "Youtm", an unfortunate precedent in a pedagogical text. The book was already successful, for a first edition had appeared in 1812 without plates; separate engravings were issued for it in 1814; and text and illustrations were issued together in the Second Edition of 1819.

to "Christ & his Apostles [*who*] were Illiterate Men". Thornton's "Tory Translation" of The Lord's Prayer (1827) is "a Most Malignant & Artful attack upon the Kingdom of Jesus", because the only spirits in which Thornton believes are taxable "Royal Gin", "not Ghosts". "This is Saying the Lords Prayer Backwards which they say Raises the devil."[62] It certainly raised the devil in William Blake.

Blake of course had long known and admired Virgil. On 23 August 1799 he had told Dr Trusler that the works of "Homer[,] Virgil & Milton [are set] in so high a rank of Art ... because they are addressed to the Imagination".* He responded with deep joy to the rural harmonies of Virgil's *Pastorals*. In his designs, he transposed Virgil's Latin landscape to comfortable rural England, even to his beloved Felpham; in one design, a shepherd walks past a mile-post engraved with "63 Miles [*to*] London", as Felpham was, and in the distance, in a fold of the hills, is a town with a Gothic spire, like Chichester.

For this transposition to England, Blake had the precedent of Ambrose Phillips, whose Imitation of Virgil's First Eclogue he illustrated. Phillips's shepherd drives his flocks "to distant *Cam*", and Blake's design set beside the river Cam shows distant spires of King's College, Cambridge.

---

* However, Blake distinguished between the bucolic music of Virgil's *Pastorals* and the martial clangor of his *Aeneid*: "Greece & Rome ... were destroyers of all Art .... Virgil in the Eneid, Book V*I*, line 848, says "Let others study Art: Rome has somewhat better to d*o*, namely War & Dominion" (*On Homers Poetry & On Virgil* [*c*. 1821]).

The cost of printing intaglio engravings was formidable, so for inexpensive works like this one (15s.) the illustrations were often engraved on wood so that they could be printed from the surface in the same print-run as the type-set text. The same economy could be achieved by Blake's method of Illuminated Printing from relief etchings on copperplates, a method which he had used commercially before only in Hayley's charitable *Little Tom The Sailor* (1800). Thornton's *Virgil* offered Blake a last opportunity to demonstrate the commercial promise of his method of relief etching.

Blake was commissioned to make seven conventional intaglio engravings of famous individuals, such as Publius Virgilius Maro and the Giant Polypheme. But far more important were the twenty new designs he was commissioned to create.

He began his series of designs for *Virgil* in his familiar method of relief etching, composing directly on the copper with acid-resist.* In them he created a bucolic night-realm defined by flecks of light beneath a hanging moon. The shepherds are clad in tights (Pl. 127), like shepherds from his own *Songs of Innocence*.

This was a bold endeavour, for commercial printing from relief etching had rarely been attempted before. It was greeted, as are most innovations by outsiders, with "a shout of derision ... by the wood-engravers. 'This will never do,' said they; 'we will show what it ought to be'—that is, what the public taste would like",† and three of the designs were copied on wood by an anonymous engraver in a form which lost almost all Blake's magic (Pl. 128).‡

Blake therefore made drawings of all his *Virgil* scenes for this unfamiliar medium of wood-engraving§ and then copied them on wood. In these, the shepherds and sages are more discreetly clad in vaguely

---

* These relief-etched prints for *Virgil* were not known before 1997, when they were acquired by R.N. Essick.
† [Henry Cole], review of Goldsmith, *The Vicar of Wakefield* "With thirty-two Illustrations. By W. Mulready", *Athenaeum* (1843) (*BR* 267). The information, like the blocks reproduced there, clearly came from Linnell.
  "This will never do" is the opening phrase of Francis Jeffrey's notorious review of Wordsworth's *Excursion* in the *Edinburgh Review* (1816).
† Blake's design illustrates a metaphor: "First, then, shall lightsome birds forget to fly ... 'Ere I unmindful of *Menalcus* grow". In Blake's drawing, the birds are larger and in the foreground, but the anonymous woodcut has reduced them to mere background.
§ Wood-engravers ordinarily drew their designs directly on the block of wood, as Linnell did with his design of Polypheme for Thornton's Virgil (*BRS* 76) and as Blake did with "The Prophet Isaiah Foretelling the Destruction of Jerusalem" (Butlin #773). However, as Blake had not previously made wood-engravings, he may have wished to proceed more cautiously. It seems probable that he made two series of designs for Virgil, one directly on the copper for his relief etchings and the other on paper which he then copied on wood.

classical frocks, but the mysterious moon-lit world of the relief etchings lives on.*

Dr Thornton was still troubled by the unconventionality of Blake's illustrations, and on 15 September 1820 he sent to Linnell a specimen of

> what Blake's Augustus—produces in the usual mode of Printing— How much better will be the Stone—provided it turns out well—it will *amalgamate* with Wood—and not injure by comparison— I long to see your Virgil transferred upon the Stone— It has one great advantage—Authority—for the Drawing—superior execution—& cheap printing—and perpetuity—

Two and a half weeks later Linnell went with Dr Thornton "to the Lithographic Press to prove a head of Virgil". Apparently there was still uncertainty as to whether Blake's woodblocks should be used at all.

Fortunately just at this time, Thornton

> meeting one day several artists at Mr. Aders' table,—Lawrence, James Ward, Linnell, and others,—conversation fell on the Virgil. All present expressed warm admiration of Blake's art, and of those designs and woodcuts in particular. By such competent authority reassured, if also puzzled, the good Doctor began to think there must be more in them than he and his publishers could discern. The contemplated sacrifice of the blocks already cut was averted.[63]

Blake's name is associated with more plates in Thornton's *Virgil* than that of any other artist or engraver. However, the prints were published with a curiously ambivalent apology: "The Illustrations of the English Pastoral are

---

*   The lines illustrated in the vignette in the text here are:

> My piteous plight in yonder naked tree,
> Which bears the thunder-scar too plain I see . . .
> Ill-fated tree and more ill-fated I!
> From thee, from me, alike the shepherds fly.

by the famous B<small>LAKE</small>, the Illustrator of *Young's* Night Thoughts, and *Blair's* Grave; who designed and engraved them himself. This is mentioned, as they display less of art than genius, and are much admired by some eminent painters."[64]

The Ancients were deeply moved by Blake's *Virgil* series, and their own art was suffused and transformed by its gentle light. Years later Edward Calvert wrote of Blake's *Virgil* designs: "They are done as if by a child; several of them careless and incorrect, yet there is a spirit in them, humble enough and of force enough to move simple souls to tears."[65] And Samuel Palmer added:

> They are visions of little dells, and nooks, and corners of Paradise; models of the exquisitest pitch of intense poetry.... Intense depth, solemnity, and vivid brilliancy only coldly and partially describe ... [*their* light and shade]. There is in all such a mystic and dreamy glimmer as penetrates and kindles the inmost soul, and gives complete and unreserved delight, unlike the gaudy daylight of this world. They are like all that wonderful artist's works the drawing aside of the fleshly curtain, and the glimpse which all the most holy, studious saints and sages have enjoyed, of that rest which remaineth to the people of God. The figures of Mr. Blake have that intense, soul-evidencing attitude and action, and that elastic, nervous spring which belongs to uncaged immortal spirits.*

These prints illustrating Thornton's *Virgil* are among the triumphs of the art of the woodcutter and of William Blake, and they were enormously influential among the Ancients and later artists, but they were largely ignored among Blake's contemporaries.

Move to Fountain Court

In 1821, Blake's "Landlord [*Mark Martin*] leaving off business & retiring to France, he moved to [*No. 3*] Fountain Court Strand ... here he occupied the first floor ... [*in*] a private House Kept by M.ʳ [*Henry*] Banes whose wife [*Sarah*] was sister to M.ʳˢ Blake".[66] Here he lived for the rest of his life, and here the Ancients visited him in his "enchanted rooms".†

---

* *BR* 271–2. Blake gave Palmer "impressions taken there [in Fountain Court], at his own press, by his own hands, and signed by him under my eyes" (*BR* 222 n1). Linnell bought the blocks from Thornton on 16 Sept 1825 for £2.2.0 (*BR* 582), and Calvert printed some of them for Linnell (*BR* [2], 1821). The woodblocks are now in the British Museum Department of Prints and Drawings.
  Blake later designed and engraved a charming plate of the "Hiding of Moses" for *Remember Me! A New Years Gift or Christmas Present [for] 1825 [and 1826]*, which was organized by R.J. Thornton.
† Samuel Palmer letter of 3 May 1860 (*BR* 565 n4).
  Fountain Court with its charming fountain is an important element in Dickens, *Martin Chuzzlewit* (1843), but this is the Fountain Court in The Temple, not the one off the Strand where Blake lived.

The building was near the bottom of a narrow, dark lane off the Strand leading to the muddy banks of the Thames. The neighbourhood was demotic, with children playing in the street and humble conveniences so close that Blake never had to go farther than "the corner of the Court to fetch his porter".* "Once, pot of porter in hand, he espied coming along ... that highly respectable man, William Collins, R.A., whom he had met in society a few evenings before. The Academician was about to shake hands, but seeing the porter, drew up, and did not know him."†

One entered No. 3 Fountain Court through a narrow doorway and climbed a wainscoted staircase with Queen Anne style balustrades to the next floor, where there were doors opening into the Blakes' front and back rooms. The panelled east room had a window looking onto Fountain Court and a door which opened onto the smaller study-bedroom.‡ "Blake often spoke of the beauty of the Thames, as seen from the [*bedroom*] window, looking 'like a bar of gold'."§ 67

George Richmond remembered that in this study-bedroom

The fire-place was in the far right-hand corner opposite the window; their bed in the left hand, facing the river; a long engraver's table stood under the window (where I watched Blake engrave the *Book of Job*. He worked facing the light), a pile of port-folios and drawings on Blake's right near the only cupboard; and on the poet–artist's left—a pile of books placed flatly one on another; no bookcase.**

On the walls of his workroom, close to the engraving table, was a lovingly executed copy of Giulio Romano's illustration of Ovid's *Metamorphoses*, and near it was Dürer's "Melancholy the Mother of Invention".††

---

* Gilchrist (*BR* 235) also says that "During one period, he, for two years together, never went out at all" except to the corner pub. Linnell's diary demonstrates that this is extravagant hyperbole, though it is true that Blake was much confined by illness during 1826–27.

† Gilchrist (*BR* 307):

> Blake would tell the story very quietly, and without sarcasm.... His habits were very temperate. It was only in later years he took porter regularly. He then fancied it soothed him, and would sit and muse over his pint after a one o'clock dinner. When he drank wine, which, at home, of course, was seldom, he professed a liking to drink off good draughts from a tumbler, and thought the wine glass system absurd ....

And see Addenda, below.

‡ Gilchrist (*BR* 565). Gilchrist (1880), I, 322, 348 says that the back room was 12′ x 13′, with the fireplace at the northwest corner at an angle. For Frederick Shields's drawing of it, see Gilchrist (1880), I, 322, 348.

§ See Addenda below.

** George Richmond to Anne Gilchrist (*BR* 566). The well-informed anonymous author of the obituary in the *Literary Gazette* (18 Aug 1827) described "his bed in one corner, his meagre dinner in another, a ricketty table holding his copper-plates, his colours, books ... , his large drawings, sketches and MSS".

†† Samuel Palmer letter of 23 Aug 1855 in Gilchrist (*BR* 565 n3). The untraced copy of Giulio Romano's Ovid is Butlin #846. Palmer speaks of "His delightful working corner ... [*with*] its implements ready—tempting to the hand" (Palmer letter of 3 May 1860 in Gilchrist [*BR* 565 n4]).

Most of Blake's pictures were in the reception room, where must also have been kept his great printing press. When the press was set up to print copies of *Songs of Innocence and of Experience* (X) and *Marriage of Heaven and Hell* (I) for Wainewright and others on paper watermarked 1825, there must have been precious little space in the Blakes' flat for anything else.

From the reception room window, one looked out onto narrow, dark Fountain Court—but Blake looked out onto vision. "'That is heaven,' he said to a friend leading him to the window, and pointing to a group of them [*children*] at play."*

Crabb Robinson, who called on Blake in Fountain Court in 1825, found him

at work engraving in a small bedroom, light and looking out on a mean yard—Everything in the room squalid and indicating poverty except himself And there was a natural gentility about him and an insensibility to the seeming poverty which quite removed the impression [*of squalor*] . . . he begged me to sit down, as if he were in a palace— There was but one chair in the room besides that on which he sat— On my putting my hand to it, I found that it would have fallen to pieces if I had lifted it, So, as if I had been a Sybarite, I said with a smile, ["]will you let me indulge myself?["] And I sat on the bed—and near him[.][68]

The poverty of the rooms—without even a bookcase—was merely a trifling outward appearance. "'I live in a hole here,' he would say, 'but God has a beautiful mansion for me elsewhere.'"†

In these enchanted rooms in Fountain Court, Blake made his drawings and engravings for Job and Dante; these rooms were The House of the Interpreter to the young Ancients; and in these rooms he sang and died.

The Distress of Blake and Job

Blake's circumstances were even narrower in Fountain Court than they had been in South Molton Street. As Linnell explained,

---

* Samuel Palmer letter of 23 Aug 1855 to Gilchrist (*BR* 566 n4). Jesus said "little Children always behold the Face of the Heavenly Father" (Blake's marginalium [*c*. 1820] to George Berkeley, *Siris* [1744], 212).

    The exterior of Fountain Court is depicted in F.W. Fairholt, "Tombs of English Artists. No. 7.— William Blake", *Art Journal* (1858) (reproduced in *BR* at p. 563), showing a three-storey red-brick building plus a half-basement and fourth-floor garrets, with an ornamental iron fence in front. The building was torn down in 1902.

† Gilchrist (*BR* 567). When "Mr. Ruddall the Flautist" called on him, Blake "told his visitor that he had a palace of his own of great beauty and magnificence. On Mr. Ruddall's looking round the room for evidence, Blake remarked, 'You don't think I'm such a fool as to think this is it'" (J.J.G. Wilkinson's account in J. Spilling, "Blake the Visionary", *New Church Magazine* [1887] [*BRS* 76]).

W.Blake inv & sc

London. as Act directs Published March 8. 1825 by William Blake N° 3 Fountain Court Strand

Proof

it was here that he began to feel the want of employment* and before I knew his distress he had sold all his collection of old prints to Mess Colnaghi & Co.— after that I represented his case to Sir Tho.ˢ Lawrence, Mʳ Collins, R.A. & some other members of the Royal academy who kindly brought it before the Council & they voted him a donation of 25£ which was sent to him through my hands & for which he expressed great thankfulness— this however was not enough to afford him permanent support & it was in hopes of obtaining a profit sufficient to supply his future wants that the publication of Job was begun at my suggestion & expense[.]†

Blake had been making designs related to Job for over thirty-five years.‡ The most important set of these Job designs were the nineteen watercolours he had made for Thomas Butts in 1805–6. They must have appealed strongly to Linnell's deeply religious nature when Blake described or showed them to him. Here was a project which could serve the spirit at the same time that it displayed Blake's genius and provided employment and support for him.

---

* When Blake made his Job engravings, he had "no larger income than some seventeen or eighteen shillings per week" (Cunningham [*BR* 499]). Had it not been "for Linnell Blake's last years would have been employed ... [*in*] making a set of Morland's pig and ploughboy subjects", as W.M. Rossetti was told in 1863, he thought by Alexander Munro (1825–71) (*BR* 274).
    Linnell also commissioned Blake to begin his plate of the engraver "Wilson Lowry" (father of Varley's wife), for which he paid Blake £25 (on 18 Aug, 10 Nov, 25 Dec 1824, 28 Jan 1825 [*BR* 587, 588, 604]); Linnell was paid £31.10.0 for the finished work, which was published 1 Jan 1825 (*BRS* 80, 122).

† Linnell letter of 3 April 1830. Linnell applied to the Royal Academy charity through William Collins on behalf of "William Blake an able Designer & Engraver laboring under great distress", and the application was approved on 28 June 1822. Henry Howard, the committee's recording secretary, "said he would give one of his fingers to design figures like Blake", according to Samuel Palmer's letter of 1864 (*BRS* 79).

‡ His great history engraving inscribed "Job What is Man That thou shouldest Try him Every Moment?" was begun in 1786 and published in 1793, and the frontispiece to *For Children: The Gates of Paradise* (1793) bears the beginning of the same inscription. In *The Marriage* pl. 5, ¶17, he wrote that "in the book of Job Miltons Messiah is call'd Satan", and he made separate watercolours of "Job and His Daughters" (*c.* 1799–1800) and of "Job Confessing His Presumption to God who Answers from the Whirlwind" (1803–5) (Butlin #394, 461).

A "book" of twenty plates, with text only for plate-captions and a title page, was not so eccentric as might at first appear. Not only had Flaxman's designs for *The Iliad* (1793), *The Odyssey* (1793), Aeschylus (1795), Dante (1802), and Hesiod (1817) demonstrated that important volumes of designs could appropriately be published without extensive text, but there was a long tradition in England of publishing suites of illustrations to the Bible independently of the text of the King James translation, which was inconveniently protected by perpetual Crown copyright.[69] A great advantage of such a publication was that no troublesome payment need be made to author or compositor; in effect, only designer, engraver, paper-maker, and printer need be paid, and for Job the two last need not be paid until Blake had finished his work as designer and engraver.

Thomas Butts generously "lent the [*Job*] Drawing[s] to Copy",[70] waiving any copyright claim he may have had as purchaser.* Linnell made tracings of the watercolours on 7–8 and 10 September 1821, Blake finished the tracings on the 10th, and he returned the drawings to Butts on the 11th.

Blake's designs derive partly from the Job tradition in illustration, which differs significantly from the account in the Old Testament. Sometimes, as in the frescos in St Stephen's Chapel, Westminster, these variants are based on the apocryphal testament of Job.[71] For instance, in the visual tradition Job was taken to prefigure Christ and even to be a bishop, and Blake shows Gothic, presumably ecclesiastical, buildings in his first and fourth Job designs. Similarly, in the testament of Job the patriarch tells his daughters to worship God in music, and indeed Job was taken to be the patron saint of music until he was displaced about 1600 by St Cecilia. In Blake's first and last designs, Job and his family are shown with musical instruments (Pl. 129).

Blake made three major additions to the suite of nineteen designs he had created for Butts in 1805–6. In the first place, at a late stage he made illuminated borders to surround the central designs. As Linnell remarked, these "borders were an afterthought, and designed as well as engraved upon the copper without a previous drawing".†* Sometimes these marginal designs are chiefly decorative (Figs on pp. 395 and 400), and sometimes they directly illustrate Job's story, as when Satan with his sword is seen in the fourth design "Going to & fro in the Earth & walking up & down in it" and in the six days of creation in the fourteenth design (Pl. 20).

---

*   Since Butts was not a publisher, presumably the copyright in the Job designs remained with Blake; the right to reproduce a design did not necessarily or perhaps even customarily belong to the owner of the object unless an explicit agreement was made at the time of purchase, as with Blake's designs for Cromek's edition of *The Grave* (1808).

†   Linnell letter of 27 Sept 1844 (*BR* 326–7). However, some pencil suggestions of borders are on the Job sketches which Blake dated "1823" (Fitzwilliam Museum, Butlin #557) and on three proofs (Rosenwald Collection, U.S. National Gallery of Art, Butlin #559).

In the second place, he added very extensive inscriptions round the designs. Most of these are from the Book of Job, but on the first and last designs he added his own interpretation of the essence of what he called "Job's Captivity":

Prayer to God is the Study of Imaginative Art
Praise to God is the Exercise of Imaginative Art[72]

These crucial hints he later erased.

And in the third place, perhaps after he had begun his engravings, he added two new designs (the seventeenth and twentieth) of God blessing Job and his wife and of Job telling his trials to his daughters; the latter copied the marvellous tempera he had made for Butts about 1799–1800. As a compliment to Butts, he gave him the watercolours of these new designs to complete his set of twenty-one Job designs.

Blake also made numerous small adaptations of his watercolours for the engravings. For instance, in the Butts watercolour of "The Sons of God Shouting for Joy", four sons of God throw up their arms in exultation, but, in the engraving, arms of other sons of God appear at the margins, implying that there is an infinite number of rejoicing sons (Pl. 20).

Apparently when the Job drawings were traced, the plan for engraving them had not yet been formulated. It was only eighteen months later that Linnell drew up a very generous

Memorandum of Agreement between William Blake and John Linnell. March 25.th 1823—

W. Blake agrees to Engrave the Set of Plates from his own Designs of Job's Captivity in number twenty,* for John Linnell—and John Linnell agrees to pay William Blake five Pounds p.^r Plate or one hundred Pounds for the set part before and the remainder when the Plates are finished, as Mr Blake may require it, besides which J. Linnell agrees to give W. Blake one hundred pounds more out of the Profits of the work as the receipts will admit of it.

    Signed J. Linnell   Willm Blake

N.B. J.L. to find Copper Plates.[†]

---

* The twenty plates specified in the Memorandum consist of the nineteen for Butts plus an added title page.

† Linnell paid £3.5.7 for eighteen copperplates in 1823 and 6s. for two more in 1825 (*BR* 602). There is no record of the cost of the last two plates; perhaps these were the two plates which had already been used for another purpose (*BBS* 195 n10) and for which Blake may have paid little or nothing. Most of the Job copperplates were made by R. Pontifex, 22, Lisle Street, Soho.

The payment for the engravings was of course inadequate for a master-piece but sufficient for the man. Blake had been paid £5.5.0 each for his out-line etchings for Flaxman's *Iliad* (1805) and *Hesiod* (1817), but for each of his finished quarto line-engravings in Hayley's biographies of Cowper (1803) and Romney (1809) he had received £31.10.0. The possibility of £100 more in royalties for Job was unimaginable for mere copy-engraving.

Linnell paid Blake a pound or two at a time, and Blake got on with the work as he was able or inclined.* The first payment for Job was £5.0.0 "Cash on acc! of the foregoing agreement", and Blake signed his receipt on the back of the Memorandum.[73] As Linnell wrote, "he was always paid before hand for what he did for me".[74] Blake had had the same arrange-ment with Butts for his watercolours of 1803–10, and it suited him very well. For his Job, Linnell paid him £45 in 1823, £53.7.9 in 1824, and £47.6.6 in 1825.[75] With his income thus assured, Blake could get on with his visions.

Linnell paid Blake occasionally not in cash but in cauldrons of coal,[76] per-haps at unpredictable intervals. Once, as Edward Calvert's son told the story, in Fountain Court,

> there came lumbering up the stairs with heavy tread an uncouth visitor who bumped at the door. Blake, somewhat disturbed, rose to open it, but with no ungentlemanly impatience, for he never knew in what shape, or under what circumstances, his angels might appear. It was, however, "the man with the coals," who, humped up with sack, gigantic and grimy, muttered out, "Are these 'ere coals for you?"
>
> ... "I believe not, my good man, but I'll enquire," and, as my father regretfully said: "they were *not* poor Blake's coals—they were for the lodger on the floor above".†

Proofs of Job were "printed by Blake himself or by M.rs Blake at his own press"‡ in his own living-room.

By the autumn of 1823 at least one of the Job plates was sufficiently fin-

---

* Linnell said that Blake's Dante designs and engravings (1824 ff.) were produced "with the express [*though apparently only oral*] understanding that ... he was doing as little or as much as he pleased for me in return [for money advanced to him]. If they had been ever so slight or few they were all I sh.d have had for what I gave him" (Linnell letter of 16 March 1831). Blake's Job was almost certainly produced on the same terms.

† [Samuel Calvert], *A Memoir of Edward Calvert* Artist (1893) (*BR* 326), paragraphing added. Stothard's son said: "on one occasion I ... met him [*Blake*] on the stairs, saying to me 'he had a battle with the devil below to obtain the coals'", and it was apparently "Leigh, the artist" who said of Blake, "he even saw the devil in his coal-cellar" (*BR* 326 n1).

‡ Tatham's inscription on pl. 7 in the British Museum Print Room (*BB* 519). Four to fifteen working proofs survive for each plate (*BBS* 195). Working proofs should be distinguished from the 215 sets of published plates on India and French paper each inscribed "Proof".

ished to show to patrons and solicit subscriptions.[77] But they were not far enough advanced to think of printing them until eighteen months later. On 4 March 1825 Linnell and Blake went to Dixon the copperplate printer to take proofs of Job, and next day they went to James Lahee at Castle Street, Oxford Market, to see if his work was of better quality.[78] They were confident enough that the work was finished for Blake to inscribe each plate: "London Published as the Act directs March 8: 1825 by William Blake N° 3 Fountain Court Strand".

However, it was not until a year later that a label was devised adding Linnell's name as publisher: "Published by the Author, 3, Fountain Court, Strand, and Mr. J. Linnell, 6, Cirencester Place, Fitzroy Square, March, 1826".* Linnell drafted an advertisement, saying that "These Plates are engraved entirely by Mr Blake with the graver only (that is without the aid of aqua fortis)."[79]

In February 1826 the plates were printed at Lahee's "by a man of the name of Freeman".[80] There were 65 French paper "Proofs", 150 India paper "Proofs", and 100 plain copies on "Drawing paper" after the word "Proof" was erased from each plate.* These proved to be enough to last Linnell for 50 years.[†]

Blake's great suite of illustrations for the Book of Job show that "The Prince of this World shall be cast out"; "Great & Marvellous are thy Works Lord God Almighty".[81] They are triumphs of design and engraving in the old style that Blake had learned in his youth and perfected with Linnell's help in his old age. But, as the great art scholar Bo Lindberg concludes: "The restoration of engraving on copper knows one name, Blake, and it died with him."[82]

A few enthusiasts sustained Linnell's judgment about Blake's Job engravings. Thomas Griffiths Wainewright wrote as soon as he received his copy:

---

* *BR* 327. To clarify the ambiguity of the imprints on the plates ("Published ... March 8: 1825 by William Blake") and on the label ("Published by the Author ... and Mr. J. Linnell ... March, 1826"), Blake wrote in his letter to Linnell of 14 July 1826:

I hereby Declare, That Mr John Linnell has Purchased of M*e*, The Plates & Copy-right of Job; & the same is his sole Property.
Witness   William Blake
Edwd Jno Chance [Linnell's nephew]

And the same day he made out a receipt:

Recievd of Mr John Linnell, the Sum of One Hundred & fifty Pounds for the Copy-right & plates (Twenty-two in number) of the Book of Job. Publishd March 1825 by Me: William Blake Author of the Work.
                                        N° 3 Fountain Court Strand
Witness: Edwd Jno Chance

In fact, by 30 Oct 1825 Blake had been paid "on acc^t of Job" £150.19.3 (*BR* 605), which is £50.19.3 more than was required in the contract.

"The plates are as exquisitely engraved as grandly conceived"; Edward Denny spoke of their "exquisite beauty and marvellous grandeur", which are "truly sublime"; and Edward FitzGerald said that they were "terrible, awful, and wonderful".[83]

But Bernard Barton reflected more accurately the taste of connoisseurs: "There is a dryness and hardness in Blake's manner of engraving which is very apt to be repulsive to print-collectors in general . . . his style is little calculated to take with admirers of modern engraving."[84]

The work sold but slowly, and five years later Linnell wrote that "the Job only paid the expenses of printing & paper".[†]

The Ancients and the Interpreter

The little group of young men and boys who called themselves the Ancients

---

* Linnell's Job accounts (*BR* 602–3) include payments for

Copperplates	£ 3.11. 7
Proofs in 1825	£ 6.10. 0
Binding [?proofs] Nov 1825	£ . 7. 6
"to Mᵣ Lahee for 150 sets of Proofs on India paper"	£ 56. 5. 0
"for 65 Setts of Job on french paper"	£ 16. 3. 0
For 100 sets "on Drawing paper"	£ 21. 0. 0
"to Freeman the workman" [customary beer money]	£ 1. 0. 0
"to Mr White for Boarding" and paper	£ 3.10. 6
For "Mᵣ Leighton for Bindᵍ & paper &c"	£ 13.17. 0
TOTAL	**£111.15. 6**

On 30 Dec 1863 Linnell wrote to the publisher Macmillan that "about 300 sets including the India proofs & French paper proofs have been printed, they were all taken from the plates when just finished" (*BR* 327).

† Linnell printed 100 more sets of Job in 1874 (*BB* 524), the last time they have been printed. India "Proof" sets (1826) were still in the Linnell family long after Linnell's death in 1882, and some, such as the ones reproduced here, were among the 68 sets of Job sold by the Linnells at Christie's, 15 March 1918, Lots 183–9.

‡ Linnell letter of 16 March 1831; in fact, the receipts for Job come to a little more than this (*BR* 408 n1), though "The Work has never yet been advertized" (Linnell letter of Jan 1830).

consisted chiefly of Edward Calvert, Samuel Palmer, George Richmond, and Frederick Tatham. In 1824, when he first met Blake, Samuel Palmer was nineteen years old, as was the impressionable Frederick Tatham; George Richmond was fifteen then; and Edward Calvert, at twenty-five, was married and self-supporting. Others on the periphery of the group included Samuel Palmer's cousin John Giles who spoke in raptures of the "divine Blake" who "had seen God, sir, and had talked with Angels";[85] Frederick Tatham's brother Arthur (born in 1809); Samuel Palmer's brother William; Welby Sherman; and the artist Francis Oliver Finch (born in 1802), who had heard of Blake when he was Varley's pupil for five years and who said that "Blake struck him as a *new kind of man*, wholly original, and in all things".*

The Ancients held monthly meetings,† and they often called on Blake in The House of the Interpreter, as if, like Christian in *Pilgrim's Progress* on his journey from the City of Destruction to Mount Zion, they "came at the house of the INTERPRETER .... I was told ... that if I called here, you would shew me excellent things, such as would help me in my journey."‡ And like pilgrims everywhere, they had their rituals of piety. George Richmond admitted "that never did he enter Blake's house without imprinting a reverent kiss upon the bell-handle which the seer had touched; nor was he alone in this homage, which was practised by all the band of friends".§

Probably the first of the Ancients to meet Blake was Frederick Tatham (Pl. 136), for his father, the architect and Baptist Charles Heathcote Tatham, had been a friend of Blake for many years. Blake inscribed *America* (B) to C.H. Tatham on 7 October 1799, and, according to Linnell's Journal, on 4 August 1824 "Mr Varley, Mr Tatham & Son Mr Blake dined with me at Hampstead".** The senior Tatham wrote to Linnell, "Can you engage Michael Angelo <u>Blake</u> to meet us at y^r Study, & go up with us?—Such a party of Connoisseurs is worthy apollo & the muses".[86] It was perhaps for this occasion that Catherine Blake inscribed a copy of Blake's engraved portrait of Robert Hawker with one of the sayings Blake had underlined in Lavater's *Aphorisms* a third of a century before:

---

* Gilchrist (*BR* 294). According to Samuel Palmer, "of all the circle perhaps, [*Finch*] was the most inclined to believe in Blake's spiritual intercourse" (letter of Jan 1863 [*BRS* 83]).

† [Samuel Calvert], *A Memoir of Edward Calvert Artist* (1893) (*BR* 295 n1). The term "Ancients" was in use at least as early as Sept 1824, when Palmer sent greetings to Linnell's children: "love to the little ancients".

‡ John Bunyan, *Pilgrim's Progress*, ed. Thomas Scott (London, 1801), Part I, 44–6. It may have been about 1824 that Blake revised his engraving of "The Man Sweeping the Interpreter's Parlour" (*c.* 1794) and began his series of watercolour illustrations to *Pilgrim's Progress*.

§ *The Richmond Papers*, ed. A.M.W. Stirling (1926) (*BR* 292 n4). The somewhat more reliable A.H. Palmer wrote that "No one else [*besides Samuel Palmer*] ever kissed Blake's bell-handle before venturing to pull it" (*BR* 292).

** Blake's *Descriptive Catalogue* (P) is inscribed: "Frederick Tatham from the Author. June 12. 1824".

M^r C Tatham

> The humble is formed to adore;
> the loving to associate

> with eternal Love
> C Blake

John Linnell wrote that at John Martin's Baptist Church "I became intimate with Mr Charles Tatham the Architect .... He took a liking to me and I was very often at his house".* Linnell introduced Blake to Charles Tatham's "Eldest son ... an artist-sculptor, portrait painter in water-colours",[87] and Frederick Tatham came to have a surprising influence upon Blake's life and reputation.

The Tathams were important to the Ancients beyond their devotion to William Blake. John Linnell recalled that

> The Elder Tatham told me with great grief of the elopement of his [*daughter*] Julia with [*George*] Richmond [who was then a visitor with others at my house] for they went to Gretna Green [*to be married*] & Mr Palmer then a beginner in life & unmarried lent Richmond fifty pounds for the purpose. When old Tatham related the affair to me as an event to be deplored I told him flatly that I thought he made a great mistake & that he might congratulate himself for that Richmond w^d I had no doubt do well and be a credit to him & the family. ["]Do you think so my dear fellow[?"] he said. ["]I am really delighted to hear you speak so confidently."[88]

The youngest and most engaging of the Ancients was George Richmond.

As a lad of sixteen [*in 1825*], he met Blake one day at the elder Tatham's, and was allowed to walk home with him. To the boy, it was "as if he were walking with the Prophet Isaiah";† for he had heard much of Blake, greatly admired all he had heard, and all he had seen of his designs. ...

On this occasion he talked of his own youth, and of his visions. ... Mr. Richmond relates that ... he would himself ... boldly argue and disagree, as

---

* Linnell Autobiography f. 79. Later "C. Tatham got tired & ashamed of being a Dissenter, thinking it hindered his advancing his son" Arthur as a clergyman (f. 80).

† According to A.M.W. Stirling (ed., *The Richmond Papers* [1926] [*BR* 293 n2]), "my father said: 'I felt like walking on air, and as if I had been talking to the Prophet Isaiah'". This may well be merely an embroidery of Gilchrist.

though they were equal in years and wisdom, and Blake would take it all good-humouredly. "Never," adds Mr. Richmond, "have I known an artist so spiritual, so devoted, so single-minded, or cherishing imagination as he did."

Once, the young artist, finding his invention flag during a whole fort-night, went to Blake, as was his wont, for some advice or comfort. He found him sitting at tea with his wife. He related his distress; how he felt deserted by the power of invention.

To his astonishment, Blake turned to his wife suddenly and said: "It is just so with us, is it not, for weeks together, when the visions forsake us? What do we do then, Kate?"

"We kneel down and pray, Mr. Blake."[89]

In April 1825 Richmond brought one of his first pictures, "The Shepherd Abel" (1825), to show to Blake, and Blake "made a careful correction drawing of the shepherd's arm in his pupil's sketch-book",[90] which Richmond inscribed: "drawn by W Blake to help me in my picture of 'Abel'. 1825".[*]

The young men were enormously impressed by Blake's powers of concentration and vision. He "once said to Mr. Richmond, 'I can look at a knot in a piece of wood till I am frightened at it.' "[91]

The oldest of the Ancients was the artist Edward Calvert, who introduced himself to Blake.[92] They became firm friends, and one evening Blake visited Calvert and his wife in their home at 17 Russell Street, Brixton. Late that night

> when Blake and Calvert were trying some etching-ground, and melting it on the fire, the pipkin cracked, setting the chimney in a blaze, and all was flame and convolution of smoke. Here was material for weird suggestion, not unacceptable to Blake, whose anxiety, however, in his kindliness of nature, was not for the fire, but that Mrs. Calvert, who had retired to bed, should not be alarmed.[†]

Of course the conflagration was put out with no damage other than to the etching-ground and the pipkin.

---

[*]   *BRS* 83; Butlin #802 1 (a); two seated figures on the same page are identified there by Samuel Palmer as "Drawn by Mr Blake. April 4th 1825".

   The only Blake writings Richmond is known to have owned (*Europe* pl. 4, ?6–7, ?*Urizen* pl. 2, "Joseph of Arimathea Among the Rocks of Albion" [E]) were probably acquired after his death, as were the drawings he acquired from his brother-in-law Frederick Tatham. The only probable exception is the picture "Drawn by Mʳ Blake to shew me what Fuselli's mouth was when a young man" (Butlin #802 2).

[†]   [Samuel Calvert], *A Memoir of Edward Calvert Artist* (1893) (*BR* 333). The event happened after May 1826 when the Calverts moved to Brixton.

   Calvert's copy of Blake's *Songs* (Y) was probably acquired after Blake's death.

The most enthusiastic and devoted of the Ancients was Samuel Palmer, a pious and conservative young artist. The memory of his meeting with Blake remained a joy to him all his life: "At my never-to-be-forgotten first interview, ... the copper of the first plate—'Thus did Job continually'—was lying on the table where he had been working at it. How lovely it looked by the lamplight, strained through the tissue paper."*

Thirty years later, he wrote to Gilchrist:

I can never forget the evening when Mr. Linnell took me to Blake's house, nor the quiet hours passed with him [*elsewhere*] in the examination of antique gems, choice pictures, and Italian prints of the sixteenth century. . . .

No man more admired Albert Dürer;† yet, after looking over a number of his designs, he would become a little angry with some of the draperies, as not governed by the form of the limbs, nor assisting to express their action; contrasting them in this respect with the draped antique, in which it was hard to tell whether he was more delighted with the general design, or with the exquisite finish and the depth of the chiselling . . . .

He united freedom of judgment with reverence for all that is great. He did not look out for the works of the purest ages, but for the purest work of every age and country—Athens or Rhodes, Tuscany or Britain; but no authority or popular consent could influence him against his deliberate judgment. Thus he thought with Fuseli and Flaxman that the Elgin Theseus, however full of antique savour, could not, as ideal form, rank with the very finest relics of antiquity. Nor, on the other hand, did the universal neglect of Fuseli in any degree lessen his admiration of his best works.

He fervently loved the early Christian art, and dwelt with peculiar affection on the memory of Fra Angelico, often speaking of him as an inspired inventor and as a saint; but when he approached Michael Angelo, the Last Supper of Da Vinci, the Torso Belvidere, and some of the inventions preserved in the antique gems, all his powers were concentrated in admiration . . . .

He loved to speak of the years spent by Michael Angelo, without

---

* Gilchrist (*BR* 282). "*It* is customary to engrave beneath the shade of silk paper, stretched on a square frame, which is placed reclining towards the room near the sill of a window", because "the uninterrupted light of the day causes a glare upon the surface of the copper, hurtful and dazzling to the eyes" (W. Nicholson, *The British Encyclopedia* [London, 1809)], III, C5ʳ).

   There was a confusion of Palmers near Blake at the end of his life: not only his disciple Samuel Palmer and Samuel's brother William but also Mary Ann Linnell's father Thomas, a Baptist in John Martin's church who dined with Blake on 18 Oct 1825 and who delivered coal to him (at Linnell's expense) on 5 May 1825 and 27 Jan 1826 (*BR* 306, 588, 589), and her uncle Benjamin of Palmer and Son, Upholsterers & Cabinet Manufacturers, who buried Blake (*BR* 342–3).

† According to Samuel Palmer: "Of Albert Dürer, he remarked that his most finished woodcuts, when closely examined, seemed to consist principally of outline;—that they were 'everything and yet nothing'" (*BR* 315).

earthly reward, and solely for the love of God, in the building of St. Peter's, and of the wondrous architects of our cathedrals.*

And Palmer said that Julio Romano's "Nursing of Jove",

is precisely the picture Blake would have revelled in. I think I hear him say, "As fine as possible, Sir. It is not permitted to man to do better." He delighted to think of Raphael, Giulio Romano, Polidoro, and others, working together in the chambers of the Vatican, engaged, without jealousy, as he imagined, in the carrying out of one great common object; and he used to compare it (without any intentional irreverence) to the co-labours of the holy Apostles. He dwelt on this subject very fondly ....

Among spurious old pictures, he had met with many "Claudes," but spoke of a few which he had seen really untouched and unscrubbed, with the greatest delight; and mentioned, as a peculiar charm, that in these, when minutely examined, there were, upon the focal lights of the foliage, small specks of pure white which made them appear to be glittering with dew which the morning sun had not yet dried up. ... His description of these genuine Claudes, I shall never forget. He warmed with his subject, and it continued through an evening walk. The sun was set; but Blake's Claudes made sunshine in that shady place.[93]

Both Linnell and Blake served as drawing-masters to Palmer. On 2 January 1825 Palmer wrote in his notebook:

I went with him [*Linnell*] to Mr. B., who also [*like Linnell*], on seeing my ... [sketch-books], gave me above my hope, over-much praise; and these praises from equally valued judgements did (God overruling) not in the least tend to presumption and idleness, and but little to pride.

He wrote to Gilchrist about a visit in May 1824 to the Royal Academy with "Blake in his plain black suit and *rather* broad-rimmed, but not quakerish hat, standing so quietly among all the dressed-up, rustling, swelling people, and myself thinking 'How little you know *who* is among you!'"†

---

[84]* Gilchrist (*BR* 282–3). For a picture of "One of the Gothic Artists who Built the Cathedrals in what we call the Dark Ages", see "Joseph of Arimathea Among The Rocks of Albion" (Pl. 15).

[85]* Gilchrist (*BR* 280). The Royal Academy made a concerted effort to exclude the ragged and the impecunious. Gilchrist wrote (*BR* 280–1):

In his dress ... In-doors, he was careful, for economy's sake, but not slovenly: his clothes were threadbare, and his grey trousers had worn black and shiny in front, like a mechanic's. Out of doors, he was more particular, so that his dress did not, in the streets of London, challenge attention either way. He wore black knee breeches and buckles, black worsted stockings, shoes which tied, and a broad-brimmed hat. It was something like an old-fashioned tradesman's dress.

Palmer loved to remember what he had learned from Blake about the great artists.

When looking at the heads of the apostles in the copy of the *Last Supper* at the Royal Academy, he remarked of all but Judas, "Every one looks as if he had conquered the natural man." He was equally ready to admire a contemporary and a rival. Fuseli's picture of *Satan building the Bridge over Chaos* he ranked with the grandest efforts of imaginative art, and said that we were two centuries behind the civilization which would enable us to estimate his *Ægisthus.**

Years later Palmer recalled:

On Saturday, 9th October, 1824, Mr. Linnell called and went with me to Mr. Blake. We found him lame in bed, of a scalded foot (or leg). There, not inactive, though [*almost*] sixty-seven years old, but hard-working on a bed covered with books sat he up like one of the Antique patriarchs, or a dying Michael Angelo.† Thus and there was he making in the leaves of a great book (folio) the sublimest design from his (not superior) Dante. He said he began them with fear and trembling.
I said "O! I have enough of fear and trembling."
"Then," said he, "you'll do."‡
He designed them (100 I think) during a fortnight's illness in bed! And there, first, with fearfulness (which had been more, but that his designs from Dante had wound me up to forget myself), did I show him some of my first essays in design; and the sweet encouragement he gave me (for Christ blessed little children) did not tend basely to presumption and idleness, but made me work harder and better that afternoon and night. And, after visiting him, the scene recurs to me afterwards in a kind of vision ... such a place for primitive grandeur, whether in the persons of Mr. and Mrs. Blake, or in the things hanging on the walls.[94]

---

* Gilchrist (*BR* 281–2). I find no such subject in the catalogues raisonnés of Gert Schiff, *Johann Heinrich Füssli 1741-1825* (Zurich: Verlag Berichthaus; Munich: Prestel-Verlag, 1994) or D.H. Weinglass, *Prints and Engraved Illustrations By and After Henry Fuseli* (Aldershot: Scolar Press, 1994).
    In his letter of June 1806, Blake wrote of being told by "A gentleman who visited me the other day", that "Mr. Fuseli ... is a hundred years beyond the present generation".
† "Once, a young artist called and complained of being very ill: 'What was he to do?' 'Oh!' said Blake, 'I never stop for anything; I work on, whether ill or not'" (Gilchrist [*BR* 233 n5]).
‡ "Trembling I sit day and night, my friends are astonish'd at me" (*Jerusalem* pl. 5, l. 16); "Tremble" and its derivatives are among Blake's favourite words.

On one occasion, Palmer persuaded Blake and the Calverts to accompany him about twenty miles from London to his grandfather's cottage in the bucolic village of Shoreham, Kent, which Palmer loved to paint. Edward Calvert's son remembered a family story that

The journey was, to the satisfaction of all parties, performed in one of those covered stage waggons of the period .... Edward Calvert and Mrs. Calvert had arranged for seats in the van belonging to Russell the carrier, whose route was from Charing Cross to Tunbridge Wells, and therein, with Blake and Palmer snugly ensconced, and—possibly on this occasion Mrs. Blake—the heavy-wheeled vehicle, drawn by an eight or ten-horse team, jogged on in the good old style. The well-kept horses were caparisoned ... with hoops and bells, and those large flapping flanges, or housings as they are called, which Palmer said were the rudiments or degenerate wings of the ancient Pegasus ....

And then came the welcome at the house, or rather cottage, with its quaint gables, heavily thatched and overgrown, such as our Samuel Palmer loved to introduce into his pictures. We see the interesting group disposed around and within the huge chimney hearth, the room having vaulted beams supporting the upper floor. In this room they sat and talked, the elder Palmer in knee breaches and gaiters—quite of the old school.

Calvert and his wife were accorded the best room the house could offer, Mr. Blake being accommodated by a neighbour over the way, while Samuel Palmer had a warm and no doubt congenial shake-down at the village bakery. The next day Blake took up his position in the far corner of the chimney, with my father and old Palmer seated opposite. They talked of the divine gift of Art and Letters, and of spiritual vision and inspiration, and of what they termed "the traverse of sympathy". And this, naturally enough, elicited from old Palmer the story of the ghost which was said to haunt a half-ruined mansion close by. ...

On the proposal of Calvert, it was agreed that the haunted premises should be visited that night, and the eerie mystery investigated. Calvert believed in adventure, and Blake believed in ghosts, and the younger Palmer believed in Blake. And so, providing themselves with candles and lanthorn, they were ready for the exploit.

The usual associations belonging to every respectably haunted house were not wanting. The wind came eddying round, "moaning through the tortuous fissures and partly dismantled windows". The moon was down, and a sense of solemnity, not to say awe took possession of Palmer as, holding the lanthorn, their weird shadows crossed each other on the broken walls.

Then ... a curious rattling sound was heard, and they hushed and listened. In reality, a tapping, grating noise was distinctly audible. Palmer was transfixed. What Blake did is unfortunately not recorded; but Calvert was curiously interested; and, following the sound, he approached an oriel window, Palmer bringing up the light. Here they discovered a large snail crawling up the mullion, while his shell oscillated on some casement glass with strange significance. . . .

The following evening William Blake was occupied at the table in the large room, or kitchen. Old Palmer was smoking his long pipe in the recess, and Calvert, as was his custom, sat with his back to the candles reading. Young Samuel Palmer had taken his departure more than an hour before for some engagement in London, this time in the coach.

Presently Blake, putting his hand to his forehead, said quietly: "Palmer is coming; he is walking up the road."

"Oh, Mr. Blake, he's gone to London; we saw him off in the coach."

Then, after a while, "He is coming through the wicket—there!"— pointing to the closed door. And surely, in another minute, Samuel Palmer raised the latch and came in amongst them.

It so turned out that the coach had broken down near to the gate of Lullingstone Park.[95]

Samuel Palmer did not dispute with Blake—"No one could imagine Palmer arguing with Blake as Richmond did"[96]—but he selected from Blake's ideas only those which were congenial to him. His evidence about Blake is not corrupt but partial. As a result of Samuel Palmer's conventional piety and rooted conservatism and of Gilchrist's dependence upon Palmer, the portrait of Blake available to the Victorians was far less radical than is congenial to the fiery spirits of the later twentieth century. Blake's ideas as reported by Samuel Palmer, particularly concerning the established Church, sound much more like the views of a High Anglican than like those of the man who in 1827 attacked Dr Thornton's "Tory Translation" of The Lord's Prayer as "Saying the Lords Prayer Backwards", as a defence of Satan "who is father & God of this World[,] the Accuser".[97]

For instance, Palmer wrote to Gilchrist: "he quite held forth one day to me, on the Roman Catholic Church being the only one which taught the forgiveness of sins; and he repeatedly expressed his belief that there was more *civil* liberty under the Papal government, than any other sovereignty . . .".* Palmer spoke of Blake's "preference for ecclesiastical governments.

---

* Palmer letter of 24 July 1862 (*BR* 321 n5). Gilchrist concludes from statements like this that Blake "had a sentimental liking for the Romish Church, and . . . would often try to make out that priestly despotism was better than kingly. 'He believed no subjects of monarchies were so happy as the Pope's'" (*BR* 42).

He used to ask how it was that we heard so much of priestcraft, and so little of soldiercraft ...."*

Palmer urged the emasculation of Blake's works which were to be printed in Gilchrist's book:

I should let no passage appear in which the word Bible, or those of the persons of the blessed Trinity, or the Messiah were irreverently connected ....

I think the whole page [*from the MARRIAGE*] ... would at once exclude the work from every drawingroom table in England. Blake has said the same kind of thing to me ....†

And Linnell wrote of Blake the controversialist:

A saint amongst the infidels & a heretic with the orthodox[,] with all the admiration for Blake it must be confessed that he said many things tending to the corruption of Xtian morals—even when unprovoked by controversy[,] & when opposed by the superstitious the crafty or the proud he outraged all common sense & rationality by the opinions he advanced occasionally even indulging in the support of the most lax interpretation of the precepts of the scripture[.][98]

Linnell and Palmer were, as W.B. Yeats said of Linnell's grandchildren, "no little troubled at the thought that maybe he [*Blake*] was heretical. I ... found it hard to get the great mystic into their little thimble."[99]

Crabb Robinson on Blake's "Wild & Strange Rhapsodies"

In the same years that the eager and impecunious Ancients were worshipping at The House of the Interpreter, Linnell and Varley were introducing Blake to altogether grander company. Varley "took Blake to Lady Blessington's house in St. James's Square to dine" among "a sort of menagerie of small [*social*] lions", Blake wearing "the simplest form of attire as then worn, which included thick shoes and worsted stockings".[100]

Among the social lions may have been "A Historical painter, of the class

---

* *BR* 42. Tatham said that "he detested priestcraft" (*BR* 530).
† Samuel Palmer letter of 24 July 1862 (BR 319). Anne Gilchrist wrote to W.M. Rossetti on 6 Oct 1862 (*Letters of Dante Gabriel Rossetti to William Allingham, 1854–1870* [1897], 259): "It was no use to put in [the *Visions of the Daughters of Albion*] what I was perfectly certain Macmillan (who reads all the proofs) would take out again. He is far more inexorable against any shade of heterodoxy in morals than in religion."

endlessly industrous yet forever unknown". When he showed Blake one of his paintings of "hopeless hugeness", Blake said politely, "Ah! that is what I have been trying to do all my life—to paint *round*—and never could."[101]

Linnell also took Blake out among the lions. Among Linnell's patrons were Elizabeth and Charles Aders,* friendly, prosperous, and generous connoisseurs at whose elegant house at 11 Euston Square he was occasionally invited to dine. The dinner at which Blake's *Virgil* designs were stoutly defended by Linnell, James Ward, Sir Thomas Lawrence, and others was at the Aders' table. Linnell took Blake with him to dine there on 6 August 1825, and Blake particularly relished "seeing again those Pictures of the old Masters" at the Aders' house.[102] It was perhaps during this dinner—

at which Flaxman, Lawrence, and other leading artists were present— [*that*] Blake was talking to a little group gathered round him, within hearing of a lady whose children had just come home from boarding school for the holidays.

"The other evening," said Blake, in his usual quiet way, "taking a walk, I came to a meadow, and at the farther corner of it I saw a fold of lambs. Coming nearer, the ground blushed with flowers; and the wattled cote and its woolly tenants were of exquisite pastoral beauty. But I looked again, and it proved to be no living flock, but beautiful sculpture."

The lady, thinking this a capital holiday-show for her children, eagerly interposed, "I beg pardon, Mr. Blake, but *may* I ask *where* you saw this?"

"*Here*, madam," answered Blake, touching his forehead.[103]

It was at a gathering such as this that "a cultivated stranger, as a mark of polite attention, was showing him the first number [*30 August 1823*] of *The Mechanic's Magazine*. 'Ah, sir,' remarked Blake, with bland emphasis, 'these things we artists HATE!'"[104]

When Linnell and Blake went again to dine with the Aders on 10 December 1825, they found among the guests Henry Crabb Robinson, who had already seen Blake's exhibition, read his *Descriptive Catalogue*, and written an essay about him. When they met at the Aders' dinner table, Crabb Robinson was even more fascinated by Blake in person than he had been when he had only heard about him and seen his works.

Thereafter Crabb Robinson sought out Blake, and he made very exten-

---

*   Eliza Aders (b. 1785) may have known Blake from childhood, for her father was the engraver John Raphael Smith. Both Coleridge and Lamb wrote poems in her album, Coleridge's entitled "To Eliza in Pain" (later called "The Two Founts"), and Blake's drawings of "Los Walking in the Mountains of Albion" and of "Christian with the Shield of Faith Taking Leave of his Companions" from *Pilgrim's Progress* (Butlin #784 and 829 20) were pasted into it.

sive records of "the wild & strange strange rhapsodies utterd by this insane man of genius".[105] Crabb Robinson's diaries give far fuller information about Blake's conversation than may be found anywhere else. Though he could see no principle in Blake's "altogether unmethodical rhapsody on art, religion",[106] Robinson's records are consonant with Blake's writings and designs. They are a treasure-house of gnomic wisdom.

Crabb Robinson called on Blake or dined with him on 10, 17, 24 December 1825, 6 January, 18 February, 12 May, 13 June, 7 December 1826 and 2 February 1827.[107] On the first of these occasions, Robinson drew Blake out to get "from him an avowal of his <u>peculiar</u> sentiments", and in his diary he "put down as they occur to me without method all I can recollect of the conversation of this remarkable man":

> He is now old—pale with a Socratic countenance and an expression of great sweetness but bordering on weakness—except when his features are animated by expression And then he has an air of inspiration about him . . ..
>
> He was shewn soon after he enterd the room some compositions of Mrs Aders' which he cordially praised And he brought with him an engraving of his Canterbury Pilgrims for Aders[.]* One of the figures resembled one in one of Aders' pictures[.]†
>
> "They say I stole it from this picture, but I did it 20 year's before I knew of the picture—however in my youth I was always studying this kind of paintings. No wonder there is a resemblance—"
>
> In this he seemed to explain <u>humanly</u> what he had done—but he at another time spoke of his paintings as being what he had seen in his visions—And when he said <u>my visions</u> it was in the ordinary unemphatic tone in which we speak of trivial matters that everyone understands & cares nothing about— In the same tone he said—repeatedly the "Spirit told me"—
>
> I took occasion to say—"You use the same word as Socrates used— What resemblance do you suppose is there between your Spirit & the Spirit of Socrates?"
>
> "The same as between our countenances—"
>
> He paused & added—"I was Socrates."

---

* He also brought *Songs* copy AA for the Aders and copy Z for Crabb Robinson. On 3 Jan 1826 Eliza Aders wrote to Linnell, "I have also to beg you, to put me in the way, of repaying Mr Blake in the way most delicate to his feelings, for the books he brought me, as it was by no means either Mr Robinsons intention or mine, to beg the books, when we ask'd for them". For her *Songs*, she paid £5.5.0 to Linnell for transmission to Blake (*BR* 591). Robinson also acquired *America* (D) and *Visions* (O) "from Blake for he thinks 1 guinea", five copies of *Descriptive Catalogue* (including ?J, ?L, N [acquired 1842], S), *Poetical Sketches* (?A [1848], ?O), and *Marriage* (K).

† The Aders collection was particularly strong in German and Flemish Renaissance paintings. Blake almost certainly knew about the collection before he saw it, for Linnell made an engraving of one of the Aders pictures in 1825–26 (*BRS* 107–8).

And then as if correcting himself[:] "A sort of brother— I must have had conversations with him—So I had with Jesus Christ—I have an obscure recollection of having been with both of them—"

It was before this, that I had suggested on very obvious philosophical grounds the <u>impossibility</u> of supposing an immortal being created—An eternity a parte post—with! an eternity a parte ante—. . .

His eye brightened on my saying this And he eagerly concurred—"To be sure it is impossible—We are all coexistent with God—Members of the Divine body—We are all partakers of the divine nature—"

. . . on my asking in what light he viewed the great question concerning the Divinity of Jesus Christ He said—"<u>He is the only God</u>"—But then he added—"And so am I and so are you—"*

Now he had just before . . . been speaking of the errors of Jesus Christ[:] "he was wrong in suffering himself to be crucified[.] He should not have attacked the gov![;] he had no business with such matters[.]"

On my enquiring how he reconciled this with the Sanctity & divine qual^s of Jesus—he said "He was not then become the father—"

Connecting as well as one can These fragmentary Sentim^s it would be hard to fix Blake's station between Christianity Platonism & Spinozism— Yet he professes to be very hostile to Plato & reproaches Wordsworth with be^g not a Xn but a Platonist[.]

[*Hume remarks that some religious speculations tend*] . . . to make Men indifferent to whatever takes place by destroying all ideas of good & evil[.] I took occasion to apply this remark to something Blake said—"If so" I said—"There is no use in discipline or education[;] no difference b^n good & evil—"

He hastily broke in on me—"There is no use in education[.] I hold it wrong—It is the great Sin[.] It is eating of the tree of the knowledge of good & evil—

"That was the fault of Plato—he knew of nothing but of the Virtues & Vices and good & evil. There is nothing in all that—Every thing is good in God's eyes—"

On my putt^g the obvious question—"Is there nothing absolutely evil in what men do"—

"I am no judge of that[.] Perhaps not in God's Eyes—"

Tho' on this & other occasions he spoke as if he denied altogether the existence of evil—And as if we had nothing to do with right & wrong— It being sufficient to consider all things as alike the work of God—(I

---

* See *Jerusalem* pl. 4, ll. 18–19:

  I am not a God afar off, I am a brother and friend;
  Within your bosoms I reside, and you reside in me

interposed with the German word "objectivity" which he approved of—) Yet at other times he spoke of error as being in heaven—

I asked ab^t the <u>moral</u> character of Dante in writ^g his Vision[;] was he <u>pure</u>?—

"<u>Pure</u>" said Blake—"Do y^o think there is any purity in Gods eyes— the angels in heaven are no more so than we. 'he chargeth his Angels with folly.'"* He afterw^d extended this to the Supreme being—"he is liable to error too—Did he not repent him that he had made Ninevah?"

... He spoke with seeming complacency of himself—Said he acted by command— The spirit said to him "Blake be an artist & nothing else. In this there is felicity[.]" His eye glistend while he spoke of the joy of devoting himself solely to divine art— "Art is inspiration[.] When Michael Angelo or Raphael or Mr Flaxman does any of his fine things he does them in the spirit—"

Bl said "I sh^d be sorry if I had any earthly fame for whatever natural glory a man has is so much detracted from his spiritual glory[.] I wish to do nothing for profit. I wish to live for art— I want nothing what^r. I am quite happy—"†

... he was continually expressing ... his distinction between the natural & the spiritual world— The natural world must be consumed—

... <u>Swedenborg</u> was spoken of— "He was a divine teacher—he has done much & will do much good[;] he has correct^d many errors of Popery and also of Luther & Calvin—"

Yet he also said that <u>Swedenborg</u> was wrong in endeavour^g to explain to the <u>rational</u> faculty what the reason cannot comprehend[;] he should have left that—

As B. mentioned <u>Swedenb</u>: & <u>Dante</u> together I wished to know whe^r he considered their visions of the same kind[.] As far as I co^d collect he does— <u>Dante</u> he said was the greater poet— He had <u>political</u> objects[.] Yet this tho wrong does not appear in Blakes mind to affect the truth of the vision[.]

Strangely inconsis^t with this was the language of Bl: about Wordsworth[.] W: he thinks is no Xn but a Platonist— He ask^d me— "Does he believe in the Scriptures?"

On my answering in the affirmative he said he had been much pained by read^g the introduction to the excursion[.] It brought on a fit of ill-ness‡—The passage was produced & read

---

*   Job iv, 18; the next sentences Blake seems to quote are not from the Bible.
†   Samuel Palmer said: "If asked whether I ever knew among the intellectual a happy man, Blake would be the only one who would immediately occur to me" (Gilchrist [*BR* 312 n2]).
‡   Robinson said later that "the preface to the Excursion He told me ... caused him a bowel complaint which nearly killed him" (letter to Dorothy Wordsworth of 19 Feb 1826).

"Jehovah—with his thunder and the choir
"Of Shouting Angels, and the Empyreal thrones—
"I pass them unalarmed."*

This pass them unalarmed greatly offend^d Blake[.] "Does Mr Wordsw: think his mind can surpass Jehovah?"

I tried to twist this passage into a Sense correspond^g with Blake's own theories but failed and W was finally set down as a pagan—But still with great praise as the greatest poet of the age—

Jacob Boehmen was spoken of as a divinely inspired man[.] Bl: praised too the figures in Law's translⁿ. as being very beautiful.† "Mich: Angelo co^d not have done better—"

Tho he spoke of his happiness he spoke of past sufferings and of sufferings as necessary— "There is suffering in Heaven for where there is the capacity of enjoyment, there is the capacity of pain" . . . .

A few other detached thoughts occur to me.

Bacon, Locke & Newton are the three great teachers of Atheism or of Satan's doctrine[.]

Every thing is Atheism which assumes the reality of the natural & unspiritual world[.]

—Irving—He is a highly gifted man[;] he is a sent man—but they who are sent sometimes go further than they ought—

"Dante saw Devils where I see none— I see only good— I saw nothing but good in Calvin's house—better than in Luther's; he had harlots—"

Swedenborg Parts of his scheme are dangerous. His sexual religion is dangerous.‡

"I do not believe that the world is round. I believe it is quite flat—" I objected the circumnavigⁿ— We were called to dinner at the moment and I lost the reply—

The Sun—"I have conversed with the—Spiritual Sun—I saw him on Primrose-hill[.] He said 'Do you take me for the Greek Apollo[?]' 'No' I said 'that (and Bl pointed to the sky) that is the Greek Apollo— He is Satan[.]'"

---

* Wordsworth, *The Excursion* (1814), xi. On 19 Dec 1814, Robinson "Took tea with the Flaxmans and read to them . . . some passages out of Wordsworth's Excursion. Flaxman took umbrage at some mystical expressions in . . . the preface in which Wordsworth talks of seeing Jehovah unalarmed" (*BR* 312 n3).

† *The Works of Jacob Behmen* With Figures [and commentary by Dionysius A. Freher], illustrating his Principles, left by the Reverend William Law, 4 vols (1764, 1772, 1781).

‡ The New Jerusalem Church which Blake joined briefly in 1789 was later riven by controversy over interpretations of Swedenborg's "sexual religion".

"I know now what is true by internal conviction[.] A doctrine is told me—My heart says it must be true—"

I corroborated this by remarking on the impossibility of the Unlearned man judging of what are called the <u>external</u> evidences of religion in which he heartily concurred[.]

... Perhaps the best thing he said was his comparison of moral with natural evil— "Who shall say what God thinks evil—That is a wise tale of the Mahometans—Of the Angel of the Lord that murdered the infant[*] .... Is not every infant that dies of disease in effect murderd by an Angel?"

Crabb Robinson called on Blake in Fountain Court on 17 December, and once again he recorded Blake's conversation in detail, though

their being really no system or connection in his mind all his future conversation will be but varieties of wildness & incongruity—...

Our conversation began ab.ᵗ Dante[.] "He was an atheist—A mere politician busied ab.ᵗ this world as Milton was till in his old age he returned back to God whom he had had in his childhood—"

I tried to get out from B: that he meant this charge only in a higher sense And not using the word Atheism in its popular meaning But he woᵈ not allow this—Tho' when he in like manner charged Locke with Atheism and I remarked that L: wrote on the evidences of Xnity and lived a virtuous life, he had nothᵍ to reply to me nor reiterated the charge of wilful deception[.] I admitted that Locke's doctrine leads to Atheism And this seemed to satisfy him—

From this subject we passed over to that of good & evil on which he repeatedly [*made*] his former assertions more decidedly—He allowed indeed that there is error mistake &c and if these be evil—Then there is evil but these are only negations—Nor would he admit that any education shoᵈ be attempted except that of cultivation of the imagination & fine arts—

"What are called the vices in the natural world, are the highest sublimities in the spiritual world[.]"

When I asked whe.ᵗ if he had been a father he would not have grieved if his child had become vicious or a great criminal He ansᵈ "I must not regard when I am endeavouring to think rightly of my own any more than other people's weaknesses[.]"

---

[*] Crabb Robinson supposes that the allusion is to Parnell's "The Hermit" (ll. 150–230, *The Poetical Works of Dr. Tho Parnell* [1796?], 46–8) in which there is a similar story, though not connected with Muslims.

And when I again remarked that this doctrine puts an end to all exertion or even wish to change anything He had no reply—

We spoke of the Devil And I observed that when a child I thought the Manichaean doctrine or that of two principles a rational one. He assented to this—and in confirmation asserted that he did not believe in the omnipotence of God—The language of the Bible on that subject is only poetical or allegorical[.] Yet soon after he denied that the natural world is any thing. It is all nothing and Satan's empire is the empire of nothing[.]

He reverted soon to his favorite expression "my visions"—"I saw Milton in Imagination And he told me to beware of being misled by his Paradise Lost.* In particular he wished me to shew the falsehood of his doctrine that the pleasures of sex arose from the fall— The fall could not produce any pleasure[.]"

I answered the fall produced a state of evil in which there was a mixture of good or pleasure. And in that Sense the fall may be said to produce the pleasure—

But he replied that the fall produced only generation & death[.] And then he went off upon a rambling state of a Union of Sexes in Man as in God—an androgynous state in which I could not follow him—†

As he spoke of Milton appearᵍ to him—I asked whether he resembled the prints of him—‡

He answerd—"All—"

"Of what age did he appear to be[?]"

"Various ages—Sometimes a very old man[.]"

He spoke of M. as being at one time—A sort of classical Atheist—And of Dante as being now with God—

Of the faculty of Vision he spoke as One he had had from early infancy— He thinks all men partake of it—but it is lost by not being cultivᵈ And he eagerly assented to a remark I made that all men have all faculties to a greater or less degree—

---

* Gilchrist cites "Palmer and other disciples" for such casual remarks as: "'Milton the other day was saying to me,' so and so. 'I tried to convince him he was wrong, but I could not succeed.' 'His tastes are Pagan; his house is Palladian, not Gothic'" (*BR* 316 n1).

† Los says, "Sexes must vanish & cease To be, when Albion arises from his dread repose" (*Jerusalem* pl. 92, ll. 14–15).

‡ In Crabb Robinson's Reminiscences (1852) (*BR* 543–4), the prints are identified as those in [Francis Blackburne], *Memoirs of Thomas Hollis, Esq. F.R. and A.S.S.* (1780): "I have seen him as a youth And as an old man with a long flowing beard[.] He came lately as an old man." Hollis has five portraits of Milton at different ages, none with a beard. Some of the plates in the book are signed by Basire, though the Milton portraits are by Cipriani.

   Samuel Palmer wrote to George Richmond in 1879 (*BRS* 84–5) that Blake told him of "one portrait of him [*Milton*] indicative of his greatness ... in Hollis's life", and Palmer persuaded himself that the bust was "the burin work of William Blake", though signed by Cipriani in 1760, "when [*Blake was*] three years of age".

When Robinson called on Blake on Christmas Eve in 1825, the novelty of Blake's conversation seemed to him less stimulating:

I read him Wordsworth's incompara[e] [*Intimations*] Ode which he heartily enjoyed—[*]
The same half crazy crotchets abo! the two worlds—the eternal repetition of which must in time become tiresome—
Again he repeated to day—"I fear Wordsworth loves Nature—and Nature is the work of the Devil— The Devil is in us, as far as we are Nature—"
On my inquiring whe! the Devil wo[d] be destroyed by God as being of less power— he denied that God has any power—Asserted that the Devil is eternally created not by God—but by God's permission. And when I [*made an*] objection that permission implies power to prevent he did not seem to understand me—
It was remarka[e] that the parts of Wordsworths ode which he most enjoyed were the most obscure & those I least like & comprehend[.]

He called on Blake again in the new year, on 6 January 1826, but

I hardly feel it worth while to write down his convers[n] It is so much a repetition of his former talk—
He was very cordial to day[.] I had procured him two Subsc[s] for his Job from Geo: Proctor & Bas: Montagu[.] I p[d] £1 on each—This probably put him in spirits, more than he was aware of—he spoke of his being richer than ever in hav[g] learnd to know me and he told M[rs] A. he & I were nearly of an opin[n] Yet I have practiced no deception intentionally unless silence be so—
He renewed his complaints, blended with his admiration of Wordsworth[.]
The oddest thing he said was that he had been command[d] to do certain things[,] that is to write abo[t] Milton And that he was applauded for refusing[;] he struggled with the Angels and was victor—
*H*is wife joined in the conversation—

Six weeks later, on 18 February, Crabb Robinson called again on Blake and

He gave me copied out by himself Wordsworths preface to his Excursion—At the end he has added this note—

---

[*] In his letter to Dorothy Wordsworth of 19 Feb 1826, Robinson was even more emphatic: "I never witnessed greater delight in any listener".

"Solomen when he married Pharoahs daughter & became a convert to the Heathen Mythology talked exactly in this way of Jehovah as a very inferior object of man's contemplation, he also passed him by unalarmed & was permitted. Jehovah dropped a tear & followed him by his Spirit into the abstract void. It is called the divine Mercy. Satan dwells in it, but mercy does not dwell in him[.]"

Of Wordsworth he talked as before— Some of his writings proceed from the Holy Ghost, but then others are the work of the Devil*— However I found on this Subject Blake's language more in conformity with Orthodox Christianity than before— He talked of the being under the direction of <u>Self</u>; & <u>Reason</u> as the creature of Man & opposed to God's grace—And warmly declared that all he knew was in the Bible but then he understands by the Bible the Spiritual Sense For as to the natural sense that Voltaire was commissioned by God to expose—

"I have had much intercourse with Voltaire and he said to me 'I blasphemed the Son of Man and it shall be forgiven me But <u>they</u> (the enemies of V:) blasphemed the Holy Ghost in me and it shall not be forgiven them—'"

I asked in what langu: Voltaire spoke[;] he gave an ingenious answer—

"To my Sensations it was English— It was like the touch of a musical key— He touched it probably French, but to my ear it became English—"

I spoke again of the <u>form</u> of the persons who appear to him[,] asked why he did not <u>draw</u> them—

"It is not worth while—There are so many the labour wo^d be too great[.] Besides there wo^d be no Use†— As to Shakesp: he is exactly like the old Engraving‡—which is called a bad one[.] I think it very good—"

I inquired abo: his writings—

"I have written more than Voltaire or Rousseau—Six or Seven Epic poems as long as Homer and 20 Tragedies as long as Macbeth[.]"§

He shewed me his Version (for so it may be called) of Genesis—"as understood by a Christian Visionary"** in which in a style resembl^g the

---

* Blake wrote in the margin (p. 1) of the copy of Wordsworth's *Poems* (1815) which Crabb Robinson lent him in Jan 1826: "I see in Wordsworth the Natural Man rising up against the Spiritual Man Continually & then he is No Poet but a Heathen Philosopher in Enmity against all true Poetry or Inspiration".

† Blake was still making Visionary Heads as late as 1825, for Varley inscribed one: "Head of Achilles drawn by William Blake at my request. 1825" (*BR* 323). In his letter to Dorothy Wordsworth of 19 Feb 1826, Crabb Robinson writes of "the constant hallucinations in which he lives".

‡ This "old Engraving" is presumably the one by Droeshout in the Shakespeare First Folio (1623).

§ Tatham wrote on 11 April 1829 that he had "often heard him say that he has written more than Milton and Shakspeare put together" (*BRS* 90), but nothing like this bulk of manuscripts has survived.

** No surviving work by Blake is significantly like a version of Genesis "as understood by a Christian visionary".

Bible—The spirit is given[;] he read a passage at random[.] It was striking—

He will not print any more— "I write" he says "when commanded by
the spirits and the moment I have written I see the words fly abo͡ṭ the
room in all directions— It is then published and the Spirits can read—
My MSS [*are*] of no further use— I have been tempted to burn my MSS
but my wife wont let me[.]"

"She is right" said I— "You have written these, not from yourself but
by a higher order[.] The MSS. are theirs not your property— You
cannot tell what purpose they may answer; unforeseen to you—"

He liked this And said he wo^d not destroy them[.]

*H*is philosophy he repeated—Denying Causation[,] asserting everything to be the work of God or the Devil[,] That there is a constant falling
off from God—Angels becoming Devils[.] Every man has a Devil in him
and the conflict is eternal between a man's Self and God— &c &c &c &c[.]

He told me my copy of his Songs wo^d be 5 Guas And was pleased by
my man^r of receiv^g this inform^n[;] he spoke of his horror of Money. Of his
turning pale when money had been offerd him, &c &c &c—

In his letter to Dorothy Wordsworth written next day, Crabb Robinson
wrote:

I have lent B: all the works [*of Wordsworth*] which he but imperfectly
knew ... there is something so delightful about the Man—tho' in great
poverty, he is so perfect a gentleman with such genuine dignity & independence—Scorning presents & of such native delicacy in words &c &c
&c that I have not scrupled promising introducing him & M^r W:
together— He expressed his thanks strongly—Saying "You do me
honour[.] M^r W: is a great man— Besides he may convince me I am
wrong about him— I have been wrong before Now" &c. Coleridge has
visited B. & I am told talks finely about him—

But Wordsworth and Blake never met.

Three months later, on 12 May 1826, Crabb Robinson had a tea and
supper party for the Flaxmans, the Masqueriers, Sutton Sharpe, and Blake.

Masq: comment^d on his opin^s as if they were those of a man of ordinary
notions— Bl asserted that the oldest painters poets were the best—

"Do you deny all progression?" says Masqu:

"Oh yes!"

I doubt whether Flaxman sufficiently tolerates Blake. But Bl: appreci-
ates Fl: as he ought.

Next week, on 17 May, Robinson

Called early on Blake[.] He was as <u>wild</u> as ever with no great novelty, except that he confessed a <u>practical</u> notion which wo- do him more injury than any other I have heard from him[.] He says that from the Bible he has learned that Eine Gemeinshaft der Frauen statt finden sollte [wives should be in common]— When I objected that Ehestand [*marriage*] seems to be a divine institution he referred to the Bible—"that from the beginning it was not so"—

He talked, as usual of the spirits[,] asserted that he had committed many murders[,] that reason is the only evil or sin, and that careless gay people are better than those who think &c &c &c[.]

Robinson apparently did not know, as Blake surely did, the context of his Biblical quotation: Jesus "saith unto them, Moses because of the hardness of your hearts suffered you to put away your wives: but from the beginning it was not so" (Matthew xix, 8).

Seven months later, 7 December 1826, on hearing of the death of Flaxman, Crabb Robinson

called on Blake, Desirous to see how with his peculiar feelings & opinions he would receive the intelligence. It was much as I expected— he had himself been very ill during the Summer and his first observation was with a Smile—"I thought I should have gone first[.]"* He then said—"I cannot consider death as any thing but a removing from one room to another—"

One thing led to another and he fell into his wild rambling way of talk— Men are born with a devil & an angel but this he himself interpreted body & Soul.

Of the old testam[t] he seemed to think not favorably—"Xt" said he "took much after his <u>mother</u> (the law) and in that respect was one of the worst of men—" On my requiring an explan[n] he said—"There was his turning the money changers out of the Temple— He had no right to do that—"

B: then decl[d] ag[t] those who sat in judgement on others— "I have never known a very bad man who had not something very good about him—"

He spoke of the Atonement[,] Said— "It is a horrible doctrine— If another man pay your debt I do not forgive it—" &c &c &c[.]

He produced <u>Sintram</u> by Fouqué[†]—"This is better than my things!"

---

* On 12 April 1827 Blake wrote to George Cumberland:

> Flaxman is Gone & we must All soon follow[,] every one to his Own Eternal house
> Leaving the Delusive Goddess Nature & her Laws to get into Freedom from all Law of
> the Members into The Mind in which every one is King & Priest in his own House][.]
> God send it so on Earth as it is in Heaven[.]

† Frédéric Baron de La Motte Fouqué, *Sintram and his Companions: A Romance*, [translated] from the German [by Crabb Robinson's friend Julius C. Hare] (1820).

Crabb Robinson's records of his conversations with Blake are wonderfully illuminating both for what they show us of Blake's ideas and for the impression they made upon a philosophically sophisticated and personally sympathetic auditor. Often Robinson could see neither method nor connection in Blake's remarks, but the fragments he reports are strikingly consistent with the ideas Blake expressed in his writings and in his designs.[*] Without Robinson's records, we would not have known that Blake thought of Dante as "A mere politician" but still a great poet or that he considered death as merely "a removing from one room to another".

These are gifts for which we cannot be too grateful. Even from the recollections of men such as Linnell and Palmer, who loved Blake better and admired him more, we have not received so much of Blake of which we should otherwise have been ignorant as we have in Crabb Robinson's diaries and reminiscences.

The Sublimest Designs from Dante

As Blake was completing his work on Job, and long before any profits from it were possible, Linnell began to cast about for ways to occupy Blake's hands and to fill his pocket—or at least to keep bread on his table.

> The way it came about was this. Although the "Job" had been paid for, Linnell continued to give him money weekly. Blake said: "I do not know how I shall ever repay you."
>
> Linnell replied: "I do not want you to repay me. I am only too glad to be able to serve you. What I would like, however, if you do anything for me, is that you should make some designs for Dante's Inferno, Purgatorio, and Paradiso."[†]

As Linnell explained, the Dante drawings "were Done for M[r] L in return for monies advanced to M[r] B. when he had no other resources. ... M[r] L's object being only to relieve the necessities of his Friend as far as he was able". "The sum [£130] however was inconsiderable compared to the value

---

[*]   George Richmond told Anne Gilchrist, 28 July 1886: "Crabb Robinson ... was a great admirer of Blake ... but Blake used to be [*word illeg*] put to torture by him — & say <u>outrageous</u> things in reply" (Bodley: MS Eng. Lett. 196, f. 135[r]). However, this seems to ignore the strong correlation between Blake's writings with most of his recorded conversations with Crabb Robinson.

[†]   A.T. Story, *The Life of John Linnell* (London, 1892), I, 231, 228. This dialogue sounds invented, and the date is uncertain, but Story may have had good evidence for both. Palmer said that he saw Blake making a Dante design on 9 Oct 1824, but the first payment to Blake explicitly for Dante is on 21 Dec 1825 (*BR* 589).

of the Drawings".* "This work ... answered the purpose of furnishing him with the means of comfortable subsistence to his death".†

The suggestion must have been delightful to Blake. He had long admired Dante, pairing him with Shakespeare as a supreme genius in *The Marriage of Heaven and Hell* and making incidental designs from his *Divine Comedy*. For instance, he depicted Count Ugolino and his sons starved to death in prison by Archbishop Ruggieri degli Ubaldini in separate designs in 1780–5, in *For Children: The Gates of Paradise* (1793) pl. 14 ("Does thy God O Priest take such vengeance as this?"), in the background of his portrait of Dante for Hayley's Library in 1801, and in a separate tempera of 1826.[108]

Of course he then knew Dante's works only at second hand. About 1800 he annotated Henry Boyd's *Translation of The Inferno* (1785), and he had heard of Dante in the original from his friends George Cumberland, John Flaxman, Henry Fuseli, and William Hayley who were fluent in Italian. Indeed, in 1793 Flaxman had made an influential series of designs for Dante which were published in 1802.

But to illustrate Dante, he had to learn medieval Italian. His first step was probably to acquire a copy of the *Commedia* in Italian with notes by Alessandro Velutello and Landino with woodcuts published by the Fratelli Sessa (there were editions in 1564, 1578, 1596) and the three-volume set of *The Vision; or Hell, Purgatory, and Paradise*, translated by Henry Francis Cary.[109] "Helped by such command of Latin as he had, he taught himself the language in a few weeks; sufficiently, that is, to comprehend that difficult author substantially, if not grammatically ...."‡

Amidst his failing health, Blake's letters demonstrate his devotion to Dante: [7 June 1825]: "I can draw as well aBed as Up & perhaps better but I cannot Engrave[.] I am going on with Dante & please myself"; ?April

---

* Linnell to Lord Egremont, 16 March 1831. Linnell continued generously that "he is now willing to part with the Drawings for the benefit of the widow & if he can obtain a price something more adequate he will engage to hand the difference to Mrs Blake".

   Details of payments &c are given in Linnell's letters to Tatham of 9 and 16 March 1831: "he was always paid before hand for what he did for me"; "it was left entirely to him to do little or much as convenient or agreeable".

† Linnell to Bernard Barton, 3 April 1830. On 25 April 1827, Blake wrote to Linnell: "I count myself sufficiently Paid [*for Dante*] If I live as I now do."

‡ Gilchrist (*BR* 290). The date when he learned Italian is given as 1820 (J.T. Smith [*BR* 475]: "at the age of sixty-three"), as 1824 (Gilchrist [*BR* 290]: "at sixty-seven years of age"), and as 1825 (*Literary Gazette* [18 Aug 1827]: "At the age of sixty-six" (but since Anon. thought Blake was 68 in 1827, this would be 1825). Tatham, with characteristic vagueness and hyperbole, says, "He read Dante when he was past 60, altho' before he never knew a word of Italian" (*BR* 527). The drawings bear on the versos a system of interlocking numbers which seem to refer to a Dante text, e.g., "No 37 next at p 71" (Butlin #812 2), but "so far it has not been possible to find any logic in either series of numbers" (Butlin p. 555).

   Linnell said that he gave Blake a copy of Cennino Cennini, *Trattato della Pittura* (Roma, 1821) and he "soon made it out" (*BB* #717).

1826: "I am still far from recovered … [*but*] Dante goes on the better which is all I care about"; 25 April 1827: "I am too much attachd to Dante to think much of any thing else."

He did not finish his drawings "during a fortnight's illness in bed!", as Samuel Palmer claimed (9 October 1824)—in fact, he never did finish them—but he did make 102 designs in a great folio book, working both at home, often ill in bed, and at Linnell's new home at Collins's Farm, North End, Hampstead. For instance, during his visit to Hampstead of 1 August 1826 "he was at work upon the *Dante*. A clump of trees on the skirts of the heath is still known [*in 1861*] to old friends as the 'Dante wood.'"*

Blake's designs depict what he called "The Angry God of this World", and he concluded: "Every thing in Dantes Comedia shows That for Tyrannical Purposes he has made This World the Foundation of All[;] the Goddess Nature Mystery is his inspirer & not Imagination the Holy Ghost."† As he told Crabb Robinson, Dante "had <u>Political</u> objects"; "<u>Dante</u> saw Devils where I see none". However, he also told Crabb Robinson that Dante's visions were true, and that he is now with God. He was, like Wordsworth, a great though misguided poet.

Blake, like most illustrators and critics, was especially fascinated by the first portion of *The Divine Comedy*; most of his drawings and all his engravings are for the *Inferno*. However, some of his most powerful designs are for the *Paradiso*, such as the one of "Dante Adoring Christ" (Pl. 131). Notice the absence of Beatrice, his constant companion in the *Paradiso* representing the Church; at last Dante approaches Christ without mediation.

The whole project was of gargantuan, uncommercial proportions, a labour of love and visionary survival for Blake. In the first place, the 102 watercolours are unfinished; had Blake lived longer, he would surely have finished these watercolours and designed more of them. In the second place, the number of engravings contemplated was large. Assuming that Blake and Linnell intended to have approximately the same number of plates for the *Purgatorio* and the *Paradiso* as for the *Inferno*, as Flaxman did in his edition of 1802, there would be over twenty plates, even assuming that no more than the extant seven would be made for the *Inferno*. In the third place, the plates were very large (*c.* 35 x 28 cm), two and a half times the size of *Job* (*c.* 22 x 17 cm)

---

*   Gilchrist (*BR* 333). In his letter of 2 July 1826, Blake told Linnell that he would come to Hampstead with "Only My Book of Drawings from Dante & one Plate shut up in the Book".

   The largest group of Dante drawings (36) is in the National Gallery of Victoria (Melbourne), and others are in the Fogg Museum (23), the Tate Gallery (19), and the British Museum Print Room (15).

†   Inscriptions on Dante Designs #3, #7. "Imagination is the Divine Body in Every Man"; "Man is All Imagination[.] God is Man & exists in us & we in him" (marginalia [*c.* 1820] to George Berkeley, *Siris* [1744], 204, 219).

and four and a half times the size of Flaxman's Dante (*c.* 13 x 16.5 cm). And in the fourth place, these were not mere outlines, like Flaxman's Dante, but finished intaglio engravings, expensive to make and expensive to print.

The beginning of such an undertaking was an act of visionary temerity. The prospect of financial gain for Linnell was effectively nil.

Blake's friends were dazzled by Blake's Dante watercolours. Frederick Tatham said that they are "such designs, as have never been done by any Englishman at any period or by any foreigner since the 15.th Century, & then his only competitor was Michael Angelo." And T.G. Wainewright exclaimed that "His Dante is the most wonderful emanation of imagination that I have ever heard of."[110]

Blake was also working vigorously on his engravings of Dante. By February 1827 he had finished four plates sufficiently to take proofs of them at his living-room press, and on 25 April 1827 he told Linnell, "I have Proved the Six Plates & reduced the Fighting devils ready for the Copper".

These were the last large plates he ever made—but they were enough to show him at his very best. The prints for Job and Dante are triumphs of the engraver's art, among the finest line-engravings ever made (Pl. 132).

Blake's disciples were equally impressed by the engravings. Samuel Palmer wrote that "nothing can be finer: they are Art in its sublime nakedness ... and in its eternal abstraction from cloggy corporeal substances. They are not of this World."[111] However, none but friends could see them during Blake's lifetime.*

Unfinished Works

Blake's designs and engravings for Job and Dante in 1823–27 were major accomplishments requiring an enormous amount of time and visionary energy, particularly for a man approaching seventy and in failing health. But during these years, he had many other projects in hand. All of them were on a smaller scale than Job and Dante, and all were left unfinished, but they indicate the persistent vigour of Blake's imagination even in his last years.

For the Sexes: The Gates of Paradise

One of these was *For the Sexes: The Gates of Paradise* (Figs on pp. 267 and 440), an extensive revision of *For Children: The Gates of Paradise* (1793).

---

* The Dante engravings were printed in 1838 (25 India paper copies), 1892 (50 copies), 1955 (20), and 1968 (25) (*BB* 544–5). They were sold at £2.2.0, which meant that Linnell had no hope of recouping from sales of the Dante prints his £130 invested in the Dante during his own lifetime.

Blake adjusted the designs of *For Children* (for instance, he added scales to Satan's belly in pl. 7 [see Fig. on p. 140]), he expanded the captions, especially on the title page, and he added "The Keys to the Gates" (Pls 19–21). The enigmatic theme is now far more explicit:

Mutual Forgiveness of each Vice[:]
Such are the Gates of Paradise

(For the Sexes pl. 2 (title page), ll. 1–2)

"Good & Evil" are identified as "Serpent Reasonings" and represented in pl. 7 by Satan rising from his fall, a "dark Hermaphrodite", "Two Horn'd" (like Moses).[112] And Satan, with star-spangled black bat wings hovering over the sleeping Man, is apostrophized in the envoi:

> To The Accuser who is
> The God of This World
> Truly My Satan thou art but a Dunce
> And dost not know the Garment from the Man[.]
> Every Harlot was a Virgin once
> Nor canst thou ever change Kate into Nan[.]
>
> Tho thou art Worshipd by the Names Divine
> Of Jesus & Jehovah: thou art still
> The Son of Morn in weary Nights decline[,]
> The lost Travellers Dream under the Hill

(For the Sexes pl. 21)

Blake probably never finished these revisions. At any rate, only five complete copies of *For the Sexes: The Gates of Paradise* are known, all seem to have been sold after his death, and some of them may have been printed then by Catherine and Tatham.

"The Everlasting Gospel"

At about the same time, he was drafting "The Everlasting Gospel" scattered in the few remaining blank spaces in his Notebook (pp. 1–4, 33, 48–54, 98, 100–1, 120). It begins with a plain statement in prose: "the Covenant of Jehovah ... is This[:] If you forgive one another your trespasses so shall Jehovah forgive you". This is enforced by the paradox that Jesus broke all the moral laws, as in *Marriage* pl. 23:

If Moral Virtue was Christianity
Christs Pretensions were all Vanity

("The Everlasting Gospel", part c, ll. 1–2)

The moral law is the code of Satan, the God of this world:

> The Christian trumpets loud proclaim
> Thro all the World in Jesus name
> Mutual forgiveness of each Vice
> And oped the Gates of Paradise
>
> ("The Everlasting Gospel", part b, ll. 24–7)

The conventional Christian, believing in the moral law, is the enemy of Christ:

> The Vision of Christ that thou dost See
> Is my Visions greatest enemy
> . . .
> Both read the Bible day & night
> But thou readst black where I read White[.]
>
> ("The Everlasting Gospel", part e, ll. 1–2, 13–14)

And God says to Christ:

> Thou art a Man[,] God is no more[!]
> Thine own Humanity learn to Adore[113]

The truth may be seen by understanding that natural vision of the world distorts heavenly reality:

> This Lifes dim Windows of the Soul
> Distorts the Heavens from Pole to Pole
> And leads you to Believe a Lie
> When you see wit*h*, not thro the Eye
>
> ("The Everlasting Gospel", part k, ll. 103–6)

"Laocoon"

Blake had gone to the Royal Academy in 1815 to sketch the Laocoon for his engraving in Rees's *Cyclopaedia*. Later he made a similar drawing with the adult clad in priestly robes,[114] and then he made a faithful engraving of the Laocoon which he surrounded by marginalia reinterpreting it (Pl. 133). The design now represents not the Trojan Priest and his sons attacked by two great serpents for impiety but Jehovah "& his two Sons Satan & Adam" attacked by the serpents "Good & Evil" or "Riches & Poverty". The subject is now art and imagination versus war and empire: "Empire Against Art".

Morality is the weapon of empire and of Rome; "If Morality was Christianity Socrates was the Savior". "Jesus & his Apostles & Disciples were all Artists". "The Whole Business of Man Is The Arts". "A Poet a Painter a Musician an Architect: The Man Or Woman who is not one of these is not a Christian". "Prayer is the Study of Art"; "Praise is the Practise of Art".

The "Laocoon" is one of Blake's most enigmatic and fascinating works, but it was scarcely designed for sale. Only two copies survive, and probably neither was sold during his lifetime.*

"On Homers Poetry [&] On Virgil"

A similarly fragmentary work is the plate etched with remarks "On Homers Poetry" (at the top) and "On Virgil" (at the bottom). The statue of Laocoon is referred to, and the same passage from Virgil is cited in *On Homers Poetry* and in "Laocoon".

Like "Laocoon", it contrasts Art and Empire. "Greece & Rome ... were destroyers of all Art"; "it is the Classics! & not Goths nor Monks [*as in Gibbon*], that Desolate Europe with Wars".

Blake printed six copies of the little work and gave or sold them to friends such as Thomas Butts and John Linnell.

The Ghost of Abel *(1822)*

Blake etched *The Ghost of Abel* on both sides of a single sheet of copper and printed copies for his friends such as Butts and Linnell. It is a tiny play dedicated "To LORD BYRON in the Wilderness" in response to Byron's iconoclastic *Cain: A Mystery* (1821).

The Ghost of Abel is "A Revelation In the Visions of Jehovah Seen by William Blake" in the form of a dialogue between Jehovah, Adam, Eve, and the Ghost of Abel, "the Accuser & Avenger Of Blood", crying "Life for Life! Life for Life!" Adam and Eve doubt the promise of Jehovah, and Satan appears, rejecting the sacrifice of "a Lamb for an Atonement":

I will have Human Blood & not the blood of Bulls or Goats
And no Atonement O Jehovah[!] the Elohim live on Sacrifice
Of Men ....
Thou shalt Thyself be Sacrificed to Me thy God on Calvary

---

* See Addenda, below.

Jehovah concludes:

> Such is My Will   Thunders
> that Thou Thyself go to Eternal Death
> In Self Annihilation even till Satan Self-subdud Put off Satan

The struggle is between the "Elohim of the Heathen" and "Elohim Jehovah", and Jehovah's triumph comes through his "Covenant of the Forgiveness of Sins".

Only five copies of *The Ghost of Abel* survive, and there is no known contemporary reference to *The Ghost of Abel* or to any of these other late writings.

Drawings for The Book of Enoch *(1824–1827)*

Blake had been immersed in the Bible all his life, and he illustrated it extensively, particularly for Thomas Butts. He also illustrated the Roman Catholic Apocrypha and the suppressed books of the Bible.[115] Consequently he was deeply interested in the publication, for the first time in a modern European language, of *The Book of Enoch*, translated by Richard Laurence (1821).*

The Book of Enoch was composed in the first century B.C. and exerted an enormous influence on the New Testament. However, it was excluded from the Biblical canon at the Council of Nicea in 325 A.D., and therefore in Europe the Book of "Enoch ... was not, for God took him" (Genesis v, 24). The Book of Enoch was preserved as a canonical book of the Bible (Metsahof Henoc) in the Church of Ethiopia, and the only complete early copies are in Ethiopic. It was discovered by the African adventurer James Bruce about 1770, and the copy he brought back to England was translated in 1821.

The part of The Book of Enoch which interested Blake and Flaxman was the tale of the Sons of God called Watchers of Heaven. The Watchers were

---

* The translation of Enoch in 1821 excited little public interest, but it was the stimulus for Thomas Moore, *The Loves of the Angels* (1823) with illustrations by Richard Westall and for Flaxman's thirteen designs for it (see "A Jewel in an Ethiop's Ear: The Book of Enoch as Inspiration for William Blake, John Flaxman, Thomas Moore, and Richard Westall", pp. 213–40 of *Blake in his Time*, ed. Robert N. Essick & Donald Pearce [Bloomington & London: Indiana University Press, 1978], where all these designs are reproduced). Extracts from The Book of Enoch had appeared in the *Monthly Magazine* (1801) (see John Beer, "Blake's Changing View of History: The Impact of the Book of Enoch", p. 173 of *Historicizing Blake*, ed. Steve Clark & David Worrall [Basingstoke: Macmillan; New York: St Martin's Press, 1994]).

   The Enoch designs (Butlin #827) were probably commissioned by Linnell, for he later owned them, and one of them is on the verso of a Dante design made for Linnell.

seduced by the Daughter of Men (the women "led astray the angels of heaven without resistance" [xix, 2]) and begot "evil spirits", ravening monsters 300 cubits high (500´) who destroyed the earth. The Watchers also told their wives the secrets of heaven. Consequently God directed his angels to bury the Watchers and their monstrous offspring beneath the earth. And in a section ignored by both Blake and Flaxman, Enoch foretells salvation brought by the Son of Man.

Blake was particularly interested in the sexual contest which echoed the one in his own *Europe*, that "Woman, lovely Woman! may have dominion".[116] In the first of his six designs, a naked Watcher with an heroic penis is surrounded by floating nude women; in the second a Watcher reaches for the vulva of a nude woman; and in the third a Daughter of Men is between two Watchers whose "parts of shame resembled horses" and give off light (Pl. 134).

In his *Marriage of Heaven and Hell* (pl. 16), Blake had written of the giant antediluvians chained to earth who are our energies. In The Book of Enoch he found an ancient prophecy which expressed his own ideas in Hebraic form. No wonder he began to illustrate it with such enthusiasm; it was deep calling to deep, vision answering to vision.

Bunyan's Pilgrim's Progress *(1826–1827)*

Pilgrim's Progress was to Dissenters, if not a manual of devotion, at least a guide and a remembrancer. From childhood Blake must have known the story: Christian with his burden on his journey from the City of Destruction through the Slough of Despond and Vanity Fair to the gates of paradise and the Shining Ones. Christian's allegorical friends Evangelist, Goodwill, Hopeful, Faithful, and Prudence and his false friends Pliable and Worldly Wisdom and his enemies Apollyon and Giant Despair in Doubting Castle were the inhabitants of vision; "Pilgrims Progress is full of it [*vision*]".[117] His little print of "The Man Sweeping the Interpreter's Parlour" (1794; refurbished *c.* 1824) was based on *Pilgrim's Progress*, as was the name The Ancients gave to Blake's apartment: The House of the Interpreter. Christian was an easy familiar of Blake's thought: "I shall travel on in the strength of the Lord God as Poor Pilgrim says".[118]

About 1825, Blake made thirty very incomplete sketches for *Pilgrim's Progress*. He gave one of the more finished of these, "Christian with the Shield of Faith" to Eliza Aders,* perhaps in the hope that she would be

---

* Butlin #829 20; the designs (on paper watermarked 1824) are for *Pilgrim's Progress* Part 1 only. In Blake's letter to Linnell of ?March 1825, the reference to "Pilgrims" ("I send the Pilgrims", plural), may refer to the *Pilgrim's Progress* designs or to copies of his print of "The Canterbury Pilgrims".

tempted to buy the series. When this hope proved vain, he seems to have abandoned the sketches, and they were extensively touched up by another hand,* perhaps that of Catherine Blake or Frederick Tatham, who added numbers and inscriptions to them.†

The Book of Genesis (1826–1827)

Probably the last work Blake began was an illuminated transcription of the Book of Genesis for John Linnell. He drafted eleven pages (including two versions of the title page) and got as far as Genesis iv, 15, carefully ruling the pages to keep the writing level and transcribing the text first in pencil and then confirming it (as far as p. 3) in green or occasionally red ink.

But of course he was not content merely to transcribe the King James translation. To the word "the ground" he added a transliteration of the Hebrew: "Adamah", and the Lord's "mark upon Cain" became a "mark upon Cain's forehead". He also added interpretive chapter-titles:

"The Creation of the Natural Man" (i)
"The Natural Man divided into Male & Female ..." (ii)
"Of the Sexual Nature & its Fall into Generation & Death" (iii)
"How Generation & Death took possession of the Natural Man & of the Forgiveness of Sins written upon the Murderers Forehead" (iv)[119]

The King James translation says that "the Lord set a mark upon Cain, lest any finding him should kill him" (iv, 15); "the Forgiveness of Sins" is entirely Blake's interpretation.

Blake also shows on his second title page Christ handing the scroll of redemption to Adam, an action which would have surprised the authors of Genesis though not the archetypal Christian interpreters of the Bible.

In his last years, Blake saw the Forgiveness of Sins everywhere, even upon the forehead of Cain, the first murderer.

---

* The designs are reproduced in, *inter alia*, Gerda S. Norvig, *Dark Figures in the Desired Country: Blake's Illustrations to The Pilgrim's Progress* (Berkeley, Los Angeles, Oxford: University of California Press, 1993), but the significance of the non-Blakean colouring is largely ignored here.

† Tatham confessed: "She even laboured upon his Works[,] those parts of them where powers of Drawing & form were not necessary, which from her excellent Idea of Colouring, was of no small use in the completion of his labourious designs. This she did to a much greater extent than is usually credited" (*BR* 534).

  The unfinished Bunyan drawings were the only series of Blake's designs remaining in Mrs Blake's hands; the others, such as the Job and Dante, belonged to Linnell. Perhaps a reason why Tatham and Mrs Blake attempted to extract the unfinished Dante drawings from Linnell—and a reason why Linnell resisted so vigorously—was because they wished to tint the drawings.

Linnell and Blake at Hampstead

On 6 March 1824, Linnell moved his family to Collins' Farm[120] in the leafy garden suburb of Hampstead to the north of London, though he kept a studio for himself in Cirencester Place:

> Mr. Linnell's part of the house ... with a separate entrance through the garden which stretches beside,—was small and humble, containing only five rooms. In front it commanded a pleasant southern aspect. Blake, it is still remembered [*1861*], would often stand at the door, gazing in tranquil reverie across the garden toward the gorse-clad hill. He liked sitting in the arbour, at the bottom of the long garden, or walking up and down the same at dusk, while the cows, munching their evening meal, were audible from the farmyard on the other side of the hedge. He was very fond of hearing Mrs. Linnell sing Scottish songs, and would sit by the pianoforte, tears falling from his eyes, while he listened to the Border Melody, to which the song is set, commencing—
>
> > 'O Nancy's hair is yellow as gowd,
> > And her een as the lift are blue.'
>
> To simple national melodies Blake was very impressionable, though not so to music of more complicated structure. He himself still sang, in a voice tremulous with age, sometimes old ballads, sometimes his own songs, to melodies of his own.[121]

Blake was devoted to Linnell—he wrote to him that "Your Success in your Profession is above all things to me most gratifying".[122]

He went to Hampstead on Sundays—"as usual"[123]—partly in order to give drawing lessons to Linnell's wife Mary Ann. Of one of these visits, Mary Ann wrote: "Mr Blake has been to see us to day [*Thursday*] instead of Sunday, and brought a Sketch Book, of Copy from Prints & which he made when about 14 ^yrs old. I have kept it to show you ...."[124] According to Gilchrist, this sketch book "was full of most singular things, as it seemed to the children. But, in the midst of them, they came upon a finished, Pre-Raphaelite-like drawing of a grasshopper, with which they were delighted."[125]

However, Blake remembered with chagrin that "in my Cousin's time ... When I was young Hampstead Highgate Hornsea Muswell Hill & even Islington & all places North of London always laid me up the day after & sometimes two or three days, with precisely the same Complaint & the same torment of the Stomach."[126] They seemed to affect him so forty years later.

"On one occasion, for instance, when Mrs. Linnell ventured to express her humble opinion that Hampstead was a healthy place, Blake startled her by saying, 'It is a lie! It is no such thing!'"[127]

These were happy visits to Hampstead, with the Linnells surrounded by their cheerful children: Hannah (who was six in 1824), Elizabeth (five), John (four), and James Thomas (two).* Blake used to take the children on his knee and recite to them poems from *Songs of Innocence*. Years later, when Hannah Linnell had married Samuel Palmer, she told her son that Palmer's residence

> lay in Blake's way to Hampstead, and they often walked up to the village together. ... [*Blake*] was a great favourite with the children, who revelled in those poems and in his stories of the lovely spiritual things and beings that seemed to him so real and so near. Therefore as the two friends neared the farm, a merry troop hurried out to meet them led by a little fair-haired girl . . . . To this day she remembers cold winter nights when Blake was wrapped up in an old shawl by Mrs. Linnell, and sent on his homeward way, with the servant, lantern in hand lighting him across the heath to the main road.[128]

Hannah told Gilchrist that

> The children, whenever he was expected, were on the *qui vive* to catch the first glimpse of him from afar. One of them ... remembers thus watching for him when a little girl of five or six; and how, as he walked over the brow of the hill and came within sight of the young ones, he would make a particular signal . . . .[129]

Half a century later, the Linnell children remembered Blake

> as a grave and sedate gentleman, with white hair, a lofty brow, and large lambent eyes ... and a kind and gentle manner. He was fond of children, and often took Mr. Linnell's little ones upon his knee, and talked to them in a grave, yet withal an amusing manner, telling them stories, and readily falling in with, and taking part in, their amusements. On one occasion, seeing the eldest girl, Hannah, busy upon a rude attempt at a face, he took

---

* When, according to his Journal, Linnell's "3ᵈ son—William [*was*] Born ½ past 3 morning" on 3 July 1826, Blake protested that the baby should not be named after him: "The Name of the Child ... Certainly ought to be Thomas, after Mʳˢ Linnells Father" Thomas Palmer (letter of 16 July 1826). The baby was therefore renamed Thomas, and the next one was called William.

the pencil, and showed her by a few deft touches how to give it the semblance of a real human countenance.[130]

As Blake's health declined, and as it became more difficult for him to get to Hampstead even by cabriolet when "Walking to & from the Stage would be to me impossible",[131] Linnell became increasingly concerned about him. He therefore proposed that the Blakes should move closer to him, either with Mrs Hurd in Cirencester Place* where he kept a studio ("Mrs Hurds I should like as well as any") or in Hampstead, where the views were better ("As to pleasantness of Prospect it is All pleasant Prospect at North End"). Linnell proposed to pay their rent, and Blake was concerned for him: "think of the Expense & how it may be spared & never mind appearances".[132]

But Blake's fear of Hampstead as an unhealthy place (at least for him) and his fear of moving in his frail state of health made the change impossible:

> I have Thought & thought of the Remova*l*, & cannot get my Mind out of a State of terrible fear at such a Step. *T*he more I think the more I feel terror at what I wishd at first & thought it a thing of benefit & Good hope[;] you will attribute it to the right Cause Intellectual Peculiarity that must be Myself alone shut up in Myself or Reduced to Nothing. I could tell you of Visions & Dreams upon the Subject[.] I have asked & intreated Divine help but fear continues upon me & I must relinquish the step that I had wished to take & still wish but in vain[.][133]

Thereafter Linnell visited Blake in Fountain Court, but Blake probably never returned to sing to the children at North End, Hampstead.

"All Strings & Bobbins like a Weavers Loom"

Blake's constitution was robust—"I believe my Constitution to be a good one"[134]—and he was rarely confined to bed. However, he was subject to alarming "Shivering fits"[†] which he thought were brought on by visits to

---

* Linnell's Journal for 7 Feb 1827: "to Mr Blake to speak to him @ living at C P". Blake's brother James lived in Cirencester Place from 1812 until his death at the end of Feb 1827 (*BR* 564).
† Letters of ?March 1825, 11 March, 19 May 1826. Shivering fits and chills are characteristics of Inflammatory Bowel Disease, especially sclerosing cholangitis, according to Lane Robson (M.D.) & Joseph Viscomi, "Blake's Death", *Blake*, XXX (1996), 36–49, the source of most of the reliable medical information here. They argue that "Pulmonary edema was probably the final and absolute cause of death, but it resulted from liver failure due to biliary cirrhosis, itself probably caused by sclerosing cholangitis", which in turn may have been "caused or aggravated by chronic copper intoxication" from breathing fumes while etching copper; "there is no evidence to prove or disprove the

the north of London. Two days after his Sunday visit to Linnell in Hampstead on 29 January 1826 he wrote:

> I am again laid up by a cold in my stomach[;] the Hampstead Air as it always di*d*, so I fear it always will do . . . When I was young . . . all places North of London always laid me up the day after & sometimes two or three days with precisely the same Complaint & the same torment of the Stoma*ch*, Easily removed but excruciating while it lasts & enfeebling for some time after[.]*

This Complaint, "precisely the same" in youth and age, he called variously "a cold in my stomach", "This abominable Ague or whatever it is", and, in medical frustration, "that Sickness to which there is no name".[135]

The attacks left him "In a Species of Delirium & in Pain too much for Thought".[136] "It began by a gnawing Pain in the Stomach & soon spread a deathly feel all over the limbs which brings on the Shivering fit [*with its accompanying deathly feel*] when I am forced to go to bed where I contrive to get into a little Perspiration which takes it quite away . . . ."[137]

All through 1825 and 1826 the attacks persisted intermittently—"I cannot get Well"[138]—until, as he told Eliza Aders on 29 December 1826, "he does not dare to leave his room by any means. *H*e had another desparate attack of the Aguish trembling last night & is certain that at present any venture to go out must be of bad[,] perhaps of fatal consequence . . . ."

Most of these medical terms and symptoms are opaque or ambiguous today, but one is perfectly transparent: "I have been yellow accompanied by all the old Symptoms".[139] This is unmistakably jaundice, an obstruction of the bile causing yellowness of the skin, constipation, and weakness.†

---

possible role of copper in sclerosing cholangitis" (pp. 44, 37, 40). The role of copper-fumes is the most intriguing and uncertain element in their argument.

They dismiss (as do I) the diagnosis of gall stones (Mona Wilson and Geoffrey Keynes) and of "a ruptured gall-bladder with attendant peritonitis" (Aileen Ward, "William Blake and the Hagiographers", p. 15 of *Biography and Source Studies*, ed. Frederick R. Karl [New York: AMS Press, 1994], with no evidence offered).

* "My journey to Hampstead on Sunday brought on a relapse" (letter of 3 July 1827).

He also thought that it was brought on by cold air: "the Chill of the weather soon drives me back into that shivering fit" (letter of 31 May 1826; see also the letter of 2 July 1826).

† Both J.T. Smith (1828) and Frederick Tatham (?1831) say that his last illness was caused by "the gall mixing with his blood"—George Cumberland paraphrases Smith: "his desease was the bile mixing with his blood—in his random way of writing" (*BR* 475, 528, 371); this diagnosis seems approximate but plausible. Smith and Tatham presumably derived their information from Catherine Blake. Gilchrist (I, 347) says that Blake "was a perpetual sufferer from ... dysentery", but there is no primary evidence for this.

The *Literary Gazette* obituary (12 Aug 1827) adds that "his ancles [*were*] frightfully swelled, his chest disordered", and fluid retained in the lungs and legs is often associated with liver failure, according to Lane & Viscomi.

He took doctor's advice, or at least doctor's medicine, but it was almost immediately followed by another attack.* As usual, the remedies he chose were his own: "I am forced to go to bed where I contrive to get into a little Perspiration which takes it quite away"; "rest does me good", but "my Plan is diet only & if the Machine is capable of it shall make an old man yet: I go on Just as If perfectly well which indeed I am except in those paroxysms".[140]

But though he was physically reduced to mere "bones & sinews[,] All strings & bobbins like a Weavers Loom",[141] he was not diminished spiritually; as he told George Cumberland on 12 April 1827: "I have been very near the Gates of Death & have returned very weak & an Old Man feeble & tottering, but not in Spirit & Life not in The Real Man The Imagination which Liveth for Ever. In that I am stronger & stronger as this Foolish Body decays."

He still received visitors. On 2 February 1827, Crabb Robinson said that

Gotzenberg[er] the young painter from Germany called on me and I accompanied him to Blake[.] We looked over Blakes Dante—Gotzenberger seemed highly gratif.[d] by the designs and Mrs Aders says G. considers B as the first & Flaxman as the second man he has seen in England— The convers.[n] was slight—I was interpreter bet.[t] them and nothing remarkable was said by Blake—he was interested apparently by Götzenberger[.][†]

Though, as Blake wrote on 25 April, "I go on without daring to consider Futurity", he still felt well enough to go to Hampstead as usual on Sunday 1 July. It was his last visit, for, as he wrote two days later, it "brought on a relapse which is lasted till now".

But though confined to Fountain Court, he was still working. "One of the very last shillings spent was on sending out for a pencil."[142] The last engraving he made was a little card for George Cumberland (Fig. on p. 439), with boys bowling hoops and flying kites, which Cumberland's son was told "represents the Seasons".[‡]

---

*   "I have been ... taking D.[r] [*Thomas*] Youngs addition [dandelion] to M.[r] [*George*] Finchams Practise" (letter of 16 July 1826). Dandelion was a folk remedy for liver problems and gall stones (Lane & Viscomi). In May? 1826 Samuel Palmer wrote that Blake "has been visited by Dr Thornton" (*BRS* 86).

†   According to Crabb Robinson's Reminiscences, Gotzenberger "said on his returning to Germany ... 'I saw in England many men of talents, but only three men of Genius Coleridge, Flaxman & Blake— And of these, Blake was the greatest'" (*BR* 536). Gotzenberger may be the channel through which colour-printed copies of *Urizen* (J), *Song of Los* (F), *Songs of Innocence* (Z), and *Visions* (R) reached the royal libraries in Vienna and Munich in the early nineteenth century, the only copies on the Continent then.

‡   George Cumberland Jr, letter of Jan 1828. Cumberland said on 3 Dec 1827 that he had "sent up [the Plate] to have a few ornaments engraved or etched round my name". When Cumberland called on Blake on 6 June 1820, he "recommended to him [*John Linnell, who had dropped in*] the Subject of Spring on a large scale" for a painting; "He likes the idea as does Blake." Blake's choice of "the

Linnell called anxiously on Blake on 11 and 17 July, and on 3 and 10 August ("not expected to live"[143]).

By this time Blake knew that he was dying, and

Some short time before his death, Mrs. Blake asked him where he should like to be buried, and whether he would have the Dissenting Minister, or the Clergyman of the Church of England, to read the service: his answers were, that as far as his own feelings were concerned, they might bury him where she pleased, adding, that as his father, mother, aunt, and brother, were buried in Bunhill-row, perhaps it would be better to lie there, but as to service, he should wish for that of the Church of England.[134]*

The paroxysms of his illness were agonizing,

Yet he was to the last cheerful and contented. "I glory," he said, "in dying, and have no grief but in leaving you, Katherine; we have lived happy, and we have lived long; we have been ever together, but we shall be divided soon. Why should I fear death? Nor do I fear it. I have endeavoured to live as Christ commands, and have sought to worship God truly—in my own house, when I was not seen of men."[144]

Though bolstered up in bed, he was of course still at work. He was interrupted by a paroxysm of his illness, but, as Tatham recorded, when

he thought he was better, . . . and as he was sure to do, [*he*] asked to look at the Work over which he was occupied when siezed with his last attack: it was a coloured print of the Ancient of Days, striking the first circle of the Earth [Pl. 54], done expressly by commission for the writer of this.* After he had worked upon it he exclaimed "There I have done all I can[;] it is the best I have ever finished[.] I hope M.ʳ Tatham will like it[.]"

Seasons" for Cumberland's card may therefore be a delicate compliment to Cumberland. Catherine charged him £3.3.0 for the plate (*BR* 583).

Cumberland said Blake was "a Man who has stocked the english school with fine ideas,—above trick, fraud, or servility" (25 Nov 1827).

* J.T. Smith (*BR* 475–6). Notice that Blake specified the Church of England service but not the Church of England clergyman.

† J.T. Smith (*BR* 471) says: "my friend F. Tatham has just informed me, that after Blake had frequently touched upon it, and had as frequently held it at a distance, he threw it from him, and with an air of exulting triumph exclaimed, 'There, that will do! I cannot mend it.'" Cunningham specifies that the Ancient of Days was coloured "three days before his death" (*BR* 502). Tatham paid £3.13.6 for it (*BR* 471). This is the copy of *Europe* pl. 1, signed "W Blake 1827", now in the Whitworth Institute, University of Manchester.

He threw it suddenly down & said "Kate you have been a good Wife, I will draw your portrait."

*S*he sat near his Bed & he made a Drawing, which though not a likeness is finely touched & expressed.[*]

*H*e then threw that down, after having drawn for an hour & began to sing Hallelujahs & songs of joy & Triumph which M.rs Blake described as being truly sublime in music & in Verse. *H*e sang loudly & with true extatic energy[†] and seemed too happy that he had finished his course, that he had ran his race, & that he was shortly to arrive at the Goal, to receive the prize of his high & eternal calling. . . . His bursts of gladness made the room peal again. The Walls rang & resounded with the beatific Symphony.

After having answered a few questions concerning his Wifes means of living after his decease, & after having spoken of the writer of this, as a likely person to become the manager of her affairs, his spirit departed like the sighing of a gentle breeze, & he slept in company with the mighty ancestors he had formerly depicted.[‡]

Shortly after Blake died, the eighteen-year-old George Richmond came in and "closed the poet's eyes and kissed William Blake in death, as he lay upon his bed, in the enchanted work-room at Fountain Court".[§]

Three days later Richmond wrote to Samuel Palmer:

---

[*] J.T. Smith says that to "his beloved Kate, upon whom his eyes were steadfastly fixed, he vociferated, 'Stay! keep as you are! *you* have ever been *an angel* to me, I will draw you;' and he actually made a most spirited likeness of her" (*BR* 471). Blake's death-bed portrait of Catherine has not been traced since 1827 (Butlin #685).

[†] J.T. Smith (*BR* 475) adds:

> On the day of his death, August 12th, 1827, he composed and uttered songs to his Maker so sweetly to the ear of his Catherine, that when she stood to hear him, he, looking upon her most affectionately, said, "My beloved, they are not mine—no—they are not mine." He expired at six in the evening, with the most cheerful serenity.

And perhaps Cunningham had some evidence for writing (*BR* 502): "He lamented that he could no longer commit those inspirations, as he called them, to paper[.] 'Kate,' he said, 'I am a changing man—I always rose and wrote down my thoughts, whether it rained, snowed, or shone, and you arose too and sat beside me—this can be no longer.'"

[‡] Tatham (*BR* 527–8, quotation marks and paragraphing added, the two sentences about "His bursts of gladness . . . beatific Symphony" transposed from the end of that paragraph); for a slightly different version by Tatham, see *BR* (2) under 12 Aug 1827. All accounts of Blake's deathbed derive directly or indirectly from Catherine Blake.
 Lane & Viscomi conclude from their diagnosis that Blake must have been "semi-comatose" during his last few days, as does Aileen Ward, but all the biographical evidence contradicts such a conclusion. For instance, the *Literary Gazette* obituary (12 Aug 1827) said he "Died as he lived! piously cheerful! talking calmly, and finally resigning himself to his eternal rest, like an infant to its sleep".

[§] *Anne Gilchrist: Her Life and Writings* (1887) (*BR* 342). Arthur Richmond said that his father closed Blake's eyes "to keep the vision in" (*BRS* 87).

Wednesday Even^g—

My Dr Friend

   Lest you should not have heard of the Death of Mr Blake I have written this to inform you—He died on Sunday Night at 6 Oclock in a most
glorious manner[.] He said He was going to that Country he had all His
life wished to see & expressed Himself Happy hoping for Salvation
through Jesus Christ—Just before he died His Countenance became
fair—His eyes brighten'd and He burst out in Singing of the things he
Saw in Heaven[.] In truth He Died like a Saint as a person who was
standing by Him Observed—*

* * *

William Blake was a Stranger from Paradise in an alien world, in the Realm
of the Beast. His real life was in the imagination, in the realms of gold. It is
not only in his paintings and his poems that he unfolds for us the realms of
gold, the paradise of imagination from which he came and in which we too
may dwell if we choose, if we use our imaginations. He also showed these
realms of gold in his life, in which he turned his back upon the Realm of the
Beast and the temporal sun and the atoms of the world. Instead he faced the
spiritual sun of imagination in which he heard the heavenly host crying
"Holy Holy Holy is the Lord God Almighty!"

   For Blake, the world of atoms, the universe of rational doubt and of
scientific proof, of Voltaire and Newton, is merely the outline of God's
glory. In his Notebook he wrote a little poem on the golden sands of paradise and the foundations of faith:

Mock on Mock on Voltaire Rousseau[,]
Mock on Mock on: tis all in vain!
You throw the sand against the wind
And the wind blows it back again

And every sand becomes a Gem
Reflected in the beams divine[;]
Blown back they blind the mocking Eye
But still in Israels paths they shine[.]

---

*   The letter ends: "He is to be Buryed on Fridayay at 12 in morn^g[.] Should you like to go to the
    Funeral[?]— If you should there will be room in the Coach. | Yrs Affection^y | G Richmond."
       "A humble female neighbour, her [*Catherine's*] only other companion, said afterwards: 'I have been
    at the death, not of a man, but of a blessed angel'" (Gilchrist [*BR* 342]), and Catherine said that Blake
    died "like an angel" (Sydney Cumberland letter of Nov 1827; Crabb Robinson Diary of 8 Jan 1828).

The Atoms of Democritus
And Newtons Particles of light
Are sands upon the Red sea shore
Where Israels tents do shine so bright

(Notebook p. 7)

The slippery sands of science and doubt are transformed by the shining tents of Israel and faith. It is not what we see that matters to Blake but how we see it. In Blake's life, we must choose between the Realm of the Beast and the Stranger from Paradise. And if we are wise, we may learn from his life, as from his poetry, to understand the "Auguries of Innocence":

To see a World in a Grain of Sand
And a Heaven in a Wild Flower[,]
Hold Infinity in the palm of your hand
And Eternity in an hour

Postscript
Blake's Shadow of Delight Alone
Catherine Blake in 1827–1831

Tremble not so my Enitharmon at the awful gates
Of thy poor broken Heart[.] I see thee like a shadow withering[1]

A Soul Divided[2]

When Blake departed from what he called "that faint Shadow Calld Natural Life", he left Catherine, his "Shadow of Delight", "an ever-weeping melancholy Shadow".[3] Catherine "adored his memory",[4] but, beyond his memory, Blake "has left nothing for his widow but a few Plates & drawings which if sold would produce nothing adequate to defray even present expenses."*

In her immediate need, Catherine turned to the faithful John Linnell, as Blake had done for so many years. On the day of Blake's death, she borrowed £5 from Linnell, probably as a down-payment for Blake's funeral (£10.18.0) conducted by Linnell's father-in-law Thomas Palmer.[5] On the day of his funeral,

---

* Linnell, "The Case of Mrs. Blake" for the Royal Academy charity (*BR* 346). "His widow is left (we fear, from the accounts which have reached us) in a very forlorn condition" (*Literary Gazette* [18 Aug 1827]).

His hearse was followed by two mourning-coaches, attended by private friends: Calvert, Richmond, Tatham [Pl. 136] and his brother . . . were of the number. Tatham, ill as he was, travelled ninety miles to attend the funeral . . . . [*Blake*] was buried in Bunhill-fields, on the 17th of August, at the distance of about twenty-five feet from the north wall, numbered eighty.*

At the wake, Catherine "set out herself the refreshments of the Funeral".[6] Over the years,

the once beautiful brunette had . . . grown . . . common and coarse-looking, "except in so far," says one who knew her, "as love had made her otherwise, and spoke through her gleaming black eyes." [Pl. 135] This appearance was enhanced by the common, dirty, dress, poverty, and perhaps age, had rendered habitual.†

Linnell arranged for Catherine to stay with him as his "housekeeper".‡ She therefore packed up her pathetically meagre belongings from the two rooms in Fountain Court: clothing, a bit of furniture,§ Blake's library** (his collection of old prints had been sold to Colnaghi about 1821[7]), his stock of his own books and prints for sale,†† scores of his drawings from as much as

---

*   J.T. Smith (*BR* 476). For the official record of Blake's burial at 1:00 p.m., see *BR* 347. The partial list of those who attended the funeral omits the name of John Linnell, either through carelessness or because Linnell was not there due to his disapproval of the Church of England service (as asserted by David Linnell, *Blake, Palmer, Linnell and Co.: The Life of John Linnell* ([Lewes, East] Sussex, England: The Book Guild Ltd, 1994), 110.
     The members of the family were not buried together in Bunhill Fields, for Catherine Wright Armitage Blake was buried "9 feet [E & W] 16 [N & S] 42. 43" in 1792, her son William was buried "9 feet [E & W] 77 [N & S] 32" in 1827, and her daughter-in-law Catherine Sophia Boucher Blake was buried "12 ft [E & W] 7 [N & S] 31.32" in 1831. The Bunhill Fields records do not indicate the locations of the graves of James Blake (1784) or Robert Blake (1787).   ·

†   Gilchrist (*BR* 237); "'never saw a woman so much altered' was the impression of one on meeting her again after a lapse of but seven years" (Gilchrist [*BR* 24], perhaps referring to Flaxman, who was in Italy from 1787 to 1794).

‡   Crabb Robinson Diary for 8 Jan 1828. Linnell wrote on 9 March 1831, "I paid [£]47 to Mrs Blake for the Funeral [£10.18.0]—the rent of fountain Court &c 20 of which . . . [*was*] for taking Care of House &c in Cirencester Place" (*BR* 404–5). A wage of £20 plus board and lodging for 7 months of "taking Care of House" is generous, at a time when many domestic-servants had neither wages nor beds of their own.

§   Some (or all?) of her furniture, sold when she moved from Linnell's (April 1828), brought only £1.10.0 or perhaps £2 ("Cash paid by J. Linnell to Mrs. Blake" [*BR* 606]).

**   Tatham said that "the possessions into which I came by legacy from Mrs. Blake" included "books well thumbed and dirtied by his graving hands, in Latin, Greek, Hebrew, French, and Italian, besides a large collection of the mystical writers, Jacob Behmen, Swedenborg, and others"; "the most thumbed from use are his Bible & those books in other languages" (*BR* 41 n4, 527). Except for Swedenborg, none of these books from Blake's library is known. The surviving copies of books Blake owned are recorded in *BB* 680–702 (44 books), *BBS* 313–25 (5 more), and "William Blake and His Circle", *Blake* (1999) (2 more).

††   For example, Catherine sold "The Canterbury Pilgrims" to Crabb Robinson and others and the prints of "Ezekiel" and "Job" plus *Songs* (W) to John Jebb (*BR* 362, 379), and Tatham acquired *Jerusalem* (E) from her.

fifty years previously, and manuscripts such as the Notebook and the Pickering Manuscript.* The bulkiest object, the great printing press, was moved to Linnell's house in Cirencester Place on 29 August,† two weeks before Catherine moved herself.

The Means to Live

Catherine told George Cumberland Jr in January 1828 that "her late husbands works she intends to prin[t] with her own hands and trust to their sal[e] for a livelihood". She and Tatham printed Blake's copperplates of *America, Europe, Jerusalem*, and the *Songs*, and Tatham wrote letters on her behalf and sometimes in her name trying to sell them.[8] Gilchrist says that

> She was an excellent sales-woman, and never committed the mistake of showing too many things at one time. Aided by Mr. Tatham she also filled in, within Blake's lines, the colour of the Engraved Books; and even finished some of the drawings [*e.g., for* PILGRIM'S PROGRESS]—rather against Mr. Linnell's judgment.‡

Their efforts to sell Blake's works were fostered by the surprising number of obituaries and biographies of Blake which appeared very quickly[9] and were noticed very widely.[10] The biography of Blake's old friend J.T. Smith ended with a poignant appeal to collectors: "his beloved Kate survives him clear of even a sixpenny debt; and in the fullest belief that the remainder of her days will be rendered tolerable by the sale of the few copies of her husband's works, which she will dispose of at the original price of publication . . .".§

However, sales of Blake's books and prints were unlikely to provide Catherine with much security, and several of Blake's friends undertook more ambitious measures. John Linnell summarized "The Case of Mrs. Blake Widow of Wm. Blake Historical Painter & Engraver"[11] for an appeal to the charity of the Royal Academy, vainly as it turned out. More effec-

---

* Linnell had already bought or been given the unique copies of *The French Revolution* and *Vala*, and the drawings for *Paradise Regained*, Job, Dante, Genesis, and Enoch.

† Linnell vainly offered it (18 Aug 1827) to Lahee, the printer of the Job plates.

‡ Gilchrist (*BR* 363–4). Joseph Viscomi describes the characteristics of Catherine Blake's colouring and identifies the copies of works in Illuminated Printing which she coloured (*Blake and the Idea of the Book* [Princeton: Princeton University Press, 1993], 133–4). She coloured *Night Thoughts* (N) (*BBS* 289), and after Blake's death she added the ornamental borders to *Songs* (W) (*BB* 423).

§ J.T. Smith (*BR* 476). In Nov? 1828, J.T. Smith wrote to Linnell: "What I have said of your worthy friend Blake I am *fully* aware has been servisable to his widow." Cunningham wrote: "She still lives to lament the loss of Blake—and *feel* it" (*BR* 504).

tively, in July 1829 Lord Egremont paid £84 for Blake's watercolour of "The Characters of Spenser's *Faerie Queen*",* a sum sufficient to secure her confidence about her financial future. She therefore withdrew her application to the Artists' General Benevolent Institution on 5 January 1830,[12] and when Princess Sophia sent her "a gift of £100 ... Mrs. Blake sent back the money with all due thanks, not liking to take or keep what (as it seemed to her) she could dispense with, while many to whom no chance or choice was given might have been kept alive by the gift".†

Catherine's Comforts

Catherine

saw Blake frequently after his decease: he used to come and sit with her two or three hours every day. These hallowed visitations were her only comforts. He took his chair and talked to her, just as he would have done had he been alive: he advised with her as to the best mode of selling his engravings. She knew that he was in the grave; but she felt satisfied that his spirit visited, condoled, and directed her. When he had been dead a twelve-month, the devoted and affectionate relict would acquiesce in nothing "until she had had an opportunity of consulting Mr. Blake."‡

In time Catherine became an icon for some Victorians,[13] largely because of her tractability. However, the picture dealer Joseph Hogarth, who bought many Blake drawings and prints from Frederick Tatham, wrote that

Mrs Blake was hardly the passive cre[a]ture here described [*in J. T. Smith's biography*]—at all events Tatham did not find her so for she was opposed to everything he did for her benefit and when she submitted to his views it was

---

* Gilchrist (*BR* 363); Catherine wrote to Lord Egremont about the picture on 1 and 4 Aug 1829 (*WBW* xxix–xxx). On 16 March 1831, Linnell offered the Dante drawings to Lord Egremont, promising to pass on to Catherine any sum he received beyond the £130 he had paid for them.

† A.C. Swinburne, *William Blake* (1868) (*BR* 345), based on information from Seymour Kirkup (*BR* [2] under 1809–1810). Catherine's polite rejection of the royal bounty may have been related to her republican sympathies.
  Tatham attempted to extract from Linnell the Dante drawings and engravings which Linnell had paid for, first on Catherine's behalf (Jan–March 1831) and then on his own (March 1833). On 27 Jan 1829 Linnell went "to Mʳˢ Blake—who sᵈ that Mʳ Blake told her [*?in a vision*] he thought I shᵈ pay 3 gs. a piece for the Plates of Dante" (*BRS* 110).

‡ Anon., "Bits of Biography. No. 1. Blake, the Vision Seer, and Martin the York Minster Incendiary", *Monthly Magazine* (March 1833) (*BR* 373–4). According to Gilchrist (*BR* 364), "Of her husband she would always speak with trembling voice and tearful eyes as 'that wonderful man,' whose spirit, she said, was still with her, as in death he had promised. Him she worshipped till the end."

always with the words she "Had no help for it"—that at last Tatham tired with her opposition threw the Will behind the fire and burnt it saying ["]There now you can do as you will for the Will no longer exists["] and left her. Early the following morning she called upon [*him*] saying William had been with her all night and required her to come to him and renew the Will which was done and never after did she offer any objection to Tatham's proceedings.[14]

If this curious story is true, it indicates an odd view of a "Will". No will for William Blake was ever proved, and legal wills cannot be as casually "renewed" as this. Perhaps Blake's deathbed wishes were written down (a nuncupative will)—though it seems unlikely that Blake would have entrusted Catherine to the financially unstable Tatham rather than to the loyal and prosperous Linnell, with whom, after all, she went to live immediately after his death.

After nine months with John Linnell at Cirencester Place, Catherine moved to 20 Lisson Grove (April 1828–early 1831) to live with Frederick Tatham "whose domestic arrangements were entirely undertaken by her",[15] and then, when this became too onerous for her, she moved to 17 Charlton Street (1831) where she lived "at a Bakers".[16]

Passing from One Room to Another

Since Blake's death, "her stomach had proved restless & painful".[17] However, "always self-negligent", "she had suffered [the severe attack of inflammation of the bowels] to run to a height before calling in medical aid."

When told by the doctor that ... [*the* Cramps & Spasms] would terminate in mortification, she sent for her friends, Mr. and Mrs. Tatham, and, with much composure, gave minute directions for the performance of the last sad details; requesting, among other things, that no one but themselves should see her after death, and that a bushel of slaked lime should be put in the coffin, to secure her from the dissecting knife.* She then took leave of Miss Blake, and passed the remaining time—about five hours—calmly and cheerfully; "repeating texts of scripture, and calling continually to her William, as if he were only in the next room, to say she was coming to him, and would not be long now". This continued nearly till the end.[18]

The Tathams put "into her trembling hands the last cup of moisture she applied to her dying lips & to them she bequeathed her all".†

---

* Resurrection men did a brisk business at the time robbing graves to supply cadavers to doctors for dissection.

† Tatham (*BR* 535). Tatham described himself and his wife as "2 whom she dearly loved, nay almost idolized, whose welfare was interwoven with the chords of her life & whose well being was her only solace, her only motive for exertion & her only joy."

Tatham wrote to Linnell on 18 October 1831 to inform him

of the death of Mrs Blake, who passed from death to life this morning, at
$\frac{1}{2}$ past 7—After bitter pains, lasting 24 hours, she faded away as the whisper of a breeze.

Mrs Tatham & myself have been with her during her suffering & have
had the happiness of beholding the departure of a saint for the rest promised to those who die in the Lord.*

Tatham said that

She was buried [beside her husband] according to her own directions at
Bunhill Fields with the same Funeral decorations as her husband which
was also her desire .... [*At her funeral, the Tathams and*] Mr Bird Painter
Mr Denham Sculptor M^r & Mrs Richmond followed ... the remains of
this irradiated Saint.[19]

Blake's Shadow had passed into the next room to join him again.

The Dispersal of Blake's Heritage

According to Tatham, "some" of "those who were ... intimate with him"
proposed in 1829 "to give forth ... biographical information" about Blake,[20]
but the only result was Frederick Tatham's sententious biographies of Blake
and Catherine,[21] which were written in part to help him sell the coloured
copy of *Jerusalem* with which they were bound.

Neither Blake nor Catherine left a will,[22] and on her death, as Tatham
said, "I became possessed of all the residue of his Works being Drawings
Sketches & Copper Plates",[23] despite the fact that Blake's sister, Catherine
Elizabeth Blake, was still alive and in want.† As Anne Gilchrist commented,

it is inexplicable, and take it how you will, an ugly circumstance that
while Miss Blake, the sole surviving relative and natural heiress to what
was left of Blake's possessions after the widow's death—while Miss Blake
I say, lived in such penury, such absolute want, that I have heard a
rumour she died of her own hand rather than continue in life on such

---

* Gilchrist adds that "She died in Mrs. Tatham's arms" (BR 410).
† On 1 July 1833, Linnell went to the solicitor George Stephen "to meet Miss Blake @ Administering to her
Brothers Effects" (*BRS* 112), but Blake's sister is not known to have received any benefit from his estate.

terms of misery*—Tatham came into possession of so large a stock of Designs and engraved Books, that he has, by his own confession, been selling them "for thirty years" and at "good prices."[24]

Tatham made a sordid, unsuccessful attempt to obtain from Linnell Blake's Dante drawings, first for Catherine Blake (1831) and then for himself (1833).[25]

After Catherine Blake's death in 1831, Tatham became "a Bankrupt or something like it".[26] He printed *America*, *Europe*, *Jerusalem*, and *Songs* on paper watermarked 1832, and then he lost the copperplates themselves. For thirty years, he sold Blake's drawings and prints.

He also became "a zealous Irvingite" and was persuaded "by some very influential members of the Sect . . . that Blake was inspired; but quite from a wrong quarter—by Satan himself—and was to be cast out as an 'unclean spirit'".[27] Edward Calvert, fearing a holocaust of Blake's manuscripts, went "to Tatham and implored him to reconsider the matter, and spare 'the good man's precious work;' notwithstanding which, blocks, plates, drawings, and MSS.,† I understand, were destroyed".[28]

Frederick Tatham was devoted to William and Catherine Blake, but the heritage of William Blake which passed into his hands was far greater than what survives today.

---

*   For evidence suggesting that Blake's sister died in penury, see *BR* (2) under March 1841.
†   Save for the Ballads or Pickering Manuscript, which he sold, and Blake's Notebook which Catherine gave to Samuel Palmer's brother William (*BB* 334); Blake had already given *Vala* to Linnell.

Appendix 1
Principal Biographies of Blake*

1806 **B.H. Malkin** (1769–1842), *A Father's Memoirs of His Child* (London: Longman, Hurst, Rees, & Orme, 1806), xviii–xli (reprinted in *BR* 421–31),[†] gives original, reliable, and important accounts of Blake's youth and early manhood apparently derived from Blake himself.

1811 **[Henry Crabb Robinson** (1775–1867)], "William Blake, Künstler, Dichter und religiöser Schwärmer" [tr. Dr. Niklaus Heinrich Julius], *Vaterländisches Museum*, II (Jan 1811), 107–31 (*BR* 432–55 in German and English), written before Robinson met Blake,[‡] is derived largely from Malkin and from Blake's writings, with a few original and important details.

1827 **Anon.** [?**William Paulet Carey** (1759–1839)], "William Blake; *The Illustrator of the Grave, &c.*", *Literary Gazette* (18 Aug 1827), 540–1 (*BR* 348–50), is an original and valuable obituary; it was largely reprinted in *Monthly Magazine* (Oct 1827) (*BR* 354–5), *Gentleman's Magazine* (1 Nov 1827) (*BR* 356–7), *New Monthly*

---

* Excluding journalistic accounts after 1830 chiefly derived from Cunningham (1830), e.g., John Gorton, "Blake (William)", *A General Biographical Dictionary* (London: Whittaker & Co., 1835; 1841; 1847; 1851); W.A. Beckett, *Universal Biography* (London: G.F. Isaac, 1836); W[alter] T[hornbury], "Blake, William ...", *The Imperial Dictionary of Universal Biography*, ed. P.E. Dove et al. (London, Glasgow, Edinburgh, Liverpool, Leeds, Aberdeen, Newcastle, Bristol, "Boston, U.S.", N.Y.: William Mackenzie, [?1863]).

† Facsimiles of the accounts by Malkin, Crabb Robinson, Smith, Cunningham, Tatham (from A.G.B. Russell's transcription) and others are given in *Nineteenth-Century Accounts of William Blake*, ed. Joseph T. Wittreich, Jr. (Gainesville, Florida: Scholars' Facsimiles and Reprints, 1970).

‡ Crabb Robinson wrote very important, largely first-hand accounts of Blake in his Diary (1810–13, 1815, 1825–28) (*BR* 223–6, 229, 231, 235, 309–18, 320–6, 331–2, 336–8, 362–3, 367–8, 371) which were revised in his Reminiscences (1852) (*BR* 535–49).

Magazine (1 Dec 1827) (*BR* 359), *Annual Biography and Obituary* (1828) (*BR* 361–2), and *Annual Register* (1828) (*BR* 362).

1827 **Anon.**, "William Blake", *Literary Chronicle And Weekly Review* (1 Sept 1827), 557–8 (*BR* 351–3), is an original obituary.

1828 **John Thomas Smith** (1766–1833), "William Blake", *Nollekens and His Times* (London: Henry Colburn, 1828; 1829), II, 454–88 (*BR* 455–76), is an important and reliable account of Blake as an artist by a friend from his early manhood.

1830 **Allan Cunningham** (1784–1852), "William Blake", *The Lives of the Most Eminent British Painters, Sculptors, and Architects* (London: John Murray, 1830; Second Edition [revised], 1830; ...) (*BR* 476–507), is a largely derivative and anecdotal biography which was enormously influential—until 1863 it was by far the best-known account of Blake. The facts in Cunningham's life of Blake which demonstrably derive from earlier sources have uniformly been engagingly embroidered, and in any Cunningham story which cannot be traced to an earlier source one must wonder which parts are fact and which invention.

1832 **Frederick Tatham** (1805–78), MS "Life of Blake" (*c.* 1832), first printed with *The Letters of William Blake*, ed. A.G.B. Russell (London: Methuen & Co., 1906) (*BR* 507–35), provides valuable information derived from his intimacy with Blake's widow but is inaccurate in petty details.

1835 **Thomas Dodd** (1771–1850), MS "William Blake" among his "Memorials of Engravers that have exercised the art in Great Britain" (*c.* 1835), is derivative and negligible; it was printed in "An Unknown Early Biography of Blake", *Times Literary Supplement*, 16 March 1962, p. 192.

1863 **Alexander Gilchrist** (1828–61), *Life of William Blake, "Pictor Ignotus"* (London: Macmillan, 1863; 1880 ...), is based on careful research particularly among Blake's friends (usually un-named); it is reliable, vastly influential, and irreplaceable.

1893 **Edwin John Ellis**, "Memoir", *The Works of William Blake, Poetic, Symbolic, and Critical*, ed. Edwin John Ellis & William Butler Yeats (London: Quaritch, 1893), I, 1–172,* is a surprisingly fictional account, including allegations that Blake was Irish.

---

* Yeats wrote: "The biography is by him [*Ellis*]. He wrote and trebled in size a biography of mine" (Hazard Adams, *Blake and Yeats* [Ithaca: Cornell University Press, 1955], 47).

1893 **Alfred T. Story**, *William Blake:* His Life Character and Genius (London: Swan Sonnenschein & Co.; New York: Macmillan & Co., 1893), is a pedestrian biography.

1907 **Edwin J. Ellis**, *The Real Blake:* A Portrait Biography (London: Chatto & Windus, 1907), is an "original" work revealing that the "real" William Blake was the son of an Irishman named "O'Neill".

1907 **Arthur Symons**, *William Blake* (London: Archibald Constable and Company Ltd, 1907), is chiefly significant for its reprints of the Blake sections of (**1**) Henry Crabb Robinson, MS Reminiscences (1852), (**2**) H.C. Malkin, *Memoirs* (1806), (**3**) Lady Charlotte Bury, *Diary* (1839), (**4**) [R.C. Smith], *Urania* (1825), (**5**) *Literary Gazette* obituary (1827), (**6**) *Gentleman's Magazine* obituary (1827), (**7**) John Varley, *Zodiacal Physiognomy* (1829), (**8**) J.T. Smith, *Nollekens and his Times* (1828), (**9**) J.T. Smith, *A Book for a Rainy Day* (1845), and (**10**) Allan Cunningham, *Lives* (first edition, 1830).

1919 **Charles Gardner**, *William Blake the Man* (London: J.M. Dent & Sons; New York: E.P. Dutton & Co., 1919), is a pedestrian biography.

1922 **Allardyce Nicoll**, *William Blake & his Poetry* (London, 1922) is a popular, ill-informed biography.

1925 **Herbert Jenkins**, *William Blake:* Studies of his Life and Personality, ed. C.E. Lawrence (London: Herbert Jenkins Limited, 1925), reprints his biographical articles (some published under the pseudonym Herbert Ives), including original material.

1927 **Mona Wilson**, *The Life of William Blake* (London: Nonesuch, 1927 . . .), is a careful biography of major importance with some original information.

1927 **Thomas Wright**, *The Life of William Blake*, 2 vols (Olney: Thomas Wright, 1929), is a curious combination of original research and garbled facts.

1933 **John Middleton Murry**, *William Blake* (London: Jonathan Cape, 1933), is an earnest attempt to describe Blake as a Marxist Christian.

1943 **Jacob Bronowski**, *William Blake, 1757–1827:* A Man Without a Mask (London: Penguin, 1943; . . . revised as *William Blake and the Age of Revolution* [N.Y., 1965 ff.]), is a valuable book which stresses Blake's social and political background.[*]

[*] See also David V. Erdman, *Blake: Prophet Against Empire:* A Poet's Interpretation of the History of his Own Time (Princeton: Princeton University Press, 1954; 1969; 1977; 1991).

1951 H.M. Margoliouth, *William Blake* (London, N.Y., Toronto: Oxford University Press, 1951) includes some valuable original materials.

1951 Morchard Bishop [i.e., Oliver Stoner], *Blake's Hayley:* The Life, Works, and Friendships of William Hayley (London: Victor Gollancz Ltd, 1951), focuses on Hayley but includes important original material relating to Blake.

1969 G.E. Bentley, Jr, *Blake Records* (Oxford: Clarendon Press, 1969), reprints all the documents then known relating to the life of Blake and his family, of major importance.

1969 Deborah Dorfman, *Blake in the Nineteenth Century:* His Reputation as a Poet From Gilchrist to Yeats (New Haven & London: Yale University Press, 1969), prints some useful new material for the period 1863–93.

1970 Joseph Anthony Wittreich, Jr, ed., *Nineteenth-Century Accounts of William Blake* by Benjamin Heath Malkin, Henry Crabb Robinson, John Thomas Smith, Allan Cunningham, Frederick Tatham, William Butler Yeats: Facsimile Reproductions with Introductions and Headnotes (Gainesville, Florida, 1970) (Scholars Facsimiles and Reprints).

1973 Suzanne R. Hoover, "William Blake in the Wilderness: A Closer Look at his Reputation 1827–1863", *William Blake:* Essays in honour of Sir Geoffrey Keynes, ed. Morton D. Paley & Michael Phillips (Oxford: Oxford University Press, 1973), 310-348, reprints some interesting new material.

1975 G.E. Bentley, Jr, "Forgotten Years: References to William Blake 1831-1862", *William Blake: The Critical Heritage* (London: Routledge & Kegan Paul, 1975), 220–69, is a supplement to *Blake Records* (1969) gathering all the material for 1831–62 then known.

1977 Michael Davis, *William Blake:* A new kind of man (London: Paul Elek, 1977), gives a responsible synopsis.

1979 Soho Kumashiro, *William Blake—sono shogai to sakuhin no subete* [*William Blake—On His Life and Works*] (Tokyo: Hokuseido Shoten, 1979); in Japanese.

1979 Jack Lindsay, *William Blake:* His Life and Work (N.Y.: George Braziller, 1979),* is concerned particularly with religious and political radicals.

---

*   The 1979 book is quite distinct from Jack Lindsay, *William Blake:* Creative Will and the Poetic Image (London, 1927), an impressionistic attempt to assess the "psychological machinery" of Blake's work.

1979 **Ryo Namikawa**, *Blake no shogai to sakuhin* [*On Blake's Life and Works*] (Tokyo: Hara Shobo, 1979), in Japanese.

1988 **G.E. Bentley**, Jr, *Blake Records Supplement* (Oxford: Clarendon Press, 1988), prints material related to Blake discovered since 1967, some of it important.

1990 **Shivshankar Mishra**, *Rise of William Blake* (New Delhi: K.M. Rai Mittal, 1990), is about criticism of Blake *c*. 1806–1979, derived chiefly from *Blake Records* (1969).

1991 **James King**, *William Blake: His Life* (London: Weidenfeld & Nicolson, 1991), is concerned with Blake's "paranoia", with no new facts.

1995 **Peter Ackroyd**, *Blake* (London: Sinclair-Stevenson, 1995, . . .), is a careful and usually accurate biography with few pretensions to originality.

1995 **Michael Phillips**, *William Blake:* Recherches pour une Biographie: Six Etudes, tr. Antoine Jaccottet (Paris: Diffusion les Belles Lettres, 1995), reprints his largely bibliographical essays preparatory to "une grande biographie du poète".

1998 **Stanley Gardner**, *The Tyger, the Lamb, and the Terrible Desart: Songs of Innocence and of Experience* in its times and circumstance Including facsimiles of two copies (London: Cygnus Arts; Madison & Teaneck: Fairleigh Dickinson University Press, 1998), concentrates usefully on the first half of Blake's life (1757–94) with special reference to charity to children in the parish of St James and to the *Songs*, with novel ancillary details.

Appendix 2
Blake's Chief Writings, Series of Designs, Exhibitions, and Commercial Engravings

Note: The place of publication is London unless otherwise identified. Dates in the left margin for Blake's commercial work are those of engraving, which may differ from the book-publication dates. Blake's works in Illuminated Printing are coloured unless otherwise specified. **Bold face** identifies Blake's writings. The rough indications of size ("folio" &c.) suggest the scale of the engraving work entailed.

1773?   "Joseph of Arimathea Among the Rocks of Albion", 4°, 1 plate after his own design adapted from Michelangelo, revised 1810–20, 12 copies, at least one printed posthumously (Pl. 15)

1777-79?   Jacob Bryant, *A New System ... of Ancient Mythology*, 3 vols (T. Payne *et al.*, [Vols I–II] 1774, [Vol. III] 1776; [Second Edition of Vols I–II] 1775), 4°, several plates were probably engraved by Blake though signed by his master Basire

1777-79?   Sir Joseph Ayloffe, *An Account of Some Ancient Monuments in Westminster Abbey* (Society of Antiquaries, 1780), part of *Vetusta Monumenta*, folio; Blake probably designed (1775) and engraved 7 plates signed by J. Basire

1777-79?   [Richard Gough], *Sepulchral Monuments in Great Britain*, I (T. Payne & Son, 1786), folio, 16 plates (n.d., signed by Basire) after Blake's drawings (1777) of monuments (Pl. 18)

1780   "Death of Earl Goodwin" exhibited at the Royal Academy

1780   *The Protestants Family Bible* (Harrison & Co. [1780–81]), 4°, 5 plates (n.d.) after Raphael

1780   William Enfield, *The Speaker* (Joseph Johnson, [1780]; 1781; 1785; 1795; 1797), 12°, 1 plate after Stothard

1780   [J.] Olivier, *Fencing Familiarized*; *L'Art des Armes Simplifié* (John Bell, 1780), 8°, 1 plate after J. Roberts

1780–82   *The Royal Universal Family Bible* (Fielding & Walker, 1780–82 [i.e., 1782–83]), 4°, 5 plates after Anon.

1781   Henry Emlyn, *A Proposition for a New Order in Architecture* ([no publisher], 1781; 1784), folio, 1 plate [after Earle]

1782   John Bonnycastle, *An Introduction to Mensuration* (Joseph Johnson, 1782; 1787; 1791; 1794), 12°, 1 vignette after Stothard

1782   Edward Kimpton, *History of the Holy Bible* (J. Cooke, 1782?; 1785?), folio, 3 plates after Stothard and C.M. Metz (2), also printed in Flavius Josephus, *Works*, ed. George Henry Maynard (J. Cooke, 1787?–1790?)

1782   *The Ladies New and Polite Pocket Memorandum-Book* (Joseph Johnson, 1782), 12°, 2 plates after Stothard

1782   "Morning Amusement" and "Evening Amusement" (Thomas Macklin), 4°, 2 plates after Watteau

1782   William Nicholson, *Introduction to Natural Philosophy*, 2 vols (Joseph Johnson, 1782; 1787), 12°, 1 vignette (printed twice) after Anon.

1782   *Novelist's Magazine*, VIII (Harrison & Co., 1782; 1784; 1792), 8°, 2 plates after Stothard for Miguel Cervantes, *Don Quixote*, tr. Tobias Smollett

1782–83   *Novelist's Magazine*, IX (Harrison, 1782; 1785; 1793), 8°, 3 plates after Stothard for Laurence Sterne, *Sentimental Journey*, Sarah Fielding, *David Simple*, and Tobias Smollett, *Launcelot Greaves*

1782   John Seally & Israel Lyons, *Complete Geographical Dictionary*, 2 vols (John Fielding, 1784?; 1787; reprinted as *New Royal Geographical Dictionary*, 1793?; 1794?), 4°, 3 plates after Anon.

1782   *A Select Collection of English Songs*, [ed. Joseph Ritson], 3 vols (J. Johnson, 1782), 12°, 9 plates after Stothard

1782   John Scott, *Poetical Works* (J. Buckland, 1782; 1786; 1795), 8°, 4 plates after Stothard

1782–83   *Novelist's Magazine*, X–XI (Harrison, 1783; 1785; 1793; 1800?; 1811; 1818), 8°, 3 plates after Stothard for Samuel Richardson, *Sir Charles Grandison*

1783   Ariosto, *Orlando Furioso*, tr. John Hoole (congery, 1783; 1785; 1791; 1799), 8°, 1 plate after Stothard

1783   *Poetical Sketches*, 8°, 76 pp., in type, privately printed, 23 copies (14 distributed posthumously) (Pl. 32)

1783   Geoffrey Chaucer, *The Poetical Works* (Bell, 1782 [*sic*]), 12°, 1 plate after Stothard

1783   Thomas Henry, *Memoir of Albert de Haller* (J. Johnson, 1783), 8°, 1 plate after Dunker

1783   "The Fall of Rosamund" (T. Macklin, 1783), 4°, 1 plate after Stothard (Pl. 30)

1783   "Robin Hood & Clorinda" (T. Macklin, 1783), 4°, 1 plate after J. Meheux

1784   "A breach in a city, the morning after a battle" and "War unchained by an angel, Fire, Pestilence, and Famine following" exhibited at the Royal Academy

1784?   *An Island in the Moon*, 8° manuscript, 32 pp. (lacking 2 or more leaves from the middle) (Fitzwilliam Museum, Cambridge)

1784   *The Wit's Magazine*, I (Harrison & Co., 1784), 8°, 6 plates after Stothard (2) and Samuel Collings (4)

1784   "Zephyrus and Flora" (Pl. 39) and "Calisto" (Blake & Parker, 1784), 4°, 2 plates after Stothard

1784–85   D. Fenning & J. Collyer, *A New System of Geography* (J. Johnson, 1785–86; 1787), 4°, 2 plates [after Stothard]

1785   Exhibited at the Royal Academy (1) "Joseph making himself known to his brethren" (Pl. 37), (2) "Joseph's brethren bowing before him", (3) "Joseph ordering Simeon to be bound", and (4) "The Bard, from Gray"

1785   [Elizabeth Blower], *Maria*: A Novel (T. Cadell), 8°, 1 plate after Stothard

1786   Thomas Commins, *An Elegy Set to Music* (J. Fentum, 1786), 4°, 1 plate after his own design

1787   "Venus Dissuades Adonis" (G. Hadfield, 1787), 4°, 1 plate after R. Cosway

1787	"Rev. John Caspar Lavater", First State (Johnson, 26 Dec 1787), First State (1 copy), Second and Third States (1801, 21 copies), folio, 1 plate after Anon.
1788?	*All Religions are One*. 24°, 10 plates, 1 copy (Huntington Library) (see Figs on pp. 131 [right], 335)
1788?	*There is No Natural Religion*, 24°, 21 plates, 13 very diverse copies (see Fig. on p. 131 [left])
1788, 1790	William Hogarth, design for John Gay, *Beggar's Opera*, etched by Blake (1788), then finished as an engraving (1790) for Hogarth's *Works* (Boydell, 1790?–1880?), elephant folio
1788	"The Idle Laundress" and "The Industrious Cottager" (J.R. Smith, 1788), 4°, 2 plates after Morland
1788	J.C. Lavater, *Aphorisms on Man*, tr. [Henry Fuseli] (J. Johnson, 1788; 1789; 1794), 12°, 1 plate [after Fuseli]
1788	J.C. Lavater, *Essays on Physiognomy*, tr. Henry Hunter, 3 vols bound in 5 (Henry Hunter, John Murray [& Joseph Johnson], 1789–98; 1810; 1792 [i.e., 1818]), folio, 4 plates after Rubens and Anon. (3)
1789?	*Tiriel*, MS, 8°, 15 pp. (British Library) plus 12 watercolours (Pl. 50) (scattered)
1789	*Songs of Innocence*, 8°, 27 plates, 26 copies (Pl. 9, Figs on title page, pp. 1, 17, 87, 98)
1789	*The Book of Thel*, 4°, 8 plates, 14 copies (Pl. 51 and Fig. on p. 363)
1790?	*The Marriage of Heaven and Hell*, 8°, 27 plates, 9 copies (Pl. 52 and Fig. on p. 447)
1790–91	C.G. Salzmann, *Elements of Morality for the Use of Children*, tr. [Mary Wollstonecraft], 3 vols (J. Johnson, 1791; 1792; 1799; 1805?; 1815?), 12°, 45 plates perhaps engraved by Blake after D.N. Chodowiecki*
1791	*The French Revolution* (J. Johnson), 8°, 20 pp. in type, 1 proof copy (Huntington) (Pl. 42)
1791, 1795	Erasmus Darwin, *The Botanic Garden* (J. Johnson, 1791; 1795; 1799; reprinted in his *Poetical Works*, 1806), 4°, 6 plates after Fuseli (2) and Blake's copies of Wedgwood's vase (4)

---

* The 10 anonymous engravings after Chodowiecki for Salzmann's *Gymnastics for Youth* (1800) are no longer thought to be by Blake.

1791   David Hartley, *Observations on Man* (J. Johnson, 1791; 1791),
            8°, 1 plate after Shackleton

1791   James Stuart & Nicholas Revett, *Antiquities of Athens*, III
            (Printed by John Nichols, 1794), folio, 4 plates after [Stuart &
            Revett]

1791   Mary Wollstonecraft, *Original Stories from Real Life*, 3 vols (J.
            Johnson, 1791; 1796), 12°, 6 plates after his own designs; re-
            engraved by Anon. in *Marie et Caroline* (Paris: Dentu, 1799) (Pl.
            43); Blake's 10 designs are in the U.S. National Gallery

1792   John Hunter, *Historical Journal of the Transactions at Port
            Jackson and Norfolk Island* (John Stockdale, 1793), 4° and 8°
            editions, 1 plate after Governor King

1792–94   John Gabriel Stedman, *Narrative of a five year's expedition against
            the Revolted Negroes of Surinam*, 2 vols (J. Johnson & J. Edwards,
            1796; 1806; 1813), 4°, 16 plates after Stedman (Pls 44–5)

1793   *Bellamy's Picturesque Magazine* (T. Bellamy, 1793), 8°, 1 plate
            after C.R. Ryley

1793   *America*, 4°, 19 plates, 16 copies (3 posthumous), 12 not
            coloured (Pls 35–6 and Figs on half-title, p. xxvi)

1793   *For Children: The Gates of Paradise*, 8°, 18 plates, 5 copies,
            uncoloured, revised, with 3 additional plates, as *For the Sexes*
            (1826?) (see Figs on pp. 29, 100, 110)

1793   **"The History of England, a small book of Engravings.
            Price 3s"**, 18? plates, 8°, no copy survives

1793   **"To the Public"**, 8°, 1? plate, no copy survives

1793   *Visions of the Daughters of Albion*, 4°, 11 plates, 18 copies (Pl.
            53 and Fig. on p. xxiv)

1793   "The Accusers" (1 copy; Second State [1793–96], 2 copies;
            Third State [1805–10 or later], 6 copies), "Albion Rose" (2
            copies; Second State [1804–18?], 2 copies), "Edward & Elinor"
            (2 copies), "Job" (1 copy; Second State [1804–18], 2 copies), and
            "Joseph of Arimathea Preaching" (2 copies) (Blake, 1793), folio,
            5 plates after his own designs

1793   James Earle, *Practical Observations on the Operation for the Stone*
            (J. Johnson, 1793; 1796; 1803), 8°, 2 plates of instruments after
            Anon.

1793   John Gay, *Fables* (John Stockdale, 1793; [1811]), 8°, 12 plates after W. Kent (5), J. Wootton (4), and H. Gravelot (3)

1793?–1818?   **Notebook**, MS, 8°, 120 pp., including "Vision of the Last Judgment" (1810?), "Public Address" (1811?), and "The Everlasting Gospel" (1818?) (British Library)

1794   *Europe*, 4°, 18 plates, 12 copies (4 posthumous), 4 uncoloured (Pls 54–6)

1794   "Ezekiel" (Blake, 1794), folio, 1 plate after his own design, First State (no copy known); Second State (post 1804 to 1818), 3 copies (see Pl. 47)

1794   *The First Book of Urizen*, 8°, 28 plates, 8 copies, mostly colour-printed (Pls 57–8, and Fig. on p. 30)

1794   *Songs of Innocence and of Experience*, 8°, 54 plates, 37 copies (9 posthumous), 11 uncoloured (see Figs on pp. 145, 146, 147, 351)

1794–95   George Cumberland, *Thoughts on Outline* (Robinson & T. Egerton, 1796), 4°, with 8 plates after Cumberland; 4 were reprinted in Cumberland's *Outlines from the Antients* (Septimus Prowett, 1829)

1794–96   Edward Young, *The Complaint and The Consolation, or Night Thoughts*, 537 **folio watercolours** (43 engraved in 1796–97) (British Museum Print Room) (for engravings, see Pls 64–70, and Fig. on p. 161)

1795   *The Book of Ahania*, 4°, 6 plates, 1 copy, colour-printed (Library of Congress) (Pl. 60)

1795   *The Book of Los*, 4°, 5 plates, 1 copy, colour-printed (British Museum Print Room) (Pl. 61)

1795   *The Song of Los*, 4°, 8 plates, 6 copies, colour-printed (Pl. 59)

1795   John Brown, *The Elements of Medicine*, 2 vols (J. Johnson, 1795), 8°, 1 plate after Donaldson

1795   Caius Valerius Catullus, *Poems*, tr. [John Knott] (J. Johnson, 1795), 2 plates after Xavier Della Rosa

1795   **Large Colour Prints** of (1) "Christ Appearing to the Apostles", (2) "Elohim Creating Adam" (Pl. 62), (3) "God Judging Adam", (4) "The Good and Evil Angels", (5) "Hecate", (6) "The House of Death", (7) "Lamech and his Two Wives", (8) "Naomi Entreating Ruth and Orpah to Return to the Land of Moab", (9) "Nebuchadnezzar", (10) "Newton", (11) "Pity", and (12) "Satan Exulting over Eve", some repeated as late as 1805, offered for sale as late as 1818

1796   **Large Book of Designs**, 4°, 8 plates from other works, 2 copies

1796   **Small Book of Designs**, 8°, 23 plates from other works, 2 copies

1796   Gottfried Augustus Bürger, *Leonora*, tr. J.T. Stanley (William Miller, 1796), 4°, 3 plates after his own designs

1796   George Cumberland, *An Attempt to Describe Hafod* (T. Egerton, 1796), 4°, 1 plate perhaps engraved by Blake

1796–97   Edward Young, *The Complaint, and The Consolation; or, Night Thoughts* [Nights I–V of 9] (Richard Edwards, 1797), folio, 43 plates after his own designs (Pls 64–70 and Fig. on p. 161); 26 copies are coloured, at least a few probably by Blake; one design copied by P. Jones in *The Seraph*, ed. John Whitaker (?1818–28)

1796?–1807 *Vala* or *The Four Zoas*, MS, folio, 146 pp. (British Library) (Pl. 80–1)

1797   Advertisement for carpets (Moore & Co., [1797]), folio, 1 plate after his own design

1797   Charles Allen, *A New and Improved History of England* (J. Johnson, 1797), 8°, 4 plates [after Fuseli]

1797   Charles Allen, *A New and Improved Roman History* (J. Johnson, 1798), 8°, 4 plates [after Fuseli]

1797   Leonard Euler, *Elements of Algebra*, tr. [Francis Horner] (J. Johnson, 1797), 8°, 1 plate after Ruchotte's medallion

1797   *Monthly Magazine*, IV (R. Phillips & J. Johnson, 1797), 8°, 1 plate after Anon.

1797–98   Thomas Gray, *Poems*, 116 **folio watercolours** for Flaxman (Yale Center for British Art) (Pls 71–3)

1799   "The Last Supper" exhibited at the Royal Academy

1799   John Flaxman, *A Letter to the Committee for Raising the Naval Pillar or Monument* (T. Cadell et al., 1799), 8°, 3 plates after Flaxman

1799   William Shakspeare, *Dramatic Works*, ed. George Steevens, 9 vols (Boydell, 1802 [i.e., 1803]; 1832), folio, 1 plate after John Opie; also issued in *Boydell's Graphic Illustrations of the Dramatic Works of Shakspeare* (Boydell, 1803?; 1807)

1799–1805   Bible 135 **folio temperas** (1799–1800) **and watercolours (1800–1805, with a few up to 1809)** for Butts (scattered) (Pls 3, 5, 37, 75–9, 130)

1800   William Hayley, *Essay on Sculpture* (T. Cadell Jr & W. Davies, 1800), 4°, 3 plates after T. Hayley and John Flaxman (2) (Pl. 83A)

1800   William Hayley, *Little Tom the Sailor* (Folkestone: The Widow Spicer, 1800), 4°, 4 plates after his own designs (Pl. 85)

1801   Henry Fuseli, *Lectures on Painting* (J. Johnson, 1801), 8°, 1 plate after Michelangelo

1801?   John Milton, *Comus*, 8°, 8 **watercolours**, the larger set (Huntington) (Pl. 86) repeated in c. 1815

1802   William Hayley, *Designs to a Series of Ballads* (Felpham: William Blake et al., 1802), 4°, 14 plates after his own designs (Pl. 92)

1802, 1804   William Hayley, *Life … of William Cowper*, 3 vols (J. Johnson, [Vols. I–II] 1803; [Second Edition of Vols I–II] 1803; [Vol. III] 1804), 4°, 6 plates after George Romney, D. Heins, Thomas Lawrence, Blake, Francis Stone, and John Flaxman (Pl. 89)

1803   William Hayley, *Triumphs of Temper* (T. Cadell & W. Davies, 1803; 1807), 12°, 6 plates after Maria Flaxman

1804[–11?]   *Milton A Poem*, 8°, 51 plates, 4 copies (Pl. 4A–B, 93–5)

1804[–20?]   *Jerusalem*, 4°, 100 plates, 8 copies (3 posthumous), 1 coloured (Pl. 110 and Figs on pp. xvii, 312, 313, 452)

1804   Prince Hoare, *Academic Correspondence* (Robson, Payne, Hatchard, & Barker, 1804), 8°, 1 plate after Flaxman

1804   William Shakspeare, *Plays*, ed. Alexander Chalmers, 9 and 10 vols (Longman, 1802–3; 1805; 1805; 1811), 8°, 2 plates after Fuseli

1805   40 **designs** for Robert Blair, *The Grave* (now scattered), mostly lost (etched by Schiavonetti [1808])

1805   John Flaxman, *The Iliad of Homer* (Longman et al., 1805–29; 1870), 4°, 3 plates after Flaxman, without text

1805   William Hayley, *Ballads . . . Relating to Animals* (Richard Phillips, 1805), 8°, 5 plates after his own designs (Pl. 97)

1805?   William Hayley, *Life of George Romney* (T. Payne, 1809), 4°, 1 plate after Romney

1805–6   *Job*, Butts set, 8°, 19 **watercolours**, 2 more added in 1823 (Pierpont Morgan Library)

1806   Prince Hoare, *Inquiry into the . . . Arts of Design in England* (Richard Phillips, 1806), 8°, 1 plate after Sir Joshua Reynolds

1806   Benj. Heath Malkin, *A Father's Memoirs of His Child* (Longman, Rees, & Orme, 1806), 4°, 1 plate designed and engraved by Blake, re-engraved by R.H. Cromek (Pls. 99–100)

1806–9   William Shakspeare, Second Folio (1632), 6 **watercolours** (British Museum Print Room)

1807?   "Enoch", lithograph after Blake's own design

1807   John Milton, *Paradise Lost*, 4°, 12 **watercolours** for the Rev Joseph Thomas (Huntington), repeated in 1808

1807?   **The Ballads or Pickering Manuscript**, 8°, 22 pp. (Pierpont Morgan Library)

1808   "Jacob's Dream" (Pl. 130) and "Christ in the Sepulchre, guarded by Angels" exhibited at the Royal Academy

1808   John Milton, *Paradise Lost*, 4°, the larger Butts set, 12 larger watercolours (9 in the Museum of Fine Art, Boston) (Pls 103–6)

1808   Robert Blair, *The Grave* (R.H. Cromek, 1808; 1813; [1870]), 4°, 12 plates after Blake engraved by Louis Schiavonetti; reprinted in Jose Joaquin de Mora, *Meditaciones Poeticas* (R. Ackermann; and in Megico, Columbia, Buenos Ayres, Chile, Peru, & Guatemala, 1826) (Pls 63, 91, 101–2, 111)

1809   *Descriptive Catalogue* (J. Blake, 1809), 8°, 72 pp. in type, 22 copies

1809   John Milton, *On the Morning of Christ's Nativity*, 4°, Rev Joseph Thomas set, 6 **watercolours** (Whitworth Art Gallery) (Pl. 68), repeated in *c.* 1815

1809–10   Blake exhibited 16 **pictures** at 28 Broad Street (his brother's hosiery shop): (1) "The Spiritual Form of Nelson", (2) "The Spiritual Form of Pitt", (3) "Sir Jeffrey Chaucer and the nine and twenty pilgrims in their journey to Canterbury", (4) "The Bard, from Gray", (5) "The Ancient Britons", (6) "A spirit vaulting from a cloud to turn and wind a fiery Pegasus", (7) "The Goats", (8) "The spiritual Preceptor", (9) "Satan calling up his Legions", (10) "The Bramins", (11) "The body of Abel, found by Adam and Eve", (12) "The Soldiers casting lots for Christ's Garments" (Pl. 76), (13) "Jacob's Ladder" (frontispiece), (14) "The Angels hovering over the Body of Jesus in the Sepulchre", (15) "Ruth", and (16) "The Penance of Jane Shore"

1810   "The Canterbury Pilgrims" (Blake, 1810–1941[?]), oblong folio, 1 plate after his own design (Pl. 103)

1811   Geoffrey Chaucer, *The Prologue and Characters of Chaucer's Canterbury Pilgrims* (Harris, 1812) 12°, 2 plates after his own designs

1812   Blake exhibited at the exhibition of The Associated Painters in Water Colours: (1) "Sir Jeoffrey Chaucer and the Twenty-seven Pilgrims", (2) "The Spiritual Form of Pitt", (3), "The Spiritual Form of Nelson", and (4) "Detached Specimens of … '*Jerusalem* …'"

1814–17   John Flaxman, *Compositions from … Hesiod* (Longman et al., 1817; 1870), 4°, 37 plates after Flaxman, without text (Pl. 112)

1815?   John Milton, *Comus*, 8°, 8 **watercolours** (Museum of Fine Art, Boston), repeated from the 1801 set

1815?   John Milton, *On the Morning of Christ's Nativity*, 8°, 6 **watercolours** (Huntington) (Pl. 87), repeated in smaller size from the 1809 set

1815–16   [*Wedgwood's Catalogue of Earthenware*] ([?Wedgwood, 1816?– 43?]), 8°, 18 plates after Blake's copies of Wedgwood earthenware

1815-19   Abraham Rees, *Cyclopaedia*, 39 vols of text, 6 vols of plates (Longman et al., 1802–20), 4°, 7 plates after Anon. (6) and Farey

1816?   John Milton, *L'Allegro*, 8°, 8 **watercolours** (Pierpont Morgan Library) (Pl. 114)

1816?   John Milton, *Il Penseroso*, 8°, 8 **watercolours** (Pierpont Morgan Library) (Pl. 101)

1816?   John Milton, *Paradise Regained*, 8°, 12 **watercolours** (Fitzwilliam Museum) (Pl. 116)

1818   "The Child of Nature" (3 copies) and "The Child of Art" (1 copy) (C. Borckhardt), folio, 2 plates after C. Borckhardt

1818–19   Smaller Blake–Varley Sketchbook, 34 leaves with Visionary Heads (now scattered) (Pl. 126)

1818–19   Larger Blake–Varley Sketchbook, 4°, 90 leaves (24 removed, one replaced), 52 with Visionary Heads (Allan Parker) (Pls 122–4)

1820   "Revd Robert Hawker" (A.A. Paris, 1820) (3 copies), folio, 1 plate after Ponsford

1820   "Mrs. Q" (J. Barrow, 1820) (15 copies plus 43 untraced), folio, 1 plate after H. Villiers

1821   *Job*, Linnell set, 8°, 21 **watercolours** (scattered)

1821?   *On Homer's Poetry [&] On Virgil*, 8°, 1 plate, uncoloured, 6 copies

1821   Virgil, *Pastorals*, ed. Robert John Thornton, Third Edition, 3 vols (F. & C. Rivington et al., 1821), 12°, 27 woodcuts by Blake after his own designs (4 after portraits by others), 1 Blake design engraved by Byfield; there is also an unpublished plate with 3 designs etched in relief by Blake (R.N. Essick) (Pls 127–8 and Figs on pp. 389, 391); Blake's drawings are now widely scattered

1822   *The Ghost of Abel*, 8°, 2 plates uncoloured, 4 copies

1824–27   John Bunyan, *Pilgrim's Progress*, 8°, 29 **watercolours** probably touched up by Catherine or Tatham (Allan Parker plus 1 in the U.S. National Gallery)

1824   *Remember Me!* (I. Poole, 1824; 1825), 12°, 1 plate after his own design

1824?   Enoch, 5 drawings (U.S. National Gallery)

1824–27   Dante, *Divine Comedy*, 103 **folio watercolours** (widely scattered) (Pl. 131)

1825   "Wilson Lowry" (Hurst, Robinson, 1825) (18 copies plus 11 untraced), folio, 1 plate after Linnell

1825   *Illustrations of The Book of Job* (William Blake & John Linnell, 1826; 1874), 4°, 22 plates without separate text (Pls 20, 128 and Figs on pp. 395, 400)

1826?   *For the Sexes: The Gates of Paradise*, 8°, 21 plates uncoloured, 9 copies (7 posthumous); a revision of *For Children* (1793) (Figs on pp. 140, 267, 440)

1826?   "**Laocoon**", 8°, 1 plate, uncoloured, 2 copies (Pl. 133)

1826–7?   **Illuminated Genesis MS**, 11 leaves (Huntington)

1826–27   *Blake's Illustrations of Dante* ([John Linnell, 1838; 1892; 1955; 1968), oblong folio, 7 plates after his own designs (Pl. 132)

Endnotes

Preface: The Purpose and Character of The Stranger from Paradise

1 G.E. Bentley, Jr, *A Bibliography of George Cumberland* (New York and London: Garland Publishing, 1975) and the edition of Cumberland's *The Captive of the Castle of Sennaar*, ed. G.E. Bentley, Jr. (Montreal, Kingston, London, Buffalo: McGill-Queen's University Press, 1991).

2 G.E. Bentley, Jr, *The Early Engravings of Flaxman's Classical Designs* (New York: New York Public Library, 1964) and David Irwin, *John Flaxman 1755–1826:* Sculptor, Illustrator, Designer (London: Studio Vista/Christie's, 1979).

3 Gert Schiff's catalogue raisonné of *Johann Heinrich Füssli 1741–1825* (Zurich: Verlag Berichthaus; Munich: Prestel-Verlag, 1973); *The Collected Letters of Henry Fuseli*, ed. David Weinglass (Millwood [New York], London, Nendeln [Liechtenstein]: Kraus International Publications, 1982); and D.H. Weinglass, *Prints and Engraved Illustrations By and After Henry Fuseli:* A Catalogue Raisonné (Aldershot: Scolar Press, 1994).

4 Shelley M. Bennett, *Thomas Stothard:* The Mechanisms of Art Patronage in England circa 1800 (Columbia: University of Missouri Press, 1988).

5 G.E. Bentley, Jr, "Thomas Butts White Collar Maecenas", *PMLA*, LXXI (1956), 1052–66; Joseph Viscomi, "William Blake's 'The Phoenix/to Mrs Butts' Redux", *Blake*, XXIX (1995), 12–15; Joseph Viscomi, "Blake in the Marketplace 1852: Thomas Butts, Jr. and Other Unknown Nineteenth-Century Blake Collectors", *Blake*, XXIX (1995), 40–68; Joseph Viscomi, "A 'Green House' for Butts? New Information on Thomas Butts, his Residences, and Family", *Blake*, XXX (1996), 4–21.

6 Gerald P. Tyson, *Joseph Johnson, A Liberal Publisher* (Iowa City: University of Iowa Press, 1979) and the discovery of Joseph Johnson's office letter-book now in the Pforzheimer Library.

7 David Linnell, *Blake, Palmer, Linnell and Co.:* The Life of John Linnell (1994).

Introduction: Paradise and the Beast

1 *Milton* pl. 37, l. 43; *Jerusalem* pl. 75, l. 20; pl. 89, l. 53

2 *Vala* p. 111, l. 24.

3 *Jerusalem* pl. 74, l. 32.

4 *Jerusalem* pl. 74, l. 16.

5 Marginalium (1798) to Watson, *Apology* (1797) p. 25.

6 Letter of 7 Aug 1804.

7 Marginalium (?1798) to Bacon, *Essays* (1798) p. 14.

8 *BR* 292.

9 Gilchrist quoting unnamed friends of Blake (*BR* 567).

10 Letter from Thomas Woolner of 1860 (*BR* 274–5).

11 Letter of 25 April 1803.

12 Crabb Robinson in 1826 (*BR* 337).

13 Draft of "London" in Blake's Notebook p. 109.

Chapter I 1720–1772: God at the Window

1 Crabb Robinson (*BR* 543).

2 Anon., "Nativity of Mr. Blake, The Mystical Artist", *Urania*, No. 1 (1825), with explanations of its astrological significance, perhaps by John Varley (*BR* 296–7).

3 [John Lambert], *An Illustrated Guide to St James's Church Piccadilly* (London: St James's Church, [1991]), 6.

4 Mark x, 14, used in the baptismal service.

5 Cunningham (*BR* 482).

6 See *BR* (2).

7 See *BR* (2).

8 *BRS* 2–8.

9 See *BR* (2).

10 Tatham (*BR* 508).

11 Tatham (*BR* 519).

12 Cunningham (*BR* 477, 480–1).

13 See *BR* (2).

14 "Blake & Son, Hosiers & Haberdashers" at 28 Broad Street are listed in *Kent's London Directory* (1793–1800), *The New Annual Directory* (1800, 1801, 1803), *Holden's Triennial Directory* (1802–4), and "Blake, James, Hosier" in *The Universal British Directory* (1790), *Kent's Directory* (1794–1800), *Holden's Triennial Directory* (1799, 1805–11), *Kent's Directory* (1801–2, 1804–8, 1810), *The New Annual Directory* (1806–13), and in *The Post Office Directory* (1812).

15 Gilchrist (*BR* 2, 3).

16 *BR* 562.

17 Smith (*BR* 465).

18 Gilchrist (*BR* 3).

19 Tatham (*BR* 509).

20 Tatham (*BR* 508).

21 Tatham (*BR* 510).

22 Smith (*BR* 457).

23 Tatham (*BR* 509).

24 Letter to Blake of Sept 1800.

25 Gilchrist (*BR* 415).

26 Letter of 1 Feb 1826.

27 Smith (*BR* 476).

28 "The Everlasting Gospel" Part e, ll. 13–14, Notebook p. 33.

29 "The Chimney Sweeper", *Experience* (*Songs* pl. 37).

30 "The Everlasting Gospel" Part d, ll. 37–8, Notebook p. 120.

31 Lodowick Muggleton, *A Looking-Glass for George Fox* (1756), 62–3 (quoted in E.P. Thompson, *Witness Against the Beast* [1993], 94).

32 Annotation to Watson's *Apology for the Bible* p. 25.

33 Cunningham (*BR* 502).

34 Crabb Robinson Diary for 9 Feb 1826.

35 Samuel Palmer (*BR* 42).

36 Samuel Palmer (*BR* 283).

37 Crabb Robinson Diary for 18 Feb 1826.

38 See Chapter IV.

39 Crabb Robinson Diary for 7 Dec 1826.

40 Crabb Robinson Diary for 10 Dec 1826.

41 Crabb Robinson Diary for 17 Dec 1826.

42 Crabb Robinson Diary for 10 Dec 1826.

43 Annotation to Thornton, *Lord's Prayer* p. 3.

44 Annotation to Bacon's *Essays* p. 14.

45 Crabb Robinson Diary for 10 Dec 1825.

46 John Saddington, *The Articles of true Faith* (1830), written in 1675 and circulated in manuscript (quoted in E.P. Thompson, *Witness Against the Beast* [1993], 73). The images are also Kabalistic.

47 *America* pl. 17, l. 191 and annotation to Swedenborg's *Divine Providence* p. xix.

48 Annotations to Watson's *Apology for the Bible*, 1, 6.

49 Letter of 22 Nov 1802, all punctuation added.

50 Letter of 14 Sept 1800.

51 Letter of 7 Oct 1803.

52 *Milton* pl. 18, l. 44.

53 Marginalium to Reynolds, *Works* p. 157.

54 W.T. Whitley, *Artists and their Friends in England 1700–1799* (London, 1928), I, 115.

55 *Survey of London Volume XXXI: The Parish of St James Westminster Part Two: North of Piccadilly* (London: The Athlone Press, 1963) 204–5.

56 Smith (*BR* 465).

57 "MR BLAKE'S NURSERY RHYME" was once with *Songs* (X) but has since disappeared; it is quoted in Geoffrey Keynes & Edwin Wolf 2nd, *William Blake's Illuminated Books: A Census* (New York: The Grolier Club of New York, 1953), 64.

58 Henry Chamberlaine, *A New and Compleat History and Survey of the Cities of London and Westminster* (London: J. Cooke [1770]), 599.

59 As in "Blind-man's Buff" in *Poetical Sketches*.

60 Such games are shown in Blake's designs for Gray's "Ode on a Distant Prospect of Eton College".

61 *An Island in the Moon* Chapter 11.

62 Crabb Robinson Diary for 10 Dec 1825.

63 See "The Freaks of Learning: Learned Pigs, Musical Hares, and the Romantics", *Colby Library Quarterly*, XVIII (1982), 87–104. Blake refers to both Learned Pigs and Hares playing on a tabor (Notebook p. 40).

64 As in Hogarth's "Gin Lane" (1751).

65 "Edward the Third", Scene [ii], ll. 10–11 (*Poetical Sketches*).

66 Letter of 21 Sept 1800.

67 Letter of 23 Aug 1799.

68 Crabb Robinson's Reminiscences (*BR* 542–3), a passage which does not appear in his Diary: Catherine Blake said, "You know, dear, the first time you saw God was when You were four years old And he put his head to the window and set you ascreaming."

69 Linnell wrote that Blake was "reprov'd by his Father for asserting" his "belief in his inspiration" (*BR* 318 n2).

70 Crabb Robinson Diary for 10, 17 Dec 1825.

71 Vision of the Last Judgment, Part x, Notebook p. 95; I have divided one paragraph into three.

72 Linnell noted his "Early talent of design 3 years old" (*BR* 318 n2).

73   Cunningham (*BR* 477).
74   Stanley Gardner, *The Tyger, the Lamb, and the Terrible Desart* (London: Cygnus Arts; Madison & Teaneck: Fairleigh Dickinson University Press, 1998), 6, with no indication of source.
75   Samuel Johnson, *The Rambler*, No. 116 (27 April 1751) in *The Rambler*, IV (London: J. Payne & J. Bosquet, 1752), 141–2, a story about an apprentice haberdasher. Of course the account is a caricature of a mechanic or counter trade ("applying all my powers to the knowledge of my trade, I was quickly master of all that could be known"), but it does show a useful patrician view of an apprentice haberdasher at work.
76   Autobiographical "Memoirs of Thomas Jones, Penkerrig Radnorshire 1803", ed. A.P. O[ppé], *Walpole Society*, XXXII (1951), 8, reporting his experience in 1767, the year Blake joined the school.
77   Marginalium to Reynolds, *Works* p. xix.
78   Autobiographical "Memoirs of Thomas Jones, Penkerrig Radnorshire 1803," ed. A.P. O[ppé], *Walpole Society*, XXXII (1951), 8.
79   Malkin (*BR* 421). Presumably Malkin means that Blake profited from these opportunities.
80   Malkin (*BR* 422).
81   *Descriptive Catalogue* (1809) ¶78.
82   Malkin (*BR* 422).
83   *BR* 283.
84   *BR* 288.
85   Malkin (*BR* 428).
86   It is quoted in his Notebook pp. 88–9.
87   This is a series of engravings of the paintings in the Vatican made long after Raphael's death in 1520.
88   Advertisement [by A.S. Mathew] to *Poetical Sketches*.
89   Tatham (*BR* 527).
90   Gilchrist (*BR* 234).
91   *Milton* pl. 28, l. 57; "The Crystal Cabinet" from the Pickering Manuscript p. 11.

Chapter II 1772–1779: The Visionary Apprentice

1   Letter of 23 Aug 1799.
2   Gilchrist (*BR* 511 n1).
3   *BR* 511 n1.
4   *Jerusalem* pl. 12, l. 26; pl. 90, l. 48.
5   As William Hayley wrote in 1789 (*BR* 556); Hayley lived in Kneller's house at 5 Great Queen Street in 1769–74.
6   Public Address, Notebook p. 51.
7   Samuel Palmer describing Blake's rooms in Fountain Court about 1824–27 (*BR* 565 n4).
8   Letter of 12 March 1804.
9   Public Address, Notebook p. 24.
10   *BR* 12.
11   *BR* 460 n1.
12   Gilchrist (*BR* 13); Goldsmith died in 1774.
13   James Boswell, *Life of Samuel Johnson* (1791), chapter called "Aetat 54".
14   Public Address, Notebook p. 58.
15   Public Address, Notebook p. 58.
16   Malkin (*BR* 422–3).
17   Butlin #1.
18   *On Homer's Poetry [&] On Virgil.*
19   Malkin (*BR* 423).
20   "To the Public" (10 Oct 1793).
21   Marginalia to Wordsworth, *Poems* p. 364.
22   *Lectures on the English Poets* (1818).
23   Lamb's letter of 15 May 1824.
24   Crabb Robinson's Reminiscences (*BR* 543–4).
25   Tatham (*BR* 509).
26   The preface [by A.S. Mathew] to *Poetical Sketches* says that the poems were "commenced in his twelfth, and occasionally resumed ... till his twentieth year", i.e., from Nov 1768 to Nov 1777.
27   "A War Song to Englishmen" l. 21, *Poetical Sketches* p. 59.
28   "The Everlasting Gospel" part d, l. 38, Notebook p. 120.
29   *BRS* 11.
30   On 26 Aug 1799, Blake wrote: "It is now Exactly Twenty years since I was upon the ocean of business."
31   As Blake said of his move to Felpham in his letter of 21 Sept 1800.

Chapter III 1779–1787: "Delighted with Good Company"

1   Upcott's Autograph Album.
2   Blake's marginalium to *The Works of Sir Joshua Reynolds, Knight*, I, 56.
3   Malkin (*BR* 423).
4   Sidney C. Hutchison, "The Royal Academy Schools, 1768–1830", *Walpole Society*, XXXVIII (1962), 130, and *Library of the Fine Arts*, III (1832), 443, 444.
5   *Descriptive Catalogue* ¶87.
6   James Elmes, *Annals of the Fine Arts*, II (1818), 359.
7   Gilchrist (*BR* 31), recounted as an anecdote "Blake used to tell".

8 Gilchrist (*BR* 31), citing a letter from "a surviving friend" about a time when Blake was "a very young man".

9 Marginalium to *The Works of Sir Joshua Reynolds, Knight* I, title page verso.

10 Gilchrist (*BR* 33).

11 J.T. Smith and Frederick Tatham (*BR* 469, 517).

12 Cunningham (*BR* 503).

13 Tatham (*BR* 517). Tatham's account of Blake's tempera technique applies to the years he knew Blake (*c.* 1824–27); Blake's early practice was probably quite different.

14 Samuel Palmer to George Richmond in Oct 1828 (*BRS* 9).

15 William Vincent, *A Plain and Succinct Narrative of the Late Riots and Disturbances in the Cities of London and Westminster . . .* with an Account of the Commitment of Lord George Gordon to the Tower (London Fielding & Walker, 1780) 35, 26.

16 Cumberland letter of 7 June 1780 (*BR* 18).

17 Gilchrist (*BR* 18); this "long remembered" story is reported by no one else.

18 *America* pl. 16, l. 176; *Vala* p. 123, l. 8; *French Revolution* l. 67, *Jerusalem* pl. 5, l. 6; *Europe* pl. 15, l. 177; *America* pl. c, l. 9; *Jerusalem* pl. 14, l. 28; *Vala* p. 58, l. 18; *Milton* pl. 24, l. 32; *Jerusalem* pl. 29, l. 82.

19 According to Anon., "John Flaxman, Esq. R.A. Professor of Sculpture at the Royal Academy", *Annual Biography and Obituary for the year 1828*, XII (1828), 21, "in early life he [*Flaxman*] was in the habit of frequently passing his evenings in drawing and designing in the company of . . . Mr. Stothard, Mr. Blake, . . . Mr. George Cumberland, and Mr. Sharp".

20 Letter of 12 Sept 1800.

21 Mrs [A.E.] Bray, *Life of Thomas Stothard, R.A.* (London: John Murray, 1851) (*BR* 19–20). This account by Stothard's daughter-in-law is supplemented by "the account of Frederick Tatham recieved from Mrs Blake" on the copy of the print in the Balmanno Collection in the British Museum Print Room ("Parkes") and by the imprecise note of "M.ʳˢ Blakes account" on the copy of the print in the Rosenwald Collection of the U.S. National Gallery (which identifies "T. Blake", "Parkes", and "the Coast of France").

22 Most of the background details here derive from "Blake's First Arrest, at Upnor Castle", *Blake*, XXXI (1997–98), 82–4.

23 The first line of a "Song" taken, like the other poems quoted just below, from *Poetical Sketches*.

24 Gilchrist (*BR* 21).

25 Gilchrist (*BR* 21).

26 *Ambulator:* or, A Pocket Companion in a Tour Round London, 9th edn (London: J. Scatcherd, 1800), 32, 33.

27 Tatham (*BR* 517).

28 Tatham (*BR* 518).

29 See the Boucher genealogy above (p. xx). At least three of her sisters had died in childhood.

30 For individuals named Bouche, Boucher, Bouchet[t], Bucher, and Du Bouchet, see *Lists of French Protestants and Aliens Residing in England 1618–1678* from Returns in the State Papers Office, ed. Wm Durant Cooper (Camden Society, 1862); David A. Agnew, *Protestant Exiles in France in the Reign of Louis XIV*, or, The Huguenot Refugees and their Descendants in Great Britain and Ireland (London: Reeves & Turner, 1871), I, 26, 28–9, 37–8, 52, 58; Eugene & Emile Haag, *La France Protestante*, 2nd edn, II (Paris, 1889), 964–5; *The Registers of the French Church, Threadneedle Street, London*, ed. T.C. Collyer-Fergusson (1916), Publication of The Huguenot Society of London, XXIII; *Registers of the Churches of the Tabernacle, Glasshouse Street and Leicester Fields, London, 1688–1783*, ed. William & Susan Minet (1926), Huguenot Society, XXIX; *Société de l'Histoire du Protestantisme Français, Table Alphabétique, Analytique & Chronologique . . . du Bulletin historique et littéraire (1852–1902)* (Paris, 1902); A.P. Hands & Irene Scouloudi, *French Protestant Refugees Relieved through the Threadneedle Street Church, London, 1681–1687* (1971), Huguenot Society, XLIX; *The Case Book of "La Maison de Charité de Spittlefields"* (1981), Huguenot Society Quarto Series, LV; *Minutes of the Consistory of the French Church of London, Threadneedle Street 1679–1692*, Calendared by Robin Gwynn (1994), Huguenot Society Quarto Series, LVIII.

For instance, John Boucher was one of the London Merchants who signed a Loyal Address against the [Catholic] Pretender in 1744 (David C.A. Agnew, *Protestant Exiles from France*, 3rd edn [1886], I, 212).

31 Agnew, *Protestant Exiles*, II, 104.

32 Hillel Schwartz, *The French Prophets:* The History of a Millenarian Group in Eighteenth-Century England (Berkeley & Los Angeles: University of California Press, 1980), esp. 216, 285.

33 Robin D. Gwynn, *The Huguenot Heritage:* The history and contribution of the Huguenots in Britain (London, Boston, Melbourne & Henley: Routledge & Kegan Paul, 1985), 68.

34   Gwynn, *Huguenot Heritage*, 68.
35   The Register of the Tabernacle in Glasshouse Street and Leicester Fields 1688–1783 in *The Publications of The Huguenot Society of London*, Vol. XXIX (1920). The Hog Lane Church absorbed other French churches in London (Reginald Lane Poole, *A History of the Huguenots of the Dispersion at the Recall of the Edict of Nantes* [London: Macmillan, 1880], 85).
36   *BR* 556–7.
37   [Charles Lamb], "The South Sea House", *Essays of Elia* (London: Taylor & Hessey, 1820), 7.
38   *Minutes of the ... French Church of London*, LVIII, pp. 85, 104, 110, 115, 118, 220, 272.
39   Gwynn, *Minutes*, 160.
40   Tatham (*BR* 517).
41   *Ambulator:* or, A Pocket Companion in a Tour Round London, 9th edn (London: J. Scatcherd, 1800), 33.
42   *BR* 6.
43   Blake's good friend Henry Fuseli told Joseph Farington on 24 June 1796 that Blake had "married a maid servant".
44   As William Hayley wrote on 3 Aug 1805, repeated almost word for word from his letter of 15 July 1802; each passage begins "perhaps".
45   Crabb Robinson Reminiscences (*BR* 542).
46   Gilchrist (*BR* 237).
47   Crabb Robinson Reminiscences (*BR* 542).
48   Gilchrist (*BR* 307).
49   Hayley's letter of 15 July 1802.
50   Tatham (*BR* 534).
51   Hayley letter of 15 July 1802; Hayley also wrote poetry for music.
52   Crabb Robinson Reminiscences (*BR* 542).
53   George Richmond (*BR* 294) "in excuse for the general lack of soap and water".
54   *Marriage* pl. 7.
55   Tatham, clearly derived from Catherine (*BR* 518).
56   Letter of 22 June 1804.
57   *BR* 569.
58   For details of Blake's Commercial Engravings, see Appendix 2.
59   There was "half a gale blowing", according to "Daily records kept at Sion House" (Stanley Gardner, *The Tyger, the Lamb, and the Terrible Desart* [London: Cygnus Arts; Madison & Teaneck: Fairleigh Dickinson University Press, 1998], 31).
60   Letter of 16 Sept 1800.
61   Tatham (*BR* 534).
62   This is the address Blake gave when he exhibited at the Royal Academy in May 1784.
63   As Fuseli told Joseph Farington about the Blakes on 24 June 1796.
64   W.T. Whitley, *Artists and Their Friends in England 1700–1799* (London, 1928), II, 282.
65   Hayley letter of 3 Aug 1805.
66   Hayley letter of 15 July 1802.
67   Seymour Kirkup to Lord Houghton, 25 March 1870 (*BR* 221); she "was as good as a servant. He had no other".
68   J.T. Smith (*BR* 459).
69   Crabb Robinson Diary for 18 Feb 1826.
70   Marginalium to Lavater, *Aphorisms* p. 210.
71   Gilchrist (*BR* 275–6).
72   Gilchrist (*BR* 276), following and perhaps paraphrasing comments by Samuel Palmer. I have divided the long paragraph into several short ones.
73   Tatham (*BR* 525). The Blakes might have expected to be able to live for about a week on a guinea.
74   Smith, *A Book for a Rainy Day* (*BR* 26–7).
75   Blake's inscription in Upcott's Autograph Album in 1826.
76   Smith, *A Book for a Rainy Day* (*BR* 26).
77   Smith (*BR* 457). The only songs Blake is known to have written at this time are in his *Island in the Moon* (?1784).
78   *BRS* 18–19.
79   Smith (*BR* 456).
80   Smith (*BR* 457).
81   Letter of 23 Oct 1804, see *BR* 68, 70–2, 99.
82   In 1806 Malkin quoted the two Songs beginning "I love the jocund dance" and "How sweet I roam'd" (*BR* 428–30); in 1811 Crabb Robinson gave "To the Muses" in German (*BR* 442); in 1828 J.T. Smith printed "How Sweet" (*BR* 457); in 1830 Cunningham gave "To the Muses", "I love the jocund dance", and parts of "Edward the Third", "Gwin King of Norway" (*BR* 478–80, 505–6); and in 1847 Robert Southey printed the "Mad Song" in his collection of anecdotes called *The Doctor*. William and Dorothy Wordsworth copied "I love the jocund dance" from Malkin (*BR* 430 n1), Tatham incorporated "How sweet I roam'd" and "Love and Harmony Combine" in his manuscript biography of *c.* 1831 (*BR* 513–14), and Crabb Robinson transcribed "To the Muses" and "How sweet I roamed" (*BR* 224 n. 3).
83   Malkin (*BR* 431).
84   *BR* 453; the original German version is on p. 442.
85   Cunningham (*BR* 479); he says that the prose is "wild and incoherent" (480).
86   Cunningham (*BR* 478).
87   Tatham (*BR* 513).
88   Cunningham (*BR* 480).
89   A.C. Swinburne, *William Blake* (London: John Camden Hotten, 1868), 8.

90 See Martha England, "The Satiric Blake: Apprenticeship at the Haymarket?", *Bulletin of the New York Public Library*, LXXIII (1969), 440–64, 531–50.

91 British Library Add MSS 36,494, ff. 357–8◦ See the letter of Candid [George Cumberland] in the *Morning Chronicle*, 21 Oct 1784, on "Mr. Taylor's Lecture on the Lamps of the Ancients", which discreetly says nothing of the explosion.

92 William George Meredith, Taylor's patron, writing on 30 Dec 1829 (*BRS* 94–5).

93 *Vala* p. 33, ll. 34–5.

94 Alexander Dyce, Taylor's long-time friend, writing about 1867–69 (*BRS* 95); I have broken up the long paragraph into several smaller ones.

95 *BR* (2).

96 *BR* (2).

97 *BR* (2).

98 *Abstract of the Annual Registers of the Parish Poor ... [for] 1783* (1784), and *Sketch of the State of the Children of the Poor in the Year 1756, and of the Present State and Management of all the Poor in the Parish of Saint James, Westminster* (1797), p. 1. The paragraphs above about the St James institutions derive from *BRS* 2–7.

99 *Sketch of ... the Poor, in the Parish of Saint James*, 3–5.

100 *Sketch of ... the Poor, in the Parish of Saint James*, 5–6.

101 *An Island in the Moon* (?1784) Chapter 11; "Holy Thursday" was modified slightly when it was printed in *Songs of Innocence* (1789).

102 For all details of the business of Blake & Son with the parish of St James, see *BRS* 2–8.

103 *Sketch of ... the Poor, in the Parish of Saint James*, 3.

104 *BR* 554.

105 Tatham (*BR* 509).

106 *BR* 558.

107 *BR* 558.

108 Tatham (*BR* 509).

109 *BR* (2).

110 Tatham says James Blake "supported his only sister" until his death in 1827 (*BR* 509).

111 Linnell's note on J.T. Smith (*BR* 461 n1).

112 Flaxman's letters of 27 Aug 1795 ("The Journeyman and the Genius: James Parker and His Partner William Blake With a List of Parker's Engravings", *Studies in Bibliography*, XLIX [1996], 208–31) and 7 Nov 1804 (*BR* 155).

113 Obituary of Parker in *Gentleman's Magazine*, LXXV (June 1805), 586.

114 Some of these details derive from Parker's will reported in "The Death of Blake's Partner James Parker", *Blake*, XXX (1996), 49–51.

115 See "The Journeyman and the Genius: James Parker and His Partner William Blake With a List of Parker's Engravings", *Studies in Bibliography*, XLIX (1996), 208–31.

116 Gilchrist (*BR* 29).

117 *BR* 603.

118 Parker's will of 1805 (see above, n114) did not mention a printing press.

119 Cunningham (*BR* 482).

120 Gilchrist (*BR* 363–4), describing Catherine's methods after Blake's death.

121 *BRS* 8.

122 Smith (*BR* 457).

123 Gilchrist (*BR* 30), one paragraph which I have divided into three. Catherine was two months older than Robert.

124 See John Heath, *The Heath Family of Engravers 1779–1878* (London: Scolar Press, 1993), I, 142.

125 For Blake's plates, see Appendix 2 here; for Parker's, see "The Journeyman and the Genius: James Parker and his Partner William Blake with a List of Parker's Engravings", *Studies in Bibliography*, XLIX (1996), 208–31.

126 As Parker wrote in his letter of 24 March 1803 to the amateur illustrated book publisher Du Roveray (see "F.J. Du Roveray, Illustrated-Book Publisher 1798–1806: [Part] III: Du Roveray's Artists and Engravers and the Engravers' Strike", *Bibliographical Society of Australia and New Zealand Bulletin*, XII [1988], 101—the essay displays Parker's diplomatic skills in reconciling Du Roveray with the striking engravers).

127 Public Address (*c.* 1811) (Notebook p. 52) speaking of a time "five & twenty years ago".

128 Smith (*BR* 457). The passage begins "soon after this period", referring to *Poetical Sketches* (1783), but as the firm of Parker & Blake was at 27 Broad Street "next door to his father's" (as Smith says) only from the end of 1784 to the end of 1785, the date of Mrs Mathew's generosity in enabling them to continue in business was probably in the spring or summer of 1785.

129 Smith (*BR* 457).

130 Cunningham (*BR* 482).

131 Fanny Burney, *Memoirs of Dr Charles Burney* (1832), I, 134, describing the area as it was about 1770. Oxford Road is now called Oxford Street.

132 Allan Cunningham, *The Life of Sir David Wilkie* (London, 1843), I, 80, describing the public house in 1805.

133 Tatham (*BR* 510).

134 Linnell (*BR* 459 n2).
135 Gilchrist (*BR* 32).
136 Linnell (*BR* 459 n2).
137 *Vala* p. 125, ll. 29–30.
138 *Vala* p. 133, l. 25.
139 Letter from Catherine Blake of 14 Sept 1800.
140 Letter of 22 Nov 1802.

Chapter IV 1787–1795: Dark Profitable Years

1 Blake speaks in his letter of 23 Oct 1804 of the "twenty dark, but very profitable years" from 1784 to 1804.
2 Last page of *Island in the Moon* (?1784).
3 George Cumberland, "A New Mode of Printing", *A New Review*, IV (Oct 1784), 318–19.
4 As Cumberland confessed in his letter of 2 Jan 1784 (British Library Add MSS 36,494, ff. 231–2), though he did not mention this defect in his printed essay on the subject.
5 Anon., *Valuable Secrets concerning Arts and Trades* ([1758], 1775, 1778, 1795, 1798, 1809, 1810), gave directions "*To engrave with* aquafortis, *so that the work may appear like a* basso relievo".
6 Public Address, Notebook pp. 58, 24.
7 *Descriptive Catalogue* ¶76.
8 J.T. Smith, amplified by Cunningham and Gilchrist (*BR* 460, 486, 32–3).
9 Gilchrist (*BR* 32).
10 Joseph Viscomi, *Blake and the Idea of the Book* (Princeton: Princeton University Press, 1993), 118.
11 See Viscomi, *Blake and the Idea of the Book*, the source of most of the information about Blake's techniques of Illuminated Printing here.
12 Letter of 12 Sept 1800.
13 Letter of 2 July 1800.
14 *BR* 531.
15 John Johnson letter of 14 June 1822 (see *BR* [2]).
16 Public Address, Notebook p. 62.
17 Notebook p. 40.
18 As Linnell had heard (*BR* 53).
19 *BR* 53.
20 Cunningham's life of Fuseli (*BR* 480 n 10); I have divided the single paragraph into three.
21 Fuseli letter of 17 Aug 1798 (*BRS* 15).
22 Smith (*BR* 467), silently echoed by Gilchrist (*BR* 39).
23 Gilchrist (*BR* 39). Tatham said that "Fuseli admired Blake & learned from him as he himself confessed, a great deal" (*BR* 531).

24 *Poetical Sketches* (E, F, S), which he sponsored, *Descriptive Catalogue* (N), *Songs of Innocence* (D), and *Songs of Innocence and of Experience* (O).
25 Gilchrist (*BR* 39).
26 Erasmus Darwin to Josiah Wedgwood, 9 July 1791 (*BRS* 10).
27 Johnson to Erasmus Darwin, 23 July 1791.
28 *BR* (2).
29 *The French Revolution* ll. 89–90, 94–6. This defence of the past is apparently based upon Edmund Burke.
30 Letter of Richard Twiss to Francis Douce, 25 Sept 1794—see *BR* (2).
31 Gilchrist (*BR* 40) was, of course, writing half a century and more after the facts. Tatham said that Blake "was intimate with a great many of the most learned & eminent men of his time, whom he generally met at Johnsons, the Bookseller of S! Pauls Church Yard[.] It was there he met Tom Paine ..." (*BR* 530), but the social intimacy which Tatham alleges is probably exaggerated.
32 [William West], "Annals of Authors, Artists, Books, and Booksellers, Letter XI: Mr. Johnson of St. Paul's Church-Yard, and his Literary Connexions", *Aldine Magazine*, I (April 1839), 204: "I knew Mr. Johnson from 1785 to 1805."
33 *BR* 40–1. Samuel Greatheed said on 27 Jan 1805 that he "understood, that, during the crisis of the French Revolution, he [*Blake*] had been one of its earnest partizans".
34 Linnell wrote notes of what he intended to tell Gilchrist about Blake's life, including Richard "Edwards Godwin, Paine, H. Tooke, &c.—Fuseli" (*BR* 318 n2).
35 *BRS* 14.
36 Gilchrist (*BR* 40).
37 Fuseli writes on 29 May 1792 of "M! Paine who is a Mechanic as well as a Demogorgon", and Hayley's reference of 1800 to Romney's painting studio as "Demogorgons Hall" "may mean that Paine had helped to fit up Romney's studio" (*BR* 46, 70 & n2).
38 Marginalia (1798) to Bishop Watson's *Apology for the Bible* (1797) pp. 12–13.
39 Watson, *Apology*, p. 1.
40 Watson, *Apology*, p. 49.
41 *BR* 41 n1.
42 *BR* 530–1.
43 Michael Phillips, "Flames in the Night Sky: Blake, Paine and the Meeting of the Society of Loyal Britons, October 10ᵗʰ, 1793", *Bulletin de la Société d'Etudes Anglo-Américaines des XVIIᵉ et XVIIIᵉ Siècles*, No. 44 (juin 1997), 100. There is no evidence that Blake met or was even

aware of the Loyal Britons mob, but their clamour and conflagration may have been apparent to his neighbours.

44   *BR* 45, quoting from Stedman's diary (then in the collection of Stanbury Thompson and now in the University of Minnesota Library). All the quotations from Stedman are from this source (see *BR* 45–51).

45   Details of Johnson's agreement with Stedman derive from Johnson's Letterbook (now in the Pforzheimer Collection, New York Public Library), which is quoted extensively in "William Blake and His Circle . . . 1995", *Blake*, XXIX (1996).

46   Stedman's *Narrative* in the form in which he submitted it to Johnson was edited by Richard Price and Sally Price (Baltimore and London, 1988).

47   E.g., in May 1796 Stedman wrote "12 letters to Blake"; none of the Stedman–Blake correspondence is known to have survived.

48   Tatham speaks of Blake's "utter detestation of human slavery" (*BR* 521).

49   Letters of 10 Jan 1802, 11 Sept 1801.

50   Letter of 26 Aug 1799.

51   *Milton* pl. a, l. 26.

52   Letter of 25 April 1803, a general statement not referring to Stedman.

53   *BR* 522.

54   Letter of 22 Nov 1802.

55   Letter of 21 Sept 1800.

56   Public Address, Notebook p. 64.

57   See *BR* (2) under 1789.

58   J. Hassell, *Memoirs of the Life of the Late George Morland* (London: James Cundee & C. Chapple, 1806) (*BRS* 9).

59   *BR* 189.

60   *BR* 136.

61   *BR* 46, *BRS* 10.

62   Flaxman letter of 7 Nov 1804 (*BR* 155).

63   Letter of 26 Aug 1799.

64   *BR* 569.

65   *BR* 55; Blake's copy of Cumberland's *Thoughts on Outline* has not been traced.

66   Letter of 26 Aug 1799.

67   See *BB* 542–4 for details; Cumberland may have given away as many copies as he sold.

68   "When Klopstock England defied" l. 8, Notebook p. 5.

69   Tatham (*BR* 522).

70   The authority for the statements about three floors plus a basement, the panelling, and the mantelpieces is Thomas Wright (*Life of William Blake* [Olney, Thomas Wright, 1929], I, 51), who "went over the house twice a few years before it was pulled down", while the information about the grates, cupboards, and the well-proportioned ground-floor rooms derives from Anon., "William Blake's Homes in Lambeth and Sussex", *Spectator*, No. 4,584 (6 May 1916), 571–2.

71   *Europe* pl. 3, ll. 23–4.

72   *Observer*, 10 Feb 1793, a reference generously pointed out to me by my friend Paul Miner, who explores its significance in his *The Bard's Prophetic Song* (MS in 1999). The reference gives no indication of which house in Hercules Buildings had the peach and rose trees.

73   Tatham (*BR* 521). Fuseli reported on 24 June 1796 that they then had no servant.

74   Letter of 12 April 1827.

75   *Jerusalem* pl. 84, l. 4.

76   *Milton* pl. 4, ll. 14–15; cp. *Jerusalem* pl. 84, ll. 3–4.

77   *Jerusalem* pl. 41, l. 15.

78   Cp. *Jerusalem* pl. 31, ll. 25–6: "Bethlehem where was builded Dens of despair in the house of bread"—Bethlehem Hospital for Lunatics moved near Lambeth, and "Bethlehem" means "house of bread" in Hebrew.

79   *Milton* pl. 20, ll. 5, 9, 10–12.

80   A.C. Swinburne, *William Blake* (London: John Camden Hotten, 1868) (*BR* 31).

81   He had "a large collection of works of the mystical writers, Jacob Behmen, Swedenborg, and others" (Tatham writing in 1864 [*BR* 41 n4]).

82   Crabb Robinson's Diary of 10 Dec 1825.

83   *BR* 38 n1.

84   *BR* 35.

85   *Minutes of a General Conference of the Members of the New Church Signified by the New Jerusalem in the Revelation* (1789) (*BR* 37).

86   *Milton* pl. 20, l. 50.

87   *Jerusalem* pl. 48, ll. 9–11.

88   Charles A. Tulk (1768–1849) told Garth Wilkinson (1812–99), who told James Spilling, who reported it ("Blake, Artist and Poet", *New Church Magazine*, VI [1887], 254), that Blake wrote "The Divine Image" "in the New Jerusalem Church, Hatton Garden" (*BRS* 10). However, "The Divine Image" was published in 1789, and Hatton Garden Church was not established until 1797; indeed the poem was probably written before the New Church was established in April 1789. However, it could have been written at one of the meetings of the Swedenborg study group.

89   *Descriptive Catalogue* ¶92–3. The picture (Butlin #660) does not survive.

90   Crabb Robinson (*BR* 452, 440).

91   Smith (*BR* 458).

92   *Jerusalem* pl. 3.
93   *Europe* pl. 16, ll. 202–3.
94   See *Tiriel:* Facsimile and Transcript of the Manuscript, Reproduction of the Drawings and a Commentary on the Poem by G.E. Bentley, Jr (Oxford: Clarendon Press, 1967); the *Tiriel* designs, Butlin #198 1–12, but only the first is reproduced there.
95   *There is No Natural Religion* pl. b12.
96   Joseph Viscomi, *Blake and the Idea of the Book* (1993).
97   *Marriage* pl. 27, ¶92, *Visions* pl. 11, l. 215, *America* pl. 10, l. 71, *Vala* p. 34, l. 79, adapted from the marginalium to Lavater, *Aphorisms*, ¶309 ("*all life is holy*").
98   "A Dream", *Songs* pl. 26, l. 16.
99   "The Little Boy found", *Songs* pl. 14, l. 4.
100 "Night", *Songs* pl. 20, ll. 12–13.
101 "A Cradle Song", *Songs* pl. 16, ll. 24, 32 (Pl. 10).
102 "The Chimney Sweeper" from *Innocence* (*Songs* pl. 12) ll. 13, 23.
103 Twenty-five copies of *Innocence* by itself survive and twenty-six more in *Songs of Innocence and of Experience*.
104 The "Introduction" to *Innocence* was printed in (1) Crabb Robinson (1811) (*BR* 443–4, 454); (2) Cunningham (1830) (*BR* 483); (3) T.F. Dibdin, *Reminiscences of a Literary Life* (1836) (*BR* 243); (4) *Monthly Magazine* (1839) (*BBS* 343); (5) *Boys' and Girls' Magazine* (July 1843) (*BBS* 157); (6) *Blackwood's Edinburgh Magazine*, LXII (Oct 1847) (from Cunningham) (*BB* #1083); (7) *Union Magazine* (1848) (*BB* #1440); (8) William Allingham, *Hogg's Weekly Instructor* (1849) (quoted from Cunningham without acknowledgement) (*BB* #803); (9) *Nightingale Valley*, ed. William Allingham (London, 1860) (*BB* #264); (10) *Folk Songs*, ed. John Williamson Piper (1861) (called "The Piper") (*BB* #284); (11) *The Children's Garland*, ed. Coventry Patmore (1862) (*BB* 340).
     "The Divine Image" was printed in (1) Malkin (1806) (*BR* 427–8); (2) *Dawn of Light* (1825) (*BRS* 83); (3) *London University Magazine* (1830) (*BR* 385 n1); (4) *New Church Advocate* (1844) (*BBS* 151); (5) *National Anti-Slavery Standard* (1842) (*Blake* [1998]); (6) J.J.G. Wilkinson in *The Human Body and its Connection with Man* (1851) (called "The Human Form") (*BB* #2971); (7) *Heat and Light* (1851) (*BBS* 151); it was copied in MS by Crabb Robinson (*BRS* 60).
     "The Chimney Sweeper" from *Innocence* was printed in (1) Cunningham (1830) (*BR* 483–4); (2) James

Montgomery, *The Chimney Sweeper's Friend* (1824; 1825) (*BR* 284); (3) *Eclectic Review* (1824) (*BRS* 80); (4) William Hone, *Every-Day Book* (1825 … 1889) (*Blake* [1998]); (5) [Amedée Pichot], *Revue de Paris* (1833) and *Revue Britannique* (1862) (*BB* #2392); (6) *National Anti-Slavery Standard* (1842) (*Blake* [1998]); (7) *National Anti-Slavery Standard* (1849) (*Blake* [1998]); (8) [Jane Laurie Borthwick], ed., *Illustrated Book of Songs for Children* (1863) (*Blake* [1995]); it was copied in MS by Crabb Robinson (*BRS* 60).
     "The Lamb" was printed in (1) Cunningham (1830) (*BR* 505); (2) Pichot, *ut supra*; (3) *Monthly Magazine* (1839) (*BRS* 342–3); (4) *New Jerusalem Magazine* (1842) (*BB* #268); (5) *Retina* (1843) (*BBS* 157); (6) *New Church Magazine for Children* (1843) (*BBS* 157); (7) *Boys' and Girls' Library* (1844) (*BBS* 157); (8) *Little Truth Teller* (1846) (*BBS* p. 157); it was given in MS by Tatham (1831) (*BR* 532).
     All the *Songs* were reprinted by J.J. Garth Wilkinson in 1839 and (in twelve copies) in 1843.
105 "To the Public" (1793) and letters of 9 June 1818 and 12 April 1827.
106 *Songs of Innocence and of Experience*, ed. J.J.G. Wilkinson (London: W. Pickering & W. Newbery, 1839), xx.
107 Letter of 25 Oct 1833 *BR* (2).
108 Crabb Robinson letter of 10 Aug 1848 (*BRS* 68).
109 Crabb Robinson Diary of 24 May 1812.
110 In a notebook of 1800–8, Dorothy and William Wordsworth copied from Malkin "Holy Thursday" and "Laughing Song" from *Innocence*, "The Tyger" from *Experience*, and "I love the jocund dance" from *Poetical Sketches* (*BR* 430 n1).
111 Samuel Palmer writing in 1862 (*BRS* 71).
112 His favourites in *Innocence* were "Holy Thursday", "Infant Joy", "The Ecchoing Green", "The School Boy", and especially "The Divine Image", "The Little Black Boy", and "Night" (letter of 12 Feb 1818).
113 Letter of 6 Feb 1818.
114 Crabb Robinson letter of 19 Feb 1826.
115 Anon., "The Inventions of William Blake, Painter and Poet", *London University Magazine*, II (March 1830) (*BR* 386).
116 *Thel* pl. 5, ll. 68–9.
117 "To the Public" (1793) and letters of 9 June 1818 and 12 April 1827.
118 *Marriage* pl. 27. Joseph Viscomi is responsible for the argument that the *Marriage* "resulted from four or five distinct and recognizably sequential periods of composition, all presumably

taking place in 1790" ("The Evolution of *The Marriage of Heaven and Hell*", *Huntington Library Quarterly*, LVIII [1996], 285), with pls 21–4 first.

119 *Marriage* pl. 27, ¶¶1–2. This Chorus is lacking from *Marriage* copy M, which disappeared from March 1918 until November 1997.

120 *Marriage* pl. 22, ¶79, ¶78.

121 *Marriage* pls 4 (¶12), 10, 7.

122 *Marriage* pl. 5 (¶17), 6 (¶22).

123 *Marriage* pl. 6 (¶23).

124 *Marriage* pl. 9.

125 *Marriage* pls 4 (¶2), 11 (¶30), 16 (¶56), 23–4 (¶86).

126 *Marriage* pl. 18 (¶66–7).

127 *Marriage* pl. 20 (¶72).

128 *Marriage* pl. 8.

129 Palmer's letter of 24 July 1862 (*BR* 319 n1).

130 *BR* 581.

131 See *BR* (2), Feb 1827.

132 There is no charge for a minister at the burying ground.

133 "To the Public" (10 Oct 1793). Catherine sold "Job" and "Ezekiel" together for £2.2.0 on 25 Feb 1830.

134 "To the Public" (10 Oct 1793).

135 Malkin (*BR* 423). Perhaps the other engraving for *The History of England* was to be from "The Penance of Jane Shore" which was painted before 1779 (*Descriptive Catalogue* ¶112), though no engraving for it is known.

136 "To the Public" (1793) and letters of 9 June 1818 and 12 April 1827.

137 "To the Public" (1793) and letters of 9 June 1818 and 12 April 1827.

138 Cunningham and Crabb Robinson (*BR* 500, 454). Robinson translated some of *America* into German (*BR* 446–7).

139 *BR* 470; Smith is quoting Richard Thomson.

140 *BR* 486.

141 "Eternity", Notebook p. 105; see the design on *Visions* pl. 3 (Fig. on p. xxiv) of Oothoon kissing the winged joy as it flies.

142 Crabb Robinson's *Reminiscences* (*BR* 548).

143 Gilchrist (*BR* 237 n3).

144 Joint title page to *Songs of Innocence and of Experience* pl. 1.

145 "Introduction" (*Songs* pl. 30), ll. 12, 8–9; "Earth's Answer" (*Songs* pl. 31), ll. 5, 14, 7, 11.

146 "The Clod & the Pebble" (*Songs* pl. 32), l. 12.

147 *Jerusalem* pl. 84, l. 11. In the *Jerusalem* design the old man is being led leftward towards a Gothic church.

148 "To the Public" (1793) and letters of 9 June 1818 and 12 April 1827.

149 *BR* 252–3.

150 "Introduction" in *London University Magazine* (1830) (*BR* 381); "The Garden of Love" in (1) Crabb Robinson (1811) (*BR* 454) and (2) *London University Magazine* (1830) (*BR* 385); "A Poison Tree" in *London University Magazine* (1830) (*BR* 385); "On Anothers Sorrow" in *Dawn of Light* (1825) (*BBS* 159); and "The Tyger" (1) in Malkin (1806) (*BR* 430–1), (2) Crabb Robinson (*BR* 444–5, 454), (3) Cunningham (1830) (*BR* 479), and (4) Pichot in *Revue de Paris* (1833) (*BB* #2392).

151 *BR* 454.

152 *BR* 429, 454.

153 *BR* 285, 286.

154 *BR* 479.

155 According to *A Concordance to the Writings of William Blake*, ed. D.V. Erdman et al. (Ithaca: Cornell University Press, 1967).

156 *Island*, last page. See "What Is the Price of Experience? William Blake and the Economics of Illuminating P[r]inting", *University of Toronto Quarterly*, LXVIII (1999), 617–41.

157 *WBW* 708. Exactly the same passage is cited by J.T. Smith (*BR* 471).

158 *BR* 470–1.

159 "To the Public" (1793) and letters of 9 June 1818 and 12 April 1827.

160 *BR* 454.

161 *BR* 500.

162 *BR* 470, 471.

163 "To the Public" (1793) and letters of 9 June 1818 and 12 April 1827.

164 *BR* 486, 487.

165 Gilchrist (*BR* 34).

166 Letter of 9 June 1818.

167 In Butlin the Small Book of Designs is #260 1–23 and #261 1–11, while the Large Book of Designs is #262 1–8. Blake dates the first copy of the Small Book "1794" and the second copy "1796".

168 #289, 292, 294, 297, 301, 303, 306, 320, 321, 313 are inscribed with some variant of "W Blake 1795".

169 Besides Butlin (1981), see Martin Butlin, "The Evolution of Blake's Large Color Prints of 1795", pp. 108–116 of *William Blake: Essays for S. Foster Damon*, ed. Alvin Rosenfeld (Providence, 1969); Martin Butlin, "The Physicality of William Blake: The Large Color Prints of '1795'", and David W. Lindsay, "The Order of Blake's Large Color Prints", *Huntington Library Quarterly*, LII (1989), 1–17, 19–41; Martin Butlin, *William Blake 1757–1827* (London: The Tate

170　Butlin #289, 291–2, 294–303, 306–7, 310–12, 316–18, 320–7.

171　*BR* 572–3; Butlin #289, 294, 297, 301, 306, 320, 323, 325. Butts also acquired #291, 310, 316, but he is not known to have owned the twelfth print, "Naomi Entreating Ruth and Orpah".

172　Butlin #301, 306; the late dates are based upon Martin Butlin, *William Blake 1757–1827* (London: The Tate Gallery, 1990), Tate Gallery Collections, Vol. 5, 82–105.

173　Butlin #320, 323, 302–3, 289, 307. "Elohim Creating Adam" is the only known copy, but it was probably preceded by one of 1795.

174　Butlin #292, 295–6, 302, 304, 307, 311–12, 318, 321–2, 324, 326–7. Five of them were probably the first pulls Blake made of those subjects (Butlin #292, 295, 311, 324, 326).

175　Letter of Frederick Tatham to W.M. Rossetti of 9 Nov 1862 (*Rossetti Papers 1862–1876*, ed. W.M. Rossetti [London, 1903], 16–17.

176　The dealer Joseph Hogarth offered #292, 295, 304, 307, 312, 318 by 1843 and #321, 327 by 1854, and Sotheby sold (for Tatham) #296, 302, 322, 324, 326 in 1862.

Chapter V 1795–1800: The Ocean of Business

1　In his letter of 26 Aug 1799, Blake writes: "It is now Exactly Twenty years since I was upon the ocean of Business".

2　Paraphrase of Fuseli's otherwise-unknown judgment of Blake's *Night Thoughts* designs in the auction by Messrs Thomas Winstanley & Co., 10 May 1826, of Thomas Edwards, Bookseller of Halifax (Halifax: Thomas Winstanley & Co., 1826), 65–6, Lot 1076.

3　Diary of Joseph Farington for 12 Jan 1797, reporting the opinion of the Royal Academician John Hoppner, who ridiculed the absurdity of the designs for Young's *Night Thoughts*.

4　Letter of 26 Aug 1799.

5　Annotation (?1798) to Bacon, *Essays* (1798), p. 14.

6　Some of the background details here derive from "Richard Edwards, Publisher of Church-and-King Pamphlets and of William Blake", *Studies in Bibliography*,

XLI (1988), 283–315, and "The 'Edwardses of Halifax' as Booksellers by Catalogue 1749–1835", *Studies in Bibliography*, XLV (1992), 187–222.

7　Auction catalogue of Thomas Edwards, 10 May 1826, repeated in the auction catalogue of Thomas Edwards, 24 May 1828.

8　Thomas Edwards, *Edwards's Catalogue* (Halifax: Thomas Edwards, 1821), Lot 3, specifying that the signature was lost through the "inattention" of the bookbinder, presumably when the leaves were mounted for Blake's designs.

9　These were seen in Traylen's bookshop (Guildford) in 1978.

10　E.B. Bentley & G.E. Bentley, Jr, "Bishop Phillpotts Library, The Franke Parker Bequest and its Extra-Illustrated [Macklin] Bible 1800", *Book Collector*, XXIX (1980), 378.

11　The 1821 catalogue says that the drawings "occupied nearly two years of the time" of Blake, and the 1826 catalogue says that Blake "was employed for more than two years" on the "Work". Perhaps the difference is due to whether one is counting the drawings only (presumably completed by the time the first engravings were dated in June 1796) or the drawings and engravings together (the last engravings are dated June 1797).

12　Tatham (*BR* 526).

13　Tatham (*BR* 526). The imprint on the Lavater plate is 1 May 1800.

14　Engraved for *Night Thoughts* (1797) p. 40.

15　Blake's watercolours in the British Museum Print Room are reproduced in black and white (with a few glorious colour examples) in somewhat reduced size and numbered in *William Blake's Designs for Edward Young's NIGHT THOUGHTS: A Complete Edition*, ed. John E. Grant, Edward J. Rose, Michael J. Tolley, Co-Ordinating Editor David V. Erdman, 2 vols (Oxford: Clarendon Press, 1980).

16　*Night Thoughts* watercolours echo designs in *No Natural Religion, Innocence, Marriage, Europe, Jerusalem*, and *Vala* (see *WBW* 5, 8, 12, 40, 96, 230, 586, 633, 1072, 1075, 1138, 1157, 1241).

17　*BR* 59. Advertisements in similar terms in *Monthly Magazine* (Nov 1796) and *Monthly Epitome and Catalogue of New Publications* (Jan 1797) specified that the price to non-subscribers would be £6.6.0 (*BRS* 12, 13). *The Monthly Epitome* ad does not mention Blake.

18　*Elucidation of Mr. Bowyer's Plan for a Magnificent Edition of Hume's History of England* (London: R. Bowyer, 1795), 30; the cost of the book derives from a prospectus entitled *Mr. Bowyer's Address to the Patrons of the Fine Arts Respecting His Splendid National Undertaking of the History of England* (London: Robert Bowyer [May 1793?]).

19   The copy on vellum in the Huntington (Butlin #334) is traced from Night the First p. 6; the copyist (not Blake) forgot to include the staff, leaving the traveller's raised hand without a function.

20   J.T. Smith (*BR* 461).

21   The price Blake received from Longman for each of his three much smaller plates for Flaxman's *Iliad* (1805) and his thirty-seven plates for Flaxman's *Hesiod* (1817) (*BR* 571, 579).

22   Letter of 12 March 1804.

23   *Monthly Epitome and Catalogue of New Publications* (Jan 1797) (*BRS* 13).

24   Edward Young, *The Complaint, and The Consolation; or, Night Thoughts* (London: R. Edwards, 1797) iii–viii. The prose sounds like that of Fuseli.

25   In early Nov 1797, Nancy Flaxman mentioned it in her letter (*BRS* 14), and on 6 Nov 1797 James Edwards billed Fuseli's friend William Roscoe £1.1.0 for the first part of *Night Thoughts* and £1.1.0 towards his subscription for the remaining parts (*BRS* 14).

26   In 1810 Crabb Robinson wrote that Blake's *Night Thoughts* "is no longer to be bought, so excessively rare has it become" (*BR* 453), and in 1801 Jean Paul Richter thought that his copy of these "herlichen phantastischen Kupferstichen" ("magnificent fantastic copper engravings") was probably the only one in Germany (*BRS* 17).

27   "Young's Night Thoughts, decorated with appropriate Designs, by Mr. *Blake*. Part I. 11.1s. Robson", *Monthly Magazine* (June 1798) (*BRS* 15).

28   The patent is in my own collection. Richard Edwards "relinquished business about 1799, on being presented by [*his brother James's most important patron and customer*] Earl Spencer to the appointment of Head Registrar of Minorca" (*Gentleman's Magazine*, XCVII [Nov 1827], 478, an obituary of Richard Edwards).

29   *BB* 645–6, 643, 645.

30   *BR* 453. Robinson also said that "the publisher ... has refused to sell the drawings, although a handsome sum was offered him for them" (*BR* 453).

31   T.F. Dibdin, *Reminiscences of a Literary Life* (London: John Major, 1836) (*BR* 243). In a letter of 15 May 1824 Charles

Lamb referred to Blake's "splendid folio edition of the Night Thoughts".

32   T.F. Dibdin, *The Library Companion* (London: Harding, Triphook, Lepard, and J. Major, 1824) (*BR* 289).

33   Edwards, *Edwards's Catalogue* (*BBS* 284).

34   Auction catalogue (10 May 1826) of Thomas Edwards, Bookseller of Halifax, sold by Messrs Thomas Winstanley & Co. (Halifax: Thomas Winstanley & Co., 1826). Similar terms were used in the auction catalogue (24 May 1828) by Messrs. Stewart, Wheatley, & Adlard of the property of Thomas Edwards, Esq.

35   *BR* 487.

36   Edward Bulwer Lytton, "Conversations with an Ambitious Student in Ill Health", *New Monthly Magazine* (1830) reprinted as *The Student* (1835 ff.) (*BR* 401–2). Bulwer Lytton's information about Blake came from John Varley.

37   See *BR* (2) under 1795.

38   See "Flaxman's 'Sports of Genius': 'The Casket' as an Illustrated Poem", *Harvard Library Bulletin*, XXXI (1983), 256–84.

39   *BRS* 14. The fact that this letter summarizes the one of March 1796 which never arrived and that the earlier letter says nothing of the Gray designs suggests that the project had not been started, or at least was not known to Nancy, in March 1796.

40   Flaxman's payments to Blake of £5.5.0 in July 1796 and £2.2.0 in early Oct 1797 (*BR* 569, 570) may be related to the Gray commission, and the payment of 3s. in early May 1797 for "Blake's book, binding" (*BR* 569) may be related to it also.

41   In the early summer of 1807, George Cumberland wrote that "Blake made 130 drawg[s] for Flaxman for 10.10—". The number is wrong—there are 116 drawings in the Gray suite—but the only suite of Blake designs which otherwise matches this description is that for Gray.

42   *BR* 41 n4.

43   *WBW* 1324. The watercolours, rediscovered in 1919 and now in the Yale Center for British Art, are reproduced full size and in colour in *William Blake's Water-Colour Designs for the Poems of Gray*, ed. Geoffrey Keynes, Kt (London: Trianon Press for The William Blake Trust, 1972). They were never engraved.

44   *BRS* 11.

45   *BR* 570.

46   *BRS* 13.

47   Thanks particularly to the amplifications and corrections to *BB* by Joseph Viscomi,

Blake and the Idea of the Book (Princeton: Princeton University Press, 1993).

48   *BRS* 14.

49   See *BR* (2).

50   Stanley Morison, *John Bell, 1745–1831* (Cambridge: Cambridge University Press, 1930), 4. The first Part of Trusler's *Memoirs* was published in 1806; the second, unpublished, Part is in the W.S. Lewis Library of Yale University in Farmington, Connecticut.

51   Letter to Cumberland of 26 Aug 1799. "Malevolence" (Butlin #341) is reproduced in *BR* at p. 60 and in Butlin (pl. 345).

52   *Paradise Lost*, Book VII, ll. 29–30; the same passage from Milton in illustration of Blake's claim to inspiration is quoted in an anonymous review of Blake's designs for Blair's *Grave* in *The Monthly Magazine* (Dec 1808).

53   The unspeakable prophet is Balaam in Num. xxiv, 13.

54   Letter of 26 Aug 1799.

55   Inscription, perhaps not by Blake, on the Tate copy of *Urizen* pl. 2 (*WBW* 240) (Fig. on p. 30).

56   *Descriptive Catalogue* ¶64.

57   "Laocoon".

58   *BR* 293–4, all one paragraph.

59   *BR* 291 n2, one paragraph.

60   Marginalium to Reynolds's *Works* third contents leaf.

61   *BR* 291.

62   Tatham (*BR* 524–5, one paragraph), giving little indication of the date (?1790s) and no indication of the identity of the young artist.

63   The first reference to the patronage of Thomas Butts is in Blake's letter to George Cumberland of 26 Aug 1799; probably Blake and Butts had met not long before this.

64   See Ian Maxted, *The London Book Trades, 1775–1800: A Topographical Guide* (Exeter: printed and sold by the author, 1980).

65   Letter of 22 Nov 1802.

66   Quoted from the MS (*c.* 1800) in the British Library Department of Manuscripts (the MS was discovered after the publication of *WBW*).

67   Letter of 22 Sept 1800.

68   Even after he had moved to Felpham, Blake wrote wistfully to Butts, "I shall wish for you on tuesday Evening as usual" (letter of 22 Sept 1800).

69   These objects, hallmarked 1792, 1794, and 1796 and "traditionally stated [*in the family*] to have been used by BLAKE", were sold at Sotheby's 19 Dec 1932 by Anthony Bacon Drury Butts, the great-grandson of Thomas Butts (*BR* 73).

70   On 26 May 1960 Mrs Camilla Israel wrote to me that her grandmother directed in her will: "I give my eight needlework pictures by Elizabeth Butts a friend of William Blake to the Trustees of the Boston Museum"; the Curator of Textiles at the Boston Museum wrote to me on 28 June 1960 that the museum did not accept them, and "The former Curator of Textiles tells me that the pictures bore no resemblance in design to the work of William Blake". A needlework panel by Mrs Butts of two hares in long grass was designed by Blake, in the opinion (there is "little doubt") of Sir Geoffrey Keynes, *Bibliotheca Bibliographici* (London: Trianon Press, 1964), 53, 54.

71   It is inscribed "Agnes | From the Novel of the Monk | Designed & Painted by Catherine Blake | & Presented by her in Gratitude & Friendship | To Mʳˢ Butts" (Geoffrey Keynes, *Bibliotheca Bibliographici* [London: Trianon Press, 1964], 50; Butlin #C1).

72   Sotheby's, 22 March 1910, Lot 446, called "William Blake's Working Cabinet", with the crest of the Butts family (in the form of a harness badge) on the outside front and the Butts coat of arms painted inside the door added by Aubrey Butts after he acquired it about 1880. When the cabinet was sold by W.E. Moss at Sotheby's 2 March 1937, Lot 284, it was "believed to have been given him [*Thomas Butts*] by Blake".

73   Butlin #410–11 (Pls 495–6); see also #412, which may be yet another variation made for Butts if Rossetti, who is the only evidence for its existence, has not confused it with #411.

74   Receipt of 15 Oct 1806 (*BR* 575).

75   Receipt of 3 March 1806 (*BR* 573).

76   In his letter of 22 Nov 1802, he sent Butts two pictures, asked "what Subject you choose to be painted in the remaining Canvas which I brought down with me (for there were three)", and reminded him that "the remaining Number of Drawings which you gave me orders for is Eighteen".

77   Butlin (p. 336) records Graham Robertson's guess that the inscriptions were made by Mrs Blake but suggests that "alternatively they may have been done while the watercolours belonged to the Butts family".

78   Butlin #193–6 (and #442, a duplicate of "Pestilence" which also belonged to Butts).

79 Letter of ?April 1826. In his *Job* accounts, Linnell recorded that Butts paid the price of a plain copy (£3.3.0) but was given a proof copy (value £5.5.0) "because he lent the Drawing to Copy" (*BR* 599).

80 *Marriage* (?1790), *Visions* (1793), *For Children* (1793), *America* (1793), *Urizen* (1794), *Europe* (1794), *Book of Los* (1795), and *Book of Ahania* (1795).

81 Marginalia to Francis Bacon, *Essays Moral, Economical, and Political* (London: J. Edwards & T. Payne, 1798) half-title, 65, 14, 84.

82 R. Watson, D.D. F.R.S., Lord Bishop of Landaff, and Regius Professor of Divinity in the University of Cambridge, *An Apology for the Bible*, in a Series of Letters, Addressed to Thomas Paine, Author of a Book entitled, The Age of Reason, Part the Second, being an Investigation of True and of Fabulous Theology, 8th edn (London: T. Evans, 1797), title page verso.

83 Marginalia to Watson pp. 1, 3, 6, 9, 2, 125.

84 Marginalia to Watson pp. 2, 8, 6, 108, 9.

85 Including 537 watercolours for Young's *Night Thoughts*, 116 watercolours for Gray's poems, 50 temperas for the Bible, and 84 drawings for *Vala*.

86 *Vala* Night the First p. 1, ll. 8–10, 13; the omitted lines are later additions.

87 *Jerusalem* pl. 36, l. 31.

88 *Europe* pl. 8, l. 92.

89 *Vala* Night the First p. 4, l. 34, a late addition adapted in *Jerusalem* pl. 13, l. 31.

Chapter VI 1800–1804: Sweet Felpham and Rex vs Blake

1 *Milton* pl. 7, ll. 5–6.

2 *Milton* pl. a, l. 26; *Jerusalem* pl. 30, l. 10; paraphrased in Blake's letter of 25 April 1803.

3 Letters of 19 Dec 1808 and 12 April 1827.

4 Letters of 22, 21, 12 Sept 1800.

5 *BR* 65, 70, 154.

6 *Letters of Robert Southey: A Selection*, ed. Maurice H. Fitzgerald (Oxford: Oxford University Press, 1912), 157.

7 Richard Dally, *The Chichester Guide* (Chichester: P. Binstead, 1831), 98:

    A rustic club was established at Felpham, and this thoroughly good-natured man [*William Hayley*] was accustomed every year to provide "*A Copy of Verses*," and to get them printed and circulated amongst members of the club and through the village; and he permitted them, with their rural band of music and their colours flying, on their annual feast-day, to parade through his grounds.

8 [Richard Dally], *The Bognor, Arundel and Littlehampton Guide* (Chichester: Printed by William Mason, 1828), 61.

9 Thomas Alphonso Hayley to his father, June 1796 and 1 June 1795: West Sussex Record Office, Add MSS 2817, #43, 35.

10 Tom Hayley to his father, 24 March 1795 (West Sussex Record Office, #30). The "immortal painter" is presumably Romney.

11 Tom Hayley to his father, 12 March 1795 (West Sussex Record Office, #28).

12 Tom Hayley to his father, 29 May 1797 (West Sussex Record Office, #63). On 17 March 1795 he told him that he had "read Greek testament" (#29). Probably Hayley taught Blake Greek and Latin in 1802 in the same way he and Flaxman had taught Tom.

13 Tom Hayley to his father, 10 March 1795 (West Sussex Record Office, #28).

14 Tom Hayley to his father, 2 April 1995 (West Sussex Record Office, #32).

15 See *BR* (2).

16 In the spring of 1797 Flaxman said that Tom may "at any future time learn to etch in two hours without costing you a Farthing" (Yale University).

17 Tom Hayley to his father, 3 March 1795 (West Sussex Record Office, #27).

18 Flaxman to Johnny Johnson, 26 March 1823 (collection of Mary Catherine Barham Johnson).

19 William Hayley, "Felpham a local Epistle to Henrietta [*Poole*] of Lavant 1814", 6 (MS in University of Texas Library), printed as "Felpham: An Epistle to Henrietta of Lavant. 1814" in [William Hayley], *Poems on Serious and Sacred Subjects. Printed Only as Private Tokens of Regard for the Particular Friends of the Author* (Chichester: Printed at the Private Press of W. Mason, 1818), 22.

20 Hayley to Samuel Rose, 7 March 1800.

21 Flaxman to Hayley, 26 March 1800.

22 Letter of 6 May 1800.

23 Letter of 2 July 1800.

24 Letters of 1 Sept (see *BR* [2]) and 14 Sept 1800, the latter from Catherine Blake.

25 Letter of 10 Jan 1802; "This from Johnson & Fuseli brought me down here" to Felpham. The context is "my dependence ... on Engraving".

26 Letter of 10 Jan 1802.

27   Letter of 1 Sept 1800 (see *BR* [2]).

28   Hayley letter of 6 July 1802; the London post reached Chichester every morning except Monday at 8 a.m. and left Chichester daily except Saturday at 4 p.m. ([Alexander Hay], *The Chichester Guide, and Directory, A New Edition* [Chichester: J. Seagrave, (?1804)], 35, correcting *BR* 103 n2).
    Blake wrote to Hayley "at Miss Pooles Lavant near Chichester" (Tuesday 16 Sept 1800), and Hayley wrote on Wednesday 18 Jan 1804 that "a Letter met me yesterday at Lavant".

29   Hayley letter of 6 July 1802.

30   Letter of 11 Dec 1805.

31   Hayley letter of 27 April 1804.

32   Letter of 30 Jan 1803.

33   As Samuel Rose said in 1804 (*BR* 143).

34   Blake's description of her "whenever she hears it [*Felpham*] named" in his letter of 16 Sept 1800.

35   Letter of 14 Sept 1800 to "My Dearest Friend" Nancy Flaxman, ostensibly from Catherine Blake.

36   On Wednesday 10 Sept they had tea with the Buttses, on Saturday 13 Sept Blake breakfasted with Mrs Butts, and on Sunday 14 Sept they were to call on the Flaxmans (Blake's letter of 12 Sept).

37   Details of the journey derive from Blake's very similar letters of 21 and 22 Sept 1800. By Hayley's advice, they came by the Petworth road (letter of 16 Sept 1800), rather than by the post-road through Lavant.

38   Letter of 21 Sept 1800.

39   In 1801 there were 536 persons in Felpham and 82 houses (Richard Dally, *The Bognor, Arundel and Littlehampton Guide* [Chichester: Printed by William Mason, 1828]). According to James Dallaway, *A History of the Western Division of the County of Sussex* (London: printed by T. Bensley, 1815), I, p. 9, in 1801 Felpham had 71 houses with 85 males and 221 females, but probably the "85" should be "285", for in 1811 there were 536 persons and in 1821 there were 581, with approximately equal numbers of males and females.

40   Dally, *Bognor* (1828), 58, 59; three of the bells are dated 1589, 1600, and 1627. Though Blake probably did not attend services in the church, he may have seen the "ancient open seats of oak", the Saxon or Norman font large enough to immerse an infant, and the "rather laughable lines on the walls" of the belfry by a "village muse" (57–8).

41   *Jerusalem* pl. 40, l. 51.

42   Russel Ash, *The Pig Book* (New York: Arbor House, 1986), 44.

43   For "Kwantok [*or* Guantok, Gwantok], Peach[e]y, Brer[e]ton", see *Jerusalem* pl. 5, l. 25, pl. 19, l. 18, pl. 32, l. 11.

44   *Vala* p. 80, l. 9; *Jerusalem* pl. 30, l. 30.

45   *Vala* p. 35, l. 15.

46   *Jerusalem* pl. 60, l. 27, pl. 83, l. 9.

47   Letter of 16 Aug 1803.

48   Letters of 22, 21 Sept 1800.

49   *Milton* pl. 44, l. 29. In Blake's designs to *L'Allegro*, "The Lark is an Angel on the wing" (*WBW* 1333).

50   Letter of 22 Sept 1800.

51   Letter of 22 Nov 1802 (alpha).

52   Letter of 22 Nov 1802 (beta).

53   As perhaps is the one in "The Fairy" (?1793), which is caught by the speaker in his hat (*WBW* 977–8)—*For Children* (1793) pl. 9 shows a boy catching a fairy in his hat. Blake illustrated Gray's "A Long Story" (1797) with a scene of "Fairies riding on Flies" (*WBW* 1326), and in his designs for *Il Penseroso* (1815) are "Fairies hovering on the air" (WBW 1338). In Lambeth "My Fairy sat upon the table, and dictated EUROPE" (*Europe* pl. 3, l. 24).

54   *Descriptive Catalogue* ¶74; *Milton* pl. 31, l. 19 and *Jerusalem* pl. 36, l. 36; *Descriptive Catalogue* ¶32; *Vala* p. 4, l. 3.

55   In his letter of 11 Sept 1801, Blake said, "by my Sisters hand I transmit" the miniature of Butts.

56   Letter of 22 Nov 1802 (beta) describing an event of "above a twelvemonth ago".

57   Letter of 22 Nov 1802 (beta).

58   Letter of 22 Nov 1802 (beta), all line-end punctuation added; the poem, "Composed above a twelvemonth ago", is the only place where Enitharmon, Los, and Theotormon appear outside the Prophecies.

59   Letter of 21 Sept 1800.

60   Letter of 12 Sept 1800.

61   Letter of 19 Oct 1801.

62   Gilchrist (*BR* 166).

63   Letter of 22 Nov 1802 (beta), punctuation added.

64   He refers to the "indefatigable Blake" in letters of 1 Oct 1801, 31 Jan, 11 March, and 15 July 1802.

65   Letter of 7 Dec 1801.

66   Hayley, Preface to *Designs to A Series of Ballads* (1802) (*BR* 93).

67   Letter of 10 May 1801. "I continue painting Miniatures & Improve more & more as all my friends tell me" (11 Sept 1801).

68   This is how the soldier Scofield identified him in accusing him of sedition in 1803

(*BR* 124), though at first "he called me a Military Painter; I suppose mistaking the Words Miniature Painter, which he might have heard me called" (Blake's Memorandum of Aug 1803).

69 He apologized in letters of 2 Oct 1800 and 22 Nov 1802 (alpha) for not having finished it.

70 Blake wrote to Butts on 11 Sept 1801: "Historical Designing is one thing & Portrait Painting another & they are as Distinct as any two Arts can be."

71 Letter of 11 Sept 1801.

72 Letter of 30 Jan 1803.

73 On 24 March 1801 she wrote: "[*A friend*] says that he always fear'd that he [*Cowper*] would suffer from the Methodists" (*BR* [2]).

74 Letter of 19 March 1801. On 15 Jan 1803 she wrote of "that distracted and distracting look which prevails in the miniature". Not surprisingly, the miniature has disappeared.

75 Letter of 20 March 1801.

76 Poem written between 10 Sept and 20 Nov 1801 in "A Collection of brief devotional Poems composed on the Pillow before the Dawn of Day 1801" (*BR* 83).

77 Letter of 11 Sept 1801.

78 Letter of 11 Sept 1801.

79 Mary Ann Linnell's letter of 1839 (*BRS* 81).

80 See *BR* (2). Marsh's journal also reports visits to Blake of 9 May and 26 June 1801 (see *BR* [2]) and gifts of white kittens to others in Dec 1801 and May 1805 ("The Journal of John Marsh", XX, 37; XXV, 10).

81 E.G. Marsh letter of 21 Feb p. 1801 (*BRS* 18–19).

82 Hayley letter of 3 Feb 1802. The title page and motto were published in *The Odyssey of Homer*, tr. William Cowper, 2nd edn, ed. J[ohn]. Johnson (London: J[oseph]. Johnson, 1802).

83 Gilchrist (*BR* 290 n2). Blake quotes Voltaire in French in his marginalia (?1801–9) to Reynolds's *Works* (1798) third Contents leaf.

84 Letter to Flaxman of 18 Oct 1801, wishing that the poem may "strike you, as it does Blake & me".

85 Hayley letter of 8 Nov 1801.

86 Hayley's letter of 18 Nov 1801. Perhaps this experience is the basis of Blake's description of Hayley "Horseback with Death" ("And his legs", l. 22, Notebook p. 22).

87 Letters to Lady Hesketh (21 Feb, 13 March 1802), to Johnny Johnson (25 Feb 1802, plus Flaxman's version), and to Flaxman (25 Feb 1802).

88 Letter of 30 Jan 1803.

89 "The Riddle Manuscript" (?1802) (*WBW* 1298).

90 Letter of 30 Jan 1803.

91 Hayley letter of 16 Dec 1802.

92 Letters of 21 Sept 1800, 10 May 1801.

93 Blake is "is most happily settled" (3 Feb 1801) and working "happily" (3 Sept, 25 Oct, 8 Nov 1801); he is "more and more attach'd to this pleasant marine village" (18 Oct 1801), and he and Catherine "regard [*their cottage*] as the most delightful residence ever inhabited by a mortal" (15 July 1802).

94 Letter of 30 Jan 1803.

95 "Mr H approves of My Designs as little as he does of my Poems" (letter of 6 July 1803).

96 Letter of 25 April 1803.

97 Letters of 10 Jan 1802, 6 July 1803.

98 Johnny Johnson letter of 3 Dec 1802.

99 When Lady Hesketh offered to send Blake a gift of £5.5.0, Hayley replied on 25 April 1803: "Whenever I make that Liberality known to Him I must contrive to do it with the utmost caution as I know his honest pride would be otherwise hurt".

100 *BR* 119, an undated letter perhaps from the spring of 1803.

101 Letter of 10 Jan 1802.

102 Hayley's preface to his *Designs to A Series of Ballads*, And founded on Anecdotes Relating to Animals, Drawn, Engraved, and Published, by William Blake. With the Ballads annexed, by the Author's Permission (Chichester: Printed by J. Seagrave, and sold by him and P. Humphry; and by R.H. Evans, Pall-Mall, London, for W. Blake, Felpham, 1802) (*BR* 93).

103 Hayley letter of 6 July 1802.

104 Hayley letter of 10 June 1802.

105 Letters to Hayley from Johnny Johnson (7 July 1802), Flaxman (27 June), and Charlotte Collins (28 June).

106 Letter of 28–9 June 1802.

107 Letters of 30 and 3 July 1802.

108 Letter of 3 July 1802.

109 Letter of 10 July 1802.

110 Letter of 19 Aug 1802 (see *BR* [2]).

111 Marginalium to Reynolds's *Works* (1798) p. 5.

112 Letter of 30 Jan 1803. On 25 April 1803 he wrote to Butts: "The Reason the Ballads have been suspended is the pressure of other business but they will go on again Soon".

113 Letter of 26 Oct 1803; Evans had been an unfortunate choice as agent, because poetry was "out of his line of business to

publish, and a line in which he is determined never to engage".

114   28 Dec 1804.

115   Flaxman letter of 25 Jan 1802.

116   Hayley letter of 13 March 1802; the same poem was sent to Joseph Cowper Walker on 25 March.

117   Hayley letter of 15 July 1802.

118   Lady Hesketh letter of 22 July 1802.

119   Lady Hesketh letter of 29 Dec 1802.

120   Letter of 30 Jan 1803.

121   Letter of 26 Oct 1803.

122   Letter of 19 Dec 1808. From the summer of 1807 to 1809, Cumberland refers to Blake's intention to publish his new method of engraving "through ... stopping lights" (*BR* 187, 188, 211–12).

123   Letter of 30 Jan 1803. On 6 July 1803 he wrote: "there is all the appearance in the world of our being fully employd in Engraving for his [*Hayley's*] projected Works".

124   Letter of 6 July 1803. "The idiot Reasoner laughs at the Man of Imagination" (*Milton* pl. e, l. 6).

125   Letter of 27 Jan 1804.

126   *Milton* pl. 16, ll. 1–2.

127   *Milton* pl. 39, ll. 6–8; "my Path became a solid fire, as bright As the clear Sun" (pl. 40, ll. 4–5).

128   *Milton* pl. 3, l. 20.

129   *Milton* pl. 12, ll. 13–14.

130   *Milton* pl. 22, l. 58.

131   Autobiography of John Marsh under 3 Oct 1800 (Huntington Library). As captain of the company, Marsh persuaded them to remain embodied on condition that there should be no more "Monthly Meetings till the ensuing Spring".

   For more information about the disgruntled Chichester Volunteers, see "Rex v. Blake: Sussex Attitudes toward the Military and Blake's Trial for Sedition in 1804", *Huntington Library Quarterly*, LVI (1993), 83–9.

132   Letter of 19 Oct 1801.

133   John Marsh's Autobiography for 16 Aug and 27 Sept 1803.

134   Muster Books and Pay Lists (War Office 12/454–65) cited by Paul Miner, "Visions in the Darksom air: Aspects of Blake's Biblical Symbolism", in *William Blake: Essays for S. Foster Damon*, ed. Alvin H. Rosenfeld (Providence: Brown University Press, 1969), 466.

   Miner, "Visions in the Darksom air", 466, cites War Office records that the Regiment was in Chichester from June 1803 to Feb 1804, but Blake's friend the musician John Marsh wrote in his autobiography that on 15 July 1803 "4

Troops of the 1ˢᵗ Regiment of Dragoons came to quarter at Chichester, having a very good Band".

135   *Jerusalem* pl. 43, l. 51; in his letter of 2 Oct 1800, Blake says that in Felpham, "the People are Genuine Saxons".

136   Letter of 6 July 1803.

137   Flaxman letter to Hayley of 24 Aug 1803; the letter contains no reference to the fracas in Blake's garden of 12 Aug.

138   In his letter of 7 Oct 1803, Blake said that "my ... good naturd Devil ... is not in the least to be blamed for the present scrape [this Soldier-like danger], as he was out of the way all the time on other employment seeking amusement in making Verses to which he constantly leads me".

139   Blake's Memorandum; perhaps the insult was to Catherine.

140   Rose's Speech.

141   Rose's Speech.

142   Letter of 16 Aug 1803.

143   In his "Complaint", Schofield alleged that Blake's "wife then told her said Husband to turn this Informant out of the Garden", which may be true. According to Blake's Memorandum, William the ostler said "the first Words that he heard me Speak to the Soldier were ordering him out of the Garden".

144   Letter of 16 Aug 1803.

145   Blake's Memorandum.

146   "*This* was his often repeated Threat to me and to my Wife", according to Blake's Memorandum.

147   Blake's Memorandum.

148   Blake's letter of 16 Aug 1803.

149   Blake's Memorandum.

150   Blake's Memorandum.

151   Blake's Memorandum.

152   Schofield's "Information and Complaint". According to Blake's letter of 16 Aug 1803, the captain's name was Leathe.

153   These are quite clear in Hayley's autobiographical account of the trial (*BR* 144–5). Long before the incident, on 2 Nov 1801, Johnny Johnson described Blake as "peaceful", and on 22 Sept 1803 he exclaimed: "What a villain of a soldier to interfere with the most peaceable of creatures!"

154   Letter of 16 Aug 1803.

155   The bonds are quoted in *BR* 127–8. In his 16 Aug letter, Blake erroneously says that Hayley's bond was £100.

156   Blake's Memorandum.

157   Blake's Memorandum.

158   Letter of 16 Aug 1803.

159   Letter of 16 Aug 1803.

160   Letter of 16 Aug 1803.

161   Blake wrote to Hayley on 19 Sept 1803,

presumably very soon after his arrival in London.

162   Letter of 7 Oct 1803.

163   Letter of 26 Oct 1803.

164   Cumberland's note of the address was made in Nov 1803 (*BR* 562).

165   On 7 Oct 1803, Blake wrote to Hayley asking "how you escaped the contagion of the Court of Justice". Seagrave, who had put up a £50 bond for Blake and had to renew it, was probably present in Petworth as well.

166   Letter of 16 Aug 1803.

167   *BR* 131; Tredcroft is there misread as "Trederoft".

168   Tredcroft's grandson, *Recollections from Seventy Years and Memoirs of My Family* [privately printed in thirty-one copies], quoted in a letter to me by Professor Roussel Sargent.

169   *Sussex Weekly Chronicle*, 10 Oct 1803. One of the rioters was named Charles Blake, and when the *Sussex Weekly Advertiser* for 16 Jan 1804 reported the result of Blake's second trial, the accused was identified as "Charles Blake, an engraver, at Felpham".

170   *Jerusalem* pl. 5, pl. 25–6; pl. 19, ll. 18–19, 23; pl. 32, l. 11; ll. 36, ll. 16–17.

171   Letter of 7 Oct 1803.

172   Linnell says that Blake "occupied the first floor" (European style) or the "second floor" (North American style) (*BR* 395, 257). See the photograph of 17 South Molton Street in *BR*, pl. LVIII at p. 563.

173   This is the account of young Martin Cregan, who visited "this happy pair" in 1809 (*BR* 214).

174   Most of Blake's works in Illuminated Printing on paper watermarked 1804, 1808, 1813, 1815, 1818, 1819, 1820, and 1821 must have been printed while he was in South Molton Street in 1803–21. As late as 13 Dec 1803, Blake writes that "my Press [*is*] not yet ... put up" in South Molton Street.

175   *Milton* pl. a, ll. 21–2; *Jerusalem* pl. 62, l. 34.

176   *Jerusalem* pl. 38, l. 42.

177   Letter of 13 Dec 1803.

178   Johnny Johnson letter of 6 Jan 1804.

179   Flaxman letter of 2 Jan 1804.

180   Lady Hesketh letter of 27 Nov 1803.

181   Lady Hesketh letters of 27 and 31 July 1805.

182   Dally wrote on 25 Dec 1803 for a transcript of "the Indictment agst Mr Blake", and Blake paid him £15 (Blake's letter of 2 April 1804).

183   Hayley letter of 1 Jan 1804.

184   Hayley's autobiography (*BR* 144).

185   Johnson's letter to the New York booksellers T. & J. Swords of 24 Feb 1804

is in the Pforzheimer Library now housed in the New York Public Library.

186   Untitled poem in Notebook p. 12. I have transposed the last stanza to the end, as in *Jerusalem* pl. 52. The poem is called "The Grey Monk" in the Ballads Manuscript.

187   Marsh's Autobiography (Huntington) (see *BR* [2]). Marsh also says that on the 10th, "Mr Hayley was to dine with us that day & his friend Mr Rose the Counsellor, Mr Dally yᵉ attorney were occasionally coming to yᵉ house".

188   *BR* 140 gives the complete list of magistrates, plus the members of the jury.

189   Rose's Speech.

190   Hayley's Autobiography (*BR* 145).

191   Gilchrist (1880) (*BR* 145), quoting an unnamed "old man at Chichester, but lately dead" who came to the trial primarily "to see Hayley, 'the great man' of the neighbourhood".

192   Hayley's MS Autobiography (*BR* 145); the passage about the bigoted old Duke of Richmond was omitted in the printed version. I have broken Hayley's long paragraph into shorter ones.

   The Duke's bitter prejudice against Blake did not prevent him from appreciating the skill of his advocate, for Rose said: "I was highly complimented by the Duke of Richmond for my Defense of Blake" (5 May 1804).

193   Letter of 14 Jan 1804. Hayley described this letter as "so full of the most cordial Gratitude & Felicity on his safe return to his anxious Wife, that no feeling Mortal can read it without Tears" (18 Jan 1804).

194   Blake's letter to Hayley of 27 Jan 1804; Rose's letter of 5 May 1804.

195   *Jerusalem* pl. 5, l. 25; pl. 8, l. 41; pl. 19, ll. 18–19; pl. 58, l. 30; pl. 90, l. 40.

196   *Jerusalem* pl. 3; letter of 25 April 1803.

197   Letter of 23 Oct 1804, describing his situation from 1784 to 1804.

Chapter VII 1804–1810: *"Drunk with Intellectual Vision"*

1   Letter of 23 Oct 1804.

2   Letter of 2 July 1800.

3   Letter of 7 Oct 1803.

4   Letters of 13 Dec 1803 and 27 Jan 1804.

5   Letter of 23 Oct 1804: "I speak with perfect confidence and certainty of the fact which has passed upon me."

6   *Marriage* pl. 17, 18, ¶65, 67.

7   *Milton* pl. 36, ll. 19–20; pl. 14; pl. 20, l. 12; pl. 44, ll. 19–20.

8   Letters of 2 July 1800, 23 Oct 1804.
9   Hayley's letter of 15 July 1802.
10 Letter of 11 Sept 1801.
11 *Vala* p. 4, l. 34; cp. *Jerusalem* pl. 13, l. 31; pl. 22, l. 24.
12 *French Revolution* l. 21; "The Clod & the Pebble", l. 4; "The Keys of the Gates", l. 10, *For the Sexes* pl. 19.
13 *Jerusalem* pl. 69, l. 3, *Milton* pl. 27, l. 9.
14 Letter of 25 April 1803. "Urizen who was Faith & Certainty is changd to Doubt" (*Vala* p. 27, l. 15).
15 "The Keys of the Gates" l. 14 (*For the Sexes* pl. 19); *Jerusalem* pl. 93, l. 20.
16 *For Children* pl. 15—see Fig. on p.267.
17 *Vala* p. 49, l. 23.
18 Subtitle of *Songs of Innocence and of Experience*, pl. 1; *Vala* p. 126, l. 20.
19 Notebook pp.10, 67.
20 Letter of 16 Aug 1799.
21 *Marriage* pl. 24, ¶88; letters of 7 Oct 1803, 23 Oct 1804. In the *Marriage*, "The Voice of the Devil" is Blake's voice—or one of his voices.
22 *Vala* p. 80, l. 29; p. 120, l. 9.
23 Butts letter of Sept 1800.
24 Letter of 4 Dec 1804.
25 Letter of 7 Oct 1803.
26 Letter of 10 Jan 1802.
27 Crabb Robinson Diary for 10 Dec 1825.
28 Letters of 16, 21, 22 Sept 1800.
29 *Descriptive Catalogue* ¶96–7. He speaks of the "enmity to the Painter himself" of "Venetian and Flemish demons" (*Descriptive Catalogue* ¶96).
30 *Milton* pl. 18, l. 44; *Vala* p. 133, l. 3; *Europe* pl. 7, l. 77.
31 Letter of 18 Dec 1804.
32 Letter of 28 Dec 1804.
33 Hayley letter of 15 June 1804.
34 Flaxman letter of 16 June 1804.
35 Flaxman letters of 7 Nov and 2 Aug 1804.
36 Letter of 22 March 1805.
37 Letter of 28 March 1805.
38 Letter of 22 Jan 1805.
39 Letter of 22 March 1805. Of these "little high finishd Pictures", the only known survivors are "The Eagle" (Pierpont Morgan Library) and "The Horse" (Yale Center for British Art). Blake drafted an advertisement for the *Ballads* in this letter, but it was not used.
40 Weller inscription (*BR* 163) and Hayley's letter of 18 July 1803.
41 Lady Hesketh letter of 27 July 1805.
42 [Samuel Greatheed], *Eclectic Review*, I (Dec 1805), 923. Greatheed had thanked Hayley on 21 Nov 1805 for "Your pretty little volume of Ballads".
43 *Annual Review* for 1805, IV (1806), 575.
44 Phillips was to pay half (£52.10.0) the

expense of Blake's engravings (£105), and Blake was to pay half (£75.10.0) of all the other publication expenses (£151.0.7), leaving Blake in debt to Phillips for £23.
    For calculations of the costs and profits or losses of the *Ballads* (1805), see *BR* (2) under June 1805.
45 Cromek letter of May 1807.
46 Ian Maxted, *The London Book Trades 1775–1800* (Folkestone: Dawsons, 1977), 18.
47 *Scots Musical Museum*, ed. James Johnson (Edinburgh & London, 1853), 456, citing "a letter of a late date".
48 Letter of 2 Aug 1804. In his Expenses notebook, Flaxman made enigmatic payments to "Cromak—[£]5" (30 March–6 April 1805) and "Cromak, Stothard's picture—5—" (June–July 1805) (British Library Add MSS 39,784 M, f. 15). "Stothard's picture" cannot be for the Canterbury Pilgrims, which was not conceived until the next year.
49 Letter of 12 Sept 1862 quoted in [Thomas Hartley Cromek], "Memorials of the life of R.H. Cromek, Engraver, F.A.S. Edin.ʰ Editor of the 'Reliques of Burns'; 'Remains of Nithsdale and Galloway Song' &c with unpublished correspondence on those works; and other papers relative to his professional and literary works. Collected and edited by his Son", MS in the possession of Mr Wilfid Warrington.
50 "English Encouragement of Art[:] Cromeks opinions put into Rhyme", Notebook p. 41.
51 Cromek letter of 17 April 1807 (*BRS* 47). "'Fit Audience find tho' few' MILTON'" is the motto Blake chose for the advertisement for his "Exhibition of Paintings in Fresco" (1809).
52 Cromek letter to James Montgomery, 30 Dec 1807 (Sheffield Public Library).
53 Cromek letter of 27 Jan 1810 (*Poems and Songs by Allan Cunningham*, ed. Peter Cunningham [London: John Murray, 1847], xix).
54 Allan Cunningham, *Poems and Songs* (1847), xix n.
55 Letter of 3 Dec 1810 (*The Letters of Sir Walter Scott*, ed. H.J.C. Grierson [London, 1932], III, 409).
56 Cromek letter of 16 Dec 1808 (*BRS* 59).
57 Cromek letter of May 1807.
58 J.T. Smith (*BR* 464). In his letter of May 1807, Cromek writes of "the 20 guineas I have paid you" for the drawings for *The Grave*, "though I am decidedly of opinion that the 12 for 'The Grave' should sell at least for 60 guineas".
    Butlin #609-17, 619–38 records thirty

drawings perhaps for Blair, but #609-10, 617, 622, 626-8, 630, 637 are untraced and may not be related to Blair, and the connection to Blair of #619, 636 is also uncertain. Nineteen of the finished drawings turned up unexpectedly in 2001. They include the twelve which were engraved, very similar to the engravings, plus 13 "Friendship", 14 "The Grave Personified", 15 A night scene like "The Garden of Love" in *Songs of Experience*, 16 Christ leading the blessed souls into heaven, 17 Two adults by an open grave, 18 Eight airborne figures, 19 "The Gambols of Ghosts". The twentieth Blair design (not in the rediscovered cache) is probably "A widow embracing the turf", perhaps exchanged for "Death Pursuing", which the Cromeks and Cunningham thought was for *Urizen*.

59 Blake asked £31.10.0 for his quarto head of Cowper for Hayley's *Cowper* (Hayley to Flaxman, 7 Aug 1803), and he estimated the price of plates for Hayley's *Romney* at £31.10.0 "if finished & if a Sketch 15 Guineas" (letter of 28 Dec 1804). For "The Vision of the Last Judgment", one of the most intricate *Grave* plates, Schiavonetti asked £63 (*BRS* 53).

60 The Royal Academy sponsors, given in Cromek's prospectuses (reproduced in *BRS* 31-3, 35-6), also included Sir William Beechey, Thomas Lawrence, Joseph Nollekens, James Northcote, John Opie, Martin Arthur Shee, Henry Thomson, and Henry Tresham. All the sponsors save Northcote also appear in the subscription list, as do eleven other Academicians: Francis Chantrey, Richard Corbould, James Fittler, James Heath, John Hoppner, Ozias Humphry, William Owen, Thomas Phillips, J.F. Rigaud, James Ward, and Richard Westmacott Jr.

61 This was the "shout of derision ... raised by the wood-engravers" when shown Blake's relief-etchings for Thornton's *Virgil* (1820): "we will show what it ought to be" (*BR* 267).

  Cromek presumably returned the white-line print to Blake, for the only known copy of it was acquired from Blake by Samuel Palmer (R.N. Essick, *The Separate Plates of William Blake* [Princeton: Princeton University Press, 1983], 49).

62 The second Prospectus of Nov 1805 is reproduced in *BRS* 35-6; it also omits the list of SUBJECTS PROPOSED TO BE ENGRAVED".

63 Hayley's translation of "Hero and Leander" by Musaeus was not published,

and no correspondence between Hayley and Blake is known after December 1805.

64 Robert T. Stothard, "Stothard and Blake", *Athenaeum* (1886) (*BR* 172).

65 Puff in *Monthly Literary Recreations* (Sept 1807) (*BRS* 53).

66 Letter of 21 July 1807 (*BRS* 53).

67 *BR* 424.

68 Both prospectuses for Blair's *Grave* of Nov 1805 specify that it was to have a "Preface ... by BENJAMIN HEATH MALKIN". Malkin may have written the account "Of the Designs" for Blair's *Grave* (1808).

69 *BR* 421.

70 *BR* 424.

71 *BR* 422, 423, 424.

72 *BR* 425-9.

73 *BR* 622, 181, 182, 623.

74 This is the probable speculation of Gilchrist (*BB* 540).

75 Butlin #528 (eight for *Comus*), 542-3 (eighteen for "On the Morning of Christ's Nativity", *L'Allegro*, and *Il Penseroso*), 667-71, 673, 675-6, 770, 806. As late as 1831 Tatham said that he had "seen pictures of Blakes in the possession of Wᵐ [*i.e., Thomas*] Butts Esqre Fitzroy Square" (*BR* 515).

76 *BR* 574.

77 Letter of 30 Nov 1865 (*BR* 220). The passage continues: "I don't think they knew Blake's value", but he offers no evidence for this somewhat surprising conclusion. Tommy Butts was seventeen when his lessons began.

78 Ada Briggs, "Mr. Butts, the Friend and Patron of Blake", *Connoisseur*, XIX (1907), 92-6. Ada Briggs was the sister-in-law of Butts's grandson. The same information is given by Mona Wilson (1927) on the authority of Mrs Colville-Hyde, widow of Butts's grandson (*BR* 175).

79 See Essick, *Separate Plates*, 213-19. The *America* copperplate, found in a secret drawer of the cabinet given by Blake to Butts, is now in the Rosenwald Collection of the Library of Congress.

80 *Milton* pl. 2.

81 Cromek placed puffs and announcements and advertisements in (1) *Birmingham Gazette* (28 July 1806) (*BRS* 42), (2) *Birmingham Commercial Herald* (28 July 1806) (*BRS* 42), (3) *The Artist* (1 Aug 1807) (*BRS* 55), (4) *Monthly Literary Recreations* (Sept 1807) (*BRS* 53-4), (5) *Manchester Gazette* (7 Nov 1807) (*BBS* 54), (6) *Literary Panorama* (Nov 1807) (*BR* 190 n2), (7) *Wakefield Star* (28 May 1808) (*BRS* 56, (8-9) *Bristol Gazette* (9, 30 June 1808) (*BRS* 56, 57), (10) *Monthly Literary*

Advertiser (9 July 1808) (*BR* 191), (11) *Athenaeum Magazine* (Sept 1808) (*BR* 191 n2), (12) *Edinburgh Review* (Jan 1809) (*BR* 191 n2), and (13) *Reliques of Robert Burns*, ed. R.H. Cromek (Dec 1808) (*BR* 213–14).

82 Letter of 17 Nov 1807 (*BRS* 55). The subscription list detailed 51 from Manchester headed by William Roscoe, 66 from Birmingham and its Vicinity, 11 from Halifax, 7 from Pontefract, 55 from Wakefield and its Vicinity, 48 from Leeds, 69 from Manchester, 7 from Newcastle-upon-Tyne headed by Thomas Bewick, 33 from Bristol but omitting George Cumberland, and 16 from Edinburgh. (The names of a number of subscribers were accidentally omitted.) Notice how many are from Cromek's native Yorkshire.

83 *Descriptive Catalogue* (1809) ¶48. Presumably Blake had simply multiplied 688 copies by £2.2.0 (the price of ordinary copies) to get £1,444.16.0.

84 *Birmingham Gazette* and *Birmingham Commercial Herald* for 28 July 1806.

85 *Monthly Literary Recreations* (Sept 1807), Cromek letter of 17 Nov 1807 (*BRS* 55), and *Literary Panorama* (Nov 1807).

86 *Wakefield Star* (28 May 1808). The text was printed by Bensley, but the engravings were pulled by an unidentified copperplate printer.

87 *Monthly Literary Recreations* (Sept 1807).

88 *Wakefield Star* (28 May 1808).

89 The five orders are: (1) The first Prospectus (Nov 1805); (2) The advertisement in the *Manchester Gazette* (1807); (3) The Prospectus in Burns's *Reliques* (Cromek, 1808); (4) The description "Of the Designs" in Blair's *Grave* (1808); and (5) The titles on the engravings in Blair's *Grave* (1808) (summarized in *BRS* 40). There is no independent evidence that Blake chose any of these orders.

90 *Songs* (I), which belonged to Thomas Phillips's son Henry Wyndham Phillips (1820–68), was believed in the family to have been a gift from Blake, presumably to Thomas Phillips (*BB* 416).

91 The portrait is dated 4 April 1807 in Phillips's book of sitters (*BRS* 45).

92 See Chapter V.

93 Allan Cunningham, *The Cabinet Gallery of Pictures* (1838) (*BR* 183). T.F. Dibdin, who knew Blake, described it as "A magnificent portrait", "a most faithful and happy resemblance", though it shows "more elevation and dignity" than Blake really possessed (*BR* 289 [1824], 243 [1816]).

94 A notice of the marriage appeared in the *Wakefield Star and West-Riding Advertiser* for 24 Oct 1806.

95 [Mrs A.E. Bray], "Reminiscences of Stothard", *Blackwood's Edinburgh Magazine*, XXXIX (1836), 753, introduced by the phrase "The following is, as nearly as I can recollect at this distance of time, the account given to me by Mr Cromek". The same information is given in paraphrase in her *Life of Thomas Stothard, R.A.* (London: John Murray, 1851), 130. There is no reference to Blake in either account. Cromek also wrote: "I give myself great Credit for thinking of such a glorious Subject" (17 April 1807).

96 Cromek's letter to Blake of May 1807.

97 A prospectus dated Feb 1807 said that it was "TO BE ENGRAVED IN THE LINE MANNER BY MR. WILLIAM BROMLEY, *In an exquisitely delicate and finished Style*" (British Library: 1890 e 2, #122).

98 Letter of 14 Feb [1807] in Yale University (Beinecke Library). The crucial year is missing in the date, but it may be confidently inferred from references in the letter to the publication of Boyd's translation of Dante (1802), the prizes offered for artistic works in memory of William Pitt (d. 1805) and Nelson (d. 1805), the founding of the British Institution (1805), Opie's first lecture at the Royal Academy (1807), and the first English publication of Flaxman's illustrations to Dante (1807) ("Longman has purchas'd the well known plates [*for Dante, first printed in Rome*], & the Public will have Flaxman's designs in a very short time"). The contemporary docket, "Mr.⁵ Flaxman 14 Feb, 1802", must be in error as to the year.

99 Undated letter in the Boston Public Library extra-illustrated copy of Mrs Bray's *Stothard*; the letter was printed in Bray and in Bennett, *Stothard* (1988). The letter must have been written in or after 1813, for it refers to the deaths of Cromek (March 1812) and of Luigi Schiavonetti (1813).

100 J.T. Smith (*BR* 464–5).

101 "Blake's Chaucer: An Original Engraving" (1810) ¶6.

102 *Descriptive Catalogue* ¶18.

103 Butlin #653; the dimensions of the print are given in "Blake's Chaucer: An Original Engraving".

104 The Prospectus of Feb 1807 says that Stothard's "Picture is 3 Feet 1 Inches long, and 10½ Inches high. The Print will be executed exactly of the same size."

105 There were illustrated editions of Chaucer by Caxton (1483?), Thynne (1532), Stowe

(1561), Speght (1602), Urry (1721), Bell's Edition of the Poets of Great Britain (1782, with fifteen plates designed by Stothard, one engraved by Blake), Tyrwhitt (1798, with plates after Mortimer [d. 1799]), plus the Ellesmere MS (late fifteenth century) (see Betsy Bowden, "The Artistic and Interpretive Context of Blake's 'Canterbury Pilgrims'", *Blake*, XIII [1980], 164–90). Blake probably used the 1687 edition of Speght for his *Descriptive Catalogue* account of his picture (see Alexander S. Gourlay, "What Was Blake's Chaucer?", *Studies in Bibliography*, XLII [1989], 275–85), the edition used in *The Prologue and Characters of Chaucer's Pilgrims* (1812) published to puff Blake's print.

106 Notebook p. 69, quoting from Dryden's adaptation of the Knight's Tale in *Fables Ancient and Modern* (1700), probably found in Edward Bysshe's *The Art of English Poetry* (1710) (*BB* 329).

107 Linnell's notes on J.T. Smith's biography of Blake (*BR* 464 n1) were made in 1855 for Gilchrist.

108 Blake's tempera (Butlin #653) passed to Thomas Butts but there is no separate receipt in which it is named (a receipt of 29 Jan 1807 for £21 "on further account" [*BR* 575] might be for the Canterbury Pilgrims), and the work appeared as if for sale in Blake's exhibition of 1809. The surviving Butts accounts end in 1810, but Butts plainly bought works from Blake after that date. "The Original reduced Drawing made to reduce the Picture of the Canterbury Pilgrims to the size of the Plate Blake afterwards engraved" (Butlin #654) stayed with Blake until his death and was acquired from his widow by Frederick Tatham, who so inscribed it.

109 *The Morning Chronicle* for 21 March 1807 says that Stothard has "just finished" his Canterbury Pilgrims painting (British Museum Print Room Whitley Papers X, 448).

110 Cromek advertised the exhibition of the picture at his house in *The Times* for 5 March 1807 (as I am told by Professor Dennis Read). On 3 April 1807, James Hopwood wrote to James Montgomery that Cromek "has for nearly two months [*Feb–March*] been exhibiting it at his House in Newman Street, and the people are still coming by hundreds in a day to see it" (Sheffield City Libraries). A review of "This admirable performance" in *The Cabinet*, I (April 1807), 90–7, says that "the Picture is to be seen, with Tickets" at Cromek's house, No. 64, Newman Street

(p. 97). According to *Bell's Weekly Messenger*, 3 May 1807, p. 141, "Stothard's admirable Picture of the Procession of Chaucer's Pilgrims is now exhibiting", and an advertisement in *The Times* for 4 May 1807 says that Stothard's Canterbury Pilgrims, now on view at Mr Lee's, perfumer, 344 Strand, is moving soon to [Cromek's house at] 64 Newman Street (British Museum Print Room Whitley Papers X, 448).

111 "And his legs", Notebook p. 22.

112 *BRS* 46, 48–9. The poem was given in Blair's *Grave* (1808), and De Quincey quoted it in his anonymous "Sketches of Life and Manners, from the Autobiography of an English Opium-Eater", *Tait's Edinburgh Magazine* (1840) (*BRS* 49 n2).

113 *BRS* 55, 57.

114 William Bell Scott in 1892 (*BR* 193). W.B. Scott's brother David wrote in 1844 that these designs "are the most purely elevated in their relation and sentiment" "of any series … which art has produced" (*BR* 194 n1).

115 See *BR* (2)

116 *BRS* 70.

117 *BR* 333.

118 "the Council of God … behold … As One Man all the Universal Family & that One Man They Call Jesus the Christ"; "the Seventh Lamp of the Almighty is named Jesus The Lamb of God" (*Vala* p. 21, ll. 1, 3–5; p. 19, ll. 10–12). The Sons of Los are the tribes of Israel (p. 115, ll. 19–21).

119 For instance, "Beth Peor" becomes "Conways Vale", and "Mount Gilead" is replaced by "High Snowdon" (*Vala* p. 21, l. 15, p. 19, l. 8).

120 *Vala* p. 104, ll. 71, 76, 78.

121 *Vala* p. 106, ll. 1–2.

122 *Vala* p. 111, ll. 18, 20, 22–4, 21). "And who shall mourn for Mystery who never loosd her Captives[?]" (p. 134, l. 17).

123 Northrop Frye, *Fearful Symmetry* (Princeton: Princeton University Press, 1947), 305.

124 168 lines in passages of 5 to 54 lines from *Vala* pp. 4, 21, 25–6, 40–2, 59, 92–3, 105, 119–20 are repeated in *Jerusalem* pl. 7, 19, 22, 29, 38, 40, 65, 67–8.

125 *Jerusalem* pl. 3; pl. 98, l. 24; his letter of 25 April 1803 refers to a poem about "the Spiritual Acts of my three years Slumber on the banks of the Ocean".

126 *Jerusalem* pl. 4, ll. 1–2.

127 *Jerusalem* pl. 4, ll. 3–5.

128 *Jerusalem* pl. 3, ¶4.

129 *Jerusalem* pl. 3, ¶4.

130 *Jerusalem* pl. 22, l. 3.

131 *BR* 229 (1811), 398 (1830).
132 BR 265–6. Copies were printed in 1820 (A, C–D), 1821 (B, E), 1827 (F), and posthumously (H–J, watermarked 1831 and 1832) (Joseph Viscomi, *Blake and the Idea of the Book* [1993], 376–81).
133 *Jerusalem* pl. 3, ¶3, pl. 12, l. 15.
134 *Jerusalem* pl. 61, ll. 24–6. "Forgiveness of Sins... is Self Annihilation; it is the Covenant of Jehovah"; "The Spirit of Jesus is continual forgiveness of Sin" (*Jerusalem* pl. 98, l. 23; pl. 3, ¶2).
135 *Jerusalem* pl. 77, ¶1.
136 *Jerusalem* pl. 30, l. 15; pl. 95, ll. 19–20.
137 Letter of 12 April 1827.
138 *BR* 347, 594.
139 *BR* 458, 463; 383; 490; 532.
140 Gilchrist (*BR* 308).
141 Letter of 9 Feb 1808.
142 Letter of 18 Jan 1808 to Ozias Humphry, with copies (Feb 1808) for the Earl of Egremont and the Earl of Buchan.
143 Letter of 20 June 1810 (*BRS* 133).
144 Dibdin, *Reminiscences of a Literary Life* (1836) (*BR* 243–4).
145 Public Address, Notebook pp. 65, 56.
146 Public Address, Notebook p. 60.
147 Dennis M. Read, "The Context of Blake's 'Public Address': Cromek and The Chalcographic Society", *Philological Quarterly*, LX (1981), 69–86, the source of all the information here about the Chalcographic Society.
148 *BR* 230.
149 *BRS* 69.
150 *BR* 623.
151 Lamb letter of 15 May 1824. Crabb Robinson wrote in 1852 that his friend "Lamb preferred it [*Blake's engraving of the Canterbury Pilgrims*] greatly to Stoddart's and declared that Blakes description was the finest criticism that he had ever read of Chaucer's poem" (*BR* 538).
152 *Specimens of Polyautography Consisting of Impressions taken from Original Drawings made purposely for this work* (London: P. André, Patentee, № 5 Buckingham Street, Fitzroy Square, and J[ames]. Heath, № 15 Russell Place, Fitzroy Square, 30 April, 1803), expanded (Printed by G.J. Vollweiler, Patentee, Successor to M. André, 1806[–1807]), with a prospectus listing terms for renting the stone and printing from it. The work was printed at the Polyautographic Office, 9 Buckingham Place, across the river in Walworth, far from Buckingham Street, Fitzroy Square.
153 Charles Dickens, *The Life and Adventures of Nicholas Nickleby* (1839), 5-6.

154 *Jerusalem* pl. 84, ll. 15-16; Blake lived in Broad Street (1757-72, 1779-1782, 1784-85), Great Queen Street near Lincoln's Inn (1772-79), and Poland Street (1785-90).
155 "Exhibition of Paintings in Fresco", ¶1.
156 The subjects for his History of England listed about 1793 in his Notebook (p. 116) include "The Ancient Britons according to Caesar" and "Boadicea inspiring the Britons against the Romans".
157 Southey in 1847 (*BR* 226).
158 *Descriptive Catalogue* ¶75, 80–2. This is clearly derived from physiognomical theories such as those of Lavater.
159 *BR* 222 n1. In 1866, Kirkup wrote: "the impression which Blake's *Ancient Britons* made on me (above all others) was so strong that I can answer for the truth of my sketch" made fifty years later (*BR* 220 n2)
160 Kirkup letter of 25 March 1870 (*BR* [2]).
161 Kirkup letter of 25 Jan 1866 (*BR* [2]).
162 *BR* 438, 451.
163 Flaxman letter of 19 Aug 1800.
164 Southey in 1847 (*BR* 226).
165 *BRS* 66, translated from the Welsh.
166 *Descriptive Catalogue* ¶10.
167 Smith (*BR* 451); *Lady's Monthly Museum* (1812) (*BRS* 69).
168 *Descriptive Catalogue* ¶97, 98, 96.
169 *Descriptive Catalogue* ¶9.
170 Crabb Robinson Reminiscences (*BR* 538). In the *Descriptive Catalogue* ¶87, Blake says that he "defies competition in colouring".
171 The date Blake added at the end of his flyer called "Exhibition of Paintings in Fresco".
172 *Descriptive Catalogue* ¶2.
173 Crabb Robinson in *Vaterländisches Museum* (1811), *Gentleman's Magazine* obituary (1827) (but not in other obituaries), J.T. Smith (1828), Allan Cunningham (1830), and Frederick Tatham (1832) (*BR* 435–41; 357; 465; 492–6; 515–6); of course Malkin, whose memoir of Blake was published in 1806, does not refer to the *Descriptive Catalogue* of 1809.
174 Crabb Robinson's Diary and Reminiscences (*BR* 225, 537). He gave one copy to Charles Lamb, sent one to a friend in Hamburg, perhaps gave one to Wordsworth, and of course kept one for himself.
175 Crabb Robinson in *Vaterländisches Museum* (*BR* 450, 452). In his Reminiscences (1852) he remarks more neutrally that "it is a very curious exposure of the state of the artists mind" (*BR* 537).
176 *BR* 465, 494.
177 Notebook p. 40.
178 *Jerusalem* pl. 3, ¶1, 2.

Chapter VIII 1810–1818: "I Am Hid"

1 Marginalium (?1808) to Reynolds, *Works* (1798) title page verso.

2 Gilchrist reporting a conversation (probably derived from Flaxman's sister-in-law Maria Denman) between Henry Frances Cary, the translator of Dante, and John Flaxman (*BR* 232–3).

3 Kirkup told Lord Houghton on 25 March 1870, "I was much with him from 1810 to 1816, when I came abroad" (*BR* 221).

4 Seymour Kirkup's conversation reported by C.E. Norton to James Russell Lowell, 24 Feb 1870 (*BR* 221 n4).

5 Seymour Kirkup to A.C. Swinburne, 30 Nov 1865 (*BR* 220).

6 Seymour Kirkup to W.M. Rossetti, 19 Jan 1866 (*BR* 221 n2).

7 Seymour Kirkup to Lord Houghton, 25 March 1870 (*BR* 221).

8 Swinburne, *William Blake* (1868) paraphrasing Kirkup (*BR* 221 n3).

9 Kirkup letter of 25 Jan 1866 (*BR* [2] under 1809-10).

10 Kirkup letter of 19 June 1867 (*BR* [2] under 1809-10).

11 Kirkup letter of 10 Feb 1868 (*BR* [2] under 1809-10).

12 Crabb Robinson Reminiscences (1852) (*BR* 536); he goes on to say that this is "what a German wd. call a *Verüngluckter Genie*".

13 Crabb Robinson Reminiscences (1852) (*BR* 537).

14 *BR* 226.

15 Crabb Robinson Reminiscences (1852) (*BR* 537).

16 [Henry Crabb Robinson], "William Blake, Künstler, Dichter, und Religiöser Schwärmer" (tr. Dr Nikolaus Henrich Julius), *Vaterländisches Museum*, I (Jan 1811), 107–31, translated back from German into English (*BR* 448, 451). The issue of *Vaterländisches Museum* with Crabb Robinson's essay on Blake is dated January 1811, though his own copy did not arrive until 28 April (*BR* 229).

17 Crabb Robinson, *Vaterländisches Museum* (*BR* 450).

18 Crabb Robinson, *Vaterländisches Museum* (*BR* 451).

19 Crabb Robinson, *Vaterländisches Museum* (*BR* 452, 453).

20 Crabb Robinson, *Vaterländisches Museum* (*BR* 453–54).

21 Crabb Robinson, *Vaterländisches Museum* (*BR* 455).

22 Crabb Robinson, *Vaterländisches Museum* (*BR* 448–9).

23 *Visions of the Daughters of Albion* pl. 11, l. 215; marginalium to Lavater's *Aphorisms* (1789) ¶630; *Jerusalem* pl. 55, ll. 36–7.

24 *Jerusalem* pl. 38, ll. 55, 57.

25 Samuel Palmer to Anne Gilchrist, Sept 1862 (*BRS* 71). This is plainly little better than rumour.

26 Public Address, Notebook pp. 56–7.

27 Marginalium (?1818) to Spurzheim, *Observations on … Insanity* (1817), 154.

28 Juninus, "On Splendour of Colours, &c", *Repository of Arts, Literature, Commerce, Manufactures, Fashions, and Politics* (June 1810) (*BRS* 62).

29 Juninus, "On Splendour of Colours, &c.", *Repository of Arts* (Sept 1810) (*BRS* 63).

30 Ker to Cumberland, n.d. (*BR* 228). It is tempting to see a connection between Ker and "Cur my lawyer" who "went to Law with Death [*Blake*] to keep our Ears on" (Notebook p. 22, ll. 25–6).

31 Cromek to Blake, May 1807.

32 *A Catalogue of the Fifth Annual Exhibition of the Associated Painters in Water Colours* (1812).

33 *BRS* 69.

34 J.L. Roger, *History of the Old Water Colour Society* (1891), I, 271.

35 C.A. Tulk's daughter Caroline Tulk Gordon (later Leigh) born 1815, writing *c.* 1860 (*BR* 250).

36 John Gibson's autobiography (*c.* 1851) (*BR* 245).

37 Lady Charlotte Bury's diary for Tuesday 20 Jan [i.e., June? 1810]. For the difficulties of the date, see *BR* 248 n2.

38 Gilchrist (*BR* 250).

39 *BR* 169, 193.

40 Gilchrist (*BR* 339); the designs (Butlin #481, 549) were repetitions of drawings Blake had made for Thomas Butts.

41 *BR* 599.

42 Anon. [perhaps C.A. Tulk], "The Inventions of William Blake, Painter and Poet", *London University Magazine* (March 1830) (*BR* 386).

43 All the *Hesiod* payments are given on *BR* 579–80.

44 Thirteen years later, after Flaxman's death, Blake sent to Flaxman's beloved sister-in-law and executrix Maria Denman on 18 March 1827 "15 Proofs of The Hesiod"; the other Hesiod proofs he has "are all Printed on both sides of the Paper … many of the backs of the paper have on them impressions from other Plates for Booksellers which he was employd about at the same time", such as Rees's *Cyclopaedia* (1816–19) and Wedgwood's *Catalogue* (1815–16).

45 *BB* 556, contract of 24 Feb 1816.

46   *BB* 560.

47   Anon., "Blake, John", *Neues allgemeines Künstler-Lexicon*, ed. G.K. Nagler, I (Munich: E.A. Fleischmann, 1835), 522: "Blake, John, Bruder William's ... stach ... die Umrisse zu Hesiod's Theogonie nach Flaxmann. Die nähren Lebensverhältnisse dieses Künstler sind uns nicht bekannt". Anon. knew no more about John Blake, engraver, because there was no more to know; indeed, there wasn't even this much.

48   *BB* 560. In that year Longman sold the "Coppers & Copyright" to Flaxman's sister-in-law Maria Denman for £50; she sold them to H.G. Bohn; and at the end of the century the plates were sold by Bell & Daldy in a fit of patriotism to be melted down for cannon (*BB* 560).

49   Percy Bysshe Shelley, "England in 1819".

50   Dibdin, *Reminiscences of a Literary Life* (1836) (*BR* 242, 243, paragraphing added).

51   *BR* 338–9, 589, 604. The offer to Chantry is undated, from Gilchrist.

52   Note by Frederick Tatham on a Wedgwood proof (*BR* 239).

53   Josiah Wedgwood's proposal to Blake in his letter of 29 July 1815 and Blake's tardy reply of 8 Sept.

54   There are notes in the Wedgwood Archives about the progress of Blake's drawings on 23 Oct, 25 Oct ("Mrs. Blake: 1 W.H. Basin 20 in. | 1 Nurse Lamp with | bason top & lip"), 5 Dec, and 13 Dec 1815 ("Mʳ Blake ... states that he shall very soon have completed Designs from all that he has" [*BR* 240–1]).

55   Wedgwood account of payment to Blake (*BR* 578).

56   Flaxman letter of 2 Jan 1804.

57   Frederick Tatham's inscription on a "Laocoon" drawing (*BR* 238).

58   Gilchrist (*BR* 238).

59   For Kirkup's letter of 25 Jan 1866, see *BR* (2) 1 under 1809–10.

60   Longman Ledger (*BRS* 72).

61   Turner, 21 Dec 1817 (*BRS* 72).

62   *BR* 257.

63   Robert N. Essick, *The Separate Plates of William Blake* (Princeton: Princeton University Press, 1983), 183–5 and Figure 79.

64   Christie's catalogue of Vine's collection (24 April 1837).

Chapter IX 1818–1827: The Ancients and the Interpreter

1   Letter of 10 Jan 1802, quoting Thomas Tickell's popular ballad "Lucy and Colin"; coincidentally the same lines are applied to Blake in Juninus, "On Splendour of Colours, &c.", *Repository of Arts* (Sept 1810) (*BRS* 63).

2   Dante Gabriel Rossetti to Thomas Woolner, 6 Dec 1860 (*BR* 274–75).

3   Anon. [?William Carey], obituary, *Literary Gazette* (18 Aug 1827).

4   Dante Gabriel Rossetti, 6 Dec 1860 (*BR* 274–5).

5   William Carey, *Description and Analytical Review of "Death on the Pale Horse", Painted by Benjamin West, P.R.A.* (London, 1817); reprinted in *Repository of Arts, Literature, Fashions, Manufactures, &c.* (1818) (*BR* 247). Carey had found that Blake "is now a resident in London".

6   Linnell, Autobiography, f. 15r.

7   Linnell, Autobiography, f. 44 (addendum numbered "44 2") and f. 48.

8   Linnell, Autobiography, f. 54.

9   Linnell, Autobiography, f. 32; he later learned that the aspirant purchaser was Mr Hope.

10   Linnell, Autobiography (*BR* 257).

11   Linnell's Journal for 10 July, 21 Aug 1818 (*BRS* 102). Leonardo's "Last Supper" is the copy in the Royal Academy.

12   Linnell's Journal for 24 Aug, 9, 11, 18–19 Sept 1818 (*BRS* 102, 103).

13   Linnell's Journal for 12 Sept 1818 (*BRS* 103).

14   C.R. Leslie, *Memoirs of the Life of John Constable, Esq. R.A.* (1843) (*BR* 258).

15   Cowper letter of 17 April 1790 in William Hayley, *Life and Posthumous Writings, of William Cowper, Esqr* (London: J. Johnson, 1803), I, 365; Blake may have seen this letter in manuscript.

16   *WBW* 1750 n2.

17   Gilchrist (*BR* 40).

18   A.T. Story, *The Life of John Linnell* (London, 1892), I, 168.

19   Butlin #692 131; this, like some other designs, has a pattern for "Counting for Geomancy".

20   Anon., "Bits of Biography. No. 1. Blake, the Vision Seer ...", *Monthly Magazine* (March 1833) (*BR* 298–9, paragraphing added).

21   Cunningham ¶36–7 (*BR* 496–7), paragraphing added. Cunningham specifies that the drawings were on two sheets of paper, framed, "the size of

22 Larger Blake–Varley Sketchbook ff. 31v, 32v.

23 Butlin #696, 752, 755.

24 Anon., "William Blake"(obituary), *Literary Chronicle* (1 Sept 1827).

25 For the argument that these were "eidetic visions", "phenomena that take up an intermediate position between sensations and images", see Joseph Burke, "The Eidetic and the Borrowed Image: an Interpretation of Blake's Theory and Practice of Art", Chapter 13 of *In Honour of Daryl Lindsay*, ed. Franz Phillip & June Stewart (Melbourne, London, Wellington, N.Y., 1964), 110–27.

26 Robert Hunt, *Examiner* (Aug 1808, Sept 1809); Blake's exhibition is "fresh proof of the alarming increase of the effects of insanity".

27 Crabb Robinson Reminiscences (1852) (*BR* 536).

28 Crabb Robinson letter of 10 Aug 1848 (*BRS* 68) and J. Forster, *Walter Savage Landor* (1869) (*BR* 229 n3).

29 Farington, Diary for 24 June 1796 (*BR* 52).

30 Crabb Robinson Reminiscences (1852) (*BR* 537).

31 Flaxman letters of 2 Jan 1804 and 1 Dec 1805; Blake himself writes of "my Abstract folly", "this spirit of Abstraction & Improvidence" (letter of 11 Sept 1801).

32 Hayley letters of 15 June 1802 and 3 Aug 1805.

33 Crabb Robinson Reminiscences; *Vaterländisches Museum* (1811) (*BR* 223, 448).

34 Crabb Robinson, *Vaterländisches Museum* (1811) (*BR* 448) and Diary for 24 Dec 1825.

35 Southey letter of 8 May 1830.

36 Crabb Robinson Reminiscences (1852), amplifying a description of 10 Dec 1825 (*BR* 539, 309).

37 Linnell letter of 3 April 1830.

38 Marginalium (?1789) to Swedenborg, *Divine Love and Divine Wisdom* (1788) p. 233.

39 Public Address (Notebook p. 57).

40 Gilchrist (*BR* 268).

41 Blake's receipt of 27 Aug 1819 (*BR* 581) for *Songs* (R).

42 Linnell's General Account Book (*BRS* 120).

43 Linnell's General Account Book (*BRS* 120); the payment for *America* (O) and *Europe* (K) is "on acc!", implying that Linnell paid more on another occasion. As the works are now coloured, presumably Blake finished them at a later date.

44 *BRS* 104–9 for originals; for notes, see *BR* 264–5, 267, 271–5, 277–8, 288, 300–1, 308–9, 332, 338, 341–2, 345–6, 350.
   Note that Linnell saw Blake on occasions not recorded here, e.g., when he took from him receipts dated 22 March 1822, 25 March 1823, and 14 July 1826.

45 *BRS* 77 n3.

46 Draft reply on the back of a letter of 2 Nov 1821 from Edward Denny to Linnell (*BRS* 77).

47 *Times* review of *Œdipus* (2 Nov 1821) (*BRS* 78).

48 Letter of 7 Oct 1803.

49 *BRS* 77. There is no record in Butlin of Denny's ownership of Blake drawings.

50 *BRS* 115.

51 Denny letter of 20 Nov 1826.

52 *The Letters of Charles and Mary Lamb*, ed. E.V. Lucas (London, 1935), II, 395, 323.

53 Samuel Palmer's recollection of seeing the Royal Academy exhibition with Blake in 1824 (*BR* 280).

54 Wainewright letter of Feb 1827 (*BR* [2]).

55 [Thomas Griffiths Wainewright], "Mr. [*Janus*] Weathercock's Private Correspondence, Intended for the Public Eye. George's Coffee House, Tuesday, 8th August 1820", *London Magazine* (Sept 1820).

56 Wainewright letter of 29 March 1826 (*BR* [2]).

57 See Wainewright letters of 28–9 March 1826 (*BR* 327 and *BR* [2]).

58 *The Marriage*, which does not appear in the lists of 9 June 1818 and 12 April 1827, was probably the same price (£6.6.0) as *Urizen* in 1827—it is the same size as *Urizen*. The price of *Milton* was £10.10.0 in 1818; it is not in the 1827 list.

59 *BR* 346.

60 *BRS* 73.

61 Thornton and Blake called on Linnell on 19 Sept 1818.

62 Marginalia to Robert John Thornton, *The Lord's Prayer, Newly Translated from the Original Greek* (1827) title page and verso and pp. 1, 10.

63 Gilchrist (*BR* 267–8).

64 *BR* 271. The work was entered at Stationers' Hall on 12 Feb 1821.

65 *BR* 271.

66 Linnell letter of 3 April 1830.

67 George Richmond to Anne Gilchrist (*BR* 566).

68 Crabb Robinson Reminiscences (1852) (*BR* 542), somewhat amplifying his Diary entry for 17 Dec 1825.

69 See "Images of the Word: Separately Printed English Bible Illustrations

1539–1830", *Studies in Bibliography*, XLVII (1994), 103–28.

70   Linnell's explanation in his Job Accounts (*BR* 599) as to why Butts was given a set of proofs (value £5.5.0), though the sum he had paid (£3.3.0) was the price of a "plain" copy.

71   This and many of the other details about Job here derive from Bo Lindberg's brilliant *William Blake's Illustrations to the Book of Job* (Abo, Finland, 1973). Lindberg says that Blake "certainly knew" the frescos, which were re-discovered behind the wainscoting in St Stephen's Chapel in August 1800 when the Houses of Parliament had to be expanded because of the addition of new Irish members consequent upon the Act of Union with Ireland (pp.138–9). The drawings are described in John Topham, *Some Account of the Collegiate Chapel at Westminster*, with engravings by Basire (London: Society of Antiquaries, April 1807).

72   *BBS* 195–6, where the first plate is reproduced. Blake repeated these two inscriptions in his "Laocoon", omitting "to God" and "Imaginative" and replacing "Exercise" with "Practise".

73   *BR* 582.

74   Linnell letter about Blake's Dante designs of 16 March 1831. The conclusion is amply supported by Linnell's account books.

75   *BR* 607.

76   Linnell's father-in-law Thomas Palmer delivered coal to Blake in Jan 1824, 5 May 1825, 27 Jan 1826 (*BR* 587–9, 604). Butts too had paid Blake in coal (*BR* 573).

77   Robert Balmanno wrote that Blake had "showed me one of the plates" when he subscribed on 15 Nov 1823 (*BR* 329, 604).

78   Linnell's Journal for 4–5 March 1826 (*BRS* 107).

79   Draft advertisement for Job (see *BR* [2] under March 1826); this advertisement was not printed. The information is repeated in Linnell's letter of 6 Aug 1838 (*BR* [2]).

80   Mary Ann Linnell letter to her husband of 9 Feb 1826.

81   Inscriptions (quoting Job) on the 17th and 22nd plates.

82   Lindberg, *William Blake's Illustrations*, 176.

83   Letters of T.G. Wainewright, 29 March 1826 (*BR* [2]); Edward Denny, 20 Nov 1826 (*BRS* 115); Edward FitzGerald, 23 Oct 1836 (*BR* [2]).

84   Bernard Barton letter of 22 April 1830.

85   [Samuel Calvert], *A Memoir of Edward Calvert Artist* (1893) (*BR* 294).

86   *BR* 288.

87   Linnell, Autobiography f. 80.

88   Linnell, Autobiography ff. 80–1.

89   Gilchrist (*BR* 293–4), paragraphing added.

90   *Anne Gilchrist: Her Life and Writings*, ed. H.H. Gilchrist (1887) (*BR* 293 n1).

91   A.H. Palmer, *The Life and Letters of Samuel Palmer* (1892) (*BR* 294); the "f" is omitted from "frightened".

92   Gilchrist (*BR* 294).

93   Palmer letter, n.d. (*BR* 314–15), paragraphing added. For a curious variant of these "Claudes", see *BR* (2) under 1780.

94   A.H. Palmer (*BR* 291), paragraphing added. The "fear and trembling" story was one which Palmer loved to tell (*BR* 291 n2, *BRS* 81).

95   [Samuel Calvert], *A Memoir of Edward Calvert Artist* (1893) (*BR* 302–3), some paragraphing added.

96   A.H. Palmer (*BR* 292).

97   Marginalia to Thornton's translation of *The Lord's Prayer* (1827), pp.10, 3.

98   Linnell's memorandum of April 1855 (*BR* 318). In this context, it should be remembered that one of Linnell's most passionately held precepts was the wickedness of male midwives (Autobiography) and that Blake believed Christianity had nothing to do with moral precepts.

99   *BR* 319 n1.

100   F.G. Stephens, *Memorials of William Mulready* (1867) (*BR* 277); the dinner must have taken place before August 1822.

101   D.G. Rossetti letter to Anne Gilchrist, *c.* April 1880 (*BR* 307); the conversation occurred "on the last occasion when the old gentleman visited me". The "endlessly industrious" painter of "hopeless hugeness" sounds woundily like Benjamin Robert Haydon.

102   Letter to Mrs Aders of 29 Dec 1826.

103   Gilchrist (*BR* 301), paragraphing added.

104   Gilchrist (*BR* 279).

105   Robinson Reminiscences (1852) (*BR* 536).

106   Robinson Reminiscences (1852) (*BR* 538).

107   These Diary entries are rephrased and occasionally supplemented in his letter to Dorothy Wordsworth of 19 Feb 1826 and in his Reminiscences (*BR* 536–49). In the passages from Robinson's Diary given below, almost all the quotation marks and most of the paragraphing have been added.

108   Butlin #207–208 (1780–85), #343 4 (1801), #806 (1826).

109   The obituary of Blake in the *Literary Gazette* (12 Aug 1827) said that he worked from "Sessi Velatello's Dante, and Mr. Carey's translation", and Crabb Robinson speaks of finding Blake on 17 Dec 1825 "at

work on Dante—The book (Cary) and his sketches both before him". According to J.T. Smith, Blake "agreed with Fuseli and Flaxman, in thinking Carey's translation superior to all others" (*BR* 475).

110 Tatham (*BR* 527); T.G. Wainewright letter, Feb 1827 (*BR* [2]).

111 Samuel Palmer letter, Sept–Oct 1828 (*BRS* 89).

112 *For the Sexes* pl. 19, ll. 8, 7, 15, 13.

113 "The Everlasting Gospel", part j, ll. 41–2, repeated in part k, ll. 75–6.

114 Butlin #681.

115 "Susanna and the Elders", The Testament of Job, and the Fourth Book of Esdras (Butlin #394, 550 15, 20, 21).

116 *Europe* pl. 8, l. 3.

117 "Vision of the Last Judgment", Notebook p. 68.

118 Letter of 4 Dec 1804.

119 Butlin #828. The leaves bear watermarks of 1821 and 1826.

120 Linnell Journal for 6 March 1824; the rent was £10 per quarter (*BR* 286, 590).

121 Gilchrist (*BR* 305).

122 Letter of ?Feb 1827.

123 Letter of 11 Oct 1825; there are other references to his Sunday visits to Hampstead in his letters of 31 Jan, 19 May 1826, and 3 July 1827.

124 Mary Ann Linnell letter of Thursday 20 Oct 1825 (*BRS* 113). The sketchbook has not been traced today.

125 Gilchrist (*BR* 306).

126 Letter of 31 Jan 1826.

127 Gilchrist (*BR* 306).

128 A.H. Palmer, *The Life and Letters of Samuel Palmer* (1892) (*BR* 292): *Songs of Innocence* "were the first poems I ever heard & ... she who repeated them had heard them as she sat at the authors knee at Hampstead" (*BR* 292 n1).

129 Gilchrist (*BR* 304).

130 A.T. Story, *The Life of John Linnell* (1892) (*BR* 305 n1).

131 Letter of 1 Aug 1826.

132 Letter of 2 July 1826. Gilchrist says that Linnell "proposed taking lodgings for him in the neighbourhood of his own cottage at Hampstead" (*BR* 338); Linnell's journal and Blake's letters do not identify where Blake was to lodge in Hampstead.

133 Letter of ?Feb 1827.

134 Letter of 31 Jan 1826.

135 Letters of 31 Jan 1826, 7 June 1825, 1 Aug 1826; he also calls it "Aguish trembling", letter of 29 Dec 1826, and Tatham calls it "a species of Ague, (as it was then termed)" (*BR* 527).

136 Letter of 16 July 1826; on 5 July 1826 he speaks of "paroxysms" of pain.

137 Letter of 19 May 1826.

138 Letter of 10 Nov 1825.

139 Letter of 3 July 1827.

140 Letters of 19 May 1826, 10 Nov 1825, 5 July 1826.

141 Letter of 1 Aug 1826.

142 Gilchrist (*BR* 341).

143 *BRS* 109; the entry has a slight sketch of Blake in bed.

144 Cunningham (*BR* 501–2); most of Cunningham's account comes from J.T. Smith, but this passage is unique—and, like all Cunningham's dialogue, probably an embroidery of fact.

Postscript
Blake's Shadow of Delight Alone: Catherine Blake in 1827–1831

1 *Vala* p. 87, ll. 41–2.

2 Hayley wrote that Catherine "is so truly the Half of her good Man, that they seem animated by one Soul" (*BR* 106).

3 Letter of 11 Dec 1805; *Milton* pl. 36, l. 31 (cp. pl. 44, l. 28); *Jerusalem* pl. 53, l. 26.

4 J.T. Smith, *Rainy Day* (1845) (*BR* 26).

5 *BR* 342–3. She probably gave a month's notice to her landlord that day, for she moved out exactly a month later.

6 Tatham (*BR* 533–4).

7 Linnell letter of 3 April 1830.

8 See, for example, Tatham's letter of 1 April 1829 (*BRS* 90–1) and the letters signed by Catherine of 1 and 4 Aug 1829 (*WBW* xxix–xxx). *America* (N), *Europe* (I), and other works were almost certainly sold to the artist James Ferguson of Tynemouth (see *BR* 363) because of letters written by Tatham.

9 There were obituaries in the *Literary Gazette* (18 Aug 1827) (the source of most of the others, sometimes verbatim), *Literary Chronicle* (1 Sept 1827), *Monthly Magazine* (Oct 1827), *Gentleman's Magazine* (1 Nov 1827), *New Monthly Magazine* (1 Dec 1827), *Annual Biography and Obituary for the Year 1828*, and *Annual Register* (1828), followed by more formal biographical essays by J.T. Smith (1828) and Allan Cunningham (1830). Some of these accounts, such as that of J.T. Smith (*BR* 468), are clearly based upon information which came from Catherine Blake.

10 There were editions of Cunningham in 1830 (two editions), 1831, 1837, 1839, 1842, 1844, 1846, 1859, 1862, 1868, 1879,

1886, 1898, and the Blake biography was reviewed or sometimes merely excerpted in *Athenaeum* (6 Feb 1830), *London Literary Gazette* (6 Feb 1830), *Edinburgh Literary Gazette* (13 Feb 1830), *Edinburgh Literary Journal* (20 Feb 1830), *Gentleman's Magazine* (Feb 1830), *Monthly Review* (March 1830), [?C.A. Tulk], *London University Magazine* (March 1830, reprinting the "Introduction" to *Experience*, "The Poison Tree", "A Cradle Song", "The Garden of Love", and portions of *Thel*), *Fraser's Magazine* (March 1830—not really a review but almost half of it is quoted from Cunningham's life of Blake), Philadelphia *Casket* (May 1830), Hartford *New-England Weekly Review* (3 May 1830), Philadelphia *Literary Port-Folio* (13 May 1830), *Zeitgenossen* (1830), *Library of the Fine Arts* (Feb 1831), and *American Monthly Magazine* (June 1831). J.T. Smith's life of Blake was reviewed in *Athenaeum* (19 Nov 1828) and *Eclectic Review* (Dec 1828).

11 *BR* 346.
12 *BRS* 96.
13 For instance, Lydia Maria Frances Child, *Good Wives* (1833–71) and Herbert Ives [Herbert Jenkins], "The Most Perfect Wife on Record", *Bibliophile* (1909).
14 Hogarth note on J.T. Smith (*BR* 374). The fact that Tatham "left her" suggests that the incident took place in 1831 when Catherine was no longer living with the Tathams.

15 Tatham (*BR* 534; *BRS* 90).
16 *BR* 567, 568.
17 Tatham (*BR* 535).
18 Gilchrist (*BR* 410), with bracketed interpolation from Tatham (*BR* 535). Clearly all Gilchrist's information comes from Tatham.
19 Tatham (*BR* 535), supplemented in brackets from Gilchrist (*BR* 410). Tatham adds: "Her age not being known but by calculation, 65 Years were placed upon her Coffin"; she was really 69.
20 Tatham (*BRS* 91).
21 *BR* 507–35.
22 On 22 March 1833, Linnell's father-in-law Thomas Palmer searched vainly for wills of William and Catherine Blake (*BR* [2]), and none is now recorded in the Public Record Office.
23 Tatham letter, n.d. (*BR* 413). He also wrote of "the possessions into which I came by legacy from Mrs. Blake" (letter of 8 June 1864 [*BR* 41 n4]), but the "legacy" was clearly oral rather than, as he implies, written.
24 *Anne Gilchrist: Her Life and Writings*, ed. H.H. Gilchrist (1887) (*BR* 416–17).
25 See *BR* 403–18.
26 Linnell letter of 18 March 1833 (*BR* [2]).
27 *BR* 417–18.
28 [Samuel Calvert], *A Memoir of Edward Calvert Artist* [1893]) (*BR* 417 n3).

Addenda: A Strange Story

John Clark Strange,* a modest but prosperous Quaker corn chandler from Streetley, near Reading, bought a number of Blake pictures at the sale of Thomas Butts Jr at the Foster auction on 29 June 1853, and he later bought more pictures from H.G. Bohn which Bohn had acquired at the Butts sale.

For some years, Strange considered collecting information about Blake and perhaps even writing a biography of him, and in the spring of 1859 he began seeking out men who had known Blake and reading books about him. His chief sources of information were Dante Gabriel Rossetti (who lent him Blake's Notebook to transcribe), William Palmer and his brother Samuel, and George Richmond. He kept detailed notes on his findings in his Journal.

He was told that Alexander Gilchrist was writing a biography of Blake but had abandoned it. When Strange met Gilchrist in 1861 and learned that Gilchrist's biography was almost complete, he gave up his own work, probably with a sense of relief.

Most of Strange's information about Blake is also given in a somewhat different form in Gilchrist (1863), for "he [*Gilchrist*] told me I had adopted the same plan he had and gone over same ground". At the very least, Strange identifies the sources of Gilchrist's information which Gilchrist had often deliberately concealed. And on occasion, Strange's informants gave him information which has not been recorded elsewhere, such as an account of Blake's nurse.

Strange's Journal was given by Peter Bindley to Mr Ray Watkinson, who transcribed it in 1975 and published excerpts from it in "A Meeting with Mr. Rossetti", *Journal of Pre-Raphaelite Studies*, IV (1983), 136–9, though he does not name the Quaker collector.

In December 2000, as *The Stranger from Paradise* was being set in type, Mr Ray Watkinson very generously sent me his transcript of the Blake portion of the Strange Journal, from which extracts appear below. The Blake

---

* He may be the John Strange who (according to the International Genealogical Index) was born 3 November 1808 in Shalston, Buckinghamshire, was married to Lydia Mullis on 4 May 1839 in Chipping Wycombe, Buckinghamshire, died on 18 December 1889 at Astwell, Brackley, Northamptonshire, and was buried on 20 December 1889 at Wapperton, Northamptonshire.

parts of the Journal will be printed in *Blake Records*, Second Edition (2002).

In the transcript below, the page references at the start of each entry identify the point in *The Stranger from Paradise* where the subject is dealt with.

pp. 19–20 When he told his father of seeing on Peckham Rye "a tree filled with angels", it was "only through his mother's intercession ... [*that he escaped*] a thrashing from his honest father, for telling a lie".

But according to Samuel Palmer, Blake did not escape a thrashing from his honest father: "When very young Blake used to go out for walks in the country & would frequently come home & describe the angels he had seen in the trees— *H*is father was so angry at first with his accounts at first [*sic*] that he treated them as falsehoods & severely whipped him several times[.]"

George Richmond said that

Blake spoke most tenderly of an old nurse[.] 'Twas to her he related his first vision—when a lad out walking at harvest time he saw some reapers on the fields & amongst them angels[;] he came home & told his friends but all of them laughed at him excepting this old nurse, who believed what he told her— He always spoke of her with great affection

There is no other biographical record of Blake's old nurse. It is at least possible that the "Nurses Song" in *Songs of Innocence* is related to her. (This was of course not Blake's first vision, which occurred when he was four years old.)

p. 28 Blake would walk in the countryside south of London "to Blackheath, or south-west, over Dulwich and Norwood hills".

Samuel Palmer said that "Blake was fond of the country & particularly of that part surrounding Dulwich, he much preferred it to Hampstead & would take long walks in that neighbourhood with Palmer pointing *from* those passages of scenery he thought most beautiful." We had not previously known that he went for such long walks as late as the 1820s.

p. 30 James Blake took his son to William Wynne Ryland with a view to apprenticing the boy to the engraver cum artist, but the boy said: "Father, I do not like the man's face: *it looks as if he will live to be hanged.*"

Palmer told a similar story, thus confirming Gilchrist's otherwise somewhat suspect account:

*W*hen he first desired to be put to an engraver to learn that art—his father took him to —— who lived in the same street but Blake was so horrified by the mans countenance that he would not be bound to him but was put with Basire[.] Blake declared the man would come to be hanged, which was actually his end— P related this in proof of his knowledge of phys-iognomy[.]

The only engraver who is known to have lived in Broad Street at this time (1768–74) was Francesco Bartolozzi, but the only engraver who is known to have been hanged was William Wynne Ryland, who was at the Royal Exchange, Cornhill in 1767–72 and in Queen's Row, Knightsbridge in 1772.

p. 91   Blake's brother about 1792 "ran way to join the army".

George Richmond said that "His brother was a coal merchant & died early", but there is no other evidence that John Blake was a coal merchant.

p. 110   "It seems somewhat unlikely that the artisan William Blake was a member of this genteel gathering of earnest liberals [*at Joseph Johnson's house*], though he was often in political sympathy with them."

Palmer told Strange:

It was likely his mind was injured by some of the companions he met at Johnson's the booksellers, where ..... [*sic*] Fuseli Commin [*?Godwin*] Paine & other such men frequently assembled—at one of these parties held at some gentlemans, the talk was upon astronomy and the distance of heavens &c .... [*sic*] one asserting so many thousand miles[,] others disputing & fixing the distance in very exact terms when Blake rising up said ["]Gentlemen I call[,] come with me & I will shew you, where I can lay my finger upon the sky, where the heaven & earth meets.["]

He told a similar story to Anne Gilchrist (*BR* 302): "Being irritated by the exclusively scientific talk at a friend's house, which talk had turned on the vastness of space, he cried out, ''Tis false. I walked the other evening to the end of the earth, and touched the sky with my finger.'"

p. 116   In 1795, "blake was mob'd and robbd".

Samuel Palmer asked Strange to "remember that I tell you the story of Blake & the robber"—but he never did, at least not in Strange's Journal.

p. 123   "Blake, for the only time in his life, *saw a ghost* ... 'scaly, speckled, very awful,' stalking downstairs towards him. More frightened than ever before or after, he took to his heels, and ran out of the house."

Strange writes:

I had a lengthy discussion with Mr P. on the nature of Blakes visions—
Mr P. on the whole thought they were seen as real objects by his outward
eyes and as such painted. said that when B was sometimes half sneered at
he would give some incredible acct as if for the sake of exaggeration—that
Blakes visions were not the same as ghosts or apparitions which appearances never but once happened to Blake—*H*e then when entering a house
saw the ghost of a friend go up stairs & in the morning precede him out
of the house which he slept in.

pp. 143–4   "There *had* been stormy times . . . when both were young; discord by no means trifling . . .. But with the cause (jealousy on her side, not
wholly unprovoked,) the strife had ceased also."
    Samuel Palmer claimed that Blake "was a very virtuous man in his life[,]
more so than anyone P, ever knew—was very fond of his wife, had no
family, and looked on marriage not quite in the light it is commonly
regarded & its sanctity &c." But we must remember that Palmer knew Blake
only in his old age and chose to believe well of him in all things.

p. 158 footnote[1]   Samuel Palmer wrote in 1862 that *Marriage* pl. 24
"gives Blake's idea of Nebuchadnezzar in the Wilderness. I have very old
German translation of Cicero and Petrarch in which . . . almost the very
same figure appears. Many years had elapsed after making his own design
before Blake saw the wood cut."
    According to Strange's Journal, "shewed me a print of Blakes; subject
Nebuchadnezzar crawling on his belly, naked covered with hair & nails
grown long, eating grass.— 'What was singular was that Blake's conception
was almost a facsimile of an ancient German print of the same subject and
which design Blake had never seen['] he declared." Since Palmer did not
own a copy of *The Marriage*, what he showed Strange must have been the
separate colour print of Nebuchadnezzar. Butlin points out that this colour
print is based on Dürer's "The Penance of St John Chrisostomus" but does
not note that this copy (Butlin #303, one of three known) belonged to
Samuel Palmer.

p. 165   According to Tatham, "*W*hile he was engraving a large Portrait of
Lavater, not being able to obtain what he wanted, he threw the plate completely across the Room. Upon his relating this he was asked whether he did
not injure it, to which he replied with his usual fun 'O I took good care of
that' ".
    Palmer told Strange a similar story:

Blake had been engaged several weeks, most earnestly, upon a plate, which was considerably advanced—but could not master a particular effect[,] worked incessantly & still not attained to his mind[;] growing enraged he flung the plate across the room in a passion—

["]*Did* you break the plate[?"] I asked him—;

["]*No*[",] said Blake quietly ["]I took care to throw it so that it should fall unbroken—["] *T*he copper was costly & Blake was poor[."]"

pp. 263–4   "in the middle of the trial, when the soldier invented something ... [*Blake*] called out '*False!*' with characteristic vehemence, and in a tone which electrified the whole court and carried conviction with it."

Samuel Palmer "said he remembered Blakes narrating his trial for treason (seditious language is stated in Hayleys Life) that when Blake was in court & some evidence was given falsely—Blake cried out in a voice & vehemency which startled the court [']'tis false 'tis false['.] *H*e had a powerful voice—*H*is wife was also present at the trial". Gilchrist gives the story as that which "Mrs Blake used afterward to tell", which makes the evidence hearsay, as Mrs Blake was not at the 1804 trial.

p. 393 footnote†   According to Gilchrist, "When he drank wine, which, at home, of course, was seldom, he professed a liking to drink off good draughts from a tumbler, and thought the wine glass system absurd".

Palmer told Strange, "He never cared to drink wine out of a wine glass he said—*If* he had wine he would like to pour it into a tumbler and drink it off at a draught".

p. 393   George Richmond told Anne Gilchrist that "Blake often spoke of the beauty of the Thames, as seen from the [*bedroom*] window, looking 'like a bar of gold'."

According to J.C. Strange's Journal, "*H*is talk was so enchanting that Palmer[,] altho' he hated London[,] when sitting with him in his rooms at Fountain Court and glancing through the windows looking over the river Blake would speak of the view in such a way that it look[*ed*] delightful to Palmer."

p. 410   Gilchrist told Blake's story of seeing "a fold of lambs" in a field, but "coming nearer, ... I looked again, and it proved to be no living flock, but beautiful sculpture". A lady sitting by him "eagerly interposed, 'I beg pardon, Mr. Blake, but *may* I ask *where* you saw this?' '*Here*, madam,' answered Blake, touching his forehead."

Palmer told Strange a similar story:

At a lady's home (whom P. named) where several were met amongst whom Blake & Coleridge—Blake was telling the company that when passing over Dulwich fields the other evening he saw a most lovely scene which he described in glowing language—and in a corner of the field were several beautiful angels wandering about—a Lady present was so struck with the description that she begged Mr Blake to tell her where the particular spot was as she would like to take her little son. when Blake remained silent & pointed mysteriously to his forehead in reply.—*The* scene had been in his brain.

Palmer adds to the story in Gilchrist the locale of the sheepfold (Dulwich) and puts Coleridge in the company. He also changes the sheep to "several beautiful angels wandering about"—but it must be essentially the same story.

p. 427   Probably no copy of "Laocoon" was sold during Blake's lifetime.

J.C. Strange wrote in his Journal, Samuel Palmer "shewed me a fine engr. of Blakes of the Laocoon with writing surrounding being Blakes sentiments on many subjects which P asking him about he had given him one of the prints saying at the same time 'you will find my creed there'".

p. 447   Tatham wrote that "some" of "those who were . . . intimate with him" proposed in 1829 "to give forth . . . biographical information" about Blake (*BRS* 91), but nothing more was known of this.

However, George Richmond told J. C. Strange: "Some years ago 4 of us who knew Blake well resolved to write down all the particulars we knew concerning him—which was done, & formed a considerable number of pages, when one of us who had the acct fell into some fanatical notions and destroyed the papers, flung them on the fire, unhappily". The four authors were probably George Richmond, Samuel Palmer, Frederick Tatham—and Edward Calvert or perhaps John Linnell. The fanatic was manifestly Frederick Tatham. This is the only evidence that such a collaborative manuscript biography of Blake was ever written—or destroyed.

Further Note to the text

p. 3   "we do not even know . . . the names of their [*Blake's parents'*] mothers"; Blake's father was "probably born about 1732".

In the Church of St Mary, Rotherhithe, under "Christnings 1722 April", was listed the baptism of "James y^c S[*on*]. of James & Eliz: Blake [*on the*] 12" of April. This is almost certainly the James Blake, son of James Blake of Rotherhithe, who has apprenticed as a Draper fifteen years later, on 14 July 1737.

No other child of this couple was christened in St Mary's, Rotherhithe, between 1714 and 1759.*

The second name of the poet's sister Catherine Elizabeth Blake came from her paternal grandmother.

Index

Works by Blake are listed under the title rather than under Blake. References to Figures and Plates are in **bold** type.

QuickBooks® All-in-One Desk Reference For Dummies®

Cheat Sheet

Speedy Keyboard Shortcuts

Shortcut Key Combination	Result
Ctrl+A	Displays the Chart of Accounts window
Ctrl+C	Copies your selection to the clipboard
Ctrl+F	Displays the Find window
Ctrl+G	Goes to the other side of a transfer transaction
Ctrl+I	Displays the Create Invoice window
Ctrl+J	Displays the Customer:Job List window
Ctrl+M	Memorizes a transaction
Ctrl+N	Creates a new *<form>* where *form* is whatever is active at the time
Ctrl+P	Almost always prints the currently active register, list, or form
Ctrl+Q	Creates and displays a QuickReport on the selected transaction
Ctrl+R	Displays the Register window
Crtl+T	Displays the memorized transaction list
Ctrl+V	Pastes the contents of the clipboard
Ctrl+W	Displays the Write Checks window
Ctrl+X	Moves your selection to the clipboard
Ctrl+Z	Undoes your last action — usually
Ctrl+Ins	Inserts a line into a list of items or expenses
Ctrl+Del	Deletes the selected line from a list of items or expenses

How to Perform Common Tasks

To perform a common accounting or bookkeeping task, use these commands. When QuickBooks displays the commands window, you just fill in the boxes and press Enter.

To Do This . . .	Choose This Command
Dealing with Customers . . .	
Invoice a customer	Customers⇨Create Invoices
Record a cash sale	Customers⇨Enter Cash Receipts
Issue a credit memo	Customers⇨Create Credit Memo/Refunds
Record a customer payment	Customers⇨Receive Payments

For Dummies: Bestselling Book Series for Beginners

QuickBooks® All-in-One Desk Reference For Dummies®

To Do This . . .	Choose This Command
Banking Activities	
Pay a bill with check	Banking⇨Write Checks
Buy inventory with check	Banking⇨Write Checks
Move money between bank accounts	Banking⇨Transfer Funds
Deposit money in a bank account	Banking⇨Make Deposit
See a bank account's transactions	Banking⇨Use Register
Reconcile a bank account	Banking⇨Reconcile
Working with Vendors	
Prepare a purchase order	Vendors⇨Create Purchase Orders
Record when items are received	Vendors⇨Receive Items or Vendors⇨Receive Items and Enter Bill
Record an accounts payable amount	Vendors⇨Enter Bills or Vendors⇨Enter Bills for Received Items
Managing Employees	
Preparing employee payroll	Employees⇨Pay Employees
Paying tax deposits	Employees⇨Pay Liabilities
Updating tax tables	Employees⇨Get Updates⇨Get Updates
Getting Financial Information	
Accounts	Lists⇨Chart of Accounts
Customers	Lists⇨Customer:Job List
Inventory	Lists⇨Item List
Vendors	Lists⇨Vendor List
Employees	Lists⇨Employee List
Managing Employees	
Profit and loss	Reports⇨Company & Financial⇨Profit & Loss Standard or one of the other profit & loss reports on Company & Financial submenu
Net worth	Reports⇨Company & Financial⇨Balance Sheet Standard or one of the other balance sheet reports on the Company & Financial submenu
Managing the QuickBooks System	
Setting up a new company	File⇨New Company
Resetting company information	Company⇨Company Information
Backing up data file	File⇨Back Up
Restoring a data file	File⇨Restore
Customizing QuickBooks	Edit⇨Preferences
Adjusting accounting data	Company⇨Make Journal Entry

Wiley, the Wiley Publishing logo, For Dummies, the Dummies Man logo, For Dummies, the For Dummies Bestselling Book Series logo and all related trade dress are trademarks or registered trademarks of Wiley Publishing, Inc. All other trademarks are property of their respective owners.

For Dummies: Bestselling Book Series for Beginners